Battle of the Little Big Horn Series
Volume Three

The Battle of the Little Bighorn
A Comprehensive Study

by
Jack Pennington

UPTON & SONS, PUBLISHERS
El Segundo, California
2001

ACKNOWLEDGMENTS

To my wife Joan
Without her by my side I would not have been able to accomplish the few things I have in life,
or the researching and writing of my account of the Battle of the Little Bighorn.

To my son Jack
whose suggestions and aid has been invaluable in checking my manuscript
and placing it on the computer in an acceptable form.

To these two I give my heartfelt thanks and my love.

Copyright 2001 by
JACK PENNINGTON

All rights reserved including the rights
to translate or reproduce this work or parts
thereof in any form or by an media.

Library of Congress Catalog Number 00-100326
ISBN: 0-912783-34-6

UPTON & SONS, PUBLISHERS
917 Hillcrest Street
El Segundo, California, 90245

Contents

	Preface	1
1	Overview	3
2	Reno's Attack Orders – Separation From Custer – Crossing Ford A	23
3	The Reno Court of Inquiry – Part I	33
4	The Reno Court Cover-Ups – Part II	39
5	Wallace, Girard, Keogh and Cooke	45
6	Sightings of Custer	55
7	Sergeant Kanipe	61
8	Trumpeter Martin	65
9	The Arikaras	85
10	Crow Accounts	91
11	Curley – Crow Scout	101
12	Sioux and Cheyenne Testimony	113
	Wooden Leg	113
	John Stands In Timber	119
	Chief Gall	125
	Chief Gall and General Godfrey	129
	Mrs. Spotted Horn Bull	142
	Red Horse	147
	Chief Hump	149
	Chief Crow King	150
	Low Dog	152
	Seven Sioux	153
	Flying Hawk	154
	Iron Thunder	155
	Flying By	155
	White Bull & Tall Bull	156
	Standing Bear	157
	Left Hand	158
	Waterman	159
	Turtle Rib	160
	Foolish Elk	160
	He Dog	162
	Joseph White Bull	165/168
	Henry Oscar One Bull	170
	Dewey Beard	172
	Chief Two Moon	173/176
	Kate Bighead	176
	Joseph White Cow Bull	182
	Cedar Coulee	186

CONTENTS

13 **Analysis of Writers' Scenarios** 193
    Curse Not His Curls by Robert J. Ege 193
    Legend Into History by Dr. Charles Kuhlman 199
    Keep the Last Bullet for Yourself by Dr. T. B. Marquis 215
    The Custer Myth–A Source Book of Custeriana, by Colonel W. A. Graham . . 220
    Evidence and the Custer Enigma by Jerome Greene 223
    Markers, Artifacts and Indian Testimony by Richard G. Hardorff . . 232
    Sole Survivor by Douglas Ellison 239
    The Custer Tragedy by Fred Dustin 250
    Custer's Fall by David Humphreys Miller 269
    Custer's Luck by Edgar I. Stewart 278
    Archaeological Insights into The Custer Battle
        by Douglas D. Scott and Richard A. Fox Jr.
    Archaeological Perspectives on The Battle of the Little Bighorn
        by Douglas D. Scott, Richard A. Fox Jr.,
        Melissa A. Connor and Dick Harmon 293
    Custer's Last Campaign by John Gray 301
    Little Big Horn Diary – Chronicle of the 1876 Indian War, by James Willert . 317
    A Critique of Captain Hughes' Letter and William O. Taylor's Book . . 342

14 **Conclusion** 353
    Appendix 1: Time Table 357
    Appendix 2 359
    Bibliography 365
    Index 369

Illustrations

Map A: Major Locations	17
Map B: Actual Routes Taken	17
Map C: Custer's Attack Plan Routes	17
Map 1 & 2: Movement of Command on Reno Creek	43
Views of Weir Peak from Valley	58
Views from Sharpshooter Ridge	71
Map 3: General locations once Custer reached the ridge	80
Views from Reno Hill	93
Views from Ford B and of Bouyer's Bluff	122
Map 4: Custer's route from Weir Point to battle area	177
Views from Weir Peak relating to Cedar Coulee	190

Preface

My first book, *The Custer Controversy – A Critical Analysis*, was shortened from the original manuscript in order to have it published. This new book represents the entire original document, which includes my analysis of additional participants (both Indian and white) as well as writers' scenarios concerning the battle and its aftermath.

I believe the lack of critical analysis of other writers' scenarios has been one of the main problems in determining what took place at the Battle of the Little Bighorn. Each writer or commentator has presented his view of what happened and used what evidence he could find to support his thesis without actually analyzing the validity of opposing evidence and then indicating on what basis he disagreed with those contradictory perspectives. In other words, to arrive at a more accurate conception of the battle one has to be objectively critical of others' viewpoints, just as they should be critical of those I support. Historians should follow a basic premise of scientists who believe the only way to find correct solutions is to tear down one another's ideas, testing them for every weakness.

The Custer Controversy expressed my hypothesis and some of the more important testimony which led to my conclusions. However, in a short version there was no feasible opportunity to present numerous facets and reasons used by participants and writers which contradicted my position as well as those that supported my scenario. Consequently, there was the need to have my full treatment published.

One benefit resulted from the shortening of my original manuscript: I was able to recognize another major cover-up at the Reno Court of Inquiry, one that I had not previously realized. It was apparent in my original study the necessity for cover-ups at the court concerning Custer's orders, and also the early sighting by Reno's troops of Custer's men on the ridge. Even though I recognized timing deviations and distortions, I failed to associate them with an actual cover-up. However, once I began to relate differences in timing statements with when they were issued, the necessity for the inclusion of the itinerist Lieutenant Wallace in the cover-ups, the variance in his accounts, and how the early division of command correlated with Indian testimony of when Reno's attack took place, along with the basic factor of Reno's initial report as indicated below, the structure of the deception gradually took shape. In no way could Major Reno and Captain Benteen or their defense go along with the earlier stated time of around 10:00 a.m. as to when Custer divided his command. Even with the "official" change to approximately 12:12 p.m., Reno and Benteen could be and were condemned for their slow reaction to gunfire from what could only be Custer's troops. Without the "official" time change there was no possibility that the need to wait for the packs or tend to the wounded could be extended to justify the late move to aid Custer. The military court could not have evaded levying court martial charges against Major Reno and, though not on trial, Captain Benteen.

I have not changed this book to incorporate the timing conspiracy except to insert the Reno Court chapter from *The Custer Controversy* into the Reno Court chapter here. That way the reader can be aware of my reasoning that there was a timing cover-up, and they should be able to do their own analysis as to whether they believe there actually was one. However, in my analysis of Chapter 17 of John Gray's book, *Custer's Last Campaign*, and in James Willert's book, *Little Big Horn Diary*, I break down the action taken by the command on the morning of the 25th, and why, to me, the "official" time represents a timing cover-up.

I do believe that anyone who accepts the "official time" represented at the Reno Court of Inquiry has to explain the following excerpts from Major Reno's letter to Captain E. W. Smith, A.D.C., A.A.A.G., Adjutant to General Terry, on July 5, 1876. If you are justifying the time differences only because of time zones (as I did), this is not enough. These officers had been in this time zone for some time, and their watches were synchronized.[1] It is also not enough to reject Indian reports of when the firing commenced because of their lack of knowledge of the white man's way of keeping time. It should also be recognized that Major Reno would have used the itinerist, Lieutenant Wallace, for confirmation or aid in making his report.

The following is a partial transcript of the letter Major Reno sent. The letter can be found in Loyd J. Overfield's, *The Little Big Horn, 1876*, (The Official Communica-

---

[1] Godfrey, *General Godfrey's Narrative; The Custer Myth,* p. 137, "We compared watches to get the official time, and separated to attend to our various duties."

PREFACE

tions, Documents & Reports with Rosters of the Officers and Troops of the Campaign), University of Nebraska Press.

The underlining is mine.

> Headquarters 7th U.S. Cavalry,
> Camp on Yellowstone River
> July 5, 1876

Captain E. W. Smith
A.D.C. and A.A.A.G.

. . . 23rd marched up the Rosebud passing many old Indian camps and following a very large lodge-pole trail, but not fresh making thirty three (33) miles; 24th the march was continued up the Rosebud, the trail and signs freshening with every mile until we had made twenty-eight (28) miles, and we then encamped and waited for information from the scouts; at 9:25 p.m. Custer called the officers together and informed us that beyond a doubt the village was in the valley of the Little Big Horn, and in order to reach it, it was necessary to cross the divide between the Rosebud and the Little Big Horn, and it would be impossible to do so in the day time without discovering our march to the Indians; that we would prepare to march at 11 p.m.

. . . About 2 a.m. of the 25th the scouts told him that he could not cross the divide before daylight. We then made coffee and rested for three hours, at the expiration of which time the march was resumed, the divide crossed and about 8 a.m. the command was in the valley of one of the branches of the Little Big Horn, by this time the Indians had been seen and it was certain that we could not surprise them and it was determined to move at once to the attack . . . .

I was ordered by W.W. Cook Adjutant, to assume command of Companies M, A, and G; Captain Benteen of . . .

. . . As we approached a deserted village, and in which was standing one tepee, about 11 a.m., Custer motioned me to cross to him, which I did, and moved nearer to his column until about 12:30 p.m. when Lt. Cook, Adjutant, came to me and said the village was only two miles ahead and running away; to move forward at as rapid a gait as prudent and to charge afterward, and that the whole outfit would support me. I think those were his exact words. I at once took a fast trot and moved down about two miles where I came to a ford of the river. I crossed immediately and halted about ten minutes . . . .

1
Overview

As an American History teacher, and like most Americans, I was aware of names associated with the settling of the West. Names such as Davy Crockett, Sam Houston, Buffalo Bill, Jesse James, Wild Bill Hickok, George Armstrong Custer, Sitting Bull, Crazy Horse, Geronimo and others difficult to find in an American History text book. I was also familiar with battles fought between the Indians and the whites. Several of the more noted ones were fought in my home state of South Dakota or neighboring states; still, I had only a cursory knowledge of them. After retiring from teaching, I found time to delve into the articles and books written about these battles along with visiting the sites where some of the encounters took place. Most of the battles, though interesting, did not stimulate a continuing curiosity or questioning as did my reading of the Battle of the Little Bighorn and visitations to the battlefield. I believe my interest was aroused by the contradictions and the failure to agree on answers among the participants and writers. As was pointed out by Edgar I. Stewart, so many of the whites who took part in the battle failed to reveal all they knew because of a sense of gallantry for Mrs. Custer or loyalty to certain officers. Stewart points out that Mrs. Custer outlived most of the participants, and many of the clarifications that might have came out, didn't. Many of the participants distorted the picture by their attempts to support or condemn certain officers, particularly General Custer or Major Reno, and by attempting to vindicate their own actions.

I found that Indian testimony is often ignored in written accounts. Some authors considered it unreliable, while others used their testimony, but placed too much emphasis on certain Indians and the statements that corroborated their own theories. The fear of punishment for having taken part in the battle affected much of Indian testimony and led to a desire to say what they believed the interviewer wanted to hear. Their testimony should be examined, as much as one's knowledge permits, within the framework of their cultural beliefs, recognizing their fears as well as the natural tendency for humans to rationalize, reiterate, agree with or follow what others have said and, in some cases, to exaggerate in recounting their own actions. I believe within this framework their veracity was as good and often better than that of the soldiers and interrogators from whom so many views of the battle originate.

In the years immediately following the battle, those searching for answers to what caused Custer's defeat concerned themselves to a large extent with attempting to either defend or blame Major Reno or General Custer. Much of the writing dealt with questions such as these: Should Major Reno have followed orders and continued his attack on the village? Was Reno a coward? Should Reno have stayed in the timber? Why did he leave the timber? Was his a panicky retreat or a somewhat disorderly cavalry charge? Was Reno drunk? Should Major Reno and Captain Benteen have moved to find and support General Custer immediately after Captain Benteen joined Reno? Should Captain Benteen have attempted to join Custer as his orders stated?

Then there are those who either blame General Custer for not following the orders they said were given to him by General Terry, and those who defend Custer's actions. They also criticize or support him for dividing his command. Most agree he failed to use proper reconnaissance and that he ignored the warning of his scouts, although Custer also has his defenders on these issues.

All these are interesting questions and are important in forming an overall picture. However, the points supporting or condemning Custer have been well covered, and although I might consider some positions more logical than others, they would not, in themselves, have compelled me to continue searching for answers to what happened to Custer.

Colonel Graham states, "But does it really matter how Custer came to the battlefield? We know he did arrive there, because he and most of his men were found there." Graham goes on to discuss different ideas of how Custer got there, then continues, "When so many who speak with authority differ with each other so completely, and the Custer story is not affected in the least, I think it proves the point of such small importance that I shall spare the reader any guesswork of my own."[1]

I disagree with Colonel Graham in several respects. I believe what happened to Custer after he left Major Reno is what provides the intrigue and thus the fascination that has and – because of the conjectural nature of any answer – will continue to promote interest in the Battle of the Little Big Horn. The other contentions about the battle were important to those involved in the events because the resolution would reflect on their military conduct and transform their careers and relationships with the major participants. These questions, though interesting, do not engender the mystery or speculation raised by the unknown events that transpired after Custer separated

OVERVIEW

from Major Reno. I would also challenge Colonel Graham's statement that the outcome was not effected by this aspect of the events. We could also say that the interpretation of Major Reno's and Captain Benteen's conduct didn't alter the inevitable outcome, but it does – and certainly should – influence the way we evaluate Custer's courage and his ability as a commander.

I continued to look for explanations why a courageous leader did not launch a recognized attack, or an orderly retreat, or at least establish a sound defensive position. This is the essential question: Why didn't he?

In attempting to find the answer, I faced other questions, many of which should have been resolved by the participants and the early writers investigating the battle. My concern centered around finding explanations that would satisfy me as to what happened to Custer after separating from Major Reno. It is not hard to understand the contradictions and contrary views presented by the participants, interested individuals, and writers regarding what happened after Trumpeter Martin left General Custer, but there is no easy solution for the contradictions in the debate over where Custer went before Martin departed. The following should not be equivocal: Where was the high point from which Custer first viewed the valley? Did he see Major Reno's troops at that time? Did Custer move along the ridge in sight of the valley or back from it? Did Custer view the valley from Weir Point? Did Custer go down Cedar Coulee?* Where did Trumpeter Martin leave Custer? What was the route Martin took back to meet Benteen? Where did the Indians fire at him?

Although imperfections of memory may have made the assessment of some of the exact locations difficult, the general route should have been clear. These were important issues that could have been clarified, and yet there are still conflicting views. It seems like the military writers, or other interested figures, should have brought together the individuals that were known to have been with Custer <u>after</u> he separated from Major Reno and moved to the ridge overlooking the valley; those being: the Arikaras who followed his trail to the ridge and part way along it; the four Crow scouts; Sergeant Kanipe, Trumpeter Martin and soldiers who professed to have been with Custer until they couldn't keep up or were sent back. To the best of my knowledge, Trumpeter Martin was never

---

*The Crow scouts' report of Custer's route and sightings as found in James Hutchins' book, *The Papers of Edward S. Curtis Relating To Custer's Last Battle*, Upton & Sons, Publishers, has to be seriously considered as an answer to the above questions.

brought back to the battlefield. Walter Camp did interview Curley and Kanipe on the battlefield, as did General Scott when questioning Curley and White Man Runs Him. However, to have obtained an accurate consensus of what happened and which route Custer followed, it would have required Sergeant Kanipe, Trumpeter Martin and the Crow scouts. Individual attempts to provide answers were unreliable, as evidenced by conflicting testimony, and were often too general in their descriptions. As I will point out when analyzing Trumpeter Martin's account, it appeared from the time of the Reno Court of Inquiry that there were those who wanted to discredit him and his statements rather than clarify them. If so, why?

A study of the Battle of the Little Big Horn seethes with contradictions. Testimony by whites is inconsistent, statements by various Indians are incompatible with one another, and even the same person often negates other remarks he has given. The one area of agreement in practically all of the testimony pertains to General Custer's character. Here we find those who support and those who criticize the General agreeing that he was a courageous and fearless leader. They also believe he was egotistical and his natural desire to defeat the Indians was enhanced by his problems with President Grant, other officers, and the military in general. Some even maintain that Custer wanted a victory in the hope it would lead him to the presidency. What this view suggests is that he needed not just a military victory over the Indians but one he could claim was specifically due to his actions.

I accepted the idea that Custer was a fearless and courageous commander, but this basic premise gave rise to a problem that bothered me: Why didn't Custer come to the aid of Major Reno? Most writers seemed preoccupied by the reverse question, or a defense of Major Reno's actions. When they did attempt to explain this paradox, I found their answers inconclusive, inadequate or illogical. My main concern then centered around General Custer <u>after</u> he separated from Major Reno. I wanted to know why there were no signs of Custer having launched an identifiable offensive move against the Indians. I found that the accepted theory was that for a cavalry to win a victory they must attack. Here we had a man who represented the epitome of this attack-orientated philosophy, but failed to make even a recognizable attempt to do so. I searched in vain for Indian testimony that would lend credence to the idea that such a movement had been made. Most writers either ignored the issue, or offered a scenario where Custer moved away from the Indian encampment or encountered an overwhelming number of Indians at the ford.

If, at the last minute, Custer realized there were too many Indians, why wasn't there any evidence, either from Indian testimony or from artifacts, that an organized retreat had been attempted? We know Custer was concerned with receiving aid via Captain Benteen and Captain McDougall; if the number of Indians confronting him prevented an attack, why didn't he retreat so he could unite his command? Indian statements indicate that initially there was not a large number of them in a position to hinder such a retreat.

Since Custer didn't launch a major attack or establish a disciplined retreat, the question then becomes: Why wasn't a sound defensive position created? Indian testimony leads us to believe there was adequate time; considering this fact, as well as the Indian's fighting habits, it seems inconceivable that Custer would not have been able to accomplish such a maneuver, especially since there weren't any signs of an attack against the Indians.

Archaeologists under the direction of Douglas Scott began excavations on the battle site in 1984, and their evaluation of the artifacts prompted them to conclude that Custer did retreat in an orderly fashion, and set up a V-shaped defensive formation which was overwhelmed by a deluge of Indians. Though their findings are extremely important, I do not completely endorse their evaluation. I agree with the archaeologists that historical interpretation has to coincide with artifactual evidence; at the same time, evidence derived from artifacts should correspond with reliable historical information. I do not believe that either the testimony of soldiers viewing the scene after the battle, Indian accounts, or the outcome, substantiate the archaeologists contention that an organized defense line had been established. The archaeologists have expressed their value judgments on different aspects of the battle, which is their prerogative. Some of those judgments are supported by historical testimony, while some are not. Where they have not been corroborated, the archaeologists, I believe, are wrong.

It was easy to develop a general hypothesis that would resolve my doubts; but if it was to have any authenticity, it was necessary to go over as much testimony of those who took part in the battle as I could find. The next step was to examine the writers who have analyzed the battle and the scenarios they have presented, particularly as it applied to the questions under consideration and whether they provided satisfactory or unsatisfactory explanations. If I was to disagree with them, I needed testimony to validate my position and a reason for rejecting theirs. I would not just accept the remarks made by whites or Indians and ignore conflicting accounts, since the same individuals often made contrasting statements. If I was to embrace some of those remarks to support my theory, then I had to explain why others were disregarded. I knew such an attempt would lead to repetitious rejections and positions that would become redundant, but it was necessary if I were to develop objective and logical conclusions. My research was done to satisfy my own curiosity and to prove a hypothesis. I did not set out to write an exciting story about the Battle of the Little Bighorn. (This is another criticism I have of some of the texts: they appear to have been written for entertainment purposes, with the idea of being marketable. Many are far-fetched scenarios with little logic or testimony to support the authors' positions. On the other hand, some accounts seemed more concerned with fulfilling the requirements of academic form than with analyzing and establishing a logical content.)

Although I differ with many writers on their opinions, I still have great admiration for the work they have done. Among them are Thomas B. Marquis, Charles Kuhlman, Daniel Magnussen, William A. Graham, Edgar I Stewart, Robert Utley, John Gray, Charles duBois, Jerome Greene, W. Kent King, Roger Darling, D. H. Miller, Richard Upton, George Bird Grinnell, Fred Dustin, R. Hardorff, Charles Eastman and the archaeologists. Anyone interested in the Battle of the Little Bighorn owes them a great debt of gratitude.

The explanations I propose are naturally conjectural and subject to criticism. Criticism which stems from objective questioning is needed for enlightenment.

Hopefully the Little Bighorn Preservation Committee can obtain more of the battlefield land so that additional excavations can take place. This might enable the archaeologists to shed more light on what happened during the battle. I also wish there were more ways to honor the Indians who fought there for their freedom.

The first book I read concerning the Battle of the Little Bighorn aroused my curiosity. It illuminated the emotions that the battle stirred throughout the country, and the many conflicting stories and exaggerations that subsequently emerged. But there was something that urged me to continue my study of the testimony, searching for a way to decipher why General Custer didn't come to the aid of Major Reno. Something more resonant than the usual simple assumptions as to why there was no sign of a major attack having been launched by General Custer and the five companies with him.

To operate successfully in battle, a cavalry must attack. This was the view corroborated by numerous testimonies, including remarks made by General Custer himself. He regarded attack and victory as synonymous. Many writers repeated this sentiment, yet provided no concrete evidence of Custer's attempt to employ this maxim.

General John McCausland, who had fought Custer in the Shenandoah Valley during the Civil War said, "The only way to fight with cavalry is with a dash – to charge ..."[2] In other words, for a cavalry to be effective it should attack, and this would be especially vital when fighting Indians. Let us look at several other statements concerning Custer and his character, as well as his perception of the Indians he planned on facing that memorable day.

Edgar Stewart wrote:

> There is another aspect to consider – Custer's character or disposition. Throughout all of his military career Custer had been distinguished by a wild and reckless bravery, which, together with an utter lack of fear, was largely responsible for the military reputation that he enjoyed. Custer on a hot trail was like a bloodhound: he could not leave it, he could not even rest until he had brought his quarry to bay.[3]

> Billings Gazette, August, 1933 – Was Custer worried about the number of Indians he would face that day? He was too astute and too experienced an Indian fighter not to have read the message so plainly pictured in the various Indian camps that the regiment had passed.

> Billings Gazette, January 6, 1934 – He had been warned by Bloody Knife, Girard, Bouyer, Reynolds and other Crow scouts. Reynolds had reported to him that the biggest bunch of Indians he had ever seen was ahead.

> Oregon Journal, August 3, 1923 – Custer informed his officers that "the largest Indian camp on the North American continent is ahead and I am going to attack it."

> Montana, Godfrey, p. 210 – "The number of hostiles caused him no concern, for he knew that a large camp could scatter as easily as a small one."

Many writers have pointed out that Custer had not the slightest doubt of the ability of his 7th Cavalry to defeat the entire Sioux nation. General Sherman declared that the attack was neither desperate nor rash in view of all the circumstances or according to the rules of Indian fighting, and that Custer "could do nothing but attack when he found himself in the presence of the Indians."[4]

I assume that General Sherman was referring to the overall move against the Indians. "Audacity, always audacity," is the motto for a cavalryman, declared General G. A. Forsyth.

The essence of these views is that Custer was fearless and courageous, that he knew he must attack in order to defeat the Indians, and he realized he would be facing an extremely large Indian encampment. It would thus seem that Custer not only had the courage and confidence to attack, but would have considered it imperative that he do so, not only to defeat the Indians but also to fulfill his pledge to support Major Reno.

These remarks seemingly make it impossible for Custer not to have launched an attack, but it is understandable if, faced with an overwhelming number of Indians, he would have decided against it for various reasons quite distinct from a lack of courage. Though many writers contend he was confronted by just such a multitude of Indians when he reached Medicine Tail Coulee, Indian testimony doesn't bear this out. So, if Custer did not face an overpowering number of Indians at the onset, but, for whatever reason, he believed he should not attack, why didn't he order a retreat back the way he came in order to unite his command? His messages via Sergeant Kanipe and then Trumpeter Martin indicated his concern for the need to accomplish this unification. There should have been signs, if such an attempt to retreat had been made, and they should have been noted by the soldiers after the battle and by Indian testimony and artifacts (which there were not).

Why? Again, I was not satisfied with the theories that confronted me. Few writers even brought up the issue, let alone gave a reasonable explanation. Whatever the cause for this great U.S. cavalry leader not to attack nor attempt an organized retreat, why didn't Custer at least establish a sound defensive position? Had he done so, Major Reno, Captain Benteen and their troops would have recognized it when they came on the scene after the battle, and there would be some record of it along with confirmation in the testimony of the Indians.

General Phil Sheridan said, "If Custer could have reached any position susceptible of defense he could have defended himself, but none offered itself in the choppy and broken ravines..."[5] This statement was made in 1876. However, Indian testimony doesn't support the idea that, initially, such a defensive position could not have been reached or established.

I proceeded to search for answers by examining authors' viewpoints in articles and books on Custer and the Battle of the Little Big Horn. I have not found any complete accounts that were satisfactory. I did gain respect for many of these writers, and I would agree with much of their presentations; but they either did not deal with my primary concerns, or there was a lack of cohesion necessary for what I considered to be logical and objective conclusions.

I believe the prerequisite to understanding what happened to General Custer and his command has to be an explanation of why General Custer did not attempt an attack on the Indian encampment by the five companies under his direct command. There was no way he could defeat the Indians or come to the support of Major Reno without doing so. It was recognized that for a cavalry to succeed it must attack. General Custer not only supported such an attack philosophy, he epitomized the type of leader necessary to carry it out. General Custer knew he was moving against an extremely large number of Indians, but this hadn't deterred him because he believed his 7th Cavalry could defeat the whole Sioux nation. **Yet he didn't attack.**

As Richard Hardorff points out, "Any attempt to reconstruct the Custer battle should naturally begin with the route followed by his troops."[6] The time and the questions raised prior to the division of the command enhanced Custer's motivation and, at least from his standpoint, the need to attack. Those earlier events and views were well authenticated, whereas those arising after the division of the command were not, so the latter were the ones which solicited my attention.

We know the last official recorded time by Lieutenant Wallace was at 12:05 P.M.* This was after they crossed the divide between the Rosebud and the Little Bighorn rivers, and the division of the command took place. The regiment was divided into battalions. Captain Benteen's consisted of three companies or troops: H, D, and K. Captain Benteen and Lieutenant Gibson were in command of H; Captain Weir and Lieutenant Edgerly with D; Lieutenant Godfrey was the officer in charge of K. After the division Captain Benteen's battalion moved out to the south toward Wolf Mts . . . and were told to "pitch in" to whatever Indians they met. Major Reno was assigned a battalion made up of Company M under Captain French; Company A, Captain Moylan and Lieutenant DeRudio; Company G, Lieutenants McIntosh and Wallace; and the battalion included the Indian scouts under Lieutenants Varnum and Hare, the interpreter Girard, Lieutenant Hodgson was Acting Adjutant, and Doctors DeWolf and Porter were the medical officers. The pack-train was commanded by Lieutenant Mathey and they were escorted by Company B, with Captain McDougall in charge. The other five companies were commanded by General Custer and were made up of Company I, Captain Keogh and Lieutenant Porter; Company F, Captain Yates and Lieutenant Reily; Company C, Captain Tom Custer and Lieutenant Harrington; Company E, Lieutenants Smith and Sturgis; Company L, Lieutenants Calhoun and Crittenden; Lieutenant Cooke was the Adjutant, and Captain G. E. Lord was the medical officer. Custer's command was generally believed to have been divided into two battalions, though <u>when</u> it was divided is subject to different interpretations. It could have happened at the division of the command, or shortly after Martin was sent back with his message to Captain Benteen. Captain Yates was in charge of a battalion made up of Companies F, C, and E; Captain Keogh was assigned Company L under Lieutenants Calhoun and Crittenden, along with his own Company I. Some believe C Company was under Captain Keogh's command rather than that of Captain Yates.

After Captain Benteen's battalion had left, Major Reno's battalion, and what I will refer to as General Custer's command, moved down what is now called Reno Creek. (Prior to the battle it was called Ash Creek or Sundance Creek.) They came to what has become known as the Lone Tepee. This was a burial tepee for a Sioux warrior who had died from wounds received at the Battle of the Rosebud approximately a week earlier. The time, according to John Gray in his book, *Centennial Campaign,* was now 2:07 P.M. Dr. Kuhlman estimated it between 2:10 and 2:15. Though this particular difference is not too important, it does illustrate the problem of estimating time. We have an established official time and then a move to a generally agreed on location; yet we have a difference of as much as eight minutes. Time is very important in ascertaining and correlating events. At a controlled gallop or canter, depending on the terrain, a horse could move a mile or more if one were to use the eight minute variance. General Miles said that at a slow or hand gallop he moved from Reno's position on the bluff to where Custer's body was found – in about 10 or 15 minutes. This is a distance of at least four miles. Even though his timing could be considered fast, a lot could happen in a few minutes. Differences in timing and distance estimates abound in testimony. They could have made a profound difference on what General Custer saw and the action he then took.

After the last official time, both the officers and the men had other things on their mind. They were not concerned with what time it was, where something happened, or what the distance between certain places was, until days,

---

*As I brought out in my book, *The Custer Controversy – A Critical Analysis*, a major cover-up at the Reno Court was changing the official time of the division of the command from 10:05 to 12:05. At the time I wrote this original manuscript I was not aware of the change. However, from the questions I pose one can see how they led to my eventual recognition that there had to be a cover-up.

months, or longer following the battle. Indians were not familiar with the white man's way of keeping time or measuring distance; their knowledge or ability to relate events in this way would not have taken place until long after the event.

Since becoming interested in this issue, I, in my own riding at home, have tried to judge the time it took and the distance traveled. Even with the aid of quarter and section lines, this task is extremely difficult. Also, after returning home from the battlefield and having been specifically concerned with distance while there, I would attempt to visualize the space between main landmarks such as Reno Hill and Weir Point, but fail to give a reliable estimate. The problem would only be worse between ephemeral points. Time and distance, in most cases, had to be a matter of opinion, thus subject to question and cross-examination.

Colonel Graham, in a letter to Captain Carter:

> You know how long military movements take. Figure it out. Could it have taken less than fifteen or twenty minutes to do the things he did?[7]

Captain Carter declared in a letter to Colonel Graham:

> I kept the time or tried to, in our Mexican raid and have said we halted to cut off the packs only a few minutes. It must have been nearly an hour if not more. Time goes "blewy" when men are exhausted and are marching night and day.[8]

This difficulty and the method with which a time sequence was often established, is best described by Lieutenant Varnum, who was the officer in charge of Custer's scouts. At the Reno Court of Inquiry, in answer to the question as to what hour of the day Major Reno's command separated from General Custer's column with orders to attack the Indians, Varnum said:

> Any statement I may make in regard to time would be a guess on my part. I have very little to base an opinion of time upon unless I connect it with someone else's statement. I thought of it a great deal, and I think it must have been two o'clock. I base my opinion a good deal on other people's opinions, compared with my own as to time.[9]

This is why we have to analyze a time sequence, and not just accept someone's testimony. Many of the time references were most certainly developed in the manner described by Varnum.

Today it is extremely hard to pass judgement on the testimony taken years ago. We cannot know these men or women, so rely on the writers who did to accurately portray their character. We should be careful even then. From our knowledge of people and the number of times we have misjudged them, we learn how evaluations of character can be misleading. As the news of Custer's defeat swept the country, special attention was paid to the participants. Newspapers looked for sensational stories, and certainly many were created. They probed for the reasons why the Indians could have inflicted such a defeat on General Custer and his elite 7th Cavalry. This search led to rationalizing and the need for scapegoats. Some attempted to blame Custer, but to many he was a hero; so the blame was transferred to Major Reno, and to a lesser extent Captain Benteen. Through all of this, it was only natural that stories were exaggerated, deeds were enhanced and cover-ups took place. I believe the Reno Court of Inquiry was particularly vulnerable to such deceptions, and since the testimony has been the source of many of the conflicting views, special attention should be used in analyzing those proceedings.

If it is hard to judge the testimony of whites, it is even harder to judge that of the Indians. These difficulties are aptly brought out by Robert Utley and Edgar Stewart. They should be recognized by any student of the battle.

Robert Utley:

> . . . very few writers indeed, have succeeded in doing more then make themselves look silly . . . the rest failed because they lacked insight into the character of Indian testimony and the manifold influences that produced distortion, incoherence and falsehood.
>
> This result sprang mainly from failure of white interrogators and red witnesses to achieve a meeting of the minds, especially when, as was usually the case, a third mind, that of an interpreter, intervened. Exact meaning is extremely difficult to convey from one language to another, and the average Sioux or Cheyenne interpreter was scarcely proficient in the science . . .
>
> The character and disposition of the Indian himself offered even greater obstacles. When telling his story, the Indian emitted a disconcerting jumble of ephemeral, non-chronological impressions. He skipped indiscriminately from one incident to another without regard to time or place. To the white mind the product was incoherence at its worst. There was the tendency to portray only what the individual narrator saw personally as applying to the battle as a whole. There was, finally, the inescapable truth that the American Indian was a showman and braggart. Boasting of great deeds in war was a time-honored custom that formed part of tribal ceremonies. Too often, as a result, the questioner was told what he wanted to hear, heavily laden with allusions to grandiose feats of heroism, instead of what actually happened.
>
> Beyond all this, Indian participants had a very sound

reason for not telling the whole truth, for now that the white man once more had them in his power, many undeniably feared reprisals.[10]

Edgar Stewart:

> The stories of the Indians who were in the hostile camp suffer from several drawbacks recorded at various times after the events, real and assumed, and by pronounced rationalization. For the Indian had learned early and from bitter experience that it was much better for him to tell what he knew his auditors wanted to hear, and if he didn't know, to keep still. Moreover many of the Indians were afraid of being punished should they admit taking part in the battle in which the Long Hair lost his life. Also, we must not forget that the Indian in a battle is an individualist and not being bound to any particular group, is free to come and go as he pleases. Indians do not have commanders and sub commanders as the white man does. Each tribe had its various warrior societies, each of whom had its chief and sub-chiefs. Some of them were great warriors, but in battle they could not give an order and have it obeyed ...
>
> Given these limitations, it is obvious that the Indians sees a battle from the point of view of an individual ... The Indian also suffers from the all too human tendency to magnify his own part in the proceedings, unless he deems it expedient for reasons of personal safety to deny participating altogether ... as a result, there are many white students of the battle who will give little credence to the hostile accounts, forgetting that in this case the Indians alone know, and also that in many ways their stories are no more unreliable than those of the white soldiers. In both cases a wholesome amount of skepticism is the essential ingredient of consideration.[11]

In attempting to determine what happened to General Custer, I believe it is necessary to establish a postulate for which you are seeking an answer. In my case that would be: Did Custer, with his five companies, launch a major attack against the Indian village? My decision must be able to provide a logical explanation not only for this question, but for the secondary factors of whether there were signs of an organized retreat or a sound defense. These answers must be able to relate to testimony, artifacts and logic.

I will begin by attempting to answer the following questions: When and where did Custer give Major Reno his orders to attack? How long did it take Major Reno to reach Ford A, cross it, reform and be ready to move down the valley? Did Custer see Reno when Custer reached the ridge? Did Custer's command move along the ridge? Did he view the valley from Weir Point? Did General Custer see Major Reno go into action? Did Custer move down Cedar Coulee? Where did Sergeant Kanipe and Trumpeter Martin leave General Custer?

These are some of the important issues to be resolved. Since so many of the explanations are tied up with testimony given at the Reno Court of Inquiry, special attention will be given to those proceedings.

I know my answers will be conjectural, but my principal criticism has been that many of these questions have not been asked – or when asked, answers have been assumed, or statements used selectively because it supported someone's theory, with no attempt made to explain why conflicting testimony was rejected. The view I present may not be what actually happened to General Custer, but it will be supported by testimony, artifacts and logic. Above all else, I will strive to make it consistent throughout.

Dr. Kuhlman expressed several opinions on what he believed was necessary to find the answer to what happened to General Custer. He said:

> ... I have sought to explain, in a systematic way, the why of the battle, not so much by dint of quotation from the sources as by subjecting these sources to a rigid analysis in order to discover what they seem to spell after all definite inconsistencies have been canceled out. It is a large order that leaves ample room for self-deception and other types of error. Sustained analysis calls for close attention and the habit of logical thinking as well as an open mind, a mind as far as humanly possible unencumbered with irrevocable convictions.[12]

I would also agree with Dr. Kuhlman that to understand why Custer, Reno, Benteen or any of the troop commanders did what they did, we must in imagination "ride at their elbows" and try to see what they saw at any given time and place. I may not know what Custer said or thought as he went along, but I believe his desire to defeat the Indians – for a myriad of reasons – had to be uppermost in his mind. So a consideration of his actions must take into account this primary motivation. When there is any doubt as to what Custer did, one should not accept a contradictory conjectural rationale. This has been done too many times, and it results in a weak attempt to blend time periods, testimony and actions.

My first priority was to correlate Reno's and Custer's movements after Reno received his attack orders. Where did they separate? How long did it take Major Reno to reach the ford, cross, move through the timber, reform and start his move down the valley? Where was Custer during this time? Testimony and writers' theories have presented varying descriptions of these questions.

OVERVIEW

Time is an essential ingredient; but after the official recorded time of 12:05 made by Lieutenant Wallace denoting the halt with the division of command following, there are only two reliable observations, and one of these is suspect. Wallace said it was shortly after 2:00 when Major Reno was summoned by General Custer and Reno crossed over Ash Creek; this time is usually considered fairly accurate. Wallace's term of reference does reveal other problems of analysis. What is meant by subjective terms as "shortly after," "not long," or "about that time"? Lieutenant Godfrey's recollection of 4:20 is usually accepted as the time Captain Benteen's battalion joined Major Reno on the bluff, or when the packs arrived, but this was merely Godfrey's opinion, formulated some time after the battle.

It is necessary to adopt some sort of timing reference, but frequently they are formed from opinions expressed by participants, making them inflexible; yet events are often placed within these time frames. Is it correct to say Major Reno had crossed Ford A, reformed and started his move down the valley by 3:05? Accepting or rejecting such time reference can change the whole picture of the events that followed, whereas the time is secondary to the correlation of events. One should also remember the perspectives on time as expressed by Lieutenant Varnum, Colonel Graham, and Captain Carter. The primary necessity is to accept a basic time reference and then attempt to correlate action and time between battalions, events and individuals.

John Gray, in his book, *Centennial Campaign*, and Dr. Kuhlman in *Legend into History*, give two of the more accepted time outlines. General Edgerly, in writing to Colonel Graham years after the battle, said the division of command took place about 10 A.M., whereas the official time is some two hours later. Captain Benteen said he returned to the main trail by 1 P.M., and although this time is accepted by duBois, most writers believe it would actually have been 2 o'clock. Benteen said his battalion moved at a trot, except for watering his horses at the morass, until they reached the point where they saw Major Reno. Edgerly said they went at a walk from the morass to the Lone Tepee. Different estimates of the distance Benteen traveled on his excursion to the left range from 4 to 14 miles. How fast should you judge that a cavalry would travel at a walk, trot or gallop, and would it be approximately correct to use that rate in estimating the 7th Cavalry's movement on that fateful day? John Gray said the standard time it would take to travel a mile at a walk would be 20 minutes, at a trot 10 minutes, and at a gallop roughly 7 1/2 minutes. DuBois, on the other hand, said that at a walk a cavalry would cover a mile in 15 minutes, at a trot in 7 1/2 and at a gallop in 5 minutes. General Miles said he walked his horse from Reno's entrenchment to where Custer's body was found in 30 minutes, and this distance is usually considered to be at least 4 miles. This would have been twice as fast as duBois had a cavalry moving at a walk, and duBois used a faster time than John Gray. General Miles said he could have covered the distance in 10 to 15 minutes at a slow or hand gallop. How much difference would the terrain make? How do you figure in the distance the horses have already traveled or their condition? How do you estimate the time to cross a stream 30 feet wide compared to 40 feet? Two feet deep or three feet? If the horses drink, how much more time is involved? These and numerous other factors could alter the time and the scenario of events.

John Gray has General Custer at the Lone Tepee at 2:07; Dr. Kuhlman at 2:10 to 2:15. John Gray puts Benteen at the Tepee at 3:13, while Dr. Kuhlman has him there at 3:35; both have Reno reaching the ford at 2:50. The distance from the divide to the morass is 4 miles by Dr. Kuhlman's estimate and 4 1/2 by John Gray's; Dr. Kuhlman has Major Reno receiving his attack orders at the Lone Tepee while John Gray has the orders being given some three miles further. All these differences suggest that though one should adopt a time reference, it is necessary to remain flexible and not depend too much on time and distance measurements unless there is a definite linkage with testimony and events.

My attempt to determine the time and place Major Reno received his attack orders led me to doubt some generally accepted assumptions. I have already pointed out that I agree with Dr. Kuhlman's concept that one should "... in imagination ride at their elbow and try to see what they saw at any given time and place." This is what I have tried to do.

Various questions arose concerning views which, because of their acceptance, have tainted the conclusions reached as to what brought about Custer's defeat. It is generally assumed that Custer did not formulate any general plan of attack until he passed the Lone Tepee; until then he supposedly did not know where the Indian village was located. Edgar Stewart said it was obvious Custer felt that the Indian encampment was located at the site of the Lone Tepee. It, of course, had been prior to the 24th, but I don't believe there is any reason to think Custer thought it was still there on the morning of the 25th. The point is then made that Major Reno had received his orders and was moving out when Lieutenant Varnum, who had been scouting ahead of the column, reported to General Custer, notifying him of a village and the proximity of a large number of Indians. This, according to Stewart, was the first reliable information Custer received on the general location of the Indian camp. Stewart maintains that at the time of the division of the command, no village had been sighted and no notable number of hostiles had been seen, and so there was obviously no plan of battle in Custer's mind; indeed, there couldn't have been any because he had not established the position or the strength of the enemy. Colonel Graham also thought Custer had no plan of battle and his information on the enemy was insufficient for him to have one until after Girard's sightings near the Lone Tepee. It was then that Custer gave Major Reno his orders to attack, and indicated that he would support him. Colonel Graham would have agreed with Major Reno that at that time, General Custer planned to follow him. It wasn't until Lieutenant Cooke came back with his message from Girard that Custer changed his plan. This has been the generally accepted version of what took place and what Custer had in mind from the division of command until either Varnum's report or Cooke's message.

This scenario is entirely possible, but I believe it is open to much more criticism than it has been subjected to. One of the first things that began to bother me were the orders given by Custer and received by Major Reno and Captain Benteen. Following the battle these orders played an essential part in the attempt to synchronize the events that were deemed necessary to protect the conduct and the actions taken by Reno and Benteen. The debate over whether General Custer did or didn't follow the orders of General Terry was important at the time, and generated a great deal of controversy in official circles as well as with the general public. But today, this issue has assumed a minor role and is important mainly as a discussion topic.

The orders that were actually given by General Custer would depend on what he believed as he moved toward the Little Bighorn. My misgivings on the subject were: Can I really imagine that General Custer traveled for some three hours without formulating any plan of action, although he realized he would be coming in contact with the enemy that day? Can we accept the supposition that Custer did not know where the general location of the Indian encampment was or its relative size? Could this be possible when Custer is usually considered one of the most competent military leaders of that period, with a good knowledge of Indians, and a respect for his scouts and the information they brought him?

Is it conceivable that Custer really did not associate or recognize from the remains of the Indian villages they had been passing, the general size of the Indian encampment they were now approaching? Mr. James Gitchell in the *Billings Gazette*, Aug. 13, 1933, believes that Custer knew there were 13 thousand Indians ahead. Gitchell also points out that Custer was "too astute and experienced on Indian fights not to have read the message so plainly pictured in the various Indian camps that the regiment had passed." According to Robert Utley, on June 23 the command passed through three abandoned campsites, and on the 24th through several others. Supposedly, Custer didn't realize these were continuous campsites and not individual ones. This may be true, but with the reports and the premonition of the scouts, it seems that Custer would have recognized the immensity of the Indian camp lying somewhere ahead.

Fred Dustin points out:

> . . . From the account of William Jackson, the young Pikuni scout, it seems that not only Bloody Knife but also Reynolds had presentiments of their coming fate. The former said to the scouts that it was as he had told Custer; this great gathering was too many for them, but he would not believe it; . . ." We are going to have a big fight, a losing fight. I know what is to happen to me . . . I shall not see the set of the sun." Jackson said that Bloody Knife's words chilled them, and that he saw Reynolds nod his head in agreement with them, tomorrow will be the end for me, too." and that he opened his war sack and began dividing his outfit, . . . This scene related by Jackson seems to have taken place the night before at the last halt when Varnum and his party left for the Crow's Nest.[13]

Dustin also observes that:

> . . . There was no lack of competent scouts: Bouyer and the Crows were the best guides and keenest observers in that whole region. It was their own hunting grounds and here they had made and received foray after foray, and were at home on every mile of territory. Neither Rees nor Crows were in the least deluded as to numbers of Dakota, for after their examinations of the abandoned campgrounds, they well knew that not far ahead there were probably two thousand warriors with their families, who, while they were simply wishing to be left alone, were not at all unready for another fight.[14]

We know Varnum and some of the scouts went to the Crow's Nest the night of the 24th, and in the early morning of the 25th saw the smoke of the village and the pony herds. Custer was informed of the sightings. He climbed up and viewed the valley through his glasses, but was supposedly unable to make out the village; thus he was skeptical of what was reported. Coughlin, in the *Cavalry Journal*, wrote that Bouyer told Custer it was the largest village which had ever collected in the Northwest, and reminded him that Bouyer had known these Indians for over thirty years.[15]

Custer had been warned by Bloody Knife, Girard, Bouyer, Reynolds and the Crow scouts that the biggest gathering of Indians they had ever seen was ahead of him. Custer, according to the *Oregon Journal*, Aug. 3, 1923, told his officers that "the largest Indian camp on the North American continent is ahead and I am going to attack it."

White Man Runs Him, a Crow scout, said he told Custer of the smoke they had seen coming from the Sioux camp. This was at the Crow's Nest. When Custer saw the village he told the Crows, "these people are very troublesome and bother the Crows and the white people. I am going to teach them a lesson today. I will whip them and will build a fort at the junction where the Little Horn flows into the Big Horn, and you Crows may then live in peace."[16] White Man Runs Him said he would have advised Custer to wait and attack the camp at night, but since they had already been observed by some Sioux, he believed they couldn't delay. The inference from this exchange is that the camp's general location was acknowledged by Custer. Red Star said that although Custer didn't see the camp at first, he later nodded to Charlie Reynolds indicating that he did.

Considering these and other similar reports, it is difficult for me to imagine Custer moving to the divide and separating his troops without considering the approximate location of the Indian camp. I cannot believe he thought it was in the location of the Lone Tepee. Custer would have known he would be facing an exceptionally large number of warriors. It is more erroneous to take the position that Custer ignored all the signs, warnings and premonitions, than it is to assume that although he was skeptical, he realized they were probably right, and at least planned accordingly. I think uppermost in his mind would have been the fear of the Indians escaping once he knew his troops had been observed. This seems to have been a predominant worry of most commanders when moving against the Indians. It was reflected in the overall plan the military was using to defeat the Sioux and bring them into the reservations. Lieutenant Edgerly, in a statement made in August of 1881, said, "The idea was that the Indians would not stand against a whole regiment of cavalry, and that as soon as they learned of our advance they would try to get away from us."[17] In this same report, Edgerly said that when Custer came down from the Crow's Nest he told the officers that the scouts had chased a small number of Indians, who had gotten away and gone in the direction of the Indian camp. Here again is a reference to the camp after Custer had viewed it and received the reports from the scouts as to where the camp was located. Although Custer could have been using the word "camp" in the context of its general direction toward the Little Bighorn, it would not have diminished his need to develop a plan of attack.

I believe Benteen's remarks are the main reason why writers have accepted the idea that Custer was unaware of the size or whereabouts of the camp. At the Reno Court of Inquiry Benteen reported, "General Custer told us that he had just come down from the mountain. He gave it to us as his belief that they were mistaken, that there were not Indians there . . ."[18] When cross-examined, Benteen said, ". . . if there had been any plan of battle, enough of that plan would have been communicated to me so that I would have known what to do under certain circumstances. Not having done that, I do not believe there was any plan. In General Custer's mind there was a belief that there were no Indians nor any village."[19]

General Godfrey, when informed by Colonel Graham of the statements given by Major Reno and Captain Benteen at the Reno Court of Inquiry to the effect that Custer did not know the location of the Indian camp, said, "I confess to considerable surprise that Reno and Benteen had testified at the Court of Inquiry that Custer expressed a disbelief in the near proximity of the village at that time. . . . I feel perfectly sure that such an expression of disbelief from the General would have made an unforgettable impression on my mind. . . . At all events, the General must have accepted the scouts' point of view, because he made their location of the village his objective."[20]

Even without Godfrey's denial of Custer's ignorance, I don't know what additional orders Benteen would have thought necessary to meet these exigencies. He was to find the valley of the Little Bighorn; if the Indians were attempting to escape he was expected to prevent it, if at all possible. He was to "pitch in" to any Indians. If he saw Indian villages he would know he should inform Custer. Benteen said his move was senseless because the Indians were farther downstream, where their presence had been reported by the scouts. He knew he wouldn't meet any Indians. Since Benteen saw the command moving down Ash Creek towards the Little Bighorn and in the direction of the Indian camp, why didn't Benteen take on an angle that would have brought him to the valley and nearer to where he knew the Indian camp to be? Instead, he not only violated orders but took an oblique direction away from the Little Bighorn, one that placed him miles behind the rest of the command. The position he took is actually more of an indictment of himself than it is of General Custer.

Several years after the battle Benteen wrote in what is now referred to as the "Benteen Narrative":

General Custer notified us that he had been on the mountain to the left, where our scouts(Crows) were all the night; that they had told him thru ... the interpreter, that they could see dust, Indians and ponies, and all that. He could see nothing through the old telescopic glass they had and didn't believe there was anything to be seen, now, strange perhaps to say, I did believe it: – another "Pre." I knew it, because, why, I'd sooner trust the sharp eye of an Indian than to trust a pretty good binocular that I always carried; and I'd gotten that from experience. However, 'twasn't my "chip in," so I said nothing.[21]

After the return from the Crow's Nest, other accounts of Custer's reaction to the warnings and sighting by the Crows suggest that although he did not see what they saw, and although he may have been skeptical, he did not say they were wrong. I believe his response to the warnings about the size of the Indian village and the number of warriors he would be facing had to do with his rejection of their fears that he could not defeat the Indians. This view is borne out by his taunting of the scouts; not that he didn't realize he would be going against, as he is credited with saying, "the largest Indian camp on the North American continent." He recognized that he would be facing a much larger force of Indians than the number of men he had in his 7th Cavalry.

The famous letter of General James Brisbin to General Godfrey also supports the fact that Custer realized, in a general sense, the large number of Indians his men would be opposing.

Brisbin wrote:

> ... That Custer knew the strength of the Indians I know, for at the mouth of the Rosebud, Gibbon and I had laid for days with our commands, and had picketed one side of the Yellowstone, while they picketed the other. ... Bradley (back from scouting) said their camp (the Indians), was 7 miles long up the Rosebud, and we all put them at l000 to a mile or 5000 souls, with 3000 fighting men, as they did not seem to have many squaws and children with them. All this Custer knew, for I told him about it, and cautioned him to be careful. It was I who suggested to Terry the putting of all the cavalry together and going himself in command ...
>
> ... when I went up to him, Custer) and said:
> "General, do you feel quite strong enough with your Seventh Cavalry to handle all the Indians you may meet? If not, myself and officers will be most happy to take service with you."
>
> He replied briskly, "The Seventh can handle anything it meets."[22]

It is difficult for me to imagine Custer not having a general plan, even if not yet consumated, by the time he crossed the divide. With all the reports that he had received, he would have been devising some sort of strategy. The division of his command, by itself, supports such a contention.

If one assumes Custer realized the probability his scouts were right and the Indian camp was located across the Little Bighorn in the general location of where the smoke and the pony herds were reported that morning, then what he did seems credible. He divided his regiment into three main fighting battalions. It is understandable, in fact one could say necessary, that he sent troops to the left because he would be concerned with the possibility of Indians escaping or setting up an ambush. Custer also would have realized that there could be Indian camps to the left of where he believed the main camp was situated. This he should have learned from the Battle of the Washita. If Benteen's battalion did not run into any Indians or their camps, they would then move down the valley of the Little Bighorn and engage in the attack on the Indian village. Custer would have wanted a good sized company to protect the packs because they couldn't be expected to keep up with the rest of the command, so he had additional men assigned to Captain McDougall's company. The other main battalions under Major Reno and General Custer would move down Ash Creek at a slow pace, in order for Benteen's battalion to have time to reach the valley of the Little Bighorn. In case Benteen ran into trouble they could come to his aid. If Benteen didn't encounter any Indians – which I don't believe Custer thought they would – then Benteen would support the attack by Major Reno and General Custer.

It doesn't require the knowledge of hindsight to visualize Custer formulating such a plan. In all probability, he conceived the plan when he divided his command. As he neared the Little Bighorn, Custer would have realized that if the terrain permitted and no Indians or camps to the south had been reported, Benteen would be coming down the valley. He would then send Major Reno across the Little Bighorn, and he himself would move along the east side and attempt a flanking attack. This would not only help in defeating the Indians, but would prevent them from escaping to the south and west. Those Indians that did escape to the west would run into General Crook's troops – which Custer did not realize had been forced to withdraw by these same Indians. If the Indians moved to the Bighorn, they would encounter General Terry and Colonel Gibbon.

As Cyrus Brady points out, Custer's plan was entirely simple:

> Reno was to attack the end of the village. Benteen was to sweep around and fall on the left of it, Custer on the

OVERVIEW

right. The tactics in the main were those which had been used so successfully in the Battle of the Washita, and were much in vogue among our Indian fighters during the Indian wars.[23]

With all the signs and information available to Custer, it is feasible that he formulated such a plan or some other strategy. The main reason others subscribe to the theory that he didn't apparently results not only from Captain Benteen's testimony that Custer didn't think there was a significant number of Indians at that location, but also from Reno's and Benteen's orders as they reported them. One should also note that the main differences as to the content of these orders were expressed by enlisted men.

I think it is quite clear to any student of history that whether from a military, governmental, business or personal standpoint, if the end product is justifiable then the means to achieve it are justified as well, even if the position may be considered unethical. I certainly believe such an attitude played a primary role in this case, not only from the military standpoint (the defense of Major Reno), but also in Benteen's need to rationalize his conduct.

Captain Benteen is probably the most outstanding character involved in the battle. He was hard-nosed, embittered, sarcastic, biting and exceptionally courageous. He looked down on most people's abilities, but supported the ordinary soldier and had more sympathy for the Indians than most other officers. He didn't like Custer for numerous reasons, but I can't see this preventing him from carrying out what he would conceive to be his orders or duty. In that same sense, I can't picture him obeying an order just because it was an order. Certainly he was a strong, unique character. I also believe he would evade, distort or lie if he thought it was necessary to achieve what he considered to be a justifiable end. I don't think there is any question that his orders came to be considered such a means – by the military, Major Reno and Captain Benteen – but to what extent is the key question.

General Custer did halt the regiment after they crossed the divide between the Rosebud and the Little Bighorn River. The time was approximately 12:05, and, shortly after, Custer divided his command into three main battalions. Captain Benteen was in charge of one battalion made up of three companies. He was given his orders and Benteen said he moved out without hearing how the rest of the command was divided or what their orders were. He was told to take his battalion and move to the left. Three companies were assigned to Major Reno, and five companies made up the troops under the direct control of General Custer. The pack train was put in charge of Lieutenant Mathey and was to be protected by Company B under Captain McDougall.

Benteen, at the Reno Court of Inquiry, said his orders were to proceed to a line of bluffs about 4 or 5 miles away. He had gone about a mile when he received additional orders to go on to the second line of bluffs. About a mile further (in his narrative he would say 15 to 20 minutes later) he received additional orders through the Sergeant Major: If he saw nothing from the second line he was to go into the valley, and then the next. Benteen said he moved at a trot, except when watering his horses after he got back on the main trail. He was adamant that no orders were ever sent to join Reno's command; in fact, he didn't even know Reno had a command because he departed before that decision was announced. In answer to numerous questions, he denied having any instructions to support Reno; neither from the left nor rear. He told the court he was "valley hunting."

Lieutenant Godfrey, who commanded K Company in Benteen's battalion, said he knew nothing of Benteen's orders. Nor did he ever mention the other orders Benteen received while on his jaunt to the left and back to the main trail. Lieutenant Edgerly of Company D did mention the additional orders Captain Benteen received, but he did not know where it happened or what they were. Company D was led by Captain Weir, who died before the Reno Court of Inquiry convened.

Colonel Graham, in his book, *The Custer Myth*, included a manuscript by Benteen, found among Benteen's papers after his death. In it Benteen states his orders, much the same as he gave them at the Reno Court. The first order he received, after moving out, was brought by the Chief Trumpeter; the second, some 15 or 20 minutes later, was through the Sergeant Major. If nothing was seen from the second line of bluffs, the order stated, he was to go on until he came to a valley. Again, the "pitch in" was to be used if he saw any Indians.

Note that Captain Benteen's battalion is usually said to have moved out at about 12:15. According to Benteen, they arrived back on the trail by one o'clock, though it is assumed he meant two o'clock. The question as to how far Benteen actually travelled on his excursion to the left has been a subject of dispute. Roger Darling, in his book, *Benteen's Scout*, has probably done the most extensive work on the route and the terrain Benteen would have followed. Benteen said:

> . . . My real, simon-pure straight orders were to hunt that valley; but I didn't know where the valley was, and thought that perhaps an opportunity might happen later

to search for it, but just then I believed I hadn't time to do it. So, shouldering the responsibility of not having found the valley, I pitched off with the battalion at a right oblique to reach the trail Custer's column had followed . . .[24]

Benteen communicated through letters with Theodore Goldin, a lawyer in Janesville, Wisconsin, who had been a private in C Company during the battle. In a letter dated Feb. 24, 1892, Benteen wrote:

> . . . Now if I had carried out to the letter the last order brought to me from General Custer by the Sergeant Major of the regiment – which was, to the effect, that if from the furtherest line of bluffs which we then saw, I could not see the valley – no particular valley specified – to keep on until I came to a valley (or perhaps the valley) to pitch into anything I might come across and notify them at once. Now I don't know how much farther I should have had to go in the direction I was headed to have found the valley of the Little Big Horn river, but think perhaps that six or seven miles more would have brought me to it. What I want you to deduce from this is: supposing I had found up that valley that Reno and Custer found down the river – how in the name of common sense was Gen'l Custer to get back to where I was in time to keep the troops from being chewed up as it were by the combined reds?[25]

Benteen, in a letter to his wife, July 2, 1876, said:

> . . . about 15 miles from an Indian village, the whereabouts of which he did not know exactly, I was ordered with 3 Co's., D, H, and K, to go to the left for the purpose of hunting for the valley of the river – Indian camp – or anything I could find. I found nothing, and after marching 10 miles or so in pursuit of the same determined to return to Custer's trail . . .[26]

Benteen had given many conflicting statements, but from the letters to his wife and Goldin, and from his report to Brininstool, there should be no question that his orders included a search for a valley; that could only be the valley of the Little Bighorn. Benteen said his orders told him if he didn't find any Indians or the valley itself, he was to return to the main trail. Yet in his "own story" he implied he violated orders in returning to the main trail, but would "shoulder" that responsibility. He also implied this when he said that he could have gone on looking for a valley indefinitely. In other words, Benteen had orders to search for the valley of the Little Bighorn, and by turning back, he wasn't following orders. In his letter to Goldin, he said it might have been six or seven miles further; but even then, depending on how far he actually went and whether he had taken the proper angle to reach the rest of the command, he could have traveled a shorter distance than he did and in much less time.

What raises suspicion is why Custer would send two messengers with much the same orders, and yet didn't send a messenger (according to the predominant view) when he supposedly found out the location of the camp or when he gave Reno his instructions to attack. I can see Custer sending the first messenger, as he may have learned from Bouyer, Varnum, some other scout or from observing the topography, that he would want Benteen to go beyond the first line of bluffs and proceed to the valley of the Little Bighorn. Custer may have thought his original orders were too restrictive. Those orders might have said that if Benteen saw no Indians beyond the bluff he could return to the main trail. But Custer soon realized that the bluffs extended to the valley, and by moving to the valley Benteen would have been in a position to prevent any surprise Indian attack from the south. If Benteen saw no Indians or encampments, he could then move down the valley in support of the rest of the command. But why would Custer have sent a second messenger so soon after that, as Benteen indicated, with basically the same message as the first? I also wonder if the Arikara, Stabbed, was sent with the Sergeant Major, or if Custer dispatched another messenger. Stabbed mentioned going to the left with a message, and Walter Camp thought it was to Benteen. I doubt if Stabbed could speak effective English, so even if it was a written message he would have accompanied a soldier.

In a letter, Lieutenant Gibson of Benteen's company said the battalion was ordered to the left in an attempt to discover whether any Indians were trying to escape up the valley of the Little Bighorn. Since Gibson was the officer sent ahead to the top of the bluffs, it would seem that he would have known what they were looking for. According to Gibson's letter published in the *New York Herald*, August 8, 1876,[27] 'if they satisfied themselves that the Sioux were not moving in that direction they were to rejoin the main command as soon as possible.'

The important question would have been what route to choose: going to and down the Little Bighorn, or returning to the main trail? It would seem foolish for Custer to want him to return to the main trail by going back to it, rather than in the direction that the primary command was moving. I think Custer would have realized that by the time Benteen reached the valley, he and Major Reno should have been in a position to launch their attack. By moving down the valley, Benteen could prevent the Indians from escaping in that direction, as well as being situated so that he could support the attack on the Indian villages.

OVERVIEW

Roger Darling, in his book *Benteen's Scout*, points out that Benteen could have seen Reno or Custer's troops from Ridge B (as noted on Darling's map of Benteen's route), down what Darling refers to as "a window of Valley 2."[28] Benteen should then have realized from the angle of the valley that Reno and Custer were moving ahead of his position. Darling believes Benteen was concerned at that time with the length of his excursion, as he had not gone that far and had no noteworthy intelligence to report. Not too far ahead is a ridge, referred to on Darling's map as Ridge C. Benteen decided to send Lieutenant Gibson to this ridge while Benteen and his battalion moved slowly down Valley 3. This would provide the horses and troops with a breather. Gibson then went to Ridge C, and in a letter to Godfrey in 1908, said that he mounted the ridgeline and had a very clear view of the Little Bighorn Valley. Thus, Darling maintains, "The last high ridge had been reached. At last Gibson had a clear and unobstructed view to the west and the Little Bighorn Valley." Gibson should then have reported his findings to Benteen. According to Darling, Benteen now had his first reliable evidence concerning the Indians; he then made his decision to return to the trail by moving on down Valley 3. This action had him taking a right oblique and reaching Reno Creek just above the morass.

In attempting to analyze Benteen's movement and decisions, the following observations by Darling should be mentioned:

> Yet, something in that ferment of thought was causing Benteen to form rigid conceptions about the geographical features in the scout area. He expressed the idea later that he knew the Indians had "too much sense to go into such rough ground": as was now confronting him at Ridge B. (fn. 59 – Kuhlman, op.cit., 82, Graham, *Myth*, 180). But this could only have been a false rationalization entrenched by later negative thinking about that day, for the ground was not "rough" except at the high ridge lines which the battalion had encountered only briefly in crossing the ridge. The Indians had moved directly through these very same valleys going to their camp along the Little Big Horn River from the fight with General Crook on the Rosebud only days before. The Indians had also camped in these valleys.[29]

> Whether the nature of the terrain figured importantly in Benteen's decision to rejoin the regiment is unclear. Ridge C and Valley 3 did not present the degree of rugged terrain described by the participants in later years. Close examination of the surface today reveals it to be quite mild. The land surface itself was not the chief determinant of the battalion fatigue.[30]

I will use Roger Darling's topographical landmarks in describing my view of Captain Benteen's excursion to the left. Captain Benteen's trail from the first bluffs to Ridge B could have been difficult and tiring for his horses. This would depend to a degree on whether there were serviceable Indian or buffalo paths through the gullies. Having ridden over this route myself with Chip Watts, a local rancher, the gullies, as they are today, would be quite demanding on horses, and certainly the battalion's movement would be slow.

Although Benteen probably moved at a comparatively fast pace over this terrain, I would expect he recognized a number of things which condemned his actions even though his decision to take an oblique and return by Valley 3 may have saved part of the command (which he used to rationalize what he did). Gibson, from Ridge C (Gibson's Lookout), should have made the following observation: Once the bluffs separating Benteen from the South Fork were crossed, there would have been little difficulty reaching the Little Bighorn. The Lieutenant said he could see the Little Bighorn and he must have known there were no Indians or camps south of Ash Creek or where they assumed the Indian encampment was situated. This knowledge, coupled with Benteen's orders to move to the Little Bighorn, and Gibson's being able to either see Custer's command or the dust they were raising in order to determine their location, along with the previous sighting of Custer's battalions and the fact that Benteen, even without orders, must have recognized that an attack on the Indian encampment was imminent, indicates that, militarily, he needed to take the following action: (1) He should have crossed the ridge. Sergeant Major Sharrow would have met him as his battalion entered into South Fork. (2) Knowing there were no Indians to the south he should not have spared his horses in angling toward the Little Bighorn and the main trail. (3) Benteen would then have moved down the Little Bighorn valley in support of Reno. Other factors would have determined the overall effect on the battle that this action would have had.

Considering the location of Ridge C and Ridge B, I believe Benteen had already made up his mind to move down Valley 3 to the main trail by the time Gibson reported back to him. Benteen would not have changed his plan, since he more than likely believed this would be as fast as crossing the bluffs to South Fork. Valley 3 would have presented him with no obstacles in reaching the main trail. I believe that either along Valley 3 or the morass was where Sergeant Major Sharrow met him with the information that Custer was about to order Major Reno to cross the Little Bighorn and attack the Indian villages. Custer

OVERVIEW

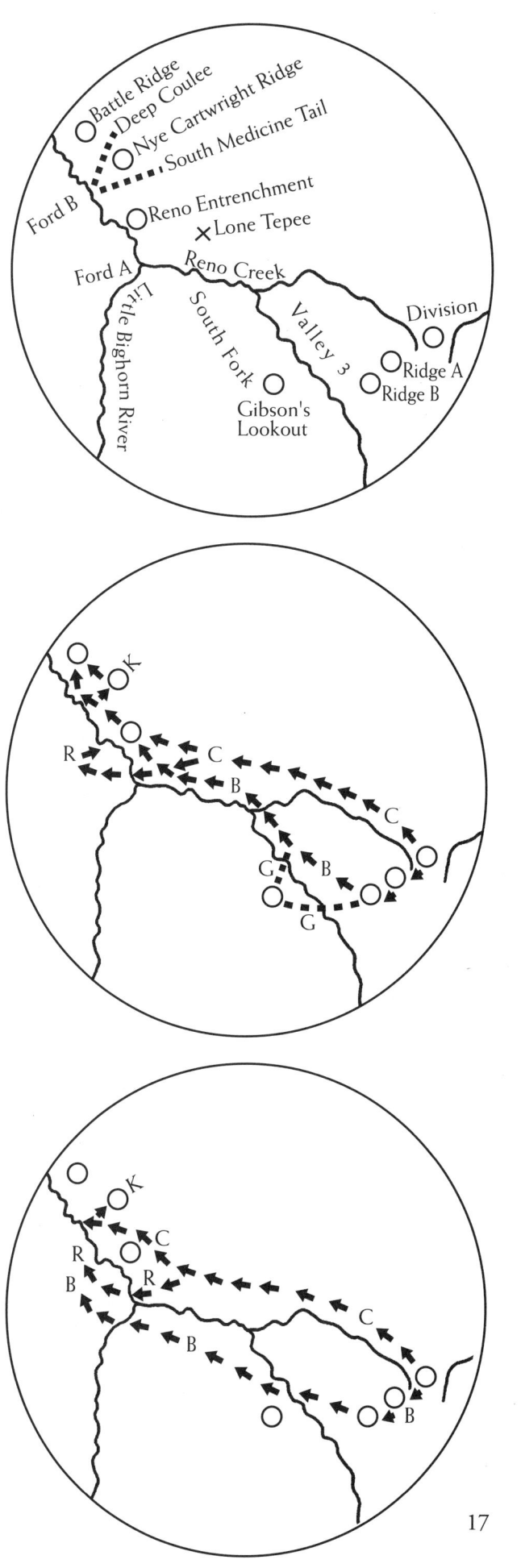

Map A

Major Locations

Map B

Actual Routes Taken

- **C** Custer
- **B** Benteen
- **R** Reno
- **G** Gibson
- **K** Keogh

Map C

Custer's Attack Plan Routes

Routes expected to be taken if there were no Indians to the south of Reno Creek or the suspected encampment location.

OVERVIEW

would have ordered Benteen to move to the Little Bighorn and proceed down the valley in support of Reno. Although I think Benteen moved at a reasonably fast pace on his movement to the left, his failure to cross over to South Fork and the slowness of his pace, once he moved back to the main trail, reflects negatively on Captain Benteen and the actions he took before joining Major Reno.

What all of these considerations suggest is that Benteen definitely violated his known orders, and they point to his subsequent rationalizations. If the terrain was a primary motive for Benteen's decision, Gibson would have reported that, once they moved from Valley 3 to South Fork, the going was comparatively easy. They could not only have followed the instructions we know Benteen received, but would have been in a position to carry through with the military reasons for such a mission: catch the rest of the command before they were attacked or reached the Indian encampment. Keep in mind that Benteen proclaimed to have known where the Indian encampment was, while accusing Custer of being ignorant of that fact.

I firmly believe that when Custer called Reno over to his side of Ash Creek, there was no question in Custer's mind that it would be necessary to give Reno his attack orders soon. Also, Custer was so concerned with winning a victory over the Indians, he would never have sent Benteen on his mission simply to get rid of him, as some writers have suggested. Custer wouldn't have allowed his personal animosity for Benteen to have overridden his desire to win a victory. There is no way Custer would have ignored an integral part of his fighting force at a time he was about to or had given Reno his attack orders. Consequently, a messenger would have been sent to Benteen (whether the messenger was Sergeant Major Sharrow or somebody else). This would be at a time when Benteen's battalion was already moving down Valley 3. This messenger should have met Benteen along Valley 3 or at the morass. The message must have indicated Custer's attack plans for Reno, and Benteen as well.

There are several other considerations that seem important. Although Benteen denied strongly that he had any inkling Major Reno even had a command, let alone orders to support him, both Sergeant Davern and Trumpeter Martin said Major Reno's orders did indicate support, not only from General Custer, but also Captain Benteen. If this was true, Custer must have given or sent orders to Benteen to that effect.

Sergeant Edward Davern of F Company testified at the Reno Court that he was Major Reno's orderly on the 25th. He said that before they moved to the river, he heard Adjutant Cooke give Major Reno an order. The order stated: "Girard comes back and reports the Indian village three miles ahead and moving. The General directs you to take your three companies and drive everything before you. Captain Benteen will be on your left and will have the same instructions. Those I believe were the exact words."[31]

Trumpeter Martin said General Custer told Lieutenant Cooke to order Major Reno "to go down and cross the river and attack the Indian village and that he would support him with the whole regiment. Custer said he would go down to the other end and drive them, and that he would have Benteen hurry up and attack them in the center."[32]

Both these reported orders to Reno suggest that Benteen either knew or was being sent such a message. I have said that it is odd that Custer didn't send a message at the time he gave Reno his attack orders, although Benteen never reported receiving one. The Sergeant Major, if sent just before or at the time of Reno's attack orders, would have to have met Benteen either along Valley 3 or at the morass – if the general time table is accepted. Lieutenant Hare said that Sergeant Major reported to him that Custer desired scouting information at the time when Hare was near the Lone Tepee and only slightly ahead of Custer's command. Sharrow would have to either have returned from taking his message to Benteen, which is extremely doubtful (even using Benteen's time reference), or, shortly after returning to General Custer, from Hare; the Sergeant Major would have been sent to Captain Benteen, which is what I believe happened.

What I suggest within a general context is the following scenario: At the divide, the bluffs to the left presented a problem for General Custer. Custer had accepted White Man Runs Him's and Bouyer's advice to move down Ash Creek to the Little Bighorn, but he was concerned with what might lie behind the bluff on his left. He needed to make sure there was no large body of Indians laying in ambush which could attack his troops as they moved down Ash Creek. He delegated Benteen's battalion to move to the bluff, and if they saw any Indians to pitch into them and wait for support. If not, he should return to the command. As the rest of the regiment started down Ash Creek, Custer could see additional bluffs extending in the direction of the Little Bighorn. He realized it would be better for Benteen to continue until he reached the valley of the Little Bighorn, so he sent his first messenger with orders to that effect. Benteen would then have been in a position to prevent any Indians from scattering in that direction. I believe this was Custer's main worry at that time. Custer would understand that by moving to the Little Bighorn,

Benteen would be in a position to prevent any flanking attack if one should materialize, and he could make sure there were no Indian camps to the south of the known encampment. Godfrey and Benteen both mentioned seeing the Gray Horse Troop as Custer's command moved down Ash Creek. Actually, Benteen's battalion was moving about 2 miles south of Custer but in the same direction, and might have joined the command before they reached the Little Bighorn if Benteen had continued on a half-right angle to the river. Although Custer may have sent two couriers, after he sent Trumpeter Voss, I think he waited until he was at or near the Lone Tepee and then sent Sergeant Major Sharrow. More than likely it was done right after Girard sighted the Indians from the knoll and said they were running. Custer probably beckoned Reno over and sent the message to Benteen. I don't believe Custer gave Reno his attack orders at that time, but I think he knew he would have to soon. Custer would have been anxious to hear from Benteen, and would not have wanted to initiate an attack until he had. What happened at the Lone Tepee would have made Custer realize he could not wait much longer before issuing such an order. I cannot imagine Custer giving Reno orders to move against the Indians and then not informing or attempting to inform Benteen of what he was going to do and what he expected Benteen to do. The Sergeant Major most likely went to some high point and saw Captain Benteen's battalion on their way back to the main trail. He probably met Benteen along Valley 3 or near the morass, and this is why Edgerly,[33] John Frett, a civilian packer,[34] and Private Corcoran of Company K[35] thought Kanipe or a Sergeant met Benteen there.

Benteen, after the battle was over, realized his mistake in not continuing toward the Little Bighorn instead of taking the oblique back to the trail. He would also have known that he should have moved much faster than he did. Benteen then had to rationalize and distort his orders from Custer. He and Major Reno must have realized that if they related their orders in their entirety, they would be blamed for the disaster that befell General Custer and his men. All Benteen had to do was to go with his initial instructions: if they didn't see any Indians he was to return to the main trail. It was hard to explain why he continued beyond the first bluff, and – since Lieutenant Gibson knew they were looking for the valley of the Little Bighorn – not to include this part of the order. Benteen then incorporated this element into the directions he was given and indicated that this is what the Sergeant Major had told him. It was necessary for him to discredit Custer, to suggest that Custer didn't have any plans, didn't know where the Indians were, didn't even believe they were ahead of him or where the scouts said they were, and that he, Benteen, didn't think there was any substance to the Custer orders he did receive. Custer was sending him on a wild goose chase looking for the Little Bighorn valley which could have been miles away, and if he hadn't been smart enough to violate his orders, the whole regiment may have been wiped out. More than likely, as can happen with any rationalization, Benteen came to believe this version himself. It certainly was necessary for him to continue to emphasize this lack of knowledge of any Custer plans, and to reject any coordination of the commands that might indicate he knew what Major Reno was doing or what knowledge Reno had of his orders.

Benteen, however, gave away his own actions in his condemnation of Custer. He criticized Custer for not believing his scouts as to the size and whereabouts of the Indian encampment; but Benteen said he did believe the scouts. By saying this he was actually indicting himself. Captain Benteen and Lieutenant Godfrey pointed out that they were aware of General Custer's movement down Ash Creek, and one could expect that Lieutenant Gibson, in going to the top of ridges to look for Indians, would have seen the dust raised by Custer's command as they moved toward the Little Bighorn and the Indian encampment. Even if we accept Benteen's rationalizing on how far he might have to go to reach the Little Bighorn, it doesn't excuse him for taking a slow right oblique which had his troops moving back from the route the command was taking. If Benteen was as ignorant of the location of the Indian camps as he claimed Custer was, this might have been defensible, but since he supposedly knew the location, the direction Benteen took was inexcusable. By the knowledge of the orders he professed to, Captain Benteen would have known the location of the Little Bighorn (and Gibson said they had). Couple this with his instructions to move to the valley, and there is no justification for having taken a right oblique.

There are two other acts which condemn Benteen's actions at this time. The first is not sending a message to Custer regarding what he had seen and the actions he was taking. The second, which Robert Utley so aptly pointed out, was the slowness of his movement, even after receiving the messages from Kanipe and Martin. Some have excused Benteen by saying he was concerned with the condition of his horses, but as Custer didn't spare his horses once he had committed the troops under his direct command to a flanking attack, neither should have Benteen.*

---

*As I have previously pointed out, Roger Darling indicated the terrain should not have been as tiring as Benteen made it out to be.

Napoleon's credo would apply: "I do not wish the horses to be spared if they can catch men."[36]

Because of their attacks on Custer and his supposed lack of planning, Benteen and Reno's statements have always been very effective in stereotyping Custer's actions. Custer's messengers were dead, and the officers would not necessarily have known or disclosed the full extent of Reno's and Benteen's orders; probably more to protect Benteen than Reno. The only other ones that may have been able to shed any light on the orders were one Indian and two enlisted men. Whether the Ree scout, Stabbed, could have or not, I wouldn't know; but Walter Camp seemed to think he had gone with a message to Benteen. He may have been assigned to go with the Sergeant Major. The other two men would have been Sergeant Davern and Trumpeter Martin.

At the Reno Court of Inquiry, Davern probably surprised them; but he was an enlisted man, and they wouldn't have worried about his testimony. As far as I know, they didn't ask Trumpeter Martin about Custer's orders to Major Reno. Martin later suggested that Custer's orders were more extensive than the Court's defense tried to make them out to be. This could account for why they did not ask Martin about these issues, as well as for their attempt to discredit him. If Martin had expressed the details he later disclosed, it would have destroyed Major Reno's case at the time.

It is important to recall that Sergeant Davern said Reno's orders indicated Captain Benteen would be on Reno's left. Trumpeter Martin reported that Custer's orders to Reno conveyed that Captain Benteen would be supporting Reno in the center, and he also included the information relating to Custer's move to flank the Indians. It has surprised me – and it is difficult to understand in reading various accounts of what took place – that these two fundamental remarks made by two witnesses not likely under any military pressure were so commonly ignored. On the other hand, two officers' denials would be widely accepted in a situation where any other opposing testimony on their part would have been incriminating, making them responsible for the defeat and the deaths of Custer and his men.

My hypothesis may be giving Custer too much credit. It is certainly speculative, but it does account for the need to send a second or third messenger, and provides reasonable conclusions to other aspects of the debate. Custer didn't get to be a general at such an early age without showing more ability than most, and as Cyrus Brady pointed out years ago, it's difficult to picture him moving for a matter of miles and hours without forming a basic plan of action.[37]

The emphasis on the lack of knowledge and planning on Custer's part centers around the need for Benteen and Reno to protect themselves from being blamed for Custer's defeat. The essence of how this could be accomplished was contingent upon their orders. As I will point out in greater detail later, there was a cover-up before and during the Reno Court. An integral part of this deception were the orders received by Major Reno and Captain Benteen. The defense at the trial would have limited the cover-up to as few individuals as possible – probably the two major figures, Benteen and Reno, plus Lieutenant Wallace. However, Wallace's involvement would have centered on his testifying that he was by Major Reno when he received his orders. Lieutenant Hodgson was dead and Major Reno needed some form of verification. Since this would not have required any great deviation by Wallace, he was, I am sure, glad enough to do it. His testimony could be considered a little white lie for the good of the corps. The defense would have been most concerned with what the officers might testify to; more than likely, Girard was correct that they would have inquiries as to how the officers felt about certain points, and put pressure on them if they thought their testimony might be damaging. Considering the enlisted man's status and the small number that were called to testify, the defense was probably not too worried about what those people would say. There may have been some trepidation in Martin's case, but it was easy enough to discredit him.

One other aspect with regard to the division of command and the orders given, which raises suspicion and should have raised more, is the statement at the Reno Court by Lieutenant Edgerly:

> ... After moving over the divide between the Little Big Horn and the Rosebud, General Custer gave the command: "Halt." I was close to him riding with Captain Benteen and Weir. I saw General Custer and Adjutant Cook dismount and make the division into battalions as I suppose with pencil and paper; and then they were announced: that Major Reno would have "A," "G," and "M,"; Captain Benteen "K," "D," and "H," and one battalion was given to Capt. Keogh and one to Capt. Yates; and Capt McDougall with one company was to be the rear guard.
>
> Captain Benteen was ordered to move to the left at about an angle of forty-five degrees and to pitch into anything he came to. Major Reno's orders were to move down the valley and attack anything he came to – those were all the orders I heard. Major Reno was not present when Benteen got his orders: he had about a hundred and twenty-five men and Reno about the same.[38]

Lieutenant Edgerly was with Captain Benteen's battalion as an officer in Company D under Captain Weir. Benteen said he received his orders and then moved out without even knowing how the rest of the regiment was divided or what orders they received. Since, at that time, Major Reno was not in command of any companies, Benteen said he did not know that General Custer had now placed Reno in charge of a battalion, let alone what orders he may have been given.

It is possible that Edgerly, realizing later that the command was divided in this way, even though he didn't actually hear it himself, felt that this was what happened and so testified to that effect. But I doubt that for several reasons. Considering the situation and Major Reno, and the fact that at the time he was not in charge of a company (which undoubtedly was why he wasn't there), he was still the next ranking officer and would have presumably been placed in some sort of command when they were going into battle. It would then have been appropriate to have read off his command first and indicated what would have been expected of him, even though he wasn't there. Also, after assigning Captain Benteen a battalion, it would be considered protocol to assign Captains Keogh, Yates and McDougall to their commands. The fact that Edgerly didn't hear any special orders for Captain Keogh and Yates is understandable, not only because Captain Benteen may have left so Edgerly followed, but because they were under Custer's direct command. Custer would not have believed it necessary to divulge any plans nor would he have been apt to know at that time just how they would be used. I believe Edgerly's memory of the orders helps confirm my belief that General Custer had a plan of action when he divided the command. One might also note that Benteen should not have left until Adjutant Cooke finished completing all of the orders.

Edgar Stewart:

> ...in the years following the battle, the orders to Benteen suffered not a little from conscious and unconscious distortion, from rationalization, and from faulty memories. What the actual orders were we do not know. We have only Benteen's word for them since all of the others—Voss, Sharrow and Cooke—died on the heights with Custer, and it would have been comparatively easy for the orders to have been misunderstood or misrepresented, either deliberately or otherwise.[39]

SOURCES

1. Graham, *Reno Court Abstract*, p. 145.
2. McCausland, *Army and Navy Journal*, July 22, 1876.
3. Stewart, *Custer's Luck*, p. 258.
4. Brackett, *Custer's Last Battle*, p. 262.
5. *Report of the Secretary of War*, 44th Congress, Vol. I, 1876-77.
6. Hardorff, *Markers, Artifacts, and Indian Testimony*, p. 9.
7. Graham, *The Custer Myth*, p. 307.
8. Ibid., p. 315.
9. Varnum, ed. Carroll, *Custer's Chief of Scouts*, p. 118.
10. Utley, *Custer and the Great Controversy*, p. 86.
11. Stewart, *Custer's Luck*, p. 432.
12. Kuhlman, *Legend into History*, p. vii.
13. Dustin, *The Custer Tragedy*, p. 101.
14. Ibid., p. 98.
15. Coughlin, *The Battle of the Little Bighorn*, Cavalry Journal, Vol. XLIII (Jan., Feb., 1934).
16. Graham, *The Custer Myth*, p. 16.
17. Ibid. p. 219, Edgerly's statement, made 18 August, 1881, at Ft. Yates.
18. Graham, *Reno Court Abstract*, p. 135.
19. Ibid., p. 149.
20. Graham, *The Custer Myth*, p. 295.
21. Ibid., p. 149.
22. Brininstool, *Troopers with Custer*, pp. 278, 279.
23. Brady, *Indian Fights and Fighters*, p. 235.
24. Brininstool, *Troopers with Custer*, p. 74, "Benteen's Own Story."
25. Graham, *The Custer Myth*, p. 194.
26. Ibid., p. 187.
27. Stewart, *Custer's Luck*, p. 319.
28. Darling, *Benteen's Scout*, p. 19.
29. Ibid., p. 26.
30. Ibid., p. 29.
31. Stewart, *Custer's Luck*, p. 327 (fn. 77, *Official Transcript*, p. 480; *Reno Court*, p. 269).
32. Graham, *The Custer Myth*, p. 289.
33. Graham, *Reno Court Abstract*, p. 159.
34. Ibid., p. 186.
35. Camp, ed. Hammer, *Custer in 76*, p. 150.
36. Ira Meistrich, *"En Avant"*, MHQ, Vol. I, Number 3, p. 47.
37. Brady, *Indian Fights and Fighters*, p. 235.
38. Graham, *Reno Court Abstract*, p. 157.
39. Stewart, *Custer's Luck*, p. 318.

2
Reno's Attack Orders – Separation From Custer – Crossing Ford A

My first line of inquiry involved the place where Major Reno received his attack orders and the time it took to reach and cross Ford A. As I have previously suggested, there is the distinct possibility that Lieutenant Edgerly was correct when he said that in assigning the companies to Major Reno, Custer gave a general order for Reno's battalion to move to the Little Bighorn, cross over, move down the valley and attack the Indian camp. Since Major Reno had not been in command of any company he was not at the meeting, but would have been informed by Lieutenant Cooke that he would be leading a battalion made up of Companies A, G, and M. Major Reno did not have any direct orders to attack at that time. The statement made by Lieutenant Edgerly – that Reno's orders at the division were to move down the valley and attack anything he came to – would indicate not only recognition of where Custer believed the Indians would be located, but also a plan of attack.

Shortly, they reached a tributary to the Little Bighorn. This tributary was called various names, but was usually known as Ash Creek (following the battle, the name was changed to Reno Creek). They proceeded down this creek with Reno on the left side and Custer on the right. After some eight miles they neared a Lone Tepee. General Custer beckoned Major Reno to cross over to his side of the stream. Girard, the Indian interpreter, had ridden to a knoll and saw some forty or fifty Indians moving toward the Little Bighorn. He reported the Indians were fleeing.* General Custer ordered his Ree Indian scouts to pursue them. This they refused, thinking they were to go alone. General Custer admonished them and then beckoned for Major Reno.

Testimony of officers and troopers during this movement of Major Reno's and General Custer's battalions down Ash Creek illustrates the problems associated with the recollection of events that at the time were not significant. They would become even more vague and jumbled because of the traumatic events that followed, as well as the period of time which elapsed before the participants were expected to recall what happened. I have found very little analysis that took place then or since concerning this period. The inconsistency of testimony is considerable, particularly due to the problems mentioned but also as a result of the cover-ups that developed from the attempts to defend or condemn Major Reno or General Custer.

By putting ourselves "by the elbow" of these men, we can understand the difficulties they faced in recalling events. It's not easy to retain when, where and how something happened a few days, weeks, or months ago, especially during a period of time one is passing through an unfamiliar area.

There are certain elements the soldiers were apt to remember since they would have stood out in their memory: Major Reno's crossing the tributary to join Custer; the Lone Tepee and its burning; Girard's sighting the Indians; Lieutenant Cooke coming to Major Reno and giving him a message after Reno crossed Ash Creek. Then, sometime after the battle, they were asked where Major Reno received his attack orders. Their answers would be reflective of these general conceptions and the opinions expressed by others.

Since I believe Reno's crossing the Little Bighorn and moving down the valley, in relationship to Custer's action, is of primary importance in determining what happened to General Custer, I will be stressing these accounts. I realize they become repetitious and seemingly redundant. However, they do bring out the need to recognize the varying interpretations during a period when the participants were not under battle conditions. One might think they would be fairly consistent in their accounts, but the fact that they aren't reveals why it is important to be wary of time-event relationships, particularly trying to place events within a chronologically exact order. It is also necessary to recognize why Custer's orders, or lack thereof, played such an important role.

It is essential to be aware of these inconsistencies in attempting to arrive at an acceptable explanation. There is the need for analysis and not just an attempt to use testimony to support a thesis or to make an interesting story. The analysis should then be coordinated with one's postulate and final conclusions.

A number of questions need to be addressed: Did Major Reno receive his orders to attack at the Lone Tepee, or <u>after</u> he had passed the tepee and moved toward the Little Bighorn? What would have been the approximate time he received the orders and when did he reach the Little Bighorn? How long did it take to cross, reform and be ready to move down the valley? These are issues one must con-

---

*One should note John Gray's doubts as to whether Girard notified Custer at this time. There are also variations as to the location of the Lone Tepee. These are not instrumental in changing ones' analysis of the overall action.

sider. However, it is more important to formulate a view of what orders Major Reno received than where he received them. The time he received them is less important than the time it took for Reno to cross the Little Bighorn and begin his move down the valley in relationship to when Custer began his move to the ridge and arrived at a position from where he could view the valley.

Lieutenant Hare, Dr. Porter, Captain Moylan, George Herendeen, Lieutenant DeRudio, Sergeant Culbertson, Trumpeter Martin, Red Bear, Lieutenant Godfrey and Sergeant Windolph were all participants in the battle who said or inferred that Reno received his orders at the Lone Tepee. Writers Robert Utley, Cyrus Brady, Colonel Graham, D. H. Miller, Edgar Stewart and Dr. Kuhlman also believe the event took place at the Lone Tepee. Daniel Magnussen and Fred Dustin use a fairly safe expression, saying it took place near the Lone Tepee. Many of the writers paid little attention to where Reno received his orders.

Of particular interest is Dr. Kuhlman's response, since he was the one who suggested that to understand the events one must "ride at the men's elbow." Kuhlman was very concerned and meticulous in ascertaining the terrain and Reno's movement on his skirmish line and in the timber, but showed little interest in Reno's movement to Ford A and his crossing. I consider the crossing a critical period in attempting to account for what happened, and it is difficult to fathom why Kuhlman did not.

Major Reno, Lieutenant Wallace, Sergeant Kanipe, and Lieutenant Varnum as participants, and John Gray in his book, *Centennial Campaign*, felt the orders were given after Reno passed the Lone Tepee. This version would also correspond to what White Man Runs Him and Curley would have indicated in their interview with General Scott, which is probably the most reliable evidence as to where the separation took place.

Since I believe there were no ulterior motives involved in whether Reno received his orders at the Lone Tepee or beyond, the major importance lies in analyzing testimony. As Dustin wrote, "it may be observed that in the matter of time and distance, there are great discrepancies in the accounts of participants; many of them educated officers."[1]

Where did Major Reno receive his attack orders? The distance between the Lone Tepee and the Little Bighorn today is usually said to be 4 1/2 miles. Both Reno and Lieutenant Wallace described Reno being beckoned by General Custer as Reno approached the Lone Tepee. When Reno crossed the tributary Lieutenant Cooke met him with orders from General Custer.

I think it would be fair to say that most of the troops were aware of Custer beckoning to Major Reno, certainly of his crossing over, and of the Lone Tepee. Lieutenant Cooke, in bringing his message to Reno about moving to the front, would have been observed by nearly all the troops. I'm sure that is the reason so many thought he received his orders to attack at that time. Major Reno mentioned passing the Arikaras, which would have been near the Lone Tepee, and Reno referred to the tumult. Girard by that time would have informed the scouts they were not expected to attack the Sioux alone, and they were preparing themselves for the battle they knew lay ahead. When Reno did receive his orders to attack, the troops were strung out in a column. They were supposedly mingling and talking with Custer's command, so not many were in a position to have seen Cooke give Major Reno his final orders. Some say Reno and Custer conversed, others that they didn't. It is worth noting that it was the officers who said they did not, while two non-attached civilians said they did. Whatever really happened, it seems that the two commands moved together beyond the Lone Tepee.

Lieutenant Wallace, part of whose job it was to keep the official time, remembers looking at his watch when Reno crossed Ash Creek: it was 2 o'clock. This would have been about 5 miles from the Little Bighorn. Wallace also said Ford A was 12 to 15 miles from where Custer divided his command. Wallace thought that Reno crossed Ash Creek nine miles from the division point. This would mean the Little Bighorn could have been from 3 to 6 miles from where Reno crossed when beckoned by Custer. We certainly know it was at least 4 miles, but the point is that it could by Wallace's reckoning be 3 miles or 6 miles. Wallace had the battle commencing at 2:30. For this to have happened, Reno would have to have gone about 6 miles, during which time he crossed a ford, moved through timber, reformed his battalion, and moved close to 2 miles down the valley – all of this in a half hour. If they had galloped the whole way, they couldn't have accomplished this. It is hard to understand how he can be that far off on correlating his timing with other events that must have taken place before Reno reached and established his skirmish line. This point is not emphasized as an indictment of Wallace, but as a way to recognize the variances and difficulties of arriving at accurate figures for timing and distance.*

Lieutenant Varnum reported to General Custer after having scouted ahead, and said Major Reno's command

---

* These timing discrepancies later caused me to realize they were brought about because of the need to change the official time at the Reno Court of Inquiry. Refer to my book *The Custer Controversy* or the chapter in this book on the Reno Court.

was moving by at a trot. At the Reno Court he said it was about a mile from the Little Bighorn, while in his *Reminiscences* he said it was 2 miles. From the various testimonies one can see that where something happened and *what* actually happened is blurred in the memory. I think the orders came after they passed the Lone Tepee, between 1 and 2 miles from the river.

Estimating time also appeared egregious because the men's watches reflected different time zones.* Wallace said his last official time notation was at l2:05, which according to him was when the halt was made and the division of command took place. Major Reno and Edgerly used 10 o'clock. I am sure some testimony mixed time references which is probably the explanation for Wallace's error previously mentioned.

Colonel Graham corresponded and talked with Edgerly years later when the Lieutenant had risen to the rank of Brigadier General, and this is what he has to say about him: "I have many letters from General Edgerly, and found him always frank in his opinions and clear in his expression of them; if he talked at all, he talked plainly and without evasion or reserve; and though he was a more reticent man then was General Godfrey, he was much more informative and far more open minded."

Colonel Graham went on to say:

> General Edgerly passed on in 1927. He was a knightly gentleman of the old school, a man of immaculate character, a loyal and courageous soldier, and an able officer. The army has not had too many like him.

Graham also pointed out that Edgerly was:

> ...wholly unbiased in his appraisals of Custer, Reno, and Benteen, though it was easy to see that he considered the latter the outstanding figure of the campaign, whose personality, courage and leadership held high the morale of what was left of the regiment after Custer's debacle.[2]

Colonel Graham wrote:

> ... as I read back this letter to General Edgerly after thirty years, I wonder that he answered at all. It showed unadulterated nerve for a junior officer to put a general officer "on the spot" on such a touchy subject; but answer it he did, and though his answer did not help at all in the time problem (it never has been satisfactorily solved) it was both direct and informative...[3]

This is an example of what I call the "army mentality." It demonstrates one of the main obstacles in finding the solution to what happened to General Custer. The military hierarchy influenced the testimony of officers, which in turn affected the written history and conventional perspective of what happened. Officers' accounts were generally more accepted than those of the enlisted men, and as far as I know, the enlisted men were never questioned by the military. From what I can ascertain, the truth rests within this psychological framework.

General Edgerly, in his letter to Colonel Graham, said that by his recollection, the separation into battalions took place at 10 a.m. He estimated the village about 15 miles from the Crow's Nest, and it would take about 4 hours to cover this area at a walk. He said the 7th Cavalry was a very fast walking regiment. This would mean Custer's command could cover a mile in 16 minutes rather than 20 minutes, which is considered the average cavalry time.

The fact that Edgerly used 10 a.m. is interesting. The official time, generally accepted, is 12:05 p.m. One has to wonder how many other times given and used would have failed to make this same adjustment.

Lieutenant Edgerly's testimony as to the orders delivered by Lieutenant Cooke at the division of command, and its conflict with the testimony of Captain Benteen and Major Reno, did not, to my knowledge, raise a question from Colonel Graham or anyone else. Maybe it was considered too "touchy" a subject for the individuals involved, but it should have been asked by someone and an explanation should have been given. Colonel Graham didn't make any attempt to question such inconsistencies or explain his reason for accepting or rejecting contradictory testimony. I realize that in his book, *The Custer Myth*, Graham is mainly attempting to collect and present memorabilia. This inconsistency is true with most writers, but Colonel Graham's relationship with Edgerly and his acceptance of Edgerly's statements without comment are prime examples of how writers approve or dismiss the conflicting remarks of major witnesses without any attempt at explanation.

Another timing sequence (showing the unreliability of categorically accepting time estimates) also involved Colonel Graham (Graham, *The Custer Myth,* p. 292). After the division of the command, Colonel Graham had Custer's troops moving at a walk until shortly after 2 o'clock when an Indian lodge was sighted; whereupon Custer bore down upon it at a trot. Girard, the interpreter, rode up on a knoll and declared the Indians were running. Graham said this was at 2:15 p.m. Immediately Custer ordered the scouts to pursue. They refused, and the Adjutant ordered Major Reno to follow and attack. Colonel Graham indicated this would have taken place

---

*The officer's time and watches were synchronized.

RENO'S ORDERS - SEPARATION - CROSSING FORD

at the Lone Tepee. The Lone Tepee, as represented by Graham and most others, was 4 1/2 miles from the ford. Graham said Reno reached the river bank at 2:30. Graham's time sequence seems impossible: How could Girard indicate the Indians were running at 2:15, Custer order the scouts to pursue, be refused, and then order Reno to attack, while Reno still had to cross Ash Creek and move alongside of Custer's column, yet somehow Reno reached the ford by 2:30? This scenario would mean that Reno covered the 4 1/2 miles in ten minutes or less.

Graham, at the time Reno was given his attack orders, pictured Benteen "probably some eight to ten miles to the left and rear."[4] Benteen should never have been over two miles to the left of the command nor over four miles in back, and considering the walking done by Custer's command before reaching the Lone Tepee, it is questionable that he was even that far behind. Benteen would have already been taking his oblique at the time Custer was at the Lone Tepee. If Benteen had not taken the oblique nor watered or taken the amount of time he did at the morass, he would have been only a short distance behind Custer or ready to cross into the valley of the Little Bighorn. This, I firmly believe, Custer envisioned and definitely acted upon.

I have nothing but respect for the tremendous work done by Colonel Graham in compiling the memorabilia of the battle. He did a commendable job in rebutting objectively prejudicial positions. My admiration for his efforts makes it all the harder to understand how he can use remarks made by leading participants without questioning their veracity, or present conflicting reports without explaining their many inconsistencies.

Why did General Custer give his attack orders when and where he did? Certainly Girard's warning that the Indians were fleeing would have had its effect, and suggests to many that the orders were given at the Lone Tepee. More likely, Custer refrained from issuing orders at the Lone Tepee; instead, he delivered them when he was within two miles of the Little Bighorn. The observations Curley and White Man Runs Him made to General Scott would have been the most accurate, because they had the most familiarity with the lay of the land. Furthermore, their move to the bluffs was made soon afterwards. Both of these conditions would brand that location in their minds. Major Reno's own recollection of his orders would have supported such a location; he would have had no reason to distort his testimony on the location where he was given his orders. But the main reason Custer would have delayed his orders to Reno before beginning his own flanking movement was his desire to hear from Captain Benteen. Custer would have wanted to be sure of the situation to the south, hoping to hear that Benteen had indeed reached the valley of the Little Bighorn. Custer would want to give Benteen as much time as possible to accomplish this task. To return to my evaluation of General Custer, in which I seem to give him more credit than his avid supporters: I believe he was intelligent, had an agile mind, and would have realized the approximate location of the Indian village and its size; consequently, Custer's actions, beginning with the division of his command, were predicated on that knowledge. Custer would not have ignored a major part of his attacking force (Benteen's battalion), and he would have been concerned for the packs and Captain McDougall's Company B. He couldn't leave the packs miles behind the rest of the command and in a position to be cut off if there had been Indians to the south. Therefore, Custer waited as long as he could to hear from Benteen before giving his orders to Reno and beginning his own flanking movement. He had to assume that Benteen was at the valley of the Little Bighorn, or would soon reach it, and then move to aid the attack.

General Godfrey in his narrative said:

> Some time before eight o'clock [a.m. of the 25th] General Custer rode bareback to the several troops and gave orders to be ready to march at eight o'clock, and gave information the scouts had discovered the locality of the Indian villages or camps in the valley of the Little Big Horn, about twelve or fifteen miles beyond the divide. Just before setting out on the march, I went to where General Custer's bivouac was. The General, "Bloody Knife," and several Ree scouts and a half-breed interpreter were squatted in a circle, having a "talk" after the Indian fashion. The General wore a serious expression and was apparently abstracted. The scouts were doing the talking, and seemed nervous and disturbed. Finally "Bloody Knife" made a remark that recalled the General from his reverie, and he asked in his usual quick, brusque manner, "What's that he says?" The interpreter replied: "he says we'll find enough Sioux to keep us fighting two or three days." The General smiled and remarked. "I guess we'll get through with them in one day."[5]

Godfrey's remarks support my view in several ways. That morning, General Custer was not denying the sightings made by the scouts at the Crow's Nest, but instead said the Indian camps had been located. Godfrey also indicated Custer's reference to the valley of the Little Bighorn, which again emphasizes his recognition of the general location of the Indian camps. When Godfrey went to the General, he said that Custer had a serious expression and was apparently "abstracted." I doubt that the General was dreaming or that his mind was in a vacuous state, as so many appear to believe was his condition as he proceeded to the Lone Tepee and beyond. It is also interesting to note who he was with; these were the Indians and scouts that most writers say Custer ignored. They were the ones that not only knew the terrain, but, as stated above, were aware of the size and strength of the Indians. Custer didn't reject the facts on the size or location of the camp; what he rejected was the notion that he would not be able to defeat the Indians.

The view that Custer didn't believe or know the location and size of the Indian camp is derived primarily from remarks made by Captain Benteen. One has to acknowledge and respect the courage, fortitude and leadership qualities of Captain Benteen. On the other hand, it is necessary to recognize Benteen's hubris, which resulted in his vituperative, supercilious and vindictive nature. This enables us to understand the need for Benteen to justify his actions, which centered around his shifting the blame to General Custer. The focus of this blame would be aimed at Custer's lack of awareness concerning the Indians' location, the number of them he would be going up against, and his orders – which didn't allow Benteen or Reno to know of his plans – and the implication that Custer didn't even have any specific plan until after he directed Reno to attack.

Edgar Stewart speculated on what General Custer saw in front of him when he called the halt after crossing the divide. He didn't know what was to the left of him, but he realized the Little Bighorn was several miles in front and the Indian camp somewhere across and to the right. Stewart said:

> The troops in a column of fours followed down the small creek which had its origin near the place where the regiment had crossed the divide and which flowed in the general direction of the smoke which the scouts said marked the approximate location of the hostile camp. This was the middle fork of Reno Creek, which empties into the Little Bighorn some two or three miles above the southern limit of the Indian camp.[6]

I don't think there is any way that a cavalry commander who had fought through the Civil War and been a part of the rise, development and deployment of the Union cavalry, could have traveled from the Crow's Nest to near the Little Bighorn without planning for a multiple pronged attack on where he expected the village to be. I would suppose that Napoleonic cavalry tactics were taught at West Point: the battles of Eylau, Jena, Austerlitz, etc.; the use of the Hussar and the Cuirassiers; Marshall Marat's tactics; even Napoleon's words: "The use of the cavalry demands boldness and ability; above all it should not be used with any miserly desire to keep it intact . . ."[7] Flanking attacks had been used by Custer and were in vogue against the Indians. During the Civil War, Custer ". . . fully realized the value of the element of surprise, and he made flanking attacks a fine-honed specialty."[8] Custer may have even reflected upon his actions during the Civil War; whatever his thoughts were, he must have had a coordinated attack planned, to the extent warranted by his lack of knowledge about the terrain.

How long did it take Major Reno, after receiving his attack orders, to move to the ford, cross, reform and be ready to move down the valley to attack the Indian village? The length of time it took Reno to reach the ford would naturally depend on where he received the orders and his gait to the ford. I will use 2:35 as the time Reno received his orders, and 2:50 for when he reached the river. This should approximate the time it would have taken him to cover a mile and a half or two miles, which then coincides with the generally accepted time of his arrival. Though, as I have previously suggested, in a military campaign a few minutes can make a great difference and affect the outcome. For my purpose, it is primarily needed to establish an operational framework.

I will assume that Major Reno, leading his battalion, came to the river at 2:50 p.m. How long did it take him to cross the ford and be in a position to move down the valley and attack the Indian village? Once again there are different estimates. Considering what an investigation of time and distance testimony reveals, it is imprudent to accept what was reported merely because "so and so" said it.

Dr. Porter thought it took 5 or 10 minutes to cross and reform.[9] De Rudio said there was no delay.[10] Lieutenant Hare said 10 or 15 minutes.[11] Major Reno thought that about 10 minutes were needed to reform after crossing.[12] Dr. Kuhlman had them arriving at 2:40–2:50, and ready to move down the valley by 3:05.[13] Edgar Stewart talked about 10 or 15 minutes.[14] (This estimate probably came about because of Major Reno's statement that after crossing the ford, they reformed in 10 or 15 minutes. Note that he didn't say how long he thought it took to actually cross.) Many participants, investigators and writers must not have thought it made much difference, because they glossed over it, but it is a critical period in attempting to determine General Custer's actions, so again I tried to follow Dr. Kuhlman's advice and place myself at their "elbow."

RENO'S ORDERS - SEPARATION - CROSSING FORD

It is important to reiterate certain statements already presented.

Lieutenant Varnum at the Reno Court of Inquiry:

> Any statement I may make in regard to time would be a guess on my part. The last time I know anything about was eight o'clock the night before. I have very little to base an opinion of time upon unless I connect it with someone else's statement. I have thought of it a great deal, and I think it must have been two o'clock. I base my opinion a good deal on other people's opinions compared with my own as to time.[15]

Colonel Graham:

> ... you know how long military movements take. Figure it out. Could it have taken less than fifteen or twenty minutes to do the things he did? He did all these things – not one right after another as if on a schedule, but as the necessity for them developed. You have had long experience in handling troops. I have had a little myself. But we both know that situations do not develop, nor are troop movements made, in an instant.[16]

Captain Carter:

> I kept the time or tried to, in our Mexican raid and have always said we halted to cut off the packs only a few minutes. It must have been nearly an hour if not more. Time goes "blewy" when men are exhausted and are marching night and day.[17]

None of these remarks were made in direct reference to the crossing, but they do apply. Reno moved down Ash Creek to the mouth of the creek. Some of the Ree scouts had passed over the Little Bighorn while others were still on this side.

Lieutenant DeRudio, in an interview with Walter Camp, said there were two fords: one was near the mouth of Ash Creek and the other somewhat south of it.[18] Jerome Greene, in his book, *Evidence and the Custer Enigma*, pointed out that the river was swollen from melting spring snows, causing Reno to divert briefly to the south before finding a suitable crossing.[19] I would think that Major Reno would have checked with his scouts when he arrived at the river – in regard to the ford and the Indians. He then decided to seek a better crossing. Reno moved to the other ford. We can assume he would have investigated it for himself, or had somebody do it for him. By the time he was ready to cross, Major Reno would have already spent a minimum of 5 minutes since his arrival at the river's edge. This was a fast moving stream, belly high to the horses. Since there were no Indians directly across the river to attack, it would be safe to say that Major Reno was more likely to remain cautious.

DeRudio told Walter Camp that when he came to the river he found Reno and Girard sitting on horses in the river, and Reno was drinking from a flask. DeRudio said he was the first man to ford the river, and as he passed Reno his horse splashed water on him. Reno then said, "What are you trying to do? Drown me before I am killed."[20]

At the Reno Court, Lieutenant Hare said that when he came to the ford Major Reno was standing on the right bank. Some of the men were watering their horses. After Hare passed through the ford and timber he fixed his gear, and when he was mounting, the first of the troops emerged.[21] In an interview with Walter Camp, he said that while Reno was watering, he went down the valley with the scouts. Hare also said the scouts pulled out just as Reno and his battalion came up. "Reno stopped here and took plenty of time to water," he observed.

John M. Ryan, 1st Sergeant "M" Company, *Hardin, Montana Tribune*, June 22, 1923:

> We arrived at the bank of the Little Big Horn and waded to the other side, and here there was a very strong current and there was quicksand about 3 feet deep. On the other side of the river we made a short halt, dismounted, tightened our saddle girths, and then swung into the saddle...[22]

Lieutenant Wallace said the command crossed in a column of two's, passed through the timber, halted and closed up. He also mentioned the horses "scattered" when they came to the ford.[23] What he meant by that I don't know, unless they bunched up or got mixed up with horses from other companies. The horses were thirsty and probably hard to handle. So we have three companies of about 40 men to a company. A horse would average 7 feet in length, and the horse following would be, say, 3 feet back. I recognize there would be bunching, etc., but one needs to establish a general picture. Captain Moylan said that when moving, the heads of the column would be 15 to 25 yards from the next company.[24] This would have differed as they crossed the ford. If Major Reno's three companies were in a column of twos, with at least 20 yards separating each company as they approached the river, they would have extended some 200 yards. They probably halted in column formation when Reno reached the ford.

The Little Bighorn was, according to Lieutenant Varnum, 25 to 30 feet wide at Ford A.[25] This measurement seems to have been accepted, although Sergeant Windolph spoke of the river being a hundred to a hundred and fifty feet wide. General Godfrey said the Little Bighorn was twenty to forty yards wide, which would be closer to Windolph's opinion. Neither Windolph or Godfrey were referring to Ford A specifically.

Private Morris said Sergeant O'Hara of M Company tried to prevent their company from allowing their horses to drink as they crossed the ford, but Morris's horse was able to.[26] From what Hare and others have said, I'm sure most of the horses did drink, supposedly as they forded the river.

For a horse to drink and to ford a belly-high stream it must have taken close to a minute. If crossing by two's, and if they could be kept in column formation (which I doubt took place), you wouldn't have over six horses crossing a 25 foot stream at one time. If we estimated a minute for 6 horses to pass through the ford, it would have taken 20 to 25 minutes for the 3 companies to have crossed.

There was a clearing on the other side, and there must have been some confusion and mingling as they emerged from the water. This was suggested by several soldiers. Lieutenant Hare spoke of adjusting his saddle blanket, as did Sergeant Ryan, and I am sure they checked their other gear and weapons. Most of them would have done so. They may have been either ordered or expected to.

As Colonel Graham said, troop movements are not made in an instant. Major Reno undoubtedly conversed with some of his officers, and some planning and passing of information would have taken place. Supposedly, Girard warned Reno during this period. Reno sent a messenger to Custer and expected a reply. After not receiving one, he sent another messenger.

From the clearing, there was timber to pass through before they reached the open valley. Several writers mention the timber without specifying its width or density. There must have been paths made by Indians and animals; but we also know troops survived in the timber along the river after Reno's retreat to the bluffs. Private James Wilbur of Company M said they went through considerable timber on the far side of the ford.[27] Sergeant Stanislas Roy mentions about 50 yards of timber on the west side of the ford[28], while Lieutenant DeRudio claims it was 200 yards wide.[29] Thomas F. O'Neill was a private with Company G, and said he remembered Ford A where Reno crossed as being at a high bank, "... on other side of river there were timber and fallen logs and took some time to get through."[30] Considerably more time would have elapsed from the period when the troops moved through the timber and regrouped.

The following chart is based on a realistic assessment of the amount of time it must have taken Reno to cross Ford A, prior to his move down the valley. It is possible that he may have taken even longer. This represents a logical time structure:

Time	Action	Number of Minutes
2:50 p.m.	Reno arrives at mouth of Ash Creek; checks ford and situation with officers and scouts. He moves to Ford A and inspects it.	5
2:55 p.m.	Reno orders officers to move their companies across the ford in column of twos; most companies water their horses.	20
3:15 p.m.	Troops dismount, check gear; some still crossing. Reno sends messenger to Custer; orders companies to move through timber.	5
3:20 p.m.	Troops move through timber and reform.	10
3:30 p.m.	They are ready to move down the valley . . .	

In my judgement, from the time Major Reno reached the ford, halted the column, checked the fords, crossed and watered, checked gear, passed through the timber and regrouped, it would have taken 40 minutes. Since this assessment is speculative, I will lower it to a very conservative estimate of 25 minutes, which is the minimum time it could have taken to perform all the tasks.

Recognize one crucial fact: I am not including the time it took Reno to reach the ford after receiving his orders from Custer. Many of the later estimates, in stating time, were made in order to synchronize events between 2:00 p.m. – when Lieutenant Wallace looked at his watch and said Reno was ordered to cross Ash Creek – and Lieutenant Godfrey's time of 4:20. Although Godfrey couldn't remember just why he looked at his watch at that moment, he did feel it represented some significant event. Later Godfrey thought it was the time the main packs arrived with Captain McDougall. Colonel Graham (fn. p. 142 – *The Custer Myth*) said he convinced Godfrey that it would have been when Benteen arrived on Reno Hill. This has generally been accepted, but one should keep in mind several things. Colonel Graham was attempting to place it into the above mentioned time-frame, which also took speculative time periods for the move to Ford A, going down the valley, the time Reno engaged the Indians, as well as his retreat to the hill. Though speculation is necessary to an extent, one has to be careful it doesn't become too rigid when using so many tentative time estimates. It becomes even more so when one uses two specific speculative times: Reno's crossing and starting his move down the valley at 3:05, with Godfrey's 4:20 as the time Benteen reached Reno Hill. Too often the two are placed into an obdurate mold.

RENO'S ORDERS - SEPARATION - CROSSING FORD

Keep in mind that Godfrey was not sure of his assessment, except that it took place after they arrived on the hill. It should also be pointed out that Godfrey's account came from a 1908 and 1921 revision of an article he had written in 1892 for the *Century Magazine,* and even then he did not change his original view that he thought that 4:20 was the time when Captain McDougall and the main packs arrived. He still wasn't sure of that; consequently, it may have been the time when Lieutenant Hare came up with several ammunition packs, when the Indians appeared to be leaving, when Captain Weir went to look for Custer, or when Lieutenant Edgerly followed with D Company. It may have been something else that seemed important at the time, that he might not have consciously remembered later. Godfrey thought it was 2:30 when Benteen joined Reno; 5 o'clock when the command moved down toward Custer; about 7 o'clock when they retreated and the Indians surrounded them.[31] As we know, many of the officers' watches were two hours behind "the official time." One has to also consider what may have happened with Lieutenant Wallace and the impossible time-frame he used, in which he may have switched from one time to the other.* The point of all this discussion is that one should not attempt to categorize a time-frame. It is necessary to fit in an event-time-event relationship, but one has to be careful how they attempt to adjust a time-event determination within a time framework.

The crossing of Ford A is an example of a time-event determination which has been generally accepted. It came about at the Reno Court of Inquiry, with Reno's and other officers' statements that it took 10 to 15 minutes. It should be looked at as an event-time-event consideration when we relate it to what Custer was doing. One knows that Reno would not say he was at Ford A 20 or 25 minutes, so it was necessary for the defense to use the shortest time which could be considered plausible. If it took Reno 25 minutes to cross and regroup, as I believe it did, where would Custer have been? If Reno's orders were correct as he stated them, shouldn't Custer have been right behind Reno waiting to cross Ford A? Major Reno said he sent a messenger and when he didn't receive a reply, he proceeded down the valley. If Custer was following, why didn't the messenger return?

If Custer and Reno separated a mile and a half from the ford, and it took 15 minutes for Reno to reach the ford and another 25 minutes to cross (a conservative estimate), what was Custer's location? Custer, according to Martin, moved several hundred yards toward Ford A, watered, then moved quickly to the ridge, about a mile and a quarter away.[32] Custer should have covered the distance in 15 minutes using a maximum time figure. If we factor in the watering time, no more then 30 minutes should have elapsed since the separation. This would have Custer reaching the ridge some 10 minutes before Reno was ready to move down the valley, and at least 5 minutes before Reno had cleared the timber. Again, this is a conservative estimate.

Looking at the situation another way, Sergeant Kanipe didn't report that Custer even stopped after the separation. Martin did mention the watering; most likely along Ash Creek or a small tributary about a mile and a quarter from the ford, which would approximate where the two battalions separated. For Lieutenant Cooke or Private McIhargey to have given Custer the information that caused him to change his plans and move to flank the Indians, Custer would have had to have waited close to 30 minutes for these messages to reach him. There is no testimony to support this possibility, while the testimony of Martin and Kanipe, along with the fact that the slower Rees would have caught up to Custer before he made his move to the ridge, refutes it. Sergeant Roy's observation of sighting Custer on the ridge at the time Reno was reforming his troops or coming into line after passing through Ford A, would have to be in error; as would the testimonies of other troopers who claimed to have sighted Custer when they were half way down the valley.

The big question in Custer's mind, as it would be in any competent commander, must have been: Where was Benteen, and why he hadn't heard from him? This was probably the reason Custer delayed his flanking movement. Custer finally realized that if he was to support Reno, defeat the Indians and keep them from scattering, he simply could not wait, but had to gamble on Benteen's location and the action Benteen would take.

Reno had to have been aware of the sighting by his troops of Custer on the bluffs above the valley. What should be recognized and has been questioned is why Reno didn't admit to such sightings. The answer seems obvious. Reno, after the battle, would have known that if he said he saw Custer on those bluffs it meant he knew Custer was moving to flank the Indians. Reno had enough difficulty justifying the statement in his report following the battle that Custer intended to support him by a flank attack. The sighting of Custer's command would have

---

*As I previously stated, reports indicate that the officers' watches would have been synchronized. The timing discrepancies are evidence of the timing cover-up. The necessity is apparent.

made it difficult to defend his decision not to continue to attack the Indian village and there would have been no justification for leaving the timber.

The above considerations suggest an event-time-event correlation which is more logically sound in its conclusion even if the exact time might be imprecise and doesn't quite coincide with the fixed time perimeter which is generally used. This hypothesis provides additional substantiation for the primary need to cover-up orders as well as time sightings at the Reno Court of Inquiry in order to support Major Reno's actions.

SOURCES

1. Dustin, *The Custer Tragedy*, p. 110.
2. Graham, *The Custer Myth*, p. 217.
3. Ibid., p. 216.
4. Ibid., p. 293.
5. Ibid., p. 136, "General Godfrey's Narrative."
6. Stewart, *Custer's Luck*, p. 321.
7. Ira Meistrick, *"En Avant!" MHQ*. Vol. 1, Number 3, p. 47.
8. Urwin, *Custer Victorious*, p. 270.
9. Graham, *Reno Court Abstract*, p. 64.
10. Ibid., p. 105.
11. Camp, ed. Hammer, *Custer in 76*, p. 65.
12. Overfield II, *The Little Big Horn, 1876*, Reno to E. W. Smith, p. 44.
13. Kuhlman, *Legend into History*, Map enclosure, itinerary.
14. Stewart, *Custer's Luck*, p. 331.
15. Varnum, ed. Carroll, *Custer's Chief of Scouts*, p. 307.
16. Graham, *The Custer Myth*, p. 307.
17. Ibid., p 315.
18. Camp, *Custer in 76*, p. 84.
19. Greene, *Evidence and the Custer Enigma*, p. 13.
20. Camp, *Custer in 76*, p. 84.
21. Graham, *Reno Court Abstract*, p. 89.
22. Camp, *Custer in 76*, p. 65.
23. Graham, *Reno Court Abstract*, p. 23.
24. Ibid., p. 77.
25. Varnum, ed. Carroll, *Custer's Chief of Scouts*, p. 119.
26. Letter from William Morris to Robert Bruce, May 23, 1928.
27. Camp, *Custer in 76*, p. 148.
28. Ibid., p. 111.
29. Ibid., p. 84.
30. Ibid., p. 106.
31. Graham, *The Custer Myth*, p. 142.
32. Ibid., p. 289.

3
The Reno Court Of Inquiry – Part I

The time of the Reno Court of Inquiry was a period in American History when scandals and duplicity in the government's dealing with and handling of the Indian situation were common. To most people, then as now, the end justified the means. As Edgar Stewart wrote about testimony in general: "... all of the rest is an excrescence gathered through the years for the purpose of maligning or defending some of the actors in the ensuing tragedy."[1]

Colonel Graham, in defending Major Reno's actions in the valley, rebutted Captain Carter's accusations by saying:

> I do not know whether you have read the testimony taken by the Reno Court of Inquiry at Chicago; but if you have, you cannot reach the conviction you now hold without discrediting the sworn statements of every military witness, who recounted what occurred in the valley. These were Wallace, Hare, Varnum, Moylan and DeRudio of the officers, and Sergeants Culbertson and Davern of the enlisted men.... You would not say that Wallace and Hare and Varnum and Moylan and DeRudio were all "cowardly poltroons," I feel sure. Yet, to be consistent, you must say either that, or they willfully and deliberately perjured themselves at Chicago in 1879, and you would not say that, either.[2]

In a general sense, I am sure Colonel Graham was correct, particularly as it pertained to the matter of cowardice and attempting to distinguish between that and being scared. On the other hand, I am just as sure that there were cover-ups. In many of the cover-ups, if the false statements had been exposed they could have been characterized by the witnesses as having been their opinions or could be considered little white lies for the good of the corps; but there were those who deliberately lied and distorted basic facts. It was with these main issues that the Defense would have been concerned, trying to decide how the officers might testify and where military pressure could be applied. Most testimony, though differing to a degree on time, place, distance, or numbers, would have been truthful and inconsequential, or could have even aided the Defense. Girard referred to one officer having been subject to military pressure, and inferred that others were also. An enlisted man's testimony, if controversial, could be discounted or overruled by Major Reno's and Captain Benteen's representatives. Trumpeter Martin, with wide recognition of his speech handicap, was easily discredited.

For those interested in the battle, the discrepancies brought out at the trial have remained throughout the years, and there has been very little attempt to analyze the proceedings. The colored testimony and deceptions have made it even more difficult to determine just what happened in a battle which, by its nature and outcome, has to rest on conjecture.

One is extremely naive if they believe there were no cover-ups or slanting of the truth, and because of the nature of the defense and prosecution, some outright lies. Any student of history is aware of numerous cover-ups organized by high officials in every branch of government as well as those in business. One should always keep in mind that the Reno Court was not an attempt to determine what happened to General Custer. For the Prosecution, it was a Janus-faced attempt to establish evidence to warrant a military court-martial for Major Reno. They disingenuously attempted to show conduct unbecoming an officer, suggesting that Reno exhibited cowardice, panic, drunkenness, and dereliction of his duty, and that because of his actions, he brought about the defeat of General Custer.

The Defense was trying to exonerate Reno from those charges. But don't forget that although the trial was being played before a military tribunal, its primary audience and purpose was to present a prima facie case to the public through newspaper accounts. In many of the essential areas necessary to determine what actually happened to General Custer, the views were distorted and pertinent questions were <u>not</u> asked, in order to protect Major Reno. Although Captain Benteen was not on trial, his reputation was at stake. And, to a certain extent, this was the same situation for the other officers. The testimony at this trial has been used as the groundwork by most writers in attempting to create their own scenarios to uncover the action taken by General Custer. The orders, the plans, the sightings of Custer, the number of Indians and at different locations, the timing, the route taken by Custer, and many other facts have been affected by this testimony. Most of the testimony can be characterized as honest attempts to recall the events; but not all, and the questionable portions are often in critical areas.

I will use the word Inquiry in the general sense, recognizing that it was a Court of Inquiry to determine if there was justification to conduct an actual trial or, in military terminology, a court martial. Defense refers to Mr. Gilbert in supporting Major Reno, and the Prosecution signifies Recorder Lee and his attempt to substantiate the need for court martial proceedings to be levied against Major Reno.

To what extent Mr. Gilbert of the Defense and Recorder Lee of the Prosecution sat down with their major witnesses and tried to determine how the witnesses should testify, I do not pretend to know. But if a certain amount of preliminary work was not done, then they were not doing justice to their assignment.

Within this framework, keep in mind that the trial was conducted by the military. The recorder and prosecutor was 1st Lieutenant Jesse M. Lee, Adjutant, 9th Infantry. On page viii of Colonel Graham's abstract of the Reno Court, Graham said, "... though a more expert interrogator than was Lieutenant Lee could doubtless have gotten more information from them [witnesses] than Lee was able to do. But he did his best ..."[3]

More important than Lieutenant Lee's presumed lack of expertise as a interrogator was the need to operate within a prescribed boundary. It is my opinion that many pertinent questions concerning sightings, orders and timing were not asked during the trial. Although I would agree in the main with the attempt by the military to absolve Reno of the charges, my position doesn't diminish any criticism of the effect the trial has had on evaluating the actions taken by General Custer. The trial was a dismal failure in this respect, and, in fact, it became the principal source for obfuscating events and thereby preventing clarification of what actually happened to Custer.

I would surmise that Mr. Gilbert had gone over critical issues with Major Reno and Captain Benteen. It became apparent that there was the necessity of a third officer to corroborate Reno's account, particularly regarding the orders he received. Lieutenant Hodgson had been in such a position, but he was killed in the retreat to the bluffs; the need for some other officer was apparent. That officer was Lieutenant Wallace. The Defense would want to know, or at least have some idea, of what the other officers would be testifying. Girard and others were probably correct that this sounding out took place at social affairs. It's hard to say how much pressure would have been applied if an officer's testimony was likely to be damaging. In most cases, although the accounts were somewhat conflicting, they would not have affected the version of events the Defense wanted to project. If they thought it might, they would probably use a reminder that the military should be protecting their own, or that the accusations against Major Reno would reflect against the 7th Cavalry. In the case Girard mentioned, it might have been necessary to apply military pressure and point out that the officer's future might be in jeopardy. The military was clearly in support of absolving Major Reno.

Colonel Graham said:

> This attempt by Mr. Whittaker to discredit the conduct and finding of the Court, even before the latter was promulgated, resulted in reviving once again all the old animosities and disputes that the Army, doubtless, had hoped would soon be buried and forgotten. But it was not to be.
>
> To let sleeping dogs lie has ever been the army policy, especially when to waken them would inevitably result in a public clamor critical to the service.

Distortions or cover-ups were used, particularly pertaining to testimony having to do with the following crucial points: The orders received by Major Reno and Captain Benteen; the location of Captain Keogh and Lieutenant Cooke as Reno moved to the ford; the number of Indians first seen in the valley; how long it took to cross Ford A; the sighting of Custer; time estimates; and the number of Indians Custer faced as he moved down Medicine Tail Coulee.

Instead of "riding by their elbow," I will attempt to sit by the elbow of Mr. Gilbert and the Defense, and Recorder Lee, the prosecutor. What were they trying to prove or disprove?

First, the Prosecution. Recorder Lee, overall, was accusing Major Reno of conduct unbecoming an officer. The main accusation he made was that Reno didn't follow orders and because of this failure, Custer and his five companies were wiped out. If Reno had attacked the village, or at least held in the timber, he would have kept a large force of Indians engaged; by retreating from the timber he released these Indians, who then squared off with Custer and caused the debacle. The Prosecution wanted to prove or indicate that Reno should have realized Custer would be attempting to aid him. They wanted to show that Reno knew Custer was aware of his predicament; that Custer saw Reno engage the enemy. If they could have Reno's officers seeing Custer and reporting the sighting to Reno, then Reno would have had to realize Custer was using a flanking movement. Thus, Reno would know Custer was on his way to aid him, and consequently he should have stayed in the timber. Leaving the timber would be evidence that Reno not only disobeyed orders, but exhibited cowardly behavior – that he panicked. They would also attempt to suggest that Reno was drunk. This last point would be used to supplement their major premise about Reno's conduct as an officer.

Captain Benteen was not the main target. His courage during the Reno entrenchment period could not be questioned, but there were those, then and since, who felt his hatred toward Custer and the slowness of his response to Custer's messages were a central factor in Custer's defeat. Therefore, Benteen himself would have recognized the importance of obfuscating orders and supporting Reno's position.

Robert Utley suggests that besides Reno's failure, Benteen "doomed" Custer's plans:

> First, Benteen dawdled on the back trail, falling far-

ther and farther behind the rest of the regiment. Sergeant Kanipe, enroute to McDougall, told Benteen about the battle taking shape ahead, but that news failed to stir the battalion's pace from a leisurely walk. When Trumpeter Martin dashed up with Custer's urgent summons, Benteen ordered a trot. Only a gallop would have been responsive to Custer's expectations, and even that pace might not have brought Benteen to Medicine Tail in time.[4]

Another malfeasance, according to the Prosecution, was Major Reno's failure – after retreating to the ridge and being joined by Benteen – to rush to the aid of Custer when gunfire was heard downstream. These allegations also affected Captain Benteen.

Mr. Gilbert and the Defense knew they must concentrate on justifying Reno for not attacking the village, but it was particularly necessary to defend his retreat from the timber. It is here that the orders Custer gave and the sightings of Custer became essential elements in their defense. They wanted to portray Reno's actions in responding to his orders as officially competent and quickly administered, focusing on such events and circumstances as: his movement to Ford A; the notifying of Custer; the move down the valley, looking for support from Custer at the rear, not aware of Custer's plans or any other orders; the need to save his troops; the charge to the ridge; not knowing the whereabouts of Custer, but, upon arrival of the packs, when he realized his wounded could be handled, his attempt to reach Custer. They would try to suggest that Custer encountered an overwhelming number of Indians even before the Indians facing Reno dispersed and became a factor in Custer's defeat. These were the essential points for the Defense to make.

With this goal in mind, Mr. Gilbert endeavored to paint the following picture: At the division of command, Major Reno is given a battalion of three companies but has no idea of any other orders. He sees Captain Benteen move to the left, but does not know for what reason. Captain Benteen is ordered to the left and moves out without hearing any other orders and without knowing that Major Reno had been assigned a battalion. Gilbert made clear that Reno and Benteen were not aware of each other's orders. Benteen did not specify clearly what his two additional orders consisted of, but he was explicit in the ferocity and intensity of his disparaging remarks about Custer and the supposed orders he received. By so doing, he seemed to have blocked any discerning questions and effectively distorted the picture of what Custer knew and planned. In fact, Benteen did such a good job of creating this impression that it has been accepted by virtually everyone from that time until now. Mr. Gilbert, the two battalion commanders, and Lieutenant Wallace, created the desired scenario in which Reno and Benteen had no idea of what Custer may have been planning, or what the other man's orders were, and Major Reno only expected Custer's support from the rear.

In the next part of Gilbert's summary of the events, Major Reno attempts to follow his attack orders as quickly and precisely as he can within the boundaries of what he considers prudent. Reno moves to Ford A, wasting no time in crossing and reforming his troops for their move down the valley. He has already realized he will be facing a large number of Indians and should warn Custer. Reno proceeds to send a courier. When he does not hear from Custer, he sends another. (It could be considered odd that they were both from Captain Keogh's company.) His orders were that he would be supported by General Custer. It is imperative that people realize this support is expected to come from the rear. Reno, in crossing the ford, has no reason to believe that Custer is not right behind him. The Defense attempted to support this point and provide ample proof by having Lieutenant Cooke going to the ford with Major Reno. When he doesn't hear from General Custer, Reno hurries down the valley to carry out his orders and attack the village. (One might think that when Reno didn't receive a reply to his message or see any sign of Custer on his back trail, he might have suspected a flanking move; but no, he still expected Custer to support him from the rear.) Though there are not too many Indians in front of him, he suspects this is the old decoy trick. When more of the Indians appear and begin to move to his left, he halts his troops and forms a skirmish line. Still no Custer! He is afraid the Indians are encircling him and beginning to flank him, so he retreats to the timber. Still no Custer! By then Custer has had plenty of time to come to his aid, so Reno must now think of his own battalion and what is best for them. He doesn't know where Benteen is or what his orders are, so he can't expect any help from him. Reno feels he can't hold out long in the timber. He must try to reach the bluffs on the other side of the river. He then makes his decision to charge the Indians, cross the river, and reach the bluffs. Though he loses a number of men, he accomplishes his objective. In a short time, Captain Benteen arrives and most of the Indians move downstream. Reno believes he must wait for the packs and prepare the wounded before attempting to locate Custer.

The Defense had several other crucial objectives. Since the condemnation of Major Reno reflected hindsight, the Defense now had to tie in several points so that Reno's actions would not be held responsible for General Custer's defeat. After the battle it became known that Custer had decided to use a flanking movement to support Reno. Major Reno, according to his accusers, should have known that General Custer, with his renowned courage and ability, would be moving to keep his promise to support him, while at the same time trying to defeat the Indians. The Defense had to prove that there was plenty of time for Custer to have reached Ford B and launch an attack, and the only way such an attack would not have taken place was that Custer met such an overwhelming number of Indians, he was forced to retreat. This would have taken place before Reno withdrew from the timber. Since the Indians didn't leave until Reno's troops reached the bluff, they would not have had time to return and be instrumental in defeating Custer. Major Reno and Captain Benteen were so preoccupied on Reno Hill that, though others may have heard gunfire to the north, they did not.

Recorder Lee, speaking for the Prosecution, also wanted the court and public to know that General Custer had been warned the Indians were not fleeing, and that Major Reno should have known Custer would have been aware of that fact. Reno's Defense, inferring that Lieutenant Cooke had gone to the ford with Reno, provided the Prosecution with the means to suggest that Reno realized Custer got the message. The Prosecution accomplished this goal by having Girard tell Reno that the Indians were not running, and that he was going back to inform General Custer. The Defense's use of the point that Adjutant Cooke was present at the ford now made it possible for Girard to have given Cooke the message and still have had time to return and join Major Reno. In a later interview with Walter Camp, Lieutenant DeRudio does give credence to Girard's account by saying he saw him talking with Major Reno in the middle of the stream.[5] At the Reno Court, DeRudio supported Girard and the Prosecution in his sighting of General Custer after Reno's troops retreated into the timber, and the claim that this was only 5 or 6 minutes before they left the timber.[6] This could then coincide with Girard's reported sighting of Custer as Reno's troops moved into the timber. From a time standpoint these sightings were important to the Prosecution, and actually were their main argument in the testimony used against Major Reno. The only person who seemed to have looked at his watch was DeRudio, who said he looked at it every 10 minutes. This would make his 5 or 6 minutes an accurate estimate of when his sighting occurred, and he said Custer was some distance south of Weir Point. If DeRudio was the officer Girard referred to in his interview with Walter Camp – the officer who failed to give him the supporting story he expected, purporting to be under pressure from the defense and military – it must not have involved his sighting of Custer. Girard might have wished that DeRudio had said he mentioned his sighting to Major Reno – that would have made it difficult for the Defense to counter the Prosecution's position – but it did support the Prosecution's main contention that Major Reno left the timber long before General Custer could have reached Ford B. Custer couldn't have gone back down, talked to his officers and men, then moved to Ford B before Reno had left the timber and removed the pressure on the Indian village, thus enabling the Indians to concentrate on Custer.

One of the interesting aspects of the trial is the way the Prosecution reverses an original position and then partly returns to it again. In order to give Girard the excuse to talk to Reno and go back to warn Custer, it was necessary to establish that a large number of Sioux were in the valley at the time Reno reached Ford A. Girard estimated the number at 1500, but as Reno moved down the valley the number was reduced, so that Reno could have been expected to charge the village.[7] But then there was the need to increase the number again; not to the point that Reno would have had justification for leaving the timber, but still enough so that when the Indians were released – because of Reno's action – they would be able to seal the fate of General Custer.

This aspect of the trial produces another dilemma which presented itself to theProsecution and the Defense. I have already mentioned it in one aspect by interrelating the play between the two sides, and the convolutions to which evidence was subjected. Recorder Lee had to concentrate on having it recognized that Custer knew Major Reno was in trouble, and Reno should have known General Custer would be coming to his aid. Besides the message to Custer, they needed some officer to have seen Custer on the ridge, but not too soon. As I have pointed out, Lieutenant DeRudio came through for them.

Since a number of troopers reported in later interviews with Camp and others that they saw General Custer on the ridge, either at the time they were reforming after crossing Ford A or part way down the valley, it is hard to believe that some of Reno's officers would not have seen Custer's command at that time.* This evidence, from a timing standpoint, would have helped the Defense, because General Custer would then have had plenty of time to reach Ford B even before Major Reno moved into the timber. However, Mr. Gilbert couldn't press the officers on this point. For the Defense to have admitted that Reno's officers saw General Custer at the time Reno's troops did, would mean they and Reno knew that Custer was executing a flanking movement and would not be supporting them from the rear; consequently their line of defense would have been weakened. From an official military standpoint, Reno

---

*Later Major Moylan claimed he did see Custer on the bluffs as the Indians began to form in front of them. Godfrey's Narrative, *The Custer Myth,* Graham, p. 141.

then should have stayed in the timber no matter what the Indian situation was.

The Prosecution's dilemma was that if the officers testified to seeing General Custer when the troops did, the blame would lie on Custer, not Reno. Custer then should have been supporting Major Reno, since he could have moved to Ford B and attacked the village while Reno was still on his skirmish line. There were no signs or testimony to bear out that such an attack had taken place. Even Varnum's sighting was too early to aid theProsecution in their accusations. It would take a sighting such as the one reported by DeRudio to support their contentions. The sighting five or six minutes before leaving the timber would fit into the necessary time frame; the other sightings wouldn't. But DeRudio would have had to have informed Reno of such a sighting for it to have been effective.

The main trouble with distorting testimony is that it leads to more misrepresentations and the creation of unsound views. One of the major distortions took place because both sides needed to have General Custer facing overwhelming odds as he moved to support Major Reno and attack the Indians. The Defense had General Custer facing so many Indians at Ford B that it prevented him from launching an attack. Such a view supported their argument that the Indians were there, even before they were released by Reno's retreat to the bluffs. The Prosecution's case, although it used later time estimates, also needed to include a large number of Indians. To further secure their timing framework they portrayed Custer moving further downstream. This ensured that when Custer was in a position to attack, the Indians leaving Reno would have had time to arrive and prevent Custer from launching a full-fledged assault. Either way, the testimony has been influential down through the years, both in judging the number of Indians and establishing what happened to General Custer.

The first sentence of the following summation by Recorder Lee is noteworthy in its wording: "We will support you." One can't help but wonder why it wasn't stated – even Major Reno referred to it – since this would have benefited the prosecution's position. Lee and the prosecution attempted to make the jury realize Reno should have expected Custer to support him, if not from the rear, then from some direction. If, according to Reno, his orders said he would be supported by the "whole outfit," then why not say Reno believed the "whole outfit" would be supporting him? The "whole outfit" would include Captain Benteen, and since Major Reno had seen him moving to the left, shouldn't Reno have also expected Benteen to be coming to assist him? One wonders why the "whole outfit" and its ramifications have been glossed over. Was this part of the overall coverup by a military tribunal to protect the military, Reno, and Benteen by not examining the extent and meaning of the orders Custer actually gave?

I believe any analysis of the Reno Court should include the basic summations of the prosecution and the defense.

Recorder Lee, in summing up the Prosecution's position, said:

> The last words from General Custer to Major Reno were, "we will support you." From the time Major Reno started to obey the order, General Custer must have been possessed of that idea, that intention; not for one moment did he forget it. His route downstream lay behind the bluffs or ridge next the river, mainly unexposed to the view of the hostile Indians. He was hurrying on at a rapid gait to strike the foe. Major Reno's support might not come from the rear but he would be supported still with the sound of Custer's guns and the cheers of Custer's men in front. . . . With Reno holding the Indians near him – Benteen coming up with 250 men and Custer striking in front, there was a glorious chance for a thrice glorious victory. Major Reno slipped his hold and all was lost!
>
> . . . The inference from the testimony is therefore perfect that the last view had by General Custer of Major Reno's command was when the latter was engaged; that he waved his hat signalling to Major Reno's command, his own cheering words to his brave men: "Courage boys." He did this doubtless with the hope of being seen by someone and then went back to his own column to make a flank attack in support of Major Reno. It is undisputed, save by opinion, that General Custer's engagement did not commence till after Major Reno had left the timber to retreat to the hill.
>
> . . . Leaving out mere matters of opinion it appears to me from all the testimony that General Custer's column never attempted a crossing at the ford "B." He must have gone around the head of that ravine and evidently sought to cross and attack the village lower down. . . . It seems conclusive that his struggle began soon after Major Reno reached the hill.
>
> The well-known capacity, tenacity and bravery of General Custer and the officers and men who died with him forbid the supposition of a panic and a rout. There was a desperate and sanguinary struggle in which the Indians must have suffered heavily. From the evidence that has been spread before this court, it is manifest that General Custer and his comrades died a death so heroic that it has but few parallels in history. Fighting to the last and against overwhelming odds, they fell on the field of glory. Let no stigma of rout and panic tarnish their blood-bought fame . . .

In his address Mr. Gilbert observed:

> The charges against Major Reno rest largely on the tes-

timony of two mule-packers, a doctor, an Indian scout, a sergeant, and an Indian interpreter.

. . . After the command was received, Reno gave the order to trot and his battalion moved down to the crossing of the river. . . . the battalion went to the other side of the river, and passing through a fringe of timber such as follows the water courses on the western prairies, halted to reform . . . Major Reno saw enough Indians who were approaching him, to judge of their numbers and their disposition. He knew as Benteen knew, as Girard says he knew, that General Custer believed the Indians were retreating, and he could fairly presume that the order he had received from General Custer had been predicated on wrong information.

. . . The Indians were certainly there in number that in the minds of military men justified the belief that they were able to overcome at one and the same time each portion of the command that then engaged them . . . The fact that Reno's withdrawal from the timber had no influence whatever upon the fate of General Custer is seen by two considerations. It is plain from the testimony that Reno was at least forty-five minutes in the timber. During that time General Custer with his command was thrice seen. Lt. Varnum saw the Gray Horse company on the bluffs above the right bank of the river about thirty minutes before Reno left the timber. He believes that Custer had certainly time to reach the point on the map known as Ford "B" before Reno reached the top of the hill. [Since Lt. Varnum said he saw the Gray Horse troop when Reno had just established his skirmish line, the Defense could have made a better case than they did.] DeRudio, who saw with straining eyes, Custer with Cooke standing on the high land overlooking Reno in the timber, states that the firing he heard down the river was almost simultaneous with Reno's reaching the top of the hill. [As shown by this statement, this is the strong point in the accusations made against Major Reno. It also brings out the dilemma for the Defense: the necessity to see Custer on the ridge fairly early, but not too soon, and without Major Reno being aware of the sightings.]

. . . Custer having promised to support Reno and having had a view of him attacking the Indians under his order, would undoubtedly in turn have charged the Indians at the first point where he could have reached them. That point was the ford "B."

It cannot be doubted by this court that the testimony that they have heard, not merely from officers of Reno's command, but also from the evidence given by Lt. Col. Sheridan, who made a careful examination of that point – that there was a proper point for General Custer to give his promised support to Reno, if it was in the power of his command to support him at all. If the mind can believe testimony and draw any inference from it, it is overwhelmingly clear that Custer had reached ford "B," where he could have crossed to the Indian village, before the Indians whom Reno was diverting by his attack in the timber could have reached that point; and from the known character of Custer for valor and bravery, it was equally plain that not withstanding the thousand Indians whom Reno detained at the upper end of the village, there were Indians at the ford "B," in such overwhelming number as to make it a matter of madness for Custer and his command to engage them there. That explains the fact of the sleeping village which Martin says Custer saw. [?]

So far then as Reno's retreat from the timber was concerned, it had no effect whatever on the fate of General Custer, for not a man nor a horse were found dead at the ford "B," [?] and the first indication that Custer had found his enemy was at least eight hundred yards below the ford on the right bank of the river.

Another consideration proves this. Custer and his men were found in such position, with such separation and with such disorder, that it proves that whatever resistance they made, brave and heroic as it was, was in the nature of a defense and not of an attack. Competent judges have shown, not merely that the struggle could not have lasted more than an hour, but that from its very beginning it was hopeless . . . .

It has not escaped the attention of the Court that when Benteen came up to the point where he afterwards joined Reno, he saw the Indians still in the bottom and that he thought they were at least eight hundred or nine hundred in number. Sgt. Culbertson, a most careful witness, fixed their number at about a thousand . . . Lt. DeRudio, who watched them from the timber in which he had remained said, that they did not retire because Reno left the timber, but because Benteen was seen to approach on the other side of the river.

The trial, I am afraid, changed and colored testimony because its real aim was not to determine what happened to General Custer, but to defend or accuse Major Reno. The end result of the trial was muddied waters, stirred up even further, making objective study and conclusions problematic.

SOURCES

1. Stewart, *Custer's Luck*, p. 319.
2. Graham, *The Custer Myth*, p. 305.
3. Graham, *Reno Court Abstract*, p. 230.
4. Utley, *Cavalier in Buckskin*, p. 187.
5. Camp, *Custer in 76*, p. 84.
6. Graham, *Reno Court Abstract*, p. 115.
7. Ibid., p. 42.

4

The Reno Court Cover-Ups – Part II*

At the Reno Court there were two primary cover-ups.** The first involved the actual orders General Custer gave Major Reno and Captain Benteen. This was the most important cover-up, due to the effect it has had on the perception of Custer's actions. Reno and Benteen attributed Custer's supposed failure to give explicit orders to his ignorance of where the Indian village was located. They even went so far as to claim that Custer did not know there was any large number of Indians in the immediate vicinity. Reno also stated that he believed Custer would follow him and support him from behind. These reasons were used to justify the actions taken by Reno and Benteen.

The second cover-up was necessary in order to explain why Reno and Benteen were late in coming to the aid of Custer after gunfire was heard downstream. Here several excuses were created. One was the distance Benteen traveled on what was later called his "wild goose chase" to the left. Benteen referred to the difficulty encountered in the terrain. Then, when they reached the ridge, there was the alleged need to wait for the packs which Benteen said were a considerable distance behind the battalion. These distortions were necessary, for it was known that the Indians facing Reno's forces left during the time Benteen's battalion joined what remained of Reno's troops. There could be no denying that both Benteen and the packs had orders to come to Custer's aid; therefore, the sound of gunfire necessitated a military move to support the troops under fire.

The cover-up consisted of several elements. Both Reno and Benteen declared that they had not heard gunfire. Though Custer's troops may have been under attack, they could temporarily take care of themselves. Reno's soldiers needed time to recover from their engagement. There was the need to take care of the wounded and prepare them for such a move.

Reno's troops were low on ammunition. The ammunition packs were six or seven miles behind Benteen's battalion and were moving slowly. The officers in command of the packs received no orders from Custer. Once the packs arrived, Reno's forces moved as quickly as possible to support Custer. By the time they reached Weir Point and could view the Custer battlefield, nothing was seen or heard from Custer's troops. The full force of the Indians then moved against them, and in order to obtain a better defensive position, they retreated to the Reno entrenchment area.

There was certainly a need to provide aid for the wounded and prepare them for a move downstream, but this could have been accomplished while the main body moved rapidly toward Custer. Thus, manipulation of timing became the primary means to cover up Reno's and Benteen's failure to act. Their conduct could not even be explained by Benteen's extended excursion period and the late arrival of the packs. A time change was also needed.

When a number of people are involved, it is difficult to be consistent. This was true of the cover-up involving the timing and the arrival of the packs. How far behind Benteen's battalion were the packs? Benteen placed them at a distance of six or seven miles,[1] but was this an accurate estimate? Did they receive orders to support Custer? Sergeant Kanipe indicated that he delivered orders for the packs to hurry, cut across country, and come to the aid of Custer. He placed the packs close behind Benteen, at a distance of about one mile.[2] Trumpeter Martin said at the Reno Court of Inquiry that he was sent by Benteen with a message to the packs, and indicated that they were not far back and were moving at different gaits.[3] Later Martin denied making this statement, and claimed that the court misinterpreted him. I believe his realization of the effect it could have on the officers, as well as his army loyalty and desire not to contradict Benteen, caused him to disavow his remarks.

Since the packs did not cut across or hurry to the aid of Custer, it was necessary for Captain McDougall and Lieutenant Mathey to deny receiving any messages. Mathey reported that the packs followed the main trail and even rested for fifteen minutes.[4] McDougall testified to hearing gunfire and seeing Captain Weir's move toward Custer.[5] This would imply an arrival on Reno Hill <u>earlier</u> than what was being portrayed by Reno and Benteen. Even Lieutenant Hare's meeting and returning with some ammunition packs would suggest a closer proximity to Benteen's battalion than Benteen proclaimed.

There seems little doubt that a cover-up was devised in order to justify their failure to move to the aid of Custer's companies. Whether they would have been able to prevent the complete annihilation of those soldiers or whether it may have caused the destruction of the total command, is a matter of conjecture. However, there can be no military excuse for not going to support Custer immediately, even if the ammo packs arrived as late as claimed.

At the time of the Reno Court of Inquiry, the second cover-up was more difficult to hide than the first, since more

---

*Part II is taken from my book, *The Custer Controversy – A Critical Analysis*. As I stated in the Preface, at the time I wrote my original manuscript I was not aware of the timing cover-up.
**There were actually three major cover-ups. The third would be the failure to point out Reno's troopers' early sighting of Custer as they reformed and were partway down the valley.

people were involved and had knowledge of the timing, gunfire and actions. The officers would have wanted to avoid any penetrating questions, not only out of a sense of loyalty, but because of the reflection on their own conduct. Captain Weir probably would have exposed the scheme, but he conveniently had died. Lieutenant Gibson could have given damaging evidence on both cover-ups, but he was not invited to testify. Captain French would undoubtedly have given detrimental statements concerning Major Reno's actions, but he was undergoing a "benzine" court martial. Sergeant Kanipe had retired but should have been called as a witness, because under any true investigative questioning his testimony would have been crucial.

Trumpeter Martin almost upset the "apple cart" by saying that Benteen sent him back to the packs and they were only a short distance behind. The attempt by the court to discredit Martin during his interrogation was apparent.* They failed to question Martin on the initial orders Custer gave to Reno and Benteen, and prevented him from testifying that Custer gave another order.[6] The court's fear of what he might reveal led to Martin's early dismissal.

The military and officers had a problem. Despite Benteen's excursion distortions, the contended distance of the packs, and McDougall and Mathey's claim that they received no messages, the evidence strongly suggested that the lapse of time was still too long from when the packs arrived to when Reno moved to investigate the gunfire. Changing the time when the division of the command took place was the only solution to their dilemma. The time frame also perplexed Colonel Graham, but he could not believe in the possibility of a military cover-up, so he failed to follow it to a logical conclusion.

It seems surprising that those investigating the battle would not have debated the slowness attributed to Benteen's movements, and then associated them with the need for a cover-up. Even if, as some believe, his battalion was to act in a reserve capacity, Benteen was too good a soldier not to recognize the urgency of the situation. The logical conclusion is that he moved at a relatively fast pace. However, neither he nor Reno had followed Custer's orders; this necessitated the first cover-up. If the orders had been exposed, both men would have been blamed for the debacle. It is understandable why Benteen used distance and terrain to account for his late arrival, while others, realizing his measurements were in error, indicated that his gait and even his enmity toward Custer were a more likely explanation.

Colonel Graham, in a letter to General Edgerly, said:

---

*When I wrote this I had only read Graham's, *Reno Court Abstract*. The discrediting of Martin became even more apparent after reading the full transcript of the trial.

It puzzles me greatly that nearly all the early accounts of the fight put its occurrence several hours earlier than do the later ones. According to the first interviews and accounts, Custer went to the Crow's Nest at daylight, the command crossed the divide and was separated into battalions about ten o'clock. Reno's fight commenced about noon, Custer's about 12:30, and Benteen joined Reno about 2:30. But Wallace's itinerary and most of the later accounts and in particular General Godfrey's story, show that Custer did not go to the Crow's Nest until after ten a.m.; that he stayed there over an hour and that the command did not cross the divide until noon . . . .

I cannot account for these discrepancies in time. I have asked General Godfrey many times; but he is unable to account for them except upon the theory that everybody was too busy to take account of the hours.

The time element has to me, however, a most important bearing, for if the fight in the valley did in fact commence at noon, and Custer's column was engaged within a half hour thereafter, it is hard to account for Reno and Benteen during the several hours that intervened before their attempt to advance down the river, which occurred, by common consent, about 5 o'clock. On the other hand, if Benteen only reached Reno after 4 p.m., and they were forced to wait for the arrival of the mules and the distribution of ammunition, it is easy to see that this must have consumed an hour or more, and so account for the lateness of the advance.[7]

The testimonies of the scouts and Lieutenant Varnum (who was in charge of the scouts), indicates that they sighted grazing ponies and smoke from the Indian village at dawn.[8] According to the Ree scout Red Star, he reported the sighting to Custer just as the sun was coming up.[9] A consensus of Lakota and Cheyenne testimony had Reno's attack taking place at mid-day. Captain Benteen's statement that he reached the main trail around 1:00 p.m.,[10] and Godfrey's that they arrived on Reno Hill by 2:30 p.m.,[11] support this earlier period.

In a letter to Captain E. W. Smith, Acting Assistant Adjutant General at the 7th Cavalry Headquarters, on July 5, 1876, Major Reno gave the following timetable of the main events:[12] The command crossed the divide about 8:00 a.m. They approached the Lone Tepee around 11:00 a.m.; about 12:30 p.m. Reno received his orders to move against the village, and by 2:30 p.m. he was on the ridge meeting Benteen. The packs arrived soon after, and Reno then moved to aid Custer. Reno admitted to hearing gunfire, but when he moved to the highest bluff (Weir Point) he saw and heard nothing, which would indicate an engagement was still taking place. By six o'clock he had retreated to Reno Hill and was battling with the Indians.

At the Reno Court there was an unaccounted two hour lapse which this scenario could not justify. It was apparent that there was a need to change this time period by extending the official duration by some two hours. This was done by delaying the division of the command until after 12:00 Noon. This deception was necessary not only to prevent a court-martial of Reno, but also the indictment of Benteen, McDougall, and Mathey, and a discredit to the other officers and the 7th Cavalry in general.

One of my primary criticisms of the proposed scenarios is their excessive reliance on establishing exact time estimates. Benteen's excursion is a good example of how difficult this is. There is no way to set either a precise gait time determination or distance measurement. Testimony differs on both matters, even without the attempt to distort facts. Roger Darling's analysis seems to be the most accurate. By his map, the distance Benteen traveled appears to be roughly eight miles from the division point to the morass.[13]

However, it cannot be judged with any degree of accuracy the actual gaits that the troops used, or how long they delayed in allowing Gibson to move to the top of the bluffs to observe, return and report. The same can be said about the troop movement once they regained the main trail. It seems acceptable that Benteen was back on the main trail by one o'clock. Between 1:00 p.m. and 2:30 p.m. they watered, traveled nearly five and a half miles, met Kanipe, Martin, and the Crow scouts, saw some fighting and burning in the valley, made decisions, and moved to Reno Hill. This would make any strict time and gait measurements completely speculative. But the timing does suggest that Benteen moved at a comparatively fast trot rather than a slow walk. It seems unlikely that Benteen, for whatever reason, would have gone as slowly as portrayed in most accounts.

In my opinion Custer would have taken the following actions: Realizing that he would soon be launching his attack on the Indian village, he sent Benteen a message to that effect. This would most likely have been at the time he summoned Reno to cross Ash Creek, or when he gave Reno his attack orders. After dividing the command, Custer moved at a fairly slow pace to the Lone Tepee in order to give Benteen ample time to accomplish his mission (i.e., reach the Little Big Horn, prevent an ambush or scattering, and make sure there were no other Indian camps). If one assumes that Custer left after dividing his command at approximately 10:15 a.m., he would have been near or at the Lone Tepee around 12:00 o'clock. Since he hadn't heard from Benteen, he sent Sergeant Major Sharrow and the Ree scout Stabbed, or a third messenger, to inform Benteen that he was about to initiate his attack on the village. Custer would presume that Benteen was nearing the Little Big Horn, and would want him to move in support of Reno. Custer would then have six companies attacking from the south, while he with his five companies attempted to encircle the village. At the Crow's Nest, Custer had expressed such a plan to his Indian scouts.[14]

Either Sergeant Major Sharrow or a third courier would have moved to a high promontory where he would have seen Benteen's battalion on its way back to the main trail. His work completed, Stabbed would have been released with a message for Custer. The courier would then have proceeded to meet Benteen. From a time standpoint, this meeting would have taken place along Valley 3 or near the morass, as reported by several witnesses, and inferred by Edgerly.[15]

(This type of analysis, which uses events to support a general time estimate, is what I refer to as an "event-time-event" determination. This method is more accurate in defining what occurred than trying to fix events in a "time-motion" analysis, as Gray and others have done. Because of the many interpolating factors, an examination of time-motion is subordinate to the correlation of events and a general time is then established.)

In regard to the second cover-up, it should be pointed out that even a quickly executed move to aid Custer by Reno's forces would not have changed the outcome of the battle. Custer's engagement did not last over two hours, and it began while Reno was still on his skirmish line. By the time Reno or Benteen could have made the necessary preparation to move, they would have been too late. This consideration does not excuse the lengthy period of inaction on their part, nor does it justify the cover-up at the Reno proceedings.

The recognition that the Indians viewed the troops on Nye Cartwright ridge, and the artifacts found there, have helped make the first cover-up more historically damaging to Custer's image. It created fanciful scenarios of an incompetent buffoon, and prejudiced the reputation of one of our great cavalry leaders. The truth is that Custer's orders and actions were sound. But even if Reno and Benteen's mistakes had never taken place, the annihilation of Custer's command would have. The success of Custer's plan hinged on the presence of Custer himself. When he was shot at the Minniconjou Ford (Ford B), his plan and the possibility of its success collapsed.

The second major cover-up at the Reno Court of Inquiry was necessitated by the need to extend the time between when Benteen's troops met with Reno's forces. This was done by changing the time of the division of the command from around 10 a.m. to 12:00 Noon. To accommodate this distortion, it was necessary to shorten the period it took Reno to cross Ford A and begin his move down the Little Bighorn valley. This apparently paradoxical extension of time on the one hand and reduction on the other was essential in manipulating how the conduct of the officers involved was perceived. The need to extend the division was required to conceal the actual length of time between the point when Benteen and the packs met Reno, and when they were known to have moved in support of Custer. The shortening of the ford crossing helped show an expeditious, competent Reno, but was primarily needed to back Reno's claim that he only expected Custer to support him from the rear. Any lengthy period in crossing the ford would have placed Custer either close behind or at a place where Reno should have recognized – even without orders – that Custer was attempting to flank the Indians. Reno should then have remained in the timber; by not doing so, he laid himself open to court-martial proceedings and the charge of causing Custer's defeat.

The shortened time used for Reno to cross Ford A has resulted in the creation of many of the erroneous and senseless actions attributed to Custer. These statements made by Colonel Graham and Captain Carter should be noted (although neither of these remarks were made in direct reference to the crossing, they do apply).

Colonel Graham:

> ... you know how long military movements take. Figure it out. Could it have taken less than fifteen or twenty minutes to do the things he did? He did all these things – not one right after another as if on a schedule, but as the necessity for them developed. You have had long experience in handling troops, I have had a little myself. But we know that situations do not develop, nor are troop movements made, in an instant.[16]

Captain Carter:

> I kept the time or tried to, in our Mexican raid and have always said we halted to cut off the packs only a few minutes. It must have been nearly an hour if not more. Time goes "blewy" when men are exhausted and are marching night and day.[17]

The Event-Time-Event Analysis

I will attempt to illustrate the effect of a shortened crossing by presenting my estimates and differentiating them from those of John Gray and the more accepted itineraries. I will use the times Reno gave in his letter of July 5, 1876,[18] rather than the later statements associated with the cover-up. I will then transpose Gray's estimates on Reno's calculations, indicating in parentheses Gray's generally accepted time using the 12:00 p.m. division rather than the 10:00 a.m. reference.[19]

I accept Gray's belief that Custer gave Reno's attack orders approximately a mile and a quarter from Ford A. It would have been 12:30 p.m. by the estimate in Reno's letter; Gray uses 2:43 p.m. Gray has Reno reaching the ford in ten minutes, at 12:40 p.m. (2:53). Although I believe it may have taken slightly longer to separate the troops and move out, I will accept his estimate.

Gray has Reno crossing in ten minutes and ready to move down the valley at 12:50 p.m. (3:03). This is the most significant timing error. I think Reno would have taken forty minutes from when he first arrived at the Little Big Horn to the point where he examined the valley, appraised the fords, made his crossing (in a column of twos), watered, moved through the timber, realigned his troops, and was ready to move down the valley. My time estimate is 1:20 p.m. Gray determined that it took fifteen minutes for Reno to travel two miles and establish his skirmish line; the time would be 1:05 p.m. (3:18). Using Gray's movement, distance and time, I would place it at 1:35 p.m. Gray employs the generally accepted time that Reno fought in the valley as thirty-five minutes. Reno would then have begun his retreat at 1:40 p.m.(3:53); I would place it at 2:10 p.m. Gray calculates that Reno's retreat to Reno Hill took seventeen minutes. It would then be 1:57p.m. (4:10); by my timetable it would be 2:27 p.m. which is roughly the same as what Reno and Godfrey first indicated. (2:30 p.m.).

The following may help illustrate the above: "A" column will represent the early division of the command as Reno brought out in his letter of July, 1876. Gray's time-motion analysis will be used except for the time of the division. "B" column represents John Gray's estimate of Reno's movements using the later "official" timing division of the command. Gray's time motion analysis is found on page 272, Table 6, and passage 290, Table 7, in his book, *Custer's Last Campaign*. "C" column is my estimate using Gray's timing except for the Ford A crossing and the early division of the command.

	"A"	"B"	"C"
Separation from Custer	12:30	2:43	12:30
Move to Ford A	12:40	2:53	12:40
Crossing Ford A	12:50	3:03	1:20
To Skirmish Line	1:05	3:18	1:35
Valley Fight	1:40	3:53	2:10
Retreat to Ridge	1:57	4:10	2:27

If we were to use the early division of the command as represented in "A" column with Gray's ten minute crossing at Ford A (as shown), Reno would have arrived even earlier on the ridge. This would make his movement downstream to aid Custer even more of a travesty, but it illustrates (as previously stated) the dilemma the defense

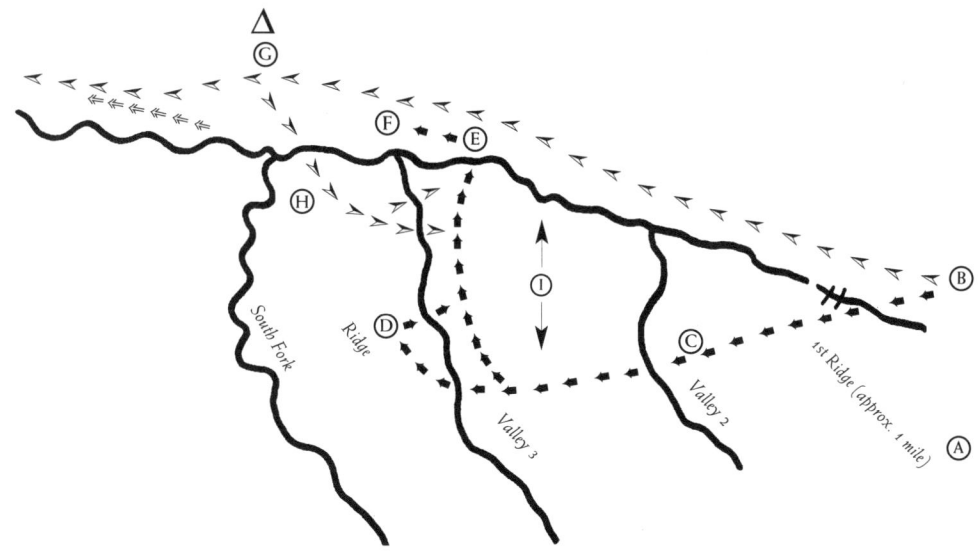

Map 1

- Command divided.
- Benteen's route (according to Roger Darling).
- Custer's route.
- Reno crossing to Custer's side of Ash or Reno Creek by the time they reached Lone Tepee.
- Benteen's route covers approximately 7 miles to where it reaches the main trail.
- Custer passed point E after approximately 6 miles.

◅ Custer's route
← Benteen's route
⇐ Reno's route after crossing Ash or Reno Creek

(A) Crow's nest
(B) Division of command
(C) Captain Benteen & Lieutenant Godfrey report seeing Custer's gray horse troop traveling on main trail (Darling)
(D) Lt. Gibson goes to high point – sights river in distance
(E) Benteen reaches main trail (Darling)
(F) Morass
(G) Lone tepee (hypothetical)
(H) Route of Sergeant Major Sharrow or a third courier, probably met Benteen at the morass or on his way down Valley 3
(I) Maximum distance separating Custer & Benteen – 2½ to 3 miles

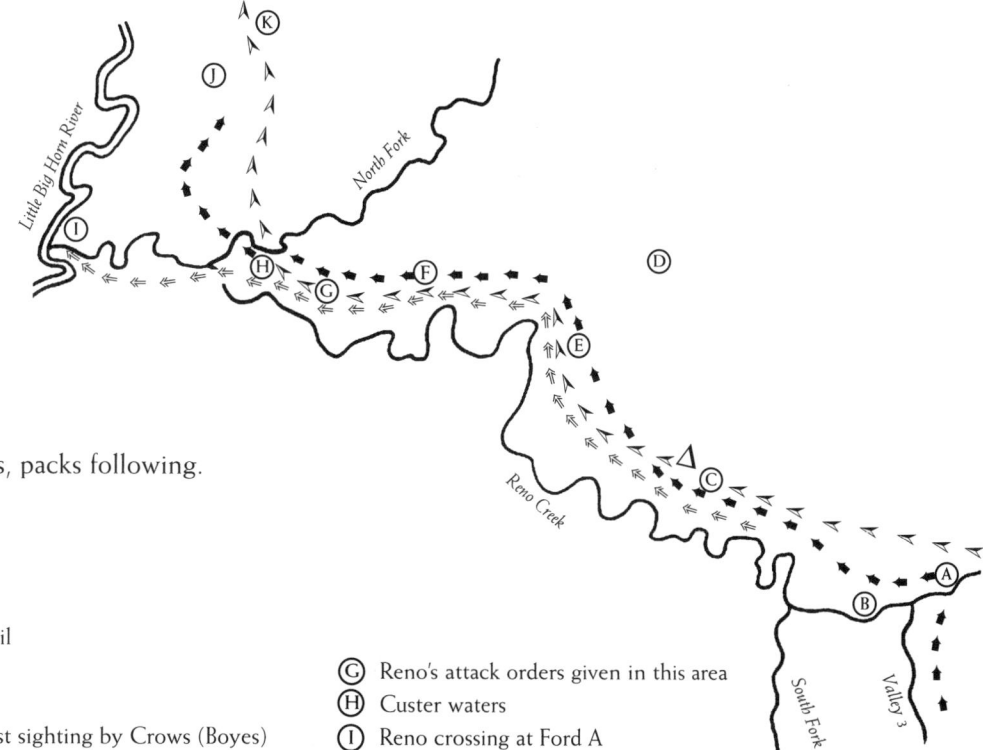

Map 2

Continuation of Map 1

Movement of 3 battalions, packs following.

◅ Custer's route
← Benteen's route
⇐ Reno's route

(A) Benteen reaches main trail
(B) Morass
(C) Lone Tepee
(D) Referred to as Custer's last sighting by Crows (Boyes)
(E) Kanipe meets Benteen
(F) Martin meets Benteen
(G) Reno's attack orders given in this area
(H) Custer waters
(I) Reno crossing at Ford A
(J) Reno's entrenchment
(K) Sharpshooter Ridge

was in; they needed both a quick crossing and yet an overall extended time. I believe my view of the crossing is more accurate, but either way, the need to change the time of the division of the command is apparent.

This provides substantial evidence that when Reno reached Ford A, his crossing would have taken longer than previously acknowledged. The only other way to account for timing errors (except for slight or immaterial ones) would be to change the appraisal of how long Reno fought in the valley. Writers, such as W. Kent King, thought this time was much shorter than generally recognized and that a major attempt at a cover-up resulted in extending it to thirty five minutes.[20] Considering the actions supposedly taken by Reno, thirty-five minutes seems a fairly accurate estimate.

The difference in time attributed to the crossing is essential in ascertaining Custer's actions. If one uses the thirty extra minutes and still has Custer reaching the ridge after Reno has started down the valley, this estimate indicates that from the time Reno and Custer separated (12:30 p.m.), Custer would have remained along Ash Creek for fifty minutes. In no way does the testimony of Rees, Crows, Kanipe or Martin support this thesis. Instead, it would mean that Custer was on the ridge before Reno began his move down the valley. This supports Trumpeter Martin's repeated claims that he did not see Reno, as well as Custer's purported remarks. This assumption would not refute the fact that at least some of Custer's and Reno's troops saw each other.* Since Martin and Custer would have been some distance ahead of the rest of the command as they moved along the ridge, they, or at least Martin, would not necessarily have seen Reno. Custer, on the other hand, may have seen Reno while observing from a high point.

These considerations reveal the need for the first cover-up. They would bear out the contention that Custer had prior knowledge of the village and had plans to attack and encircle it. He undoubtedly would have expressed this intention in orders to Reno and Benteen, as was implied by Davern[21] and specified in Martin's recollections.[22] Statements made by Privates O'Neil and Donohough would also give credence to this view. When O'Neil was asked where he expected Custer to support Reno he said, "I think the general's command would cut through from the other end of the village." Private Donahue, in a letter to the *Bismark Tribune* stated, "Reno was to be supported by Benteen."[23] With Reno still engaged in the valley, Custer would have had more than enough time to reach Ford B while the Indian village was in a state of near panic. Clearly Custer would have wanted to synchronize his attack with Reno. I believe Custer, as he observed the Indian encampment and the surrounding terrain, realized that all five companies would not be effective in attacking at Ford B. He would then have planned to lead Yates' battalion in such an attack, while sending Keogh's battalion to Luce Ridge to act in a reserve role – a common cavalry practice. From there, Keogh would have been in a position to take several actions: Come to Custer's aid if needed, help prevent the Indians from scattering, and direct and give orders to Benteen when he arrived. This supposition is backed by the time of the Indian sightings on Nye Cartwright, and the fact that Calhoun and Keogh were the only two commanders found with their companies.

When one factors in Custer's psyche, this is the logical action for him to take – not an indecisive failure to attack which so many scenarios have suggested. Evidence supports the contention that Custer reached the ford while Reno was still engaged in the valley, and that he was subsequently shot there – an event which resulted in a disorganized retreat that ultimately led to the destruction of his command. It was the shooting of Custer at the ford and not any faulty planning or actions on his part that brought on the debacle.

SOURCES

1. Brininstool, *Troopers with Custer*, p. 79.
2. Hammer, ed. Camp, *Custer in 76*, p. 93.
3. Graham, *Reno Court Abstract*, p. 131.
4. Ibid., p. 189.
5. Hammer, ed. Camp, *Custer in 76*, p. 70.
6. Gray, *Custer's Last Campaign*, pp. 336, 337.
7. Graham, *The Custer Myth*, p. 215.
8. Carroll, ed., *Varnum, Custer's Chief of Scouts, The Reminiscence of Charles A. Varnum*, p. 62.
9. Graham, *The Custer Myth*, p. 21.
10. Ibid., p. 180.
11. Ibid., p. 142.
12. Overfield II, *The Little Bighorn, 1876*, Reno to E.W. Smith, pp. 43, 44, 45.
13. Darling, Roger, *Benteen's Scout*, See Darling's map.
14. Graham, *The Custer Myth*, p. 33.
15. Graham, *Reno Court Abstract*, p. 159.
16. Graham, *The Custer Myth*, p. 307.
17. Ibid., p. 315.
18. Overfield II, *The Little Big Horn, 1876*, Reno to W. W. Smith.
19. Gray, *Custer's Last Campaign*, Table 6, p. 272; Table 7, p. 290.
20. King, W. Kent, *Massacre, The Custer Cover-Up*, p. 13.
21. Stewart, *Custer's Luck*, p. 327; Officers Transcript, p. 480, Reno Court, p. 269.
22. Graham, *The Custer Myth*, p. 289.
23. King, W. Kent. *MASSACRE: The Custer Cover-Up*. Custer Trail Series, Vol. III, El Segundo: Upton & Sons, p. 182.

---

*The failure of Major Reno to report such sightings is an integral part of both the first and second cover-up. It should be considered the third major cover-up. Note addendum.

5
Wallace, Girard, Keogh and Cooke

The distortions and cover-ups at the Reno Court tainted later attempts to determine what happened to General Custer. Testimony that was used to protect Major Reno and Captain Benteen contorted and falsified an already difficult and murky picture, making it even more of a quandary. It became very difficult to sift through the conflicting remarks and evidence to arrive at logical conclusions.

Benteen's diatribe against Custer, along with his and Reno's evasion as to what their orders consisted of, prompted most people to think that Custer had no plan of attack or knowledge of where the Indians were. Benteen's and Reno's portrayal of Custer was willfully contorted to protect the latter and to justify the actions of the former.

As I suggested in examining the testimony from the Reno Court of Inquiry, the defense needed someone to verify the orders Major Reno received from General Custer. Reno's adjutant Lieutenant Hodgson had been killed. Company officers had not been in a position to know what the orders were, so could not provide any validation. But Lieutenant Wallace, who had the job of itinerist, was unattached and could play such a role. Mr. Gilbert, the defense counsel, would want as few officers as possible directly involved in the formation or discussion of stratagems. Mr. Gilbert would have known that much of the testimony would be conflicting, jumbled and confusing, but this would not hurt his client except in a few specific areas. His two main witnesses would have to be included in briefings to make sure their stories coincided in the critical areas. Wallace would be brought into this inner circle to corroborate evidence, particularly Reno's orders or lack thereof. This was necessary because I don't think Wallace was at Major Reno's side until he reached the ford, the skirmish line, or possibly not at all.

Why do I believe Wallace was not with the Major, as both he and Reno professed? First, what baffles me is why so many questions were not asked and the answers not found at a time when it would have been possible to do so.

At the Reno Court of Inquiry Lieutenant Wallace said:

> I was riding near Major Reno and with his battalion . . . There was no announcement made to Reno as to junction with Benteen that I know of . . . I was riding to the left of Lt. Hodgson, Reno's adjutant, and he to the left of Reno . . . It was the understanding of all the other officers to whom I talked that General Custer was to support Reno . . . Reno moved off at a gallop till we came to the crossing; there we came to a walk and the horses scattered . . . Lt. Cook and Captain Keogh went with us toward the ford. I heard them talking as we rode along. I thought at the time they went with us into the fight . . . Reno received the orders to charge about 2:15 p.m. . . . I don't know where Lt. Cook and Capt. Keogh turned back. I saw them within a half mile of the ford A. . . . [Reno] moved over [Ash Creek] with his battalion and the two [Custer and Reno] moved along 10 to 15 yards apart . . . The heads of the columns about opposite each other. . . . There was some mingling together of the men . . . Some of General Custer's officers started (toward the river) with us . . . .[1]

Major Reno's testimony offers the following version of events:

> He called the officers together and I attended of course [after the Crow's Nest] . . . He said the Indian scouts reported a large village – that he did not believe it himself . . . About <u>10 o'clock</u> Lt. Cook came to me and said, the General directs that you take specific command of Companies "M," "A," and "G." I said "Is that all?" I made no further inquiry . . . Captain Benteen had started to the left . . . I had no instruction as to him.
>
> Shortly after, Lt. Cook came to me. "General Custer directs you to take as rapid a gait as you think prudent and <u>charge the village</u> afterward and you will be supported by <u>the whole outfit</u>. . . .My Adjutant, Lt. Hodgson, was on my left and Lt. Wallace on his left. . . .He came up and said, laughing, that he was going as volunteer aide . . . He proceeded to carry out my orders . . . At the time I was in the timber I had not the remotest idea where either the pack train or Benteen's column were. . . . There was no plan communicated to us. . . .If one existed the subordinate commanders did not know of it. . . .At the time I left the timber I did not see Benteen's column, nor had any intimation that Benteen was to support me in my attack on the bottom . . . the only expectation of support I had from the order, I received, was from the rear . . . I had no reason to believe that General Custer would support me in any other manner than from the rear . . . <u>in my opinion there was no other way</u> . . . <u>an attack on the flank would not have been a support under the circumstances, though I may have stated in my report that he intended to do so</u> . . . I did not know where Benteen was; he might have gone . . . when I said in my report that General Custer meant to support me by a flank attack, it was a conviction formed after the fight. <u>I did not see how it was possible, on account of the high bank on the other side, for support to come from the flanks</u> . . . <u>There was no communication to me that Custer's command had been sighted from the timber</u> . . . [my underlining][2]

Note the repetition of questions concerning orders, support, Reno's lack of knowledge about Benteen's actions, his not having seen or been informed of Custer being sighted on the ridge, and, in other parts of his testimony, questions pertaining to Girard. Reno's statement that he had no idea that Benteen was to support him in his attack in the valley could certainly infer this was a common conception.

Both Lieutenant Wallace and Major Reno state that Wallace was by Reno's side. Wallace's remarks indicate he was with Reno from the time the command was divided.

Varnum said he reported to Custer as Reno was moving out at a trot, toward Ford A:

> Lt. Varnum asked General Custer where they were going and the General said, "To begin the attack." I asked instructions and he said to go with them if you want to. Lt. Hare and I and my whole party started at the trot. Lieutenant George D. Wallace, a classmate of mine and dear friend and old roommate, was riding at the head of the column with the General. He was acting topographical officer. I called back to him "Come on, Nick, with the fighting men. I don't stay back with the coffee coolers." Custer laughed and waved his hat and told Wallace he could go and Wallace joined me. It so happened that his troop G and my A were with the advancing squadron under Major Reno. We put the spurs to our horses and crossed the river with the command and then pulled out ahead, with the scouts, guides, etc. The valley was full of Indians riding madly in every direction. We advanced rapidly down the valley, the Indians retiring before us for about a mile, Wallace, Hare and myself riding together.[3]

Here we have two good friends who were both competent officers. It is unlikely that Lieutenant Varnum would have had an ulterior motive in giving testimony that differed from that of Wallace. Presumably Varnum was not even aware of what statements Wallace gave to the Reno Court. Was Varnum lying for some unknown reason, or was he merely mistaken? Were Wallace and Reno lying, misunderstood, or misinterpreted? Since Wallace and Reno's words were taken at the Court of Inquiry, they should not have been misrepresented. It would seem to justify the conclusion of Captain Carter, Girard, and others, that officers gave testimony to protect Reno. There was no reason for Varnum to concoct such a story, and unlikely that he would have simply forgotten what happened. Obviously the participants would have had difficulty in recalling just where, when, or who was involved in every event, especially if it did not seem significant at the time. But Varnum's statement to Wallace and his description of Custer's reaction do not appear to be something that he just imagined. A careful study of the testimony, particularly the remarks made at the Reno Court, indicate that Varnum was credible.

It is easy to understand the difficulty the participants had in recalling just where, when or who was involved in events, especially in regard to those that did not seem significant at the time. One might question if Lieutenant Wallace moved down the valley with Lieutenant Varnum and the scouts – certainly Mitch Bouyer did not – yet Varnum had him doing just that, in the revised draft of his testimony. However, his statement to Wallace and the reaction of General Custer seemed to go beyond what Varnum might imagine or mistakenly think took place. As I continued to study testimony and particularly remarks made at the Reno Court of Inquiry, I came to believe Lieutenant Varnum. I recognized the need of the Defense to have an officer who could verify the orders Major Reno received. I noted the number of questions that dealt with the orders: where Reno expected the support to come from, whether he knew where Benteen was, etc. The death of Lieutenant Hodgson created the need for such an officer, and Wallace, being the itinerist or topographical officer and not being assigned to any company, would be the logical choice. With the one exception of Lieutenant Edgerly's contradictory statement, Captain Benteen had been left to interpret his own orders, and with his vehement attack on Custer and the instructions he received, Benteen seemed to have effectively diverted any penetrating questions. The prior death of Captain Weir could have aided him in accomplishing this goal, as could the absence of Lieutenant Gibson from the proceedings. Reno was the focal point of the inquiry, and there was a need for another officer to back up his statements on what his orders consisted of. The only real contradiction to either Reno's or Benteen's orders did or could have come from two enlisted men, Sergeant Davern and Trumpeter Martin. Recorder Lee said in his summation, referring to the civilian mule packers' testimony: "as to matters of fact . . . [it] is as good as that of anyone, however exalted, until it is contradicted."[4] This, one realizes, is an idealistic, not a realistic assumption, certainly not from a military standpoint where civilian and even an enlisted man's testimony would not have carried the weight of that of the officers. Using Lee's remarks one could say an officer's contradiction would prevail over an enlisted man's. This attitude does point out, however, the need for an officer to be near enough to Major Reno to support what he said his orders were.

Other remarks then fell into place. For example, Wallace's contention that Reno galloped to the ford, when we know the front of the column close to Reno trotted most of the way. He and Varnum galloped to catch up and pass Major Reno's battalion, in order to reach the ford ahead of them. This galloping – possibly even the perception of seeing some of Reno's troops galloping to regain their company or the rear companies in order to catch up with the front – compelled Wallace to say that they galloped to the ford. Dr. Porter's statement comes to mind, "I was at Major Reno's side when he received his attack order. He was at the head of his command and Lt. Hodgson, I think, was with him. Do not remember seeing Lt. Wallace."[5] Dr. Porter, who was condemned by the Defense, seems to be more straightforward in his answers than most. Because of Wallace's assignment, he should have accompanied General Custer. If Wallace was riding alongside him, he would have been aware that Custer signaled Reno to cross Ash Creek, and the time when the event took place.

Bouyer could not have been with Varnum unless all other testimony is incorrect. It's very odd that Varnum would have mentioned him, as it would seem that anyone connected with the battle, especially those associated with the scouts, would have heard accounts of what happened to Mitch Bouyer. Girard indicated he went back and warned Cooke, recrossed, and followed Reno's command. This would not have placed him with Varnum. I believe portions of Lieutenant Varnum's testimony are untrue. Either he was mistaken or expanding on his story. Yet I also believe he was probably the military officer Girard referred to as having his testimony subjected to military pressure. Since Girard was the interpreter of the Ree scouts, and Lieutenant Varnum was the officer in charge of the scouts, they would have worked together. Varnum, after leaving Reno's skirmish line in the valley, moved into the timber and was with Charlie Reynolds and Girard. Varnum was reported to have attempted to stop the "panicky" flight of Reno's troops to the bluff, until he was rebuffed by Reno. At the trial Varnum did not reveal this fact, although he did so in his book, *Custer's Chief of Scouts*.[6] There is also the possibility that he reported the sighting of the Gray Horse Troop on the ridge to Reno. Either accusation would have been extremely damaging to Major Reno's case. Varnum's statement concerning the number of Indians in the valley at the time Reno was moving down, may have been a subtle way of supporting Girard's claim. The statement contradicts other officer's remarks, the action taken by the Rees, as well as Lakota and Cheyenne accounts of the events.

I believe the Defense thought at first it would be to their advantage to play on the conception that Lieutenant Cooke and even Captain Keogh went to Ford A with Major Reno. Since Reno would be leading his troops, substantiation by another officer was necessary to support the two officers' move to the ford, and Lieutenant Wallace was used for that purpose. I realize that Wallace's suggestion that the two officers were with them may have been an error of memory, of which there were many examples during the trial. Initially, I couldn't see why the Defense used it, because it seemed questionable that Cooke ever went as far as the ford; certainly Girard and the prosecution could, and did, use it to their advantage. That Cooke went to the ford with Reno, and Girard sent a message to General Custer by way of Cooke, has been accepted by most every writer I have read. Several questions directed to Major Reno as to whether Girard informed him that he was going to warn Custer indicated it was a salient point for the Prosecution.

I have assumed the following: there were various remarks to the effect that some thought Lieutenant Cooke and Captain Keogh had gone to the ford with Major Reno. The defense thought they could use this fact in order to make it appear that Reno had every reason to believe that General Custer was right behind them, and this would back Reno's contention that Custer would be supporting him from the rear, as Cooke and Keogh would never have gone as far as the ford otherwise.

I presume the belief came about because at the time General Custer sent Major Reno his orders, by way of Lieutenant Cooke, both commands were proceeding at a slow pace and were close together. As Lieutenant Wallace said, the troops were mingling. Captain Keogh went with or joined Cooke when he delivered the attack orders. Keogh probably rode a short distance with Reno until all the men had rejoined their companies and then returned to his company or battalion. Cooke rode a little farther, and when Reno recrossed the tributary he was sitting on his horse by the crossing, ready to return to Custer, and admonished some of the riders. Like so many events, this would not have been significant in itself; but after the battle some men placed Cooke at the ford rather than the tributary. Wallace, for example, said, "Lt. Cooke and Capt. Keogh went with us toward the ford. I heard them talking as we rode along. I thought they went with us into the fight..."[7] Wallace doesn't say he knew they went to the ford with them and I would agree they went part of the way, so he would be on fairly safe ground. He, of course, would not have heard them if he was not with Major Reno. If, as Wallace said, they were galloping, it is doubtful, even if he had been with Reno, that he would have heard them. This then is an example of where the Defense thought they could capitalize on the conception some of the troops had, and it also indicates Wallace's involvement in the deception.

Dr. Porter said that after Reno received his orders, "The Adjutant rode back and Reno went on to the crossing. I do not recall seeing Girard there..."[8]

Sgt. Culbertson: "As we were crossing the <u>tributary</u> [my underlining] to the Little Big Horn, while on the way to the crossing ford, I heard Adjutant Cook tell the men to close up; there was hot work ahead for them."[9]

James Wilber, in an interview with Walter Camp: "Cook sat on bank on his horse. We were galloping fast, and just as we got to the river Cook called out: 'For God's sake men, don't run those horses like that; you will need them in a few minutes.'"[10]

Edgerly, in an interview with Camp: Edgerly says Cooke and Keogh went to ford with Reno; that they actually crossed. As Keogh was in charge of a squadron of Custer's battalion (and Yates the other) it was not so necessary that he be with his company. . . .Edgerly thinks Custer really intended to follow Reno into village, but that when he got near the river he changed his mind.[11]

General Godfrey in his narrative: "both Captain Keogh and Lieutenant Cook were at this crossing for a short time. Reno now sent word to Custer that he had everything in front of him, and that the enemy was strong . . ."[12]

Why would I accept the statements that indicate Lieutenant Cooke and Captain Keogh were not at Ford A rather than those that said they were? One reason is that they are more logical. Edgerly's explanation as to why Keogh could have left his company and battalion, although possible, is unlikely and lacks plausibility. My main reason, however, is that having them going to the ford dealt with the quintessence of the case for the Defense and the need to develop supporting evidence to back their positions. The main point the Defense was attempting to make, for this particular time period, would be a short and incorrect version of Reno's orders in which Reno is only expecting Custer's support from the rear. Along with this fact is Reno's supposed lack of knowledge of Benteen's whereabouts and orders. Having Captain Keogh and Adjutant Cooke going to the ford with Major Reno would then suggest that Custer was planning on supporting Reno from the rear.

When Major Reno's troops were passing Custer's, Lieutenant Varnum asked Custer where they were going. Custer answered, "To begin the attack."[13] This would mean that the only reason Keogh and Cooke would have gone to the ford with Major Reno would have been that Custer was expecting to support Reno from the rear. The defense would need to corroborate those positions and Lieutenant Wallace was the only officer in a position to do so. Wallace, more than likely, was made to believe these were only little white lies and he would be giving them not only to aid Major Reno, but for the good of the army and the 7th Cavalry. All he had to do, besides verifying a shortened version of the orders, was to say he was with Reno rather then with Custer when the orders were given, and since he ended up with Major Reno's command this was no great distortion of the truth. Then, his other white lies were merely expressions of opinions – that he thought Captain Keogh and Adjutant Cooke had not only gone to the ford with them but had gone into battle alongside of them. Wallace would also support the need for Reno to leave the timber, and when they reached the ridge he again supported Reno in saying he, too, hadn't heard any gunfire from Custer's location.

Wallace's testimony at the Reno Court on these issues provided additional evidence of his involvement with the inner circle stratagems of Reno's Defense team. Wallace, along with Reno and Benteen, were the only officers to indicate that they did not hear any significant amount of gunfire to warrant a concern for Custer's predicament. Wallace in his testimony at the Reno Court as to whether firing could be heard said, ". . . whether the firing could be heard I don't know. I did not hear any, though others will testify they did."[14]

Contrast this with statements made by his friend, Lieutenant Varnum: "I had borrowed a rifle of Lieutenant Wallace and had fired a couple of shots at long range and as I handed the rifle back to him I heard the firing and said, 'Jesus Christ, Wallace, hear that! And that!' Those were my words."[15] In a letter to his father written July 4, 1876, he said that the men on the bluff had known "from the fearful firing at the other end of the village that someone was getting it hot and heavy up there."[16]

Following this line of reasoning a little further, there is no doubt that firing was heard and it could only have meant one thing: either Custer's troops were attacking or under attack. What would your answer be to the following questions: Did Wallace hear gunfire? Did Captain Benteen? Did Major Reno? Remember that Reno in his July 5, 1876 report to Captain E. W. Smith said, "We heard firing in that direction and knew it could only be Custer."[17] Since they were the only three at the Reno Court who indicated they didn't hear gunfire – or only such a small amount it didn't create any fear that Custer might be in danger – should this have raised a question, by an unbiased military court and prosecution, as to why these three didn't hear the degree of gunfire others professed hearing? Should they have asked: Could there be a cover-up? Besides the gunfire, there were orders from Custer to 'come quick to his aid, that there was a big village': Did Reno and Benteen fail in their military duty, which may have resulted in the death of Custer's battalions? Do you believe it would have justified a military court martial? Since it didn't result in one, does it indicate complicity on the part of the military tribunal? Do you think, by not hearing gunfire, the distance and difficulty

Benteen supposedly faced on his "wild goose chase" to the left and the 7 miles the packs – according to Benteen – were trailing his battalion, might indicate a recognition by the Defense for the need to shorten the time between Benteen's arrival on Reno Hill and the attempt to investigate the sound of gunfire? Because of conflicting testimony, might this not require an "official" time change?

Add to this Lieutenant Varnum's contention that Wallace was with Custer and not Reno when Reno received his orders and started for the ford, and you have the elements that helped me formulate and corroborate my belief that a cover-up on these particular points took place.

Lieutenant Edgerly and Lieutenant Godfrey were with Captain Benteen, and so their reports are hearsay and resulted from the testimony at the Court of Inquiry and inferences made by Lieutenant Wallace, the Defense, and, in this case, Girard and the Prosecution. Private James Wilber indicated they were galloping. Because of the terrain, this more likely would have taken place at the tributary crossing than when reaching the ford.

What is odd, from my elbow position, is the idea that the warnings to Custer that the Indians were strong in front of Reno and not running, supposedly caused Custer to decide not to support Reno from the rear but to flank the Indians. I would think the reverse would be true, and if he had been planning to flank the Indians he would have changed his mind and thought it imperative to support Reno from the rear. The terrain to his right would not have been inviting for him to expect to coordinate a flanking attack, which is why Reno said he hadn't expected Custer to use a flanking maneuver. Custer would also be leaving the packs exposed and an area open for the Indians to move into. What I can't see is the generally accepted hypothesis that Custer was planning on supporting Major Reno from the rear, but the messages he received from Reno and Girard caused him to move to the ridge and attempt a flanking movement. Considering that the messages would have indicated Reno could have been under attack momentarily and that Custer lacked knowledge of the terrain and the distance he might have to go to accomplish the move, it would have been foolish. If he had been informed by Bouyer as to the distance and the terrain, it still would have been unwise for him to choose that option.

I also find it difficult to assume that a sighting of 40 to 50 Indians along the ridge by Kanipe would have caused Custer to change his plan of support. Custer might have sent a company after them, or the Crows to investigate, but not to go chasing up an incline with 5 companies.

If Custer had received any messages from Girard or Cooke via Girard, then the only way I could see him not coming to the aid of Reno from behind is if he had already reached the ridge when the messages arrived. This would mean he had already planned such a move and it wasn't precipitated by the reports. On the ridge he would have seen that the Indians were not an immediate threat to Major Reno and he would have proceeded with his attempt to co-ordinate a flanking attack. This view would support my contention that Keogh and Cooke would not have gone to the ford.

The above reasoning helped confirm my belief that Custer planned a flanking attack at the time he gave his original orders, at the division of the command. They would not have been inflexible, which is one reason he wouldn't have divulged them. Custer must have realized a lot could change by the time they reached the Little Bighorn. Captain Benteen may have needed support or the Indians could have confronted Custer as he moved down Ash Creek. Custer wouldn't have expected to start a flanking movement until he came close to the Little Bighorn and received word from Benteen. There is ample evidence that Custer accepted the scouting reports as to where the Indian camp was located, even though he may not have seen it himself. Custer would have been anticipating his own moves as well as those of the Indians. I can't see a man who was appointed to the rank of General at 23 with the commendations and the exploits credited to him, going from 8 a.m. to at least 2:15 P.M. without a conceived plan of action. General McClellan who wrote of Custer during the Civil War, says that, ". . . his head was always clear in danger and he always brought me clear and intelligible reports of what he saw when under the heaviest fire. I became much attached to him."[18] General Pleasonton indicated that the young officer had a talent for gathering and reporting important intelligence. He also said, "Custer is the best cavalry general in the world."[19]

Another reason why I don't believe Keogh or Cooke went to the ford with Major Reno is the conflicting testimony given by Girard. It has been accepted that Girard took a message to Lieutenant Cooke that the Indians were not running. I doubt that he did. I may be giving the Prosecution of Major Reno too much credit, but with the assumption made by the Defense that Cooke and possibly Keogh went to the ford with Reno, I believe they saw an opportunity to use it to their advantage. Girard's dislike for Reno, coupled with his being the major witness for the Prosecution, his connection with the scouts, his ability to move freely, and the general problems of memory, would all make Girard an ideal candidate for such a ploy. We have to remember that within a militarily prescribed formula, the Prosecution was playing not only to a military jury but also to the public. Lieutenant Cooke was killed with General Custer, so if any information was passed on to Cooke and to Reno – which in this case would be the fact that the Indians were not running – there should be no doubt General Custer would have been aware of Reno's situation and would be hurrying to his assistance (note Recorder Lee's summation). Reno should then have been expected to put the two facts together. He would have known Custer would have no trouble supporting him from the rear, and when that did not happen, Reno should have realized that Custer must be planning to aid him from another direction. Custer would have been counting on Reno to follow his orders. Since Major Reno did not do this, the blame for the defeat of General Custer must rest squarely on Reno's shoulders.

As I have stated before, the importance placed on establishing the court's awareness of these facts can be found in Recorder Lee's summation:

> ...The last words from General Custer to Major Reno were, "we will support you." From that time Major Reno started to obey the order, General Custer must have been possessed of that idea, that intention; not for one moment did he forget it....Major Reno's support might not come from the rear, but he would be supported...With Reno holding the Indians near him – Benteen coming up with 250 men and Custer striking in front, there was a glorious chance for a thrice glorious victory. Major Reno slipped his hold and all was lost.[20]

Why do I believe Girard never gave Lieutenant Cooke a message?

Fred Girard was the Indian (Ree) interpreter and from what I have read, a fairly knowledgeable person. At one time he had been accused by Major Reno of stealing government supplies. Whether he was guilty or not I do not know, but it certainly embittered him toward Reno and the feeling was mutual. This fact has to be considered when viewing his testimony. I think he would not have been above stretching or distorting the truth if it could be used to reflect negatively against Reno.

Girard said in an interview with Camp in 1909:

> ...When we got across the river, one of the Indian scouts called out that the Sioux were coming to meet Reno. Gerard exclaimed, "Hell, Custer ought to know this right away, for he thinks the Indians are running. He ought to know they are preparing to fight. I'll go back and inform him." And so he went back and met Cooke at the knoll 1/2 or 3/4 miles east of the ford. It was probably about 75 or 100 feet high, but right in the mouth of the valley. The trail passed to the right of it. When Cooke saw him coming up he said: "Well, Gerard, what is the matter now?"

> I told him that Reno and his battalion had forded and that the Indians were coming up the valley to meet him, and I thought the General ought to know that the Indians were showing fight instead of running away...I turned and rode back toward the river, and before I reached it met a mounted soldier hurrying east. (McIhargey)

> After fording, went ahead and rode behind command with Charlie Reynolds. Ree scouts were up ahead of the line of soldiers and over to the left. When got up near point of timber, the Rees espied a considerable herd of ponies over in the foothills to the left of the valley, perhaps 1/2 mile distant. They made for these and tried to drive off the whole herd, but a band of Sioux got there nearly as soon as the Rees, so that the latter succeeded in getting away with only part of the herd....[21]

At the Reno Court of Inquiry, Girard testified:

> We lost sight of Custer's column after going about a mile, when we arrived near a knoll, right at the river bank. Before crossing the river the scouts on my left called attention to all the Indians coming up the valley. I called Reno's attention to it, and thought General Custer should know about it and rode back toward the knoll meeting Col. Cook. I told him and he said "All right, I'll go back and report." As I came back from reporting to Col. Cook I could see Reno's command going down to where they dismounted and threw out a skirmish line.[22]

I had reservations in accepting Girard's story because there were too many inconsistencies between his accounts. Why didn't Girard say in the Camp interview that he had warned Reno, and why wouldn't he have mentioned Reno's response and other particulars? Reporting the sighting to Reno was the crucial element of the situation. Then there were other important questions: Was the knoll right at the river bank or 1/2 or 3/4 mile from it? Did the scouts inform Girard before or after he crossed the river? These discrepancies might be considered natural if not for the fact that within the context of his overall testimony there were many other loose links.

If Girard was informed before he and the scouts reached the river, why would he have gone to the river to tell Major Reno? One would think that Major Reno would receive the information away from the river. Lieutenant Hare said the scouts reached the river half a mile ahead of the column. If Girard's later interview with Camp was correct, and the information was passed after they had crossed the river, shouldn't Girard have tried to confirm the sighting, and expected Varnum or Hare to bring such a warning to Major Reno? If the situation as indicated by Girard's actions was so imminently dangerous, why did Varnum, Hare and the scouts move down the valley without seemingly being aware of this threat? It would be expected that some of the scouts that were later interviewed might have mentioned it. At this time, according to their accounts, they were mainly interested in capturing Sioux ponies. It would certainly be odd to have them move after the ponies if that many Sioux had been spotted only a short way down the valley. No one else mentioned the Indians moving to attack or threatening them at this time, including the Indians.

Lieutenant Hare said a Sioux, with the ponies the Rees went after, fired on them. Hare also said he didn't know that Cooke and Keogh went to the Ford A with Reno.[23] Dr. Porter saw a few Indians and a great many ponies.[24]

Sergeant F.A. Culbertson recalled: "When we went down to the crossing... saw no Indians... some dust."[25]

Captain Moylan did not see Girard talking to Reno. Moylan did not even recall seeing Girard at the ford, and he saw no Indians threatening, although he said he was in a position to see them.[26]

Other questions came to mind. At the Reno Court, Girard said his scouts informed him before crossing the river, and the scouts were ahead of Reno's troops. If Lieutenant Cooke was behind the Major but went to the ford, why did Girard have to ride back to inform Adjutant Cooke? If Girard met Cooke at the knoll right by the river and Major Reno had not yet crossed over, how did Reno cross the river so fast, and, as Girard said, was moving down the valley by the time he got back.

Before they reached the Little Bighorn, even Girard referred to being able to look down the valley. Captain Benteen later saw some of Major Reno's troops and Indians in the valley. The Indians saw Captain Benteen's troops. Shouldn't Reno have been able to see down the valley, or been concerned when checking out the first ford before moving to Ford A? No one mentioned such a concern as they crossed the ford or while regrouping.

Since Captain Moylan was leading A Troop and they were the closest behind Major Reno, wouldn't he have noticed Girard, if he met Major Reno? Since he didn't see Girard, might that not mean Girard was already across the Little Bighorn with Lieutenant Varnum and Hare? Was Moylan merely covering for Reno? Varnum thought Girard was with him, but he could have been mistaken, as this is the type of fact one could easily forget. In his recollection of Mitch Bouyer being with him, he was certainly in error. On the other hand, Girard could not have made such a mistake about going back to warn General Custer. If he didn't go back, he knew he didn't, and he would have to invent the story.

Major Reno, at the Court of Inquiry, denied that Girard ever communicated such a message to him. Reno said, "I received no communication from Girard at Ford A, he had no right to speak to me officially. I had had trouble with Girard, and discharged him because I thought he was stealing from the government."[27] In cross examination Reno again said, "I received no communication from Girard at the crossing; I would not have believed it if I had. I should have listened to him, but I repeat I should not have believed him."[28] Isn't Major Reno saying there was no Indian threat at that time? If there had been an Indian threat, shouldn't Reno have been notified of it through various sources?

Lieutenant DeRudio, in his interview with Camp, puts Girard and Major Reno in the middle of the Little Bighorn together, and Reno taking a drink (which Girard never mentioned). DeRudio said he himself was the first of Major Reno's command to cross the stream. This does not mean the scouts had not crossed. As I have pointed out, if Girard had been warned by his scouts before they reached the river, Reno should have been behind him; certainly Girard would not have had to go ahead and meet Reno in the middle of the stream. Nor is it likely, considering the feeling between them, that Reno would be taking a drink with Girard present, nor that he would do it in front of his troops. He might have been taking a drink of water, but DeRudio said it was whiskey.[29] This sighting by DeRudio raises the question of his reliability.

Girard said that after warning Adjutant Cooke, he returned and Major Reno was already moving down the valley.[30] If one accepts this part of Girard's story, then the knoll had to be the 1/2 to 3/4 mile east of Ford A, and Reno's command must have been across or almost across the ford when he started back. Girard would not have had to follow Reno if the knoll and Adjutant Cooke had been as close to the river as he indicated in his court testimony, and he wouldn't have received the information from the scouts before he reached the river. Girard said he rode behind Reno as they moved down the valley, and that he was with Charlie Reynolds. It was nice of Charlie to wait for him. However, since Reno moved down the valley at a comparatively fast pace, it strikes me as odd how Girard and Reynolds could have then caught up with the command, met Dr. Porter, Herendeen and Bloody Knife, had a drink, dismounted and "just then the skirmish line was being drawn up, and the Indians were moving up."[31] Girard also indicated he saw the scouts going after the Sioux ponies and the Sioux chasing them.[32] With all the dust that was being stirred up, and the Rees who were chasing the Sioux ponies already about half way down the valley ahead of the troops, it is somewhat surprising he would notice all these events unless he was nearer to Lieutenant Varnum and the scouts. It might have been possible, but the point raises more doubts.

George Herendeen, the scout sent with General Custer by General Terry, is the only one to corroborate Girard's statement that the scouts warned Major Reno at the time he started to cross the Little Bighorn. It's somewhat strange that Lieutenant Varnum, with whom Girard should have been, and who was in command of the scouts, did not deliver such a warning to Reno.

Girard, at the Court of Inquiry asserted:

> When I first came to the ford where Reno crossed and turned the knoll, I had a full view down the valley. The bottom was alive with Indians, at least 1500 of them. When we got in the woods, [after moving down the valley.] I was astonished that there were not more around, and having seen Custer down there and no more attacking us. I think they had discovered him and went to intercept him.[33]

This is a good example of how the Prosecution attempted to use the warning that the Indians weren't running; and if one considers their large numbers, it is easy to imply that since they were not there when Reno moved into the timber, the Indians were already concerned with stopping Custer. The implication would be that Reno should have continued to exert pressure on the camp, and should have followed orders. By not doing so, he was responsible for Custer's encounter with an overwhelming number of Indians, which led to his defeat.

This account, which stipulates the presence of 1500 Indians in the valley, does not correlate with what Varnum, Hare, Reno, other officers, the scouts or the Sioux indicated in their testimony or interviews. Mr. Gilbert did recognize that it could be used to their advantage in defending Reno. He pointed out in his summation:

> The large number of Indians, about 1500, seen by Girard to be advancing up the valley to meet Reno while at the ford; the dust behind them indicating a still larger number in their rear, and to intercept his crossing and the support he expected to reach him, told to the practiced eye of an Indian fighter the story of an Indian ambush . . .[34]

In his court testimony Major Reno denied having received a report from Girard, thereby implying the absence of an Indian threat at that time. If Reno thought there were 1500 Indians in the valley, it is extremely doubtful that he would have moved on down the valley without further word from Custer. Reno was not an experienced Indian fighter, but he would have been aware of the decoy practice of the Indians. Reno didn't say he saw any such number of Indians until after he was attacked on the hill. In this context one has to commend the Defense for recognizing the need to use the sighting by Girard to sustain their arguments that Reno's decision not to continue his attack was the correct one. It would be clear that Girard did not make the statement in order to back Reno's action.

Girard in his interview with Camp brings out his bitterness toward Major Reno. He mentions that the Defense attempted to influence him; he points out that he said things on the stand they objected to, and he didn't think some of his testimony had even been recorded:

> When I got to Chicago, Reno sent for me very hospitably and had me talk with his lawyer. This fellow tried to pick out of me what I was going to testify to, but I talked only in general terms. After awhile Reno came in and Gilbert said to him in an undertone: "This man is all right; he knows nothing that is damaging." After I got on the stand, I told some things that did not set very well with them, and Gilbert tried all manner of tricks, browbeating etc., to get me to contradict myself and at time our tilts at each other were rather bitter. I understood from inside sources at the time that much that passed between us was not going to be permitted to go on record.
>
> After I came off the stand, a commissioned officer of the 7th Cavalry with whom I was on very friendly terms, who was at the Little Big Horn, took me aside, grasped my hand and said" Gerard, I want to congratulate you for telling the truth so fearlessly and for maintaining your story unshaken. When I go on the stand I will tell them a few things that I know." I replied by saying: 'I am wondering whether you will or not.' He said: "Well, just wait until you see."
>
> Shortly after this he and I were together when a porter came up with a note which he opened and later said: 'An invitation to a champagne supper.' I said: "Yes and it will also be a blanket for you."
>
> In due course he was called as a witness, and I heard his testimony, and upon meeting him later I said: "Well, I noticed that when they got you on the stand you were not as well informed as you intended to be." and he replied: 'Well, Girard, they have got the whip over us; they have some things in the pigeon holes that could be used to make me feel rather uncomfortable, and I thought there was no use trying to stand against the whole gang by myself.'
>
> Gerard said the general understanding among all whom he talked with confidentially was that any officer who made himself obnoxious to the defense would incur the wrath of certain officers in pretty high authority in certain department headquarters farther west than Washington and not as far west as St. Paul. There was much dining and wining all the time the trial was going on, and he knew the whole object was to compromise certain of the witnesses.[35]

Girard did not explain what he believed the officer and others should have made clearer. His recorded testimony concerns the command's movement to Ford A and Reno's actions in the valley. Girard tried to indicate that by Major Reno's leaving the timber, the Indians were able to confront General Custer. This point was effectively offset by the Defense to support their own contentions. The Prosecution, to support their case, would show that Reno should have realized the message delivered by Girard to Cooke and the sightings of Custer's command by Girard and DeRudio, made it clear that Custer was not supporting him from the rear, but from another direction. Reno should have either continued his attack or held out in the timber.

It's important to mention Girard's claimed sighting of Custer, as he related it to the Reno Court:

> As I was about to go down into the timber at point C, [Reno's skirmish line] I looked up and saw what I took to be General Custer's column. It was at about the letter D in the word command on the map; [D was on Reno Hill] . . . at the rate it was moving, I think it would have traveled about 2 to 2 1/2 miles by the time Major Reno reached the top of the hill. (The witness here indicated the point of advance by figure 2.) [Figure 2 would be near Weir Point – which would still have left Custer some distance from Ford B, and Major Reno would have already retreated to Reno Hill.][36]

Although I may be reading too much into what the Defense and the Prosecution were attempting to do, I can't help but believe that the essence of their strategy can be summarized in the following assumptions pertaining to Cooke's purported move to Ford A, with Reno's and Girard's sighting and warning that the Indians were "not running."

The Defense strongly suggested that Lieutenant Cooke and Captain Keogh moved to the ford with Major Reno. This scenario would certainly emphasize and reinforce the Defense's main premise: Reno, in moving to attack the Indians, believed he would be supported by General Custer from the rear, otherwise Cooke and Keogh would not have moved to the ford with him.

The Prosecution, on the other hand, was attempting to suggest that Major Reno knew General Custer was aware of his predicament and would be moving to support him (from whatever direction), so Reno should have followed his orders. Their primary attack on Reno's actions was to object to his leaving the timber, by which action he removed the threat to the Indian encampment, enabling the Indians to leave Reno, tipping the scale and causing Custer's defeat.

Girard and the Prosecution realized they could use the Defense's story of Lieutenant Cooke and Captain Keogh moving to the ford. They subsequently created Girard's warning to Major Reno in which he told Reno he was going to let Custer know the Indians were not running. By doing this, Girard and the Prosecution planted in the minds of both the jury and the public the idea that Reno knew Custer was aware the Indians were ahead of Reno and threatening; consequently, Reno should have known Custer would be moving to support him, if not from the rear, then from some other direction. Reno denied that Girard informed him and insisted he still expected Custer to aid him from the rear. What then becomes important in the Prosecution's case was the sighting of Custer on the ridge and the necessity for this event to be as far back as possible for timing purposes. Girard accomplished this by saying he saw Custer near Reno Hill, but there was nothing in the record to indicate he told Major Reno about it. It would be a little too much to expect that he could have talked to Reno a second time; hence, the need for an officer to have seen Custer.

I thought the commissioned officer whom Girard referred to as having had his testimony subjected to military pressure must have been either Lieutenant Varnum or Lieutenant DeRudio. They both testified after Girard. At first I believed it was DeRudio, for several reasons. One was DeRudio's background and personality; another, the fact that his testimony appeared to be more supportive of Girard. I then realized the latter argument actually pointed to Varnum. This conclusion coupled with the recognition that Girard and Varnum worked together during the campaign, made me realize it could just as easily have been Varnum. DeRudio did support Girard, in that he was the only officer who professed to seeing Major Reno and Girard together at the ford. He was also one of the few officers that believed Reno should have held out in the timber. His late sighting and location of Custer, in comparison to Varnum's, would be basic to the premise and supposition that Reno had fled to the bluffs before Custer could have reached Ford B, an act which released the full force of Indians to confront and defeat Custer.

If one assumes Girard did try to let General Custer know the Indians were not running away, which of his accounts should be accepted? We can probably discount his court testimony as to the knoll being right along the river bank and meeting Adjutant Cooke there. If this were true, he would have been able to get back before Reno had regrouped on the other side. We can also disregard the stories that have Adjutant Cooke and Captain Keogh going to the river and even crossing; Girard would not need to go back, and certainly he would not follow Reno down the valley at the distance he described.

If I accept Girard's account of delivering a message to Cooke, I must then reject accounts of Custer coming within two or three hundred yards of Ford A, for the general's battalion should have been in sight of Girard when he went back to warn Custer, even if the knoll and the Adjutant were near the river. When Reno reached the ford, Custer should have been noticed by officers and men as they were waiting to cross, and someone would have mentioned this sighting.

In answering nearly all the questions, witnesses would have given their opinion without coercion, and there would naturally be honest differences. If a witness belonged to the military and didn't particularly agree with Reno's conduct, he undoubtedly tempered his criticism. Even the key witnesses in the important issues such as orders, sightings of Indians and Custer, timing and distances, would have to change their testimony only slightly – My orders "said" or "only said"; I "saw" or I "didn't see"; I "heard' or I "didn't hear". The decision would depend on whether the witness believed Reno should be indicted or cleared. In the trial, the end often justified the means. The Defense would have spent time with their key witnesses and the Prosecution with theirs. There were cover-ups. No matter how rationalized, white lies are still lies.

Distortions lead to confusion and unsound conclusions. Just look at the footnotes in the books and articles written about the battle: Reno Court, Reno Court, Reno Court. In one sense a person can say that single events in themselves are not that important: it is not important whether Cooke went to the ford, or whether Custer was seen by Girard and DeRudio between Reno Hill and Weir Point when they said they did. However, the overall picture of what happened to General Custer is definitely affected by the sum of these elements.

I have explained the reasons why I don't think Girard went to warn Custer. When linked with the underlying feeling Girard had toward Major Reno, the Prosecution's need for such an action in order to be successful, and Girard's role as their key witness, the deduction that he never went to warn General Custer is logical. Some of the reasons are not too important in themselves; but combined, they influenced my conclusion that either Girard or Frederick Whittaker, separately or together (with Recorder Lee in no position not to go along), concocted the story presented during the trial. What bothered me most in reading Girard's testimony was that it wasn't questioned. According to everyone I have read, Girard warned Cooke and Cooke must have then told Custer. Possibly these accounts are correct, but in looking at the list of deviations Girard made, I can't understand why they were accepted without being debated. I found this attitude in many sources: the author is supposedly attempting to determine what happened to Custer, but the writing amounts to no more then presenting opinions or attempting to entertain the reader. Throwing together a number of quotations without analyzing or explaining the conflicting testimony does not help formulate a logical explanation as to what occurred. The question of whether Girard went to Lieutenant Cooke with his message to General Custer, and whether the message was accepted is crucial to establishing a proper timing sequence. The orders and the timing of the sightings were the essential points around which the trial revolved as it pertained to General Custer. When they were distorted, so was the history and image of the General.

SOURCES

1. Graham, *Reno Court Abstract,* pp. 13, 34.
2. Ibid., pp. 211– 228.
3. Varnum, ed. Carroll, *Custer's Chief of Scouts,* p. 64–65.
4. Graham, *Reno Court Abstract*, p. 250.
5. Ibid., p. 66.
6. Varnum, ed. Carroll, *Custer's Chief of Scouts,* p. 67.
7. Graham, *Reno Court Abstract*, p. 24.
8. Ibid., p. 66.
9. Ibid., p. 127.
10. Camp, *Custer in 76,* p. 148.
11. Ibid., p. 55.
12. Graham, *The Custer Myth,* p. 139.
13. Varnum, ed. Carroll, *Custer's Chief of Scouts,* p. 64.
14. Nichols, Ronald H., ed., Reno Court of Inquiry, p. 35.
15. Ibid., p. 160.
16. Barnett, Louise, *Touched by Fire,* p. 294.
17. Overfield, Loyd J. *The Little Big Horn, 1876,* p. 45.
18. Urwin, *Custer Victorious,* p. 48.
19. Ibid., p. 278.
20. Graham, *Reno Court Abstract*, p. 257.
21. Camp, *Custer in 76,* p. 231.
22. Graham, *Reno Court Abstract,* pp. 36, 38.
23. Camp, *Custer in 76,* p. 65.
24. Graham, *Reno Court Abstract*, p. 62.
25. Ibid., p. 62.
26. Stewart, *Custer's Luck,* p. 332; *Reno Court,* pp. 368, 341.
27. Graham, *Reno Court Abstract*, p. 223.
28. Ibid., p. 226.
29. Camp, *Custer in 76,* p. 84.
30. Graham, *Reno Court Abstract*, p. 38.
31. Ibid., p. 39.
32. Camp, *Custer in 76,* p. 232.
33. Graham, *Reno Court Abstract*, p. 42.
34. Ibid., p. 247.
35. Camp, *Custer in 76,* pp. 237-238.
36. Graham, *Reno Court Abstract*, p. 44.

6
Sightings of General Custer

At the Reno Court of Inquiry one of the more important and intriguing issues were inconsistencies concerning the sightings of General Custer. Within a general framework, the Prosecution was attempting to show that Major Reno should have realized that General Custer knew his predicament, and, even though he was not supporting him from the rear, that he would be coming to his aid from some direction. They hoped Girard's story of telling Reno that the Indians were not running, and that he was going to inform Custer, would convince the jury as well as the public that Reno should then have known Custer would be moving to his aid. In light of these facts, Reno should not have retreated from the timber, a move which caused Custer's defeat.

Since Major Reno would not, at the time, have been sure General Custer received Girard's or his own message, this could not be considered concrete evidence. Reno denied even knowing Girard was going to take a message to Custer. There were attempts to say Reno had received messages from Custer as Reno was about to or was moving down the valley, but these were never substantiated.

The Defense continued to insist that Girard never talked to Major Reno, that Reno only expected support from Custer from behind. He knew nothing of Captain Benteen's orders or whereabouts, so could not have expected support from him.

If there had been any egregious contradictions among the officers' testimony, I think we can be assured they would have been brought into line. Major Reno received his attack orders, moved to the Little Bighorn, quickly crossed over, recognized that the Indians were down the valley in strength and, as a dutiful officer, sent messages to that effect to General Custer. Not receiving a reply, and wondering where Custer might be, he proceeded to carry out his orders and moved down the valley.

Timing is extremely important. For the Defense, Reno's crossing the Little Bighorn and beginning his move down the valley had to be undertaken in a comparatively short time; otherwise Reno should have been aware, even then, that Custer was not behind him.

The Prosecution must have realized that Reno's version of the events was not very convincing. However, with Captain Benteen backing Reno, and vowing that he knew nothing of Reno's orders and was just lucky to have come along when he did, the Prosecution was somewhat stymied.

The next important move by the Prosecution would be to try to tie in sightings of General Custer with Reno's troops, for then Reno would have had to have known General Custer was moving to the north and would not be expected to support him from the rear. I would assume the sightings by Reno's troops would have been common knowledge to both sides. Since Custer moved along the bluffs (although an attempt to cover this fact was also made), it would seem natural he would have been observed by some of Major Reno's battalion. We know enlisted men said they did see Custer and his command. The question would be: Why weren't they called as witnesses? The answer goes back to the concept of a controlled court: certain questions were not asked, and certain witnesses were not called.

Thomas F. O'Neill, a private with Company G, in 1919 recounted to Walter Camp that he remembered Ford A, where Reno crossed, as a high bank:

> The trail split and went around a little rise of ground on which some of the Rees were sitting holding a council. . . . on other side of river there were timber and fallen logs and took some time to get through. When about half way down to where skirmish line was formed he saw Custer and his whole command on the bluffs across the river, over to the east, at a point which he would think was about where Reno afterwards fortified, or perhaps a little south of this. Custer's command was then going at a trot.[1]

Henry Petring, a private with Company G, said:

> . . . while in the bottom going toward the skirmish line, I saw Custer over across the river on the bluffs, waving his hat. Some of the men said: "There goes Custer, He is up to something for he is waving his hat."[2]

Sergeant Stanislas Roy of Company A, a Medal of Honor winner, reported:

> . . . after passing ford we formed in line and while forming I heard some of the men say "There goes Custer." He could be seen over on hills to our right and across the river.[3]

Red Star, Boy Chief and Strikes Two were Ree scouts who reported seeing Custer on a bank near where Hodgson's stone stands. These Rees then moved along the valley ahead of Major Reno's troops.

O'Neill's account of the problem in moving through the timber should be remembered in establishing the time it took Major Reno to cross the ford and regroup. More than likely, O'Neill saw Custer on the ridge somewhere between Reno's entrenchment area and Weir Point, the same as the others. Since O'Neill said he saw the whole command, the lead company could have been near Weir Point, and Custer may have been on Weir Point.

SIGHTINGS OF GENERAL CUSTER

Sergeant Roy's men noticed the Custer column as Reno's men were formed into line after they had moved out of the timber. This version is plausible from the sighting standpoint, as some were apt to be looking over the whole scene around them. Custer's five companies would have been moving along the ridge so they could have been seen and, in fact, should have been. Henry Petring said that on the way to the skirmish line he looked up and sighted Custer waving his hat. I would think Petring's sighting may have also been at the same time as Roy's; if it was shortly afterward, he may have seen Custer on Weir Point, which would coincide with my time analysis.

What is peculiar is that the officers, when reforming or moving down the valley, did not report seeing Custer on the ridge. One would think they would have heard their men shouting and pointing to where they saw Custer. However, none, at the time of the trial, seemed to recall seeing Custer. Nor were they asked. It is quite apparent that such a sighting could be characterized as contradictory to the portrayal of events desired by the military, and so the officers conveniently failed to remember seeing Custer on the ridge.

It's not hard to find the explanation for this lack of testimony about sighting Custer. For the Defense, it has created a paradoxical situation: they would have liked to acknowledge that Custer was sighted on the ridge at the time of regrouping, or moving down the valley, because it would have meant that Custer had plenty of time to come to Reno's aid by way of Ford B. Reno's retreat from the timber would then have had no effect on Custer being defeated. The dilemma was that Reno would then have known Custer was moving to support him, but not from behind. Reno should then have stayed in the timber, as he would have realized that leaving it would not only violate his known orders, but could also jeopardize the plan of General Custer.

What makes the situation even more interesting is that the Prosecution was also confronted with a paradoxical situation. They wanted the troops and the officers to testify that they spotted Custer on the ridge; but, if they reported seeing him when reforming, or as they moved to the skirmish line, it would have meant that Custer had time to launch an attack on the Indians before Reno retreated from the timber. This would have taken away their main charge against Reno. The Prosecution's only applicable maneuver was to have them see Custer on the ridge, but not as early as the troops said they saw him. Girard was able to provide one testimony of the sighting, but, without an officer's backing, it would not have been effective. The Prosecution needed an officer to have also seen Custer. Lieutenant Varnum said he saw the Gray Horse Troop on the ridge, but he didn't associate it with Custer. His sighting took place as Reno established his skirmish line and he had the location of the Gray Horse Troop fairly close to Weir Point. Since Custer could easily have reached Ford B while Reno was still fighting in the valley, this sighting would not aid the Prosecution. It did aid the Defense and was used in Mr. Gilbert's summation to the effect that Custer had time to attack the Indians at Ford B. Lieutenant DeRudio then said he saw Custer only 5 or 6 minutes before Reno left the timber. He also said he looked at his watch every 10 minutes, so his time estimate should have been fairly accurate. His sighting was near Weir Point, but it meant that General Custer could not have reached Ford B; consequently even more time would be allowed for the Indians facing Reno to have returned and become the decisive factor in Custer's defeat.

DeRudio's testimony could have been decisive against Major Reno (as could Varnum's), but to have accomplished this he would have had to let Reno know that he saw Custer on the ridge. This he didn't do, or at least he did not testify to that effect. DeRudio's testimony, though not helping the Prosecution accomplish their objective, has influenced writers and their opinions as to what happened to General Custer.

I don't think DeRudio saw General Custer just before Major Reno left the timber, and his testimony was used in a way which he hoped would aid the Prosecution. Here's the justification for my theory: Lieutenant Charles DeRudio said, in his testimony, that General Custer diverged to the right, and Major Reno went ahead four or five miles to the river, at a trot. He also said he only saw a few Indians before he crossed the river, and they were going down the creek. DeRudio said there was 200 yards of timber passed through after crossing Ford A. Moreover, he thought they were on the <u>skirmish line</u> for not more than ten minutes before they moved into the timber. DeRudio's skirmish and timber time estimates, along with Girard's, were much shorter than most. DeRudio's may have been a veiled form of support for the Prosecution. He then said:

> Pretty soon Lt. Wallace directed my attention to Indians coming in on the other side of the woods. I started over with five or six men to see. The woods made a horseshoe loop and had a clearing inside. I crossed the clearing and saw some Indians through the woods, downstream. We stood there about ten minutes, when the trumpeter of my company came and said, "Lieutenant, here is your horse." "They are leaving the timber, Lieut."...DeRudio looked and saw a party of Indians coming into the timber and the men with him all fled.[4]

Under direct examination at the Court, DeRudio said:

"I did not see General Custer's column at all; but while I was in the woods, General Custer, Lt. Cook and another man I could not recognize came to the highest point on the right bank, just below where Dr. DeWolf was killed. It was not under the bluff. The bluff is very narrow there – hardly wide enough for a horse to stand. He was about 1000 yards from me. (The witness here designated by the figure 7 on the map the point where he saw General Custer.) It was probably five or six hundred yards down the river from the hill afterwards occupied by Major Reno. I saw them only five or six minutes before Reno's retreat.[5]

...The point where I saw General Custer was about three to three and a half miles from the middle ford "B." I was then standing on the bank of the creek. This was six or seven minutes after the command went into the timber, it left five or six minutes later.

...I recognized General Custer and Lt. Cook by their dress. They had blue shirts and buckskin pants. they were the only ones who wore blue shirts and no jackets: and Lt. Cook besides had an immense beard. The third man I did not recognize and he may have been an orderly.

General Custer had a birdseye view of the whole situation there; he could not see all of the village, but could see most of it: but after he left, there was no further opportunity for him to see us. The middle ford "B" was the first opportunity to cross and support us by flank attack."[6]

There are a number of things which make his account noteworthy, and compel me to dispute his sighting. Since he knew how narrow this location was, it would mean he took note of it <u>after</u> the battle. If this was near where Dr. DeWolf was killed, there would have been opportunities for nearly a mile to observe the valley and Major Reno. Before this happened, DeRudio said, General Custer, Lieutenant Cooke, and another man he couldn't recognize, came to the highest point of the bluff and waved their hats and made motions as if cheering. Whether looking from the valley or the ridge, there is no question that the highest point is Weir Peak. DeRudio referred to the bluff being very narrow – hardly wide enough for a horse to stand – but apparently three of them managed to make it. Since many of these estimates are expressed in relative terms, I wouldn't use them to dispute DeRudio's observations, if other parts of his story had been sound. There are two major points I cannot accept in DeRudio's accounts. One is the question of what he saw and how he justified it, and the other is related to the matter of timing.

To begin with, from that distance it would be impossible to determine the identity of General Custer and Adjutant Cooke solely on the basis of the blouses they were wearing and Adjutant Cooke's beard. Many believed Custer was wearing his buckskin jacket, and although I think he was wearing a blue shirt, for DeRudio to perceive that it was a blue shirt and not a jacket seems implausible. I don't believe Custer changed from his buckskin jacket until after he passed the Lone Tepee, and I doubt if DeRudio would have seen this take place. This element would be a minor flaw in the testimony; but his knowledge that it was a shirt and not a jacket, and his recognition of Cooke from his beard, at that distance, definitely is not. It is doubtful he could perceive what anyone was wearing. To have been able to distinguish what he claimed he saw from the distance he estimated at about a 1000 yards would be difficult enough; but from the timber, the distance to the point he refers to is nearly a mile. Earlier in the day he had given his glasses to General Custer. In his testimony, he never said that he was looking through glasses. Recognizing Cooke by his beard makes his story even more absurd. Anyone can go outside and see if it is possible to determine what someone is wearing or if a man has a beard, even a flowing one, from the distance of one mile; and this without the dust, gun smoke and fires that hung over the area at the time.

Captain Carter, referring to Lieutenant Varnum's sighting of the Gray Horse Troop from the skirmish line, a sighting involving roughly the same distance, had this to say: "Varnum must have been far sighted to have seen a gray troop at the distance he gives. It was difficult to tell the color of horses a half mile away, especially if there was dust."[7]

If someone couldn't make out a company of similar colored horses from that distance, how could one possibly distinguish a blue blouse from a jacket, or determine whether a person had a beard or not? However, I disagree with Captain Carter's point that Varnum could not have been able to distinguish a company of similar colored horses. If Varnum had recognized two gray horses on the ridge, I would question his statement; but a company would, by the way they rode, indicate they were soldiers and not Indians, and the mass of gray would suggest that it was the Gray Horse Troop. Troopers indicated that between the time of regrouping and moving down the valley they saw Custer's command on the ridge. Here again, it would be the way the cavalry moved in contrast to the Indians which enabled them to be identified. Seeing Custer wave, I believe, was likely an embellishment, probably stemming from their having heard Martin say that Custer waved, as they knew he often did.

The second major point in discrediting DeRudio's sighting is timing. If we were to accept DeRudio's statement, it would be necessary to discount the sighting by Sergeant Roy at the time of regrouping, and by the other troopers who viewed Custer's command on their way down the valley. These were not officers, and if I were Colonel Graham or

1. Bluffs as seen from the direction of Reno's skirmish line. Weir Peak is on the left. For Reno's troops to have seen Custer's men on the ridge, or for Lt. Varnum to have seen the Gray Horse Company, they would have to have been moving along the ridge and not back from it.

2. Picture taken approximately 200 yards from the base of the hill. It is impossible to recognize the figure on the hill. Neither his appearance or clothes are distinguishable.

Magnussen I might disclaim their sighting because of the fact they were enlisted men. However, because of the Reno Court cover-ups by officers, we should give their sighting more credence. I do accept that after crossing at Ford A, some of Reno's troops saw Custer's troops on the ridge, just as Sergeant Kanipe reported seeing Reno's troops moving down the valley. From the time Reno's troops came out of the timber until they set up their skirmish line, at least 15 minutes would have gone by.

Lieutenant DeRudio said he checked his watch every ten minutes.[8] He is the only one, if he can be believed, who did this. But even if he had checked the time, he would still have the problem of remembering what it related to. His problem could have been similar to that of Lieutenant

Godfrey, who had a clear remembrance of an important event taking place at 4:20, but was not sure which event it was.

Let us assume that after fifteen minutes of riding down the valley, Major Reno's men got off their horses, gave them to every fourth man, possibly moved forward a hundred yards, fired on the enemy for a time, then moved to the timber. Certainly another 15 minutes should have passsed. Lieutenant Varnum supposedly saw the Gray Horse Troop moving during the setting up of the skirmish line. When the troops entered the timber, 25-30 minutes have gone by from their first reported sighting of Custer, after crossing the ford. The troops were probably in the timber at least 20 minutes, but let's use DeRudio's estimate of 12 minutes. DeRudio said he would have sighted Custer some 5 or 6 minutes before Reno left the timber, so I'll add conservatively another 6 minutes. We now have 30-35 minutes from the first reported sighting of Custer on the bluffs. Custer would still not have left the ridge if DeRudio's claimed viewing location was correct. Custer would have come down from this high point, and if other accounts are correct, talked briefly to his men before they moved off the ridge. DeRudio would expect us to believe that Custer is on the ridge, being witnessed for some 35 minutes (add another 10 minutes to that before the troops left the ridge). We might want to speculate that Custer viewed the valley from Weir Point (if that is not the location DeRudio is indicating), so we could add another 5 or 10 minutes. This would amount to roughly a period of 40 minutes to nearly an hour (without using the generally accepted time Reno was in the timber) that Custer's command was on the ridge.

In attempting to determine the time it would have taken to go from Major Reno's entrenchment position to the place some 4 miles away where Custer's body was found, General Miles said he was able to cover the distance at a walk in 30 minutes, and at a slow or hand gallop in 10 to 15 minutes. E. Curtis gave about the same time estimate.[9]

The distance between Reno's entrenchment area and Weir Point is a little over a mile, and should have been covered in 7 to 10 minutes. In the time table I am using, one should also remember that General Custer may have been on the ridge for some time, when Sergeant Roy made his first sighting. So to contend that General Custer was on the ridge for a minimum of 40 minutes to an hour, stretches things so far that only one of two things could account for it: either DeRudio testified falsely, to aid the Prosecution's charges; or, if he saw Custer at all, it was when Reno's enlisted men did (or he may have seen several troopers waving from that location when he was in the timber). Even if this was true, to use the sighting in this manner would indicate he was attempting to aid the Prosecution, providing them with an account they desperately needed if their main charges against Reno were to have any substance. Though DeRudio's sightings did not sway the tribunal, they have clouded the public perception of Custer and the scenarios of the events presented by many.

I might add that Sergeant Roy's and the troopers' sighting of General Custer, and Lieutenant Varnum's sighting of the Gray Horse Troop, do coincide in a logical event-time-event sequence.

One other pertinent point is that in a letter published in the *New York Herald,* in July of 1876, and alleged to have been written by Major Brisbin, DeRudio doesn't mention sighting Custer, nor does he do so in a later interview with Walter Camp. This conspicuous absence appears odd to me.

Captain Benteen made several comments about DeRudio, who had been in his company at one time. I realize Benteen had a biting tongue, but his view of DeRudio is worth noting. On the 24th of June, Benteen observed:

> It wasn't far from twilight then, so, after getting supper Keogh came over to my bullberry bush, . . . and the crowd was listening to one of the Italian patriot, DeRudio's recitals, of his hair breath 'scapes with Mazzini, or some other man, in some other country, all of which I rudely interrupted . . .

In a letter to his wife on July 4, 1876– Benteen said: DeRudio was supposed to have been lost, but the same night the Indians left their village he came sauntering in dismounted and accompanied by McIntosh's cook. They had hidden away in the woods. He had a thrilling romantic story made out already, embellished, you bet![11]

In a letter to his wife on July 24, 1876: Benteen wondered if his wife had heard the rumor that Moylan, Gibson, and DeRudio showed the white feather. "Moylan heard of it and threatened vengeance . . . I think had DeRudio made as good use of his eyes as 15 or 20 of the men did . . ."[12]

My earlier remarks about Colonel Graham and Daniel Magnussen being able to repudiate the sightings by enlisted men because they weren't officers, requires further explanation. In his book, *The Custer Myth,* Graham refers to an article from the *Greensboro* [N.C.] *Daily Record* of April 27, 1924.[13] The article recounts an interview with the former Sergeant Kanipe, and is characterized by numerous errors which could probably be attributed to the interviewer, or Kanipe's age. In discussing these errors, Graham provides an explanation that is both enlightening and disappointing. He says that the main inaccuracies in Kanipe's story were characteristic of most of the enlisted men's accounts made during the 1920s.[14] If Colonel Graham had said it was characteristic of most of the accounts made during the '20s by officers and enlisted men, I might have agreed; but to pin this label on just the enlisted men illustrates the attitude I referred to earlier as the "army mentality." The obvious errors made by officers, even after the battle, along with the cover-ups, as well as later errors and fantasies, by not one but several officers, should prevent anyone from pointing the finger at any single class of soldier.

Magnussen believes Custer separated his command as he was moving to the ridge. The fact that Sergeant Kanipe and Trumpeter Martin did not realize this took place can be attributed to their being enlisted men. Magnussen explains that "this was not their concern. When [Kanipe and Martin] were sent back from the head of the column, they would hardly have known that two companies under Captain Keogh were proceeding in the same direction as their column but on the other side of the ridge. Not knowing the composition of the command, it would stand to reason that these enlisted men would not therefore note the absence of two companies in their rearward rides."[15]

Magnussen would have us believe that the two were just a couple of dumb enlisted men. Martin, riding right next to Custer, would never have noticed them separate; but one might expect that Custer would have called the commanders together and given them orders – at least Captain Keogh. This, supposedly, would not have made an impression on an enlisted man, nor would he have noticed the two companies move to the right. According to Magnussen, Custer maintained control of both battalions. Martin then wouldn't have noticed the troops and dust clouds to their right. It would never have occurred to him that there were only three companies behind Custer, and the other two companies might be the cause of the dust and banners to their right.

When I read such accounts I have to question the objectivity and the analytical ability of the writer, particularly as it pertains to his evaluation of officer's testimony.

I recognize that my analysis is based on the assumption that Mr. Gilbert, Recorder Lee and their key witnesses realized the importance of timing with regard to the crossing of Ford A, the positions on the skirmish line and in the timber, as well as the importance of sightings and Custer's orders. I may be giving them more credit than is due. On the other hand, too many writers have ignored and failed to question all of the inconsistencies, never exploring the consequences of the need for the Defense and the Prosecution to present or hold back certain information related to the details of their case. I don't think that the Prosecution and the Defense were so obtuse that they didn't realize the important ramifications of remarks. They would have tried to either bring them about or block them.

To ignore Girard's charges made against the Defense, or even the accusation of Custer's biographer, Frederick Whittaker, only lead to a distorted picture of what took place. During the Reno Inquiry, Frederick Whittaker said: "Reno and Benteen were inseparable; and Reno's counsel, . . . made up a happy trio. They ate and drank together at all times . . ."[16]

Whittaker went on with a number of vicious accusations not worthy of being repeated, but to believe that witnesses for either side would not have slanted their remarks, covered up facts, or lied when they deemed it necessary, is extremely naive.

In analyzing the roster of witnesses, their testimony, and the choice of questions, it must be taken into account that both the Prosecution and the Defense (as well as the tribunal), represented the military operating within the overall framework of a board of inquiry. A verdict against Reno would have resulted in a military trial and continued public scrutiny; consequently, they would have wanted Reno cleared of his charges, and for those charges to be put permanently to rest.*

SOURCES

1. Camp, ed. Hammer, *Custer in 76,* p. 106.
2. Ibid., p. 133.
3. Ibid., p. 111.
4. Graham, *Reno Court Abstract,* p. 106.
5. Ibid., p. 114.
6. Ibid., p. 115, 116.
7. Graham, *The Custer Myth,* p. 315.
8. Graham, *Reno Court Abstract,* p. 107.
9. Graham, *The Custer Myth,* p. 311.
10. Ibid., p. 178.
11. Ibid., p. 300.
12. Ibid., p. 187.
13. Ibid., p. 247.
14. Ibid., p. 250.
15. Thompson, *Narration of the Little Bighorn Company,* Magnussen, p. 124.
16. Graham, *The Custer Myth,* p. 328.

---

*Note Appendix 2, Part B – The questioning of Trumpeter Martin.

7
Sergeant Kanipe

Sergeant Kanipe was one of two known couriers sent by Custer after separating from Major Reno, and his testimony is important to analyze. There appears to be little doubt that Kanipe was sent back with a message from General Custer to Captain McDougall to hurry up the packs. It is generally accepted that he met Captain Benteen approximately one mile west of the Lone Tepee. Both Captain Benteen and Sergeant Kanipe seemed to agree on that point, although Lieutenant Edgerly and troopers Corcoran and Lynch thought the meeting took place near the watering area (morass), which could make a four mile difference. From a timing sequence, as well as the general statements, it appears that a spot just west of the Lone Tepee was the actual location.* The issue on which Benteen and Kanipe didn't agree is how far back McDougall was. Benteen said the distance was about 7 miles.[1] Kanipe, however, had the lead mules at the Lone Tepee and McDougall only a half mile behind them.[2] From Kanipe's estimate, the pack train would have been a mile behind Benteen and strung out for another half mile. This distance would correspond to Trumpeter Martin's statement at the Reno Court of Inquiry. If this was true, such a scenario would help substantiate the slowness with which Benteen's battalion was moving, especially since this was about the same distance the packs were behind Benteen at the morass.

What pace did Captain Benteen take as he went from the watering hole to Reno Hill? Lieutenant Edgerly had them walking, although he said that after receiving the urgent message delivered by Trumpeter Martin they increased the pace to a fast walk. Captain Benteen said the battalion was moving at a trot the whole distance, except when watering, and Lieutenant Godfrey had them galloping a good portion of the time. And, Colonel Graham criticized trooper testimony; Private Morris said Private Moeller of Benteen's troop stated they walked all the way and heard gunfire when watering.[3]

Kanipe said he reported to Captain McDougall, yet both Lieutenant Mathey and Captain McDougall deny receiving messengers. To use a polite euphemism, somebody must have been mistaken.

Sergeant Kanipe said he passed a half dozen or more Rees with Sioux ponies about the time he met Benteen, which according to his account, was in the vicinity of the Lone Tepee. Captain McDougall testified that 8 or 10 Indians passed with about 15 ponies shortly after he left the burning tepee. If these were the same Indians, his testimony would create additional questions, but it would substantiate Kanipe's as well as Martin's original Reno Court account of McDougall's proximity to Benteen. One realizes there were undoubtedly several groups of Rees leaving the area with captured ponies. Most of them should have left by the time the packs, according to Benteen's estimate, reached this location; but not if the packs were close behind Benteen and just west of the Lone Tepee.

Commenting on an article attributed to Sergeant Kanipe, found in *Contributions to the Historical Society of Montana*, IV, 1903, Edgar Stewart said:

> Although Lt. Mathey and Captain McDougall each insisted that the Sergeant did not report to him, the train, in obedience to the orders which Kanipe brought, ceased to follow the trail of the regiment and cut straight across country toward the bluff where the Sergeant said he had left the five troops of Custer's command.[4]

However, Lieutenant Mathey's testimony at the Reno Court would seemingly deny that the packs cut across country. Mathey said:

> ... after passing the tepee two or three miles I saw somebody coming; one I remember was a half-breed. I asked him if General Custer was whipping them, he replied in the negative, adding that the Sioux were too many. I stopped the head of the column and sent back word to Captain McDougall that there had been fighting and I would wait for him to bring up the rear. when it came up we went ahead after a halt of about 15 minutes.[5]

Colonel Graham was correct in condemning Sergeant Kanipe's story in the *North Carolina Daily Record*, Greensboro, N.C., April 27, 1904, as it contained many errors which should have been pointed out. However, his condemnation of all later accounts by troopers was not appropriate, particularly if one considers Graham's reverence for General Edgerly, which apparently made him blind to contradictions and apparent errors in Lieutenant Edgerly's testimony. These were made shortly after the battle and should have raised questions for Colonel Graham and others.

Sergeant Kanipe said he saw some 60 or 70 Indians on the bluffs north of where Reno entrenched. After they were pointed out to General Custer, Kanipe said the column immediately turned and moved to the bluffs. There

---

*One should note that authorities differ on their view of the location of the morass and the Lone Tepee. I am referring to Benteen's and Roger Darling's description of where the morass was located.

were certainly Indians in the area (Wolf Tooth's band, and probably others), but I can't help wondering if Kanipe saw any or at least as many of them as he claimed. Martin did not recall seeing any Indians at that point, which would indicate there was no great emphasis on the supposed sighting, if it indeed took place. The Crow scouts that previously had moved to the bluffs did not mention any Indians either.

Walter Camp believes these Indians were the ones that signaled Chief Gall.[6] However, Gall offered so many stories that it is difficult to know just which one Camp would be referring to. When attacking Major Reno during his retreat to the bluffs, Gall was warned of Custer's imminent attack. He then claims to have alerted the others, and they left Reno to move downstream. If this is the signal Camp is referring to – which seems the only possibility – then it would not correlate with either timing or testimony.

Walter Camp says Kanipe was very positive and emphatic in expressing his recollection that Custer and all his men proceeded north along the bluffs, so far west that they had a full view of Reno's men and the Indian village all the time. This version contradicts Godfrey and other writers who speculate that Custer moved back from the ridge and out of sight. Camp quotes Kanipe saying:

> ... when Custer's men saw Reno charging northward on opposite side of river, Custer's men broke into rather wild disorder – began waving arms, yelling and urging their horses ahead at break neck speed. In this wild run many of the men got in advance of Custer and the last word Kanipe heard Custer utter were; 'Hold your horses, boys, there are Indians enough down there for all of us.' [I believe this statement by Custer would indicate he had just come down from Weir Point from which he had seen part of the Indian camps. It also coincides with what Martin brings out.] Shortly after this Kanipe was sent back to carry word to McDougall.[7]

Camp also records Kanipe having said:

> ... he (Custer) turned square to the right, increasing our speed, and General Custer did not leave his five companies. He rode right in front of them all the time. The command never halted, nor did Custer ever leave his five companies from the place up on the divide where he divided his regiment until after I got my orders to go back; and when the command got up on the bluff where the Indians were supposed to have been seen we could see across the valley, see Reno, and his three companies, about thirty-five Indian scouts going right to the Indian camps. We could see the Indian camp plainly.[8]

Since Sergeant Kanipe and Trumpeter Martin were the last two known soldiers to have been with Custer, a comparison of their statements should be undertaken. One important similarity – which, as far as I know, was never examined to any extent – was the position of the packs when they met Benteen along Reno Creek. Kanipe and Martin placed them close behind Benteen, whereas Benteen had them several miles back. Both men said Custer's command went near the edge of the bluffs rather than farther back, as many others have speculated. This appeared to be the scope of the similarities in their testimonies. In describing subsequent events, Martin had the troops moving in a column formation while Kanipe portrayed them in a line. Martin said he didn't see Major Reno in the valley, whereas Kanipe did. Martin had Custer going to several high points; Kanipe didn't mention any. They both have the troops waving and cheering; however, Kanipe depicts them doing this after seeing Major Reno, while Martin said they cheered and waved after Custer came down from the high point and told the troops they had caught the Indians "napping." This is said to have happened just before they left the ridge. Certainly the way questions were asked and the answers taken down could account for the differences, but I also think the following conjectural analysis may be fairly close to what actually took place.

It would seem natural that due to their respective locations in the command, the timing and observations of the two witnesses would differ. Was Custer's command traveling in line or column formation? More than likely both. Considering the terrain, after the companies had watered near the junction of Reno Creek and the North Fork tributary, they could have left in a line formation. However, after they had reached the ridge, it became necessary to pass onto it by columns. It can be reasoned from Curley's and Martin's testimony that they reached the ridge by moving to the south side of Sharpshooter Hill, which could have necessitated going to a column formation. Kanipe, in looking back, would be more apt to remember the move to the ridge, while Martin remembered how they were traveling once they reached the ridge and later as they departed in their move to Medicine Tail Coulee.

While the troops finished watering, regrouping and preparing to move out, Custer would have gone ahead. Custer had a fast walking horse, and he was anxious to see the valley, the Indians, Major Reno's position, and to receive a report from Mitch Bouyer. This would have been a typical maneuver Custer had used during the Civil War: to dash ahead of his command to reconnoiter. It could be expected of him to use it at this time. In this scenario,

Custer converses with Bouyer, is seen by the Rees, then moves back to meet members of his staff. Major Reno has not left the timber, so Martin, when viewing the valley, does not see him. The command then arrives, moves onto the ridge in a column formation, which becomes strung out some distance behind Custer. The command proceeds along the ridge. As they near Weir Point, Major Reno begins his rapid move down the valley. Custer, Martin, and probably the adjutant and battalion commanders, have reached Weir Point and view the Indian encampment, which is still not aware of the soldiers. Custer comes down from the high point. He now knows the route and the place where he wants to attack the camp, and he is aware that he will be doing so shortly. By that time, if not earlier, Custer must have recognized the need for the packs to move quickly toward him, so they either wouldn't remain along Ash Creek, as their prior orders may have stated, or so they wouldn't follow Major Reno's trail across the Little Bighorn. Consequently, Custer orders Captain Tom Custer to send a messenger to Captain McDougall. Tom Custer sends Kanipe. The troops, who have just seen Reno, are dashing up and Custer tells them to slow down. He informs them there will be plenty of Indians but they have caught them "napping." (In his testimony, Kanipe reported hearing Custer telling the troops to slow down, but hadn't seen Custer go to any high point.) Major Reno is now setting up his skirmish line. Martin didn't see Major Reno when on the high point, and associates the cheering with Custer's announcement. Martin, somewhat below Custer while on Weir Point, hears the officers wonder where the Indians are and remembers that one remarked they may be hunting buffaloes.[9]

Though this scenario is speculative, it does back up two main points which should be derived from an analysis of Martin's and Kanipe's testimony. Martin didn't see Major Reno's troops in the valley, which means he arrived on the ridge and proceeded down it some distance ahead of the rest of the command. It also means that Reno had not left the timber when Custer first arrived on the ridge. During the command's move along the ridge they do see Reno, and since the Rees, as Kanipe implied, are still in the lead, it would mean the troops are only part way down the valley. This version, I believe, is not only logical but can be synchronized with a proper timing sequence, one which has Reno setting up his skirmish line as Custer's command leaves the ridge. It also allows Lieutenant Varnum, looking up from the skirmish line, to see the Gray Horse Troop as they are moving off the ridge.

I believe the following points or questions can also be drawn from Sergeant Kanipe's accounts:

First, Kanipe was sent back with a message for Captain McDougall to hurry the packs. We know Kanipe delivered the message to Benteen, but we don't know if he did to Captain McDougall or Lieutenant Mathey. What I consider to be odd – if Kanipe delivered the message – is that, as far as I know, he makes no mention as to what he told them or what they may have asked about Reno or Custer, nor does he recall any verbal exchange or reaction, which certainly must have occurred. If McDougall or Mathey received such a message, why did they rest for 15 minutes after passing the Lone Tepee, as Mathey stated at the Reno Court?[10] It would appear they made no special attempt to reach General Custer, and were either resting or moving along the main trail when Lieutenant Hare reached them.

Looking at the situation from a different perspective, one may wonder whether Captain McDougall and Lieutenant Mathey said they didn't receive any messages from General Custer because they were part of a cover-up. Obviously the packs played an important part in Major Reno's and Captain Benteen's reason for the delay in moving to aid Custer or find out what may have happened to him. If the packs were as close behind as Sergeant Kanipe claimed, then there is no reason why they shouldn't have arrived on Reno Hill shortly after Benteen's battalion. Captain McDougall's remarks – that Captain Weir was still in sight when he arrived on the hill – would more likely support Kanipe's contention, at least as it pertained to the location of the packs.[11] One should also consider that if McDougall or Mathey admitted to receiving any messages – either from Sergeant Kanipe or Trumpeter Martin – they would have placed themselves in the position of not following orders. These are questions which should have been asked in search for a definitive answer.

Second, Kanipe's statements corroborates testimony that Custer's command moved along the ridge overlooking the valley.

Third, Kanipe saw Reno's troops moving down the valley but does not suggest they were engaged, although they could have been before Kanipe or Custer left the ridge.

Fourth, the fact that Kanipe was sent back with a message for Captain McDougall would mean that Custer was still not aware that Benteen was back on the main trail. This implies Custer was expecting Benteen to move down the valley in support of Major Reno. It seems inconceivable that Custer would have ignored or forgotten a major component of his fighting force to the extent that he not only failed to include them in his attack plans, but would not even have notified Benteen of the attack at the time he issued his orders to Major Reno. The number of messengers we know Custer sent should, in itself, preclude such a notion. W. Kent King, in his book, *Massacre: The Custer Cover-Up,* suggests that Benteen was placed in a reserve role, but I do not agree with his explanation. King believes that from maps and scouting reports, Custer was aware of the location and the number of Indians he would be facing. This is probable, but had Custer known these facts, he would not have expected Major Reno with his 3 companies to be the sole attacking force from the south. Rather, he would plan on 6 companies attacking from the south while his 5 companies attempted a flanking movement.

SOURCES

1. Brininstool, *Troopers With Custer,* p. 79.
2. Camp, Custer in 76, p. 93, footnote 11.
3. Brady, *Indian Fights and Fighters,* p. 404.
4. Stewart, *Custer's Luck,* p. 398.
5. Graham, *Reno Court Abstract,* p. 189.
6. Camp, *Custer in 76,* p. 97.
7. Ibid., p. 97.
8. Ibid., p. 92.
9. Ibid., p. 100.
10. Graham, *Reno Court Abstract,* p. 189.
11. Camp, *Custer in 76,* p. 70.

8
Trumpeter Martin

Giovanni Martini, known as Trumpeter John Martin, was the last living white man to see General Custer alive. Martin, Custer's orderly on the 25th, riding next to the General, was sent back with a message to Captain Benteen: to hurry. Martin's testimony is instrumental in ascertaining Custer's moves until he engaged in battle, yet his comments have been the most ignored, maligned and neglected of any of the major witnesses. In my opinion, the essence of Martin's story never changed. His accounts are as reliable as any I have analyzed. If he had a fault as a witness, it was his attempt to please the interviewer, a problem similar to that of some Indian witnesses, but for different reasons. Martin didn't understand the English language too well; he may have often misinterpreted questions, and, I would assume, like most people under those circumstances, would have hesitated to ask for clarification. His answers could also be easily misinterpreted. He realized, and, unlike most other witnesses, admitted that his knowledge of distance and timing could be wrong. As far as I know, Martin never went back to the battlefield (which both the military and writers of the time should have insisted upon); nor was he ever asked the questions he should have been asked. I have been to the battlefield enough times to know how hard it is to remember the precise location of the prominent terrain characteristics such as a dip, a ravine, or a bluff, and the relationship of one point to another. The recollection would be even more difficult if your mind was preoccupied with being shot, losing your horse, or a hundred-and-one other things having nothing to do with the location and exact nature of the terrain features. I think Martin's whole career indicated a conscientious, patriotic, solid type of character; certainly not a genius, but a person of unquestionable integrity and reliability. His testimony, compared to those of others, is responsible and consistent on major points. When it is not, the discrepancies are due to his misinterpretation of the question, the interviewers' misrepresentation of his answer, or his inability to remember just where a particular hill or a ravine happened to be, possibly having confused it with another. His retraction of a message taken to the packs, I believe, was due to his loyalty to Captain Benteen.

The attempt to discredit Trumpeter Martin took place at the Reno Court of Inquiry. Martin couldn't be completely ignored and the trial officials were fearful of his testimony, particularly as it related to the orders and messages sent by Custer. With his linguistic difficulties, it was easy to defame his intelligence, and within that framework, his character.*

The success of this campaign against Martin, along with later comments by Benteen, allowed writers and others not only to ignore his testimony but to cast unwarranted aspersions on what he said, and, in turn, has prevented objective analysis of what happened to General Custer. The following comments by Dr. Kuhlman and Dr. Stewart are good examples of how Martin has been treated.

Dr. Kuhlman says:

> ... To this might well be added the further observation that, had it not been known that Benteen was back on the trail, Martin would not have been sent at all, for he was little more than a boy, spoke and understood English with difficulty, was relatively inexperienced, and not too intelligent. If Benteen was thought to be still on his scout, far away in rough ground, an experienced sergeant with a good horse would have been sent.[1]

In *Custer's Luck,* Edgar Stewart observes:

> Martin, the lone surviving participant, gave two versions of what happened. According to the traditional account, Custer summoned him and said:
> "Orderly, I want you to take a message to Colonel Benteen. Ride as fast as you can and tell him to hurry. Tell him it is a big village and I want him to be quick, and to bring the ammunition packs." He didn't stop at all when he was telling me this and I just said 'Yes Sir' and checked my horse, when the Adjutant said, "Wait, orderly, I'll give you a message," and he stopped and wrote it in a big hurry in a little book and then tore out the leaf and gave it to me."
>
> However, Martin told the Reno Court of Inquiry in 1879 that after going down a ravine that led to the river Custer told the adjutant to send a message to Captain Benteen and to go as fast as he could over the same trail that the five companies had followed. If there was no danger and Martin had time, he was to return; otherwise he was to join his own troop and report to Lieutenant Cooke when he did return.
>
> Martin was a green Italian lad – he had been a drummer boy with Garibaldi at Cillafrance and had been in the U.S. only a few years – and his intellectual and language difficulties were many; indeed, this is not the only incident of which he gave different accounts at different times.[2]

---

*Note Appendix 2, Part B.

In answer to Benteen's questions about what had taken place, the trumpeter replied that the Indians had "skidaddled" and, by his language, gave the very definite impression that the troops were in possession of the Indian village. Martin, in his account, however, says that he told Benteen that the Indians he saw were running and that he supposed that by this time Custer had charged through the hostile camp. Although he told the Court of Inquiry that he said nothing about Reno's battalion, because Benteen asked no questions about it, he later said he was going to tell Benteen about seeing Reno's men in action, but did not get a chance to do so, for just then Benteen pointed out that his horse was severely wounded. Even this did not jog Martin's memory, for he not only did not tell Benteen of the Reno action in the valley, but also neglected to inform him of the ambush and attack upon Custer's command. All of which adds up to the conclusion that Martin not only had language difficulties but was also lacking in general intelligence and justifies Benteen's statement that he was a "thick-headed, dull-witted Italian, just as much cut out for a cavalryman as he was for a king."[3]

What we see, on careful examination in the writings of Kuhlman and Stewart, is not an indictment of Martin, but of the writers themselves. I have found more discrepancies in the accounts of major officers, sergeants, and interpreters than I have in Trumpeter Martin's statements. We must look for consistency in basic areas, and we must allow that not every word, every ravine, every estimate of distance or time is going to be the same. Since there were so many errors in everyone's testimony, one should be questioning why Martin was singled out for such detrimental remarks. One also has to wonder why Benteen centered his barbs on Custer and Martin.

Let's go back to Dr. Kuhlman's accusations. Martin was assigned to ride with Custer on a day which everyone recognized would most likely be eventful and important; only a competent person would have been assigned for the duty. One could also assume that anyone with the experience Martin had in Italy, who possessed the ability and perseverance to make it to America and learn the language fairly well, would not be completely lacking in intelligence. One might question how much better Benteen, Kuhlman, or Stewart would have spoken Italian after three years in Italy. Martin had some knowledge of drums and bugles, and later became a sergeant in the U.S. Army. He must not have been too incompetent. In both Kuhlman's and Stewart's observation, he was classified as a mere boy, which he wasn't. Martin was 25 years old at the time – older than most of the troopers, and older than Custer when the latter became a general. He had been with the 7th Cavalry several years, and had been with Custer's expedition to the Black Hills. Martin came to the U.S. in 1873 and enlisted in the U.S. Army. Before that, when only fourteen, he had joined and fought with Garibaldi. I would say he had more experience than most of the troops.

Leaving out his denigration of Martin, Dr. Kuhlman, I believe, was correct. When Martin was sent back, Custer had already dispatched three couriers that we know of: Trumpeter Voss, Sergeant Major Sharrow and Sergeant Kanipe. Dr. Kuhlman's reasoning that if Custer still thought Benteen was searching for the valley of the Little Bighorn, he wouldn't have sent Martin alone, was probably true, although not because he wasn't a sergeant. Trumpeter Voss was sent soon after Benteen had left and so was still in sight; if not, there was little danger of encountering Indians or not finding Benteen. It is Kuhlman's reasoning that makes me believe that when the Sergeant Major was sent, he may have been accompanied by the Ree scout, Stabbed, as Custer would not have been sure where Benteen was. Kanipe was sent by himself since Custer realized there was little danger and knew where the packs would be. Kuhlman's reasoning is also behind my belief that the Sergeant Major reported back <u>after</u> Kanipe had left but <u>before</u> Martin was sent back. Because of the Sergeant Major's report, Custer realized Benteen had returned to the main trail, and the packs and Captain McDougall's company should be moving toward him. Knowing the Indians were preoccupied with Reno in the valley, Custer would believe that Martin could make it through. What I am opposed to in Dr. Kuhlman's report are his observations which convey a condescending view of Martin as an inferior and unreliable witness, an attitude which has allowed his testimony to be brushed aside.

Both Kuhlman and Stewart use Captain Benteen's reference to Martin as a thick-headed, dull-witted Italian, which destroys his credibility as a witness; yet both of them knew Benteen downgraded others and had flippant remarks to make about almost everyone from officers to enlisted men. A foreigner, because of his language problems, is often judged in that way, but as Private Windolph would have said, "before the battle we kidded Martin but not afterwards."[4]

Stewart's use of the passage in which he discredited Martin is, to me, inexcusable. First and foremost he didn't quote all of Martin's testimony to the court. What Martin said was:

> . . . we went more to the right from the ridge and down to a ravine that led to the river. At the time General Custer passed the high place on the ridge, or a little below it,

he told his Adjutant to send an order back to Captain Benteen, I don't know what it was. Then the Adjutant called me . . .[5] *

Stewart interprets this reference to a message as the one Martin received and carried to Captain Benteen, and he believes Martin received it when moving down to the ravine which led to the river. The ravine would be South Medicine Tail Coulee. As I have indicated, Martin never said this. He testified that after he passed the high place on the ridge, which would most likely be Weir Point or below it, Custer told the Adjutant to send a message back to Benteen. Martin claimed to be unaware of the content. This was probably the message taken by Sergeant Kanipe. Martin possibly caught Benteen's name being mentioned, so thought the message was for Benteen. Martin didn't even know who had taken the message, let alone what it said. We might remember that Martin asserted that he never knew Kanipe took any messages. The location would coincide with the place where Kanipe said he received his message. Then, when they got to the ravine which led to the river, Martin was given his message. If one studied the testimony instead of merely quoting excerpts, this would be apparent. In it, Stewart suggested that Martin couldn't be trusted because he had said that Custer gave him his orders verbally and then Cooke wrote them down. But at the Reno Court, Martin didn't mention receiving verbal orders from Custer and said he didn't know what the orders were. (Martin was referring to the orders taken by Kanipe.) He claimed to have been instructed by Cooke to take the written order to Benteen and come back if he could. Stewart, it seems, distorted the facts. It appears the Defense did not quiz Martin as to what orders were given, which supports my view of the Defense's concern with the question of orders and what Martin might reveal. Martin's testimony is clearly incomplete, and Stewart should have considered what Martin told Walter Camp: that at the Reno Court they didn't want him to tell all he knew. Stewart should have been disputing the actions of the court, rather than Martin's testimony.

The second passage written by Stewart is even more uncalled for and unsavory. First, it supports my general objection to many historical articles and books, where too often footnotes seem to be used to impress people with how objective and factual the writer is. Without careful analysis, footnotes can be meaningless and can actually prevent the formulation of a proper hypothesis. For example, I could use statements made by Hitler, Goebbels or Goering, and they certainly wouldn't make my conclusions correct as to what was happening in the world in 1939. In his book, *Custer's Luck*, Stewart has done a masterful job of compiling and putting together memorabilia in a tremendously interesting way. It is when he attempts to draw conclusions from this panorama of memorabilia that he actually impedes the knowledge and understanding which he should be illuminating. His berating of Martin doesn't add to our perspective on what happened to Custer, but instead prevents us from paying the attention we should to the key figure in the investigation. It is one thing to examine Martin's remarks critically, as they should be; it is another to cast aspersions on his intelligence and thereby on anything he has said. This is not the way one develops an objective analysis. There is not one officer whose testimony I cannot question at some point, and in many cases I know with certainty their account could not have been true.

Instead of accepting Lieutenant Edgerly's comments, Stewart should have questioned them. For example, the issue of what Martin said about Custer charging in and killing everybody, when elsewhere he denied it, especially since the remarks are so similar to those made by Kanipe.[6] With Edgerly's contrasting views of what happened on other essential points, one might think he could have been confused about what really happened, particularly since Benteen, when he received the message, was several hundred yards ahead of his troops, and it would appear that Captain Weir and Edgerly were either close to Benteen or moved up when they saw him receiving the messenger. I wonder how close Edgerly would have been to the troops when Martin joined them or was sent back to the packs? I think the behavior ascribed to Martin is not compatible with the impression one would have of his character or condition at that time. It is not that Edgerly's comment should not be included, but Stewart should not present it as an accepted fact.

Before portraying Martin as a green lad, Stewart should have considered the circumstances of the situation. He should have remembered Martin had just traveled some eight to ten miles at a fast pace (since Custer had started his move to the ridge). His horse had been injured, and they were both exhausted. He was appearing before an officer, after having accomplished his mission. Major Reno's situation was not that serious when he saw him, and Martin might have been thinking of his own close call; yet because he didn't blurt out or interrupt the officer, he was labeled a dull-witted, unintelligent person. Possibly Stewart should have wondered why Benteen wasn't more concerned, and asked some penetrating questions

---

*Note John Gray's more complete recording of the questioning in my analysis of Gray's book, *Custer's Last Campaign*.

about what was happening, which he didn't. Benteen supposedly didn't even bother to ask Major Reno anything specific about Custer when he arrived on the hill, and neither of them was curious enough to ask Martin any questions during that time. Using Stewart's own reasoning, this failure must have made them a pair of unintelligent, dull-witted officers. To cap it off, Stewart then accused Martin of not reporting that Custer was being ambushed. There is no evidence, either from Martin's statements, from the Crow scouts, or the Sioux and Cheyenne, that there was an ambush.

To return to analyzing testimony, Stewart and others should have also had more questions about the packs and their location, and the reasons why Captain McDougall didn't remember receiving any messenger. It would be more productive to probe these issues instead of sympathizing with Benteen's excuse for not bringing up the ammunition packs, particularly if they were as close as Martin and Kanipe indicated and Mathey's testimony implied. Certainly if Benteen's gait was no faster than Edgerly said it was, they wouldn't even have had to slow down. They seemed to accept Major Reno's need for ammunition packs but not General Custer's. The primary concern of the orders was for Benteen to hurry, which he didn't do. Custer and Cooke were not in a position to think through the various implications of their message, but their concerns were legitimate.

There are discrepancies in Martin's accounts, but with the exception of the orders to McDougall, they are minor and natural. This is in contrast to definite errors, conflicts and inconsistencies in the testimony of major witnesses which did not even raise an eyebrow.

John Martin continued to serve in the army, and rose to the rank of sergeant. His career does not mark him as an intellectual; however, the consistency of his remarks as shown even in Colonel Graham's account, written shortly before Martin died, belies the accusations made against him.

Captain Benteen's ability to create an image which prevented attempts to analyze a person or a situation is remarkable. Benteen was able to credit a great general with inability to recognize existing signs and warnings and failure to have formulated any plan of action until practically in the Indian village. Then he imposed on Martin the stigma of a dumb Italian so one needn't accept anything he said.

Instead of casting doubt and adding to the ubiquitous view of Martin, what Stewart should have gained from Martin's remarks made at the Court of Inquiry is that Martin went as far as Medicine Tail Coulee with General Custer before he was given the message to Benteen. Trumpeter Martin's testimony is indispensable in analyzing what happened to General Custer until he engaged the Indians. There are four main accounts Martin gave that I will examine: one at the Reno Court of Inquiry, two given to Walter Camp, and one given to Colonel Graham. Before doing so, keep in mind Martin's comment to Camp about a statement he did *not* make at the Court:

> He [Martin] did not tell this at the Reno Court of Inquiry for it was not desired that he should tell all he knew and said. That, afterward, he never was invited by officers to discuss what he knew of the battle and never volunteered.[7]

This supports other testimony and indicates how objective and concerned the court was with what really happened to Custer. The Inquiry was a cover-up of Major Reno's and Captain Benteen's actions.

Martin at the Reno Court:

> ...At the tepee, on the right side of the river, Major Reno's column took off to the right. It was at a ravine; we could see hills on both sides. We remained on the right side of the river and went on the jump all the way: ...General Custer did not go near the river at all: he halted only once, at a little creek to water the horses for about five minutes. We were there about 10 minutes altogether, and the General directed the commanders not to let the horses drink too much.
>
> He left that watering place and went about three hundred yards in a straight line; then turned to the right a little and traveled four or five hundred yards and there was a big bend on the hill; he turned these hills and went on top of the ridge. All at once we looked on the bottom and saw the Indian village; at the same time we could only see children and dogs and ponies – no Indians at all. General Custer appeared to be glad to see the village in that shape and supposed the Indians were asleep in their tepees.
>
> We could see the bottom from the ridge but could not see the timber because it was under the hill – nor anything of Major Reno's column.
>
> I rode to the left and rear of General Custer, and about two yards from him. That was my position as an orderly.
>
> The gray horse company was in the center of the column. We could see the river while on top of the ridge, but after we went down a ravine we could not see the river or timber or anything else. We heard no firing as we went down.
>
> General Custer's column moved always at a gallop. It was about a mile and a half from the watering place to the point on the ridge where we could see the village. After he saw the village, he pulled off his hat and gave a

cheer and said "Courage, boys, we will get them, and as soon as we get through we will go back to our station."

... we went more to the right from the ridge and down to a ravine that led to the river. At the time General Custer passed the high place on the ridge or a little below it he told his Adjutant to send an order back to Captain Benteen. I don't know what it was.

Then the Adjutant called me. I was right at the rear of the General. He said "Orderly, I want you to take this dispatch to Captain Benteen and go as fast as you can." He told me if I had time and there was no danger to come back, but otherwise to remain with my company which was with Captain Benteen.

My horse was tired and I went through as fast as he could go. The Adjutant told me to follow the same trail we came down.

After I started back I traveled five or six hundred yards, perhaps three quarters of a mile, and got on the same ridge where General Custer saw the village. I looked down and saw that Major Reno's battalion was engaged. I went on to about three or four hundred yards above the watering place and met Captain Benteen. I delivered my dispatch to him and told him what Lt. Cook had told me. Capt. Benteen read the dispatch and put it in his pocket and gave me an order to Capt. McDougall to bring up the pack train and keep it well up.

Capt. Benteen asked me where General Custer was. I said I supposed that by that time he had made a charge through the village. I said nothing about Major Reno's battalion. He did not ask about it.

When I left General Custer he was going ahead: the Adjutant stopped to write the dispatch. It took me three quarters to an hour to get back to the ridge and saw Reno in action before I met Benteen. I went at once to Capt. McDougall about 150 yards. He was in front of his troops, and the packs were pretty well together. I delivered my message and joined my company.

After delivering of Custer's dispatch to Benteen, he moved a little faster. The packs were coming on – some walking, some running, some trotting.

We followed General Custer's trail till we got on the same ridge where I saw Reno engaged. About the time we got there we saw Reno's battalion retreating to the same side of the river we were on. We joined Reno, and the packs came up in about fifteen minutes. After the packs were all up, we moved down the river in about one and a half hours. I was right in front of the column and could see the Indians after we got to the head of the first ravine. We halted then and Captain Weir wanted to take his company down the stream to see General Custer. He went a little to the right and came back again. The Indians were leaving General Custer and coming back to us, firing; the bulk of them came to where we were. The column then turned back as it was in a bad position; the Indians were on both flanks and the ravine was very deep and we could not go through. We took position a little farther down the stream from where we first saw Major Reno.

Cross Examination:

I judge it was <u>about noon</u> when General Custer and I were on the ridge and saw the village. I did not see General Custer after that. His command was galloping when I left. When I saw the Indian village there was no dust at all; just dogs and children playing around the tepees. I was sent back from about ravine that Custer went down toward the river. (here the witness designated the point by marking the figure 8 on the map.)

After I saw Major Reno engaged, I traveled about two miles to Captain Benteen. It took about three quarters of an hour to come back with Benteen's command.

I was about an hour and a half going from Custer to Benteen and about three quarters of an hour back to the ridge. I can't say how long it took; two or three hours. I judge I went about five miles, but I cannot judge the time and distances. I do not know. [These are attempts to confuse him with questions concerning different time and distance estimates. This is even more apparent when reading the full transcript.]

Re-direct examination:

<u>The ridge from which General Custer and I saw the village is the highest point around there. I met Captain Benteen before I got as far as the tepee; was not in sight of it.</u> [My underlining. This would indicate the Lone Tepee was farther from the river than some believe.] I don't think I crossed Reno's trail at all. I can only guess at the time. I had no watch.[8]

There is no doubt that some of Martin's distances and timing are off, but Martin admits to that. What creates problems in Martin's testimony is his use of the terms "ridge," "higher ground," "high point," and "highest point." Just where Custer came onto the ridge is not known. Sergeant Kanipe and Trumpeter Martin both stated the command proceeded along the ridge. They could see the valley and some part of the village as they moved. What Martin saw on the high point could become intertwined with what he saw when they came onto the ridge and moved to the high point. This would be natural. One has to examine Martin's other interviews; as he said, they did not want him to tell all he knew at the Reno Court, nor did they afterward ask him to divulge what he knew.

From his testimony I can see no reason to accept the accusations levied against Martin that he was so mixed up as to be disqualified as a reliable witness. I do believe that either the recorder, at times, mingled Martin's answers, or the questions were asked in such a manner that his answers appeared to have been mixed chronologically.* It would seem the officials asked him numerous questions pertaining to time and distances which they knew he wouldn't be able to answer in a consistent manner. However, no one else was able to either. They also didn't ask key questions they should have, or if they did, they were not recorded in the abstract.** I don't know of any questions pertaining to the orders Benteen or Major Reno received; nor of any curiosity as to when or where Martin may have seen Sergeant Major Sharrow; or how far from Ford B he was when he was sent back; or whether he and Custer viewed the village from Weir Point; or whether the Adjutant at first went with Major Reno . . . one could go on and on. Though some of such questions may have been irrelevant to the Inquiry, many of them would have been pertinent, and if they could not be asked then, they should have been asked later.

One of the primary direct and indirect accusations against Major Reno – which also affected Captain Benteen although he himself was not under scrutiny – was the failure of Reno and Benteen to go to the aid of General Custer as soon as many thought they should have. It is necessary to realize that although Benteen was not officially on trial, he certainly was, <u>unofficially</u>. If his orders gave any indication that he was to aid Reno, especially if he had been expected to move down the Little Bighorn, and he had not followed these instructions, one can imagine the repercussions this failure would have produced. If Reno knew what his orders were, as stated by Sergeant Davern and confirmed in a later interview with Martin, Reno's case would have been easily decided. This is why the orders received by Major Reno and Captain Benteen were so important, and why the one person who could destroy their whole case was Trumpeter Martin. For him to have insisted - as he later did - that he heard an order to Reno that Benteen was to support him, and with the implication that Benteen had similar orders, would not only destroy the case for Reno but would indict Benteen as well. It is no wonder that the Defense (and also the Prosecution, representing the military), uncertain what answers he might give and perhaps aware that such orders had been received, simply tried to confuse and discredit Martin.

There is one phase, crucial to the case, where someone was lying. It involved the question of where the packs were in relation to Benteen's battalion when the messages sent by Custer and delivered by Sergeant Kanipe and Trumpeter Martin were received. Another related question is whether these messages were delivered to Captain McDougall. Martin said Benteen sent him back with orders to Captain McDougall and the packs. Benteen and McDougall denied that a message was sent and received. The fact should also be noted that McDougall denied receiving any message delivered by Kanipe. It is hard to imagine Martin fabricating such an answer or the Court misinterpreting Martin, as he later claimed. This could have helped the Prosecution but certainly not the Defense, so it is unlikely they would have allowed it to be recorded without Martin having said it.

The accusations levied against Reno, and indirectly affecting Benteen, focused on their failure to move to the aid of Custer at a time when it may have been possible to have prevented the destruction of Custer's five companies. Reno's and Benteen's defense centered around their inability to hear gunfire. An even more important factor was the need to wait for the packs: their proximity to Benteen's battalion and Reno Hill became crucial. This aspect would have made a difference in their time of arrival. It would also affect the timing of Lieutenant Mathey and Captain McDougall's reaction, and the timing of Reno's ability to move to support Custer. The time in question has been a matter of dispute.

Once again Benteen's remarks – in this case his denial of giving any order to Martin – and his estimate of how far back the packs were, has generally been accepted, then and now, without questioning. The issue of the arrival of the packs, though not affecting Custer or his actions, would still have been essential in its effect on Major Reno's case and, inferentially, on Benteen. It also suggested another area which needed to be examined but was covered up instead. Was Martin's testimony true, or was he misinterpreted, as he later claimed, in that he never said he took a message to Captain McDougall from Captain Benteen? What is odd is that the arrival of the packs and Captain McDougall's location fit in with Sergeant Kanipe's remarks made in a later interview with Walter Camp, and actually coincide with what Lieutenant Mathey suggested in his testimony. (I have indicated this in analyzing Sergeant Kanipe's remarks.)

It's understandable that the Defense would not want to involve any more officers than necessary in the cover-ups. Major Reno, Captain Benteen, and for minor substantiation, Lieutenant Wallace. (Wallace changed to a major conspirator when I recognized the necessity for, and his part

---

*Appendix 2:Part B. Further corroboration of this type of questioning is given by Gray in his book, *Custer's Last Campaign*, 336, 337. (see also my analysis of Gray's book.)

**They are not asked or recorded in the full proceedings of the Reno Court of Inquiry.

1. A view from Sharpshooter Ridge looking back to Reno Creek. Reno Hill is on the right. This photograph shows the route I believe Custer's command took coming on to the ridge. They may have moved in a line formation, but here they most likely would have changed to a column.

2. A view from Sharpshooter Ridge looking toward Weir Point. If Custer came to the ridge on the south side of Sharpshooter Hill, he would have wanted to move to Weir Peaks for a better view, so that he could locate the best and quickest route to the Indian villages. With villages to the left, he would not have gone down Cedar Coulee, the head of which starts just below Sharpshooter ridge.

in the official time change.) They were probably the only officers involved, and there was probably a general warning not to be too critical of Major Reno's actions. Wallace was the one officer who supported Reno and Benteen in saying he did not hear any gunfire downstream. Edgerly's remarks concerning orders given at the divide could have been damaging, but unless the Prosecution took advantage of them, which they didn't, they could be ignored. The officers, in spite of their dislike for Major Reno, would have realized the necessity to not mention that they had seen Custer on the ridge early in their move down the valley. Trumpeter Martin was the only possible stumbling block for the Defense, but they didn't want to take a chance in exerting pressure (outside of warning him not to say too much), or attempting to get him to see the overall plan of the Defense and convince him to comply with it. Instead the Defense chose to simply not ask him pertinent questions, knowing that, with his language problem, it would be easy to discredit him, if need be.

As I have said, the two items that were important to the Defense, and which Martin's testimony could affect, were the orders Custer gave to Major Reno and Captain Benteen, and the situation with the packs. The packs, in one way, were not so much a problem for Major Reno as they were for the three other officers: Captain Benteen, Captain McDougall and Lieutenant Mathey. Ex-Sergeant Kanipe was a private citizen at the time of the Inquiry and was only involved in an indirect way. It was known that he carried a message from General Custer to Captain McDougall, and he met Captain Benteen, who sent him on back to McDougall. Captain McDougall denied receiving any message. The problem one faces here is the location of the packs. Sergeant Kanipe said he reached Captain Benteen a short distance west of the Lone Tepee, and that when he went back to Captain McDougall, he was only a short distance east of the Lone Tepee. At the Reno Court we have Martin saying the packs were west of the Lone Tepee. Then, Benteen, according to Martin's court testimony, gave Martin a message to take to McDougall, and he was only 150 yards behind Benteen.[9] Lieutenant Mathey denied receiving any message from Custer, but otherwise he did indicate they were west of the Lone Tepee,[10] and so his account could coincide with those of Martin and Kanipe. Kanipe maintained his position in interviews with Walter Camp some years afterwards, while Trumpeter Martin denied, at these later dates, going back to Captain McDougall. I believe Martin was a good, honest, reliable individual, but I also recognize that he was a good soldier. His record proves that. I would assume that Martin realized later that his statements reflected on Captain Benteen and the other officers, and placed the blame on the Court and their misinterpretation of what he had actually said.

These are some of the questions that should have been asked and definitive answers determined at that time. Did Sergeant Kanipe lie when he said that he took his message to Captain McDougall, or did Captain McDougall? Did Mathey? Did Captain Benteen? Was it just a general mix up? Did the court, indeed, misinterpret Martin? Were the packs near the Lone Tepee when Sergeant Kanipe came with his message, and to the west of the Lone Tepee when Martin came with his? Was Captain Benteen correct that the packs were 7 or 8 miles back? Was Martin's answer one reason his testimony was discredited?

Here are several of Captain Benteen's answers and views:

Reno Court:

> It would have delayed me an hour and a quarter to wait for the packs to come up after I got the Martin order. I did not send him to the pack train (Martin); if he went there he did so on his own.... I am convinced that when the order brought by Martin reached me General Custer and his whole command were dead. It was then about three o'clock.[11]

Benteen in his Narratives, written after 1890:

> ... John Martini, the trumpeter, bringing this dispatch, was a thick headed, dull witted Italian, just about as much cut out for a cavalryman as he was for a king: he informed me that the Indians were "skidaddling" . . . so much of the Italian trumpeter's story hadn't "panned out."[12]

Captain Benteen at the Reno Court:

Q. Where was the pack train at that time? [When he viewed Reno's troops retreating.]
A. I judge about 7 miles back.
Q. How far down the river was the furthest point reached by any company under Major Reno?
A. About half a mile below that highest point.
Q. Did you examine what was supposed at that time to have been his trail? [Custer's]
A. On the morning of General Terry's arrival, I asked for permission to saddle up my company and go over to the battlefield of General Custer. I did so and followed <u>down the gorge</u> thinking that was the route taken by General Custer on the 25th of June. [my underlining]
Q. Describe your movement to that point [the highest point – Weir Point], the location of the country and everything you saw?
A. That was my first sight of the village after I arrived at that high point. That was the only point from which

it could be seen, and I saw, as I supposed, about 1800 tepees.
Q. When you met Trumpeter Martin, did he report to you on which side of the river General Custer's column was?
A. Not at that time. He did after we had reached that highest point, at the figure "7". He then pointed out the place from which he had been sent back.[13] [According to Martin, Benteen told him it was about 600 yards from Ford B.]

Benteen's Narratives:

I sallied after Weir, and about 3/4ths of a mile lower down, from the top of the highest point in the vicinity, saw Weir's troop returning.[14]

Again we find that the phrase "highest point" means Weir Point. There are various high points in the area, but when the highest point on the ridge is referred to, it invariably means Weir Point.

The essential question is: Why is Benteen, after 1890, still attempting to berate and discredit Martin? Even if Martin did say the Indians were "skidaddling," it would not justify Benteen's failure to follow orders. If the packs were as close as Martin and Kanipe said they were (and by Lieutenant Mathey's account they must have been), then Benteen should have sent Martin or someone else back to the packs, which is what I believe he did. If we add to this the fact that Martin's statement at the Reno Court was too explicit to have been misinterpreted, then the evidence seems overwhelming in suggesting that Martin was sent back to Captain McDougall. One way or the other, Benteen should have sent someone; the excuse that Sergeant Kanipe had already taken such a message would still not justify Benteen for not sending an even more urgent message. Actually Benteen should have sent an officer to hurry and bring up some of the ammunition packs, as Lieutenant Hare, a short while later, was said to have done.

The evidence, as I have read it, indicates the packs were not an hour and a quarter, or 7 miles, behind Captain Benteen, as he maintained. Benteen was rationalizing his actions and putting up a smoke screen by criticizing Martin. This was a deception to excuse his own inaction and his failure to follow orders, just as he criticized Custer in order to remove the blame for defeat from himself. I firmly believe Benteen consciously, or subconsciously, thought he was to blame for the tragic outcome of the battle.

Martin said that after receiving the message from Custer, he traveled some 3/4 of a mile back to the same ridge where General Custer had viewed the village.[15] A crucial point is that he could not have passed two soldiers and Boston Custer and have needed to tell them where the General was, if Custer had gone down Cedar Coulee. There is no way Boston Custer would not have seen the command before, or as he started down Cedar Coulee. Five companies would have been strung out for nearly 400 yards; so even if the command had reached Medicine Tail Coulee, Boston Custer would not have had to wonder where the General was. However, if Custer had gone down Middle Coulee (the Gorge), the distance and the terrain (Weir Point) in particular would have prevented Boston Custer from seeing the command.

Captain Benteen claimed that Martin told him the Indians were "skidaddling," whereas Martin said he told Benteen that he thought Custer would have made a charge through the village by that time. In every report and interview, Martin suggests that this is what he would have expected Custer to have done. This is also what the troops felt Custer would do; and although later Martin remembered seeing some elements of Custer's command that he believed were retreating, the answer he gave at that time was a natural one. Even if he had used the term "skidaddling," it was what he could have expected to happen, and it certainly should cast no negative reflection on Martin, as it has been made to do. "Skidaddling" is a word that fits Benteen's vocabulary more than that of a person having difficulty with the English language.

Martin was sure he didn't see Major Reno's troops, and that the village was quiet, with no dust or Indians moving around. This recollection would indicate that Major Reno had not yet engaged the Indians, since all reports agree that once they did, the village erupted. Martin's claim that he didn't see Reno's troops, and his continued insistence on this point through the years, suggest that he did not use it as a subterfuge. It is difficult to assume that he could not have noticed Reno's troops, or that he would not remember Custer mentioning or pointing them out.

On re-direct examination, Martin said the ridge from which he and General Custer saw the village is the highest point in the area.[16] This assertion would indicate that they viewed the village from Weir Point.

I believe the evidence Martin gave at the Reno Court bears out five main conclusions: (1) Martin did not see Major Reno while on the ridge. (2) The village was peaceful, so Reno hadn't engaged the Indians by the time Custer left the ridge to move down a coulee. (3) Custer did view the village from Weir Point. (4) Martin was with Custer when he reached Medicine Tail Coulee. (5) Custer did not go down Cedar Coulee.

Martin was interviewed by Walter Camp in 1908 and 1910, and Colonel Graham would have communicated

TRUMPETER MARTIN

with him not long before his death in 1922. I will attempt to break the interviews into two parts: the first covering the period that ended when he left General Custer with his message to Captain Benteen, and the second dealing with his return to Benteen and their move to Reno Hill.

From Walter Camp's interview in 1908:

> Trumpeter Martin, Orderly for Custer on June 25, 1876... did not see Indians on the ridge... when Custer separated from Reno. Says that before Custer reached high ridge he marched in column of twos with gray horse in center of column.... Custer never left his command to ride to the high point to wave his hat, as is sometimes reported. When Custer was on the high point his whole command was there with him, sitting on their horses. [This discredits those who believe his command stopped in Cedar Coulee and Custer then went back to the high point to view the Indian village.] As soon as the command left this high point everybody passed out of sight from Reno's position and went down the hollow toward dry Creek. [This would have the command stopping on the ridge and supports Varnum's sighting of the Gray Horse Troop as it was about to leave the ridge.] I do not remember seeing Mitch Bouyer or the Crow scouts at this time. They might have been somewhere in the vicinity and I did not see them.
>
> ... Martin says Custer trail passed along where Reno retreated to. Then Custer halted command on the high ridge about 10 minutes and officers looked at village through glasses. Saw children and dogs playing around the tepees but no warriors or horses except few loose ponies grazing around. There was then a discussion among the officers as to where the warriors might be and someone suggested that they might be buffalo hunting, recalling that they had seen skinned buffalo along the trail on June 24.
>
> Custer now made a speech to his men saying "We will go down and make a crossing and capture the village." The whole command then pulled off their hats and cheered. And the consensus of opinion seemed to be among the officers that if this could be done the Indians would have to surrender when they would return, in order not to fire upon their women and children. Then command "Attention" "Fours Right" "Column Right" "March" was given and the command went forward down off the hill and then "Column left" and whole command passed down ravine toward dry creek. Did Custer follow the bottom South Coulee all the way and make turn into Medicine Tail [Coulee] or cut across the hill? No, Custer followed Coulee all the way.
>
> Martin thinks he continued about 1/2 mile farther when Cooke halted and wrote message to Benteen and gave to Martin, and then Custer spoke to Martin and said: "Trumpeter, go back on our trail and see if you can discover Benteen and give him this message. If you see no danger come back to us, but if you find Indians in your way stay with Benteen and return with him and when you get back to us report."[17]

Camp's interview in 1910:

> Custer first halted on Weir's hill and took a look at village (from this point he could see only about 1/3 of it (Hunk and Blackfoot villages – WMC). Martin says whole column passed over the high ridge from which they could plainly see village and children and dogs in it. Martin says he was with Custer after he passed the high ground and left him just as the command started down a ravine to get off the bluff, somewhat to the right of highest ground and about 1000 feet from it.
>
> Here (after Weir Hill) he turned column to the right and went down coulee to Dry Creek... and turned to left and followed Dry Creek (MTC) straight for the village.... About half way down to Little Bighorn we came into full view of the village. (The first time he had seen the south end of it – WMC)... Martin was seemingly confused at this point. [He possibly saw the north end but may have thought it was the south end. He would have had to have been fairly close to Ford B if he saw the Cheyenne camp. However, it would support Marquis and Kuhlman, as well as my view of the camp's location.][18]

When Martin said that Custer never left his command to ride to the high point to wave his hat, and that his command was with him, he contradicted the testimony of those who claimed that Custer left his command some distance to the east, rode to the high point, then waved his hat to encourage Major Reno or to warn him, since Reno was supposedly engaging the Indians at that time. Martin also agreed with Kanipe, who stated that the whole command moved along the ridge right behind Custer.

Martin said he didn't see Mitch Bouyer or the scouts. Curley mentioned they were behind General Custer as he moved down the ridge. If the Rees, who said they saw Custer with Curley and Black Fox were correct, it was apt to have been when Custer first reached the ridge. Custer, we can assume, wanted to talk with Bouyer, and Bouyer would be expected to have reported to Custer. If the exchange did take place, as I believe it must have, why didn't Martin report or mention seeing Bouyer?

I believe there are possibly two answers, involving the following line of reasoning: On other campaigns, Custer often moved some distance ahead of his troops. Custer's Vic was reported to have been an exceptionally fast-walking horse; we know troopers were having a difficult time keeping up with Custer. Custer's Crow scouts and Mitch Bouyer had already moved to the ridge and the General would be anxious to see the valley and know what Mitch Bouyer had to report. Consequently, it would be natural to surmise that Custer may have been some distance in front of the rest of his command, including his orderly, Martin. Custer could have spoken briefly to the scouts and then moved on or back to where the troops were moving to the ridge. This is the type of event which, if not specifically referred to in a question, could have been forgotten or not mentioned. The second possibility is that Martin thought Camp was referring only to the time they were at Weir Point, and since he was not asked specifically about the period just before that, it wouldn't necessarily mean he didn't see or meet them as they came on the ridge.

No matter when Custer arrived on the ridge, he could see the valley, grasp the situation and would have continued his move downriver. Kanipe indicated, and Martin implied, this sort of movement until Custer reached the high point. From there, they could view part of the village and see that it was still peaceful. In all of his accounts, Martin portrayed the village in this manner. There were not many braves around, mainly children and dogs. There is a consensus in all Sioux and Cheyenne accounts that this is how the village appeared until Reno's troops commenced firing. Once the firing began, the village erupted, and in no way could this have been the scene they described. If Reno had already set up his skirmish line and engaged the Indians, the officers would not have been wondering where the warriors were. According to Martin, however, they viewed a peaceful camp, which meant that Reno had not yet engaged the Indians. This would place Custer's move to the ridge ahead of Reno's move down the valley. Curley reported the same picture of the village in several of his interviews. Those who ignore Martin's testimony, or, in discrediting him, believe themselves absolved from the need to provide an explanation of why they think Martin did *not* see a peaceful village, should propose some better reasons than the ones I have read.

Following Custer's viewing from the high point, Martin said, Custer waved and talked to his men, who then waved and cheered. Sergeant Stanislas Roy claimed that after passing through the timber and while coming into line, some of Major Reno's troops looked up and saw Custer's men moving along the ridge. I would speculate they would have done so as General Custer, Martin and the General's staff were moving to Weir Point. Reno's troops, who saw Custer when they were about half way down the valley, would have seen them during the period when Custer's troops were still moving along the ridge, as Custer was observing the Indian camps from Weir Point. If my conjecturing is right, when he first went to Weir Point, General Custer may have seen Major Reno's troops as they began their move down the valley. It was during this time that Custer's and Major Reno's men saw each other. Possibly, as Kanipe reported, Custer's troops began waving their arms, yelling and urging their horses ahead at break-neck speed.[19] The first of Custer's command, probably Company C, may have met General Custer just after he came down from Weir Point. Some of the troops dashed by Custer and he warned them to "hold your horses…" This, according to Walter Camp's interview with Kanipe, was just past the high point.[20] Kanipe was then sent back with his message to Captain McDougall. This version would support Martin's belief that a message was sent back at this time. It would most likely mean that C Company was at the front of the command with the other companies strung out behind. During that time, Major Reno halted his troops and formed his skirmish line. Lieutenant Varnum looked up and saw the Gray Horse Troop as it was moving off the ridge, while the front of Custer's command was on its way down Middle Coulee. This scenario fits into a logical time sequence, has testimonial support, and gives a general view of what would have taken place.

Whether Custer saw Reno's troops or not, he must have known they were, or would be, moving down the valley. Even if Martin was correct in his recollection that they thought the warriors were absent, or whether they assumed they were sleeping, would not make any difference in determining Custer's reaction. Martin remembered some officer saying that if they could capture the village and the warriors returned, they would surrender in order to save the women, children and old people. This remark means that Custer wanted to attack the village as quickly as possible.

Should we assume that, in this situation, Custer would move away from the village by going down Cedar Coulee, or would he take a shorter and quicker route down Western Coulee or Middle Coulee? There is little doubt as to what his decision would be. If Custer's "Column Right" moved the troops into Cedar Coulee, then the "Column Left" was issued right after, and those orders served to move the command around Weir Point into Middle Coulee (the Gorge). The fact that there was no question, right after the battle, that Custer moved through and beyond Weir Point, is further support for this contention.* Custer had to locate the best and quickest route to reach the village. This would have led him to Weir Point. He then needed to determine which of the routes available would enable him to reach and attack the village most quickly. This could have been Western Coulee, or Middle Coulee, but not Cedar Coulee. Even the summations at the Reno Court for both sides would support such a premise.

Martin reports that he continued about 1/2 mile farther when Cooke wrote and handed him the message to take to Benteen. At a half mile farther from Weir Point, Custer would have been close to Medicine Tail Coulee, by way of Middle Coulee, and a little over half way down Cedar Coulee. If Martin meant that he went a 1/2 mile down Medicine Tail Coulee from Cedar Coulee, it would have left him close to a mile from Ford B. A half mile down Medicine Tail Coulee from Middle Coulee would have placed him about 600 yards from Ford B. This would be the distance Benteen told Martin had separated him from the ford after Martin pointed out to him the place where he had received the message.

There are some differences between Martin's interview with Camp in 1910 and his 1908 account, but they are not major. In the 1910 interview Martin said it was at Weir Point that Custer first halted and looked at the village, whereas he referred to the location as the "high point" in 1908. The message is clear: Martin does mean Weir Point in both cases. This contention is corroborated by his cross-examination statement at the Court of Inquiry.[21] Since Custer's primary concern, as he moved along the ridge, would have been to get a better view of the village and find the best and quickest route to attack it, there is only one place that fulfills this requirement, and that is Weir Point.** There shouldn't be any question as to whether Martin confused Weir Point with some other location, as Martin had been with Benteen and H Company when they moved to Weir Point, and established a position near there before falling back to Reno Hill.[22] It is the one place that stands out between Reno Hill and Last Stand Hill. With testimony as well as logic to back up such a move, it is difficult to understand how so many claim Custer never went to Weir Point.

When Martin used the term "highest ground," I believe he meant the ridge which extends from Reno Hill to Weir Point and down the western side of Middle Coulee to Medicine Tail Coulee. The high ground of Middle Coulee turns to the right as it reaches Medicine Tail Coulee, so the topography would comply with Martin's description. Martin could have meant that they moved to the right from this higher ground or bluff and started down Medicine Tail Coulee, and he went with Custer for another 1000 feet. This hypothesis coincides with what I believe he meant in his 1910 interview. It would be a natural route for Custer to have followed. Custer may have cut over to Western Coulee, but I don't think this is what Martin is saying, although Martin would have cut across this ridge on his way back. I realize this is a speculative scenario; what bothers me is that speculation wouldn't be necessary if the right questions had been asked.

Martin indicated that when they turned left, they followed Medicine Tail Coulee straight toward the village. He then said that about half way down to the Little Bighorn they came into full view of the village. According to Martin, it was the first time they had seen the south end of the village, and Camp felt Martin was confused. Martin, according to Camp, also suggested that he had not seen the village when he started back with his message. Without knowing how the questions were phrased, it is hard to judge the matter with certainty; but it seems fair to assume that the important part of his answer wouldn't be effected. Martin's statement does substantiate the contention that he was with Custer when he reached Medicine Tail, and that they moved toward the Little Bighorn. Martin would need to have been within about 600 yards of the Little Bighorn; before this point he would have been cut off by Bouyer's Bluff to the south and the bluff or cut bank on the north side of Ford B. Martin's statement that about half way down to the Little Bighorn they came into full view of the village is clear-cut and indicates movement as well as the sense of sight. Unless Martin was lying, it amounts to a definite statement of fact rather than an opinion or an answer to a general question. One might also realize that if Custer went down Middle Coulee, then halfway down Medicine Tail Coulee would place Martin in a location where he could see the village. However, if the command went down Cedar Coulee, then half way down Medicine Tail Coulee would still not put them in sight of the village.

In Graham's account of the events, Martin has Major Reno being called over to the right side of Ash Creek, near the Lone Tepee, and receiving his attack orders shortly after. Martin is then reporting that Custer told Reno he would go down to the other end and he would have Benteen hurry up and attack the Indians in the center.

---

*Henry Weibert, who spent most of his life going over the battlefield (sometimes with metal detectors), didn't believe Custer went down Cedar Coulee. See page 113, *Sixty Six Year's in Custer's Shadow*.
**Note Benteen's reference to this point in a letter to Mr. Goldin in 1892. Benteen – Goldin Letters, *The Custer Myth*, p. 195.

As I indicated, in examining the Reno Court, this is a very important point, and the only other person to describe such an order was Sergeant Davern, Major Reno's orderly, who said Reno's instructions were, "To take your three companies and drive everything before you. Captain Benteen will be on your left and will have the same instructions. Those I believe were his exact words."23*

Trumpeter Martin was not asked, during the Reno Court Inquiry, if he knew what Major Reno's orders were. Recorder Lee should have been aware of the importance these orders were to his case, and it is difficult to understand why he wouldn't have asked Martin questions pertaining to Reno's orders. Colonel Graham may blame Recorder Lee for being a poor interrogator, but I am more inclined to believe that disregarding such a basic and essential part of the case was intentional and reflected the military's preoccupation with preserving an image of an impartial Court, but without prying too deeply into a case which might tarnish the image of the officers involved.**

In dismissing the latter part of Reno's orders as reported by Davern and later by Martin, Dr. Kuhlman points out that they would imply Custer already knew the approximate location of the village; "... an implication which is obviously untenable since Custer did not as yet know of the existence of the village." (Kuhlman, *Custer and the Gall Saga*)***

Keep in mind that Major Reno said, in his report to the Adjutant General to General Terry (made on July 5, 1876 and referring to the night of the 24th): "... at 9:25 P.M. Custer called the officers together and informed us that, beyond a doubt, the village was in the valley of the Little Big Horn."24 This statement coupled with the scouts' sighting of the village the following morning, is additional proof that Custer was aware of the general location of the Indian encampment and, in all probability, had thought of plans to attack the camp.

I don't think there was any question in Custer's mind as to where the Indian village was. Custer wouldn't have given his attack orders if he wasn't sure; and in Davern's explanation of the orders, Custer supposedly referred to the location of the village. The words Martin used would indicate that Custer either was going to, or did in fact, send a messenger back; the same can be said about Davern's remarks. In both statements it is possible, and probable, that the messenger had already been sent. Both these testimonies support my contention that Sergeant Major Sharrow or someone else was sent to Benteen about that time.

In his account, Martin told Colonel Graham he merely said they went down to a big ravine that led to the river; but, here again, this could only have been Medicine Tail Coulee. Martin said it was about a mile from where they had gone up on the hill. Recognizing the problem with distance that Martin admitted having—and other participants also seemed to have—a mile from Weir Point, going down Middle Coulee, would have the command entering Medicine Tail Coulee. This, by itself, would not prove Custer went down Middle Coulee, nor would it indicate just where Martin was sent back, but it would be supporting existing evidence.

Martin's account of his movement, once he had been given the message to Benteen, is also important in determining whether the above conclusions are correct. Martin's Reno Court testimony dealt mainly with his estimates of time and distance, factors which he admitted he wasn't sure of. Therefore I will examine mainly his Walter Camp interviews and his account presented to Colonel Graham.

This point of the Walter Camp interview from 1908 continues after Martin had received the message to take to Captain Benteen and had started back:

> ... Martin started back on trail before got up the hill (that is up to high point where whole command had halted – WC) he heard heavy firing to his right. It might also have been Reno's fire which he heard as that would have been to his right. He afterward supposed [firing] was at Ford B. After this he met Boston Custer going to join the command. When Martin got to top of the ridge he looked down on village and saw Indians charging like swarm of bees toward the ford, waving buffalo hides. At the same time he saw Custer retreating up the open country in the direction of the battlefield. (Camp – he did not tell this at the Reno Court of Inquiry as it was not desired that he should tell all he knew and said that afterward he never was invited by officers to discuss what he knew of the battle and never volunteered to do so.) The Indians were firing straggling shots. About this time, Martin was fired on by Indians on the bluffs between him and the river: they hit his horse on hip, and blood spattered on Martin's back. Martin says he met Boston Custer after his horse was hit and that Boston Custer called attention to the fact that his horse was limping.

---

*After reading King's book, *Massacre: The Custer Cover-Up*, on page 181-182, several others are mentioned.

**King also supports this premise with statements later made by Prosecutor Jesse M. Lee and inferred by the absence of Lieutenant Gibson as a major witness, pp. 54, 85, 147, 179.

***King believes the maps being used by Custer and other officers were more accurate and extensive than the maps later presented, which according to King were part of a cover-up. Chapter 3: King also realized that Custer had to have formed some plan of battle enroute, p. 180.

Martin now rode fast and met Benteen on Benteen Creek and came back with him. Martin says when he gave message to Benteen, Benteen asked: "Where is General Custer?" Martin said: "about 3 miles from here." Benteen said, "Is (Custer) he being attacked or not?" and Martin said: "Yes, (he) is being attacked" and said no more. Martin is positive that he did not tell Benteen . . . that Indians were "skidaddling." Ask Martin if, when he returned and did not see Reno, if he saw any Indians where he afterwards learned Reno to be. No – saw neither Indians nor Reno nor any fighting.

. . .After Martin got to Reno Heights, did Benteen or Reno consult him to direction of Custer? "No."

. . .Martin says that when General Terry came up on the 27th, Terry took him to the spot where Martin started back from Custer with the message, and Martin described the ground and incidents to him precisely.[25]

Martin states that when he reached the top of the ridge and looked down, "he saw Indians charging like a swarm of bees toward the ford, waving buffalo hides. At the same time, he saw Custer retreating up the open country . . ." This description would synchronize with what I consider to be a proper timing sequence. It would be ten to fifteen minutes after Martin started back; Custer had reached the ford and his troops were now retreating. This scenario would coincide with accounts of White Man Runs Him, Curley, and White Cow Bull. The Crows, according to White Man Runs Him, saw Custer go to the ford and then retreat. Curley saw Indians going to attack Reno, and others going toward the ford and Custer. White Cow Bull, a Sioux, reports that the Indians were moving to aid him and the few other Sioux and Cheyenne who were at the ford and were facing Custer. The time of these sightings and Reno's move into the timber should then be occurring together as Martin has suggested. Custer had left the ridge just before Reno set up his skirmish line; his command moved to the ford and then retreated while Reno was still on his skirmish line. Martin's statement to Benteen that Custer was being attacked would also indicate that Custer had reached Ford B while Reno was still engaged in the valley. These considerations suggest again that comparing events is more important than attempting to place relative time estimates of those events into a given framework. Time estimates, naturally, differ to such a large degree that any attempt to do that distorts the picture and prevents the investigator from understanding what actually transpired.

I believe the essence of this part of Martin's testimony supports my positions and resolves certain lines of inquiry: (1) Custer reached Ford B and was retreating before Reno left the timber to move to the bluffs. (2) Custer moved down the "Gorge" or Middle Coulee and not Cedar Coulee. (3) It addresses my basic question: Why did Custer make such a quick retreat from a village that by all Indian accounts would have been in a near state of panic? One could not expect a more ideal situation for an attack to take place.

Martin said that in moving to the ridge he heard firing on the right and afterwards thought it was Custer at Ford B. The timing would be about right if Martin left Custer some 600 yards from the ford. Just after Martin left, I believe, Custer would have assigned Captain Keogh's battalion to a reserve status. Though Custer may have done this a short time before, it is something he should have done and would have during this period. Major Reno, in moving down the valley, would have thought of using one of his companies in a reserve role and it certainly was a common cavalry tactic. Paddy Griffith, a senior lecturer at the Royal Military Academy at Sandhurst, England, writes in his book, *Battle Tactics of the Civil War*: "Typically a regiment kept back a mounted reserve of about a quarter of its number, ready to charge when the moment was right."[26] I would think at West Point they would have studied Napoleon's tactics and those of Marshall Joachim Murat who was recognized as one of the greatest cavalry leaders. "Heavy cavalry . . . they were held in reserve until exactly the right moment in a battle . . . Marengo, Austerlitz, Eylau, and Friedland were just a few of the engagements where heavy cavalry effectively determined the outcome."[27]

I would calculate that at this stage, with how the village must have appeared, two things would be uppermost in Custer's mind. First, he would see the need to attack in order to aid Major Reno and to gain control of the village and defeat the Indians. Secondly, viewing the village and the movement within, he would be concerned that the Indians might still escape to the west. I would then assume he would have ordered Captain Keogh and his two companies, I and L, to move back to the ridge behind them and from there to judge the course of the action, either coming to their aid or, if it appeared the Indians were going to escape to the west or north, to move to prevent this. I don't believe the separation took place earlier, for then Martin would have known about it (unless because of the lack of pertinent questions he failed to mention it), although Custer may have made the decision at Weir Point.

Boston Custer becomes fairly important in trying to determine what happened to General Custer. Martin gave several different versions of his meeting with Boston

Custer. In 1908 Martin told Walter Camp that he met Boston Custer before he got to the top of the ridge. Apparently Martin was fired on by the Indians and his horse was hit before he met Boston Custer; Boston called attention to Martin's horse limping. In the 1910 Walter Camp interview Martin said:

> ...I kept on up the north and south coulee and soon met a mounted man whom I recognized as one of C Troop, but whose name I did not know. He inquired where the command was, and I told him down the coulee quite a distance and that he had better fall back to get the pack train, as he would likely be cut off by Indians before reaching the command, but he kept on. After this I met Boston Custer. On his way to Benteen with the message he met first Boston Custer on the bluffs and farther along on the bluffs two enlisted men who were together and inquired for Custer's command. This is another good proof that Custer hesitated and stopped some considerable time after he came in sight of village. About meeting Boston Custer, when going back with message and after, he heard firing. Told him he had better look out as there were Indians around and Boston Custer said: "Well I am going to join the command anyhow..." It would seem that if the meeting of Boston Custer was a fact Custer must have remained some time in vicinity of ford or else Boston Custer must have cut a big circuit and joined command on the high ground. However, it might have been Reno's firing that Martin heard, in which case Boston Custer may have had time to overtake the general before reaching Ford B. The meeting of Boston Custer and the fact that he died with the General can hardly be reconciled by any other explanation.[28]

In his account for Colonel Graham, Martin said:

> Just before I got to the hill I met Boston Custer. He was riding at a run, but when he saw me he checked his horse and shouted "Where's the General?" and I answered, pointing back of me. He dashed on. This was the last time he was ever seen alive.[29]

However, in the 1910 Camp interview Martin pointed out that he didn't follow dry Creek all the way back to coulee running north and south but cut across the high ground.

> When I got up on the elevation I looked behind? Met Boston Custer half way between medium coulee and Weir Hill.... met the two men ... After this I heard a volley and looked back and saw Custer retreating from the river.[30]

Although all three coulees generally run in the north-south direction, actually only Western and Middle Coulee could be characterized as such. Cedar Coulee lies in much more of an east to south direction. Martin's statement that he met Boston Custer half way between medium coulee and Weir Hill would be additional proof that Martin was going up Middle Coulee and Custer had gone down Middle Coulee. If this was the only reference, there could be a semantic dispute; but with all the other available evidence this version seems definitive. Camp seemed to believe that the meeting with Boston Custer and the two other soldiers was proof that Custer halted for some time. It is hard for me to accept Camp's reasoning. If Martin had left Custer, as he later stated, some 600 yards from the river, Custer would have probably moved at least another four or five hundred yards toward the ford. There may have been some hesitation as he approached the ford. Mitch Bouyer probably reported to him at that time and Custer would have informed his commanders of any particular plans, such as having Keogh's battalion hold back or move to Nye CartwrightRidge. By this time Martin would have met Boston Custer at a place about half way to Weir Point. Martin would warn Boston Custer about firing that had taken place. Although it is not clear exactly where Martin was fired upon, he did indicate it took place before he reached Boston Custer.

The impression we get from the one report is that Boston Custer informed Martin that his horse was limping and he had blood on the back of his shirt. I think the account Martin gave Colonel Graham more likely describes what actually happened. I believe it was Benteen who informed Martin that his horse had been shot, and Martin is merely stating that it happened before he met Boston Custer. He later realized this was why Boston Custer said his horse was limping.

Martin's statement to Camp that he did not follow Dry Creek (MTC) all the way back to coulee running north and south but instead cut across the high ground,[31] is also informative. I have mentioned before that I believe by high ground Martin meant the ridge that runs from Reno Hill to Weir Point and down Middle Coulee to Medicine Tail Coulee, and I think this statement supports my belief. It also helps corroborate my view that Martin left the command about 600 yards from Ford B. He then angled to the southeast across the high ground separating West Coulee and its entrance into Medicine Tail Coulee from Middle Coulee. Martin then moved back on the trail Custer made coming down from Weir Point and ran into Boston Custer, who as we know, would have been following Custer's trail. After Boston Custer asked where the General was, Martin answered by pointing back and saying: "Right behind the next ridge you'll find him."[32] If

TRUMPETER MARTIN

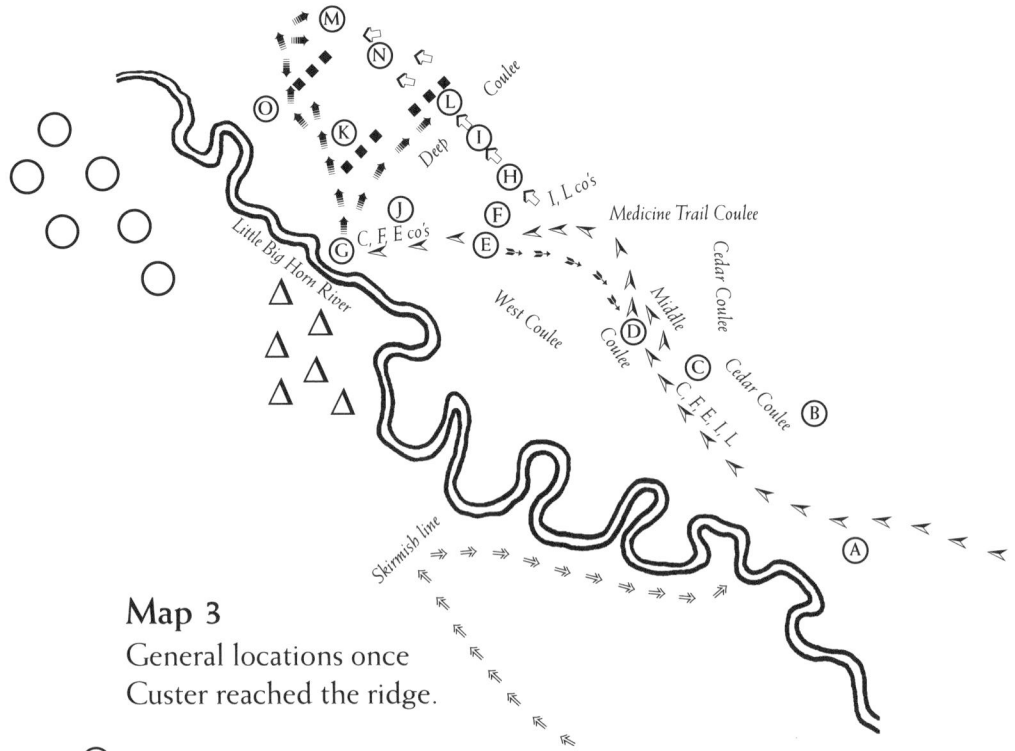

Map 3
General locations once Custer reached the ridge.

- Ⓐ Reno Hill
- Ⓑ Sharpshooter Ridge
- Ⓒ Custer's troop alignment as they approached Weir Point
- Ⓓ Weir Point
- Ⓔ Martin given message to Benteen
- Ⓕ Keogh's battalion sent to Luce Ridge in reserve
- Ⓖ Ford B — Minneconjou Ford
- Ⓗ Luce Ridge
- Ⓘ Nye Cartwright — Blummer Ridge
- Ⓙ Retreat of Yates' battalion C, F, E companies
- Ⓚ Retreat of Yates' "main element"
- Ⓛ Calhoun Hill
- Ⓜ Last Stand Hill
- Ⓝ Battle Ridge
- Ⓞ Deep Ravine

- ⊰ Custer's route
- ⇀ Martin's route back to Weir Point
- ⇨ Keogh's battalion I & L companies move in reserve
- ⬅ Companies retreat from Ford B
- △ Indian villages on the 25th of June
- ○ Indian villages on the 26th of June
- ■ Rear guard action (semi-skirmish positions)

we take Martin literally, his statement fits in exactly with what I think took place. Martin had left Custer some 600 yards from the ford and moved to the southeast across the high ground and into Middle Coulee. From Weir Point this high ground runs slightly to the northwest and then curves to the northeast as it enters Medicine Tail Coulee. Martin cut across this high ground where it curves to the northeast and then met Boston Custer at the time when the General should have been back of the ridge behind Martin.

Many writers believe Martin was sent back several hundred yards after leaving the high point, and differ on what the "high point" was. The above comments by Martin should have dispelled such views, or at least forced those who held them to explain in a constructive way why they disagree with Martin's account, without accusing him of being a dumb enlisted man or employing some other irrational excuse. If Martin was sent back after going only two or three hundred yards from the high point, regardless of which coulee they went down, he wouldn't have had to answer a question about Custer's location because the command would still have been in sight. Martin would only have gone some 150 yards before meeting Boston Custer, and there is no way the rear of the command would have been out of sight. Most writers seem to have accepted that Custer went down Cedar Coulee, supposedly because someone else accepted it as fact. I have only found one writer who at least gave several reasons to support such a view, and I will deal with these later.

In the Graham account, Martin described his impression of looking down the valley:

> . . . I saw Reno's battalion in action. It had been not more than ten or fifteen minutes since the General and I were on the hill, and then we had seen no Indians. But now there were lots of them, riding around and shooting at Reno's men who were dismounted and in skirmish line. I don't know how many Indians. There were a lot of them. I did not have time to stop and watch the fight; I had to be on to Colonel Benteen; but the last I saw of Reno's men they were fighting in the valley and the line was falling back."[33]

The major significance of Martin's account in both his interviews with Camp and Graham is that Custer would have reached Ford B while Reno was still on his skirmish line.

In the 1910 interview with Walter Camp, Martin says that Benteen followed Custer's trail:

> . . .We marched on General Custer's trail and when we got up this ridge from where I saw Major Reno fighting...we saw Major Reno's command and the Major himself, the men still retreating on the bluffs.

> Commenting on Martin's account, Camp observes: "He says the packs got up to Reno in 10 or 15 minutes behind Benteen, and in another place he says 3 hours. Says it was 1 1/2 hours after McDougall reached Reno Hill before the whole command went in direction of Custer."[34]

Camp's statement casts unnecessary doubts on Martin. I believe Martin's account to be an example of the difficulty he may have had in interpreting just what the meaning of a question might have been. We know that 3 hours is wrong; however, considering Kanipe's and Martin's testimony, the question is how close to being correct the 10 or 15 minutes might be.

The testimony pertaining to the packs varies greatly from person to person. It's not clear where they were in the valley when Sergeant Kanipe and Trumpeter Martin came across them; when they arrived on Reno Hill; or how long it was before all the command moved to where they thought Custer might be. The central question is: If Major Reno had moved sooner, would Custer have lost all five companies? It is odd that more perceptive questions were not asked and more definitive conclusions arrived at. Instead, one finds various answers and time estimates with seemingly little effort to collect and coordinate them in a meaningful way.

Three main reasons are usually given to explain the length of time it took Major Reno to move to where he knew General Custer had gone. The first attributes the delay to not hearing gunfire (which everyone else seems to have heard). Major Reno, Captain Benteen and Lieutenant Wallace maintained they didn't hear, or were unaware of gunfire of any amount necessary to solicit concern for General Custer. One should relate their statements to the one Reno made to General Terry's adjutant general on July 5, 1876. This statement should also be factored into an analysis of the Reno Court of Inquiry. Major Reno in this report said, ". . . almost at the time I reached the top, mounted men were seen coming toward us, and it proved to be Colonel Benteen's battalion . . . We heard firing in that direction and knew it could only be Custer."[35] The second reason given by Reno is that he had to wait for the packs to arrive. The third is his concern for the wounded. The time it took to prepare them for such a move was also tied in with the rationale for the need to wait for all the packs and Captain McDougall's company.

The first packs that Lieutenant Hare brought back with him came up shortly after Major Reno and Captain Benteen joined forces on the hill; and though it may have been longer then Martin's estimate suggests, it is not a major error. One should also note the similarity between Martin's testimony and Sergeant Davern's, the other enlisted man. The main questions should have dealt with the inconsistencies in the testimony surrounding the packs and the reasons for the multiplicity of different versions of the events. How much of a cover-up was associated with the packs? It would appear from Lieutenant Hare's and Captain McDougall's interviews with Camp that the two of them arrived at about the same time. This would support the view that the packs were much closer behind Benteen then he made them out to be.

Let's look at some of the different time estimates and accounts given to see how they compare with Trumpeter Martin's statements.

Lieutenant Hare's 1910 interview with Walter Camp, *Custer in 76*:

> Benteen came up about 10 minutes after Reno got to top of bluffs . . . About 10 minutes later Hare went for ammunition. Pack train around a mile from Reno Hill . . . Hare was gone about 20 minutes. He saw Co. D advancing toward Custer.

Captain Thomas McDougall – in charge of packs – letter to Camp, 1909:

> Hare met pack train about half mile east of Reno Hill . . . Came up to Reno about 4:00 p.m. . . . On hill about 1 1/2 hours before starting to find Custer . . . McDougall said D Troop had gone out but were still in sight. [If this was true he must have reached the hill much sooner than many say he did.] . . . Wasted some time before Reno attempted to move to meeting with Custer. (p. 70)

General Godfrey in his "Narrative": *The Custer Myth*, p.142:

> Thought it was about half past two when we joined Reno. About five o'clock command moved down toward Custer . . . McDougall came up with pack-train and reported firing . . . looked at watch at 4:20. Thought it was when Pack Train came up.

Official Transcript, 1064:

> Although Reno later went so far as to say that after the packs came up he formed the command in three columns . . . started downstream . . .

Stewart, p. 402, referring to the above statement:

> "Was undoubtedly pure rationalization, concocted in an attempt to justify his conduct."

Bozeman Avant–Courier of July 7, 1876:

> . . .reported that the attack on Custer began "about 3 p.m. and lasted about three hours in the judgment of Major Reno who heard the first and last volleys of the firing."

Reno Court of Inquiry: *Reno Court Abstract,* Graham, pp. 216, 221 – Major Reno:

> "I went to the river after Benteen's arrival . . . I was gone about a half hour. [to find Hodgson] . . .In about an hour the packs arrived . . . I heard no firing from down river till after we moved out in that direction and then only a few scattering shots. I thought they were from the village."

Reno Court of Inquiry, *Reno Court Abstract,* Graham, p. 21– Lieutenant George D. Wallace:

> "Whether their firing could have been heard I don't know. I heard none. It was well on to an hour before the pack train got up, guarded by McDougall."

Reno Court of Inquiry: *Reno Court Abstract,* Graham, p. 139 – Captain Benteen:

> "I have heard officers disputing about hearing volleys. I heard no volleys. About half hour after our arrival on the hill, Capt. Weir sallied out in that direction in a fit of bravado, I think, without orders.

Reno Court of Inquiry, Proceedings ed. Ron Nichols, Testimony of Sergeant Edward Davern, pp. 352-353:

> Q. Did you see his column come up? [Benteen's]
> A. No, I did not, but I saw the pack train come up soon after I got on the hill.
> Q. How soon after the pack train came up did the whole command move down?
> A. About two hours after the advance of the pack train came up.

Again, it is interesting that enlisted men (not apt to be part of any cover-up) report a shorter period of time between Benteen's arrival and when the packs came up, and a longer period before the movement toward Custer takes place.

One might note that Benteen refers to volleys and not gunfire.

As previously stated, Martin may not have been correct in his estimates, but the differences are not great and they don't reflect an attempt to cover up the actions, which is obvious in the testimonies of Reno, Benteen, and Wallace.

Several other comments made by Martin should be

brought out. In his 1910 interview with Camp, Martin said (p.104):

> [After joining Benteen] . . . we turned to the north along the bluffs just above the river and there met three Crow scouts who pointed out Reno's men who were now retreating across the bottom.

This account certainly agrees with most reports, and would indicate that Curley was not with the three Crows. It also substantiates Reno being in action on his skirmish line or in the timber at the time Custer reached Ford B. It seems that Martin's general statements are quite accurate and it is only when he gets into time and distance estimates that errors arise, but this is no different than the testimony of most other witnesses.

Martin also pointed out (pp. 104, 105):

> . . . It has been asserted by some writers of late years that Custer's command never got nearer the river than where he was found dead, but I know this to be incorrect, for I myself was with General Custer when he was much nearer the river than is the point where he was found dead, and I saw him and his command right down on the flat within a few hundred yards of the river, retreating from it. Until late years no one ever seemed to doubt the fact that Custer <u>went to the river</u> at the place which I state . . .
>
> . . . I showed (on June 27) Benteen where I left with note from Custer and <u>Benteen estimated the distance to be 600 yards from Ford B.</u> [my underlining]

The above statement corroborates my belief that Custer went to Ford B and that he never went down Cedar Coulee. If Martin was returning by way of Cedar Coulee, it would have been out of his way to have gone to the ridge near Weir Point. Such a step would be time-consuming as well as dangerous. He would have stayed in the coulee until he met Custer's trail near Reno Hill and then continued on the trail toward Reno Creek. Coming back by way of Cedar Coulee would not have allowed Martin to have seen Custer's troops retreating along the flat in Medicine Tail Coulee or Keogh's battalion moving to Nye Cartwright Ridge (if that is who he saw).

As I have previously suggested, Martin's leaving Custer some 600 yards from the ford coincides with other topographical references made by him. Martin does indicate he was close to Benteen when moving with Co. H to Weir Point. At the Reno Court, Benteen said that from Weir Point, Martin pointed out from where he had been sent back.[35] Benteen did not mention the 600 yards but I see no reason to reject Martin's claim. Benteen does remark that he didn't believe Custer got any closer then 3 furlongs from the ford which would be the approximate distance he is quoting to Martin.

The essence of Martin's testimony could be summarized in the following points:

1. Custer moved along the ridge and viewed the Indian village from Weir Point.
2. Custer saw a peaceful village from Weir Point.
3. This meant that Reno had not engaged the Indians at that time.
4. Custer then moved off the ridge, going down Middle Coulee to Medicine Tail Coulee.
5. Major Reno had engaged the Indians by the time all of the command had left the ridge.
6. Custer's command did not go down Cedar Coulee.
7. Martin was with Custer when the command reached Medicine Tail Coulee.
8. Martin was sent back with his message to Benteen when Custer was roughly 600 yards from Ford B.
9. Custer had reached Ford B while Reno was on his skirmish line.
10. The packs were not far behind Benteen.
11. Reno's movement toward Custer took place some 2 hours after the packs had arrived.

In my view, Martin is the most honest among the main witnesses. It is obvious that many others attempted to justify their actions, or believed they had, to either support or accuse someone else. Martin's testimony should be the focal point of any analysis of what happened to Custer; instead, it has been ignored or discredited.

The following are the last few paragraphs of his account to Colonel Graham, and I believe they portray both character and intelligence:

> I admired General Custer very much; all the men did. He was a fighter and not afraid of anything. But he tried to do more than he could that day. They were too many for us, and good fighters, too. They had better weapons than we had and they knew the ground. It is lucky that any of us escaped alive. I don't think we would but for the fact that they heard that General Terry was coming.
>
> I am an old man now and have served the United States a long time since I came from Italy in 1873. I enlisted in 1874 and was in the army thirty years. My memory isn't as good as it used to be, but I can never forget the battle of the Little Big Horn and General Custer.
>
> I have two sons in the army, and one of them is named for the General, I want them both to be as good soldiers as their father was.

It's a long time since I rode with Custer to his last fight – forty six years – but I still have the old trumpet that I blew officer's call with the morning of that fateful day, and still have a lively recollection of, as I have a deep affection for, my old General.

John Martin
Sergeant, U.S. Army, Retired[36]

SOURCES

1. Kuhlman, *Legend into History*, p. 94.
2. Stewart, *Custer's Luck*, p. 340.
3. Ibid., p. 386.
4. Windolph, *I Fought with Custer*, p. 83.
5. Graham, *Reno Court Abstract*, p. 130. (Addendum: Note John Gray's more complete recording of the question in my analysis of his book, *Custer's Last Campaign*.)
6. Graham, *The Custer Myth*, "General Godfrey's Narrative," p. 140.
7. Camp, *Custer in 76*, p. 101.
8. Graham, *Reno Court Abstract*, pp. 129-132.
9. Ibid., p. 131.
10. Ibid., p. 189.
11. Ibid., p. 150.
12. Graham, *The Custer Myth*, p. 180.
13. Graham, Op. Cit., pp. 148, 154.
14. Graham, *The Custer Myth*, 181.
15. Graham, *Reno Court Abstract*, p. 130.
16. Ibid., p. 132.
17. Camp, *Custer in 76*, pp. 99–102.
18. Ibid., pp. 102–105.
19. Ibid., p. 94.
20. Ibid., p. 97.
21. Graham, *Reno Court Abstract*, p. 132.
22. Brininstool, *Troopers with Custer*, p. 81 (Benteen after moving to Weir Point made this statement, "From my position was my first sight of the village, and the only point from which it could be seen.").
23. Graham, *The Custer Myth*, p. 289.
24. *Report of the Secretary of War,* 44th Congress, Vol. I, 1876-77, p. 32.
25. Camp, *Custer in 76*, pp. 101, 102.
26. Griffith, *MHQ*, "Civil War Cavalry: Missed Opportunities", Vol. I, No. 3, p. 47.
27. Meistrich, *MHQ*, "En Avant", Vol I, No. 3, p. 47.
28. Camp, *Custer in 76*, p. 104.
29. Graham, *The Custer Myth*, p. 290.
30. Camp, op. cit., p. 104.
31. Ibid., p. 104.
32. Graham, *The Custer Myth*, p. 290.
33. Ibid., p. 290.
34. Camp, *Custer in 76*, p. 104.
35. *Report of the Secretary of War,* 44th Congress, Vol. I, p. 32.
36. Graham, *The Custer Myth*. p. 291.

9
The Arikaras

The Arikaras, or Ree scouts, were considered enlisted men, but not soldiers. Varnum was the officer in charge of the scouts and he was assisted by Lieutenant Hare. Girard was the interpreter for the Rees, and Charlie Reynolds also acted as a scout and interpreter. Six Crow scouts were assigned to Custer's command. Mitch Buoyer was their interpreter and served as a scout himself. The Arikara stories are important sources in attempting to answer questions concerning Black Fox and Curley, and the relative positions of Major Reno and Lt. Colonel Custer.

Indian testimony has often been discredited. However, I found it as good as that of the whites. In both cases, cover-ups had to be considered, but for different reasons. The Arikaras were told to go with Major Reno. Though they operated under Varnum and Hare, their movements were disorganized. Their insructions were to run off Lakota horses, so they actually operated on their own. There were some who crossed the Little Big Horn while others apparently did not. Varnum referred to their disappearance once the battle commenced, but some remained and were involved in the action throughout. Bloody Knife (Custer's favorite scout and a half-breed), Bob-tailed Bull and Little Brave were killed. The two Crow scouts, Half Yellow Face and White Swan, along with the Ree scouts Young Hawk, Goose, Red Foolish Bear, and Forked Horn were forced to remain in the valley until they were able to join Reno on the bluffs. A number of them drove off Lakota ponies, others remained until things began to look hopeless and then left. All in all they did what they were expected to do. There were also five Lakota scouts with the Arikaras, and three half-breeds.

I believe Red Star's account of the message he brought to Custer, following the Crow's Nest sighting of the Indian encampment, is very important in determining what took place that day. It should be examined and explained by those who think General Custer did not believe the location of the Indian camp until he received a message from Girard, or Reno.

From the Crow's Nest, Red Star brought General Custer the message that the Sioux camp had been sighted. The General, along with Red Star, Girard, Bloody Knife, Bob-tailed Bull, and Little Brave went to the Crow's Nest. Charlie Reynolds came to meet Custer. They climbed the hill and Charlie pointed out where Custer was to look. They viewed for some time and then Girard joined them. Red Star then stated:

Girard called back to the scouts: "Custer thinks it is no Sioux camp." Custer had thought Charley Reynolds had merely seen the white buttes of the ridge that concealed the lone tepee. Charlie Reynolds then pointed again, explaining Custer's mistake, then after another look Custer nodded that he had seen the signs of a camp. Next Charley Reynolds pulled out his field glasses and Custer looked through them at the Dakota camp and nodded his head again... Then the scouts sat down and one of the Crow scouts, Big Belly, got up and asked Custer through the interpreter what he thought of the Dakota camp he had seen – Custer said: "This camp has not seen our army, none of their scouts have seen us." Big Belly replied: "you say we have not been seen. Thse Sioux we have seen at the foot of the hill, two going one way, and four the other, are good scouts, they have seen the smoke of our camp." Custer said, speaking angrily: "I say again we have not been seen. That camp has not seen us, I am going to carry out what I think. I want to wait until dark and then we will march, we will place our army around the Sioux camp." [my underlining] Big Belly replied that plan is bad, it should not be carried out." Custer said: "I have said what I propose to do, I want to wait until it is dark and then go ahead with my plan."

Red Star, as he sat listening, first thought that Custer's plan was good. The Crow scouts insisted that the Dakota scouts had already seen the army and would report its coming and they would attack Custer's army. They wanted him to attack at once, that day, and capture the horses of the Dakotas and leave them unable to move rapidly. Custer replied: "Yes it shall be done as you say." The army now came up to the foot of the hill and Custer's party rode down and joined the troop.[1]

This is additional proof that Custer knew where the camp was and that he planned to move against it that day. The testimony suggests his idea of encircling the camp, and it also shows Custer listening to and being influenced by his scouts. I can't help believing that his move to the Little Big Horn was predicated on the idea of making sure he would not be surprised by any Indians on his left. He wanted to send Major Reno's battalion to attack the camp from one direction, while trying to flank it himself; Benteen (if he found no Indians on his left) would reach the Little Big Horn and move down the valley in support of Reno. Custer would have six companies moving against the Indians from the south, and he would take five companies and move to the north in order to support Reno, attack, defeat and prevent the Indians from scattering. The packs would be protected by Captain McDougall's enlarged company and probably would have been expected to hold along Ash Creek until given further orders.

THE ARIKARAS

Little Sioux also testified that Custer told them the soldiers would charge the camp and the scouts would run off the horses. Custer's statements did not suggest he was uncertain about the camp's presence or location up ahead. Custer might not have been sure he had seen it, but his words and actions indicate he accepted what his scouts had said and had made plans to attack the camp. I think orders had everything to do with how Major Reno and Captain Benteen justified their actions. They realized the importance of the orders right after the battle and they continued to use their version to rationalize and defend their behavior.

There were at least three Arikaras who were unable to keep up with General Custer's command. One was Little Soldier, later interviewed by Camp. He said:

> "I had a good looking horse but he was lazy. Starting at the lone tepee we began the charge. My horse was slow and I was left behind..."
>
> A messenger [Camp suggests the messenger was from Major Reno and either McIlhargey or Mitchell] met the General and Custer took off his buckskin coat and tied it behind his saddle. Custer rode up and down the column talking to the soldiers. The soldiers cheered and some tied handkerchiefs around their heads and threw hats away ... They gave a big cheer and went ahead, but my lazy old horse straggled behind. I was a long way behind the soldiers. There were other stragglers between me and Custer. The ones nearest to me were White Eagle and Bull.
>
> "Stabbed was behind, came up behind me and explained that he had been out with a message to soldiers over to the east."[2]

Little Soldier said that starting at the Lone Tepee the soldiers began the charge and he then fell behind. I wouldn't call it a charge, but Custer probably picked up the pace during this time. Camp wasn't correct in assuming that the messenger was from Major Reno. Reno supposedly sent his messengers back after he crossed the ford. I would speculate that the messenger Little Soldier referred to arrived before Custer reached the Lone Tepee. This messenger could have been Sergeant Major Sharrow returning from speaking to Lieutenant Hare. Since Custer hadn't received a scouting report from Hare, he had sent the Sergeant Major to obtain one. The Sergeant Major reached Hare before Custer got to the Lone Tepee. Hare said Custer's column was not too far behind. During this period there was a movement of some Indians toward the Little Big Horn and their main village. During the Reno Court Inquiry,[3] Hare would have reported that movement and possibly said the scouts had not seen any Indians to the south. This would then clear Custer so he could go ahead with his plan of attacking the Indians. In fact, because of their fear of the Indians scattering, it would make it more imperative. Custer then had Reno cross Ash Creek and take the lead. Custer, not having heard from Benteen, would have been concerned as to his whereabouts but would have expected him to be nearing the Little Big Horn. Custer would then have sent a courier to Benteen expressing that he was or would be sending Reno to cross the Little Big Horn and move against the Indian camps, and that when Benteen reached the Little Big Horn he should move in support of the Major.

The courier Custer sent could have been the Sergeant Major, and he may have sent the scout Stabbed with him in order to help locate Benteen. Although it is pure speculation, I can visualize Sharrow and Stabbed going to some bluff or hillock and seeing Benteen's battalion moving back to the main trail along Valley[3]. Stabbed would have been sent back since his part of the mission was accomplished. Sharrow more than likely sent a message to Custer indicating Benteen was returning to the main trail.*

Although Benteen indicated his orders were to move to a valley – and there could be only one valley Custer was referring to – he would have known better than to comment on any additional part of his instructions. There wouldn't have been any questions concerning his orders until after the battle. Even if he received the orders after turning back to the main trail – considering what happened to Custer – there was no way that Benteen would admit that his orders indicated Major Reno would be sent across the Little Big Horn to attack the Indian camp, and he himself was to support him by moving down the valley. That would have meant that Benteen could not excuse his inaction and the odium of defeat would have been focused on him.

In my mind there is little question that both Benteen and Reno knew Custer planned a flanking attack. The result of what happened to Custer's five companies would have made it quite apparent to Benteen that he should have moved quickly to the valley and supported the attack. Benteen saw the initial move of Custer's command as they started down Ash Creek, and Lieutenant Gibson would have been aware of their subsequent movement.** (Gibson was the officer Benteen sent to the top of the bluffs to look for Indians and the valley.) Benteen's subsequent actions are indefensible: he was vehement about Custer's lack of plans and failure to acknowledge the scouts' reports on the location of the Indian village, while claiming that he himself realized they were indeed correct. Benteen had to, and did, take the position that his orders were only to

---

*I don't believe Sergeant Major Sharrow could have reached Captain Benteen at the location projected by Darling and made it back to Custer in time to have been sent to Lieutenant Hare. (Darling, Benteen's Scout, page 12.)

**Roger Darling, in his book, Benteen's Scout, points out these sightings.

continue in search of some unknown valley, and if it wasn't for his great intuitive move back to the main trail, even Major Reno, the packs, and everybody else would have been lost. This rationalization then justified his not continuing to search for this valley he couldn't see.* However, it was also necessary to make his orders vague and the valley his only objective. This placed the blame on Custer, specifically focusing on his not heeding the scouts and his lack of planning and orders, thus removing the burden from Benteen's shoulders.

Those supporting Benteen, and those refuting this position, could say that if his orders stated what I suggest they did, then Benteen could have revealed their real contents. Benteen could have said in his defense that because the terrain was rough and he had no idea how far he might have to go, and since he recognized the urgency of the orders, he decided it would be best to return to the main trail. These orders indicated he was to support Reno, so when he found Reno on the bluff he was merely following instructions and, considering the situation, was justified in staying with Reno.

This hypothetical scenario might be reasonable except for several factors. It would not relieve the dilemma facing Major Reno, for he then should have remained in the timber. Nor would it excuse Reno and Benteen for not moving immediately to aid Custer. Benteen would also have been indicted for his actions. There would have been no excuse (horses, men, distance, terrain, whatever) for not hurrying to support either Reno or Custer, and we know that Benteen did neither. He took so much time at the morass that Captain Weir became impatient with him.[4] Robert Utley has pointed out that he didn't hurry, even after receiving Sergeant Kanipe's message – directed to the packs but indicating an urgent need for aid. Nor did he do more than move out at a trot when Trumpeter Martin arrived with a message directed to him, and which one would think might have brought on at least a canter.

Though I am guessing, it is a logical speculation. The testimony of Sergeant Davern and Trumpeter Martin would support the existence of more complete orders to both Major Reno and Captain Benteen. Custer's failure to have informed the packs and Benteen, through his messages, via Sgt. Kanipe and Trumpeter Martin, that he was planning on flanking the Indians, indicates, to me, that they already knew his plans. Walter Camp attempted to justify Benteen's actions of not rushing across country to aid Custer, because there was no notice of where Custer was, and that he only said "to come on." I believe the reason there wasn't any notice was because Custer knew that Benteen and Reno realized, through his prior statements and orders, that he was planning on flanking the Indians. The questioning of Martin by the Court clearly illustrates their concern that questions would not be asked pertaining to the orders Custer gave to either Benteen or Reno. My question is why? The only answer seems to be the court's fear that they would portray Reno's and Benteen's knowledge of Custer's plan to flank the Indians. Lt. Edgerly's pronouncement of Custer's orders,[5] given at the division of the command, if issued in the sequence and manner Edgerly reported, would have made Benteen aware that Custer was planning on sending Reno to attack when they came to the Little Big Horn. This would mean that Benteen knew that Custer planned to have Reno cross the Little Big Horn and move against the Indians. Any orders directing Benteen to find the valley of the Little Big Horn would indicate that he was to make sure there was no Indian threat in that direction. After realizing that no threat existed he should have moved to support Reno. This would be a natural extension of such an order, even if not put into words. Davern was not likely to have been in on any cover-up at the Reno Court, so his testimony would not have been subject to any military pressure. Edgerly's implications were apparently ignored by the court, as they were afterwards by Graham and others who should have asked for a clarification.

The scouts that went with Reno were mostly Arikaras, but there were also five Sioux, two Crows, and three half-breed scouts. Some of the scouts crossed the Little Big Horn ahead of Major Reno's troops and then continued to lead the way toward the Indian camps. I have divided these scouts into two groups, one on the left and the other on the right. Of these scouts, as I previously stated, Bloody Knife, Bob-tailed Bull, and Little Brave were killed. The two Crow scouts, Half Yellow Face and White Swan, along with the Ree scouts Young Hawk, Goose, Red Foolish Bear, and Forked Horn, were forced to remain in the valley until they were able to join Reno on the bluffs. Strikes Two, Little Sioux, Red Bear, One Feather, Boy Chief, and Red Star were also with Reno in the valley. According to Red Bear, Black Fox was with them.[6] Little Sioux also reported seeing Black Fox with Forked Horn.[7] There were three half-breed scouts: the two Jackson brothers, and Billy Cross. Those scouts that were reported not to have crossed the river with Reno were: Stabbed, Bull-in-the-Water, Red Wolf, Strikes-the-Lodge, Charging Bull, White Eagle, Bull, Soldier, and some indicated Black Fox. Pretty Face, who had been assigned to the packs, joined the other Rees on the ridge. White Cloud, a Lakota scout, is referred to by Red Bear, and as many as four other Sioux scouts are

---

*W. Kent King in his book, *The Custer Cover-Up,* and Roger Darling's *Benteen's Scout,* also bring out Benteen's knowledge of where the Little Big Horn valley was.

listed without any real knowledge of their actions. Of the Rees and Sioux scouts stated as being present there are at least six not accounted for. Lt. Hare said, "about half way down the valley (my emphasis), some of the Rees (these, I believe, would have been the scouts that were present, but later were not accounted for) took after a herd of Sioux ponies. An Indian with these ponies turned and fired on the Rees, but they chased him and captured some of the ponies and ran them off."[8] I think these Rees crossed the river and retreated down the back trail with the captured horses, and were the Indians that Sgt. Kanipe reported seeing when carrying his message to Captain McDougall. This is why Walter Camp had difficulty in accepting Kanipe's account, as he realized the time Kanipe reported passing the Rees would not coincide with that of when the known Rees left with captured ponies.

The Ree scouts on the left came under attack at the same time as Major Reno's troops, and many of them were with Reno until rescued by Colonel Gibbon's men. Those on the right, Little Sioux, Red Star, Boy Chief, and Strikes Two, being nearer the Little Big Horn, saw several Sioux women across the river. They crossed the river after the Sioux women, and then saw the Lakota horses on the flat and went after them. Reno must have been about to, or had just established his skirmish line, as there was very little fighting noticed at the time, and the Rees said the village was just beginning to stir. However, the valley fighting was going on as they drove the horses up the bluffs at the place where the flat narrowed and the ridge extended into their path. In trying to adjust time with events, I would say this must have been at least fifteen minutes after they had crossed the river after the women. Little Sioux said they were fired on by soldiers on the ridge as they drove the Sioux horses to the bluff. Little Sioux's account found in Libby's *Arikara Narrative*, and in Hammer's *Custer in 76*, vary, and, though twisted, are important. I believe the soldiers firing on them from the bluff were a rear guard established by Custer when leaving the ridge. Varnum, probably some fifteen minutes earlier, had seen the Gray Horse Troop when they were about to leave the bluff. At least twenty minutes earlier, the slower Rees should have reached the ridge, since they claim to have seen Bob-tailed Bull far out to the left, which would have been before Reno's men established a skirmish line. Stabbed, seeing the soldiers further down the ridge, moved ahead of the slower Rees in order, I believe, to deliver a message from the Sgt. Major that Captain Benteen was back on the main trail.

Little Sioux said that, when driving the captured horses on the flat, he heard firing to his right, and also to his left, and more faintly some firing from behind.[9] The firing to his right would have been from the Reno engagement; that on the left would appear to be from Luce or Nye Cartwright Ridge and most likely soldiers firing at Wolf Tooth's band; and the lesser fire would be the first coming from Ford B. This would mean Reno's skirmish line was being set up near the time the four Rees crossed the river and saw the Lacotah ponies. It would support the position that Reno was just starting down the valley when Custer was at Weir Point, and Custer was going down the Gorge as Reno continued his move down the valley. Lt. Varnum then saw, as Reno was setting up his skirmish line, the Gray Horse Troop. Fifteen minutes later, the Rees were driving the Sioux horses along the flat, Captain Keogh's men were firing at Wolf Tooth's band, and Custer was arriving at Ford B. The rear guard fired on the Rees driving the horses, and were told by Stabbed that they were their scouts. The slower Rees, along with some of the scouts that had not crossed the river then, met the four Rees driving the captured horses. At this time the rear guard, who had already sent a courier to Custer with Stabbed's message, was moving downstream to report to Custer on Major Reno's actions. Sgt. Major Sharrow would have or was about to catch up to them. Strikes Two mentioned passing a sergeant, who I believe – because of what I assume was the location and timing – was not Sgt. Kanipe but Sgt. Major Sharrow.

The three Crows, and possibly Curley, fired on the Indian village from Bouyer's Bluff as Custer with three companies moved to the ford. Custer's troops retreated from the ford and the Crow scouts fled. Curley, further back, went along the ridge and passed the soldiers making up the rear guard, and also saw the Arikara scouts with the captured ponies, as he reported in his General Scott interview.[10] The other Crows, moving back from the ridge, did not see Reno's retreat until they reached Reno Hill. Here they joined Curley, and then met Red Bear and White Cloud. Curley separated and went to the river; the others saw Red Star and then Benteen. Naturally this is speculative, but I believe it is a logical deduction from the reports of the four Crows and the Rees.

The four Rees, after driving the captured horses to the ridge and being joined by the other Rees that had not crossed over, herded the captured horses back some distance. Considering where they must have come onto the ridge, it would seem likely that they drove the captured horses down Cedar Coulee. Many of them changed horses, then left the remaining horses with Charging Bull, Bull, Red Wolf, and White Eagle. The others went to the top of the coulee where, as Little Sioux reported, he looked west for about two miles and saw high sloping hills covered with Sioux, at the top of which were some soldiers lying down firing at these Indians. I would assume they were looking at fighting taking place along Calhoun Ridge. Little Sioux then looked to the south where he saw Indians about three miles away, moving here and there along a hill. This would most likely be considered the hill (ridge) above the valley, just before Reno's men retreated to the bluffs. We know these Rees joined them, so I assume they then saw Reno's men arriving on the bluffs, Captain Benteen's battalion moving in that direction, and the packs not far behind. The scouts went back to the ridge, and as reported by Little Sioux, Strikes Two, and Soldier, they saw some of Reno's men still retreating, and Lacotahs riding about the the dead bodies across the river and shooting into them. The scouts mentioned were Little Sioux, Bull-in-the-Water, Strikes Two, Red Star, Boy Chief, One Feather, Stabbed, Soldier, and Strikes-the-Lodge.

Red Bear, after fleeing the valley, spoke of Major Reno:

> ... Then, at their head he saw Reno, with a white handkerchief tied about his head, his mouth and beard white with foam, which dripped down, and his eyes were wild and rolling. The Soldiers with Reno took Red Bear for a Dakota and aimed their guns at him, but he rode in close to Reno and struck him on the chest with his open hand, crying "scout, scout." ... They all then fired at the Dakotas higher up on the ridge without taking aim, ... Red Bear rode up to the top of the ridge and saw a Dakota scout, White Cloud, riding up from the river, and he told Red Bear that the Arikara scouts had driven off a number of Dakota horses and they were to return but they had not yet come back. Then White Cloud said to Red Bear: "Let's go back where the scouts are with the horses." ... they came to a little hill and from there they saw four riders coming toward them; they thought they were Dakotas ... The riders were really Crow scouts and they seemed to recognize Red Bear ... The Crow scouts said that two of their number had been killed on the ridge and they were going there and then would come back ... Red Bear and White Cloud waited for them for a long time. Then Red Bear said to White Cloud: "The Crow scouts will not return. Let us go back to Reno." They went back and found Reno with his soliders still there. Just then, the scouts who had taken fresh horses, came back. After awhile, the other scouts came in with the herd of captured horses, about forty in number. Where Reno was, the soldiers were on higher ground, and the scouts were down the slope about ten rods off. Stabbed was riding about on horseback making a speech. He said: "What are we doing now, we scouts? We ought to do what Custer told us to do if we were defeated. He told us to fall back to the Powder River where the rest of the scouts are and the wagons and provisions," ... reached the Powder River camp. Here they found the party led by Strikes Two ... [11]

Red Bear, who had been with the scouts on the left, and subsequently retreated to the ridge, saw Reno, and then White Cloud. He and White Cloud saw the four Crow scouts. Since they talked to them and knew them, it would be hard to deny there were not four. Benteen must have been near. Kanipe would have met Benteen some distance back, and Trumpeter Martin should now have been with Benteen. They would be moving close to where they first saw the valley and Reno's troops.

Red Bear's account, according to which he saw the four Crow scouts and spoke to them, indicates that Curley was with White Man Runs Him, Goes Ahead, and Hairy Moccasin. This version would coincide with Curley's interview with General Scott and supports my assertion that this is the most accurate of the Curley interviews as it is substantiated by others. From a time standpoint we now have Reno's troops moving to the top of the ridge in their retreat from the valley.

After Red Bear saw the four Crows, Curley left the others and went for water and met Black Fox. Curley, in his interview with General Scott, indicated leaving the other three Crows; and Black Fox's statement to Red Star, Boy Chief, and Strikes Two would support the idea that the meeting with Curley took place near the mouth of Reno Creek.[12] They then left to obtain the hard tack, and most likely met the packs. During this time, Red Star saw Curley and Black Fox together. Red Star saw the other three Crows and reported seeing Black Fox and Curley. The Crows then met Benteen and went to the ridge with him.

There are several important points to consider in this context. It is fairly well substantiated that at least three of the Crows fired down on the Sioux from the bluff above Ford B or Bouyer's Bluff – this, in a straight line, is some three miles away from where they would have met Red Bear and White Cloud. They would not have followed a straight line, so the distance traveled would most likely have been even farther. This point offers additional support to the contention that Custer was at Ford B before Reno began his retreat.

Red Star, Boy Chief, and Strikes Two said that after they got back to the mouth of the Rosebud the next morning they saw Black Fox, who said that he and Curley got together near Reno Ford.*

After Red Bear and White Cloud joined the other Rees

---

*Note Gray's account in his book, *Custer's Last Campaign*, p. 103, where he disagrees with the Arikaras that Curley and Black Fox got together near Reno Ford, or that they were ever together. See also, my analysis of Gray's view. See further interpretation of this issue in Chapter 13, my examination of Fred Dustin's book, *The Custer Tragedy*.

along the ridge, the four Rees who had stayed with the captured ponies returned with them. Some time had now gone by and Reno's troops made their attempt to locate Custer. This is where a statement by Lt. Hare would apply. He said, as Reno's troops were moving to check on the firing heard from downstream (Custer's), he saw the Rees on the ridge. Most likely this is when Stabbed was telling the Rees that their job was done and that they should fall back to the Powder River base camp. I assume that as they began to leave they saw the Sioux forcing Reno's soldiers to retreat back to what became known as the Reno entrenchment area. Stabbed divides the Rees into what the writer, John Gray, in his book, *Custer's Last Campaign*, refers to as the "rear guard" and the "horse herders." The "horse herders" consisted of the following Rees: Bull-in-the-Water, Charging (Rushing) Bull, Red Wolf, White Eagle, Red Star, Pretty Face, Red Bear, and Pta-a-te (Lacotah scout). The "rear guard" was made up of Strikes Two, Stabbed, Soldier, Boy Chief, Strikes-the-Lodge, Little Sioux, Ga-roo (Lakota Scout), E-esh (Lakota Interpreter), and Bull. As Gray points out, the "rear guard" reached the camp on Powder River before the "horse herders."

The Rees went back along the path they entered, and the sun was just going down when they were six miles beyond the Lone Tepee. I believe the timing correlates with the events as I think they took place.

A speculative resumé of events would be: Most of Custer's five companies had already left the ridge when the slower Rees arrived on the bluffs following Custer's path. Custer would have assigned a rear guard. Reno would have been part way down the valley. Stabbed went ahead of the slower Rees and caught up to the rear guard, delivered a message from the Sgt. Major, and prevented them from continuing to fire on the Rees driving the captured ponies. Timewise, Custer's troops were encountering the Indians, as noted by Little Sioux in his statement, that while still on the flat and driving the captured horses, he had heard firing to the right, left, and behind. Later, Custer's perceived action and timing would also coincide with Little Sioux's sightings from a rise above Cedar or Medicine Tail Coulee that indicated Custer's troops were engaged along Calhoun Ridge. His sighting of Indians along the bluffs to the south would suggest that Reno's troops had not yet reached the ridge. However, the Rees decided to return, after seeing Reno's men arriving on the hill, and Captain Benten and the packs moving in Reno's direction. They were there for some time; but when the troops moved out to check on the firing previously heard from the Custer battlefield, Stabbed would have told the Rees they should leave. By this time Reno's troops were already retreating, and Stabbed, realizing the Sioux would see them and attempt to recapture their horses, set up a "rear guard," while the Rees with the captured ponies – the "horse herders" – took off.

Although the Arikaras' accounts are jumbled and hard to decipher, I do believe they support the following view of what took place: (1) Custer did have a plan of attack, the essence of which had six companies crossing the Little Big Horn and moving down the valley, while Custer took five companies in an attempt to flank the Indian encampment. (2) Custer accepted the general location of the Sioux camp. (3) Custer talked with, listened to, and even changed his plans on the advice of his scouts. (4) Reno's attack occurred after Custer himself had left the ridge. (5) Red Star was misinterpreted, and only said that he saw Black Fox and Curley together near the ford, and this is what Goes Ahead agreed to. However, Red Star would have seen, before or just after crossing the Little Big Horn and starting down the valley, the four Crows, Bouyer, and Custer together near where the Hodgson marker was placed. This indicated that Custer was on the ridge before Reno began his move down the valley. (7) Curley's stories of being with Custer when he was attacked were wrongly interpreted. (8) Custer's and Reno's troops began fighting approximately at the same time. (9) The Crows were able to return from Bouyer's Bluff to Reno Creek by the time Reno was retreating from the valley, which would prove that Custer's move to Ford B took place before Reno fled the timber.

SOURCES

1. Graham, *The Custer Myth*, p. 33.
2. Hammer, Kenneth, ed., Walter Camp, *Custer in 76*, p. 187.
3. Libby, O. C., *The Arikara Narrative of the Campaign Against the Hostile Dakotas*, June 1876, p. 120.
4. Graham, *The Custer Myth*, p. 41.
5. Nichols, R. H., ed., *Reno Court of Inquiry – Proceedings of a Court of Inquiry in the case of Major Marcus A. Reno*, p. 439.
6. Libby, *The Arikara Narrative*, p.122.
7. Ibid., p. 150.
8. Hammer, ed., *Custer in 76*, p. 65.
9. Libby, *The Arikara Narrative*, p.152.
10. Ibid., p. 131.
11. Graham, *The Custer Myth*, p. 41.
12. Ibid., p. 39.

10
Crow Accounts

There were six Crow scouts assigned to General Custer's 7th Cavalry when he moved out on his fateful mission. The Crows had been enemies of the Sioux for years and were noted for their courage. These six had enlisted with Colonel Gibbon and were under command of Lt. Bradley, but volunteered to go with General Custer and his 7th Cavalry. They were Half Yellow Face, who was the leader, White Swan, White Man Runs Him, Goes Ahead, Hairy Moccasin and Curley.

Mitch Bouyer went along as interpreter and scout. He was considered one of the best scouts in the country, and knew the topography of the region. He was a half-blood Sioux and could speak Sioux, Crow and English.

After passing the Lone Tepee, Half Yellow Face and White Swan were sent by General Custer to the ridge, but misunderstood their orders and joined Major Reno when they saw him moving to Ford A. They were in the fight in the valley and on the hill. White Swan, in particular, received recognition for his bravery. Private Dennis Lynch of F Company told Walter Camp that when the Sioux made a charge during the fighting on Reno Hill, White Swan, even though he had been wounded, in the valley, would drag himself out to where he could get a better shot at the Sioux; then, in a little while, he would drag himself out again. Lynch said Swan was wounded five or six times.[1]

When Half Yellow Face and White Swan failed to move to the ridge and went to join Major Reno instead, Mitch Bouyer and the other four Crow scouts went to the ridge. Some said an Arikara, Black Fox, went with them.

Like that of other Indians, the Crows' testimony is difficult to analyze. At times they might interpret a question differently than intended; the phrasing of the question could make a difference in their response, and so could the interpreter's understanding of their answer or his reporting of it. Writers have pointed out the desire of many Indians to say what satisfied the person asking the questions. The ill feeling which developed between the three Crows and Curley also has to be recognized and considered.

D. H. Miller states:

> White Man Runs Him, Hairy Moccasin and Goes Ahead could have refuted Curley's story, for they had been far closer to the action, had seen Custer fall, and had stayed a little longer near the doomed command. They were now in disfavor with the 7th Cavalry survivors for having "deserted" Reno Hill the evening of June 25th . . . They were a long time getting back in the Army's good graces. Hero of the hour, Curley, was whisked off to Washington to be wined and dined and feted as the "sole survivor of Custer's Last Stand. [Miller goes on to say] Significantly, as the Army's guest, he was given no chance to return to his people before leaving for the Nation's Capital. The authorities were taking no chances on having their growing legend watered down by more authentic accounts.[2]

The three scouts' stories would have been affected by their recognition of the accusations of cowardice levied on them for leaving Major Reno, and also General Custer. As Curley's imaginary accounts of what happened escalated – picturing himself deeply involved in the actual fighting alongside Custer and only leaving at the final moments on orders from Mitch Bouyer – so grew the resentment of the three Crows toward Curley. The Crows would certainly have been aware of the heroism and martyrdom whites bestowed on Custer, particularly the stories extolling his courage as he stood practically alone at the end, fighting to the last. Is it any wonder the scouts would *not* have told the whites they saw Custer shot at Ford B? If they had, would the interpreters have accurately relayed it to the interviewers? And if so, would it have been properly recorded?

There seems to be general agreement that Half Yellow Face and White Swan were sent to view the valley from the ridge, but went with Reno instead. Then, Mitch Bouyer, Goes Ahead, White Man Runs Him, Hairy Moccasin and Curley went to the ridge. The only account at variance with this one is the *Arikara Narrative*, where Goes Ahead said there was an Arikara scout with them.

As to the question of where the Crows and Custer came onto the ridge, no exact location has been established. There seems to be agreement that, for Custer, it was north of where Reno later entrenched, and some have suggested it was close to where the Hodgson marker is now located. Testimony of the Crows and others as to where Custer waved his hat and his troops cheered seems to vary. There appear to be two specific places where Custer viewed the valley. The first would be where Custer came on the ridge and could see the valley. This would be north of Reno's entrenchment. The second place would be farther down the ridge at a location where the village could be seen more clearly. This location, since it is often referred to as "the high point" and "highest point," must be Weir Point, as it is certainly the highest point along the ridge and would undoubtedly have given the best viewing location. Some writers question this identification, but I think an objective consensus would support it.

White Man Runs Him, in his interview with General Scott in 1919, which was made with Curley also present, pointed out where Major Reno and General Custer would

CROW ACCOUNTS

have separated.[3] This is the most specific testimony as to where the separation would have occurred that I have come across. This part of the interview took place on Ash Creek, later known as Reno Creek.

White Man Runs Him said that General Custer came down Reno Creek to a little flat about a mile and a quarter north of where the creek flows into the Little Big Horn. Custer stopped for a short rest, and from there he sent Half Yellow Face and White Swan to the ridge to view the situation. According to Curley, who also pointed out the flat, the two scouts were almost at the foot of the hill when the trumpeter sounded a call and the left wing started moving. This was Major Reno's battalion. The two scouts turned to the left and joined Reno. Then, Mitch Bouyer, White Man Runs Him, Curley, Hairy Moccasin and Goes Ahead went to the top of the ridge. This testimony would indicate that Reno and Custer separated about a mile and a fourth from Ford A. If it was not so, I assume General Scott would have made some correction of the distance. Custer more then likely watered during this rest and shortly after moved to the ridge. I don't think any testimony would have Custer waiting in this location for another twenty-five to thirty minutes for a message from Girard or Reno before moving to the ridge.

We are faced then with a definite contradiction in White Man Runs Him's account, which was probably due to the way it was recorded or interpreted. (General Scott interview) White Man Runs Him said:

> They went on ahead and Custer followed. He said this was about 9:15 a.m. (old time). Custer moved slowly and took his time and stopped occasionally. He did not leave that place until Reno had started skirmishing. Reno was fighting long before Custer moved. That was about 1:00 p.m. I went with Custer as far as Custer Creek and then came back with the other scouts. We met some soldiers (Reno's men) [Benteen's?] on our way to the pack train. We were up on the hill with Reno all the afternoon.[4]

Fred Dustin's interpretation of the one sentence in which White Man Runs Him said, "I went with Custer as far as Custer Creek and then came back with the other scouts," may be correct, but not necessarily. Dustin thought the statement was made by Curley and not White Man Runs Him. Dustin took the literal sense because White Man Runs Him said "I" instead of "we."[5] However, White Man Runs Him could have said "I" because he felt he had gone with Custer to Medicine Tail Coulee, which in the general sense is true. He said so in more appropriate words under direct questioning. Dustin should have explained, if his version was correct, why Curley would then say that he went back with the other scouts, since Dustin seemed to accept the Curley stories that he went with Bouyer to join Custer.

Although some disagree, I believe that Curley and Black Fox were the ones Lieutenant Mathey referred to in the context of meeting the packs. Mathey thought that one was a half breed, possibly Curley, or Black Fox could have been mistaken for one.

White Man Runs Him's interview was misinterpreted and parts of it were left out, causing a number of distortions. It is also characterized by a lack of strict chronology, which is so often apparent in Indian accounts. Where White Man Runs Him says that around 9:15 they (the scouts) went on ahead, he undoubtedly is referring to the time right before the division of the command. (Note his timing reference.) The slow tempo of movement and occasional stops would also indicate General Custer's movement after the division. The slow tempo supports my view that Custer lingered in order to allow Benteen time to accomplish his mission. White Man Runs Him would not have said this, had he been referring to Custer's move to the ridge. Adding a few words to the record of the interview would make it similar to the other scouts' accounts. When White Man Runs Him says Custer did not leave that place until Reno had started skirmishing, we could use "Weir Point" instead of "place"; or, when he says Reno was fighting long before Custer moved, we could add to "Ford B", and we would have a picture that coincides with what the other scouts said and what White Man Runs Him described elsewhere.

There are differences in testimony, sometimes even by the same scout, as to where Custer first viewed the valley, how he moved along the ridge, and where he moved down to Medicine Tail Coulee. There is also difference in their view as to whether General Custer saw Reno engaged before he moved out of sight of the valley. I believe this reflects their relative position with Custer's companies, and the fact that while Custer had left the ridge, all of his companies had not.

Hammer's book, *Custer in 76*, records various interviews made by Walter Camp, and in it Goes Ahead says that Custer had gone out of sight behind the bluff quite some time before Reno's fight began.[6]

Following are some other statements made by the scouts:

> White Man Runs Him told Camp that Custer sat on the bluff and saw all of Reno's valley fight. That the three Crows then went as far as Medicine Tail Coulee with Custer and then were given permission to go back.[7]

> Hairy Moccasin in the *Tepee Book* said Custer and his command were a short distance behind the scouts. Custer had told them to go on top the high hill ahead, which was a high point just north of where Reno later entrenched.

1. Photograph taken from Reno Hill. Ford A or Reno Ford in background.

2. Same area as the first photo, but to the left. A comparison of the two photographs indicates why Custer moved to the ridge along the route shown in photo 2. It explains why the sighting of Custer's troops by Reno's took place after Custer's soldiers reached the ridge. The photos also suggest why Custer's troops could have moved in a line formation after watering, until they reached the ridge.

3. Photograph taken from Reno Hill looking toward Sharpshooter Hill and Weir Peak. Shows general terrain configuration. If Custer came to the ridge on this side of Sharpshooter Hill, with no clear view of the villages and the route to reach them, he would have gone to Weir Peaks.

From there, they could see the village and could see Reno fighting. The battle was over in a few minutes.[8]

Hairy Moccasin, in a Camp interview in 1911, said Custer's command, as well as Bouyer and the four Crows, saw Reno's fight in the valley.[9]

Curley in his account to Camp on July 19, 1910 has Bouyer and the Crows ahead of General Custer's command. He says Custer did not see Reno's fight. He says Mitch Bouyer and myself did. When Reno's fighting, no one but Mitch Bouyer with me. Before got to Crow Hill [Bouyer's Bluff], Bouyer waved hat to Custer from here. Saw Reno fighting from Edgerly peaks [Weir Point].[10]

Curley, when interviewed by General Scott, described General Custer moving to the right of the scouts as he came on the ridge and waving his hat to men at the bottom of the hill, who also waved and cheered. Custer kept going on the ridge and the scouts followed. Curley said they galloped their horses when moving after Custer.[11] This is why, along with other supporting testimony, we can assume that White Man Runs Him was referring to the movement along Reno Creek, where we know the command did move slowly at times. Lieutenant Varnum mentioned that Custer was moving out at a walk when Reno's troops were passing them on their way to Ford A.

Hairy Moccasin, in his interview found in the *Tepee Book*, appears to be referring to the time when the command was moving along Reno Creek and Custer sent the two Crows to the ridge but they went with Reno instead, forcing Bouyer to take the other four Crows and go to the ridge. Here one sees the lack of chronology in the record. We know that when the scouts reached the ridge, Major Reno's troops were not in action. What we have is a relative statement of time, which does not give us a correlated or clear picture of what was taking place.

Hairy Moccasin's view, as expressed to Walter Camp, that Custer's command saw Reno engaged in the valley, supports my earlier contention that Custer's command moved off the ridge and did it during the time Reno went into action. If the scouts were following the command, it conforms to my theory that the last of the command would have seen Reno form his skirmish line. One should keep in mind that the last of the five companies could have moved off the ridge – depending on numerous factors – five or more minutes after General Custer had left. This could have been ten or more minutes from the time when Custer was viewing the Indian village from Weir Point. During that time Reno could have moved most of the way down the valley. This scenario would correspond to the sightings of Custer by Reno's troops, Lieutenant Varnum, and the sighting of Reno's troops as reported by Sergeant Kanipe.

With the various exploits attributed to him, Curley remains a special enigma. One wonders how many of the stories he was even aware of, since he didn't understand English and was not able to read. How many interpreters fabricated what they knew the officers or writers wanted to hear? The other Crows certainly didn't like his being feted and given special recognition while they were being condemned. They could not help but be aware of the different adventures and actions Curley was being credited with, which they knew were untrue.

Later I will relate some of these stories and explain why I disagree with them; at this time I will only examine Curley's interview with General Scott. I believe this is Curley's most accurate account for it concurs with what could be called the essence of the other Crow scouts' reports, and it also agrees with the accounts of the Rees and of Trumpeter Martin.[12] The main question is why this part of the testimony was recorded and interpreted in a more accurate way than other Curley accounts. It could be due to a number of reasons, among which are the following: He was interviewed at the same time as another Crow scout, as well as Feather Earring, a Sioux. He, or more likely the interpreter, may have been influenced by General Scott's rank and his expertise with the sign language which might have affected the way Curley was questioned and his answers were recorded. The most important reason could have been the presence of two interpreters. Whatever the explanation, this particular version does coincide with other accounts and with what I consider a logical sequence of events.

As in everyone's testimony, there are time and distance differences and questions that are difficult to answer. Which hill did Custer go on? Did he wave from several locations? Did he see Reno engaged? Which coulee did Custer go down? From the standpoint of the Crow scout, the primary unresolved matter is just where they separated. Some of these issues are not too important, but the question of whether General Custer actually reached Ford B is a basic point on which writers disagree, often because Curley, in different interviews, had Custer both going and not going to the ford.

In the General Scott interview, Curley had Custer moving down the ridge to a certain spot, then turning to the right in a northerly direction and going down one of the coulees.

Curley goes on:

> When Custer reached the river, we turned. By the time Custer reached the river, Mitch Bouyer said he was going down to Custer and his men, and for the rest of us to go back to the pack outfit. Being on the hill [ridge or bluffs] we could see Reno retreating and was well to the foot of the hills.[13]

This is where Curley's account differs from so many of his other stories. In those he indicated that he went with Bouyer and joined Custer, and the other scouts went back or already had done so. I attribute the difference to the interpreter or recorder and not Curley. The other scouts said that Curley left them before they reached the bluff above the ford. This inconsistency also raises questions. Why does Curley say to General Scott they were all together and left together when usually he didn't make this claim, and why would the other scouts, if Curley was with them at that time, say he wasn't?

In general, what Curley said was true and his testimony fits into a rational timing sequence. I think Custer would have reached the river in roughly 15 to 20 minutes – and more than likely sooner – after he left Weir Point. Curley would be referring to seeing Reno in retreat, anywhere from the time soon after he left Bouyer's Bluff (if he went that far), back to where I assume he met the Rees and, in particular, Black Fox. In timing, even a few minutes could make a great deal of difference in what was seen or what action was taken. In his case, the estimate could vary some twenty minutes. It means that Major Reno would have been fighting in the valley about forty minutes.

Curley and the General Scott interview continued:

> The Arapahoe [Arikara] scouts of Custer had some of the Sioux horses and brought them across the river just below the ridge on the east side. We also met two groups of soldiers on the ridge just north of where Reno made his stand. He came back past the Arapahoe scouts but do not know what became of them afterwards. The Sioux did not follow Reno across the river at first. Their attention was turned to where some Crow and Arapahoe Scouts were surrounded in some woods on the west side of the river. We stopped while they were doing this. Things looked bad, so we thought we had better hunt safety.[14]

For Curley to have known all these facts, he must have been in the vicinity, or talked to a good many of the Rees, and incorporated their accounts into what he told General Scott. This would be improbable, if only from the timing angle and the difficulty of coordinating it with his own actions. The Rees said the capturing of Lakota horses occurred before the soldiers set up their skirmish line, as the village was just beginning to stir. By the time they had crossed the river, Major Reno would have been in action. The Crows, or at least Curley, would have seen the Ree scouts who were driving Sioux ponies.

It would appear that Curley saw the Ree scouts as they moved beyond the ridge with captured Lakota horses. Since I doubt that Curley went as far as Bouyer's Bluff with Bouyer and the other three scouts, we have the problem of associating time with statements and known events.

The scenario, as I envision it, would be this: Curley saw the Ree scouts who were with Strikes Two as they drove, or were changing to, the captured Lakota horses. This would be some time after Curley and Bouyer were on Weir Point and viewed a peaceful village, and after Custer's five companies had left the ridge. Curley may have been with, or soon sees, the other Crow scouts who were returning from firing on the Indian village from Bouyer's Bluff. They continue together and encounter White Cloud and Red Bear. They then leave during which time Curley separates from the others, and while going toward the river he comes across Black Fox. The other three Crows see Red Star, then Benteen's battalion, and notify him of the soldiers on the ridge. They then go with Benteen to the ridge.

The soldiers who fired on Strikes Two and his Ree companions were the same ones that Curley recalls, which poses several intriguing questions. We know the soldiers who shot at the Rees and Strikes Two were either the last of Custer's command to leave the ridge, stragglers, or a rear guard. I would favor a rear guard. If they were stragglers, it would depend on the number of men associated with the term "groups" (a couple, ten, more?). There were reports by Thompson and several others joining Reno, but not that many; nor would the time of their arrival coincide. There were ten men of Company F unaccounted for, as reported in the book *The Little Big Horn, 1876*, compiled by Loyd J. Overfield II. These men could have been a rear guard since it was a common practice to establish one.

According to Major Reno, twenty-nine men were missing from the Custer battlefield. Some of those may not have been located until later, and there were reports of several troopers' bodies being found at some distance from the battlefield. This might account for a few of the twenty-nine, but not most of them.

Evan S. Connell in his book, *Son of the Morning Star*, offers the following remarks:

> Watson and Thompson were not the only men who failed to keep the deadly rendezvous. Quite a few soldiers assigned to Custer's battalion somehow appeared on Reno's hilltop, but with so many officers and non-commissioned officers dead it became impossible to learn why or when these men defected. For instance, twenty-four men from Captain Yates' F Company joined Reno while the rest died with Custer. This is particularly strange. It might not be puzzling if Yates' company had formed the tail of the column because one man after another could lag behind and ease out of sight, but it appears that Yates may have been leading the way. Certainly he was not the last in line. How could twenty-four men desert in the shadow of old Iron Butt himself? And had they stayed to fight– along with other defectors– might these companies have survived?[15]

These troops, if members of F Company, must have been under orders to act as a rear guard. They could have had a multi-purpose assignment: to pick up stragglers, to warn Custer of any Indian activity in the rear, to check on Reno's action, to aid the packs, and to look for Benteen. The troops that did fire on the Rees, if they remained on the ridge, and did join Reno's troops, would have done so at a time when they were in disarray, having just retreated to the hill, followed by Benteen and then the packs. This would have been a time of confusion, and so they may not have been noticed. Still, it is difficult to explain why no questions were asked of them or why they didn't, at some time, explain their actions. Were they part of a cover-up? If so, would it be for personal reasons, or were they attempting to protect Reno's officers or both?

If these men didn't speak up and it was, indeed, for personal reasons, they may have believed their failure to rejoin Custer's command would brand them as cowards. Since they would have also seen the Indians facing Reno and the Indian encampment, did they believe it would be the better part of valor to join Reno? If there was a cover-up to protect the officers, it would likely have been because they did inform the officers of Custer's predicament. The orders they had been given may have been revealing, because they might have known what Custer had expected and what orders he had administered. There is the distinct possibility that they hadn't seen any action or fighting, which they believed was not common knowledge. There still would have been numerous questions they should have been able to clear up. Their absence, if true, suggests the possibility of a cover-up.

If they were a rear guard, assigned for the purposes I previously mentioned, one would assume that when Stabbed met this "rear guard" the command was still moving to, or had just reached, Medicine Tail Coulee. The guard would probably have sent a courier with Stabbed's message to Custer. The Sergeant Major (or a third courier sent to Benteen) was probably close behind Stabbed. He would have moved faster and undoubtedly angled to the ridge. The Ree scouts' statement that they talked to a sergeant should be noted. The Sergeant Major then reported to Custer, who, on receiving the news that Benteen was back on the main trail, would have immediately sent Martin with his message to Benteen.

The accounts of soldiers being on the ridge at the time mentioned by Strikes Two and Curley, along with the reports of missing men, generate interesting lines of inquiry that were seemingly never investigated or a definitive answer made.

Curley's claim that he was aware of what the Rees were doing, and that he was with, or even near, Custer, before Custer's command reached Last Stand Hill, must be treated as a fantasy. The fact that Curley knew that the Sioux did not, initially, follow Reno across the river, would indicate he is either relying on other testimony or his own sighting. For him to have such knowledge and not have been there is inconceivable. Curley goes on to say he left the other Crow scouts and went toward Ford A. Curley could have met the other three Crows as they moved back from Bouyer's Bluff and gone down off the ridge with them. The four Crows meet Red Bear and White Cloud. After leaving them, Curley separated and moved toward the river and met Black Fox. Reno's men were retreating and Curley would have noticed the Sioux fighting around some timber where Young Hawk and some other scouts were. The other three Crows met Red Star, and then, Captain Benteen's battalion, as Benteen and others reported, and followed them to Reno Hill.

When leaving Bouyer's Bluff, the three Crows would most likely have moved back by way of coulees, and so would not have been aware of just what was happening to Major Reno, as Curley seems to have been. This would tend to support my belief that Curley never went as far as Bouyer's Bluff. Curley's realization that the Sioux did not pursue Reno across the river and were concerned with Young Hawk and his companions, places him near the scene, and, as the timing meshes with other accounts, it is unlikely that Curley had woven his facts together from talking to the Rees.

Continuing with the General Scott interview, from the point where Curley remarks that they believed "they better hunt safety," he goes on to say:

> They then turned and followed the ridge, going east toward the Rosebud. I left the others and traveled toward the mouth of Reno Creek in a southwest direction. The others yelled to me and asked where I was going. I answered "I am going down to see if I can reach the river and get some water." They said, "Come on: do not go that way, it is dangerous there." but I did not listen to them. After traveling as far as where Custer had crossed Reno Creek to go on the ridge, I turned up (east) Reno Creek toward the buttes and met the pack train. The outfit was about three miles up the creek when I saw and met the pack outfit. I went on down to the mouth of the Little Horn. The Arapahoe scouts came from near the Gros Ventres, down on the Little Missouri River.[16]

This could mean it was Curley and Black Fox who met Lieutenant Mathey. The timing would be correct and the location would support Mathey's version. Though Curley would not have understood Mathey's question, it is possible that Black Fox did and could have answered him. It is apparent that some of the Arikaras did understand and were able to speak English.

According to this account, Curley was not with the other three when they met Benteen, which would have happened as Curley moved to the river. If Curley had been with the other three at that time, he would have gone to the ridge with them.

Curley and Black Fox could have left the area by moving to the northeast rather than going back to the Lone Tepee and the trail where they came in. Curley mentioned moving to the butte above where he met the packs, and he could have left by moving from there to the northeast. Curley and Black Fox may have seen the end of the Custer battle.* Then, realizing that Custer was surrounded, Curley and Black Fox went close to the present location of Busby to pick up the hard tack. Afterwards they separated, with Curley going to the mouth of the Little Horn.

One should note that when White Man Runs Him speaks of Curley leaving them on Reno Creek, the wording might suggest he is referring to the time before they even arrived on the ridge, when he undoubtedly meant the time after they returned from Bouyer's Bluff and moved on down to Reno Creek.[17] Since we don't know the order of the questions asked, and their relationship to those posed before, what can be deduced is that White Man Runs Him is indicating that Curley left them on Reno Creek and wasn't with them when they were on the ridge with Major Reno. This chronological and contextual problem could account for Goes Ahead's statement in the *Arikara Narrative*, which suggests that Black Fox was with them. It is more plausible that Curley met him as he returned from being with Custer. Some Rees said that Black Fox crossed over the river with Major Reno, and others thought he didn't. I believe he did, but either way he would have been in a position to join Curley at this time.

In his answers to questions by General Scott, White Man Runs Him indicates this disregard for chronology prevalent in so many Indian accounts. White Man Runs Him said:

> The first time we stopped on the bluff was when Mitch Bouyer left us to go to Custer, and before we returned to Reno, those nearest began to run. [This would imply that some of Custer's men began not just a retreat but a panicky one.] Custer's men did not fire at all on this side. Custer believed that Reno's command was all killed because they were retreating into the bluff and the dust was flying and they were retreating so fast. I saw him go that far. The Sioux were right across the river. Then Custer fired. That was the first firing Custer did. If it wasn't for Mitch Bouyer, most likely I would be there with Custer, buried, but Mitch Bouyer told us to go back.[18]

What one can conclude from White Man Runs Him's statement that Custer's men didn't fire until they reached the ford, is that this would not have been true if there were a large number of Indians waiting for him. The few Sioux and Cheyenne there would not have presented a target until the troops reached the ford.

The statement also illustrates the Crows' attempt to justify their leaving by saying that Custer saw Reno's retreat; but Custer still retreated, and they would have stayed if they hadn't been ordered back.

I am certain that Custer did not see Reno retreating to the bluff, as the timing would not be right, nor would it coincide with a consensus of testimony, including White Man Runs Him's. If it happened that way, White Man Runs Him would not have been able to have returned to Reno Creek and met Benteen. White Man Runs Him continues:

> There was only three of us. Hairy Moccasin, Goes Ahead and myself. We did not see Curly. Mitch Bouyer told us to go back. He said "You go back to the pack train and let the soldiers fight." We went back and met some soldiers and soon after that the pack train was there. If those soldiers hadn't turned back and been reinforced by the pack train they would all have been killed. The Sioux were coming up fast. Curley would have been one of the live ones because he was with the Arikarees and the horses. There were older men with me and they all said my story was true as much as they could remember in all the excitement; but I did not see Curley at all when he went back to the pack train. The Arapahoes said they took the horses and went on to Rosebud junction (near Lame Deer) When they left with the horses they hurried and by evening they were where the Rosebud flows into the Yellowstone. They said Curley was with them.[19]

White Man Runs Him again offers a partly twisted description (for which the recorder may be partly to blame), but I believe a fairly accurate one. He indicates going back and meeting some soldiers, which would coincide with what Benteen said. The three Crows move to the bluffs and join Major Reno. Then, White Man Runs Him's account may be either referring to Reno's retreat from the timber, or Major Reno's move to Weir Point, and his conviction that if they hadn't turned back, they would all have been killed. At that time, Curley was already with the Arikaras and they had left, so Curley would have been safe. This account is more consistent and rational than those of most whites accounts. It also portrays the Crows' resentment. The three Crows were condemned for leaving Reno and Custer whereas Curley, who had left both of them even earlier, had been celebrated and transformed into a hero.

The Custer Myth, p. 17, White Man Runs Him's interview with General Scott, which took place at the mouth of Medicine Tail Coulee, 4 miles from Reno's entrenchment, Ford B:

---

*Note: Chip Watts and I, through glasses, were able to see Last Stand Hill from Ridge B.

Q. How far down here did Custer get?
A. Right down to the river.
Q. How far did they come?
A. They came down the ravine to the river here and started back.
Q. What did the scouts do then? Where was Mitch Bouyer?
A. He was on the point there.
Q. Where was Curley?
A. He was back on the ridge.
....
Q. Did you see Reno go up on the bluffs then?
A. No. I saw him fighting across the river but didn't know he had retreated to the bluffs.

White Man Runs Him, at Ford B, showing the exact location, indicated that Custer went down to the river. White Man Runs Him, at the time the events took place, would have been on Bouyer's Bluff only a few hundred yards away. He would certainly have been able to recognize Custer. The actions of both the scouts and Custer would indicate there was no large number of Indians waiting in ambush. Asked about Curley, White Man Runs Him said he was back on the ridge. This would bear out my view that Curley, after Weir Point, may have gone part of the way with them, or in that direction; but during this time Bouyer would have told Curley he should go back. Curley would most likely have stayed and seen the other Crows fire on the village, observed two men fall into the river, and the action of the Sioux in moving to Reno as well as the beginning of their move toward Custer's troops. It could be expected the route Curley took back to Reno's entrenchment area would have differed somewhat from that of the other scouts. They could have come together near Reno Hill and then met Red Bear and White Cloud. During this time, Curley moved, as he said, toward the Little Bighorn while the other three met Red Star and then Benteen. They would have warned Curley when he left. One must keep in mind that the statements can be quite vague. This was a period of excitement, and to remember accurately everything that happened would have been impossible.

White Man Runs Him then made a salient remark concerning Reno's action in which he indicated he saw Reno fighting in the valley but didn't know he had retreated. It contradicts the statements I have quoted before as well as those made by Hairy Moccasin. Those remarks would have Custer watching Reno's action in the valley and knowing of his retreat. Even without this comment by White Man Runs Him, it is unacceptable to believe that Custer watched Reno's fight in the valley and knew of his retreat. For one thing, the following scenario would have had to have taken place: Custer spends at least forty minutes watching Reno without taking any action, which for the General would have been impossible. Custer would then have gone to Medicine Tail Coulee, moved to Ford B and began his retreat, at which time the three Crows would have left. During that time, and before starting back, the Crows would have seen Reno retreating. Reno would have to have left the timber some time before. In fact, the Sioux and Cheyenne would have been returning to attack Custer, and the bluffs would have been filled with Indians. The Crows would then have been forced to move to the south and east and still would have been lucky to have made it back. From a time standpoint, to subsequently be able to meet Red Bear and then Captain Benteen and move to Reno Hill with Benteen – arriving shortly after Reno himself – is utterly impossible. What this indicates is that Custer reached Ford B while Major Reno was still fighting in the valley and Custer's troops started to retreat before Major Reno's. This would be supported by Ree accounts.

I think we can rule out White Man Runs Him's reference to Custer having watched Reno's retreat and credit it either to a misinterpretation of the question, an error in the recording of his answer, or attribute it to an attempt to justify the three Crows' actions. It is easy to perceive in White Man Runs Him's statements the Crows' bitter feeling toward Curley, and to understand the resentment they felt in knowing that Curley had left before them; yet, he was honored while they had been denounced.

Curley in answer to questions posed by General Scott:

Q. Where was Custer when you saw Reno come across?
A. Over the divide to the right of the first entrenchment. Custer saw the camp from the highest point on the ridge to the right of the first entrenchment. He just saw Reno going down the valley but did not see him come back.
....
Q. Where did he [Reno] cross coming back?
A. I do not know, I was not there to see them.[20]

The highest point on the ridge is Weir Point, from where Curley said Custer viewed the camp. Curley again implied that although Custer saw Reno going down the valley, he did not see him go into action. Curley said he was not there to see where Reno crossed coming back. According to Graham, Curley told General Scott that from the hill they saw Reno retreating and also that he saw where Young Hawk, White Swan and others were fighting.[21] Here again one finds a jumbled chronological picture. This is one of the more important timing considerations. It played a major role in the analysis of the battle, and although the picture is not clear, I believe several assumptions can be made. One should first recognize the difficulty of putting the time of events into a set mold. Curley's statement about "being on the hill" could mean any point from Bouyer's Bluff to beyond Reno Hill. Curley mentioned seeing the fighting around the timber where Young Hawk, White Swan and the others were. This most likely would have taken place after Curley left the other Crows, moved down toward Reno Creek (when he told the others he was going to the river to get a drink) and probably met Black Fox. Captain Benteen, from this general location, appeared to have seen similar fighting taking place.

The most important implications and corroborating factors brought out in the General Scott interview establish a specific event-time-event relation. The first of these would be that Custer left the ridge to move to Medicine Tail Coulee shortly before Reno was establishing his skirmish line. The second, and even more important association, is that Custer's troops retreated from Ford B before Reno's left the timber; but, in a comparatively short time, both troops would have been in the process of retreating.

I see no possible way that Reno could have retreated before Custer reached Medicine Tail Coulee and Ford B, as many writers have portrayed the events, and the Prosecution attempted to prove at the Reno Court of Inquiry.

Frank B. Linderman talked to Pretty Shield, one of the wives of Goes Ahead, about the battle. Goes Ahead was dead when this interview took place. Pretty Shield said:

"My man, Goes Ahead, White Man Runs Him and Hairy Moccasin were ahead of Son of the Morning Star (Custer) and his blue horse soldiers. Half Yellow-face, who was my uncle, and carried the pipe (commanded) and Curley were with the Son of the Morning Star. Curley said that he was sick, and I guess he was . . .

My man, Goes Ahead, told me that he felt afraid when he saw so many lodges. He, with the two others, Hairy Moccasin and White Man Runs Him, turned here, going up the creek that white men called Reno. They met (Custer) coming down the creek, and told him what they had seen . . . She pressed her fist against her forehead, and bent her head, tst, tst, tst. He would not listen, she murmured. "And he was brave; yes, he was a brave man."

"Two-bodies, a half breed interpreter, listened," she went on . . . He spoke to (Custer) saying, 'you can get safely away.'

But the soldier chief wanted to fight, because he had to die. And this made others die with him," she added speaking slowly and with deep feeling.

"My man, Goes Ahead, told me that (Custer) drank too often from the straw covered bottle, and that as soon as Two-bodies told him that he might yet get away he made a big mistake by dividing his blue horse-soldiers into three parties, sending two of them away from him . . ." [Custer was not known to drink hard liquor, so there was probably something else in the bottle.]

Pretty-Shield was deeply affected here. She stood up, leaning over the table. "It was now that my man . . . stripped himself for battle . . . and it was now that the little chief, Reno, went away as he had been ordered, with all of the Arikara wolves. (scouts) White Swan and Half-Yellow Face went with them by mistake, and it was now that Curly, who said he was sick, ran away. Ahh, I know these things were true, because my man was there and saw them happen.

"Reno . . .

"My man, Goes Ahead, was with Son of the Morning Star when he rode down to the water, with Two-bodies on one side of him, and his flag on the other – and he died there, died in the water of the Little Big Horn with Two-bodies, and the blue-soldier carrying his flag.

"When he fell in the water, the other blue soldiers ran back up the hill. It was now that my man, Goes Ahead, ran fast. He told me that the fighters were so many, and so crazy, that in the thick dust and powder smoke, anybody might easily have run away. So he, White Man Runs Him, and Hairy Moccasin, ran when they saw Son of the Morning Star fall into the water.

. . . "Ahh," she sighed, suddenly relaxing, "My man, Goes Ahead, told me that he was afraid; and yet he did not run away until he saw Son of the Morning Star fall down from his horse into the water of the Little Big Horn. He told me that when he fell, the blue horse-soldiers ran back up the hill. He took me to the place, and showed me exactly where Son of the Morning Star fell into the water, with Two-bodies and the flag, where he himself started to run away, and where he stopped to fight with the packers. "Yes" she said, her voice trailing off to a murmur, "my man, Goes Ahead, was afraid that day; but he did not lie to me, the monument that white men have set up to mark the spot where Son of the Morning Star fell down, is a lie. He fell in the water," she whispered, as though to the – of her man, Goes Ahead . . .

Linderman goes on to say: "Having business of my own at the traders store, I followed Pretty Shield there; and was glad that I did, because her short visit had inspired an Indian of about sixty years to talk to the trader about her man Goes Ahead. He was saying in pidgin English, when I entered, "and he showed me where he and White Man Runs Him, and Hairy Moccasin ran up a little creek that is there, where they found the packers with their pack train, and I stopped to fight, he went on "yes," he said, and when I was a young man I knew Big Nose, a Lacota who told me that he, himself, killed General Custer and that the General fell in the water, with his half breed interpreter, a man that the Crows called Two-bodies. His white name was Mitch Bouyer, I guess."

There was more, most of little importance, except the telling of finding the bodies of 4 cavalrymen six miles from the battlefield – the man declaring his father had been one of the Crows who found them. "One of these dead men was an officer; he said, thus strengthening Pretty Shield's story . . . and yet I was glad to get his uninvited corroboration.[22]

Pretty Shield's story supports the main conclusion I have derived from the Crow's testimony: that Custer did lead his troops down Medicine Tail Coulee to Ford B. It would also indicate a quick retreat from the ford. Pretty Shield would have noted or implied that Mitch Bouyer was also shot at the ford, but with the sighting of Bouyer's body in Deep Ravine as well as the recent indication of his body having been buried below Last Stand Hill, it would seem more likely that he jumped off his horse when Custer was shot and the Crows back on the bluff thought that he too had been hit. White Cow Bull's description of the men who were shot doesn't fit that of Mitch Bouyer.

The facts from White Man Runs Him and Curley's interview with General Scott coincide with the testimony of the Rees, Martin's, sighting by Reno's troopers, Lt. Varnum's and also White Cow Bull's story. The following points become apparent from the Crow accounts:

1. General Custer moved to the river at Ford B.
2. There was a quick retreat by the troops.
3. The Indians were surprised by Reno's and Custer's troops.
4. The village was peaceful just before or during Custer's move off the ridge.
5. When Custer moved off the ridge, Major Reno was establishing his skirmish line or just about to.
6. Reno was still on his skirmish line or in the timber at the time Custer reached Ford B.

Some discredit the Scott interview because General Scott said Curley accused White Man Runs Him of lying and he had to tell them not to interrupt each other. Considering the ill feeling between the two Crows, a certain amount of disagreement could be expected. However, I am sure General Scott would not have released the interview if it didn't correspond to the answers given by Curley and White Man Runs Him. There is no way that the interview, in essence, would not have represented the statements made by the two. As I brought out before, it would likely be a more accurate interview than many others (especially Curley's) because of General Scott's knowledge of the sign language and the fact that there were two interpreters.

The quintessence of Curley's and White Man Runs Him's interview with General Scott is their seeing General Custer move to the river at Ford B or the Minneconjou Ford. They would have been close enough to know it was General Custer and not some other officer. In other words, the people who say Custer went to the river were the people who were in a position to know whether he did or not. In later interviews, Trumpeter Martin was very indignant with writers for saying Custer hadn't got close to the river, because he knew that he had been with Custer nearer to the river than they said he had gone. I believe Martin was an honest soldier, and when he said Captain Benteen indicated he left General Custer about 600 yards from the ford, I'll take his word for it. Yet many writers have gone against the testimony given by the Crows and Martin without any real evidence apart from their conjectural opinions and unsubstantiated reports by Curley's interpreters. In order to cogently disagree with evidence, you must indicate exactly where and why it can't be supported, but you cannot just ignore the facts or brush them aside as too many writers have done.

If I am to follow my own advice, I must deal with Curley's other accounts which have been accepted and used as the basis for various scenarios.

SOURCES

1. Camp, ed. Hammer, *Custer in 76,* p. 140.
2. Miller, D. H., *Custer's Fall,* p. 159.
3. Graham, *The Custer Myth,* p. 13.
4. Ibid., p. 13.
5. Dustin, *The Custer Tragedy,* p. xv, A Prelude.
6. Camp, *Custer in 76,* p. 178.
7. Ibid., p. 178.
8. Graham, *The Custer Myth,* p. 25.
9. Camp, op. cit., p.177.
10. Ibid., p. 166.
11. Graham, *The Custer Myth,* p. 13.
12. Ibid., pp. 13, 14.
13. Ibid., p. 14.
14. Ibid., p. 14.
15. Connell, *Son of the Morning Star,* pp. 280, 281.
16. Graham, *The Custer Myth,* p. 14.
17. Ibid., p. 14.
18. Ibid., p. 15.
19. Ibid., p. 17.
20. Ibid., p. 17.
21. Ibid., p. 14.
22. Linderman, *Red Mother,* pp. 223-247

11
Curley – Crow Scout

Graham, *The Custer Myth,* pp. 7–11:

The first recorded mention of scout Curley as a 'raconteur' is contained in a report to . . . Lt. Maguire, by Sergeant James E. Wilson, who was aboard the steamer 'Far West' at the mouth of the Little Big Horn, 28th June, 1876:

"An Indian scout named 'Curley,' known to have been with General Custer," says the report, "arrived about noon with information of a battle, but there being no interpreter on board very little reliable information was obtained . . ."

But in sharp contrast to the above is the Arikara Narrative, which at page 208, in the course of a sketch of James Coleman, a trader who peddled whiskey to officers and soldiers of the Little Big Horn expedition, states:

After Custer's defeat, Coleman was on the boat with Terry at the mouth of the Little Big Horn, when Curley appeared on the east bank . . . Curley held up his hand with a rag in it, and they waved him aboard. He wore a cloth about his head, a black shirt, a breech-clout, and moccasins. . . . Coleman saw Curley make one sign, the sleep sign, once. Then a crowd of officers and men cut off his view, George Morgan, a squaw-man translated Curley's sign and speech. He reported Curley said he crawled two miles wrapped in a Sioux blanket; that Custer's command was wiped out and that Reno was in great danger.

The Coleman-Morgan "Curley" story, set out above, was probably the genesis of the Curley myth, which, despite the statement of Tom LeForge (reported by Dr. Marquis in his "Memoirs of a White Crow") that he interpreted Curley's story for Lt. Bradley shortly after the battle, and that Curley said: "I did nothing wonderful – I was not in the fight, "the myth grew and grew and grew" until the marvelous tales of Curley and his miraculous escape from death with Custer became not only incredible but fantastic; even absurd and ridiculous.

"But the "standard" Curley story, as first printed by the Helena *Herald* did not satisfy the disciples of Munchausen, . . .

. . . Other Indians, learning of these wondrous tales, said that Curley was a liar. but if he really authored them (which I take the liberty to doubt), . . . As for myself, I am inclined to credit LeForge's statement to Marquis above referred to <u>as to what Curley said to him</u>, but I have been unable to discover any statements or report by Bradley of such an interview . . .

"My reason for believing that Curley disclaimed having done anything wonderful because he was not in the fight rests upon the description of his meanderings as found in the statement of the Arikara scout Red Star . . . and the official report of Col. M.V. Sheridan of 20 July 1877 which clearly indicates that neither Curly nor Half Yellow Face, both of whom accompanied him to the battlefield in 1877, were able to furnish any information of value concerning Custer's fight, Sheridan being convinced that Curley "had run away before the fight really began," and that "the greater portion of his tale was untrustworthy."[1]

Curley's story as it appeared in the Helena *Herald*, 15 July, 1876:

"Custer fell upon the highest point of the field; and around him, within a space of five rods square, lay forty-two men and thirty-one horses. The dead soldiers all lay within a circle embracing only a few hundred yards square." (Lt. Bradley)

. . . But when the command returned to the Yellowstone they found there a Crow scout named "Curley" who, as verified by Major Reno, rode out with Custer on that fatal day.. He alone escaped, and his account of the battle we give below. . . .

"Custer, with his five companies, after separating from Reno and his seven companies, moved to the right around a base of a high hill overlooking the valley of the Little Horn through a ravine just wide enough to admit a column of fours. There were no signs of the presence of Indians in the hills on that side of the Little Horn, and the column moved steadily on until it rounded the hill and came in sight of the village . . . Custer appeared very much elated, and ordered the bugles to sound a charge, and moved on at the head of his column, waving his hat to encourage his men. When they neared the river, the Indians, concealed in the undergrowth on the opposite side of the river, opened fire on the troops, which checked the advance. Here a portion of the command were dismounted and thrown forward to the river and returned the fire of the Indians. During this time, the warriors were seen riding out of the village by the hundreds, and deploying across his front to his left, as if with the intention of crossing the stream on his right, while the women and children were seen hastening out of the village in large numbers in the opposite direction.

During the fight at this point, Curley saw two of Custer's men killed who fell in the stream. After fighting a few moments here, Custer seemed to be convinced that it was impracticable to cross, as it only could be done in column of fours, exposed during the movement to a heavy fire from the front and both flanks. He, therefore, ordered the head of the column to the right, and bore diagonally into the hills, downstream, his men on foot, leading their horses. In the meantime the Indians had crossed the river (below) in immense numbers and began to appear on his right flank and in his rear; and he had proceeded but a few hundred yards in the new direction . . . when it became necessary to renew the fight with the Indians who had crossed the stream. At first the command remained together, but after some minutes fighting it was divided, a portion deploying to the right, so that when the line was formed it bore a rude resemblance to a circle, advantage being taken as far as possible of the protection afforded by the ground. . ."[2]

I would agree overall with Colonel Graham's summation, particularly as it pertained to the Coleman-Morgan story versus the Wilson and Leforge accounts.

The first part of the newspaper report appears to be fairly accurate, in comparison to the rest of the article. I believe this is because Curley saw this part of the action. It is also supported by the other Crow scouts as well as the Sioux warrior White Cow Bull and the Cheyenne, Bobtail Horse.

Though the story is vague as to Custer's exact route to the ford, it does have him going there, and, if only because of its narrow width, it would appear Custer went down Middle Coulee and not Cedar Coulee. Custer's troops come under fire from Indians concealed on the other side, but there is no mention of hundreds of Indians lying in wait, only an indication that hundreds are seen moving to the ford. Women and children are seen leaving the village, which they would have been doing since they had become aware of Reno's attack. Several soldiers were killed in the stream – another similarity to White Cow Bull's and Pretty Shield's story. Thus we have corroboration by Indians fighting on both sides in the battle. Custer, according to the article, "seemed to be convinced that it was impracticable to cross," so the head of the column bore to the right and diagonally into the hills downstream. Again one should note how this corresponds to what White Man Runs Him said and to White Cow Bull's account. This would mean the troops went along South Medicine Tail toward the ford but moved to the north in retreating. They would have traveled along North Medicine Tail, crossed the western part of Calhoun Ridge and proceeded along Greasy Grass hill. I believe the account then uses "right" when they meant that the Indians were moving down from the troops on the left. This is the direction from which more of the Indians could have been seen by those troops at the ford, and where the Indians would have been likely to reverse their move toward Reno. As the troops retreated, they crossed the ford and were on the right flank and to the rear as the article suggests.

I agree with the statement that at first the command remained together but after some minutes of fighting was divided, one part circling to the left and another to the right. As the troops retreated many were on foot and leading their horses. This was true of those troops nearer the ford who were apt to have dismounted in order to fire more effectively. A number of the horses became unmanageable and broke or were turned loose. Many of the troops in the trailing companies remained on horseback as they moved to the ford and would have retreated toward Keogh's battalion. This would include the Gray Horse Troop, and that is why it became so prominent in Indian accounts. Keogh's battalion may have been back on Luce Ridge, but now were on Nye Cartwright and moving to North Medicine Tail (also referred to as Deep Coulee), while engaging in long distance fire in support of the retreating Yates battalion.[3] I believe what they are reporting is that the Indians fired on Yates' battalion as they retreated across western Calhoun Ridge and Greasy Grass Knoll toward the cemetery area and Last Stand Hill, and at some of the horsemen of Yates' battalion moving toward Keogh's men; they were also firing at Keogh's battalion moving to support Yates.

This news story is a good example of how the first part of Custer's movement and retreat is liable to be accurate because Curley was in a position to see parts of the retreat which are also substantiated by the other scouts. The main question which is not addressed is why Custer would have thought it impractical to cross here at a critical time when he could see women and children fleeing the village in confusion and near panic. A column of fours would restrict the cavalry in crossing, but once they were in the midst of the tepees this would not be that much of a handicap, especially if one considers the Indians' method of fighting. Custer could not have calculated finding a better location to attack, and if his mind was now focused on seeking a defensive position he would have retreated back to the bluffs he had just came across. There he could have expected aid and, as, the article suggests, they had not seen any sign of Indians at that location. Though Custer's move to the ford would not have synchronized in the way he may have wanted with Major Reno's attack, it would have been close to accomplishing it. The retreat appeared quite disorganized and there must be a reason to explain why it was so. Based on my knowledge of Captain Yates, Captain Tom Custer and Lieutenant Smith, if they were still in control of their companies, there would have been signs of an organized retreat rather than the chaotic dispersal that the evidence in the form of artifacts and testimony indicates took place.

The Helena *Herald* article continued:

> ... on other parts of the field than his own, Curley is not well informed, as he was himself concealed in a deep ravine, from which but a small part of the field was visible.
>
> The fight appears to have begun, from Curley's description of the situation of the sun, about 2:30 or 3 o'clock p.m., and continued without intermission until nearly sunset. The Indians had completely surrounded the command, leaving their horses in ravines well to the rear, themselves pressing forward to attack on foot... .they made several charges on all points of Custer's line, but the troops held their positions firmly, and delivered a heavy fire, and every time drove them back. Curley says the firing was more rapid than anything he had ever conceived of, ... The troops expended all the ammunition in their belts, and then sought their horses for the reserve ammunition carried in their saddle pockets.
>
> As long as their ammunition held out, the troops, though losing considerably in the fight, maintained their position in spite of all the efforts of the Sioux. From the weakening of their fire towards the close of the afternoon the Indians appeared to believe that their ammunition was about exhausted, and they made a grand final charge, in the course of which the last of the command was destroyed, the men being shot, where they laid in their positions in line ... Custer remained alive through the greater part of the engagement, animating his men to determined resistance; but, about an hour before the close of the fight, received a mortal wound.
>
> Curley says the field was thickly strewn with the dead bodies of the Sioux who fell in the attack number considerably more than the force of the soldiers engaged. He is satisfied that their loss will exceed 300 killed, besides an immense number wounded. Curley accomplished his escape by drawing his blanket about him in the manner of the Sioux, and passing through an interval which had been made in their line as they scattered over the field in their final charge ...
>
> In most particulars that account given by Curley of the fight is confirmed by the position of the trail made by Custer in his movements, and the general evidence of the battlefield. Only one discrepancy is noted, which relates to the time when the fight came to an end.
>
> Officers of Reno's command, ... say that no fighting was going on at that time- between five and six o'clock.[4]

This is a typical example of a news story marred by errors which significantly distort the picture. One can see the problem interpreters or reporters have with the Curley interviews. Curley more than likely gave the same account he had given before, but this would not be enough to make a good story of what happened. The journalists would see the necessity to make up a story which would be sensational enough to be newsworthy.

If Curley didn't know what was happening elsewhere, he certainly learned a lot by the time of the General Scott interview as to what Reno and the Rees were doing. We know the troops didn't run out of ammunition. The number of Indians killed was way too high, and with the dust, confusion, and excitement, Curley would not have had any idea how many that was. As writers have pointed out repeatedly, the use of a blanket would only have drawn more attention. Stories such as this may make for interesting reading, but they are certainly inaccurate and misleading.

The most important of the Camp-Curley interviews would be the one in 1908 which took place at the battlefield:

> On Sept. 18, 1908, the Crow Curley, scout with Custer on June 25, 1876, accompanied me on a visit to the vicinity of the burning tepee and from there back over Custer's route to the battlefield. On this day, he, with three other Crows, were with Mitch Bouyer, two other Crow scouts; White Swan and Half Yellow Face, were with Gerard. At this time Curley was 20 years old.
>
> He directed me to the site of the big Sioux camp, all of which, with the exception of the lone tepee ... had been moved in advance of Custer's arrival. This was located on the north side of Benteen Creek (Walter Camp also identifies Benteen Creek as Reno Creek. It is identified by Indians as Ash Creek and by Lt. Godfrey as Sundance Creek) about 4 miles from the Little Big Horn, on a wide and smooth piece of ground gently sloping toward the Creek. When we arrived on this ground, Curley drew my attention to rotten pieces of wood lying about, which he said had been carried there by the Sioux for their camp fires ...
>
> The site of the burning tepee he could not locate exactly, ... His means of identifying the locality was a high rocky bluff, from which he with Mitch Bouyer and three other Crow scouts, had been watching the Sioux with field glasses all that forenoon before the arrival of Custer's command ...
>
> From this point he went with Custer's battalion as it came along, and when Custer diverged from Reno's trail, about 1 1/2 miles from the river, Bouyer and his four Crows went with Custer. Custer's route from this point was directly across the country, on the crest of a long ridge running to the bluffs and coming out about 500 ft. north of the Reno Corral.[5]

This version would coincide with another report in which Curley seems to suggest that Custer's command came on the ridge just south of Sharpshooter Hill. This is why, if they had been in a line formation as Kanipe stated, it would have been only when progressing to the ridge; as they moved onto the ridge, they would have shifted into a column formation.

> ... From here Custer passed along the crest of the bluffs for full 3/4 mile, in full view of river and of the valley across it. Custer hurried his men, going at a gallop most of the time. Reno and his command were plainly seen by Custer's whole command while marching this 3/4 mile.[6]

This three quarters of a mile would have taken them to Weir Point. Sergeant Roy reported that Reno's troops saw Custer's troops on the ridge while they were realigning.[7] Martin said he didn't see Major Reno's command at that time. There would not be any reason why Curley or his interviewers would distort facts about Custer's move to this point. The discrepancy could be and probably is tied up with a timing difference and illustrates the closeness between Major Reno's move down the valley and General Custer's move along the ridge. Curley said the scouts were following Custer at that time, so they were probably aware of Reno beginning his two-mile jaunt down the valley. At the same time, Custer, more then likely, did not wait for the whole command to gain the ridge but would have moved some distance ahead to Weir Point. Trumpeter Martin would not have been aware of Reno beginning his move down the valley, nor possibly did Custer. The position of the command, combined with the dust and topography could have effectively blocked off any view of Reno's troops. However, one could expect that the scouts as well as Kanipe and many of Custer's men saw Reno's battalion.

Curley goes on – or one should say, Hammer, who compiled Walter Camp's notes:

> ... On the first line of bluffs back from the river there are two high peaks marked "A": on the map,...(fn. 3 – ... Camp uses the terms Reno peaks, Edgerly peaks, and Weir peaks interchangeably.) now called Reno peaks. For some distance south of these there is a high ridge running parallel with the river but not so high as the peaks. Custer's command passed into the valley of a tributary of Reno Creek (fn. 4 – this reference to Reno Creek and later references are confusing and misleading. Camp almost undoubtedly was referring to Cedar Coulee as the tributary and by Reno Creek he was referring to Medicine Tail Coulee.) just behind this ridge and the peaks and went down it going in a direction directly north and coming out into the bed of Reno Creek about a mile from its mouth at Ford B.[8]

Why Hammer believed that Camp was referring to Cedar Coulee I wouldn't know. It seems quite obvious that he meant Weir Point, which is at the end of this ridge; General Custer went down these peaks, directly north. The place "directly north" can only be the Middle Coulee or the "Gorge," given Curley's use of the word "north" after he left Weir Point, although Middle Coulee lies in a northeast direction and away from the Indian village. If Custer had taken Cedar Coulee he would have come although out a good mile and three quarters from Ford B, whereas Middle Coulee comes into Medicine Tail Coulee about a mile from its mouth or Ford B.

Curley's 1908 report continues:

> From the moment Custer's command commenced to descend this tributary of Reno Creek, it passed out of view of Reno's battalion, but Bouyer and his four scouts kept to the left of Custer, on the crest of the high ridge and peaks, and at all times could command a view of the river and the bottoms beyond. Before Bouyer got to the peaks, he left three of his Crow scouts behind, with orders to watch the Indian camp in the valley opposite and any movement of Indians in Custer's rear. Taking Curley with him, he passed on and over the peaks, and then on a course parallel with that of Custer (directly north) until they came down into the bed of Reno Creek, where they met Custer about a 1/2 mile from the river.[9]

One point which is not clear in any of the accounts – and often involves contradictory statements in the testimony of the same individual – is the question of whether the Crows separated, and, if so, where? I think there is credence to what Curly told Camp in the interview. The following may have taken place: Custer arrived on the ridge several hundred yards ahead of the rest of his command. He spoke briefly to Bouyer and the four Crow scouts, then moved back to meet his troops as they arrived on the ridge. The command then followed Custer down the ridge. Bouyer, on Custer's advice, told the three Crows to follow the command and check on any Indian action to the rear of the troops. Bouyer and Curley moved on to Weir Point just after Custer's lead companies had moved off the ridge. After the command left, the three Crows joined Bouyer and Curley. More than likely, somewhere between Weir Point and Bouyer's Bluff, Curley was told to go back. However, he remained in the vicinity. Curley then must have been aware of Reno's action in the valley, the Crows firing on the village (it is possible he was still with them), Bouyer going down to meet Custer, and Custer moving to the ford. It is also possible that he witnessed the beginning of Custer's retreat. Curley then left, either with the other scouts, or on his own, but, one way or another, they ended up together near Reno Hill. Curley – or I should say his interpreters – are fairly honest in describing events that Curley witnessed while on the ridge. They disagree on whether the three Crows went as far as the bluff overlooking the ford. One interpreter has Curley saying: "These three Crows were with Bouyer and me as far as the Bluff at the cut bank just south of Ford B and about 1500 ft. from that ford." According to Curley's interpreter, then, the three Crows "turned tail" and he went with Bouyer to meet Custer.[10] I don't believe Curley altered his statements, but if he was to be made a hero there was no way he could be allowed to have turned back while on the ridge: that would mean that Curley had done nothing more than the other scouts who were being censured for their actions. Curley would not only have done nothing more than the other scouts, but, actually less, as he would have left before they did. The only solution for the interpreters, recorders and reporters was to have Curley going with Bouyer to meet Custer. They coordinated information about what Curley had seen from the ridge with what was perceived to have happened afterwards to General Custer. Curley, of course, would have to have been ordered to leave the battlefield before the end came, otherwise, he would have stayed with Custer. As views of the battle changed, so did Curley's accounts. This is apparent in the records, for in early versions Custer goes to the ford with his troops, but in later accounts only a company or two are sent by Custer and he never goes to the ford himself. I think one is fairly safe in saying that Curley didn't change his story; his interpreters did.

The last sentence in his 1908 interview gives additional support to the idea that Custer went down Middle Coulee and not Cedar Coulee. According to Curley, he and Bouyer went along a course parallel with Custer's and directly north, until they came to Medicine Tail Coulee, or what Camp is calling Reno Creek. Although we don't find any of the coulees which run directly north, Middle Coulee from Weir Point is more apt to fit this description. If Custer was moving down Cedar Coulee, Bouyer could not have been going along the crest of the ridge to Bouyer's or Crow's Bluff and referred to it as " directly north" while moving parallel to Custer's command.

> When they got to the top of the first of these peaks, they looked across and observed Reno's command was fighting. At the sight of this, Bouyer could hardly restrain himself and shouted and waved his hat excitedly for some little time. Undoubtedly, Bouyer is the man seen by some in Reno's command to wave his hat, for Custer never went to the high peaks or high ridge; and when the hat was waved Custer was entirely out of sight from Reno's position and must have been for several minutes.[11]

The scouts, as they moved along the crest of the ridge, should have observed Major Reno's move down the valley, and indicated they had in their interviews. Consequently, Curley's contention that Mitch Bouyer and he went to Weir Peak and noticed Reno fighting in the valley substantiates the position. Curley maintained in most of his interviews that Custer, who would already have left the ridge, did not see Reno fighting. On the other hand, it does conflict with another part of Curley's testimony in which he and Bouyer observed a peaceful village. Both observations could be true, depending on how long they remained on Weir Peak.

In the interview, Curley contended that Custer's command moved along the high ridge. I believe the scouts were trailing the command. As brought out before, the three may have been ordered to bring up the rear while Bouyer and Curley moved to Weir Point during the time the command was leaving. They would not necessarily have been aware of Custer going up Weir Point. This could also have been the case with Sergeant Kanipe. Trumpeter Martin maintained he did not see the scouts at that time, and his statement would also bear out such a view.

I don't particularly see why Reno's engagement would cause Bouyer to become so excited, and I would question his response unless there could have been a pre-arranged signal for Custer to know Reno had engaged the enemy. I can't see Bouyer reacting so strongly for an extended period of time just because Major Reno had gone into action. It appears to be more of an attempt to correlate Curley's story with the hat waving credited to Custer. It is also difficult to understand why Camp or Hammer believe that this is what Reno's troops saw, because the soldiers at that time must have been setting up their skirmish line and actually engaging the Indians. It's hard to imagine them gazing around in those circumstances. The troopers said they saw Custer either before they started or on their way down the valley. This version would not coincide with Lieutenant Varnum's sighting of the Gray Horse Troop. From a time standpoint, it would be closer to Lieutenant DeRudio's observations; however, DeRudio said he recognized not only Custer and his blouse but also Adjutant Cooke and his whiskers.

The Camp interview continues:

> ... After Bouyer and Curley joined Custer, the command passed rapidly down to Ford B. As soon as the soldiers came in sight of the village, the Sioux gave voice to a "heap big yell, like dog," as Curley expressed it, and

when Custer's soldiers got close, there was "heap shoot, bang! bang! The troops did not dismount here, and some of them rode into the river before stopping and turning back. Curley saw one soldier gallop across the river just below the ford at great speed, pass up the bank, through the Sioux posted along it, and come out into full view on the open ground beyond the ford. The Sioux defending the ford he observed to be all dismounted. He afterwards learned that these were men who did not have time to get their ponies, which were grazing back on the hills west of the village.[12]

All of this Curley could have seen from one of the peaks or ridges, and, in fact, it actually discredits his own account of being with Bouyer and Custer. There are reports that one soldier did cross into the village, go through it, and ended up with Major Reno. This would indicate that, initially, the number of Indians by the ford was small and the main body of their forces was still going toward Reno, although the reverse movement should have been starting by that time. It is surprising that this daring, lone trooper was never questioned. In his interview the next year, Curley mentions a noncommissioned officer who crossed into the village and was killed there. A similar story is found in other reports. The reference to the Indians defending the ford being dismounted because they had not been able to get their ponies would support the view that an element of surprise was involved, and that Custer's move to the ford took place shortly after Reno's attack.

> When Custer withdrew from the ford, he proceeded down the river for some distance and then struck out for higher ground in column of fours, going direct to the point where markers are found at the southeast point of the battlefield. Before they got to this point, Mitch Bouyer lost his horse. Indians were now in front and in the ravines on both sides, and a strong force of Indians were coming up in the rear. Curley says the command was being driven like a herd of horses, and the only thing that could be done was to charge the enemy in the direction that was thought to be the most advantageous to go and then only to have them close in on all sides. The front was driving the Indians and the rear was being driven. In ascending to the elevation now marked by slabs for Calhoun and Crittenden, an attempt was made to cover the retreat until some kind of a stand could be made. Men were left at the Finley marker, and some of the troops dismounted just beyond this, Curley staking his horse with the rest. The dismounted men then tried to drive the Indians from the gulch ahead, but the men left in the rear were quickly killed, and the advance of the Indians from that direction was hardly checked at all.[13]

In reading the rest of Curley's account, one might wonder how he managed to return to his horse.

Curley does not suggest that there was any sign of an attack or an organized retreat by Custer. Even in the last stages of the battle, Indians fell back from what were only attempts to escape by a comparatively few men. A mounted move back toward the packs and Benteen would have caused the Indians to fall away from in front of the advancing troops, and like Major Reno's retreat from the timber, it might have cost a number of lives, but with some organization and discipline it was feasible. An organized defensive retreat should have enabled the troops to establish a defensive position in several areas which they could have held. The odd twist is the condemnation of Major Reno, the questioning of his ability and effectiveness as an officer, the criticism of his failure to attack and to organize a proper retreat, while very little criticism is aimed at General Custer. Attack and retreat are basic military maneuvers. Major Reno was not considered to be one of our great military leaders, whereas General Custer certainly was. Yet in these versions of the events we find General Custer neither conducting an attack, nor organizing a retreat. Why?

> ... Custer stopped at this point for a brief space of time, and what was decided upon had to be done in great haste. There was a hurried conference of officers, and Bouyer told Curley that the subject of conversation was to the effect that if the command could make a stand somewhere, the remainder of the regiment would probably soon come up and relieve them. Personally, Bouyer did not expect that relief would come, as he thought the orders would be to charge straight ahead, drive the Indians from the ravine and try to find more favorable ground. For a moment or two the fire of the Indians slackened in this direction, and it was thought the plan could be carried out, when a large force of warriors swept around that corner, as if in anticipation of the intentions of the soldiers, and the scheme had to be given up. There was then "heap shoot, shoot, shoot" ... It was now plain that no advance could be made in the intended direction, and Custer struck out westward, it being understood that some of the soldiers (probably Calhoun's troop) would try to hold the ground at this corner.[14]

I can't envision this scene. The troops had been retreating for over a mile, with Indians on all sides, and now they hold a conference and supposedly decide to either attack or find an area where they could set up an adequate defense. Indians get in front of them, so they don't attack. They are still, supposedly, together and organized, and led by an attack-orientated commander who knows that to be effective a cavalry should be on the offensive; he also knows that Indians have fallen back from such moves; but again, this great cavalry leader fails to launch an attack. They then, supposedly, strike out westward which would be, to a degree, in the direction where Curley has said the troopers in the rear were being killed, and also toward the place most writers identify as the location of the Indian encampment. If General Custer was still in control of organized troops at this time, it is impossible for me to believe he would not have launched an attack or retreated to the area of Nye Cartwright or Luce Ridge, and depending on the situation at that stage, either continued toward the packs or set up a defensive position. Curley even mentions their concern and hope for the rest of the regiment to come to their aid. They had to have been aware by then of the overwhelming number of Indians they were facing, and the movement Curley describes would only benefit the Indians. There is no mention in the accounts of any firing from Nye Cartwright or Luce Ridge. It is only in later revisions such as Curley's death-bed stories given by Russell White Bear, that Custer is crossing these ridges. What Curley, through his interpreters, related to Camp seems to be based on knowledge of where bodies were found and suggests the creation of fictional events related to various Indian stories.

Curley says, however, that the men would not stand, all who could do so either going for their horses or running in the direction of the general retreat, which was headed for the highest ground, now occupied by the monument. In doing so they had to run the gauntlet of a fire from the ravine full of warriors to the northward and a large force of Indians shooting over the long ridge extending westerly to the monument. Curley said that while on the way to where the Calhoun marker now stands, a few men had started in the direction of the monument along the south side of the ridge, but as the Indians charged up from the direction of the river these men were driven over the crest and fell in with the line of retreat.

Most of the men able to do so had now followed the line of retreat down the gully and diagonally up the slope toward the monument. In this the men with the gray horses appeared to be keeping well together, but it seemed to him that the other companies were getting badly mixed up.[15]

It is remarkable that when others were seemingly giving in to panic amid the dust, confusion and excitement, Curley could be so well in command and able to distinguish what was going on.

Mitch Bouyer now turned to Curley, saying that Tom Custer had suggested that the scouts had better save themselves if they could. Bouyer advised Curley to try it, and Curley said he told Bouyer he would do so if he (Bouyer) also would try it. [How courageous of Curley.] Bouyer declined by saying that he was too badly wounded, and he would have to stay to fight it out, although he believed they would all be killed. Curley now decided to stay no longer. He turned around to look for his horse and there he found a hand-to-hand encounter. As for him, the Sioux were a little too quick and he saw a warrior running off with his horse at the end of the lariat. Just then a wounded Indian was shot off his pony. Catching the warrior's horse and taking his Winchester and belt of cartridges to replace his own weapon, which was dirty and working badly, he mounted and rode out. The mass of Indians had now charged around on the flanks of the retreating soldiers, and Curley, by riding around the corner as though one of the charging Indians and giving voice to the Sioux yell or war cry, passed out without being recognized and was soon in a ravine out of sight. He went up the right hand ravine (to the right of Godfrey's spring), and stopped to look back only twice. He estimates that his last look at the battlefield must have been one half hour after leaving, and the soldiers were still fighting.... He traveled on a wide circuit and met the steamer *Far West* lying at the mouth of the Little Big Horn, where he got aboard and remained for several days.[16]

I will only go over parts of Curley's interview with Camp on August, 3rd and 4th, 1909:

"... While we were here, Custer's command hove in sight galloping right down the coulee toward the river. Bouyer now said he would cut across and meet it, and he started down off the east slope of the bluff and I with him.... Here Hairy Moccasin, Goes Ahead, and White Man Runs Him got away when Mitch Bouyer went down to see what Custer intended to do, as Custer was coming down Dry Creek. Then the 3 Crows skipped out without leave and went south along bluffs. This was the last I saw of them until I met them on the Yellowstone some weeks later...."

Custer's route, according to Curley: Custer left coulee of Dry Creek 900 ft. east of its mouth and struck the river 1,000 ft. downstream from its mouth. It is about 900 ft. further to the first high cut bank. It appeared to Curley here that Custer would charge across into the village, but the west bank was thick with dismounted Sioux, and back in the village hundreds of mounted ones were coming up. Good many soldiers got nearly into the water and one got across and was killed in the village. He was some noncommissioned officer. The hot fire then impressed Curley with the idea that it would be necessary for Custer to retreat and he did so, going in a direction downstream and quartering back upon the high ridge.[17]

The above directions are vague. Curley may have been separating the mouth of South Medicine Tail Coulee from that of North Medicine Tail or Deep Coulee. The command would then have moved back along the cut bank, but this would be a retreat on the part of the troops and by so doing Custer would suggest that he had no plans of attacking elsewhere. It is difficult to picture Curley being down among these troops and having such a firm grasp on the whole scene of events. One should note that in Curley's story the Indians are now thick on the other side of the ford, which would mean they were not concealed. Curley's testimony is contradicting not only his own accounts but also those of the Sioux and Cheyenne.

> While Custer's firing at the cut bank was in progress, I saw no large body of Indians fording, but as soon as we began to retreat they must have swarmed across both above and below us, for we had not proceeded one-third of the way to the ridge before the Sioux were thick upon both our right and left flanks firing into us heavily...Going up from the river, Sioux on all sides except front. Mitch Bouyer told me to keep out of the skirmish as much as possible as they might wish to send me with a dispatch to the other troops.[18]

With all the Indians in the rear and on both sides and no Indians in front, it seems that the troops would have proceeded back toward the packs or moved to Nye Cartwright or Luce Ridge to set up a defense.

> ...I escaped by riding to the right and front, through dust and powder smoke, pulling over my head a cape made by cutting up blankets, which I had tied to my saddle [Curley did not lose his own horse but found one when leaving. Picked up a Sioux blanket separately, Curley left and came south nearly to Dry Creek] Then ...turning the point of the hill (where Sergeant Butler was found). As I did this, I passed a dead Sioux who had been killed by the fire of the soldiers on their retreat up from the river. I dismounted quickly and seized his gun. [What kind of gun did he take from the dead Sioux and what did he do with his own? Took Winchester, threw his own away] "and cartridge belt. Further on, and on the north slope of the coulee of Dry Creek, rather out of view from the battle in progress. I caught up with a loose Sioux pony which I led along with me until I came to the steamer."[19]

As Graham and others have noted, Curley's pulling a blanket over his head would have drawn attention instead of producing the opposite effect. It is a little hard to visualize Curley cutting holes in his blanket with the Sioux and Cheyenne around him. In his 1908 interview, Curley claimed that he became engaged in hand-to-hand encounter with a Sioux warrior, and either this Sioux or some other escaped with his horse. However, in 1909, Curley maintained that he didn't lose his horse but did gain a Sioux pony after he left the scene of the battle. I am not sure just where Godfrey's spring is, but my impression would be that in his 1908 version Curley moved away from the battle by going more to the east, whereas in 1909 he appeared to be going to the southeast. In the 1908 account, a wounded Sioux apparently was shot off his horse where Curley had left his own, so he was able to take the dead man's horse. In the 1909 version Curley, after leaving the battle scene, found a Sioux pony which he took back with him to the steamer. The dead Sioux from whom Curley, according to his 1909 interview, picked up the gun, was near where Sgt. Butler's body was found. The Sioux was, reportedly, shot during the soldiers' retreat from the river. This is hard to accept, considering Curley's account of the route followed by the retreating soldiers, although there is always the possibility he could have been killed by long distance fire.

> Curley's story explains why troopers found dead were so mixed up, members of Troop C being found on all parts of the field. This was a puzzle to Knipe until he heard this story. Daniel Knipe who had carried a message from Custer to McDougall, was with Walter Camp on the battlefield.
>
> Curley's story has been both believed and disbelieved. As to the disbelief, I have never heard or seen in print the least particle of reliable evidence to prove that he was not in the beginning of the fight, as he states. His story throughout agrees with other authentic accounts.[20]

I don't know what Camp considers to be the other authentic accounts. I realize anyone familiar with the battlefield could fabricate a story which could sound authentic. However, Curley's would appear more authentic if, in the numerous interviews, his story would have remained essentially the same.

As I have previously said, Curley's accounts of the events, until Bouyer went down to meet Custer, generally coincide with other accounts and are consistent in themselves. But from that point on, they vary from interview to interview. Walter Camp should certainly have been aware of these discrepancies and should have given his explanation for the inconsistencies.

Curley interview, July 19, 1910 – Fred Old Horn, Interpreter:

... How much of Reno's battle did Curley see? Did he see Reno's retreat? "Yes, saw retreat and Bouyer then gave signal to Custer. Custer and Tom Custer returned signal by waving hats, and men cheered." Hairy Moccasin, White Man Runs Him and Goes Ahead must have left Bouyer before Reno's battle ended because while Reno was retreating they were down near Ford A. (Camp undoubtedly meant Ford B) I therefore think that (Curley) and Bouyer went from bluff down in to Medicine Tail Coulee to meet Custer. Did Custer remain any length of time? "No, kept going right on." Also, whether Custer stopped in Medicine Tail Coulee any considerable length of time? What he was doing there etc., or why he was waiting? "Did not stop."[21]

I don't think it is possible for Bouyer to have seen Reno's retreat. One should recall Curley's statement in another interview that Bouyer saw Reno engaged, and that he was excited and waved his hat for some time. This was after Custer had left the ridge and gone out of sight of Major Reno. Custer should not have taken over fifteen minutes to have reached the ford or Medicine Tail Coulee. For Bouyer to have seen Reno establish his skirmish line, then his retreat, and still meet Custer a half mile from the ford would mean Reno could not have been fighting in the valley over ten minutes. This would have been impossible.

According to Camp's notes, Hairy Moccasin, White Man Runs Him and Goes Ahead would have left Bouyer before Reno's battle ended, because, while Reno was retreating they were down near Ford A. Hammer felt that Camp had made a mistake and meant Ford B; but this was not an error on Camp's part. It bears out what I have just mentioned that Bouyer could not have seen Reno's retreat. It is a timing sequence which would mean that at the time Custer reached Ford B, Reno would still have been on his skirmish line or in the timber. As is obvious from General Scott's interview with White Man Runs Him and Curley, as well as Arikara testimony, the Crow scouts would have been in the area of Reno or Ash Creek at the time Reno's troops reached the bluffs. Their meeting with Captain Benteen would further support this version.

In his work, Camp asks several questions for which he should have insisted on receiving an answer; something it appears he didn't do. The questions are: What was the formation in retreating up from the river, column or skirmish line? What officers did Curley see on this retreat and where was he, in front or rear? What was Custer doing down by the river and how long did he wait down there? "No time at all" was the reply to the last question, but the other two were never answered. In fact, a number of other more pertinent questions should have been asked.

"Did he see any soldiers on top of Greasy Grass hill while he was on the flat or at any other time? "Yes, 10 or 15 went up and along the ridge, probably guides or flankers, When whole command was at Finley, the volleys were fired, and they were fired at the Sioux who were closing in."

Curley got away to 4 markers at extreme southeast. While here the Indians were killing soldiers over by Finley, and all soldiers halted there. Sioux were on all sides shooting. Soldiers were dismounted and leading horses and firing at Sioux best they could. Sioux were all along on Custer Ridge. Mitch Bouyer said "You had better leave now for we will all be cleaned out." . . . "Bouyer told me to ride out through the coulee over to the east. Bouyer had just been talking with General Custer and Custer's brother Tom, and then he came and told me this."

From where Curley left at the 4 markers, the bearing to coulee up which he rode is N81 deg. E or 9 deg. north of east natural bearings . . . When I rode out, there were no Sioux in front. I had a cape and cap made of a blanket and threw it over my head and rode out in disguise. The Sioux gave chase, but my horse was too fast, and they did not pursue far and I soon got away from them. Not sure they knew me to be a Crow. I rode up the coulee to the head of it and over the distant ridge. I had my own gun, a Winchester, and leggin's on."[22]

This indicates Curley was moving out to the northeast, which would not place him near where Sergeant Butler's body was found, or the dead Sioux he previously referred to. His disguise must not have been too effective. He did not state in the other Camp interviews that he was chased by the Sioux. Nothing is said about his hand-to-hand encounter or his horse being taken by the Sioux. Now he appears to have his own gun, not the one he picked up from the Sioux, and he does not have an extra horse.

One more interview with Curley needs to be included in my discussion. It is with a Crow friend and an interpreter used by General Scott in his interview with Curley and White Man Runs Him. The Indian was Russell White Bear. In this case the exchange of information wasn't exactly an interview. Curley and White Bear were friends, and this account, according to White Bear, was Curley's last before he died. There are two similar letters written by White Bear, one according to Colonel Graham was to a mutual friend, and the other to Fred Dustin. Graham includes these in his book, *The Custer Myth*. In his accounts, White Bear mentions several comments which coincide with views expressed by Dustin and other writers at that time. For example, Curley said that:

Custer, after leaving Major Reno's command and on

reaching Medicine Tail Creek, halted his command, and here the men rearranged their saddles. Custer at this point gave a trooper a paper and after a brief conversation the trooper rode away heading north. This trooper rode a sorrel-roan horse.[23]

In White Bear's letter to Dustin, the same "last story" differs: the soldiers didn't stop directly after they entered Medicine Tail Coulee, but only after they had moved down the coulee and made several maneuvers. White Bear, in his letter, doesn't give the direction taken by the courier. It appears to me that White Bear was including a messenger in Curley's account only because by that time the Frank Finkel story had appeared, and so his reference to the messenger could be used to give further credence to Curley's stories.

In the Dustin letter, Russell White Bear has Curley saying:

> He (Custer) did not ask Bouyer or me about the country [I presume to justify Custer going down Cedar Coulee] and seeing we were a long way from the valley – Custer – turning left rode down Medicine Tail. After riding awhile, he halted the command – then the Gray Horse Troop left us and started down the creek – when we turned north – crossing Medicine Tail Creek going on the hills north of the creek – here the command halted again . . .[24]

Note that Bouyer and Curley would now have come down Cedar Coulee with Custer, or they must have traveled some distance up Medicine Tail Coulee to have reached the command from the bluff above Ford B. So how was Bouyer able to signal Custer who would have been close to two miles away and separated from him by ridges? In his previous statements, Curley maintained that Bouyer not only signaled but was able to recognize General Custer and Captain Custer. Now Custer doesn't move to the ford. One writer after reading White Bear's "last story," stated that Curley on his death bed was, finally, not misinterpreted, as he had been for years, when he said that Custer moved to the ford without stopping.

White Bear continues:

> Custer wrote a message and handed it to a young man – on a sorrel roan horse – who galloped away. Bouyer called to him and said – 'Curley, you better leave us here,' he said. 'You ride back over the trail a ways and then go to one of the high points' – pointing eastward over to the high ridge east of the Custer Hill . . .[25]

All the fighting and retreating which was discussed in Curley's other accounts is now absent. One should take special notice of how Curley's accounts changed over the years to reflect the revision of writer's scenarios. At first Custer supposedly went to the ford; then, in later years, some writers suggested that Custer didn't go to the ford, but instead crossed Medicine Tail Coulee. Others claimed that only the Gray Horse Troops were sent to the ford. These changes are reflected in Curley's interviews.

Initially, there was the desire to make a hero out of Curley, and to do this it was necessary to insure his presence with Custer through as much of the action as possible. This was more than likely the work of the interpreter or the recorder, rather than Curley. It was quite easy to build a fairly sound general picture which would match the locations of where bodies were found with the accepted view of what had transpired. The trouble was with a small number of details which would not fit the overall scenario, and they were often adjusted to make them noteworthy or to improve the impact of the story.

This is why one has to be careful in accepting only supporting statements of a scenario without relating it to other testimony by the same person. One also has to relate those to accounts by others in order to develop a logical version of what happened. This view must correlate with time, distance and artifactual evidence, and then one must add psychological factors in order to present a picture which although conjectural, would stand up to any logical sequential examination.

I believe that Curley's accounts are fairly accurate until the time when he and Bouyer go down to join Custer. Even the first part of the retreat, in some interviews, could be close to what actually happened, but as seen from the ridge before moving back to Reno Creek, and not from within the midst of the command. As with other testimony, timing and exact locations can be imprecise but the overall picture should fit within the above framework. Curley's statements are believable until he or others attempt to portray him as being with General Custer during the actual fighting. Then the accounts become too varied and are undoubtedly reflecting the view of the person responsible for the interviews. Whether Curley is responding to the interviewer or the interpreter who would be more aware of the interrogators views, is irrelevant. As I have said, I believe General Scott's is the only accurate interview describing what happened to Curley that day. It correlates in terms of timing, distance and sequence of events with the testimony of the other Crows, Rees, Trumpeter Martin and troopers.

The most obvious reason for rejecting Curley's accounts of being with Custer during the initial phase of the battle is his uncertainty as to whether he rode his own horse or not when he left. There are a number of things a person could become confused about in the course of a battle, but whether you rode the same horse upon leaving the battle as when entering it, is not something one would hesitate about if the truth was being told.

I think there was a good possibility that Curley met Black Fox along Reno Creek, near the Little Bighorn, and they then moved northeast. From a high hill they saw the last phase of the fighting around Last Stand Hill. Interpreters then used some of Curley's remarks in a context of their choice. For example, they placed Curley's viewing from a high hill at the time he left Custer, when, in fact, it transpired when Curley fled from the Reno Hill area.

This scenario would also be supplemented by the time difference between when the three Crow scouts, White Man Runs Him, Goes Ahead and Hairy Moccasin left the Reno entrenchment area and were seen early in the morning of the 26th by General Terry's and Colonel Gibbon's troops, and when Curley reached the steamboat (in the same location) but in mid-afternoon or 24 hours after leaving Custer's command. The question then raised by Dr. Marquis, in his account, *Rain-in-the-Face and Curley, The Crow,* is certainly appropriate: Why did it take Curley more than 24 hours to reach the steamboat when it was less than eight miles from the battlefield?[26] Particularly, when most reports would have Curley intent on carrying a message to the Terry-Gibbon forces. However, if Curley had met Black Fox near the mouth of Reno Creek, and they then went after the hard tack, this could account for the difference; it certainly is strong supportive confirmation for my view of Curley's actions.

SOURCES

1. Graham, *The Custer Myth*, pp. 7-9.
2. Ibid., pp. 10-11.
3. Miller, D. H., "Echoes of the Little Big Horn," *American Heritage* (June, 1971; Miller, *Custer's Fall*, p. 131.
4. Graham, *The Custer Myth*, p.11.
5. Hammer, ed., *Camp, Custer in 76*, p. 155.
6. Ibid., p. 156.
7. Ibid., p. 112.
8. Ibid., p. 156.
9. Ibid., p. 157.
10. Ibid., p. 162.
11. Ibid., p. 157.
12. Ibid., p. 158.
13. Ibid., pp. 157-158.
14. Ibid., p. 158.
15. Ibid., pp. 158-159.
16. Ibid., p. 159.
17. Ibid., p. 162.
18. Ibid., p. 162.
19. Ibid., p. 163.
20. Ibid., p. 164.
21. Ibid., pp. 166-167.
22. Ibid., p. 167.
23. Graham, *The Custer Myth*, pp. 18-19.
24. Ibid., p. 19.
25. Ibid., p. 19.
26. Marquis, *Rain-in-the-Face and Curley, The Crow*, np.

12
Sioux and Cheyenne Testimony

Wooden Leg
Cheyenne
Book by T. B. Marquis

Page 216: The Cheyenne horses were put to graze on the valley below our camp. Horses belonging to other tribes were placed at other feeding areas on the valley and on the bench hills just west of the combined Indian camps. Boys from each tribe guarded their horse bands. An occasional riding horse was picketed near to or within each camp circle. . . . particularly among the policemen, who picketed a horse for ready use.

I had no thought then of any fighting to be done in the near future. We had driven away the soldiers on the upper Rosebud, seven days ago. It seemed likely it would be a long time before they would trouble us again. . . . I was eighteen years old, and I liked girls.

That night we had a dance . . .

"Let's go and dance awhile with the Sioux girls."

Four of us went to the neighboring camp, that of the Arrows All Gone Sioux.

. . .At the first sign of dawn the dance ended.

. . .When I awoke I went into the family lodge . . . My brother Yellow Hair and I went together (to swim). Other Indians, of all ages and both sexes, were splashing in the waters of the river. The sun was high, the weather was hot. . . . we came out and sought the shelter of some shade trees. . . . Before we knew it, both of us were sound asleep.

Page 217: . . . My brother too awakened, and we both jumped to our feet. A great commotion was going on among the camps. We heard shooting . . . the shooting was somewhere at the upper part of the camp circles. It looked as if all the Indians there were running away toward the hills to the westward or down toward our end of the village. Women were screaming and men were letting out war cries.

We ran to our camp and to our home lodge . . . Women were hurriedly making up little packs for flight. Some were going off northward or across the river without any packs. Children were hunting for their mothers. Mothers were anxiously trying to find their children. . . . I hastened on down toward where had been our horse herd. I came across three of our herder boys. One of them was catching grasshoppers. The other two were cooking fish in the blaze of a little fire. I told them what was going on and asked them where were our horses. They jumped on their picketed ponies and dashed for camp, without answering me. . . . Two other boys were driving them toward the camp circle. I was utterly winded from the running . . . I walked on back to the home lodge.

My father had caught my favorite horse . . . I quickly emptied my war bag and set myself at getting ready to go into battle. . . . "Hurry," he urged me.

I was hurrying, but I was not yet ready. . . . I got my paints and my little mirror.

. . . I combed my hair. It properly should have been oiled and braided neatly, but my father was saying, "Hurry," . . . In a moment afterward I was on my horse and was going as fast as it could run toward where all of the rest of the young men were going. My brother had already gone . . .

The air was so full of dust I could not see where to go. . . . I was led out around and far beyond the Uncpapa camp circle. Many hundreds of Indians on horseback were dashing to an fro in front of a body of soldiers. The soldiers were on the level valley ground and were shooting rifles. Not many bullets were being sent back at them but thousands of arrows. . . . I went on with a throng of Sioux until we got beyond and behind the white men. By this time, though, they had mounted their horses and were hiding themselves in the timber. A band of Indians were with the soldiers . . . Most of these Indians had fled back up the valley. Some were across east of the river . . . .

Our Indians crowded down toward the timber where were the soldiers. More and more of our people kept coming. Almost all of them were Sioux. . . . But we stayed far back while we extended our curved line farther and farther around the big grove of trees. . . . Sioux were creeping forward to set fire to the timber.

Suddenly the hidden soldiers came tearing out on horseback, from the woods. I was around on that side where they came out. I whirled my horse and lashed it into a dash to escape them. All other of my companions did the same. But soon we discovered they were not following us. They were running away from us. They were going as fast as their tired horses could carry them across an open valley space and toward the river. We stopped, looked for a moment, and then we whipped our ponies into swift pursuit. A great throng of Sioux also were coming after them. My distant position put me among the leaders in the chase. The soldier horses moved slowly, as if they were very tired.

Wooden Leg's account, as related by Marquis, agrees with those of both Indians and whites. From the Indian standpoint the surprise is very evident: all of the tribes were concerned with Major Reno's troops, and the Indians' individualism is apparent. (Wooden Leg wasn't looking for orders from White Bull, Two Moons, Gall or any chief.)

Since the Cheyennes were the farthest camp and Wooden Leg was delaying, most warriors who were ready had moved toward Reno's troops and were concerned with their strength. Many were undoubtedly still chasing their horses and some were in their tepees; Wooden Leg was young and could move faster than most. It also seems that Custer was on the ridge and viewed the peaceful village before Reno moved onto his skirmish line, because by all accounts - not only Wooden Leg's - the village erupted after Reno commenced firing. If Wooden Leg could do all the things he did after he heard the firing, certainly Custer should have been able to move to the ford while Reno was still in the timber.

The timing of this phase is interesting. Probably the initial firing which awoke the village took place between the Indian scouts and the Sioux. Still, at least twenty minutes had to have elapsed by the time Wooden Leg went back to his home lodge, then to the horse herd, walked back, braided his hair, partly painted his face, got on his horse and rode to where the fighting was. According to Wooden Leg, Reno was still on his skirmish line. If Curley was correct, as I believe he was, in claiming that Custer himself had moved off the ridge by the time Reno established his skirmish line, it would seem that Custer had plenty of time to reach the ford by the time Reno moved into the timber. Lieutenant Varnum's sighting of the Gray Horse Troop would also suggest a close timing between Reno's setting up his skirmish line and Custer's moving off the ridge: the difference could only involve a few minutes. Wooden Leg's recollection of the difficulty in seeing because of dust and the setting of fires should be considered, especially in DeRudio's account.

An important aspect of Wooden Leg's testimony which has to be considered in analyzing what happened to Custer, is the reaction of the Indians when Reno's troops broke out of the timber. This type of reaction – falling back from the initial break out – is apparent in other battles involving Indians, besides including those on the 25th and 26th. A charge or an attack with five companies would have been noted in Indian testimony; that it wasn't, means that a major attack was never launched. I also believe that those who try to discount Wooden Leg's accounts of the troops appearing to commit suicide, must acknowledge his honesty in indicating his own fear and that of other Indians, and must note those instances where he gives credit to certain soldiers for their bravery.

It should also be recognized that a disorganized retreat can be created and move in a certain direction with merely the appearance of Indians when troops realize they are up against overwhelming numbers. The reactions of the Indians and Reno's troops in the valley are relevant to establishing a view of what happened to Custer in three ways. The first is the effect on the Indians if an attack was launched by Custer against an already frightened village. The second is the effect on Custer's troops when Custer was wounded or killed at the ford. Coupled with the sight of the size of the Indian village and the recognition of the number of Indians they were up against, it would have caused a disorganized retreat which once started would force the troops to the north without the engagement of a significant number of Indians. The third is the possibility of a well-organized retreat. With proper organization, the troops should have had no trouble in retreating back along the path they had come and have been able to join forces with the rest of Custer's command.

". . . You are only boys. You ought not to be fighting. We whipped you on the Rosebud. You should have brought more Crows or Shoshones with you to do your fighting. . . ."

Page 222: Three soldiers on horses got separated from the others and started away up the valley, in the direction from where they had come . . . [Wooden Leg describes how one was killed, one escaped into the timber while the other finally got off his spent horse and was killed in some timber. Wooden Leg reports how bravely he fought. These three may have been the ones One Bull mentioned.]

. . . I returned to the west side of the river. Lots of Indians were hunting around there for dead soldiers or for wounded ones to kill. I joined in the search . . . The warriors were doing this. No old people nor women were there. They all had run away to the hill benches to the westward. Now I felt brave. I jumped upon my horse and went again to fight whatever soldiers had gone up gulches and a backbone ridge to the top of a steep high hill. Indians were all about them. Shots were going toward them and coming from them. I had been there only a short time when somebody said to me:

"Look! Yonder are other soldiers!"

I saw them on distant hills down the river and on our same side of it. The news of them spread quickly among us. Indians began to ride in that direction. Some went along the hills, others went down to cross the river and follow the valley. I took this course. I guided my horse down the steep hillside and forded the river. Back again among the camps I rode on through them to our Cheyenne circle at the lower end of them. As I rode I could see lots of Indians out on the hills across on the east side of the river and fighting the other soldiers, there. I do not know whether all of our warriors left the first soldiers or some of them stayed up there. I suppose, though, that all of them came away from there, as they would be afraid to stay if only a few remained.

Not many people were in the lodges of our camp. Most of the women and children and old Cheyennes were gone to the west side of the valley or to the hills at that side.[Writers should take note as to where the non-combatants fled.] . . . My father was the only person at our lodge. I told him of the fight up the valley. . . . "You have been brave, . . . You have done enough for one day . . ." He turned loose my tired horse and roped my other one from the little herd inside the camp circle. . . . As he was doing this I was making some improvements in my appearance, making the medicine for myself . . . Then I looked a few moments at the battling Indians and soldiers across the river on the hills to the northeastward. Some were yet coming along the hills from where the first soldiers had stopped. The soldiers now in view were spreading themselves into lines along a ridge. The Indians were on lower ridges in front of them, between them and the river, and moving on around up a long coulee to get behind the white men. [He is seeing more than he actually would have at that time – dust and the terrain would have prevented it.]

. . . We forded the river where all of the Indians were crossing it, at the broad shallows immediately in front of the little valley or wide coulee on the east side. We fell in with others, . . .As we approached the place of battle each one chose his own personal course. All of the Indians had come out on horseback. Almost all of them dismounted and crept along the gullies afoot after the arrival near the soldiers. Still, there were hundreds of them riding here and there all the time, most of them merely changing positions, but a few of them racing along back and forth in front of the soldiers . . .

. . . Although it was natural that tribal members should keep together, there was everywhere a mingling of the fighters from all the tribes. The soldiers had come along a high ridge about two miles east from the Cheyenne camp. They had gone on past us and then swerved off the high ridge to the lower ridge where most of them afterward were killed. while they were on the far-out ridge a few Sioux and Cheyenne had exchanged shots with them at long distance, without anybody being hurt. Bobtail Horse, Roan Bear and Buffalo Calf, three Cheyenne and four Sioux warriors with them were said to have been the first of our Indians to cross the river and to go meet the soldiers. Bobtail Horse was an Elk warrior, . . . They had been joined afterward by other Indians from the valley camps and from the southward hills where the first soldiers had taken refuge. (pp. 226, 228, 230)

Wooden Leg doesn't explain why all of the Indians didn't pursue Reno's forces as they crossed the river and moved to the top of the bluffs. He himself did cross over. He mentions nothing of sighting Captain Benteen's troops. Wooden Leg crossed back over, looked for wounded or dead soldiers, then recrossed the river and moved north of where Reno's troops were. These maneuvers must have taken quite some time and they had to take place at least an hour after Wooden Leg heard the first shots which had awakened the village. Yet according to the picture Wooden Leg is portraying and Marquis has accepted, at that time Custer was still moving some distance back from the river. If this was true, it is no wonder Custer's troops were wiped out. Wooden Leg then recrossed the river and moved back to his camp circle where he talked to his father, painted himself, got another horse, and moved to the river. He crossed it and went another mile and a half where he entered the battle.

For the timing sequence to correlate, if Wooden Leg is giving a reasonably accurate picture of what took place, he would have to have seen a movement of Keogh's battalion when he was north of Reno on the bluff and first saw these other troops, at the time when Yates' battalion had already retreated around the cut bank. This must have taken place at least thirty minutes after Custer had been shot. It would have been another twenty to thirty minutes before Wooden Leg joined in the battle; an additional thirty minutes elapsed before Custer's troops were killed and the battle was over. Such an estimate would approximate most of the Indian testimony.

Wooden Leg had heard that Bobtail Horse, Roan Bear, Buffalo Calf and four Sioux had been the first to go and meet Custer's troops. It's too bad Wooden Leg or Marquis didn't ask Bobtail Horse for more details. If they did there is no record of it. Since Wooden Leg, like other Indian witnesses, doesn't mention the names or events often given so much importance in the testimony of the whites, such as the exploits of Gall, White Bull or One Bull, his account suggests a behavior which is typical in much of the testimony, particularly that of the Indians: during a battle you remember only that which directly affected you, and unless you are curious enough to question others and absorb what they say, all you remember is what you did. The testimony of Wooden Leg does support White Cow Bull's story in that he mentions the same names as White Cow Bull when the latter recalls who was with him at the ford.

It is apparent from both artifacts and testimony that there weren't many casualties during the time the troops on Luce and Nye Cartwright Ridge were moving to Calhoun and Battleridge. At first there were not many Indians, but their numbers were steadily increasing. Custer would have hoped or known that Benteen was not far behind him, and McDougall not far behind Benteen. Reno might also be in a position to help. Custer was supposedly a great cavalry leader and must have known that the object of a cavalry is to attack. He realized that the Indians would fall back from a charge, just as, in fact, Wooden Leg and the others did when Reno first broke from the timber. Since we are assuming Custer's command is intact at this time, why isn't there evidence of either a major attack, a sound defensive stand, or an offensive or defensive retreat to join Benteen? We must either condemn Custer or assume this is not the correct scenario. Since there are no signs that any of these scripts relate what actually took place, then the question should be, what scenario of the events would coordinate testimony, artifacts, logic and psychology?

Page 231-232: After the long time of the slow fighting, about forty of the soldiers came galloping from the east part of the ridge down toward the river, . . . the Indians ran back to a deep gulch. [Evidence that even an overwhelming number of Indians would retreat from a charge.] The soldiers stopped and got off their horses when they arrived at a low ridge where the Indians had been. Lame White Man, the Southern Cheyenne chief, called us to come back and fight.

. . . the Indians began jumping up, running forward, dodging down, jumping up again, . . . right away, all of the white men went crazy. Instead of shooting us, they turned their guns upon themselves. almost before we could get to them, every one of them were dead. They killed themselves.

The Indians took the guns of these soldiers and used them for shooting at the soldiers on the ridge. I went back and got my horse and rode around beyond the east end of the ridge. By the time I got there, all of the soldiers were dead. The Indians told me that they had killed only a few of those men, that the men had shot each other and shot themselves. . . .

I raced my horse to hurry around to the hillside north of the soldier ridge. The Indians there were all around a band of soldiers on the north slope. . . . About that time, all of this band of soldiers went crazy and fired their guns at each other's heads and breasts or their own heads and breasts. all of them were dead before the Indians got to them . . .

Page 236: A soldier on a horse suddenly appeared in view back behind the warriors who were coming from the eastward, as fast as he could make his horse go. It seemed he must have been hidden somewhere back there until the Indians had passed him. A band of the Indians, all of them Sioux, I believe, got after him. I lost sight of them when they went beyond a curve of the hilltop. I suppose, though, they caught and killed him. [If this was true, it would appear to fit what might have happened to Sergeant Butler.]

Seven of these last soldiers broke away and went running down the coulee sloping toward the river from the west end of the ridge. I was on the side from them, and there was much smoke and dust, and many Indians were in front of me . . . It was said that these seven men, or some of them, killed themselves, I do not know . . .

The number forty keeps coming up in Indian testimony in reference to those troopers who left the ridge. I don't know who first suggested the number, but it seems to have been accepted, even though I'm sure nobody counted the troops. What's intriguing is that most Indians do not say anything about how those soldiers met their end. Wooden Leg and Kate Bighead mention suicide, but what is particularly interesting is that they claim the troops were on a ridge when they committed suicide – there is no reference to their moving into a deep gully. Wooden Leg does mention that the Indians took their guns. How did the bodies get in Deep Ravine (or even Cemetery Ravine) if the soldiers didn't die there? Some troopers reported finding bodies on the edge of the gully, but most imply they were all found down inside and suggest that there were signs of attempts to get out. Such signs would favor Deep Ravine over Cemetery Ravine. If most of them shot themselves, would this not have been apparent to Reno's and Gibbon's soldiers? Would they have thrown all the bodies into the gully? Would a later burial party have buried them in line? Was there a cover-up?

Wooden Leg doesn't mention White Bull, Crazy Horse, Gall, or any of Reno's troops as they moved to Weir Point:

Page 241: [Noisy Walking] . . . he had been hit by three different bullets, one of them having passed through his body. He had also some stab wounds in his side.

Page 242: [Lame White Man] – A bullet had gone in at his right breast and out of his back. He also had many stab wounds.

Page 252: The Sioux likewise were disposing of their dead . . . All of the camps were being moved. This was in accordance with a regular custom among the Indian tribes. When any death occurred in a camp either from battle or from other causes, right at once the people began to get ready to move camp to some other place. The Cheyennes selected a camping spot down the river about a mile northeastward. The Sioux all began moving northwestward and back from the Little Bighorn toward the base of the bench hills west from the river. In the new locations, all of the camps except the Cheyenne were west of the present railroad and highway.

This is an important point as it would effect the action and the view of the camp circles. Most accounts, both past and present, have the camp circles located in, if Wooden Leg was correct, a combination of the first and the second day. Writers have used this image of the camp location as the reason Custer moved farther to the north. I have always believed this was a significant factor and could not understand why it was not determined with certainty. Both Dr. Marquis and Dr. Kuhlman had extensive contacts with the Indians and went over the terrain numerous times. They believe the movement took place. One wonders why more Indians didn't refer to it, but it could be an example of how certain events would not have been considered important by them. Since whites didn't seem to be curious or think it was that crucial, it is no wonder the Indians didn't. In some Sioux testimony there is a suggestion of moving tepees but no definite statements. If this indeed happened, the fact could also have played a major role in determining the number of Indians, and it would suggest Dr. Eastman may have been more correct in his estimate than most others.

Page 262: (the following day they discovered the Indians scouts they had killed, were not Crows or Shoshones but Corn Ree Indians) . . . Now there began to be talk that maybe these soldiers were not the same ones we had fought there (Rosebud Creek). Or, perhaps they had added the Corn Indians to their force since that time. There were different opinions on the matter.

Page 263: . . . Three different soldiers, among all of the dead in both places of battle, attracted special notice from the Indians. The first was the man wearing the buckskin suit and who had the colored writing and pictures on his breast and arms. Another was the black man killed among the first soldiers on the valley. The third was one having gold among his teeth. We did not understand how this metal got there.

Page 272: . . . (third day after the battle) . . . All of the Waist and Shirt men wore elk teeth hanging from their ears. After we had smoked and visited a while, he said: " I think the big chief of the soldiers we killed was named Long Hair. One of my people killed him. He has known Long Hair many years, and he is sure this was him. He could tell him by the long and wavy yellow hair."

This was the first time I ever had heard of any such person as Long Hair. The news was interesting to me at first, but after I had thought a few moments about it the story seemed not very important. I recalled myself having seen at least three soldiers having long and light colored hair.

. . . A great council was held at the Greasy Grass camp that night. Chief of all the tribes were there. . . . At this council I heard an Uncpapa Sioux war chief say: "Long Hair was big chief of the soldiers. I saw him there, and I killed him. I know it was him. I could not mistake the long and wavy yellow hair."

I did not hear anyone else during that time make claims of knowing who was the soldier big chief. . . . There was some talk, though, that all of those soldiers had been chosen specially for their bravery and had been sent out direct from Washington. It was generally agreed that whoever was the big chief of them, he must have been the big chief of all of the white man soldiers in the world.

[If the soldiers were chosen for bravery and there had been as many suicides as Wooden Leg indicated, it is odd that this wasn't mentioned by the chiefs. Of course, it could have been, and Wooden Leg failed to state it. One can't help wonder if there was any mention of Custer, since we know he wasn't wearing his hair long at that time. These are statements one would have expected to have been said when the Indians heard they had fought a chief named Long Hair.]

At this council I heard chiefs of the different tribes announce the number of their killed. . . . Total deaths, about 30. [Dr. Marquis felt this was due to the extensive suicide among the soldiers.]

Thirty years after the great battle against Custer there was a gathering of Indians and white people at the Little Bighorn.

(Dr. Dixon did the interviews) Page 352: Little Wolf said to me: "Tell him Custer killed himself, and see if he becomes angry." but I did not say anything about that. Other Indians, at other times, had tried to tell of the soldiers killing themselves, but the white people listening always became angry and said the Indians were liars, so I thought it best to keep quiet. Other questions came:

"Did you see Custer?"

"I suppose I did, but I do not know. I think that no Indians there knew anything about him being with the soldiers."

Page 375: . . . For a long time there was disagreement as to the length of time we had been at the battle camp before the Custer soldiers came. some said we had been there only one sleep, others said two sleeps. This dispute was settled though, several years ago . . .

Page 376: For fifty years we old Cheyennes talked of Bear Coat, or General Miles, as having been big chief of the soldiers who came up the Little Big Horn valley the next day after the Custer battle.

. . . I never had heard of any of General Custer's relatives having been killed with him, until our present white man doctor friend told us about the two brothers and brother-in-law and the nephew. He tells us also that General Custer's body was not cut up. I do not know why he was spared, if such was the case. I never heard of any favoring of any dead man there. I do not know of any reason for intentional difference in treatment of them.

It was not then known to us who was the chief of these white man soldiers. It was not known to us where they had come from. We supposed them to be the same men we had fought on the Rosebud. I never heard of any Indian at that time guessing as to who he may have been. It made no difference to us.

I have been told that certain different ones of Indians have claimed special honor for having killed Custer himself. All such men are only boasting to get attention. There was no talk of this kind during the hours and days right after the battle. If there had been, all of us would have known of it. I tell you again; none knew anything about Custer being there. The few Southern Cheyennes and the few Sioux warriors who had seen him in earlier times did not learn until many weeks later that he had been killed in this battle. It was weeks or months later when the most of us first learned that there ever was such a man. The white people, not the Indians, told us.

I think in general these statements by Wooden Leg are true. However, he is not consistent. He had already mentioned a Sioux who believed that the chief of the soldiers was Long Hair, and who was also referred to at the Council that was held a few days after the battle. I agree with Wooden Leg's observation that those who said they killed Custer were mainly those boasting and trying to bring attention to themselves.

The question of whether Custer's body was mutilated or not was never resolved. Many thought the body may have been mutilated, but the fact was not mentioned to spare Elizabeth Custer's feelings. However, I have not read of any soldier's account which stated it was. The extent of the Indian mutilations of other bodies has varied in troopers' comments.

Page 379: Of the thirty Indians killed in both fights, I believe about half fell from the bullets of the Custer men. Of these fifteen or so killed by the Custer men there were more of them fell during the first close fighting, when Lame White Man led us and himself was killed, down toward the river, than fell at any other section of the field. The soldiers in the entire battle with the Custer men could have killed a great many more of us, if their whisky had not made them go crazy and shoot themselves. I do not know just how many of them we killed, but I believe the number was not more than twenty or thirty, all together.

I believe that at this stage of the fighting the only time when troops were closer to the river could have been the moment when the supposed forty made their attempted escape. Neither Wooden Leg, Kate Bighead or any other Indians have indicated that these troopers subjected the Indians to any amount of fire before they committed suicide or were killed. I would assume that Wooden Leg is suggesting here that most of the Indian casualties occurred during the last charges they made at the soldiers on Last Stand Hill. (Possibly Wooden Leg is referring to the "suicide boys.") It wouldn't have been whiskey that affected the troops, but it supports the supposition that there was little organized defense, and it sheds light on the mental state of the soldiers.

Page 383: I am not ashamed to tell that I was a follower of Sitting Bull. I have no ears for hearing anybody say he was not a brave man. He had a big brain and a good one, a strong heart and a generous one. In the old time I never heard of any Indians having spoken otherwise of him. If any of them changed their talk in later days, the change must have been brought about by lies of agents and soldier chiefs who schemed to make themselves appear as good men by making him appear as a bad man.

Page 380: None of the Custer soldiers came any closer to the river than they were at the time they died. When the first Indians went out and met them, and exchanged shots with them, these soldiers were riding along the ridge far out northeastward. (TBM – Many Custer rifle shells have been found scattered along this high far-out ridge, by J. A. Blummer and other residents.) They kept moving westward along its crest until they spread out on the ridge lower down, the ridge where the most of the battle took place. After about an hour and a half of the slow fighting at long distance, the group of forty soldiers who rode down from the ridge along a broad coulee and toward the river were charged upon by Lame White Man, followed at once by many Cheyennes and Sioux. This place of the first Indian charge and the first sudden great victory is inside of the present fence around the battlefield and at its lower side.

A reinforcement of the supposition that Custer's troops never came closer to the river than Wooden Leg suggests is found in many Indian accounts, and is natural considering when they arrived on the scene from fighting Reno. The accounts mainly portray the few Indians who faced Custer's troops at the ford, and they suggest that Indians were primarily concerned with recounting their own exploits rather than formulating a sequential view of the battle.

John Stands in Timber
Cheyenne Memories
with Margo Liberty and
the assistance of Robert M. Utley

John Stands in Timber died on June 17, 1967, as the book, *Cheyenne Memories,* was being printed. Margo Liberty wrote the following about John Stands In Timber and why she felt his views were important:

Page 7: For despite the thoroughness with which the field has been discussed by other writers, John has made an important contribution to Cheyenne historiography. Its value lies in three characteristics that mark the pages that follow.

First, John has given us old material from new sources and new material from these same sources. His informants add material unrecorded by Grinnell, Marquis, and their contemporaries. Some of the stories of Cheyenne raids on many tribes, for example, have never been told before. And the account of the suicide boys at the Battle of the Little Bighorn, not even hinted at in the voluminous literature of this tragedy, may provide a major new clue to the controversial sequence of events by which General Custer and his command met disaster. Similar fragments of Cheyenne history and legend appear throughout this book for the first time in print.

Page 9: . . . John has given us the history of the Cheyenne as they themselves recall and interpret it. Grinnell's informants provided episodic views of small segments that he himself wove into a meaningful whole. Wooden Leg told the story of his life to Marquis and thus recorded one man's memory of an eventful era. But John has summed up the past for all his people. For a generation he has been their acknowledged historian.

Page 191: The attack of General George Custer on the Cheyennes and Sioux . . . , did not surprise the Indians as much as many people think . . . They knew the soldiers were in the country looking for them, and they expected trouble, though they did not know just when it would come. My grandfather Lame White Man, . . .

But they were not ignorant on the other side either. A Crow, White Man Runs Him, told the Cheyennes that they were watching the Indians and knew pretty well where the other was. [fn. 3 – . . . The Indian scouts were not watching the Sioux and Cheyennes, but they probed the hostile trail far enough in advance to know where it led. They made no secret of their misgivings, but Custer was confident of his ability to defeat any force that might oppose him. His only fear was that the enemy would escape.]

Page 192: . . . They had decided not to start anything, but to find out what the soldiers were going to do, and to talk to them if they came in peacefully.

. . . They also decided that the camp should be guarded by the military societies, to keep individual warriors from riding out to meet the soldiers. It was a great thing for anyone to do that – to go out and meet the enemy ahead of the rest and they did not want this to happen. . . . Bunches of them rode to ten or fifteen stations on both sides of the river, where they could keep good watch. About sundown they could be seen, all along the hills there. [fn. 5 – . . . since male status depended on war honors, a young unproven group always existed that was potentially dangerous in its tendency to put personal goals above tribal warfare . . .]

Soon after they had begun patrolling, my step-grandfather's friend Big Foot came to him. "Wolf Tooth," he said, "we could get away and go through...and meet the enemy over on the Rosebud . . ."

. . . They saw a bunch of them start across to the east side of the river and another bunch on the hill between the Reno and Custer battlefields. [fn. 6 – . . . The high hill on the east side of the river now known as Weir Point.] Many more were posted on the high hills at the mouth of Medicine Tail Coulee . . . [Indian police] After sundown they [Wolf Tooth's band] took their horses way up on the west side of he river and hobbled them . . . They got safely to the other side and hid in the brush all night there so they would not be discovered.

In the meantime, there was some excitement in the camp. Some of the Sioux boys had just announced that they were taking the suicide vow, and others were putting on a dance for them at the end of the camp. This meant they were throwing their lives away– they would fight till they were killed in the next battle. . . . A few Cheyenne boys had announced their decision to take the vow at the same time, so a lot of Cheyennes were up there in the crowd watching. Spotted Elk and Crooked Nose are two who remembered that night and told me about it. Both of them have been dead for a long time now. . . .

. . . but Spotted Elk said later there were not more than twenty. They remembered the Cheyenne boys that were dancing: Little Whirlwind, Cut Belly, Closed Hand and Noisy Walking. They were all killed the next day. None of them knew for sure that night that the soldiers were coming the next day. They were just suspicious.

The next morning the Indians held a parade for the boys who had been in the suicide dance the night before. Different ones told me about it. One was my grandmother Twin Woman, the wife of Lame White Man, . . . [fn. 7 – . . . No other Indian informant has reported the suicide vow and its execution, although mention has been made of brave warriors who charged into the soldiers to begin the hand-to-hand combat. That the account is not corroborated does not necessarily discredit it. The story is plausible and researchers may well have failed to question those Sioux and Cheyenne who knew of it . . . .]

> While the parade was still going on, three boys went down to the river to swim
>
> . . . some riders in war clothes came along the bank yelling and shooting. Then somebody hollered at them, "The camp is attacked by soldiers!" . . . They had to run quite a distance to get his brother's horse. Then they rode double to join the women and children where they were watching the beginning of the fight. [fn. 9 – . . . Meanwhile, Reno . . . fought defensively...for about 45 minutes . . .]

Page 197: Meanwhile, after the parade ended, my grandmother said a man named Tall Sioux had put up a sweat lodge, and Lame White Man went over to take part in his sweat bath there. It was just a little way from the tepees. She said they had closed the cover down a couple of times – they usually did it four times in all, pouring water on the hot stones to make steam and the second or third time the excitement started in the valley above the village.

She did not see which way the soldiers came, but there were some above the village. And some more came from straight across the river.

The map used on page 196 does not show the lower end of the village opposite Medicine Tail Coulee but appears, as so many others, to represent the lower end across from Last Stand Hill. In the statement, little distinction is made between the time of Reno's and Custer's attack.

> Wolf Tooth and Big Foot had come out of the brush long before then. At daylight they could see the Indian patrols still on the hills, so they waited for some time. They moved along, keeping under cover, until they ran into more warriors and then some more. Close to fifty men had succeeded in slipping through and crossing the river that way. They got together below the creek that comes in north of the present highway 212 and were about halfway up a wooded hill there when they heard someone hollering. Wolf Tooth looked back and saw a rider on a ridge a mile below them, calling and signaling them to come back. [fn. 12 – According to J. W. Vaughn, who covered this ground with Stands In Timber, the party of warriors got about four miles east of the present museum, to a hill north of Highway 212.] (pp. 197, 198)
>
> They turned and galloped back, and when they drew near, the rider began talking in Sioux. Big Foot could understand it. The soldiers had already ridden down toward the village. Then this party raced back up the creek again to where they could follow one of the ridges to the top, and when they got there they saw the last few soldiers going down out of sight toward the river – Custer's men. Reno's men had attacked the other end already, but they did not know it yet.
>
> As the soldiers disappeared, Wolf Tooth's band split up. Some followed the soldiers, and the rest went around a point to cut them off. They caught up there with some that were still going down, and came around them on both sides. The soldiers started shooting. It was the first skirmish of the battle, and it did not last very long. The Indians said they did not try to go in close. After some shooting both bunches of Indians retreated to the hills, and the soldiers crossed the south end of the ridge where the monument now stands. [fn. 13 – This skirmish took place on the high ridges between Medicine Tail and Deep Coulees, east of the ford across the Little Big Horn and not far from the stone marker denoting where the body of Sergeant James Butler was found. Mr. Vaughn, who very kindly wrote me some explanation of his work with Stands In Timber added: "Many people did not believe me when I said the fighting began at this place; they all thought it was down below, at a ford in the river. ...but finally Mr. J. W. Vaughn went there with me taking a metal detector, and we found many shells. He was the first one to accept my story. . . . They believe in books, but I know the actual experiences of those like my grandfather were true. They told me over and over, and I have been to the place I don't know how many times."] (p.198)

This account suggests the following scenario: The group of Indians were four miles east of the present location of the museum when they were signaled to come back. They went back a mile and met the warrior who told them that soldiers had moved toward the village. If the account is true, what I believe they then saw was Keogh's battalion. Because of their location the Indians would not have been aware of the separation of Yates' and Keogh's battalions. This would support Custer having sent Keogh's battalion to Nye Cartwright Ridge immediately after he had sent Martin with his message. Wolf Tooth's band moved down and through ravines and up slopes in which they caught glimpses of Keogh's troops. They fired on them, and would not have been aware that Yates' battalion had already been to the ford and was retreating, just as they were not aware of the Reno battle that was in progress. In the mind of Wolf Tooth's Indians, this was the first action involving Custer's troops, whereas Keogh's battalion could already have been moving to aid the retreating Yates' battalion.

> The soldiers followed the ridge down to the present cemetery site. Then this bunch of forty or fifty Indians

came out by the monument and started shooting down at them again . . . but they were moving on down toward the river across from the Cheyenne camp. Some of the warriors there had come across, and they began firing at the soldiers from the brush in the river bottom. This made the soldiers turn north, but they went back in the direction they had come from, and stopped when they got to the cemetery site. And they waited there a long time – twenty minutes or more. [fn.14 – Utley:] The commonly accepted thesis is that Custer conducted a desperate fighting retreat northward along the main battle ridge and dismounted the remnant of his command with him for the "last stand" at the north end of the ridge where the monument now stands. Stand In Timber thus contradicts this version by having Custer skirmish lightly to and beyond the north end of the ridge, approach the river, withdraw to where the national cemetery now is, and finally fall prey to converging hordes of warriors. This construction is as tenable as the other. Earlier, while approaching Medicine Tail Coulee after viewing the enemy camp for the first time, he had sent his orderly trumpeter with a summons to Captain Benteen and the ammunition train, and he may well have attempted to delay his attack on the village in hopes that reinforcements would arrive.

This part of the testimony is credible and even probable if one recognizes the natural errors that would inevitably occur in remembering and translating. The general pattern could have been true. What the account suggests took place, coincides with other Indian testimony as well as artifactual evidence. Even though one realizes that the Indian accounts have to be evaluated carefully, with full consideration given to the various concerns mentioned by writers, there is usually a thread of truth which one can discern. Part of this account seems to correlate other testimony about troop movement to the ford while other parts do not. Again, the question of the Cheyenne camp location becomes important. (It is odd that direct questions concerning this were not asked of Stands In Timber. Without questioning it would have been natural for them to refer to the second day's location) The move to the cemetery, then back toward the river, and then again to the cemetery is difficult to imagine if the Cheyenne camp was where the map and certain of John Stands In Timber's statements imply. Nor is the long waiting period. Contrary to Utley's conviction that this account is as tenable as others, I don't believe that one can accept the message to Benteen and the additional moves to the north as compatible with the notion that the troops were attempting to wait for Benteen and the ammunition. It is possible they may have waited for Keogh's battalion to join them, but by now Custer would have known that he was up against and exceptionally large number of Indians displaying a bold front. If his concern, therefore, was to unite with Keogh or Benteen and the slow moving ammunition packs, he would not have moved to the north, and he certainly would not have waited in an untenable position for some twenty minutes.

Page 200: Wolf Tooth and his band of warriors had moved in meanwhile, along the ridge above the soldiers. Custer went into the center of a big basin below the monument and the soldiers of the gray horse company got off their horses and moved up afoot. If there had not been so many Indians on the ridge above they might have retreated over that way, either then or later when the fighting got bad, and gone to join Reno. But there were too many up above, and the firing was getting heavy from the other side also. [fn. 16, RU – This would explain the scattering of bodies found between the monument and the river. They were members of Lieutenant Algernon E. Smith's Company E and Captain Thomas W. Custer's Company C.]

Page 201: . . . It was hard work to keep track of everything at the two battles. A number of Indians went back and forth between the two, but none of them saw everything. Most of them went toward the fight with Custer, once Reno was up on the hill. Wolf Tooth said they were all shooting at the Custer men from the ridge, but they were careful all the time, taking cover. Before long some Sioux criers came along behind the line calling in the Sioux language to get ready and watch for the suicide boys. They said they were getting ready down below to charge together from the river, and when they came in all the Indians up above should jump up for hand-to hand fighting. That way the soldiers would not have a chance to shoot, but be crowded from both sides.

The idea was that the soldiers had been firing both ways. When the suicide boys came up they would turn toward them, and give those behind a chance to come in close. The criers called out those instructions twice. Most of the Cheyennes could not understand them, but the Sioux there told them what had been said.

The statement that men were firing from the ridge but were careful and taking cover, seems to be a peculiar way of saying that they retreated from the ridge, which they had to have done when the troops moved to the ridge. The number of Indians on the ridge would also indicate a later stage of the battle than Stands In Timber implied.

In reading Stands In Timber's account, one has to assume he is giving the version of what happened as he remembers it related to him. One must consider that the Indians who gave him this information would, like any-

1. The view back from Ford B on the Indian side. The cutbank Yates' "main element" retreated behind. One can see why most Indians, if not reaching the ford in the first few minutes, would not have seen troops at the ford. Whereas Keogh's battalion, moving along the ridge in the background, would have been seen by the Indians.

2. Ford B from the Indian side. The ford would have been wider, deeper, and flowing faster at that time.

3. A view from South Medicine Tail Coulee showing Bouyer's Bluff.

one else, have a jumbled memory of the exact times and places, but in general, would have been giving their true impression of what transpired, allowing for certain personal embellishments. As in other testimony, one has to be careful not to place too much emphasis on a particular sentence or assertion. There had to have been a good deal of movement and action that these Indians were not aware of, as well as the expected blurring of memory concerning the actions they were personally involved in.

The first part of Stands In Timber's account, which dealt with general events, should be fairly accurate as there is no reason to believe the tellers would try to deceive Stands In Timber. One can then accept these events as having indeed taken place. The early part coincides with

Indian actions known from other accounts. How Stands In Timber describes young warriors who, having learned of soldiers on the Rosebud, went to harass or attack them while the older Indians would have set up patrols to prevent them from doing so. Many parts of this account are corroborated by artifactual evidence – certainly the firing by troops on Luce and Nye Cartwright ridges. One then has to at least consider the account as true.

Wolf Tooth's band would have been to the east of Luce and Nye Cartwright ridges when they fired on the troops from a distance. Stands In Timber had the band of forty or fifty splitting at that time but later indicated they got back together. We can assume that they moved down the ravines leading to Battleridge and came out near where the monument now stands. It is doubtful if they would have been able to have kept the troops in view during this movement; possibly they saw troops at intervals. On reaching Battleridge they saw troops moving toward the river and the trees.

Wolf Tooth's band was called back from the area east of what is now Highway 212 to the place from which they fired on the troops – more than likely Luce Ridge – then from there moved to where they appear near the present monument site. This maneuver had to have taken between twenty and thirty minutes, at a minimum. Since, as I believe, Custer and Yates' battalion had reached the ford, I would speculate that the firing by Wolf Tooth's band took place approximately at the same time Custer's troops were at the ford and Yates' battalion began their retreat. I don't think Captain Keogh had moved to Nye Cartwright Ridge until after Martin was sent back. Custer then made his move to the ford. Some mounted elements of Yates' battalion would have attempted, or could have joined Keogh's battalion, near Battleridge. There also would have been movement by Keogh's battalion toward the retreating Yates' battalion, and all of these maneuvers would have been interpreted variously by the Indians.

When Wolf Tooth's band reached the ridge by today's monument, Keogh's battalion may have been out of sight as they moved through Deep Coulee. The Indians then saw the retreating Yates' battalion. It would have been possible for some of the mounted troops to have retreated as far as Battleridge and then along it, but the "main element" probably passed more between the ridge and Greasy Grass hill. At the time Wolf Tooth's band reached the ridge and looked down, the troops were moving toward the river and timber, and the number of Indians was increasing along the opposite bank of the river. This development caused the troops to move back toward the cemetery area and establish a skirmish or defensive line along what I call the South Retreat Line and the archaeologists refer to as the South Skirmish Line. Firing could then have taken place here for some time before the troops fell back to Last Stand Hill. Only a small number of troopers were killed during that period. The Gray Horse Troop was noted and remembered because of the horses and not because they were the only ones involved. Wolf Tooth's band moved down from the ridge and most likely back to the area north of the present monument when the troops made their move to the ridge. It was about that time that Crazy Horse and his Indians arrived. They shared with others the information concerning the suicide boys. Keogh's battalion had reached Calhoun Hill and Battleridge but was under attack by both the Indians that crossed at the ford and caused the Yates' battalion to move to the north and west, and those who were arriving from the Reno battle area.

Since other Indians have not mentioned the warning of the attack by suicide boys – assuming such warning was given – it would seem that the few Indians receiving it would have been those on the north and eastern side of the ridge, and the warning would have come from Crazy Horse's followers. According to Indian accounts they were late in arriving and they could have been in a position to have known of such plans. Such a view would substantiate Utley's footnote 7 mentioned above, in which he believed that the suicide boys would have been of the Oglala tribe.

The fact that Stands In Timber doesn't mention that the troops attempted escape to the river, something brought out by most Indians who fought below the ridge, supports my view that they had retreated back to an area north and east of Last Stand Hill, and so were not aware of this movement. It also confirms the general observation many writers have made of Indian testimony: they are aware of what they did but not of what anyone else did, or if they are, they don't mention it. Wolf Tooth's band then is involved in the last part of the fighting around Last Stand Hill but they say and know little of what happened to Calhoun and Keogh's companies.

> Page 201: So the suicide boys were the last Indians to enter the fight. Wolf Tooth said they were really watching for them, and at last they rode out down below. They galloped up to the level ground near where the museum now is. Some turned and stampeded the gray horses of the soldiers. By then they were mostly loose, the ones that had not been shot. The rest charged right in at the place where the soldiers were making their stand and the others followed them as soon as they got the horses away.
>
> The suicide boys started the hand-to-hand fighting,

and all of them were killed or mortally wounded. When the soldiers started shooting at them, the Indians above with Wolf Tooth came in from the other side. Then there was no time for them to take aim or anything. . . . Some started to run along the edge under the top of the ridge and for a distance they scattered, some going on one side and some the other. But they were all killed before they got far.

At the end it was quite a mess. They could not tell which was this man or that man, they were so mixed up. Horses were running over the soldiers and over each other. The fighting was really close.

. . . Yellow Nose was in there close . . . the dust was so thick he could hardly see. [Yellow Nose then counted coup – Yellow Nose was mentioned by White Cow Bull and also in Grinnell's book, *The Fighting Cheyenne*, where other more noted Indians were not. One should always keep in mind the dust and the difficulty in seeing when analyzing accounts.]

. . . After the suicide boys came in, it didn't take long – half an hour perhaps . . .

Another thing many of the Cheyennes said was that if Custer had kept going – if he had not waited there on the ridge so long – he could have made it back to Reno. But probably he thought he could stand off the Indians and win.

Page 203: One of the dead is my brother-in-law, and we will have to go over and get his body. It was my grandfather, Lame White Man. So they went across to where he was lying. He did not have his war clothes on him. They thought he was an Indian scout with Custer – they often fought undressed that way. And his scalp was gone from the top of his head. Nearby was the body of another, Cheyenne, Noisy Walking. They were the only ones to have the places marked where they were found.

. . . Lame White man was the oldest Cheyenne killed and the only Cheyenne chief. I heard that the Sioux lost sixty-six and the Cheyennes just seven, but there might have been more. Four Cheyenne had been killed outright and the others badly wounded. Two died that night and one the next day. These were the dead: my grandfather, Noisy Walking, the son of White Bull or Ice; Roman Nose, the son of Long Roach; Whirlwind, the son of Black Crane; Limber Bones, Cut Belly; and Closed Hand. Closed Hand, Cut Belly, Noisy Walking and Whirlwind had been suicide boys. They were all young men . . . . The four suicide boys were all killed or mortally wounded near the site of the last stand, as was Lame White Man.

Page 205: . . . The Cheyenne warrior Wooden Leg, in his book, told about my grandfather being killed. He said he recognized the body by the shirt and war bonnet, but he was mistaken. Lame White Man did not have anything on but a blanket and moccasins. He had not even had time to braid his hair. That was why the Sioux thought he was a scout for Custer, and scalped him. Wooden Leg said some other things he took back later. One was that the soldiers were drunk, and many killed themselves. I went with two army men to see him one time. They wanted to find out about it. I interpreted. They took him some tobacco and cash and other things, and we asked him if it were true that the Indians said the soldiers did that. He laughed and said there were just too many Indians. The soldiers did their best. He said if they had been drunk they would not have killed as many as they did. But it was in the book.

Stands in Timber's statement does not indicate that Wooden Leg denied the troopers didn't take their own lives. Wooden Leg merely said that they probably weren't drunk. Supposedly the notion that soldiers were drinking came from their actions, particularly the way some of them ran down the hill and fired in the air. It would seem natural that the Indians may have thought this meant the men were inebriated. Wooden Leg's comment that there were "just too many Indians" was true. The context in which the statements were made is unclear, but Wooden Leg would have realized how the army felt about the suicide issue, and it appears they were bribing him with gifts. Wooden Leg's remark that "the troopers did their best" was no great concession or reversal of the suicide question. It would seem that Wooden Leg merely outmaneuvered his interrogators and availed himself of their gifts. He prevented the army and government's ire from being leveled against him, and only conceded that the troopers were not drunk.

Stands In Timber's grandmother would not necessarily have known if Lame White Man, after escorting her to a place of safety, did not go back and prepare himself for battle. This ritual appeared to be quite important for Indians. It seems odd that Stands In Timber refers to not having anything on but his blanket and moccasins. How and why did he wear a blanket, especially on a hot day? He wasn't then undressed in a way they should have mistaken him for a Ree. His being scalped would refute Wooden Leg's story that Lame White Man was wearing a war bonnet, unless it was lying beside him. These are questions which one way or the other would not necessarily refute either testimony.

Page 207: They should mark more places on the battlefield, from the Indian side. They told me some of the stories over and over for many years, and remembered where things happened. I have marked many of the places myself with stones, but it's getting harder for me to find them now. . . . One is at the Reno field where a young Sioux boy charged the soldier line and was killed, following an older warrior. He was the one who lost his brother in the Rosebud fight and did not want to live any longer. [fn. 32 – Two large rocks still mark this place, one to the left and one to the right of a small draw near the marker for Thomas Meador. Stands In Timber's sources for this story were Little Sun, a Cheyenne, and White Dress, an Oglala Sioux from Pine Ridge reservation . . . .]

Chief Gall
Hunkpapa

Chief Gall is believed to have led the Indians flanking Custer's troops on the south. The question of his late appearance and the individual fighting habits of the Indians, including the number of major and minor chiefs involved, should be considered in his accounts.

Chicago Newspaper Account – "Tenth Anniversary of the Battle of the Little Bighorn" – 1886:

> He told all he knew without restraint. His dignified countenance spoke truthfulness, and there is little doubt but that the true history of that dreadful day is at last known . . .
>
> We saw the soldiers early in the morning crossing the divide. When Reno and Custer separated, we watched them until they came down into the valley. A cry was raised that the white men soldiers were coming, and orders were given for the village to move immediately. Reno swept down so rapidly on the upper end that the Indians were forced to fight. Sitting Bull and I were at the point where Reno attacked. Sitting Bull was big medicine. The women and children were hastily moved down stream where the Cheyenne were camped. The Sioux attacked Reno and the Cheyennes, Custer, and then all became mixed up . . . As soon as Reno was beaten and driven back across the river, the whole force turned upon Custer and fought him until they destroyed him. Custer did not reach the river but was met half a mile up a ravine now called Reno Creek. [Medicine Tail Coulee] They fought the soldiers and beat them back step by step until all were killed. . . . The soldiers got shells stuck in their guns and had to throw them away. They then fought with little guns – pistols. The Indians were in coulees behind and in front of Custer as he moved up the ridge to take position . . . .
>
> The first two companies, Keogh and Calhoun, dismounted and fought on foot. They never broke, but retired step by step until forced back to the ridge upon which all finally perished. . . . Keogh's company rallied by company and were killed in a bunch.
>
> ". . . The warriors directed a special fire against the troopers who held the horses while the others fought. As soon as a holder was killed, by moving blankets and great shouting the horses were stampeded, which made it impossible for the soldiers to escape. Afterwards the soldiers fought desperately and hard, and never surrendered. "They fought strong – they fought in line along the ridge . . . When Reno attempted to find Custer by throwing out a skirmish line, Custer and all with him were dead.
> ". . . Some soldiers got away and ran down a ravine, crossed the river, came back again, and were killed."
>
> The news account, in describing Chief Gall, would have said: Early in the day the great Sioux Chief Gall went over the entire field and described in an intelligent and straight forward manner the exact place in which Custer's command was destroyed. Curley, the Crow scout, who was, in reality, the only survivor of all who marched into the valley of the Little Big Horn with Custer, was also present, but Gall turned his back on Curley and said: "He ran away too soon in the fight." Gall is a powerful, fine looking specimen of the red race. 46 years old, and weighs over two hundred pounds. He first appeared reticent and was inclined to get sullen, but when he stood on the spot which formed the last sight of Custer on earth his dark eyes lightened with fire, he became earnestly communicative, and he told all he knew without restraint. His dignified countenance spoke truthfulness, and there is little doubt but that the true history of that dreadful day is at last made known.[1]

This account was written for public consumption and is a good example of why it has been difficult to establish with certainty what happened. The acceptance of the account suggests that Indians must have believed the whites to be quite gullible. Most writers mention how the Indians who took part in the defeat of Custer were prone to fear what they said to whites and so would often say what they thought the interrogators wanted to hear. The "courage displayed by all troopers" is a good example of this attitude. I am sure there were many acts of courage, but I am just as sure there were examples of panic and suicide. I think one should also keep in mind Two Moon's trip to Washington, years later, where he spent some time explaining what a great chief he was and what went on during the battle. When, after the meeting, Black Wolf said to him, "You are the biggest liar in the whole Cheyenne tribe," Two Moons laughed and replied: "I think it is not wrong to tell lies to white people."[2] I am sure this statement reflected the opinion of a great many Indians.

If the Indians watched Custer cross the divide, the village would have been alerted and preparing to move, and actually would have been moving by the time Reno began his drive down the valley. Overall, Indian testimony seems to agree that the village remained peaceful – there was swimming, playing, and sleeping – until Reno's troops actually fired on the village. If Gall and Sitting Bull were at the point of attack, and if Gall was the warrior he was made out to be, he would have participated in the fight with Reno's troops. (In one of his versions he said he did not.) It is generally agreed he did. One should take note of where he said he was when he realized the village was attacked. His account in this interview differs on this point from his other testimony. In the interview Gall refers to Sitting Bull as "big medicine," in contrast to his later derogatory remarks. Gall also indicates that Reno was beaten back across the river, at which time the major force of Indians attacking Reno would have left. In other words, Gall would have been involved with Reno for at least 45 minutes before being warned of the Custer attack. He then apparently returned some three miles to where Custer's troops were. This maneuver would have taken a minimum of twelve minutes. Custer should have been at the ford and in a position to attack the Indians some fifteen minutes after Major Reno began firing on the encampment. This would mean that before Gall was in a position to contact any of General Custer's troops, at least fifty-five minutes would have gone by since the first firing between the Indians and General Custer's troops took place. Thus, a good deal of action would have transpired before Gall arrived on the scene. He would not have any direct knowledge of just where Custer's troops had been. Most Indians would not have seen Custer at the ford, and since Indians didn't sit down after the battle and attempt to chronologize the various events and would not be apt to know what went on in another part of the battlefield unless a particular friend told them, Gall's statement that Custer didn't reach the river has to be questioned. When Gall got there, the troops had all reached Calhoun Hill and Battleridge. One can only wonder where the troops had been for the past hour if they had not gone to the river. Why, if they didn't get within a half mile of the river and the Indians came out to meet them, was there no sign of an attack having taken place? Why, if not attacking, didn't they move to Luce Ridge or Weir Point and establish a defensive position. Since we know they were concerned with Captain Benteen and Captain McDougall, why wasn't there a determined effort to join them?

Anyone attempting to form a hypothesis as to what happened to General Custer has to credit some testimony and discredit others, especially when conflicting remarks are given by the same individual. This seems particularly true with Chief Gall and the Crow scout Curley. As I have suggested elsewhere, Curley's interviews are fairly accurate until the time he and Mitch Bouyer move down the bluff and join General Custer. After that incident, his stories vary to such an extent that his account has to have been adjusted in order to incorporate the view of the events that was prevalent at the time. To me, Chief Gall's accuracy is also suspect. Gall reported that the Indians in the camp knew Custer was coming but did not get excited until Major Reno attacked. Their knowledge of Custer's approach (outside of a general recognition that there were troops in the area) can be rejected, but the absence of action fits in with other Indian testimony and should be accepted.

His recognition of Lieutenant Calhoun's and Captain Keogh's companies offering more resistance is also generally accepted, and his denial of any knowledge about the firing on Luce and Nye Cartwright ridges would reflect his late arrival. It is very difficult to believe that soldiers would run all the way down a ravine with the number of Indians supposedly present there, then go across the river, come back and be killed. This feat would be next to impossible even if they were on horses. Since I don't believe Gall was in the Custer battle until the final stages, it may be that he heard of some troops crossing into camp; this is what some witnesses claim happened when Custer went to the ford. Since he was not there in person, he was not sure of just when or how it happened. It would be another indication that an attack was planned and started.

One should note that Gall said Custer was defeated by the time Reno's troops moved to Weir Point.

The following account was in the St. Paul newspaper in July of 1886:

> ... Any one present with Gall at the Custer battlefield on the morning of July 25 last could see at a glance the Chief was telling the truth, the whole truth, and nothing but the truth. When he stood on the spot from which Custer gazed his last on earth, and glanced up and down ..." My two squaws and three children were killed there by pale faced warriors, and it made my heart bad. After that I killed all my enemies with the hatchet."

Many new facts were brought to light by the visit of the chief who was the leading factor in the destruction of Custer and his troopers; and many popular errors were corrected which were about to go down into history as indisputable truths. The new points brought out were: That Sitting Bull personally had little or nothing to do with the fight . . . His prowess as a fighter is simply a creation of the white man's brain and nothing else. . . . If he has any latent fighting qualities, or abilities as a great leader, his kinsmen don't know it nor does anybody else. Crow King was really the adjutant general of the campaign, and Gall was unquestionably the leader who executed the details and led the 'young bucks on.' Another correction was made of the popular error that General Custer actually reached the Little Bighorn. General Custer was attacked three-quarters of a mile back from the river, near the crest of the ridge lining the coulee he was descending, and was forced back step by step, at right angles to his former course, to the summit now crowned by the battle monument where all finally perished. Gall went with the writer and pointed out the exact spot where General Custer stood in person when he was attacked. The brave cavalry leader some 300 or 400 yards ahead of his command alone with his orderly, was slowly descending this coulee toward the river; and near the high knoll where Benteen came in sight of the Custer field later on, his pace became slower and his actions more cautious, and finally he paused altogether to await the coming up of the command. This was the nearest point any of Custer's party ever got to the river. Gall says that he (Gall) had three Indians with him and that he sat down on a mound some six hundred yards away, in full sight of the troops, and watched the soldiers file slowly down the ravine . . . Gall is of the of the opinion that when Custer slowed his pace and finally halted, the latter began to suspect he was in a bad scrape. From that time on, Custer acted on the defensive. Poor Custer! He could have saved his well mounted command by flight, but such a thought was no doubt farthest from his mind in that trying moment. The false supposition that the soldiers were not seen until they crossed the divide was also corrected by Gall, who avers that both Reno and Custer had been watched for some hours before they separated to make their respective attacks. . . . Gall says that only two companies of Custer's command kept any sort of formation at all and from all that could be gathered from the Indian, coupled with what was read from the ground as from an open page, it would appear that Calhoun's men died fighting as skirmishers, while Keogh rallied his company which was all killed in a bunch. The other companies broke, were shot down individually as they fled in confusion from the field. Considering the point where Custer was first attacked, it would also seem that Calhoun's and Keogh's troops were the first to fall, being nearest the original point of attack; and that General Custer and the others, retreating step by step, were the last to die on the summit where the monument now stands. As a matter of fact, the true conditions of affairs was exactly the opposite. . . . He says Calhoun, Keogh and Crittenden were the last ones to fall in the day and Calhoun and Keogh taken on both flanks, . . . had nothing else to do but fight it out in line until the last trooper had fallen in his tracks . . . that the Sioux particularly the old men, women and young bucks held Reno in check, while the Cheyennes did all the bloody work at the lower end of the field . . .[3]

The disparagement of Sitting Bull is an error that, in itself, discredits Gall's testimony and makes it suspect. His statements clearly reflect his intentions to secure a position at the Agency. I am sure there are a lot of things Sitting Bull could be criticized for, but he didn't get to his position by doing nothing, and he wouldn't have kept that position after the battle if he were afraid to fight. Indians did not receive eagle feathers to wear for being cowards.

The inaccuracies in a newspaper story should not be fully blamed on Chief Gall; he didn't necessarily say what was written. One of the first sentences expresses naivete and an attempt at story enhancement as the author states; you can tell at a glance that the interviewee was telling nothing but the truth. A good salesman offering a poor product can make one believe it is the best in the world. Anyone's testimony should be analyzed critically.

Any reader of Indian accounts would know they had no real leader, so either the writer or Gall tried to create a false impression. Gall was certainly aware of this even though the writer may not have been. The distortion however, added impact to the story and has enabled Gall to maintain that position over the years.

I have already dealt with the question of why Gall or other Indians may have thought that Custer didn't reach the river. For most of the Indians this would have been a natural conclusion.

As it progresses, Gall's story becomes even more fantastic. Gall went with the writer to the exact spot where Custer was killed. Since it is questionable the Indians knew they were fighting Custer, and Gall by his own accounts was opposing Calhoun and Keogh, one can only wonder how he was able to pick out the exact spot. Gall has Custer in the lead of his troops by some 300 or 400 yards; he saw a few Indians on his left so he waited for his command. At that time Gall was sitting down with three companions some 600 yards away. He must have been so furious after his wife and three children were killed that he took his hatchet and left the Hunkpapa camp. He then crossed the river with his three companions and sat down and saw Custer moving down the coulee. His heart must have been "so bad" that he was afraid of what he might do. He didn't go with the other Hunks to attack Reno's troops that had killed his wife and their three children.

Since, according to the writer, he was the main leader against Custer, he must then have gone back to get his followers or maybe he just waited until his warriors came to attack Custer. As, according to the story, he was in charge of executing all the details, he was probably sitting on the mound, planning strategy.

Then the reader runs into the dichotomy that persists not only in that writer's report of Gall's testimony, but in many other accounts, which is the picture I've drawn and will keep drawing as it is central to arriving at any sound view of what General Custer did. We have a courageous, experienced leader who knows that for a cavalry to win victories they must attack. He also knows that to win he must attempt to coordinate his offensive with that of Major Reno. Reno is under attack and needs aid which he has promised to give him. He knows furthermore that if he doesn't act quickly the Indians may scatter. So, what does he do? According to the account, he retreats and goes on the defensive. Yet Gall has not mentioned any great number of warriors waiting for Custer; he merely indicated that there were some Indians near Weir Point. Gall also said that Custer's troops could have escaped, which would mean they could have gone back and united the command. We know Custer was concerned about bringing the command together because of the messages he sent. Does he then retreat to the south? No, he retreats to the north. According to Gall, he is concerned with defense. Although Custer fears attacking with his five companies, he must not be worried about what might happen to Reno with his three. Custer apparently knows that Reno is now in the timber, and of course Reno can hold out indefinitely, so it doesn't matter if Custer takes another half hour or so before he attacks.

Somewhere along the lines of this conjectural narrative one had better start condemning Custer for displaying ignorance and utter lack of judgement. Again, one should realize that even in this hypothetical scenario with the proper organization and discipline, it wouldn't have been difficult for Custer to have seen the Indians moving toward him in time to set up a sound defense. But, supposedly, there was no sign of either a major assault or anything resembling a sound defense, contrary to the efforts of some writers to create one.

Gall reports that only two companies kept any sort of formation. Considering the dust and excitement along with the Indians' lack of knowledge of army organization, it would seem odd that Gall refers specifically to two companies. This information would appear to have been learned later, although it is true that Calhoun's and Keogh's companies seem to be the only two that attempted to establish skirmish positions. Gall, in his report, has the other companies fleeing in confusion. They were shot down individually; although they reached the high point, they were prevented from fleeing any farther. This account differs from the one printed in the Chicago paper, according to which all troops fought bravely, retreating step by step. The St. Paul version suggests that if Custer was alive, as Gall and writers claimed, he was with Captain Yates, Lieutenant Smith and Captain Tom Custer, and they all either fled or were not able to keep control of their companies. Gall maintains that Custer and those with him were killed before Calhoun, Crittenden and Keogh. According to Hardorff, Gall, in an interview with Barry in 1886, said: "...soon we came up to some of them to the east of where the rest were. We either killed or ran over these and went on down to where the last soldiers were. They were fighting good. The men were loading and firing, but they could not hit the warriors in the gully and the ravine. The dust and smoke was black as evening. Once in a while we could see the soldiers through the dust..."[4] Given these conditions it must have been rather difficult for Gall to identify General Custer in the way he describes it in the St. Paul paper. The above statement does not indicate that Calhoun's and Keogh's troops were the last to be killed.

The St. Paul account goes on to ask questions of Gall:

"How soon after Reno charged did Custer come down the valley?"

Gall: "We saw all at one time before they separated. When Reno charged, the women and children were moved downstream, and when the Sioux bucks drove Reno on top of the bluffs, everybody came down and fought Custer. All the Indians were mixed up then." The question was asked again but no satisfactory answer was given.

"Did Custer get near the river?"

"No."

"Then how come the dead bodies of soldiers on the river's bank where we think the white chief crossed or attempted to cross?"

Gall's answer came without a moment's hesitation.

"They were soldiers who fled down another coulee, crossed the river lower down, were chased up stream again toward the village, driven back into the river and killed on this side."

"Did you fight Reno?"

"No, I only fought the white men soldiers down this way."

"Then you know nothing of what happened at the upper end of the village?"

"No, I was down among the Cheyenne looking after horses when the first attack was made on our village."[5]

According to the Chicago paper interview, Gall was in the Hunkpapa village talking with Sitting Bull, while in this account he is in the area of the Cheyenne village, which would be a mile or so away. Gall finds out about his wife and the death of his children, but he doesn't go upstream to fight Reno. He avoids the question relating Reno's attack to Custer's movement. This could have aided in the crucial determination of the timing sequential relationship between the commands. Gall wouldn't have been expected to know the answer, if he was attacking Major Reno, but should have, if he was where he said he was. Gall must have then waited for the Hunkpapas to return from attacking Reno since they were the warriors he claimed to have led. The soldiers who supposedly fled down a coulee and crossed the river and then recrossed it before being killed accomplished a remarkable feat. They were able to move down a coulee through all the Indians, cross the river, pass through the Indians moving along the river, and still were able to recross at Ford B, the major Indian crossing. It must have been true, though, because Gall didn't hesitate in his answer.

One important point should be considered. The question pertaining to bodies found at Ford B appeared to be accepted by the 7th Cavalry officers present and by Gall. In answering the question, Gall said the soldiers fled down a ravine and crossed lower down and then moved upstream toward the village. This explanation would give support to Wooden Leg's, Marquis', and Kuhlman's view that the Cheyenne camp was closer to Ford B during the battle than maps generally indicate.

SOURCES

1. Graham, *The Custer Myth*, p. 88.
2. Marquis, *Wooden Leg*, p. 360.
3. Graham, *The Custer Myth*, pp. 89, 90, 91.
4. Hardorff, *Markers, Artifacts, and Indian Testimony*, p. 53.
5. Graham, *The Custer Myth*, p. 92.

Chief Gall and General Godfrey

General Godfrey (then Lieutenant Godfrey) has been one of the few officers who wrote about the battle, giving his own account of what took place. One of the primary reasons for him to change his first opinions of what happened to Custer would be his interviews with Chief Gall, at the battlefield in 1886 and shortly afterward at Standing Rock Agency, under the auspices of Major McLaughlin and his wife. Godfrey was in charge of K Company, part of Captain Benteen's battalion. He preserves these interviews with Chief Gall in his book, *Custer's Last Campaign;* and they are also found in Graham's book, *The Custer Myth*, under the heading *General Godfrey's Narrative*. Since many of his remarks are worth noting, I will include them at this time, in connection with those given by Chief Gall:

> It was well known to the Indians that the troops were in the field, and a battle was fully expected by them; but the close proximity of our column was not known to them until the morning of the day of the battle.
>
> [Benteen's march] During this march on the left we could see occasionally the battalion under Custer, distinguished by the troop mounted on gray horses, marching at a rapid gait.[1]

This statement helps support Lieutenant Varnum's contention that he was able to see the Gray Horse Troop from Reno's skirmish line, even though some, such as Captain Carter, believed he would not have been be able to distinguish them from that distance. It also indicates that Custer and Benteen were not so far apart that Benteen could not have came to Custer's aid and, if Benteen had carried out his assignment. He could have assisted in the attack, as I believe Custer planned. Finally, the statement explains why the Indians so often referred to the Gray Horse Troop.

Godfrey continues, with Major Reno receiving his orders, moving to Ford A, crossing, and beginning his move down the valley. At that time General Custer moved to the right, separated by the line of bluffs. Major Reno went down the valley, set up his skirmish line, moved into the timber and then began his retreat.

Godfrey goes on to say:

> While Reno remained there, his casualties were few. The hostiles had him nearly surrounded, and there was some firing from the rear of the position by the Indians on the opposite bank of the river. Owing to the noise of the firing and to the absorbed attention they were giving to the command . . . The hostile strength pushed

Reno's retreat to the left, so he could not get to the ford where he entered the valley.

[Captain Benteen's battalion had moved back to the main trail and had received the messages delivered by Kanipe and Trumpeter Martin. They were now approaching Ford A.]

We were forming in line to meet our supposed enemy, when we came in full view of the valley of the Little Big Horn. the valley was full of horsemen riding to and fro in clouds of dust and smoke, for the grass had been fired by the Indians to drive the troops out and cover their own movement. On the bluffs to our right we saw a body of troops and that they were engaged.... There was a short time of uncertainty as to the direction in which we should go, but some Crow scouts came by, driving a small herd of ponies, one of whom said "Soldiers" and motioned for the command to go to the right.[2]

Godfrey may have confused meeting the Rees, who had ponies, with seeing the Crow scouts; however, the Crow scouts did pick up some Sioux ponies either before or after leaving that evening. It is too bad Godfrey didn't realize, at the time he wrote the book, the importance of knowing the number of Crows, their identity, and of noting a few more details concerning them.

> ... Following his directions, we soon joined Reno's battalion, which was still firing. Reno had lost his hat ... and appeared very much excited. Benteen's battalion was ordered to dismount and deploy as skirmishers on the edge of the bluffs overlooking the valley. Very soon after this the Indians withdrew from the attack ...
> A number of officers collected on the edge of the bluff overlooking the valley ...[3]

One should note several things. It took only a short time to move from an area close to where Reno and Custer separated to reach the bluff. The troops were firing, and the Indians left shortly after. I think we can assume the Indians were also firing. For Chief Gall to hear what Iron Cedar or the Indian women were saying, he would have had to be very close to them or a definite lull would have been taking place in the fighting. Godfrey indicated the Indians didn't leave until after Benteen reached the bluffs. In his magazine account, this is where Captain Godfrey mentioned Captain Moylan criticizing General Custer for not having kept his command together and attacking. This reference was later deleted.

> ... At this time there were a large number of horsemen, Indians, in the valley. Suddenly they all started down the valley, and in a few minutes scarcely a horseman was to be seen. Heavy firing was heard down the river ... some of Reno's men had seen a part of Custer's command, including Custer himself, on the bluffs about the time the Indians began to develop in Reno's front. The party was heard to cheer, and seem to wave their hats as if to give encouragement and then they disappeared behind the hills or escaped further attention from those below. Major Moylan thinks the last he saw of Custer's party was about the position of Reno Hill ...
> It was about this time that Trumpeter Martini left Cook with Custer's last orders... It is possible, yet probable, that, from the high point, Custer could then see nearly the whole camp and force of the Indians and realized that the chances were desperate; but it was too late to reunite his forces for the attack. Reno was already in the fight and his (Custer's) own battalion was separated from the attack by a distance of two and a half to three miles. He had no reason to think that Reno would not push his attack vigorously; if he did, he certainly would provide that such a failure should not turn into a disaster.[4]

Why didn't Moylan and Godfrey note this sighting at the Reno Court? Since such sightings took place early in Reno's move down the valley, Reno must have known Custer would be attempting to reach him and should have pushed his attack, or at least remained in the timber.

Captain Moylan, at the Reno Court, almost put his foot in it. The following question could and should have elicited the incident of his own sighting:

Q. State what the general belief was as to where the remainder of the command of the 7th Cavalry was at any time from the period Major Reno's column was engaged in the timber up to the time it reached the top of the hill?

A. The first that I heard of General Custer's command was after I got on the hill where it was rumored among the men that it had passed down on that side of the river.

You would think Moylan's answer would have solicited a follow up question as to why it was so rumored. However, such an inquiry would have led to either outright lies or questions which would have brought about the indictment of Major Reno. Instead, the question (in order to obtain the proper response), was:

Q. But at the time you were moving down this bottom and engaged in the timber and in going back to the top of the hill, was there any belief as to where the balance of the command was? What was your opinion?

A. My opinion was that it was on the rear of our trail and was coming to our assistance.

Does this answer correlate with the above comment by Godfrey? Do you think it might infer the suppression of evidence regarding early sightings of Custer's command on the ridge?

The testimony of seeing General Custer waving his hat and the men cheering is found in a number of statements including Chief Gall's. It illustrates a process where somebody makes a statement, then somebody else repeats it, and soon one is used to verify the other. This part of the testimony probably came about because of what Martin and Kanipe said about Custer waving and the troops cheering. It may have been possible to have seen and distinguished a waving Custer at some point on the ridge, but the different accounts of where it happened brings out questions of timing and veracity. It is doubtful if troops riding down the valley, amid the dust and the noise made by the horses, soldiers, and Indians, and at such a distance, would have been able to hear the soldiers cheering or recognize Custer waving. It is more likely such a sighting occurred when Reno's troops were reforming after crossing Ford A and having passed through the timber.

Godfrey, after mentioning the troops, and that Captain Moylan saw Custer near Reno Hill, said that Trumpeter Martin left Custer about that time. If so, Martin should have joined Benteen after he had left the morass and before he reached the Lone Tepee, and he shouldn't have been fired on by Indians. Sergeant Kanipe should have met Benteen at the morass, or right after he left. This version does not coincide with Kanipe's, Martin's or Benteen's recollections.

Godfrey said Custer could then see nearly the whole camp and the full force of Indians. He realized the chances were desperate but it was too late to go back. Reno was already in the fight and he was two and a half to three miles away. Godfrey believes Custer had no reason to think Reno would not push his attack vigorously – a commander doesn't expect the failure of his lieutenant – but if he had, he certainly would have made provisions that such a failure didn't turn into a disaster. In saying Custer had seen the full force of the Indians, he should have known that Reno had no hope of successfully attacking such a force with only three companies. Godfrey's suggestion that a commander knowing the plight of his lieutenant wouldn't allow such a disaster to take place, is actually a condemnation of Custer, for he states that Custer moved further away from both Reno and the support he was sending for, instead of going to Weir Point to determine the nature of the situation and then taking the quickest way to attack the Indians and aid Major Reno.

During a long time after the junction of Reno and Benteen we heard firing down the river in the direction of Custer's command. We were satisfied that Custer was fighting the Indians somewhere, and the conviction was expressed that "our command ought to be doing something or Custer would be after Reno with a sharp stick." We heard two distinct volleys which excited some surprise, that "Custer was giving it to them for all he was worth." I have but little doubt now that these volleys were fired by Custer's orders as signals of distress and to indicate where he was.[6]

Volleys were reported not long after the junction, probably fired by Captain Keogh's or Lieutenant Calhoun's order but not by Custer, and not necessarily as signals. It seems odd that a patrol was not sent out right after the Indians had left. Perhaps they didn't because of being afraid of committing all of the troops at that time. Hearing the firing – and contrary to Reno's, Benteen's and Wallace's assertions, I am sure they did – and still not exhibiting more concern for themselves, seems very poor strategy. It would appear to indicate the condition many of Reno's troops were in, as well as Reno himself. It makes one wonder how many Indians the troops thought they were facing. It may be that the fear of being led into a trap was so great they felt they had to wait until all of them were ready to move. S. L. A. Marshall, one of our foremost historians, says in his book, *Indian Wars*:

> ... any experienced observer of the impact of combat stress on men's power must hoot at the idea. When troops hit bottom, knowing the extreme of physical and emotional exhaustion, no act of will may restore energy or super-induce group action. Only rest, with preferably a few winks of sleep, will initiate recovery. Reno was incapable of doing other than he did and so were his people.[7]

Although I am no military expert, I am afraid I can't agree with Marshall. Benteen's and McDougall's troops had not been subject to any combat at that point, and I do not believe the period of time or the panic and fear exhibited by some of Reno's troops in their retreat was such that they couldn't have acted; nor is there evidence that they didn't recover quickly once they reached the bluffs and were met by Benteen's battalion and the packs. If Reno was incapable of responding to the sound of gunfire, Benteen should have assumed command. I would have thought that Benteen's orders from his commander should have taken precedence over any orders from Reno. It may have been prudent for them to have waited, but a reconnaissance patrol would have been a necessity.

The need for Reno and Benteen to say they didn't hear

the firing at a time when everyone else did, would, in itself, indicate their recognition that more direct action should have been taken.

> [Weir starts downstream with Edgerly following with Weir's company.]
>
> ... Weir, from the high point, saw the Indians in large numbers start for Edgerly, and signaled for him to change his direction, and Edgerly went over to the high point, where they remained, not seriously molested, until the remainder of the troops marched down there; ...
>
> McDougall came up with the pack-train and reported the firing when he reported to Reno. I remember distinctly looking at my watch at twenty minutes past four, and made a note of it in my memorandum book, and although I have never satisfactorily been able to recall what particular incident happened it is my impression, however, that it was the arrival of the pack-train. It was about this time that thirteen men and a scout named Herendeen rejoined my command.
>
> My recollection is that it was about half-past two when we joined Reno. About five o'clock the command moved down toward Custer's supposed whereabouts.[8]

Again 'high point' is used to indicate Weir Point, underscoring its importance for viewing the surroundings.

If Godfrey was using the official time, they could not have reached the bluff by 2:30. Criticism was levied on Martin for using a similar time period between their arrival and their move to search for Custer.*

Godfrey continues:

> Looking toward Custer's field, on a hill two miles away we saw a large assemblage. At first our command didn't appear to attract their attention although there was some commotion observable among those nearer to our position. ... While watching this group the conclusion was arrived at that Custer had been repulsed, and the firing was the parting shots of the rear-guard.**
>
> ... and the horsemen converged toward our position.

---

*This time would coincide with that of other officers as well as Indians who believed Reno's attack took place around mid-day. Whether the official time was a colluding measure or not is hard to determine and is not essential to my study. King in his book, *Massacre: The Custer Cover-Up,* believed it was. He tied it in with falsifying the time Reno was engaged in the valley. I would differ in believing that if there was subterfuge, it would have been used to cover-up the time Benteen and then the packs arrived on the ridge with Reno's move to locate Custer.

    Addendum: When shortening this manuscript in order to publish my book, *The Custer Controversy,* I realized the function and importance timing played in the overall picture of events.

**Establishing a rear guard appears to have been a common practice. This gives credence to the supposition that the soldiers seen by Little Sioux and possibly Curley may have been a rear guard.

> the command was now dismounted to fight on foot. Weir's and French's troops were posted on the high bluffs and to the front of them; my own troops along the crest of the bluffs next to the river; the rest of the command moved to the rear, as I supposed to occupy other points in the vicinity, to make this our defensive position ... I was a little startled by the remark that the command was out of sight. At this time Weir's and French's troops were being attacked. Orders were soon brought to me by Lt. Hare, Acting Adjutant, to join the main command. I had gone some distance in the execution of this order when, looking back, I saw French's troop come tearing over the bluffs, and soon after Weir's troop following in hot haste. Edgerly was near the top of the bluff trying to mount his frantic horse ... The Indians almost immediately followed to the top of the bluff, and commenced firing into the retreating troops, killing one man, wounding others and several horses. They then started down the hillside in pursuit. I at once made up my mind that such a retreat and close pursuit would throw the whole command into confusion, and, perhaps, prove disastrous. I dismounted my men to fight on foot, deploying as rapidly as possible without waiting for the formation laid down in tactics.
>
> ... Our fire in a short time compelled the Indians to halt and take cover; but before this was accomplished a second order came for me to fall back as quickly as possible to the main command. Having checked the pursuit, we began our retreat, slowly at first, but kept up our firing. After proceeding some distance the men began to group together, and to move a little faster and faster and our fire slackened. The Indians were being heavily reinforced, and began to come from their cover, but kept up a heavy fire. I halted the line, made the men take their intervals, and again drove the Indians to cover; ... When we got to the ridge in front of Reno's position I observed some Indians making all haste to get possession of a hill to the right. I could not see the command, and I knew that that hill would command Reno's position ... This movement was executed, strange to say, without a single casualty.[9]

This is one of the more enlightening accounts and it should be applied to the part of the battle involving Custer. It also points out the importance of Weir Point. If someone wanted to view the area, this is where they would go. It is difficult to believe Custer would not have taken advantage of this location. Reno's command moved up, over and around Weir Point, and so did the Indians. Certainly Custer's troops could have passed through it or around it. I would not hesitate to criticize Custer if he hadn't used Weir Point to observe the village and determine the best route to reach it. One should also note that Godfrey felt

Weir Point was to be used as a defensive position. Custer's command would certainly have found it better than Battleridge.

Anyone studying or attempting to determine what might have happened to General Custer and his troops should carefully consider the action of Companies M, D, and K. Captain Weir was a veteran who, according to Benteen, had been attempting to show how "bravado" he was, and Captain French was recognized for his bravery, supposedly even by the Indians for his retreat from the timber, but they couldn't control their troops and they panicked. The number of Indians facing them was not great at that time, yet the mere sight of the numbers coming to attack them would have had its effect on their action. Is it so hard to visualize this same thing happening to Custer's troops?

Lieutenant Edgerly's horse became frantic – even a veteran horseman can have difficulty with his mount. Godfrey realized and noted the effect Weir's and French's retreat might have had on the troops, possibly throwing them all into confusion. Godfrey was able to dismount, deploy and establish a concentrated fire. This seemed to have been a recognized method when faced with such odds and conditions. Reno, though criticized by some for not continuing to move against the village, used this tactic when he first met the Indians and was condemned for not doing so in his retreat from the timber. One should note the effectiveness of the method when employed properly. Then, as Godfrey's company again began to retreat, he faced the difficulty of preventing his troops from becoming demoralized. Although the number of Indians was increasing, the retreat was still taking place without a great deal of Indian opposition, plus Godfrey had a large supporting group not far behind. When Godfrey regained control of his troops, they were again able to drive the Indians to cover. Keep in mind that in this retreat, which caused two companies to flee and not regain their composure until their return with the rest of the command, there was firing on both sides, sometimes quite heavy, but the troops suffered only one casualty and it is doubtful if the Indians suffered many more, if any at all.

Similar considerations can be applied to General Custer's situation. If General Custer went to the ford and was shot, the effect that would have followed is not difficult to imagine, particularly if his shooting is coupled with the sight of the village and the Indians, now coming toward the troops. When they started to retreat, it would be difficult to control the soldiers, particularly if their company commanders had gone to Custer's side and were still there when the retreat began. The troops trying to escape – recruits and veterans alike – would have difficulty in controlling the horses of both the men who were still mounted and those who had dismounted. Such a scenario would also help explain why Keogh's battalion, in reserve, had stayed intact. The volleys heard by Herendeen in the valley and the several shots heard after Reno and Benteen had reached the bluffs, I would think, came from Keogh's battalion as they moved along Luce and Nye Cartwright Ridges, or when they reached Calhoun hill. It is also possible that a volley came from the soldiers firing from the area of Greasy Grass and the South Retreat Line. These shots more than likely were to aid the retreating troops, but could have had a secondary purpose of sending a hopeful signal to the rest of the command. If it is a fact that casualties were first found some distance back from Ford B, they should be related to the retreat from Weir Point.

> . . . Soon after all firing had ceased the wildest confusion prevailed. Men imagined they could see column of troops over on the hills or ridges, that they could hear the tramp of the horses, the command of officers, or even the trumpet-calls . . . Occasionally they (Indians) fired volleys at the command.[10]

Possibly this statement should be taken into account with DeRudio's sighting of whom he thought was Custer and Cooke, claiming to recognize Cooke from his sideburns. The use of the term "volleys" as being fired by the Indians should be noted.

> [From Reno's entrenchment – Benteen's charge.] . . . A large body of Indians had assembled at the foot of one of the hills, intending probably to make a charge, as Benteen had divined, but they broke as soon as our line started . . . [Another example of the Indians recoiling from a charge.]

In this narrative of the movements immediately preceding and resulting in the annihilation of the men with Custer, I have related facts substantially as observed by myself or as given to me by Chief Gall of the Sioux. His statements have been corroborated by other Indians, notably the wife of "Spotted Horn Bull," an intelligent Sioux squaw, one of the first who had the courage to talk freely to any one who participated in the battle.

In 1886, on the tenth anniversary, an effort was made to have a reunion of the survivors at the battlefield. Colonel Benteen, Captain McDougall and Edgerly, Dr. Porter, Sergeant Hall, Trumpeter Penwell, and myself met there on the 25th of June . . . through the personal influence of Major McLaughlin and Mr. Farribault, of the agency, both of whom are perfectly trustworthy and are familiar with the Sioux language.[11]

One should remember, particularly with the various statements attributed to Gall, that this was in 1886, four years before the killing of Sitting Bull. The testimony looks like an attempt to denigrate Sitting Bull and to elevate Gall's position and control at Standing Rock. I am sure Gall had an understanding of what the whites thought had happened and what they wanted to hear.

> General Custer separated from Reno...a ridge of high bluffs and the river separated the two commands, and they could not see each other. On this ridge, however, Custer and staff were seen to wave their hats, and heard to cheer just as Reno was beginning the attack; but Custer's troops were at that time a mile or more to the right.[12]

I don't know what Godfrey meant by Reno just beginning his attack: whether he referred to his beginning move down the valley or at the skirmish line. It is possible that Reno's troops saw Custer's and believed they saw the General waving, particularly afterwards when the supposed sighting coincided with Martin's testimony. Hearing from a mile away would be difficult enough if you were sitting in the valley on a quiet morning, but under the conditions that existed it would seem impossible. It's too bad they didn't insist on bringing Martin to the tenth anniversary celebration. These officers and others with all their concern and speculating as to where and what happened to Custer had one man who could have cleared up questions that still arise, but, of course, in their view he appears to have been just a semi-literate Italian, and, on top of that, an enlisted man. They should have had him retrace his steps and show where he left Custer and what route Custer took, what hill or high points he went up, what coulee he took to reach Medicine Tail. The fact that they didn't makes one doubt their overall ability and certainly the validity of their speculative conclusions.

> ... From this place Custer could survey the valley for several miles above and for a short distance below Reno; yet he could only see part of the village; he must, then, have felt confident that all the Indians were below him; hence, I presume, his message to Benteen. The view of the main body of the village was cut off by the highest point of the ridge, a short distance from him. Had he gone to this high point he would have understood the magnitude of his undertaking, and it is probable that his plan of battle would have changed. We have no evidence that he did not go there. He could see, however, that the village was not breaking away toward the Big Horn Mountains. He must, then, have expected to find the squaws and children fleeing to the bluffs on the north, for in no other way do I account for his wide detour to the right. He must have counted on Reno's success, and fully expected the "scatteration" of the non-combatants with the pony herds. The probable attack upon the families and the capture of the pony herds were in that event counted upon to strike consternation in the hearts of the warriors, and were elements for success upon which General Custer fully counted in the event of a daylight attack.[13]

It's very hard to understand and accept this line of reasoning. Godfrey seemingly based it on his interviews with Chief Gall and Mrs. Spotted Horn Bull, as well as Indian testimony which states that General Custer didn't reach the ford. Godfrey surmised that Custer, looking down from the ridge, realized that the Indians were not breaking camp or moving to the Bighorn Mountains. Custer's prognosis was that the Indians, when attacked by Major Reno's troops, become so frantic that the non-combatants would attempt to scatter, causing consternation amongst the warriors and enabling Custer to defeat them. Since Custer could not see them scattering to the west, they must have been attempting to escape to the north. (I will ignore for the moment testimony from Wooden Leg and other Indians who stated the non-combatants moved west to the foot-hills after Reno attacked.) Custer could have checked this hypothesis if he had gone to the high point a short distance from where he was. This he apparently didn't do, according to this scenario. He was sure his hypothesis was right, and Reno, with his roughly 120 men, would be successful against the Indians, so it wasn't necessary. One wonders how many Indians Godfrey believed Custer thought Reno would be facing. Certainly not two or three thousand – could it even have been a 1000? Whatever that number, Custer must have been quite sure of himself, for again he didn't think it necessary to go the short distance to Weir Point for a positive evaluation of the situation. Godfrey then had Custer striking out to the northeast down Cedar Coulee and away from the village. Custer must not have thought there was any urgent need to support Reno or to strike the village and create even more consternation. If this indeed was the reasoning for the action Custer took, then, as I have said, in the context of so many other decisions, Custer is credited with making, he deserved to be defeated.

I think Custer was faced with only one alternative at this point, either from a logical or military viewpoint. He should have realized that Reno was attacking, or was going to attack, a peaceful village, and that this action would cause distress among the inhabitants. He must have recognized the necessity for his troops to attack the village while the warriors were primarily focused on Reno, and the non-combatants were concerned with each other and thinking of "scatterating" but as yet unable to accomplish it. If Custer could strike the village quickly enough during that period of frenzy it would create even more havoc. If he could bring up Captain Benteen and Captain McDougall to enter the scene soon after, this would add even more confusion for the Indians, and they then might be able to defeat even a village of that size.

To accomplish this goal, Custer would need to know more about the village and the best route to take. He would then go the short distance to the only place along the ridge from which he could assess the situation.* That place would be Weir Point. Once there, he would have realized that the Indians were not scattering and that the quickest way to reach the village was not by Cedar Coulee. He would have then moved his troops down one of the other coulees. This would have brought him to Medicine Tail Coulee, by which time Custer would know that Major Reno had attacked and the village was engaged in frantic activity. It now would be obvious that he should send a courier to Captain Benteen. Custer, by that time, would have known Benteen was back on the main trail, and rather than moving to aid Reno he would want Benteen to angle across in order to strike the Indian camps, and to bring some ammo packs with him. Custer would have realized he couldn't attack in line, and the trailing battalion would not be effective in a column formation. He would still be focusing on his two primary objectives: first, to attack the villages in order to stir up more panic and defeat the Indians; and second to prevent the Indians from scattering. Both of these objectives could be aided by placing Capt. Keogh's battalion in reserve. The topography supported such a move as the ridges to the east would have provided such a vantage point. Keogh was probably given additional orders for Benteen when he and the packs arrived. Custer could have envisioned that Benteen's arrival, followed by that of the packs along with a strong additional company under McDougall, would provide the *coup de grace*.

I would expect a superior military commander such as Custer to come up with a plan at least similar to this; one that would reflect a logical course of action, considering what I believe Custer was aware of and had seen happen.

Godfrey continues:

> When Reno's advance was checked, and his left began to fall back, Chief Gall started with some of his warriors to cut off Reno's retreat to the bluffs. On his way he was excitedly hailed by "Iron Cedar," one of his warriors, who was on the high point, to hurry to him, that more soldiers were coming. This was the first intimation the Indians had of Custer's column; up to the time of this incident they had supposed that all the troops were in at Reno's attack. Custer had then crossed the valley of the dry creek, (MTC,) and was marching along and well up the slope of the bluff forming the second ridge back from the river and nearly parallel to it. The command was marching rapidly in column of fours, and there was some confusion in the ranks, due probably to the unmanageableness of some excited horses.[14]

Gall has now returned to his attack against Reno, and I think his testimony is plausible. Contrary to what other interviews suggest, he believes that the Indians didn't know Custer and Reno separated. It certainly meant they were not waiting in ambush for General Custer. Depending on the interview, Gall was supposedly warned of Custer's attack either by women or by Iron Cedar. How Iron Cedar was able to get the message through to Gall before the lull took place is difficult to perceive. The high point would appear to be Weir Point. I don't believe most of those Indians actually engaged in the fighting during Reno's retreat would have known about Custer's attack and began a move against him until the sighting of Captain Benteen's troops or some other event that caused them to stop their main pursuit. Most Indians do not mention Gall informing them of Custer, although it would have been possible that he initiated the response. One might recall that according to Godfrey the Indians left after Benteen arrived on Reno Hill. I would imagine that some Indians left earlier, while the last of them did so at that time. It is also worth noting that Godfrey mentions the confusion in Custer's column, suggesting that it was probably due to difficulties in managing horses. This remark brings out the problem of controlling horses even when the troops were not under direct attack from the Indians. At the time Gall first viewed Custer's command, Custer had probably been shot at least thirty minutes earlier. Custer's "main element" in the retreat from the ford would more than likely not have been in sight from Gall's or Iron Cedar's location. They would have seen Captain Keogh's battalion as they moved along Nye Cartwright Ridge, and would have witnessed the confusion caused by some of the retreating mounted troops coming in contact with either Keogh's battalion or by firing on Indians that had crossed the ford, firing on Wolf Tooth's band of Indians, Keogh's troops beginning to move toward the retreating Yates' battalion, or most likely by a combination of all of these.

---

*Note Benteen's observation after moving to Weir Point: "From my position was my first sight of the village, and the only point from which it could be seen." Brininstool, *Troopers with Custer*, p.81.

The accepted theory for many years after the battle, and still persisted in by some writers, was that Custer's column had turned the high bluffs near the river, moved down the dry (Reno's) Creek, (MTC) and attempted to ford the river near the lowest point of these bluffs; that he was met by an overpowering force and driven back, fighting to the position on the ridge. The numerous bodies found scattered between the river and ridge were supposed to be the first victims of the fight. I am now satisfied that these were men who either survived those on the ridge or attempted to escape the massacre.[15]

Custer's route was as indicated on the map, and his column was never nearer the river or village than his final position on the ridge. The wife of Spotted Horn Bull, when giving me her account of the battle, persisted in saying that Custer's column did not attempt to cross the ford, and appealed to her husband who supported her statement. On the battlefield, in 1886, Chief Gall indicated Custer's route to me, and it then flashed upon me that I myself had seen Custer's trail. On June 28, while we were burying the dead, I asked Major Reno's permission to go on the high ridge east or back of the field to look for tracks of shod horses to ascertain if some of the command might not have escaped. When I reached the ridge I saw his trail, and wondered who could have made it, but dismissed the thought that it had been made by Custer's column, because it did not accord with the theory with which we were then filled, that Custer had attempted to cross at the ford, and this trail was too far back, and showed no indication of leading toward the ford. Penwell was my orderly and accompanied me. It was a singular coincidence that in 1886 Penwell was stationed at Fort Custer, and was my orderly when visiting the battlefield. Penwell corroborated my recollection of the trail.[16]

On Godfrey's map this trail is too far back. It is bad enough to accept testimony by some Indians, particularly those that were not on the scene because they were attacking or viewing the fighting with Major Reno, and to ignore testimony to the contrary by Martin, the Crow scouts and other Indians. It is certainly not an objective way to arrive at a conclusion. Since Godfrey had gone back to check if there were troopers who may have escaped, it seems odd that he didn't follow them even if the hoof prints pointed in the direction of Battleridge. A trail could be made by shod horses escaping or being driven or ridden by Indians. If these hoof prints represented the movement of five companies, there shouldn't have been any question that they were made by Custer's command. It is difficult to imagine that in two days the Custer scenario would have been so engraved on the officers' minds that other considerations would not have been examined.

The fact that both officers and enlisted men believed that Custer moved to the ford is important as it represents their view of what would have been the logical move by Custer, and it could have been implemented by signs that were later not remembered or stated. If Godfrey and Penwell had seen shod tracks along Nye Cartwright or Luce Ridge they would have the support of artifactual evidence as well as Indian sightings, which Godfrey's do not. To believe that Custer would have then moved even farther away from the ridge where he first viewed the Indians and their encampment seems preposterous; but if Custer did so, Godfrey should have reserved his main criticism for Custer rather than Reno.

> The ford theory arose from the fact that we found there numerous tracks of shod horses, but they evidently had been made after the Indians had possessed themselves of the cavalry horses, for they rode them after capturing them. No bodies of men or horses were found anywhere near the ford, and these facts are conclusive to my mind that Custer did not go to the ford with any body of men.[17]

This is an example of irrational thinking. Godfrey condemned Reno for falling back into the timber and then not holding there – he knew they were being attacked by a large number of Indians and yet suffered few casualties until their retreat. Godfrey, in writing this account, must have just finished describing Major Reno's movement to Weir Point, and Captain Weir's and French's retreat under fire, and he portrayed his own company as preventing the retreat from becoming disorganized. The retreat covered over a mile and yet suffered only one major casualty. However, he based his opinion of what happened to General Custer on the fact that no bodies of men or horses were found at the ford (despite some claims to the contrary), and on the testimony of Gall, Mrs. Spotted Horn Bull, and Godfrey's own sighting of some shod hoof prints.

His refutation of the sighting of Custer going to the ford by others is borne out by these facts. Godfrey supported Gall's contention that the Indians knew nothing of General Custer's movements until after the attack by Major Reno which forced them to respond. One might then conclude that because of the bluffs on both sides of the ford the Indians would not have been aware of Custer until his troops were a short distance from the ford. Consequently, one could assume that Custer was not faced with many Indians when he first came into the vicinity of the ford. Therefore the question is: Why didn't Custer attack? According to Godfrey, the question is: Why weren't there signs of an attack if Custer had gone that far? A major attack would certainly have left more bodies and all the Indians would have been aware of it. It is difficult to conceive why Godfrey, who had witnessed the flight of Captain Weir's and Captain French's companies, and had difficulty in controlling his own company – primarily due to the sight of the Indians, and with very little gunfire at the beginning – would not have suspected there was a disorganized retreat.

What would have caused such a chaotic situation? It's not hard to visualize that Custer's troops, upon seeing the size of the village and the number of Indians turning to meet them, would experience concern and even fear. One might speculate, however, that even then the troops would have followed Custer and attacked unless something else happened. I believe Godfrey and others should have at least raised this question. The only plausible explanation would be that something significant happened to Custer. If we factor in the sight of an increasing number of Indians moving toward the troops to the cry that Custer had been shot, we can easily imagine the effect this development could have had on Custer's soldiers. Another component could have been the recruits, along with the difficulty in controlling the horses. These elements offer all the necessary ingredients for a disastrous retreat to take place. Custer's soldiers had certainly more reason to react that way than Reno's troops had for their panicky retreat when they left the timber. There is testimony supporting the view that such a retreat took place. The only element I believe was absent was an obtuse General. Consequently, the question that should have been raised is whether something happened to General Custer.

Do Godfrey and others assume that just because Custer's body was found back on the ridge, he had not or could not have been shot at the ford? Whites may not have concerned themselves with leaving the dead or wounded to the extent that the Indians did, but the one body that would not have been left behind was General Custer's. For Custer advocates to advance scenarios in which Custer delays the attack, does not attack, or fails to establish an effective defense, is incomprehensible.

To believe that the bodies found near Ford B were those of the men who attempted to escape through the formation of two or three thousand Indians, and not of those who fell in a retreat to Battleridge, is to me an example of illogical thinking.

> As soon as Gall had personally confirmed Iron Cedar's report he sent word to the warriors battling against Reno, and to the people in the village. The greatest consternation prevailed among the families and orders were given for them to leave at once. Before they could do so the great body of warriors had left Reno and hastened to attack Custer. This explains why Reno was not pushed when so much confusion at the river crossing gave the Indians every opportunity of annihilating his command. Not long after the Indians began to show a strong force in Custer's front, Custer turned his column to the left . . .[18]

Godfrey seems to forget that according to him the Indians left after Benteen's battalion had joined Reno. Though I think a good many had left before, there would still have been enough to have attacked Reno's troops. Such a view is supported by the testimony of those Indians who said that the sight of Benteen's troops moving toward Ford A was what prevented them from continuing to move against Reno. Then they heard the warning of Custer's troops and began, as the word spread, to move back to meet the new threat.

I don't know where Gall received Iron Cedar's report or how he managed to confirm it, since confirmation should have taken some time. Be that as it may, he then supposedly sent word to the village whose inhabitants then appeared to become distraught. However, they became upset when Reno first set up his skirmish line and fired into the village. Godfrey should also have realized that this event took place a long time after Custer had been up on the ridge, and according to Godfrey he would have seen that the Indians were not going toward the Big Horn mountains, which meant that they must have been moving to the northern bluffs. Again, it's too bad that Custer, according to Godfrey, didn't go that little distance to Weir Point to inspect what the Indians were doing before he moved several miles to the northeast to get on the ridge that Godfrey claims he went to in order to obtain the same information. Now Custer is said to have turned his column to the left and moved down toward Battleridge, and yet we still have no artifacts or testimony to suggest that he attacked or established a sound defensive position.

> . . . and advanced in the direction of the village to near a place now marked as a spring, halted at the junction of the ravines just below it, and dismounted two troops, Keogh's and Calhoun's, to fight on foot. These two troops advance at double-time to a knoll, now marked by Crittenden's monument. The other three troops, mounted, followed them a short distance in their rear. The led horses remained where the troops dismounted. When Keogh and Calhoun got to the knoll, the other troops marched rapidly to the right; Smith's troop deployed as skirmishers, mounted, and took position on a ridge, which, on Smith's left, ended in Keogh's position (now marked by Crittenden's monument) and, on Smith's right, ended at the hill on which Custer took position with Yates and Tom Custer's troops, now known as Custer's Hill, and marked by the

monument erected to the command. Smith's skirmishers, holding their gray horses, remained in groups of four.

The line occupied by Custer's battalion was the first considerable ridge back from the river, the nearest point being about a half mile from it. His front was extended about three fourths of a mile. The whole village was in full view. A few hundred yards from his line was another but lower ridge, the further slope of which was not commanded by his line. It was here that the Indians under Crazy Horse, from the lower part of the village, among whom were the Cheyennes, formed for the charge on Custer's Hill. All Indians had now left Reno. Gall collected his warriors, and moved up a ravine south of Keogh and Calhoun. As they were turning this flank they discovered the led horses without any other guard then the horse-holders. They opened fire on the horse-holders – that is yelling, waving blankets, etc.; in this, they succeeded very soon, and the horses were caught by the squaws. [Or possibly they escaped to the east making tracks that Godfrey saw on the 27th.] In this disaster, Keogh and Calhoun probably lost their reserve ammunition, which was carried in their saddle-bags. Gall's warriors now moved to the foot of the knoll held by Calhoun. A large force dismounted and advanced up the slope far enough to be able to see the soldiers when standing erect, but were protected when squatting or lying down. By jumping up and firing quickly, . . . In the meantime Gall was massing his mounted warriors under the protection of the slope. When everything was in readiness, at a signal from Gall the dismounted warriors rose, . . . The maddened mass of Indians was carried forward by its own momentum over Calhoun and Crittenden down into the depression where Keogh was, with over thirty men, and all was over on that part of the field.[19]

The above account, except for the beginning, seems quite plausible. I do not agree with the view that Custer moved to Battleridge from further east. Keogh's battalion would have done so, although not in the manner described by Godfrey. Neither do I believe that a defense was set up in the way he describes. This part of Godfrey's account of what Gall said is credible to a degree because if Chief Gall participated in the events, as I believe he did, it would be in that area and at that time. Most of the rest of Gall's interviews, except for his participation in the attack on Reno, is speculation on his part, and if he actually said some of the things that were eventually printed, they would have been outright distortions. Godfrey's attempt to reconcile his version derived from the shod hoof prints with Gall's belief that Custer didn't go to the ford, forced him to sketch a new outline of Custer's actions.

My view of what actually took place is different. I believe that Keogh's battalion moved along Nye-Cartwright Ridge, providing protective fire for Custer's retreating, disorganized troops. They then moved across Deep Coulee and probably dismounted, as was the cavalry custom, sending the horses into a gully to the east. Calhoun's company attempted to establish a skirmish line in which they provided fire against the increasing number of Indians that by now included those who had been fighting Reno. Probably the volleys heard by Reno's troops took place at that time. Gall would have been one of the major chiefs in that area. The "main element" of Yates' battalion was now moving to Battleridge from below Last Stand Hill. The Sioux warriors and Gall moved around Calhoun's troops and more than likely ran into the horses which they proceeded to run off. Then, in the area which is now called Henryville (after Henry rifle shell casings found there), they fired on these troops and then charged and overran them. According to Wooden Leg, during that time some troops, at least from Keogh's company, made an attempt to move to Last Stand Hill. This might have solicited the charge by the Indians which overran them. (The sighting and placing of the Gray Horse Troop in the location on the ridge that Godfrey and various Indians reported, is due to being the third company in the move to the ford. They, in the retreat that followed, were more apt to have stayed mounted, and have moved more toward Keogh's battalion and then on to the ridge.)

In the meantime the same tactics were being pursued and executed around Custer's Hill. The warriors, under the leadership of Crow King, Crazy Horse, White Bull, "Hump," and others, moved up the ridges on his right flank and back of his position. Gall's bloody work was finished before the annihilation of Custer was accomplished, and his victorious warriors hurried forward to the hot encounter then going on, and the frightful massacre was completed.

Smith's men had disappeared from the ridge, but not without leaving enough dead bodies to mark their line. About twenty eight bodies of men belonging to this troop and other organizations were found in one ravine nearer the river. Many corpses were found scattered over the field between Custer's line of defense, the river, and in the direction of Reno's hill. These doubtless, were of men who had attempted to escape; some of them may have been sent as couriers by Custer. One of the first bodies I recognized and one of the nearest to the ford was that of Sergeant Butler of Tom Custer's troop. [Sergeant Butler was a member of L Company.] Sergeant Butler was a soldier of many years experience and of known courage. The indications were that he had sold his life dearly for near and under him were found many empty cartridge-shells.[20]

I don't agree with the contention that Sergeant Butler's body and location provide support to the theory, presented by Godfrey and others, that Butler was sent as a courier by Custer. In fact, the contrary is more probable. It is hard to believe that an individual sent from Battleridge could cover at least a mile with what most writers have said were three thousand Indians in that neighborhood, and to advance either on foot or horseback to the point where the body was found. This might have been possible but seems extremely unlikely. The Indians speak of several soldiers who attempted to escape, and, in particular, one who they thought would get away, but, just before the Indians were going to turn back, he shot himself. This would not have been Sergeant Butler, since he was a member of Calhoun's company. I would favor Wooden Leg's account over any I have read. Toward the end of the battle he apparently saw a soldier mount his horse to the south and east of the Indians and take off with a band of Sioux chasing him. We can picture him or his horse getting shot, but continuing to fire on the Indians until killed.[21]

I do believe that the 28 soldiers, primarily of E Company, and the last seven or ten men the Indians refer to, were attempting to escape. The curious aspect is why those attempting to escape would move toward where most writers have said the main Indian camp was located rather than to the southeast. Again the exact location of the Indian camps could have played a part if they were located where Wooden Leg claimed they were. Possibly the fact that Gall, Crow King, and the Sioux Indians to the south and east were more likely to have been mounted, and thus noticeable, while the Cheyenne and Sioux fighting below Battleridge were dismounted and hiding in the grass and ravines. This might have suggested to the escaping soldiers that the latter presented a better gamble. More than likely the attempt to escape was a spontaneous move affected more by the soldiers' position than by a thoughtful decision.

What is hard for me to understand in Godfrey's scenario is why Custer would move from east of Battleridge to Battleridge, leaving I and L Companies on foot, and then move with three mounted companies along the ridge without deploying and establishing a sounder defense. Since Custer would have been in a position to see the movement of the Indians as they crossed the river and as they moved against him, it would seem that he would have established his defense while farther to the east, or made a move back to the south, or set up a much more effective defense along Battleridge. As Dr. Marquis and others pointed out in a different context, a small body of troopers, set in a good defensive position, could hold out against large number of Indians, even with ratios greater than found here. The movement of Custer's troops has all the appearance of a disorganized retreat. What we have here is forty-odd men found around Custer's body, with three company commanders whose troops are found scattered in various locations – not what one could call an organized defense. Neither do the Indian accounts of the battle suggest another appraisal of the situation.

The fact that General Custer was shot in the temple in addition to the wound he suffered at the ford, could indicate that he shot himself or that one of his soldiers did in order to avoid letting a wounded Custer be captured by the Indians. He, of course, could also have been shot by the Indians. Powder burns would not have been mentioned and in fact their presence has been denied. However, considering the conditions of the bodies, it is doubtful if they would have been noted even if there were any signs of them.

> . . . The Indians say if Reno's position in the valley had been held, they would have been compelled to divide their strength for the different attacks, which would have caused confusion and apprehension, and prevented the concentration of every able-bodied warrior upon the battalion under Custer; that, at the time of the discovery of Custer's advance to attack, at the time of Reno's retreat, this order was being carried out, but as soon as Reno's retreat was assured the order was countermanded, and the squaws were compelled to return with the pony herds; that the order would not have been countermanded had Reno's forces remained fighting in the bottom. Custer's attack did not begin until after Reno had reached the bluffs.[22]

Godfrey should have tried to be consistent, or at least explain why he wasn't. According to him, Gall, when attacking Reno in his retreat from the timber, was hailed by Iron Cedar who had sighted Custer's troops. Gall personally confirmed Iron Cedar's report and then sent back word to the village and the non-combatants were ordered to leave. By most estimates, Major Reno would have been on his skirmish line and in the timber for forty-five minutes. The retreat, before Gall was hailed by Iron Cedar, would have taken at least 5 minutes, and it would have taken another 5 before Gall could have confirmed it. We now have a period of 55 minutes during which Gall is concerned with Major Reno. Custer, who had been sighted when less than fifteen minutes away from the ford, had been moving to the east and north for forty minutes longer than it would have taken him to actually have attacked the Indians. Now, the Indians who have been concentrating on Reno become aware of General Custer so they leave Reno. It would take them a minimum of ten minutes before they could make contact with Custer, even if he had stayed close to the Indian encampment and they had galloped their tired ponies all the way. I think one could safely say that it would have been at least an hour after Custer should have attacked the Indians when this contact would have been made. What do all these facts signify to Godfrey? That if Reno hadn't left the timber, Custer more than likely wouldn't have been defeated. Does Godfrey blame Custer for not going to Weir Point and observing the quickest route to the Indian camps? No. Does he blame Custer for moving as far to the north and east as Godfrey believed he did? No. Does he blame Custer for not launching a major attack against the Indians? No. Does he blame Custer for not retreating to meet the rest of the command? No. Does he blame Custer for not deploying his five companies in a sound defensive pattern? No. Whom does Godfrey blame? Reno. Why? Because, according to Godfrey, he should have stayed in the timber, even though he was being surrounded, and even though Custer had not launched an attack on the Indians when he could and should have done so, and although he was unaware of just where Custer was or when the General would come to his aid. Instead Godfrey says, Reno retreated to the bluffs and because of this he is to blame for Custer's defeat.

According to Godfrey, Custer's attack did not begin until after Reno had reached the bluffs. I don't know of any attack that took place at that time. Custer's decision to dismount Keogh's battalion and move the other companies to Battleridge is not the sign of an attack. Since it was close to an hour after Reno set up his skirmish line before reaching the bluffs, it should have been apparent to Custer that he needed to attack the Indians, and to be effective he should coordinate his action as quickly as possible with Reno's attack. Then his failure to do so some fifteen minutes after Lieutenant Varnum saw the Gray Horse Troop on the bluffs above Reno's skirmish line should be an indictment not of Reno's actions but of Custer's. Major Reno can be criticized for a number of actions but not for the defeat of Custer.

Dr. Eastman in referring to the Reno part of the battle said:

> Gall, Crow King, Black Moon and Rain-in-the-Face now joined the young men; this encouraged the latter so much that no sooner had Lone Bull given the war whoop for the charge thanthe soldiers retreated . . .
>
> Just as the forces under Gall, . . . made their famous charge, the lower (north) end of the camp discovered General Custer and his men approaching. The two battles were fully two and one half miles apart.[23]

I don't think it is possible to set the timing exactly, but Dr. Eastman's account would make it difficult for Gall and others in the attack on Reno to believe there was no action until they reached the Custer battlefield.

Mari Sandoz states in her book, *The Battle of the Little Bighorn*:

> From up the stream, hidden by the first line of ridges rode Gall, the Hunkpapa, with Crow King beside him, their followers strung out behind. Gall had been leading a charge to cut off Reno's retreat to the bluffs with the fierceness of a wounded grizzly, the man wounded, too, in his most vulnerable spot; his wife and children dead in the Hunkpapa village. But one of Gall's warriors on a high point had signaled to hurry down the river. Another, a bigger bunch of soldiers was riding fast against the lower villages and had already crossed the dry little valley that was South Medicine Tail Coulee. Turning in his fury, Gall whipped his horse along, his mourning tatters flying out behind him, his rifle across the withers of his lunging horse, ready . . .[24]

This passage, of course, smacks of a popular writer's style, not that of a historian. It seems to be true that Gall's wife and children were killed during Reno's initial firing. This is why, it appears, Gall didn't participate in fighting Reno when the latter was still on his skirmish line or during a portion of his stay in the timber; a period, according to testimony, of a minimum of thirty minutes. Several statements attributed to Gall and explaining where he was when he first heard of Reno's attack, could account for a seeming late arrival on the Reno scene. It is hard to imagine the signaling, whether from Iron Cedar or from hearing the women during the actual run to the river because of the dust, confusion and noise. If it indeed took place, it must have happened at the end or during a lull. This scenario, however, requires an additional time period, before those attacking Reno could have come in contact with Custer's troops. Sandoz follows the assumption of so many writers in not considering this time lapse: she believes Custer crossed South Medicine Tail Coulee without going down it. If one can credit Gall's account of his own actions, Sandoz should also have Gall riding to the attack brandishing his hatchet and not having a rifle across his horse's withers.

In *Custer on the Little Bighorn*, Dr. Marquis condemns Agent McLaughlin in affecting Gall's statements to discredit Sitting Bull. Agents, during that time, often attempted to give power to Indian chiefs they believed they could work with and put down or discredit others. Agent McLaughlin has been accused of creating a situation which brought about the death of Sitting Bull in 1890. One should certainly consider this accusation in analyzing Gall's accounts. Gall might have known the views of McLaughlin and Captain Godfrey, and could have been trying to mold his testimony so that it would agree with theirs. Marquis also points out that Godfrey's informants are agency Indians.[25]

Marquis said:

> Among these six tribes (that were at the Little Bighorn) were about 25 warrior societies. Each society had one leading chief and about nine minor chiefs. So in the Custer battle there were about 25 leading warrior chiefs and 225 minor chiefs. But, even so, whatever fighting he did was as an individual as was the case with every other warrior there. He may have had a great influence as an adviser or as an exemplar, but he had no authority to give orders.[26]

Compare the depiction of Gall as a general director of the Indian warriors with what he himself said to Francis Holley, a magazine writer. This statement was published in 1890. The magazine in which it appeared was an obscure one, but that writer's report of what Gall said is in perfect natural accord with Indian warriors ways. Therefore, it is convincing. This is what he said. "I can't say that I or anyone was in command. I was sitting in my lodge and all at once I heard the cry sounded. "They are coming," and everybody rushed for their guns and horses. When I went for my horse they were running away. As soon as I caught them my plan was to try and head off the soldiers from the creek, so I circled around on the outside for that purpose. Everybody was fighting and pretty soon I heard women on the hill calling, "Daycia! Daycia!" (Here they are!) Then I saw some soldiers in that direction, and the women running that way too and we kept circling around and around them. I caught a lot of soldier's horses and hurried with them to my lodge, but when I got back every man was killed."

This simple narrative was probably the same, in general tenor, as was told by Gall to whatever other interviewers sought his own spontaneous story – and had it interpreted truthfully. He would have told it in the same way to all those who believed him.[27]

One can't help wondering what Agent McLaughlin may have told Gall before he sent him to the ten year battlefield reunion. One thing which strikes me in Gall's testimony to Holley, and which appears in so many Indian remarks, is their concern for capturing the soldiers' horses, and then going back to the village with them. This time, when Reno's attack came, Gall describes sitting in his lodge, and there is no mention about his wife and children being killed. This version does support other accounts claiming that he participated in the attack against Reno. This question is a good illustration of the chronological and spatial difficulties one encounters in Indian testimony, particularly in those accounts that don't reflect interviewers' prodding or embellishments. In this story, apparently it wasn't Iron Cedar but Indian women who made Gall aware of Custer. Gall acts as if he were able to see some soldiers, a point which is questionable, but which may just reflect the time and distance problem found in testimony. According to this account, Gall wasn't the great leader of the attack that overwhelmed Calhoun and Keogh, and he was not even there when those on Last Stand Hill were wiped out.

I would accept the following points from the various Gall accounts: (1) The Indians were surprised by Reno's attack. (2) Gall fought against Reno before he joined the attack on Custer's command. (3) The Indians did not know Custer and Reno had separated until Custer's troops were sighted. (4) Gall wouldn't have been aware of Custer's actions until Gall neared Battleridge, at which time Custer's troops were not near the river. (5) Gall participated in some fighting near Calhoun Hill.

I do think Gall's account of Calhoun's and Keogh's action, as well as the actions of Indians in that area of the field, is likely to be fairly accurate. If Gall left with some horses, as he stated to the writer Holley, it was probably at the time the Indians scared off the horses of Keogh's battalion, which would suggest that the defeat of the remaining troopers on Last Stand Hill took a comparatively short time.

SOURCES

1. Graham, *The Custer Myth*, pp. 137, 138.
2. Ibid., pp. 140, 141.
3. Ibid., p. 141.
4. Ibid., pp. 141, 142.
5. Edited by Ron Nichols, *Reno Court of Inquiry*, Proceedings of a Court of Inquiry, in the case of Major Marcus A. Reno, p. 235.
6. Op.Cit., p. 142.
7. Marshall, *Indian Wars*, p. 162.
8. Graham, *The Custer Myth*, p. 142.
9. Ibid., p. 143.
10. Ibid., p. 144.
11. Godfrey, *Custer's Last Campaign*, pp. 63, 64.
12. Ibid., p. 64.
13. Ibid., p. 64, 65.
14. Ibid., pp. 65, 66.

15. Ibid., p. 66.
16. Ibid., pp. 66, 67.
17. Ibid., p. 67.
18. Ibid., p. 67.
19. Ibid., pp. 67, 68, 69.
20. Ibid., p. 69.
21. Marquis, *Wooden Leg,* pp. 236, 237.
22. Godfrey, *Custer's Last Campaign,* pp. 72, 74.
23. Graham, *The Custer Myth,* p. 96, Extract from the *Sioux Narrative,* by Dr. Eastman.
24. Sandoz, *The Battle of the Little Bighorn,* p. 117.
25. Marquis, *Custer on the Little Bighorn,* pp. 106, 107.
26. Ibid., p. 109.
27. Ibid., pp. 109, 110.

Mrs. Spotted Horn Bull
Hunkpapa

Mrs. Spotted Horn Bull's account was used by Captain Godfrey to back up his theory. Colonel Graham in his book, *The Custer Myth,* uses the story she gave to the *St. Paul Pioneer Press* in 1883, and also one recorded by Major Mclaughlin in 1908-09. Keep in mind that the *St. Paul Pioneer Press* story on Chief Gall, was for the most part, a fabrication. The St. Paul and Chicago papers, although listening to the same testimony, did not come out with similar interpretations. At the end of the St. Paul paper's story on Mrs. Spotted Horn Bull, the authors said:

"... the squaws' story was told straight-forwardly and, beyond question, she believes every word. Neither she nor her husband had the slightest idea the account was to be published, and the appearance of a pencil and note book would have been the signal for a sudden cessation of the flow of conversation."[1]

I would doubt that contention. Since the interviewers didn't have tape recorders, the reporter must have had a photographic memory. Godfrey also mentioned the intelligence of the woman and his belief in the truthfulness of her account. I wouldn't question Mrs. Spotted Horn Bull's intelligence, but I would not be so certain of her reminiscence veracity. I think she, as is true of many people, liked to hear herself talk, and that characteristic is often mistaken for intelligence. In reading various Indian testimony, I can't help wondering, if after an interview, they didn't have a good chuckle about how the white man would accept anything they concocted.

Colonel Graham: "One of the most interesting and graphic eyewitness accounts of the battle is that of Mrs. Spotted Horn Bull, the cousin of Sitting Bull – a woman of the Hunkpapa Sioux noted for her intelligence and her eloquence. Her story first appeared in the St. Paul Pioneer Press of May 19, 1883, at which time she was accompanied by her husband as an active participant in the combat.

The story is important because in 1886, she repeated its substance to General Godfrey, who in the 1908 revision of his 1892 "Century" article, several times refers to this Indian woman as a corroborator of Chief Gall, . . . met his (Custer's) advance, and demonstrated the manner in which they first repulsed, then surrounded, and quickly exterminated the entire command."

These remarks are indicative of how often Indian statements are used as if they were facts, even after the writers have pointed out that one must be wary of Indian reports. As I indicated in my discussion of Gall's varying accounts, only general conclusions should be drawn from this type of testimony, and even then one has to be careful with those.

Graham continues: It is important too, because twenty-five years later when 60 to 65 years of age, she again retold the story to Major James McLaughlin, a former Indian agent at Standing Rock who knew her well; and who set forth the tale in her own words in his great work *My Friend the Indian,* first published in 1910. Here is the story in its original form, told when her memory was fresh, the events of which she spoke but seven years past and while her warrior husband, who was killed with Sitting Bull in 1890, was still in his prime, and sitting beside her, aided in the narration.[2]

Considering the problem the whites had in recounting the events, or agreeing on them just after the battle and at the Reno Court of Inquiry, along with the confusion she admits took place, seven years seems like quite a long time. I can imagine numerous instances of story telling when the battle was brought up at various Indian gatherings, and Mrs. Spotted Horn Bull doesn't appear to be a woman who would have been outdone by anyone. Consistent repetition of exaggerations tend to make one believe them after a certain amount of time.

Pioneer Press, May 19, 1883: . . . and it is boldly asserted that a smarter woman does not breathe among the Sioux today than Mrs. Spotted Horn Bull . . .

In the comfortable parlor of Major McLaughlin, . . . Mrs. McLaughlin, whose knowledge of Sioux is perfect, interpreting, . . . and her husband . . . the Major . . . prefaced the talk . . . It turned out later that her story of the

Little Bighorn had been often told . . . It is impossible to describe how animatedly the woman spoke . . .

The Sioux were not particularly proud of their victory, (over Crows some seven days before the Custer fight) . . . she said the Crows numbered thousands, her husband grunted a stomachic dissent. [This in itself portrays a person who got carried away in her story telling and should have made her account suspect.] . . . The bodies of the seven Sioux . . . town of tepees, which soon spread for nearly five miles along the river, and on its western bank. [Again an exaggeration] . . . To test the accuracy of Tatanka's memory, she was plied with questions, every one of which she answered readily, and finally, drawing herself up with dignity, said: "Why shouldn't I know the place? It is part of my country."

. . . A general description of the area is given and a map. [As in the Gall report by the St. Paul paper – if you want to judge whether a person is truthful it depends on how quick they give their answers. Her map is not accurate as to the tribes' locations or the configuration of the bluffs.]

The Indian woman continued her account . . . by saying that very early in the morning of the day of the fight seven Cheyennes started southeast to join Spotted Tail. Five of them, it would seem, got through all right, but early in the morning two rode to the brow of the bluffs and signaled with blankets that white troops in large numbers were advancing rapidly. The troops seen by the scouts were Custer's, for immediately after the signals, and while the camp was in commotion, Reno's command came up, unseen by most of the Indians, from the south and on the western side of the river, and opened fire. The white men were dismounted and the narrator told how one man was left behind to take care of four horses, as is the custom in dismounted fighting on the frontier. The camp as said, was in the wildest commotion and women and children shrieked with terror. More than half the men were absent after the pony herd.[3]

Mrs. Spotted Horn Bull indicates that a sighting of Custer's troops first alerted the camp. Whether she is referring to Custer's battalions or the whole command is not clear. Since there is no other Indian confirmation to suggest the camp became excited while the command was still advancing along Ash Creek, her statement would appear to mean that they first saw Custer's two battalions on the bluffs. Other Indian testimony is consistent in referring to the firing by Reno's troops as the signal that awakened the villages.

Mrs. Spotted Horn Bull suggests that the troops dismounted and every fourth man held his and three other troopers' horses. However, it is extremely doubtful if she was in a position to have seen this at the time. As with so much of her testimony, this statement appears to have been based on hearsay evidence and later knowledge of what happened.

The man who led those troops must have been drunk or crazy. He had the camp at his mercy and could have killed us all or driven us away naked on the prairie. I don't believe there was a shot fired when the men commenced to retreat. (Her husband qualified this by saying, "Not much firing by the Indians.") But when they began to run away they ran very fast, and dropped their guns and ammunition. Our braves were surprised by this time, and killed a good many when they crossed the plain to the river.

Mrs. Spotted Horn Bull's account is replete with inaccuracies. It's difficult not to doubt most of it, especially since many of her statements do not have supporting evidence in other testimony, artifacts or logic. She often appears to be carried away with her own storytelling. The Indian camp was not at the mercy of a hundred and twenty some men. Her husband had just said that he thought there were 5000 warriors and the reporter would have agreed. I think other testimony clearly indicates that the Indians were surprised by Reno and the unexpected attack did throw the camp into a turmoil. One does wonder how Girard came up with 1500 Indians in the valley before Reno had crossed Ford A. However, for Reno's attack to lead to a defeat of the Indians, it would have taken a simultaneous attack from another direction while this first excited reaction was still taking place. If another attack was not launched in another fifteen to thirty minutes, there would have been little chance of success. However, if such an attack were undertaken, with Benteen coming on to the scene shortly after, being followed by McDougall's company and the packs, it would have been possible to defeat the Indians. The effect would have been bolstered if Custer had placed Keogh's battalion in reserve. They then could have swung to the north, possibly crossing at the Cheyenne ford. This maneuver could have created the panic and the scattering which would have allowed the troops to have been successful.

The condemnation of Major Reno reflects the knowledge the Indians currently had of what the whites were saying. This was during the period when Major Reno apparently was the scapegoat, and was accused not only of cowardice but drunkenness.

Interview continued: [the troops] were seized with a panic greater than that among the Indians themselves. That the latter was very decided, however, was proven by the fact that the warriors hurriedly returning with the quickly rounded herds, met many fugitives from the camp and feared the worst on their own return.

The Reno retreat and its consequent slaughter was scarcely ended before the blare of Custer's trumpets told the Sioux of his approach. But they were prepared for him.[4]

At this point I believe Mrs. Spotted Horn Bull's timing is inaccurate; either that, or Custer, after Martin left, waited thirty minutes or so before making his presence known to the camp. If Custer did that, he certainly should be criticized and deserved the defeat which was handed him. It's difficult to accept this scenario in which Custer left Reno, moved as quickly as reported, was seen on the ridge by the troops in the valley, was still moving fast when Martin left him, but then stopped until Reno had retreated to the river and suddenly decided to let the Indians know he was there by blaring his trumpets. I don't know where Mrs. Spotted Horn Bull was during that period, but I don't think she would have been in a position to have coordinated events that happened two and a half miles apart. Her account lacks objectivity and merely reflects the fact that she was a person who liked to talk.

> ... The men quickly crossed the river, and by hundreds galloped to his rear, out of range at first, but taking advantage of coulee and mound, soon hemming him in constantly narrowing circles. Mrs. Tatanka mounted her pony and rode to the first bench behind her camp, where she could get a good view of the hills beyond. She saw the troops come up, dismount, each fourth man seized the bridles of three horses besides his own, the rest deploy and advance on the run toward the river. She saw the terrible withering fire which greeted the approach from the willows on the Indian side of the stream and laughs as she said; "Our people, boys and all, had plenty of guns and ammunition to kill the new soldiers. Those who ran away left them behind."[5]

In this part of the account, the Indians are prepared; they cross the river and they hem Custer's troops in. Every fourth man in the troop dismounts, and they advance on the run toward the river amid withering fire. The Indians supposedly have all these guns they picked up from Reno's retreat. (To the extent indicated, something they could not possibly have done.)

Mrs. Spotted Horn Bull clearly likes to use the image of the fourth man holding the other three's horses. Her account goes from bad to worse. It reflects an understanding of the whites' view of what happened and an attempt to blame Reno but not Custer. The account paints a picture of Indians crossing the river by the hundreds, galloping to Custer's rear, then hemming him in and circling in an ever narrowing coil. But then, the soldiers get off their horses and rush toward the river. The interviewers should have inquired – since they were doing such a good job of investigating – where this took place: at Ford B, Deep Coulee, Cheyenne Ford? Where were the Indians that had encircled Custer? The troops were met by devastating gunfire at the river crossing and were hemmed in: Did they then make it back to Battleridge or is she portraying the escape attempts that took place near the end of the battle?

From the time the Indians attacking Reno had picked up weapons and returned to the village, over an hour would have gone by since Reno had set up his skirmish line, and at least forty minutes since Custer could have arrived at Ford B.

> Slowly trotting north, along the outskirts of the encampment, she noted the Indians who had crossed, getting closer to the troops. She watched the latter – those who were left of them – retreat to their horse and mount; she hears the yells of her kindred and the shouts of the whites; but soon, as the former grew plentier and the latter fewer, she could distinguish little, save here and there an animated cluster of men and horses. Slowly her pony jogged down the stream, and she reached the Miniconjou camp on the extreme left – not an hour's ride – she said not one white soldier was visible on the field. Of horses there were plenty ... less than fifty minutes and more than five lives to the minute! ... the only way the Indians knew they had killed the Long-Haired Chief was by his buckskin coat trimmed with beaver, which they found on his person.[6]

This part of the account reflects a desire to impress, as well as awareness of what the whites had already contended. It is certainly questionable if Custer wore his buckskin coat during the battle. If he did, it is doubtful the Indians would have known that he wore one or would have distinguished him from others who also wore buckskin. It is quite clear, I believe, from overall testimony, that the Sioux had no idea it was Custer they were fighting.

Mrs. Spotted Horn Bull, while jogging slowly downstream – "not an hour's ride" – and taking this all in, would need to have started south of the Hunkpapa camp, since she claimed to have seen what happened to Reno. As she moved downstream she would not have been able to see what took place because of bluffs, tepees, trees and dust, until she arrived near the far end of the camp. This is assuming the camp was situated as most maps show it. The village on this far end would not have been the Miniconjou circle but the Cheyenne.

Possibly the inconsistencies and questionable statements in this account should be based on the St. Paul paper.

Major McLaughlin's account, 1908-09:

> [Graham] A long recital, filled with dramatic imagery so characteristic of Indian speech, it differs but slightly in substance, from the Pioneer Press report of 1883. Her placement of the various tribal circles is not quite the same, nor does she mention the seven Cheyenne who left the camp in the early morning of June 25, . . . Her later version says that Custer's column was first discovered when six to eight miles distant by some women and children who were digging Indian turnips on the east side of the river. As in the Pioneer Press story, she makes it clear that Reno's attack was a complete surprise, which, had it been both timely and pressed home, might well have crippled the power of the Sioux; but Reno attacked prematurely, before Custer was in striking distance, thus enabling the Indians to concentrate on Reno first: and having routed him, on Custer, whose command was met with overwhelming force and soon obliterated.
>
> [Mrs. Spotted Horn Bull goes on to say,]
> . . . [Reno] They fought a few minutes, and the men . . . bore them down and slew many of them . . . and Long Hair was still three miles away. . . . The shadow of the sun had not moved the width of a tepee pole length from the beginning to the end of the fight. [Custer]
>
> Down the Greasy Grass river . . . across from the camps of the Cheyenne and Sans Arcs, there is an easy crossing . . . From Long Hair's movements the Sioux warriors knew . . . the lower end as Reno struck it from the upper end.
>
> From across the river I could hear the music of the bugle and could see the column of soldiers turn to the left, to march down to the river to where the attack was to be made. All I could see was the warriors of my people. They rushed like the wind through the village, going down the ravine as the women went out to the grazing ground to round up the ponies . . . .[7]

If Mrs. Spotted Horn Bull was, as she indicated, viewing the Reno fight or even in the area of the Hunkpapa village, she would not have been in a position to have seen Custer's troops when they turned to the left, regardless of which coulee they had come down. She may have been in a position to have seen Keogh's battalion move off Nye Cartwright Ridge, but that would have taken place later.

> Our chiefs and the young men rode quickly down to the end of the village, opposite as to the hill upon which now stands the great stone put up by the whites where Long Hair fell. Between that hill and the soldiers was a ravine which started from the river opposite the camp of the Sans Arcs and ran all the way around the butte.

> To get to the butte Long Hair must cross the ravine but from where he was marching with his soldiers, he could not see into the ravine nor down to the banks of the river.[8]

Godfrey probably thought Mrs. Spotted Horn Bull was referring to an area beyond Battleridge and to the east of it. However, she would not have been able to see beyond Nye Cartwright and Battleridge. She indicated a desire by Custer to move to the river, but being a Hunkpapa she was not in a position to see what happened. Consequently she glided over that part (something common in Indian testimony). While most of the Hunkpapas supposedly crossed at Ford B, she refers to seeing the warriors crossing farther downstream. This statement dates her arrival and leaves a sequential and chronological gap in her account.

I believe she is indicating seeing Keogh's battalion during the time they were crossing Deep Coulee from Nye Cartwright to Battleridge in their attempt to aid the retreating Yates' battalion. Yates' "main element," many on foot, were already out of sight, having moved around the cutbank, across Greasy Grass Knoll and the western part of Calhoun Ridge toward the river and trees. This maneuver resulted in a picture similar to the one portrayed by John Stands In Timber, although Wolf Tooth's band would not have been aware of the separation of the two battalions. Mrs. Spotted Horn Bull would not have returned from the Reno fight during that stage of the action. Some of Yates' mounted troops moved toward Keogh's battalion as they crossed Deep Coulee, creating a collapsing and interspersing effect noted in many Indian accounts. The sight of Keogh's battalion reaching Battleridge more than likely caused Yates' "main element" to also move to Battleridge in hopes of uniting and forming a defense. I would visualize Yates' retreat as being inchoate with some rear guard action. Artifacts, testimony, as well as logic would support a move along this line.

> The warriors of my people . . . and opposite the opening into the ravine. Soon I saw a number of Cheyenne ride into the river, then some men of my band, then others, until there were hundreds of warriors in the river and running up into the ravine . . . And I knew that the fighting men of the Sioux, many hundreds in number, were hidden in the ravine behind the hill upon which Long Hair was marching, and he would be attacked from both sides . . .[9]

It seems Mrs. Spotted Horn Bull would now have the troops moving along Battleridge. The Indians could not have been hiding in the ravines east of Battleridge without the troops along the ridge being aware of it, from a topographical as well as a temporal standpoint. If they had, her testimony would be used to contradict Godfrey's theory, for Custer should have been aware of them from the ridge to the east.

> Pizi (Gall) and many of his young men had re-crossed the Greasy Grass river after the white men had been driven off or killed in the earlier engagement . . . where he with some of our warriors had been shooting at the soldiers, who were chased to the hill, . . . When Pizi re-crossed the river, women followed his party, and we heard him tell . . .[10]

This statement would indicate several points. One would be that Gall participated in the attack on Reno and had crossed to the east side, and then re-crossed with women following him. Mrs. Spotted Horn Bull indicates that she was there. This statement would place her near Reno's fight in the valley and would account for her not knowing what happened to Custer's troops during the initial period when he first surprised the village. Her later behavior is typical of the Indians who were fighting Reno: by the time they got back, there were gaps in their knowledge of what took place, and it wasn't important enough, at the time, for them to have sat down and asked other Indians to find out just what happened. They then threw in general statements or ignored the event which took place during the time lapse.

> . . . The Indians fought the soldiers with bullets taken from the first party that attacked the village, and many rode horses captured from the white men, who had fled to the hill. [This riding of army horses should be considered in reference to Godfrey's sighting of shod tracks which led him to believe Custer's troops moved farther to the east, whereas it may have been Indians on cavalry horses.]
> . . . Then the men of the Sioux nation, led by Crow King, Hump, Crazy Horse, and many chiefs, rose up on all sides of the hill, and the last we could see from our side of the river was a great number of gray horses.[11]

To characterize Mrs. Spotted Horn Bull's account, one would have to say that it is interesting but inconsistent, although the earlier account in the St. Paul paper is even worse because the reporter clearly embellished the testimony in order to make a better story. Godfrey, in his book, says that Mrs. Spotted Horn Bull persisted in claiming that Custer's column did not attempt to cross at the ford and she appealed to her husband who supported her statement.[12] She did indicate a movement of Custer's column toward the river, but did not specify exactly where this occurred. Her own movement to the north would make it appear it was in the area of Ford B.

The vagueness of Mrs. Spotted Horn Bull's accounts preclude their use to authenticate anything unless it would be the element of surprise in Reno's attack and Gall's participation in that stage of the battle. She doesn't mention Gall in referring to the main chiefs who defeated Custer, possibly because of her relationship to Sitting Bull. Alternatively, her failure to mention Gall could support the view expressed by Francis Holley and quoted by Dr. Marquis, according to which Gall was taking some captured horses across the river and by the time he returned the battle was over. Mrs. Spotted Horn Bull's account would tend to support the contention that the attack by Reno created a panic in the camp. Her statements about Reno and the implication that she heard Gall when he re-crossed the river would indicate that she had moved to where she saw the last of the Reno battle. This would mean she would not have been able to have viewed the Custer battlefield until Custer's troops had been in action for a period of time. She may, as other women supposedly did, have helped to mutilate Reno's dead, which would further have delayed her return to the Custer battle area.

SOURCES

1. Graham, *The Custer Myth,* p.85.
2. Ibid., p. 81.
3. Ibid., pp. 82-84.
4. Ibid., p. 84.
5. Ibid., p. 85.
6. Ibid., p. 85.
7. Ibid., p. 85.
8. Ibid., p. 86.
9. Ibid., p. 86.
10. Ibid., p. 87.
11. Ibid., p. 87.
12. Godfrey, *Custer's Last Campaign,* p. 62.

Red Horse
Sioux Chief
Extract from Report of Colonel W. H. Wood, February 27, 1877

I was one of the lead council men. On the morning of the attack, myself and several women were out about a mile from camp gathering wild turnips. Suddenly one of the women called my attention to a cloud of dust arising in the neighborhood of the camp. I soon discovered the troops were making an attack. . . . We ran for the camp and when I got there I was sent for at once to come to the council lodge. . . . We had no time to consult one another as to what action we should take. . . . We gave directions immediately for every Indian to take his horse and arms; for the women and children to mount their horses and get out of the way and for the young men to go and meet the troops.

Among the latter was an officer who rode a horse with four white feet. The Indians have fought a great many tribes of people, and very brave ones, too, but they all say that this man was the bravest man they had ever met.

I don't know whether this man was General Custer or not; some say he was. I saw this man in the fight several times, but did not see his body. It is said he was killed by a Santee, who still holds his horse. This officer wore a large-brimmed hat and a buckskin coat. He alone saved his command a number of times by turning his horse in the rear in the retreat. . . . The Indians call him "the man who rode the horse with four white feet."[1]

Red Horse in 1881 gave his story to Assistant Surgeon McChesney:

. . . I and four women were a short distance from the camp digging wild turnips . . . Among the soldiers was an officer who rode a horse with four white feet. (Dr. McChesney's memoranda says this officer was Captain French.) . . . I saw two officers looking alike, both having long yellowish hair.[2]

Once again we hear the statement that Indians were taken by surprise. Certainly a chief and head council member would be on the alert (not out digging turnips) if they were concerned and knew troops were fast approaching. As the chief indicated, they did not have time to talk. This view is found in too many testimonies by Indians not to be accepted. You can see in Red Horse's statements the desire to say things he knows the white interviewer wants to hear, a general recognition of what the whites thought had happened, and a conflict with what he remembers did happen. When Red Horse testifies to the bravery of the man on the horse with four white feet, one tends to suspect that he had heard of Custer riding a horse which many referred to as having four white feet. The long hair and the buckskin also convey this association with Custer. Private Morris of M Company indicated Captain French's bravery.[3] Captain French's portrayal of his own actions in the retreat from the valley was similar to that given by Red Horse. Captain Godfrey's account of the retreat of French's company from Weir Point would not support this conclusion, although some reports say French was not with his troops at that time. The long hair and buckskin jacket appear in various Indian testimony and in most cases, I am sure, these attributes are used for effect. We know Custer's hair was not long and it is doubtful he was wearing a buckskin jacket.

. . . An Indian started to go to Red Cloud agency that day, and when a few miles from camp he discovered the dust rising. He turned back and reported that a large herd of buffalo was approaching the camp. . . . a short time after he reported this the camp was attacked by the troops, . . .

The women and children fled immediately down Greasy Grass Creek . . . The troops set fire to the lodges. all the warriors then rallied and attacked this command in an overwhelming force, and drove them in confusion across the creek . . . the creek was very high and swift... and several of the troops were drowned. After driving this party back, the Indians corralled them on top of a high hill and held them there until they saw that the women and children were in danger of being taken prisoner by another party of troops (Custer's) which just then made its appearance below.[4]

Red Horse in 1881 said: On a hill the soldiers (Reno's) stopped and the Sioux surrounded them. A Sioux man came and said that a different party of soldiers had all the women and children prisoners. Like a whirlwind the word went around, and the Sioux all heard it and left the soldiers on the hill and went quickly to save the women and children.[5]

Testimony such as this suggests that the Indians had many chiefs with little authority during the battle. Still, many writers tend to give Gall or some other leader the same authority we grant our commanders. Red Horse doesn't say that Gall received the information of Custer's approach from Iron Cedar, and they then followed Gall and attacked Custer. Red Horse's statements concerning the warning against Custer capturing the women and children would indicate that Custer had moved toward the village. Red Horse's map also showed Custer's troops moving to the river. Red Horse may have known this was the consensus of the white man's view at the time of the inquiry, and merely went along with it. However, one has to consider his statement as more accurate than later testimony. Red Horse's statement resembles the first accounts of Curley and others. It is true that in the period of the first few years right after the battle an Indian would be more inclined to be afraid of what the whites might do to him. It is also true that through an interview he can be made to recall things he wouldn't have otherwise remembered or lead him into answers he believes are desired. This is why it is important to take a consensus of accounts and temper them with logic.

> The attack was made on the camp about noon. [This would be the common time reference made by the Indians.] The troops it appears, were divided, one party charging right into the camp. We drove them across the creek. When we attacked the other party (Custer's) we swarmed down on them and drove them in confusion. The soldiers became panic-stricken, may of them throwing down their arms and throwing up their hands. No prisoners were taken. All were killed. . . . These troops used very few of their cartridges . . . It was with captured ammunition and arms that we fought the other body of troops. [Mrs. Spotted Horn Bull undoubtedly got her battles and time mixed up.][6]

Outside of two soldiers, by all white reports, Reno's troops didn't charge into the camp nor would they have set fire to the lodges, which makes this statement hard to interpret. Since Reno's troops came close to the camp – particularly a few tepees – they might have been close enough for Red Horse to make this assertion. The confusion and panic of Custer's troops should be noted.

> The Sioux took the guns and cartridges off the dead soldiers (Custer's) and went to the hill on which the soldiers were, surrounded and fought them with the guns and cartridges of the dead soldiers. Had the soldiers not divided I think they would have killed many Sioux. The different soldiers (Custer's) that the Sioux killed made five brave stands. Once the Sioux charged right in the midst of the different soldiers and scattered them all, fighting among the soldiers hand to hand.
>
> One band of soldiers was in rear of the Sioux. When this band of soldiers charged, the Sioux fell back, and the Sioux and the soldiers stood facing each other. The Sioux went but a short distance before they separated and surrounded the soldiers. I could see the officers riding in front of the soldiers and hear them shouting. Now the Sioux had many killed. The soldiers killed 136 and wounded 160 Sioux.
>
> The soldiers charged the Sioux camp farther up the river. A short time after the different soldiers charged the village below.[7]

Because Indian accounts tend to be disconnected, it is difficult to piece them together. Red Horse refers to Custer's troopers firing their guns "but little," and to the Indians using these guns against Reno's troops. He suggests that Custer's troops were also being foolish, as they panicked and tried to surrender. He then points out five brave stands. This part of the account is questionable. It is possible that after Custer was shot, in the confusion that followed, with the number of Indians increasing and forcing the troops to the north, some soldiers panicked. The same could be said of some of Reno's troops. On the other hand, Keogh's and Calhoun's companies as well as the "main element" of Yates' battalion could and undoubtedly did make some brave stands. Toward the end it would also be natural for a certain amount of panic to set in. The recording of this phenomenon in Red Horse's testimony could appear uncoordinated yet reflect what actually happened.

Red Horse talks about five brave stands. When the Indians are counting numbers – the number of troops or companies, the number killed or the number escaping, or, as in this case, five brave stands – I become wary of placing too much emphasis on accuracy. There undoubtedly could have been five, more or less, brave stands. One could have been at Calhoun Hill, possibly at Greasy Grass Ridge, along the South Retreat Line, another could have been in the area of Keogh's company, and at Last Stand Hill. However, since it would have been impossible for Red Horse to have taken part in all of them, and with the dust and confusion making it difficult to see, it sounds like he may have been trying to make up to the whites for his other statements referring to panic and confusion.

Red Horse mentions a band of troopers behind the Sioux. It is difficult to determine just when and where this situation occurred. Most accounts by Indians mention the troops that broke away from the ridge. The Indians at first fall back but then close in and either they kill the soldiers or, in some Indian accounts, the soldiers kill themselves. Indians in this case speak of forty troopers, a number which most whites believe refers to the members mainly of E Company whose bodies were found in or beside Deep Ravine. Their attempt to escape from the ridge could and has been referred to as a charge.

If this charge happened earlier, Red Horse may have been thinking of Keogh's battalion which, while moving from Luce and Nye Cartwright ridges, would have been in the rear of Indians who had crossed the ford and were forcing Yates' battalion to the north. Since artifacts on these ridges do indicate Custer's troops moved across them. This could be the group Red Horse was referring to. Outside of sighting troops on these ridges, very little Indian testimony indicates firing or action taken by them until they reach battleridge.

Red Horse says that the Indians suffered 136 dead and 160 wounded. I wonder if he didn't say thirty-six killed, but the interpreter thought he must have meant 136 because most whites at that time thought the Indians must have suffered more than later testimony indicated.

The Indian charge which split the troops would corroborate the testimony of White Bull and others. According to Red Horse, Custer charged the Indian camp a short time after Reno but he gave no explanation of why his troops then retreated.

SOURCES

1. Graham, *The Custer Myth*, pp. 56-60.
2. Ibid., p. 61.
3. Brady, *Indian Fights and Fighters*, p. 403.
4. Graham, *The Custer Myth*, p. 60.
5. Ibid., p. 61.
6. Ibid., p. 60.
7. Ibid., p. 62.

Chief Hump
Miniconjou
1881 – Testimony

The sun was about at meridian when the fight began. That was the first we knew that the white warriors were coming. They attacked the Uncpapas first. . . . The Indians gave way slowly, retreating until they got their horses and got mounted. Just as soon as they got sufficient force – for our warriors were rushing to help them as fast as they could – they drove the white warriors back, and they retreated. They were Reno's men. I had a horse that I could not manage. He was not mine, and was not well broke; so I went to where the horses were, and caught a horse that I could manage better, and when I had caught him and mounted, the other party of white warriors charged. The Indians by that time all got together, and it seemed, the way Custer came, that he started to cut off our retreat, not appearing to know where Reno was, or that he had retreated. When the Indians charged on the long-haired chief, his men became confused, and the Indians had the long-haired chief and his men surrounded. Then our chiefs gave the "Hi-yi-yi" yell, and all the Indians joined, and they whipped each other's horses, and they made such short work of killing them, that no man could give any correct account of it. The first charge the Indians made they never slacked up or stopped. They made a finish of it. The Indians and whites were so mixed up that you could hardly tell anything about it.

The first dash the Indians made my horse was shot from under me and I was wounded – that above the knee and the ball came out at the hip, . . . and I fell and lay right there. The rest of the Indians kept on horseback, and I did not get in the final fight.[1]

It is interesting that in many interviews Reno's attack and retreat seem to take up very little time. However, one could say much the same for the Custer fighting. The timing doesn't seem to fit in with later testimony by Indians or whites. Both Sioux and Cheyenne mention how confused things were, which is natural enough, and possibly this confusion caused the events to blend together. The time of arriving on the battle scene would explain many of the differences. Sioux accounts have many of the Sioux on horseback throughout, whereas the Cheyenne leave their horses and move up through the gullies and ravines. Again, disorder and turmoil amongst the troops is depicted.

Frank Houston said of Hump's story that he liked it best as an account of Custer's end: "No man could give any account of it. They never slacked up – they made a finish of it." They did.[2]

Chief Hump's testimony would certainly not indicate any organized defensive stand.

It is odd that later so many seem to give such clear accounts of what happened – comparatively speaking.

SOURCES

1. Graham, *The Custer Myth*, p. 78.
2. Ibid., p. 78.

Chief Crow King
Hunkpapa
1881 – Interview in Ft. Yates
Leavenworth Weekly Times

We were in camp and not thinking there was any danger of a battle, although we had heard that the long-haired chief had been sent after us. . . . One came back and reported that an army of white soldiers was coming, and he had no more then reported when another runner came in with the same story, and also told us that the command had divided, and that one party was going around to attack us on the opposite side.

The first attack was at the camp of the Uncpapas tribe . . . The Indians retreated – at first slowly, to give the women and children time to go to a place of safety. Other Indians got our horses. By that time we had warriors enough to turn upon the whites and we drove them to the hill and started back to camp.

Then the second band of white warriors came. We did not know who was their chief, but we supposed it was Custer's command. The party commenced firing at long range. (Indicating nearly a mile.) We had then all our warriors and horses.[1]

Crow King's report that the camp was warned of the division of the command before Reno's attack implies an early move to the ridge by Custer. Custer's failure to attack by the time Reno retreated to the bluffs, and the fact that he was still a mile from the Indians after they had returned from attacking Reno, raises a basic question: What was Custer doing for the last hour?

> Crow King continued: . . . Sitting Bull and Crazy Horse were the great chiefs of the fight. Sitting Bull did not fight himself, but he gave orders. We turned against this second party. The greater portion of our warriors came together in their front and we rushed our horses on them. At the same time, warriors rode out on each side of them and circled around them until they were surrounded. When they saw they were surrounded, they dismounted. They tried to hold on to their horses, but as we pressed closer they let go their horses. We crowded them toward our main camp and killed them all. They kept in order and fought like brave warriors as long as they had a man left.
>
> When we charged every chief gave the cry, "Hi-yi-yi." When this cry is given it is a command to all the warriors to watch the chief, and follow his actions. Then every chief rushed his horse on the white soldiers, and all our warriors did the same, every one whipping another's horse. There was great hurry and confusion in the fight. No one chief was above another in that fight. It was not more than half an hour after the long-haired chief attacked us before he and all his men were dead.
>
> Then we went back for the first party. We fired at them until the sun went down.
>
> . . . Long Hair sent us word that he was coming to fight us, . . . No warrior knew Custer in the fight. We did not know him, dead or alive. When the fight was over the chiefs gave orders to look for the long-haired chief among the dead, but no chief with long hair could be found.

Crow King said that if Reno had held out until Custer came and then fought as Custer did, that they would have whipped the Indians. . . . He expressed great admiration for the bravery of Custer and his men, and said that the fight impressed the Indians that the whites were their superiors and it would be their destruction to keep on fighting them. Both he and Low Dog said that they did not feel that they would be blamed for the Custer fight or its result.[2]

Frank Houston's comments on the 1881 stories of Low Dog, Hump and Crow King are interesting. As Colonel Graham said: "He knew more about Indians – and in particular the Sioux – than anyone with whom I ever came in contact." He was a squaw-man and lived with the Indians a good portion of the time between 1866-81.[3] Some of his comments are worth noting:

> I judge that Reno (as one of his 'skippers' later told me) became rattled but he didn't stampede, and saved his command by pushing up the bluffs. That the battalion did stampede, I concede, but our people (i.e. the Indians) had 'put the fear of God' into the men...
>
> Among the Sioux, Horse (i.e., Crazy Horse) ranked as Senior (like a ranking Major General) of the four principal chiefs . . . That is to say, he was of equal rank with the late Roman Nose, Red Cloud, Spotted Tail and others.
>
> Bull (i.e., Sitting Bull) I think was a 'water pourer': only seven of them at a time amongst all the Lakota Nation – equivalent to Cardinals of the Church of Rome.
>
> As to Bull's cowardice: he had as much place in a battle as General Pershing would have had in a trench raid. His job was to make medicine to make the hearts and action of his people "strong" during a fight as well as before. As a Strong-Heart he had fought well and taken horses and scalps. After he became a medicine man, he was to fight only in great emergencies.
>
> Crow King's account (mentally edited by him) is good except that they knew the Yank command had divided. This I doubt, as I was told Custer's attack was a surprise. Rain told me, and, as he and I were friends I believe it. Crow's statement that if Custer had joined Reno the Indians would have been whipped is all "bullcon", told to

please the querist. Not an Indian there but was confident that Bull's prophecy would be fulfilled and that they could lick all hell and creation.

You have been in a battle. It's a melee, then you know how everything is confusion like a disturbed ants nest, or a pig in a girl's boarding school, only more so. . . .[4]

Even though Crow King indicates they were warned that the command had divided, it is questionable whether the Indians noticing the division would have known any more than the whites about what Custer was going to do: but it would be a natural statement afterwards. The element of surprise is still there in his testimony. As I indicated, I don't think Crow King saw the beginning of the Custer "attack." When he got to the point where he was taking part or could observe the battle he saw Calhoun and Keogh's companies providing long distance protective fire, more than likely from Nye Cartwright Ridge or in crossing Deep Coulee.

Crow King said it was not more than a half hour after Custer attacked that all of his men were dead. The half hour time is probably close to being correct if one altered the statement to say that after Crow King arrived on the scene the battle lasted only a half hour. If we accept the half hour time as correct, it would be necessary to explain what Custer had been doing the previous hour (at least) since Reno attacked.

A salient part of Crow King's remarks is his statement, "Then we went back for the first party." If taken literally, it suggests that Custer was defeated when they went to attack Reno's forces on the hill. Further investigation should have led to other questions, such as: How long after Custer had been defeated did this other attack take place?

Like other Sioux engaged in the fighting, south and east of Battleridge, Crow King claims they were on horseback. There is a common belief today, perpetuated by guides at the battlefield, that the Indians were all on foot. The belief is based on certain Indian testimony and Benteen's remark that he only noticed two dead Indian ponies on the field. Whether Benteen was correct or not is suspect: at least three Indians interviewed claim their horses were shot from under them. However, the Cheyenne and Oglala's moving up from below Battleridge seemed to have been on foot, and though testimony indicates many Sioux southeast and east would also have been on foot, there would have been a large number on horseback if indications by Crow King and others are true.

The lack of dead ponies can be explained in two ways. First, Indians crossing at Ford B were apt to have gotten off their horses to be more effective and protected while following the retreating Yates' troops and firing on Keogh's battalion. The same could be said of those Indians who then crossed the river below Last Stand Hill. The Indians fighting Reno, who then moved to the battlefield, were more likely to have remained on horseback. Those Indians are also the ones who claim the battle ended sooner. Undoubtedly when they first arrived they would have stayed outside of effective rifle range but remained on their horses. By that time the situation was quite hopeless for the troops and the final attempts to escape took place. Some of the soldiers moved along Battleridge to join those troops on Last Stand Hill. This led to the final charge by the Indians, many of whom were still on horseback. As the Indians point out, this part of the action lasted only a few minutes, and one could expect there was little effective firing from the troops.

The second reason would reflect the disorganization, confusion, lack of a sound defense, difficulty of controlling their horses and the fear and panic on the part of many of the troops. This situation produced poor shooting, and the late arrival of Indians on horseback returning from the Reno battle resulted in few Indian ponies being killed. This explanation is supported by Indian claims that they obtained much unused ammunition, although one realizes that the bulk of the ammunition would have been taken from horses that broke away. If the troopers had established any sort of defense, many more Indians would have been killed along with their ponies.

The supposed great bravery displayed by Custer's battalions, I certainly do not believe. The above discussion would indicate one reason why. When there is as much evidence to the contrary in Indian testimony and you recognize what took place with Reno's retreat from the timber and from Weir Point, to believe Custer's troops would have reacted differently becomes absurd or naive. But if such bravery was standard among Custer's five companies within a tactical retreat, an organized defense should have been established which in no way would have been penetrated in the time period portrayed. There were probably many examples of bravery, but also many of fear. If I were an Indian testifying at that time, I am sure I would have been aware of what the whites thought; I would see their attempts to portray Custer as a brave hero who fought to the end; and I would know of the accusations levied at Major Reno. My statements would have reflected the same attitudes, as so much of the Indian testimony did.

I don't know what message the Indians may have had from Custer in the days preceding the battle. They had certainly heard from the agencies or the war department, but I doubt if Custer's name was attached to any of the messages, especially considering how recently he had been put back in charge of the 7th Cavalry.

SOURCES

1. Graham, *The Custer Myth*, pp. 76, 77.
2. Ibid., pp 77, 78.
3. Ibid., p. 79.
4. Ibid., pp. 80, 81.

Low Dog
Oglala
1881 – Testimony given at Ft. Yates
Leavenworth Weekly Times

. . . We did not know that the white warriors were coming after us. I was asleep in my lodge at the time. The sun was about noon. I heard the alarm but I did not believe it. I thought it was a false alarm. I did not think it possible that any white men would attack us, so strong as we were. . . . When I got my gun and came out of my lodge the attack had began at the end of the camp where Sitting Bull and the Uncpapas were. The Indians held their ground to give the women and children time to get out of the way. By this time the herders were driving in the horses and as I was nearly at the further end of the camp, I ordered my men to catch their horses and get out of the way, and this time my people went to help them, and the less able warriors and the women caught horses and got them ready, and we drove the first attacking party back, and that party retreated to a high hill. Then I told my people not to venture too far in pursuit for fear of falling into an ambush. By this time all the warriors in our camp were mounted and ready for fight, and then we were attacked on the other side by another party. They came on us like a thunderbolt. I never before nor since saw men so brave and fearless as those white warriors. We retreated until our men got altogether and then we charged upon them. . . . As we rushed upon them the white warriors dismounted to fire, but they did very poor shooting, but their horses were so frightened that they pulled the men all around, and a great many of their shots went up in the air and did us no harm. The white warriors stood their ground bravely, and none of them made any attempt to get away. After all but two of them were killed . . . Then the wise men and chiefs of our nation gave out to our people not to mutilate the dead white chief, for he was a brave warrior and died a brave man, and his remains should be respected.

Then I turned around and went to help fight the other white warriors, . . . I got back to our camp. They were all dead. Everything was in confusion all the time of the fight. I did not see General Custer. I do not know who killed him. We did not know till the fight was over that he was the white chief. We had no idea that the white warriors were coming until the runner came in and told us. . . . No white man or Indian fought as bravely as Custer and his men . . .

This ended Low Dog's narration, given in the hearing of half a dozen officers some of the Seventeenth Infantry and some of the Seventh Cavalry.

The question was asked, "What part did Sitting Bull take in the fight?" Low Dog is not friendly to Sitting Bull. He answered with a sneer: "If some one would lend him a heart he would fight." Then Low Dog said he would like to go home.[1]

This is a good example of testimony that can be debated from several standpoints. One, the Indians now know the feeling the whites had for Custer and his troops. Two, in a gathering such as this they would have been leery of saying anything derogatory against them. Any statements about the bravery of Custer and his men should be taken with a grain of salt, for there is too much evidence to the contrary. I would assume Low Dog was in the clash with Major Reno at the time Benteen was sighted, and he would have been concerned they might run into an ambush if they continued their attack. Low Dog's contention that Custer attacked like a thunderbolt would have been said for effect, as there is no sign of where this attack would have taken place and there is no Indian testimony supporting it. Low Dog indicated they recognized the leader without knowing it was Custer and that is why they didn't mutilate his body. Yet while recognizing this leader, he tells about confusion and dust, and does not mention any outstanding figure. I cannot see the chief's passing down such a declaration under the existing conditions. Rather, his testimony represents an attempt to placate his audience made up of military officers.

Several important points keep appearing in Indian accounts. Both Major Reno and General Custer's attack caught them by surprise. Most of the Indians from the different tribes would have been moving to or preparing to attack Reno. The Indians interviewed did not participate in the initial attempt to stop Reno; most of them didn't seem to become engaged until Reno retreated. It is possible that since there wasn't a great deal of contact, and the Indians were primarily engaged in preparing, and then moving to the area and around the troops, they glossed over that period. The troops would naturally emphasize it more as it affected what they subsequently did, and was also important in examining Reno's actions. It is clear that the Indians attacking Major Reno heard about General Custer's move against the village at the time Reno's troops were in the process of crossing the river in their retreat to the bluffs. They then moved back and attacked General Custer when his troops were already on or near Battleridge. This leaves very little testimony to explain what Custer was doing from the time the village was first aware of his troops until the Indians attacking Reno had returned and first saw or made contact with General Custer's battalions.

Low Dog's reference to going to the Reno battlefield after being engaged with Custer's troops would imply that by then Custer's battle was over.

SOURCES

1. Graham, The Custer Myth, pp. 75-76.

Seven Sioux
Standing Rock, July 24, 1876,
Interviewed by Capt. J. S. Poland, 6th Infantry

. . . Runners brought news of the approach of cavalry. The dance was suspended and a general rush . . . for horses . . . Their narrative of Reno's operations coincides with the published accounts: how he was quickly confronted, surrounded, how he dismounted, rallied in the timber, remounted and cut his way back over the ford and up the bluffs with considerable loss; and the continuation of the fight for some little time, when runners arrived from the north end of the village, with the news that the cavalry had attacked the north end of the same – three or four miles distant. The Indians about Reno had not before this the slightest intimation of fighting at any other point. A force large enough to prevent Reno from assuming the offensive was left and the surplus available force flew to the other end of the camp, where, finding the Indians there successfully driving Custer before them, instead of uniting with them, they separated into two parties and moved around the flanks of the cavalry.

They report that he crossed the river, but only succeeded in reaching the edge of the Indian camp. After he was driven to the bluffs the fight lasted perhaps an hour. Indians have no hours of the day, and the time cannot be given approximately.

They report that a small number of cavalry broke through the line of Indians in their rear and escaped, but was overtaken, withing a distance of five or six miles and killed.

. . . the general outline of this Indian report coincides with the published reports. The first attack of Reno's began well on in the day, say the Indians. They report about 300 whites killed. They do not say how many Indians were killed . . .

. . . then the attack on Major Reno was vigorously renewed. Up to this attack, the Indians had lost comparatively few men, but now, they say, their most serious loss took place.[1]

A report such as this is illuminating. It was taken a month after the battle so the events were fresh in the participants minds. It is accurate in many ways writers still commonly ignore or discredit. The report indicates a delay even after Reno reached the bluff before the Indians knew of Custer's movement against the village. This version seems credible as it agrees with the reports by Godfrey, Wooden Leg and others. It also stresses the role of the surprise element in the cases of both Reno and Custer.

The report infers Custer's movement to Ford B and the conceivability that he actually crossed the river. It is possible that some of his troopers did. The report also states the Indians who first met Custer and brought about his retreat were those still in the villages or just starting to move toward Reno. When the Indians arrived from attacking Reno they made two major moves to flank the troops, who by that time should have been on or near Battleridge. I would surmise that the first Indians to meet Custer moved across the ford and then along Deep Coulee. While some of them engaged Keogh's battalion, others followed Yates' battalion over Greasy Grass Ridge. Most of those Indians probably got off their horses to fight on foot. Some moved farther downstream and crossed the river below Last Stand Hill, and would have moved on foot through the grass and ravines. The testimony, in agreement with Gall, Crow King, and others, suggests that the Indians arriving from the Reno battle made two major flanking movements. One, which included Crow King and Gall, moved up North and South Medicine Tail Coulees to flank on the south Keogh's battalion, which had by now moved to Battleridge. The other flanking move was made by Crazy Horse and his followers who advanced to the north or Yates' battalion. These forces then surrounded the troops. It is easy to visualize how the sight of the Indians returning on horseback from fighting Reno would have affected the already demoralized troops. Subsequently, this last stage of the battle lasted only a short time, according to the account of these late arrivals.

Since so many of the Indians who have been interviewed participated in the attack against Reno, most of their accounts show a lack of knowledge of Custer's move to the ford and mainly deal with the fighting after the troops had reached Battleridge.

The above report is inclined to be more honest in not reflecting later Indian knowledge of the whites' perspective on the battle, where one can sense their understanding of the importance of representing Custer's troops as courageous and the acceptance of accusations against Major Reno and his actions. Later accounts are also characterized by the enhancement of stories to give notoriety to those Indians who were engaged in the final actions, and to those who said they recognized or saw Custer, particularly if they suggested his bravery or claimed knowledge of his death. These distortions grew more and more pronounced with the passage of time.

The seven Indians must have been afraid of possible action against them for having taken part in the battle. That is probably why their statements are rather general. They indicate that Crazy Horse and Black Moon were the two principal Indian leaders.

The report that a small number of cavalry broke through but were overtaken and killed within five or six miles does correlate with some Indian accounts. This could account for at least some of the missing troopers.

If the major loss of Indians came from the attack on Reno after Custer's troops were wiped out, it would support my belief that Custer was shot at the ford; his troops became disorganized and no effective defense was established. Supposedly few Indians were killed in the battle and if most of those died during the fighting around Reno Hill, there could not have been any defense worthy of the name established on Battleridge.

SOURCES

1. Graham, *The Custer Myth,* pp. 45, 46.

Flying Hawk
Oglala
1907 – Interview with Judge Eli S. Ricker

Flying Hawk with others left the pursuit of Reno after he had gone to the hills, and as the Indians had some wounded, they went down into their camp with the wounded; then they crossed the river and attacked the soldiers on Calhoun Hill. There were also a lot of Indians who had followed the river down from Reno without going to their camp, and these also crossed the river and attacked Calhoun Hill.

Flying Hawk was with the leaders and could see (all). The Indians had crossed the river above Calhoun Hill before Custer left the second ridge. The soldiers saw the Indians in the creek leading to the river and then Custer came down off the second ridge and went up onto Calhoun Hill . . .

The half-blood Brule, Standing Bear, confirmed the essentials of Flying Hawk's statement, adding that the "second ridge" was the near ridge back from the river. However, neither one, nor any of the other Indian sources, mentioned any of the combat activity on Nye Cartwright, which undoubtedly occurred as confirmed by the artifacts found there.[1]

Flying Hawk could not have seen "all." He was not there to see the early part of Custer's movement to the ford or his retreat. This is substantiated by his lack of knowledge of the firing which took place along Luce and Nye Cartwright Ridges. His is the typical view of so many of the Indians who had been fighting Major Reno. They were not in a position to see most of Yates' retreating battalion. What they did see, I believe, was Keogh's battalion moving from Nye Cartwright Ridge to Calhoun Hill and Battleridge. They interpreted this sighting to be all of Custer's troops, for, by the time they went into action around Calhoun Hill, most of Yates' battalion had moved to Battleridge, and the Indians assumed that all of Custer's troops had moved along those eastern ridges and then on to Calhoun Hill and Battleridge. The Indians were not aware of the early shots by Keogh's battalion as they moved from Luce to Nye Cartwright, providing long-distance gunfire against the Indians who were forcing Yates' battalion to the north. Keogh's battalion had also fired at Wolf Tooth's band. The Indian flanking movements prevented the effective linking up of the two battalions.

SOURCES

1. Hardorff, Markers, Artifacts, and Indian Testimony, p. 30.

Iron Thunder
Brother to Hump
1881 – Testimony

. . . The tepees were close together, . . . I did not know anything about Reno's attack until his men were so close that the bullets went through the camp and everything was confusion. The horses were so frightened we could not catch them. I was catching my horse to join the fight. When I caught him and was mounted, our warriors had driven the white men off and were running after them. Then I followed the way they went, and I saw a lot of horsemen – Indians – crossing the river, and went after them. I followed them across the river, and before I overtook them, going up the hill, I found an Indian lying dead. I knew him . . . The whites were still firing back at us. Just as I arrived where our men were, the report came to us that another party was coming to attack us. We could not see them from where we were. The report was that they were coming to head off the women and children from the way they were going, and so we turned around and went towards them. Our men moved around in the direction of a circle, but I cut across to a knoll and looked up the river and saw them coming down. The day before the fight I had come back from a war party against the Crows . . . and by the time I got half-way back to where Long Haired Chief and his men were my horse was so lame I could go no further. I was nearly two miles away when the Indians charged Long-Haired Chief and his warriors. You could not notice the difference in the sun from the time when Custer was charged until he was done away with.[1]

This testimony reiterates the element of surprise by both Reno and Custer. Iron Thunder's account is typical of those which were given by Indians fighting Reno. They did not see Yates' battalion but they saw Keogh's battalion as it moved to Battleridge. Therefore, Iron Thunder's impression was that once the troops reached Battleridge, the fight lasted only a short time. Such a view would contradict those scenarios which claim Custer set up a defensive position and waited for Benteen, and would imply that Custer's troops had been defeated long before Reno's troops moved to Weir Point.

SOURCES

1. Graham, *The Custer Myth*, p. 79.

Flying By
Miniconjou
1907 – interpreter: Mr. Claymore

Some Sioux who had lost horses came in and reported Custer coming on trail, and Custer showed up not long after Custer's soldiers got here – Some of Indians thought it might be Custer. Had not been looking for soldiers in that direction.

Soldiers attacked Hunkpapa tepees first. All Indians that had ponies went out to help Hunkpapa fight Reno, and some were dismounted. Battle with Reno lasted only a short time, and my horse was shot. Soldiers went through timber and retreated to the river. My horse shot and I went back to village for another horse. Hunkpapas and Minne squaws had been taking down tepees during Reno's fight.

As soon as Reno retreated more soldiers (Custer's) were in sight from village farther down the stream. The soldiers had four or five flags. Custer acted as though would cross and attack village.

When I got to Custer, Indians had been fighting quite awhile. Some of the soldiers let horses go early in fight. Soldiers did not charge after I got there. We crossed over at all points along river as quick as we could and found Custer already fighting Indians and driving Indians back toward the river, but when we got over in great numbers, Custer was soon surrounded. The soldiers then got off horses and some let them go, and we captured a lot of them. I captured one myself. . . . After came back from taking horses to village, I came to gully east of long ridge and many soldiers already killed.

. . . Says Custer's soldiers kept together all the time and were killed moving along toward camp. Killed all way along. Some soldiers still had horses at that time. During fight, gray horses and others were mixed up. Did not make any stand except in one place where Custer killed at end of long ridge.

Soldiers had plenty of ammunition when killed. Indians closed in, and at last part of battle soldiers were running through Indian lines trying to get away. Only four soldiers got into gully toward river. Battle against Custer alone lasted about half the afternoon. Did not recognize Custer until some time after the battle and all the soldiers killed. Soldiers excited and shot wild. We lost only a few men. Four Minneconjou killed.[1]

Flying By would not have been present during Custer's first contact with the Indians. There has been no other testimony to imply that Custer was able to drive the Indians back except for the instance where the 28 or 40 made a dash for the river, and the Indians fell back in front of them. It could be the Indians retreated when Keogh's battalion moved to Calhoun Hill. Joseph White Bull referred to being driven back when fired on by mounted troops near Calhoun Hill. Flying By doesn't indicate any charge, although he implies panic on the part of soldiers. Nor does he suggest there were any soldiers fighting in the gully, although we supposedly know more than four were found in Deep Ravine. If Flying By is referring to Deep Ravine, his account would support Kate Bighead's view that the 28 were killed on the ridge just north of Deep Ravine. Again, one finds testimony showing that the Indians seemed to be just as concerned with capturing horses as they were with defeating or killing soldiers. Flying By has the Custer part of the battle lasting a longer period of time than others do, but he is also displaying an awareness and inclusion of the earlier retreat and not just the last stage of the fight.

SOURCES

1. Camp, Hammer, *Custer in 76*, pp. 209, 210.

White Bull & Tall Bull
Northern Cheyenne
interpreter: Thaddeus Redwater

White Bull:

Did not learn of soldiers until Reno attacked. Did not get into Custer fight until it was nearly over. Says (and so does Tall Bull) that many of Custer's soldiers acted like men intoxicated or beside themselves, as they fired into the air without taking aim.

Tall Bull:

Cheyenne village at north end of camp just as I have it.... Cheyennes did not learn soldiers coming until Reno attacked. The Sioux must have known of approach of soldiers but Cheyenne did not.

After returning from Reno, women going over east to get on high ground to overlook Reno fight discovered Custer coming. Custer got into flat near Ford B within easy gunshot of village, and Indians drove him back.

By the time I got there Indians had driven soldiers to first rise (where Foley lay), and they were going up the ridge to right of Custer coulee and Indians driving them.

The men who had not horses to go to Reno first began the attack on Custer and I did not see the first of it. Soldiers did not make any charge on Indians during the Custer fight. He is very clear that Custer was driven farther and farther back from the river. Soldiers fell back from the river. Some mounted and some on foot and not in very good order. Heard the volleys. The first was at the beginning of the fight at C (Finley marker). The last was at G. Gray horses all mixed up with bays.

I was near H3 and heard a big war whoop that soldiers were coming. Soldiers came on foot and right through us into deep gully, and this was the last of the fight, and the men were killed in this gully. Tall Bull says that some of the men who ran from the edge of the ridge to the gully were firing their guns at random.[1]

Once again, the element of surprise. Custer got to the flat which is just off from the ford. Since the Cheyenne were closer to the ford they were more likely to hear of such action. Tall Bull makes two main points in his account: he indicates that the retreat from the ford was not executed in very good order and he claims that there was no attack on the Indians. So the main question remains: Why not? There is the element of surprise and there doesn't seem to be many Indians waiting for General Custer. Why then is there no sign of a major attack? Tall Bull does indicate there was a final escape effort on foot, and it appears to have been the soldiers usually associated with E Company. His is one of two accounts that I have read in which the troops went into Deep Ravine and were killed there. Tall Bull doesn't say how they were killed, which is odd since he was in that vicinity. The inference, I believe, supports Wooden Leg's and Kate Bighead's accounts. It would seem the soldiers could have put up a good fight from that position, but there are no accounts that verify it. The question of artifactual evidence becomes important. Did Tall Bull say the bodies were found in the gully because he knew this is what the whites maintained? One should note in all of these accounts that there are no references to establishing skirmish lines below Last Stand Hill.

Tall Bull's indication that volleys were fired by the troops would support my view that at least part of Yates' battalion moved around the cutbank and across Greasy Grass Ridge; most likely the firing denotes rear guard action by the troops. This firing is also supported by artifacts.

The report that gray and bay horses were mixed together was mentioned several times by Indians, and it could signify several possibilities. One would be the disorganization on the part of the troops. Benteen's reference to the lack of sorrels among those found on the battlefield, combined with Indian reports that many of the troops dismounted when firing across the ford and during the retreat, could signify the order of companies as they approached the ford. C Company, riding sorrels, were apt to have been the lead company since they were more likely to have been in a position to fire on the Indians across the ford. Consequently, they would have had difficulty firing and controlling their horses, so they would have dismounted. One should also recognize that this scenario suggests that something happened at the ford to prevent a mounted attack from crossing. Be that as it may, it would mean F Company (bays) and E Company (grays) were behind. Those two companies would have been able to stay mounted with fewer problems in controlling their horses, at least at first. C Company members were more likely to be the troops who would have released their horses while firing or retreating on foot. Such action accounts for the few sorrels being found on the battlefield. As they retreated on foot they would have moved across western Calhoun Hill, as the artifacts attest. E Company, being the trailing company of Yates' battalion, would have more likely moved farther toward Keogh's battalion and Battleridge.

SOURCES

1. Camp, Hammer, *Custer in 76*, pp. 211-213.

Standing Bear
July, 1910

Says Black Bear and several others, early in morning of June 25, were up on divide going off on a visit, and as they proceeded they crossed the trail of the Sioux leading into valley of Little Big Horn.... upon closer inspection, they discovered a fresh trail of shod horse tracks on the older trail.... and one of them proposed they ride back to the top of the divide and take a look around, which they quickly did. From this point they could see the smoke of Custer's camp to their left, and away off to their right, high up among some trees, a small party of men, apparently scouts (Varnum's party). From this I take it that the shod horse tracks on the old trail which they discovered was the trail of Varnum in advance of Custer. They then retraced their steps to high ground, and here it was that Varnum saw them.

Says that Custer's dust was seen approaching the village over low ground to the east, down a kind of dry coulee. As soon as the soldiers came in sight they halted and apparently were preparing for a charge. All this time the Ogalalas were getting ready. Finally the soldiers advanced very near to the river, but before they could cross were engaged by the Indians and forced back to the ridge where the main fight took place.

Says as soon as Custer came in sight and halted, some of the Indians crossed over, but he advanced against this resistance nearly to the river before it became strong enough to check him.

Says that the Indians first prepared to fight were the ones camped farthest from the river. While Reno's battle was going on, Crazy Horse was getting his warriors ready, and, before they were ready, the other soldiers appeared. Crazy Horse, however, took time to consult the medicine man and invoke their spirits. This he did very cooly and he delayed so long that many of the warriors became impatient.

Was on the bluffs (where Knipe saw Indians), and Custer went down coulee into Medicine Tail and crossed over to Custer ridge in full view of village. Custer's soldiers did not fire into village. On my map should change places with Minneconjou and Sans Arc camps. Ogalalas were not on the river at all but over toward bluffs to west of Brule and Sans Arc. Custer's men did not fight by companies but all were together all the time. Could not make him say different. His recollection clear on this point. The Gray horses mixed in the rest and but few horses got beyond Keogh. Nearly all killed or captured before got farther then this.

Keogh is the first place where any of the soldiers stopped to fight. Those between Custer and river were soldiers running toward river on foot. Between Calhoun and monument there were Indians both sides of river as soldiers went along. The soldiers killed between Custer and river were men trying to make the river, and they were killed in the deep ravine.

At the time of the battle and while in the vicinity, no Indian recognized Custer's body, nor even supposed they had been fighting Peoushi. He saw the three Indian scouts killed with Reno and one of these they took to be a Sioux.[1]

Standing Bear's account is useful and informative. We can assume the following: Standing Bear took part in the Reno battle. He said he was on the bluff where Kanipe had seen the Indians. In passing Weir Point he saw what he thought was the Custer command moving off Nye Cartwright Ridge, although what he actually saw was Keogh's battalion. He noted that they then moved to Custer or Battleridge. Standing Bear said they didn't fire on the village; the troops were too far away. Standing Bear could see the troops, after leaving Nye Cartwright, come on to Calhoun and Battleridge. He, however, does mention that Custer advanced nearly to the river before he was forced back, which somebody undoubtedly told him. In making such a statement he doesn't seem to realize he is giving a paradoxical account. As Standing Bear continued to view the battlefield he saw the fighting around Calhoun Hill and as he got closer he could tell Custer's troops were scattered along the ridge, with no particular grouping or skirmish lines. The horses were also mixed with grays and bays together, which further illustrates the confusion prevailing at the time. He also refers to escape attempts, with soldiers running toward the river on foot being killed in Deep Ravine. I believe Standing Bear and other Indians have difficulty in remembering the several escape attempts that appear to have taken place. They often seem to mix up the last group with the larger group which left earlier and was made up mostly of E Company troops. This would be natural considering many of the Indians were not directly involved with fighting below the ridge. This lack of direct involvement along with the excitement, dust and confusion often led to recounting hearsay or vague impressions of the events.

I believe Standing Bear's account does, when analyzed, support the idea that there was a division of Custer's command into the two battalions: one which moved to the ford and one to Luce and Nye Cartwright Ridges. Most of the Indians who fought Reno saw Keogh's battalion as it passed over Nye Cartwright Ridge, and then moved through Deep Coulee to Calhoun Hill and Battleridge. By the time they reached the scene, Yates' battalion had also reached Battleridge; so, to them, there was no division of the command. The division is mentioned by those who were at the ford, such as Indians like White Cow Bull. One should notice in Indian reports the complete lack of any skirmish positions or stands below Last Stand Hill, whether along Cemetery Ravine, Deep Ravine or what the archaeologists referred to as the South Skirmish Line. Also apparent and worth noting is the disorganization of Custer's troops as well as Standing Bear's belief that Custer was not recognized.

It would appear from Standing Bear's account that Crazy Horse did not take part in at least the initial attack against Reno in the valley. It can be inferred that Custer appeared shortly after Reno's attack.

SOURCES

1. Camp, Hammer, *Custer in 76*, pp. 214, 215.

Left Hand
An Arapahoe warrior
1920 – Interviewed by Colonel Tim McCoy

I was in the battle of the Little Big Horn where General Custer was killed. There were four other Arapahoes with me.

. . . The first attack was made at the south end of the village when the sun was there (9:00 A.M.). The soldiers fired a few shots, but when we rushed toward them, they became frightened and started back across the river. Many of them lost their horses and had to swim across. They climbed up on a high ridge and built a barricade. . . .

When the sun was straight (about noon) we heard shooting at the lower end of the village, and knew it must be more soldiers. I went down through the village and crossed the river with a large party of Sioux and Cheyenne. We Arapahoes had all gotten separated during the first fight.

The soldiers were up on the ridge and the Indians were all around them. There was lots of shooting all around, and the Indians were all yelling. Everyone was excited. The hills were swarming with Indians, . . . I saw an Indian on foot, . . . thinking he was one of the Crow or Arikara scouts with the soldiers I rode at him, striking at him with a long lance which I carried. He fell over a pile of dead soldiers. Afterward I found he was a Sioux, and the Sioux were going to kill me because I had killed their friend. . . . As I came up on the ridge, one soldier who was on the ground, handed me his gun. I took the gun and did not kill him, but some Sioux who were behind me killed him . . .

Once I saw Custer. He was dressed in buckskin. It was almost at the end of the fight. He was standing up and had pistols in his hands shooting into the Indians. I did not see him again until it was all over. I walked around and saw him lying there. He was dead. Most of the soldiers were all dead, but some still moved a little. When the sun was there (pointing to a position indicating about 3 P.M.) all was over; not a white man was alive.[1]

The time element is undoubtedly wrong; Reno could not have attacked at 9 A.M. However, if you estimate the noon period for the beginning of the fighting (say 1 to 2 P.M.), and Custer's battle ending by shortly after 3 P.M., I believe this would be close to encompassing the proper time period.

Left Hand states he was fighting Reno, and it wasn't until noon that they heard shooting at the other end and knew other soldiers were there. By then, they had been fighting Major Reno for three hours. It wasn't messengers, but gun fire that caused them to learn of Custer's attack. The Custer battle then lasted three hours and was over by 3 P.M.

It is remarkable that, in all the excitement, Left Hand supposedly recognized Custer, since the consensus of testimony would indicate that the Indians didn't identify him. I wonder if an Indian who knew Custer could have distinguished him during the battle.

SOURCES

1. Graham, *The Custer Myth,* pp. 111, 112.

Waterman
An Arapahoe warrior
1920 – Testimony given to Colonel Tim McCoy

We heard shooting at the upper end of the village, and we all went that way. The soldiers had crossed the river and were coming toward the camp. At that time the sun was there (position indicating 9 A.M.) There were not many soldiers and I knew they would be beaten because there were too many Sioux and Cheyenne. The soldiers went back across the river where they dug some pits. The Indians kept shooting at them for a long time. After awhile we heard shooting at the lower end of the village, and, knowing it must be another body of soldiers, we started down there as fast as we could. The soldiers could have forded the river at that point, because we crossed over and drove them up the hill. They left their horses and the Indians took them. . . . This left the soldiers on foot completely surrounded by Indians.

The soldiers were on the high ground, and in one of the first charges we made a Cheyenne Chief named White Man Cripple was killed. Two Moon then took charge of the command of the Cheyenne and led them during the fight. During the early part of the fight, I was with some Indians in a small gulch below the hill where the soldiers were, but later we moved up the hill and closed in on the soldiers. There was a great deal of noise and confusion. The air was heavy with powder smoke, and the Indians were all yelling. Crazy Horse, the Sioux Chief, was the bravest man I ever saw. He rode closest to the soldiers, yelling to his warriors. All the soldiers were shooting at him but he was never hit. . . . The soldiers were entirely surrounded, and the whole country was alive with Indians. . . . A few soldiers tried to get away to the river, but were killed by some Indians there. . . . I only know of one soldier that I killed. It was just at the last of the fight when we rushed to the top of the hill and finished all that were still alive. I killed him with my gun, but did not scalp him because Arapahoes do not scalp a man with short, only long hair.

When I reached the top of the hill, I saw Custer. He was dressed in buckskin coat and pants and was on his hands and knees. He had been shot through the side and there was blood coming from his mouth. He seemed to be watching the Indians moving around him. Four soldiers were sitting up around him, but they were all badly wounded. All the other soldiers were down. Then the Indians closed in around him, and I did not see any more . . . The next time I saw Custer he was dead, and some Indians were taking his buckskin clothes. The Indians were quarreling each trying to take the clothes away from the other.[1]

The surprise factor is indicated here also. Custer is said to have attempted to cross the river. Waterman's sighting of Custer when the General reached the hill is questionable. I think testimony indicating Custer was not wearing his buckskin coat is sounder than its opposite. Most of those claiming that the General was wearing a buckskin jacket are Indians who appear to be enhancing their stories (since the reports had Custer wearing buckskin, they use this fact to verify what they supposedly saw or did). It is hard to imagine that in the heat of battle Waterman would notice where Custer was hit. If Waterman was in a position to see this event, and since he said that Custer and the four soldiers sitting around him were the only ones left alive, he wouldn't have tried to finish them or count coup. The number of Indians who supposedly knew Custer and were able to pick him out in all the smoke, dust, excitement and confusion is quite amazing. It is even more astonishing when you realize that many Indians didn't even know that the leader of the whites was Custer. There is a correlation between the time interviews were conducted and their contents: in those given right after the battle; few Indians claim knowing or having recognized Custer, whereas in later interviews he is not only liable to have been recognized, but numerous Indians imply they were responsible for his death, or in Waterman's case, were nearby when it occurred.

SOURCES

1. Graham, *The Custer Myth,* pp. 109, 110.

Turtle Rib
Miniconjou

The fighting started against the camp of the Uncapapa. He was asleep when the soldiers were first reported in the valley but got in before the fighting stopped and killed one of the Rees. He saw other Rees getting away with a drove of Sioux ponies. The fighting against Reno did not last long. He could not say how many minutes but only a few.

He did not see the fighting at Ford B, but when he passed back through the village to go against the soldiers on the high ground across the river the women were stampeded and the children were crying. They said soldiers had come over the hill from the east and had been driven back. When he got up with the soldiers; there was a running fight with some soldiers on foot. Those who kept their horses seemed to be stampeded. Some were going back toward the monument, and some were trying to ride back the way they came. Those on foot seemed to be the coolest and fought the hardest. No stand was made except at the end of the long ridge and here the bay and gray horses were all mixed together. There was a big dust, and the Indians were running all around the locality much excited and shooting into the soldiers. He saw one soldier ride across a hollow and try to get away. He was the third Indian to give chase. The soldier rode like the wind and appeared to be getting away from them, when he killed himself. He could not recall the direction in which the soldier went.

When he returned, the fight was nearly over. The Indians were up close, and the soldiers were shooting with pistols. He saw some of the soldiers shoot each other. The Indians were all around. Some of them shot arrows and, in the smoke and big dust, hit their own men. . . . The Indians had many killed and wounded. . . . He never heard the number of Indians killed...The Indians did not stop to scalp or mutilate soldiers. What the squaws did after this he did not know, . . . The Indians did not recognize Custer fighting or afterward among the dead.[1]

I firmly believe that a number of soldiers committed suicide and the only question is how many. I realize the Indians would have soon learned the reaction of the whites to such accusations (as brought out by Wooden Leg) and they would not have mentioned them or, if they did, the facts would not be recorded by the interviewer or the writer. Yet, considering the soldiers' belief that they would be tortured if taken alive, and the hopelessness of the situation they faced, suicide would have been a natural reaction and choice for many of the soldiers. Enough Indian accounts have suggested the fear or panic on the part of the soldiers, which has usually been tempered with the choice of words such as frightened, scared, confused, acting as though drunk, firing in the air, etc.

A number of Indians refer to the soldier on the fast horse who appeared to be escaping and then shot himself. This story has generally been accepted by whites who will not accede that others would have done the same. If a soldier committed suicide under conditions where he appeared to be getting away with a good horse still under him, then certainly other soldiers would have done the same when realizing there was no chance of escape and no other alternative except to face the Indians who had killed their wounded companions. Turtle Rib is one of the few to point out that some of the soldiers on Last Stand Hill did commit suicide.

I think that when Indians suggest that Custer was not recognized during the battle, if for no other reason than the conditions in the battlefield, their views are more realistic and credible than those who say Custer was identified and then come up with various stories which differ to a large extent and therefore must be considered fictional.

Turtle Rib's story would support the hypothesis of a short period of fighting once a large number of Indians who had attacked Reno arrived on the scene.

SOURCES

1. Camp, Hammer, *Custer in 76,* pp. 201, 202.

Foolish Elk
Oglala Sioux
Interpreters: Louis Roubideaux, Mr. Shaw

Foolish Elk said he was an Ogalala Sioux 54 years old, and, on the day of the Custer, battle fought with Crazy Horse. He appeared to be the opposite of what his name might imply, as I found him to be a man of more than average intelligence . . . He is a man of genial disposition and has a general reputation for honesty and truthfulness. . . . He talked without hesitation, seeming to have his recollections well in mind, and apparently he had no fear of telling all he knew.

. . . They arrived at the village the day before the battle (June 24). There was then some kind of vague report that soldiers were coming but they did not know whether it was the command of their recent enemy, Crook, or

Custer whom they knew as "Long Yellow Hair."... There was not much concern about the soldiers, as the Indians thought they had enough men to whip any force that would come against them ...

On June 25 the fighting started at the Uncapapa tepees ... On the part of the Indians there was no organized resistance, but men from all the tribes who happened to have their horses grabbed up their guns and went up the river to join in the fight. The fight did not last long, and before the larger part of the Indians could get there, they had chased the soldiers out of the river valley and up into the bluffs. The soldiers retreated across the river at the nearest point they could reach and seemed to be in too much of a hurry [what a nice euphemism] to take their back track to the ford where they had gone into the valley.

Before the Indians had decided what they would do with these soldiers who made the first attack, a force of soldiers was seen coming from the east. These men sat on their horses and fired across the river into the village without getting into it. He afterwards heard that one man rode his horse over into the village and was killed, but he did not see him.[1]

Foolish Elk indicates that the larger number of Indians hadn't reached Reno when he retreated from the timber, but were either on their way or in preparation. His statement that Reno was in too much of a hurry to take the back trail would support Wooden Leg in implying that the troops could have retreated successfully if they had been organized enough to have tried.

Foolish Elk was not there at the time but he heard that Custer's troops had moved to the river. Two elements were prominent in most of the Sioux testimony: the movement to the river by Custer's troops, and the preoccupation of the warriors with Major Reno. The Indians were not sitting and waiting for General Custer, so why wasn't a major attack launched? "These men sat on their horses and fired across the river into the village without getting into it." Why didn't they attack? After all, that command was led by the courageous Custer, not Reno.

The Indians were now getting their horses in from the hills and soon came up in large numbers. Some crossed the stream farther down and others crossed the ford and followed on after Custer in overwhelming numbers.

Foolish Elk brings out two very important points: (1) He indicates Custer came to the river and fired across it but did not get into the village. (2) That Indians were still getting horses in from the hills and were soon there in large numbers. This would mean Custer's move to the river occurred fairly soon after the Reno fighting commenced.

Foolish Elk continues: They could not see how such a small force of soldiers had any chance to stand against them. The Indians were between Custer and the river and all the time coming up and getting around to the east of him, passing around both his front and rear. Custer was following the ridges and the Indians were keeping abreast of him in the hollows and ravines. Personally, he was with the Indians to the east, or on Custer's right. Custer charged the Indians twice (probably at Calhoun and at the monument or in gully toward river from monument) but could not drive them away, and then the battle became furious. It did not appear to him that a stand was made by Custer's men anywhere except at the monument. He was in the gully and saw the soldiers killed on the side hill (Keogh) as they "marched" toward the high ground at end of ridge. They made no stand here but all were going toward the high ground at end of ridge.[Indicating Custer did not send out companies from Last Stand Hill and the two battalions were attempting to come together.] The gray horses went up in a body; then came bay horses and men on foot all mixed together. The men on the horses did not stop to fight, but went ahead as fast as they could go. The men on foot, however, were shooting as they passed along. When the horses got to the top of the ridge the gray ones and bays became mingled, and the soldiers with them were all in confusion. The Indians were so numerous that the soldiers could not go any further, and they knew they had to die.[2]

I agree with Camp on the two charges expressed by Foolish Elk. One of the two attacks more than likely took place near Deep Coulee and involved Keogh's battalion or Calhoun's company as they moved to Battleridge. This move in a northwest direction would have been toward the Indians moving up from the ford. The other charge could have been the 28 or so attempting to escape toward the river. The Indians, subject to confusion and the change of meaning in retelling, could have referred to both as attacks.

Although some would believe Foolish Elk's recounting of the grays, bays, and dismounted men moving to the top of the ridge refers to the command's movement along the ridge, I will differ with such interpretation and present the account as it supports my hypothesis of the events that took place.

Foolish Elk was an Oglala and, as he indicated, was with Crazy Horse. Thus, he must have been to the north and east of Custer's troops during the encircling process. John Stands In Timber was not aware that Custer divided his troops and placed Captain Keogh's battalion in reserve; he believed Custer's troops moved below Last Stand Hill to where the cemetery is now located. I calculate they moved to Battleridge when they saw Keogh's battalion approaching the southern end of the ridge. The two battalions attempted to link up with each other but by that time the Indians were so numerous, they made the maneuver impossible.

Foolish Elk conveys several elements which I believe support my view. What stands out in Foolish Elk's memory is the image of the Indians stopping Keogh's linkage drive; but he also notices and is involved with the position of Yates' "main element" as they move from the cemetery area to the ridge. He notes the grays moving to the top of the ridge, then the bays and men on foot. Many of the Gray Horse Troop are still mounted, due to the fact that they were the rear company as Custer moved to Ford B. F Company on bays are at that time next in line and would also have been apt to have stayed mounted, at least a large number of them. One gets the impression from Indian accounts that there were fewer bays than grays. If that is true, the reason for the disparity could be that Yates assigned some of them to rear guard duty as the command moved from Weir Point to Medicine Tail Coulee. They could be the ones Curley refers to and also the Rees (note my analysis of Arikara testimony). They might also be the missing ones mentioned by Reno, or the soldiers some Indians say escaped but were killed some distance from the main battle scene.

C Company, which could have been the lead company as they reached the ford, would have dismounted to be able to fire more effectively on the Indians across the ford. They would have had difficulty in maintaining control of their horses, and so many of the animals broke away or were turned loose. This could account for DeRudio's sighting of sorrels ridden by Indians, and the fact that few sorrels were found on the battlefield.

When Yates' battalion's "main element" reached the top of the ridge already in disorder, the number of Indians attacking Keogh's troops caused them to become even more mixed up, disoriented and panicky. I believe it would have been at that time that some troops, predominantly of E Company, made their attempted escape to the river in what Foolish Elk called a charge. The fighting on Last Stand Hill was intensified as Calhoun's company was also overrun and more Indians moved against Last Stand Hill. Then the Indians began breaking through the troops as described by Joseph White Bull, He Dog, and others. There was a last desperate attempt by a few troopers to escape and the battle was over.

Foolish Elk's last sentence ". . . and they knew they had to die," may have been a subtle way of indicating that many saw no alternative but to commit suicide.

On the day of the battle no Indian recognized Custer, either alive or dead. On the next day one of the Uncpapa men who knew him recognized him from his features, and later his horse was recognized among the captured animals. This was the sorrel horse "Dandy" with white face and white feet.[3]

There are different reports concerning Custer's horse. Some say he was found dead on the battlefield while others claim he was captured. It is odd the Indians would know Custer's horse. The horse described would have been Vic, not Dandy, and Custer would have been riding Vic.

SOURCES

1. Camp, Hammer, *Custer in 76*, pp. 197, 198.
2. Ibid., 198, 199.
3. Ibid., 200.

He Dog
Oglala
Interpreter: William Berger

70 years old – . . . When fought Crook, Oglala village was on Sundance Creek, not far from Little Bighorn. A bluff with pines on it near by. [this must have been at the lone tepee.]

Indian in lone tepee was a Sans Arc, a brother of Turning Bear. He was shot through bowels in Crook fight . . . The reason we did not pursue Crook was that we were too far from our villages which were not only a long distance off but were strung out over much country. Did not pursue Crook because afraid Crows and Shoshones would get at our village.

It has always been an argument among Sioux whether second or third day after we moved camp to Little Bighorn that Sioux, part of seven Sioux saw Custer's dust. These Indians did not come back and warn village but made a circle around the soldiers and went on southeast to the agencies. Fast Horn was the Indian whom Varnum saw from the Crow's Nest, and he got back to village only a short time before Reno appeared. . . . Did not expect to fight here as Crook had gone away . . . More Hunkpapas than any other tribe. Minneconjou next. Hunk and Blackfeet together had 600 or 700 lodges. (Thinks 1800 lodges in whole village is about right.) Did not see any white man among Sioux. In my camp there was a Canadian half breed who spoke very good English as well as Sioux.

> When Reno approached, the Hunks went out ahead, mostly on foot, and I was slow in getting my horse. The Hunks went up to point of timber and held the soldiers back. I was on hill to west of Reno's skirmish line, and Indians were getting ready for word to charge in a body on soldiers in timber. Sioux had not all got there yet, but Indians from all tribes – all that could get horses and get there. Just as we charged, the soldiers left the timber in two bunches on their horses as fast as they could ride up the river. Chased Indian scouts from timber to river also and killed some of them. Saw Benteen coming and quit pursuing Reno.[1]

More than most Indian accounts, this one focuses on a certain time period before Reno left the timber. He Dog's account brings out the element of surprise, and suggests that warriors from all tribes, if they could get hold of a horse, went to face Reno. Not all of the Indians managed to get there by the time Reno retreated from the timber. This is apparent in other Indian testimony.

> I went back to Hunkpapa camp, and then we looked and saw other soldiers coming on the big hill right over east. They kept right on down the river and crossed Medicine Tail Coulee and onto little rise. [The first rise above flat south of the mouth of Medicine Tail where Foley was found.] Pointed distance as same from his office to tank so that it agrees with my map exactly (about 600 ft.).

> Here Custer's line was scattered all along parallel with river from Foley and Butler. When Custer passed near to Ford B, he was moving as though to reach the lower end of our camp. (It is my opinion that the 5 men killed on hill by cut bank opposite village were at the head of the column and were met by Indians moving up the river.) The Indians had left the camp over west to get ready. There was no fighting while Custer down near the river but a few shots down there. No general fighting, fifteen or twenty Sioux on east side of river, and some of soldiers replied, but not much shooting there. Did not hear Custer fire any volleys.[2]

He Dog points out that the sighting of Benteen's column caused the Indians to pull up and not continue their pursuit of Reno's troops. I do not agree that the five killed near the cutbank would have been at the head of the column; I think they were killed in the retreat from the ford as outlined by White Cow Bull.

I consider He Dog's report an excellent example of what took place with the Indians who were involved in the attack against Reno. When Reno retreated from the timber they pursued him to the bluffs. They sighted Benteen's battalion and halted their pursuit of Reno, at which time they learned other soldiers were threatening the village. They then returned to the village and saw troops on Nye Cartwright Ridge. Yates' "main element" had already retreated around the cutbank and the troops were out of sight as they moved toward the present cemetery area. He Dog and the others saw some of Yates' battalion who were still in Deep Coulee and Keogh's battalion as they moved along Nye Cartwright in an effort to reach and support Yates' troops. The Indians, including He Dog, then crossed and moved to attack the troops. By then Keogh's battalion had reached Calhoun Ridge and the hogback. Calhoun's company attempted to establish skirmish positions. At that time the "main element" of Yates' battalion was moving to Battleridge and made an attempt to link up with Keogh's battalion, but the troops were too disorganized to accomplish the linkage or to establish a sound defensive position. That part of the fighting lasted only a half hour or so before the troops were overwhelmed.

After the battle, as they tried to relate their battlefield exploits, Indians dwelled on the Reno fighting and the last stages of the battle involving Custer. There was some mention of troops reaching the ford and firing on the village, but many would not have heard these accounts and those that did, if they were not actually involved in the events, would not necessarily have mentioned them in their later interviews. Some Indian witnesses did recount seeing Indian warriors who had already crossed the ford, but they assumed the warriors went to meet the troops they saw on Nye Cartwright, which in their minds represented all of Custer's command. Others merely related, as He Dog did, that there was some firing at the river but not much, and few Indians were there. What most Indians saw and remembered were troops moving from Nye Cartwright across Deep Coulee to Battleridge and the fighting that ensued. This was a disorganized period and the Indians were not aware of separate battalions, nor did they know that some of Custer's troops had reached the ford while others had been placed in reserve. Neither were they aware that while some troops were on the ridges to the east, others had already reached the ford and retreated around the cutbank to below Last Stand Hill, from where they then moved to Battleridge. Standing Bear's paradoxical account is a good example.

Although many Indians were not fighting Reno, they were either on their way or making battle preparations. By the time most of those Indians became aware of Custer's troops and moved to the Miniconjou Ford, Yates' battalion had already retreated. We have to remember that to see up South or North Medicine Tail Coulee one has to be opposite the ford or even to have crossed it.

One should also keep in mind the following: Custer's command was seen by Reno's troops on the ridge above the valley before Reno went into action. Reno was engaged for roughly forty minutes while in the valley before he retreated from the timber. His retreat to the river would have taken 15 minutes before the Indians pursuing him left. (Evidence could be used to substantiate an even longer period.) It would have taken another 15 minutes for those Indians to have reached Ford B to where they were in a position to view Custer's command. We now have over an hour in which Custer would not have moved over 2 to 2 1/2 miles, according to those scenarios. Custer could have reached the ford and attacked the village in 15 minutes. What was Custer doing for over 45 minutes? Again, we need to point out this was Custer, not Reno.

> Says location of Foley is right and he the one who shot himself. Before the fight started, we drove him up a slope to a ridge (Keogh) and over to other side of it. Soldiers mounted all time and kept going right along. All together all time. Did not fight by companies. Indians all along Custer ridge, and Custer went down along hollow by Keogh.
>
> At this time, Indians all around. At first gray horses all together but after got on hill mixed up with other horses. Fighting started at Finley and kept up all along. At Keogh is where Crazy Horse charged and broke through and split up soldiers into two bunches. Horses stampeded toward river, getting away from soldiers. There was no charge by Custer's (men) on ridge during fight. Custer's men at end of ridge, did not run out of ammunition. Found ammunition on dead soldiers.
>
> When the men rushed from Custer's last stand toward river, the dismounted ones took to the gully, and the mounted ones tried to get away to the south toward Finley. Line H to C mounted soldiers trying to get away when they ran toward gully, Foley rode out of fight from H. [corroborates 28 dead men in the gully.]
>
> Fight with Custer did not last much more than an hour, as nearly as I can estimate it.... Cheyennes were very brave in this fight and took a leading part. The bloodthirsty ones got tired of scalping before came to Custer's group. Never knew about Bustard killed in village....
>
> After killing all of Pecushi's soldiers, we attacked the other soldiers and had them cut off and surrounded on the high bluffs...
>
> The number of Indians killed at Little Big Horn was between thirty and forty...[3]

He Dog's testimony reflects the view of others who were fighting Major Reno, and is one of the more instructive accounts. Some of the details should be emphasized. He Dog refers to Custer's move against the village, but since little fighting took place and he was not involved, he barely mentions it. He is aware of the troop movement on Nye Cartwright Ridge, but when he arrives the troops are mainly along Battleridge. He does recount fighting that developed along Calhoun Hill.

There are two essential points He Dog makes in his account. One is his claim that "there was no fighting while Custer down near the river but a few shots down there."[4] With his report, and those others which mention Custer by the river, it is apparent there were comparatively few Indians and little action at that time. But what was the reason?

The other point is that there are no accounts of companies moving to establish skirmish lines or having set up skirmish lines once Custer is on Battleridge. The archaeologists and writers who present this scenario must not only have artifacts but testimony to support it. Indian accounts of troops leaving Battleridge do not suggest that any skirmish lines were undertaken; there were only escape attempts. What makes one wonder is the void surrounding the fate of those trying to escape. We know they were killed. How?

He Dog supports other statements of the escape attempt by a trooper who nearly succeeded and then killed himself. He says the trooper was Foley and he was with those trying to escape near the end of the battle. He Dog says that 28 soldiers were found in the gully. This number supports army figures, but he is one of the few Indians who places the dead soldiers there. It would seem that a good many artifacts should have been found in and around the gully, if that's where the troops fought and died. There haven't' been many. Why?

He Dog infers that Custer was defeated before Reno's troops were seen at Weir Point.

SOURCES

1. Camp, Hammer, *Custer in 76*, pp. 205, 206.
2. Ibid., pp. 206, 207.
3. Ibid., pp. 207, 208.
4. Ibid., p. 207.

Joseph White Bull
1932 – The Chief was eighty three when Vestal interviewed him

It was not yet sunup when he stepped out of his wife's tipi in the Sans Arc Sioux camp circle, loosened the picket ropes of the family horses and drove his ponies to the river for water. . . . When the horses would drink no more he drove them north of the camp to graze, left them and went home for breakfast. Later he returned, trying to keep them in a bunch about a hundred yards west of the river. . . . White Bull remained herding the horses without a thought of any danger, . . . It was not yet time for the midday watering when White Bull, watching his horses north of the camp, heard a man yelling the alarm. Immediately he jumped on his best running horse, a fast bay, and ran his ponies back to camp. Before he reached it everyone in camp had seen the tower of dust coming from the south, and below it the blue shirts of the soldiers . . . .

All through that great camp was the confusion of complete surprise. Old men were shouting commands and advice, young men running to catch up their horses, women and children streaming away to the north afoot and on horseback, trying to escape the soldiers. They abandoned their tents, snatched up their babies and called their children, White Bull saw young girls clutching shawls over their frightened heads, fat matrons puffing and perspiring, old women shriveled as mummies, hobbling along with their sticks, trying to save themselves . . . White Bull then sped up river hard as he could ride to the camp of his uncle, Sitting Bull, . . . By the time he arrived, the women and children had fled, and about a thousand warriors were gathering to resist the troops, whose bullets were already crashing through the tipis too high to hurt anyone. When White Bull reached the south end of the great camp, he saw a lively fight going on in the open, where the Ree and Crow government scouts were trying to run off the Sioux ponies. Everything was smothered in a great cloud of smoke. Immediately after, the soldiers dismounted and formed a line in the open facing the north . . .

(Reno leaves the timber and flees to the bluffs.) Just then the foremost Indians halted and White Bull heard some one behind him yelling that troops were coming from the east toward the north end of the camp three miles down-river. White Bull was near the water and turned downstream with the rest to meet the new danger. Some of the Indians rode through all of the camps and crossed the stream below them to block Custer's advance. White Bull and many other crossed almost at once, streaming up the ravine to strike Custer on the flank. As he advanced he saw Custer's five troops trotting along the bluffs parallel to the river. White Bull saw there would be a big fight. He stopped, unsaddled his horse, and stripped off his leggings. He thought he could fight better so.[1]

In this account the surprise and the effect on the camp are similar to most Indian testimony. Those Indians attacking Major Reno learn of Custer after the lull as Reno moves to the bluffs. Nothing is said of sighting Benteen. This is 56 years after the battle and it's not expected that his memory be exact. Too many things might have influenced his perspective over the years. Custer would have been, as he said, roughly three miles away. There had to be time for the signal to reach them after Custer was first sighted. It would take ten to fifteen minutes for him to have reached the vicinity of Custer. I believe his statement of five troops would have come from hearing later that Custer had five troops; it is improbable that at the time, with the dust, chaos, limited visibility and probable lack of knowledge about troops, he would have ascertained that there were five companies. It could just as well have been more or less. Since we know many of the warriors didn't attack Reno, they would have moved against Custer's troops immediately after the first firing. Before that event, Custer was aware of the size of the village and the number of warriors he would be facing, and yet he continued to move to the north and away from the support he sent for. I think the only reasonable answer to explain this behavior is that White Bull saw Keogh's battalion as it moved in support of Yates' retreating battalion.

> White Bull . . . rode up the ravine with a great horde of warriors. Most of Custer's five troops of cavalry had passed the head of the ravine by the time White Bull was near enough to shoot at the soldiers. From where he was, the soldiers seemed to form four groups of mounted men, heading northwest along the ridge. He was shooting at the group in the rear. (Lt. Calhoun's command.)
>
> . . . The soldiers fired back from the saddle. Their fire was so effective that some of the Indians, including White Bull, fell back to the south. Soon after the white men halted. Some of them got off their horses to fight. By this time the Indians were all around the soldiers . . . When White Bull was driven out of the ravine by the fire of Lt. Calhoun's men, he rode south and worked his way over to the east of that officer's command, and there joined a party of warriors with Crazy Horse.[2]

Vestal may be interjecting the officers' names, although, by the time of the interview, I am sure White Bull was familiar with them, just as he was aware of the various views of the battle held by the whites. He also had been honored on the battlefield by the whites. These points should be remembered when interpreting his testimony.

White Bull mentions riding up one of the ravines with a great number of Indians after the troops had passed the head of the ravine, which would mean they had left Luce and Nye Cartwright ridges and were moving to Battleridge. I believe most of the Indians would have crossed at Ford B, but some had moved along the bluffs after Reno's engagement, others had already crossed the river below Last Stand Hill. Then, coinciding with White Bull's movement, Crazy Horse and his followers went farther downstream. They crossed the Little Bighorn and moved to encircle the troops from the north. Supposedly, Calhoun's troops firing from the saddle, were so effective that the Indians, including one of the bravest, White Bull, fell back to the south. (As I point out elsewhere, this could be the attack and falling back which is mentioned by some Indian witnesses.)

Assuming the events happened the way White Bull remembers, and Custer's two battalions were still under disciplined order, as most writers believe they were, why didn't they engage in an effective, or at least a recognizable, attempt to retreat to where they knew their support was? Either one has to condemn Custer, or assume that the troops had become disorganized. Custer and his officers would certainly have recognized the need to retreat and would have wanted to move back and unite with the rest of the command. What would have prevented them from taking such action? Not the Indians, if they indeed fell back from gunfire by Calhoun's company. They might have been strong enough to have prevented the troops from reaching their goal, but the attempt should have been made if the soldiers were orderly and under officer control. So why were they disorganized? Once a retreat starts, the soldier's psychology changes, as evidenced by Reno's troops in their retreat from the valley and by D and M Companies from Weir Point. It then becomes necessary to have a strong leader, such as Lieutenant Godfrey in the retreat from Weir Point. I believe such leadership would have been exhibited by General Custer or any of his major officers, if they had been in a position to have done so. However, the three commanders who would have been instrumental in conducting such a retreat were not with their companies. Why? Keogh and Calhoun were with their troops, and it's one of the basic reasons I believe they had been placed in a reserve role, and sent to Luce or Nye Cartwright Ridges before Custer moved to the ford with Yates' battalion. What then prevented a disciplined retreat and an attempt to join the four known companies and the ammunition supply necessary to hold our for any length of time against the number of Indians the soldiers knew they were facing? This is the most important question pertaining to that stage of the battle.

> . . . By this time a large number of Indians were gathering around Calhoun's troops. They were particularly numerous south of him. The troopers at the tail of the column were falling back along the ridge, leaving their dead and wounded behind them, trying to join forces with Keogh's troop. Keogh's men were fighting on foot.
> . . . 'this time I will not turn back'; and charged at a run on the fleeing troopers of the last company. . . . this charge seemed to break the morale of the survivors of Calhoun's troop. They all ran to join Keogh, every man for himself, afoot and on horseback.
> By that time the last of Calhoun's men had joined Keogh's troopers, and all together they were falling back northwestward along the ridge to their comrades of the third group. A bugle blared. Those soldiers who still had horses were mounting.
> He saw a mounted trooper left behind; his horse had played out . . .
> Some troopers were left afoot. . . .
> The remnants of Calhoun's and Keogh's troops had now joined the troopers around Custer to the north and west near where the monument is now. The fourth mass of soldiers (the commands of Capt. G.W. Yates, Captain Tom Custer, and Lt. A. E. Smith) was then below these down the hill toward the river. The air was full of dust and smoke.[3]

White Bull does not indicate what number of troopers were mounting their horses or just where they went. This could have been the 40 or 28 men that some Indians referred to, even though the soldiers are often described as being on foot. Wooden Leg and Kate Bighead claim they were on horseback. According to He Dog, Foley was with that group and came close to escaping, before he shot himself. If this was true, we know the others on horseback did not get that far; so the question of just how they died is unclear.

White Bull states that, from some distance to the south, he saw Custer's formation in four groups to the northwest along the ridge. He then locates the fourth group lower down from Last Stand Hill, which would suggest that they moved off Battleridge to that lower point. I doubt if White Bull could actually see from where he was because of the lay of the land and the circumstances in general. He may simply be recounting what he heard of troops in that location. His account supports John Stands In Timber's report. These soldiers were not there when White Bull made his move through the troops on the hill, so they must have moved to Last Stand Hill some time before. There is no mention by other Indians of what the archaeologists call the South Skirmish Line during the late stage of the battle.

By this time all the troopers on the hill had let their horses go. They lay down and kept shooting . . . bays, sorrels, and grays were running in all directions. [In contrast to other accounts sorrels are mentioned. It is to be expected there would be sorrels even if the other reports were in essence true.] Many of the Indians stopped shooting and chased these loose horses. . . . White Bull – caught only one sorrel . . . immediately afterwards White Bull's horse was shot down. . . .

Then for a time all the soldiers stood together on the hill near where the monument is now, ringed in by the Sioux, dying bravely one by one . . . only a few remained alive.

. . . White Bull lay in a ravine pumping bullets into the crowd around Custer. . . . He was one of those who shot down this group in which Custer made his last stand.

All this time White Bull was between the river and the soldiers on the hill. The few remaining troopers seemed to despair of holding their position on the hilltop. Ten of them jumped up and came down the ravine toward White Bull, shooting all the time. . . . The eight remaining soldiers kept on coming, forcing White Bull out of the ravine onto the ridge. . . . Suddenly he stumbled and fell . . . he had been hit by a spent ball.

. . . At the time he stopped fighting, only ten soldiers were on their feet. They were the last ones alive. the fight began before noon and lasted only about an hour, he says . . .

Makes-Room made his son White Bull lie down under a shade there and sent for Sitting Bull. Sitting Bull put 'wounded medicine' on White Bull's ankle. . . . the herald was calling out that the camp must be moved to where the people were. The women went after their tipis and moved them. . . . Then White Bull asked for his horse. They brought it and helped him upon its back. He crossed the river to get his leggins and the saddle he had left there, and afterwards went over the battlefield to see the dead . . . On the hilltop he met his relative Bad Soup (Bad Juice). Bad Soup had been around Fort Abraham Lincoln and knew Long Hair (General Custer) by sight. The two of them found Custer lying on his back, naked. Bad Soup pointed him out and said: 'Long Hair thought he was the greatest man in the world. Now he lies there.' They did not scalp Custer, because his hair was cut short.[4]

When he charged through the soldiers alone, White Bull would have gone from the east side of the ridge to the west side, since he was between the river and the soldiers on the hill. This would indicate that the three companies he previously referred to as being below the hill must have been wiped out or retreated some time earlier to Last Stand Hill. This inference would support my theory of what took place. Not many bodies were found below Last Stand Hill, particularly if you disregard the 28 or so who tried to escape, and the final 10 men.

Since the Gray Horse Troop was the middle company as they moved to Medicine Tail Coulee, but became the rear company in the move to the ford, they were more likely to have stayed mounted. This fact could explain why so many Indians related seeing the gray horses. The troop was memorable not only because of their distinctive color, but also because in their retreat they would have been in sight of the village for a longer period of time. They were apt to have moved toward Keogh's battalion, and would have remained mounted during part of their move along the ridge. As with so many other Indians, White Bull mentions those attempting to escape at the last. He also claims that Bad Soup recognized Custer. White Bull doesn't mention shooting him or any other officer, nor does he indicate that Bad Soup found Custer's curls and the map. After White Bull's death, Vestal maintained that White Bull had told him he killed Custer. Vestal promised to keep it secret until White Bull died. As old as White Bull was at the time of the interview, it is strange that he would still have feared punishment for saying he killed Custer.

One of the key statements White Bull made, and a few other Sioux implied, is the movement of tepees to where the people were. It would suggest a move to the northwest of the camp, which places the Cheyenne village near Ford B at the time of the attack, and helps substantiate Marquis' findings. The implication of this statement would be to discredit those who believe Custer moved farther north because of the location of the village. One should also note the number of Indians who claim that Reno's attack took place at midday.

SOURCES

1. Vestal, *Warpath*, pp. 191-195.
2. Ibid., p. 195.
3. Ibid., p. 195-197.
4. Ibid., p. 198-203.

Joseph White Bull
Miniconjou
Interview by David Humphreys Miller

My most memorable meeting with him took place in 1939 at his log house in the Indian settlement at Cherry Creek, on the Cheyenne River Indian Reservation in South Dakota.

Throughout most of his lifetime White Bull was, without doubt, the most illustrious warrior of the entire Sioux nation. Twenty-six years old at the time of the Custer fight in '76. . . .

". . . My father Makes-Room, hereditary chief of my tribe. My mother was Good Feather Woman, sister of Sitting Bull, so the great chief was my uncle.

. . . At the Little Bighorn, White Bull, armed with a seventeen shot Winchester, fought first against Reno's force and then rode off to join the battle against Custer.

Little bunches of Lakotas and Cheyennes were riding into the ravine . . . We were behind the soldiers as we got up on the ridge, and we began to shoot at them. Some of them got off their horses and hid behind them to shoot back at us.

Lakotas were riding all around, shooting at the soldiers, who didn't go farther along the ridge . . .

The soldiers were divided into two bunches. [In Vestal's interview White Bull spoke of the five companies and four groups. Here he is undoubtedly referring to later in the battle.] I galloped my pony in between the two bunches and kept close to his neck until I rode clear around one of the bunches and circled back to Crazy Horse. I shouted to him . . .

I started to circle the soldiers again. This time Crazy Horse and the others followed. Some of the soldiers ran like scared rabbits, and we rode after them. One soldier was riding a black horse . . .

One of the soldiers blew on a bugle. The others began to get on their horses. I dared Crazy Horse to lead a charge against them. He refused so I rode out alone and came up behind a soldier on a bay horse. . . . I rode down two soldiers . . . Crazy Horse struck both of these men after I did.

. . . The soldiers who were still alive got off their horses and lay down to shoot. I charged through them twice. They were firing up in the air and acted as though they were drunk. A brave Lakota rode up and chased away their horses. Soon bays and sorrels and grays were running everywhere. Many Lakotas stopped shooting and began to chase these loose horses. I caught a sorrel horse. Just after that my pony went down with bullets in his shoulder and ribs. So I had to fight on foot.

. . . Not many soldiers were left alive by this time. We surrounded them and kept shooting them down. They acted like drunk people. Some of them shot wildly into the air, not hitting any of us. The army was crazy to have sent such a small band of soldiers against us, anyway. They could never have beaten us in the fight. [I don't think one can discount Indian testimony of soldiers being out of control or that many Indians at this stage of the battle were still riding horses. If the Indians were so strong they should have overran Reno's troops as well. That they didn't reflects the Indian fighting methods, and points out that if Custer's troops had set up a defense they would have held out much longer than they did.]

One soldier still alive toward the last wore a buckskin coat with fringes on it. I thought this man was leader of the soldiers, because he had ridden ahead of all the others as they came along the ridge. [Since he was back in a ravine south of Calhoun's troops at the time, Custer should have been moving along the ridge; with the dust and confusion, let alone the firing which caused him to move east of the ridge and join with Crazy Horse; it is amazing he was able to take this all in.] He saw me now and shot at me twice with his revolver, missing me both times. I raised my rifle and fired at him, he went down. Then I saw another soldier crawl over to him. The leader was dead.

By the middle of the afternoon all the soldiers were dead. The fight lasted only a short time. [In White Bull's Vestal account the fighting started around noon and lasted "only about an hour."] . . . (DHM – All Indian informants agreed that the action against Custer's command on the ridge occupied the time it took for the sun to travel the width of the shadow of a tepee pole across the ground. By actual measurement this turned out to be almost exactly twenty minutes.) [Though other Indians have reported such a time period, I would question this just as I have questioned the time given by whites for certain actions to have taken place. I don't think any Indians were checking their tepee poles. If White Bull did all the things he has credited himself with, there is no way he could have accomplished them in twenty minutes. I, however, don't believe— once the troops reached Battleridge—and this would include Keogh's battalion, that it lasted over an hour, if that long.]

My cousin Bad Soup (Bad Juice) was stripping the soldier I thought had been the leader and held up the buckskin coat.[One should note in White Bull's Vestal quote (page 239) Custer was naked - no mention of Bad Juice stripping the body. The body would have been stripped by that time.] He looked in the pockets of the coat and brought out some papers with pictures on them (maps). In one of the pockets he found coils of long yellow hair. But the dead leader had his hair cut short.

"Onhey!" Bad Soup cried, "That man there was Long Hair Custer. He thought he was the greatest man on earth, but he lies there now. And he cut his hair so he wouldn't be scalped!"

He was the leader who tried to kill me. But I had killed him.

The old man looked both relieved and vaguely troubled. After several moments he said: "I never told this to anyone before. I was afraid the white man would hang me or lock me up for a long time, if they knew I had killed Long Hair. Hecetuyelo. So be it." (DHM – White Bull apparently told the late Stanley Vestal much the same story. See Vestal's article, "The Man Who Killed Custer." in American Heritage, February, 1957.)1

White Bull's story emphasizes again that those engaged against Reno did not return to fight Custer until his troops had reached Battleridge. There would have been action for some time before, as artifacts and testimony attest. I think once the troops reached Battleridge, the Indians were soon encircling them and the battle did not last long (although twenty minutes is too short an estimate). White Bull's account supports my view that no real defensive position was established.

I am sure White Bull was quite a warrior, but the question is, how big a braggart? I do believe that Indians, whether interviewed at that late date or earlier, would have had a certain antipathy toward the whites, and even though they appeared friendly, they would not feel any compunction about twisting a story. White Bull could have, indeed, noticed and shot a person in a buckskin coat, who acted like a leader, but the person would not necessarily have been Custer. Certain elements make his story unlikely and questionable. From this version of White Bull's account of the shooting, we expect the bullet wound to be a frontal one, whereas with both of Custer's wounds the bullet entered the side of his body. Also, White Bull was slightly wounded at the end of the battle by a spent bullet. He was taken back to the camp where they sent for Sitting Bull, who doctored his wound. After that, White Bull went back to where he left his leggings, which was south of the battlefield, and from there to the battlefield, where he met Bad Soup. He doesn't mention anything about the Reno engagement, which should have been taking place. It would seem, by this time, the women or warriors would have stripped Custer's body. His story certainly conflicts with White Cow Bull's report of the Cheyenne women and their recognition of Custer's body. That story is confirmed by other Indians, White Bull's is not. Although the event could have taken place after White Bull and Bad Soup were there, it is still doubtful.

With all the concern of the whites as to who killed Custer, it is amazing some Indians didn't mention White Bull. It's hard to believe that, following the battle, when Indians were recounting their deeds and not thinking of later retribution, which might be inflicted by the whites, White Bull and Bad Soup would not have pointed out that Custer was the leader and that White Bull had killed him. This should have been quite an honor, and White Bull was not an ordinary warrior whose story might be ignored.

I doubt if Custer was wearing his buckskin jacket. There is substantial testimony indicating he had taken it off and tied it behind his saddle. However, Godfrey and many others believe he was wearing it. In reading various writers I often have the impression that they think the Indians didn't hear what the whites thought happened, and so would not have constructed or slanted their stories accordingly. We realize other officers besides Custer wore buckskin. If Custer wasn't wearing his and it was tied behind his saddle bags, then the story of looking in his coat and finding the map and his curls would have been fabricated. I don't know what happened to Custer's curls when he cut them off, so it may be possible that he had them in his coat pocket.

Stories of certain Indians killing Custer have been linked with and used to refute the idea that Custer committed suicide. Several letters to the editor, which appeared in the Autumn, 1959, issue of *Montana: The Magazine of Western History*, are especially noteworthy. In rejecting the Custer suicide theory, Mr. du Mont, who was then president of the Massachusetts Arms Collectors, points out the difficulty right handed Custer would have had in firing his pistol into the left side of his head. He also observes that at such short range, the bullet would have caused more damage than the reports indicate. This view sounds reasonable. It would seem highly doubtful Custer shot himself. If my theory is correct, he would not have been able to. If he was still alive, which I believe possible, he could have been shot by one of his men so that a wounded Custer would not fall into the hands of the Indians.

In another letter in the same issue, Reginald K. Laudin of Moose, Wyoming, an interpreter of the Indian dance and mores, points out his belief in the White Bull story as told to Vestal and Miller. Laudin says, "One reason I felt that White Bull's story could be that of the last moment of Custer is that the old man told me he took the pistol away from the man he was fighting and shot him in the head with it."2

In determining White Bull's credibility, one should take into account the different versions attributed to him. Did he shoot Custer with his own rifle or did he take Custer's pistol away and shoot him with that, as Laudin claimed? This is not a distance or time judgment. It requires consistency in the basic storyline, since it involves an individual who not only saw the man for a period of time but also fought him hand to hand.

As to the White Bull story, Laudin also brought out:

> I did not mention how I got it from him. A friend of mine and I were visiting a group of old-timers near Rapid City one summer. Several were veterans of the Custer fight, including White Bull. We asked them one time who they thought had killed Custer. Without hesitation the entire group indicated White Bull, whereupon he told the story as I, and, later Vestal, recorded it.[3]

As I previously observed, this appears to be a later version of an episode which should have been common knowledge to most Indians participating in the battle. They would have seen it take place or heard about it in the recounting of deeds. It's hard to imagine White Bull and Bad Soup not having boasted about what happened, particularly since it involved the leader of the troops. Why didn't Wooden Leg, John Stands In Timber or other Indians relate such an event?

Laudin believes the Indians would not have indicated White Bull unless it was true; yet it's debatable if they would have disagreed at the time. Another statement by Laudin in the same letter should also be considered and included in the analysis:

> Another thing, if Indians had seen Custer kill himself they would not have touched his body. His body, being unmutilated has been one of the reasons for believing the suicide story. Otherwise, had they known who he was, most Indians would have cut him to pieces. The Sioux customarily cut up the body of a brave enemy, not entirely for spite (as they might have, had they known Custer) but because of an old superstition similar to that of weir-wolves, that such an enemy could return in invulnerable form. By cutting them to pieces, there was less chance of such a return. A suicide would not have been regarded as brave and the body would have been shunned.[4]

If Custer was the brave leader who stood out from the others and whom White Bull fought, why wasn't his body inflicted with such damage? As I have already stated, the fight would have taken place near the end of the battle and should have been observed by many. If Bad Soup and White Bull recognized him as Custer and believed he had cut off his curls in order to escape being scalped, then according to their mores, and psychologically, their natural reaction would have been to scalp and mutilate him.

If we accept Laudin's explanation as to what would have been done to Custer's body if the Indians had realized he was the leader of the troops, or if they credited him with outstanding bravery, why wasn't he so defiled? Certainly White Bull's story does not provide an answer, and appears to be an example of boasting for effect. By the time he viewed the body, it should have been stripped and maimed. There is a possibility that if White Bull had, indeed, fought someone, it could have been Tom Custer, whose body was said to have been badly mutilated. Tom Custer was certainly noted for his bravery and he could have led the fighting on Last Stand Hill.

It is conceivable, as some have postulated, that Custer's body may have been disfigured, but the soldiers refrained from admitting it because of Elizabeth Custer. If so, this would also refute White Bull's account. However, I believe Custer's body was not mutilated – an assumption that helps substantiate my interpretation of events. I believe that Custer was severely wounded at the ford and played no part in the rest of the fighting. He was not recognized by the Indians after the battle with the exception of the Cheyenne women and perhaps a few others. To most, the sight or name, Custer, would have meant nothing, so there was no need to pay special attention to his body. I do believe the Cheyenne women, the awl, and White Cow Bull's story are plausible, not only because it fits into my view of what happened, but because it is supported by testimony or other Indians.

SOURCES

1. Miller, *American Heritage,* June, 1971.
2. Laudin, *Montana: The Magazine of Western History,* Autumn, 1959. p. 51.
3. Ibid., p. 47.
4. Ibid., p. 48.

Henry Oscar One Bull
Interviewed by D. H. Miller

Chief Henry Oscar One Bull was the first Indian veteran of the Battle of the Little Bighorn to pose for me and tell me his version of the Custer fight. I located him at the Indian pageant south of Rapid City, South Dakota, in the mid-1930's. As a nephew, adopted son, and bodyguard of the great Sioux Chief Sitting Bull, he had held an elevated position in the hierarchy of Indian command . . . the last hereditary chief of the Hunkpapa tribe.

. . . In the summer of 1938 I made my annual visit to

the Crow Indian Fair at Crow Agency, Montana.... To my delight I found that One Bull and his family were among them. Since the Custer battlefield was a short drive from our camp. I was determined to take advantage of the Chief's presence and invited him to show me over the fighting ground, step by step. He gladly complied ... Back in camp he told me his story, conversing, as usual in Sioux.

It was the time when ponies are fat. During a sun dance we held on Rosebud Creek ten days earlier, my uncle, Sitting Bull, had offered a hundred pieces of his flesh to Wakantanka (Great Holy Spirit) and had been granted a vision of white soldiers without ears falling upside down into camp. He told me that his vision was a promise of a great victory yet to come. Three days later, we beat Gray Fox (General George Crook) in a fight on the Rosebud. But my uncle said an even greater victory was coming.

The night before the fight with Long Hair. Sitting Bull went out to the ridge where the monument now stands. He sang a thunder song, then prayed for knowledge of things to come....

I was twenty-three that summer and had been a warrior a long time. Another Hunkpapa named Gray Eagle and I were Sitting Bull's special bodyguards.... that morning I took the family horses to the river.

At midday I went back to the pony herd and drove the horses to the river for the noon watering. Just then I heard shooting near the Hunkpapa camp circle. I knew our camp soldiers (police) did not allow offhand firing. So I recognized the shots as a warning of some kind of danger. I quickly caught my best pony... Not far away I saw dust rising and heard iron-shod hoofs pounding against loose rocks. I raced back to the tepee I shared with my uncle.

The Hunkpapa camp was in an uproar. Warriors were rushing around to catch their ponies. Women were screaming and children were crying and old men were shouting advice as loud as they could. Then the women and children began to run off to the west, not taking the time to strike their tepees or to carry off belongings.

I reached the tepee ahead of my uncle... He...then took his own rawhide shield out of its buckskin case and hung it over my shoulder. This shield was both for protection and to be used as a badge of the chief's authority.

... Many young warriors gathered around me. I raised my uncle's shield high so they all could see it. Then I led them out to meet the soldiers.

... One Bull soon discovered that any talk of peace with Major Marcus A. Reno's attacking troopers was out of the question. Soldiers now on the firing line began shooting as soon as they saw the raised shield. Ree Indian scouts, ... were trying to capture the huge herd of Sioux ponies west of the camp. Chief Black Moon rode up with a large force of Hunkpapa camp police to save the pony herd. One Bull rallied his warriors for a charge.

The Sioux onslaught began suddenly, sweeping back the Ree scouts and halting Reno's advance. Black Moon's Hunkpapas hit Reno's exposed flank. As One Bull told me:

The soldiers were mixed up. Some got off their horses, except for every fourth man, who held the horses for the other three. Then they ran on foot trying to get into the timber along the river. I raised my uncle's shield again and led another charge to chase them. They were turning to shoot at us, but we rode right into them, chasing them into the river. We killed many on the river bank and in the water. [One Bull gets the skirmish line, the timber, and retreat strung together, which, after so many years, could be expected, and is also typical of Indian accounts. He does mention an advance by Reno after the initial Indian contact.]

I rode up behind one soldier and knocked him over with my war club. Then I slid off my pony and held the soldier's head under water until he was dead. I killed two more soldiers in the water.

A Hunkpapa warrior named Good Bear Boy was riding alongside me and was suddenly shot off his horse. Black Moon fell about the same time. He was dead, but Good Bear Boy was only wounded ...

I saw many soldiers struggle across the river and climb out on the far bank. They ran to a high butte (now called Reno Hill), and from there they kept shooting at us. Some of them dug holes in the ground and got into these holes or behind their saddles so we couldn't hit them. I ordered warriors to surround the butte so the soldiers couldn't get away. I wanted to starve them out ... [One Bull appears to be mixing time periods and incidents. It is doubtful if he is drowning soldiers and still able to note and accomplish the other things he mentions. He is placing too much emphasis on his direction of events.]

Bullets were flying all around, but I saw that Good Bear Boy wasn't able to crawl back to camp. He was shot through both thighs and bleeding heavily. So I jumped off my pony long enough to help Good Bear Boy climb on. Then I leaped up behind him. I heard my pony scream. A bullet had struck his hindquarters. I took Good Bear Boy back to camp ...

... My uncle looked worried ... "Nephew, you are wounded. Go to the women and have your wounds treated."

So I laughed, saying I wasn't wounded and telling him about Good Bear Boy.

"You have done well. You put up a good fight. Now go defend the women and children and old ones. More soldiers may come."

I did as he ordered and joined our people west of the camp. Soon after I reached them, I saw more dust across the river. A second band of soldiers was riding down a coulee toward the ford by the Miniconjou camp circle. Another alarm went up. I saw a handful of warriors racing to the ford to meet them. Then more warriors left the soldiers surrounded on the butte and galloped over to head off the second attack. They chased these new soldiers out of the coulee and up onto a long ridge. More of our warriors, mostly Ogalalas and Cheyennes, were waiting for these soldiers at the end of the ridge and caught them in a trap. They were all wiped out in a short time. My brother, White Bull, later said the leader of the second band of soldiers was Long Hair Custer.[1]

One Bull has to be wrong in his timing, which would be normal for someone his age. He claims that he was involved in Reno's retreat, was at the crossing, drowned one soldier, killed two others, and saw troopers remove their saddles and dig holes. One Bull goes on to contend that he picked up Good Bear Boy and went back to camp, left him there, and started to chase three soldiers before he was called back by Sitting Bull. One Bull talked to him, decided to go west of the camp where most of the women and children were, and then saw Custer's troops moving down Medicine Tail Coulee – all of which contradicts most of the testimony and timing calculations.

Timing is essential for an understanding or analysis of events. I have pointed this out before and will continue to do so. We know that Custer left the ridge approximately when Reno set up his skirmish line. Reno was said to be on his skirmish line and in the timber for at least 35 to 40 minutes. It should have taken another 15 minutes for the troops to reach the river and cross, and somewhat longer for most of them to move up the hill.

If One Bull, after hearing the initial firing which awoke the camp, went back, got through the melee, went to Sitting Bull's tepee, obtained the shield, then moved to meet an advancing Reno, I think the 35 to 40 minutes before Reno retreated from the timber is a fair estimate. The same calculations can be applied to Wooden Leg's and other Indian accounts. He must have been in the camp at least five minutes and then taken another five to reach the villagers west of the camp, especially if he was in a position to see Medicine Tail Coulee. This would be roughly an hour and a quarter since Custer left the ridge. If Custer had gone by a direct route, down either of the first two ravines, he should have reached the ford in less than 15 minutes. With another 5 or 10 minutes thrown in for good measure, Custer should have reached Ford B in twenty five minutes, which would still put Reno in the timber. To say that Custer didn't go to the ford during that time, you would have to ignore – or dismiss out of hand – the accounts of Martin, the Crows, Pretty Shield, the Sioux White Cow Bull, as well as many of the Sioux and Cheyenne that participated in the attack against Reno. Martin saw Custer close to the river, and the Crows claimed he went to the river. They never suggested that Custer waited somewhere for over 40 minutes. Neither the Crows nor Martin would have been able to make it back to where they met Benteen, if we apply One Bull's timing sequence.

One Bull does recall seeing only a handful of Indians rushing to the ford to meet Custer. I am sure there were a good deal more before those around Reno reached the area.

One Bull must not have entered the fight against Custer. His story does support the surprise factor, and suggests that Custer wasn't initially faced with overwhelming odds at the ford or by an ambush.

SOURCES

1. Miller, *American Heritage*, June, 1971.

Dewey Beard
1935 – Interviewed by D. H. Miller

I first heard of Dewey Beard in 1935 on the Pine Ridge Reservation. Assured that he had participated in the fight against Custer, I also learned that he had taken part in other Indian white conflicts, including the Massacre at Wounded Knee in 1890.

. . . I was almost eighteen that summer . . .

Hump, Fast Bull, and High Backbone led my tribe. Crazy Horse headed the Oglala. Inkpaduta led the Santee, Lame White Man and Ice Bear led the Cheyenne. But the greatest leader of all was the chief of the Hunkpapa – Sitting Bull.

. . . I slept late in the morning of the fight. . . . So when I got up, the camp women were already starting out to dig for wild turnips. . . . I walked to the river to take a cool swim, then got hungry and returned to the tepee at dinner time.

I climbed Black Butte for a look around the country. I saw a long column of soldiers coming and a large party of Hunkpapa warriors, led by Sitting Bull's nephew, One Bull, riding out to meet them. I could see One Bull's hand raised in the peace sign to show the soldiers that our leaders only wanted to talk them into going away and leaving us alone. But, all at once, the soldiers spread out for attack and began to fire, and the fight was on. I caught my favorite war pony . . . and raced back to camp to get ready for battle.

I had not time to paint Zi Chischila properly for making war, just a minute or so to braid his tail and to daub a few white hail spots of paint on my own forehead for protection before I galloped out on the little buckskin . . . We all turned when we heard shooting at the far side of the village nearest the Miniconjou camp circle and rode fast to meet the new danger. I could see swirls of dust and hear shooting on the hills and bluffs across the river. Hundreds of other warriors joined us as we splashed across the ford near our camp and raced up the hills to charge into the thickest of the fighting.

This new battle was a turmoil of dust and warriors and soldiers with bullets whining and arrows hissing all around. . . .

Then a Lakota named Spotted Rabbit rode unarmed among us, calling out a challenge to all the warriors to join him. He shouted, "Let's take their leader alive!" I had no thought of what we would do with this leader once we caught him; it was a daring feat that required more courage and much more skill than killing him. I dug my heels into my pony's flanks to urge him on faster to take part in the capture.

A tall white man in buckskin kept shouting at the soldiers and looked to be their leader. Following Spotted Rabbit, I charged toward this leader in buckskin. We were almost on top of him when Spotted Rabbit's pony was shot from under him. Zi Chischila shied to one side and it was too late. A Minniconjou named Charging Hawk rushed in and shot the leader at close range. In a little while all the soldiers were dead. The battle was over.

The soldier chief we had tried to capture lay on the ground with the reins of his horse's bridle tied to his wrist. It was a fine animal, a blaze-faced sorrel with four white stockings. A Santee named Walks-Under-The-Ground took that horse. Then he told everyone that the leader lying their dead was Long Hair; so that was the first I knew who we had been fighting. I thought it was a strange name for a soldier chief who had his hair cut short . . .[1]

The only thing to really gain from Dewey Beard's interview (beside the entertainment the story provides) is corroboration of the fact that the Indians were caught off guard and the battle was short. The list of those who claim to have killed Custer keeps growing. While these Indians are supposedly attempting to capture Custer, and the General is finally killed by Charging Hawk, where are Crazy Horse, Joseph White Bull, Gall and the suicide boys? Captain Yates, Captain Tom Custer, Lieutenant Smith and Adjutant Cooke must have been killed before that happened, since they didn't play much part in the fighting, according to Dewey Beard. Why was Tom Custer's body mutilated more than most? Since the Indians would usually try to kill the leader - and from different reports Custer appears to have stood out as such - it's odd that his horse wasn't hit by some bullets or arrows. Considering the position of Custer's body in relationship to other soldiers, I wouldn't have wanted his horse Vic crashing around above me. It must have been difficult for Custer to fire effectively with the horse tied to his wrist. Again, we have a description of Custer wearing a buckskin shirt and Vic with four white feet. From this account, as well as some others, it's difficult to understand how any of the Indians didn't know immediately that they were fighting Custer.

SOURCES

1. Miller, *American Heritage,* June, 1971.

Chief Two Moon
Cheyenne
From *McClure's* Magazine, September 1898

. . ."Two Moon does not like to talk about the days of fighting, but since you are to make a book, and the agent says you're a friend to Grinnell (George B. Grinnell), whom the Cheyenne, Blackfeet, and Gros Ventres love and honor, I will tell you about it – the truth. It is now a long time ago, and my words do not come quickly.

. . . We were very glad to think we were far away from the white man.

"I went to water my horses at the creek, and washed them off with cool water, then took a swim myself. I came back to the camp afoot. When I got near my lodge, I looked up the Little Horn toward Sitting Bull's camp. I saw a great dust rising. Soon Sioux horsemen came rushing into camp shouting 'Soldiers come! Plenty white soldiers.'

. . . "I got my horse, and rode out into my camp" . . . "I rode swiftly toward Sitting Bull's camp. There I saw the white soldiers fighting in a line. Indians covered the flat. They began to drive the soldiers. The air was full of smoke and dust. I saw the soldiers fall back and drop into the river-bed like buffalo fleeing. They had not time to look for a crossing. The Sioux chased them up the hill, where they met more soldiers in wagons, and then messengers came saying more soldiers were going to kill the women and the Sioux turned back. Chief Gall was there fighting. Crazy Horse also.

"I then rode toward my camp, and stopped squaws from carrying off lodges. While I was sitting on my horse, I saw flags come up over the hill to the east like that (he raised his finger tips). Then the soldiers rose all at once, all on horses, like this (he put his fingers in column of fours). They formed into three branches (squadrons, with a little ways between). Then a bugle sounded, and they got off horses, and some soldiers led the horses back over the hill.

"Then the Sioux rode up the ridge on all sides riding very fast. The Cheyennes went up the left way. Then the shooting was quick, quick, pop-pop-pop – very fast. Some of the soldiers were down on their knees, some standing. Officers all in front. The smoke was like a great cloud, and everywhere the Sioux went the dust rose like smoke. We circled all round them – swirling like water around a stone. . . . soldiers shouting. . . . He rode a sorrel horse with white face and white fore-legs. I don't know who he was. He was a brave man.

"Indians kept swirling round and round, and the soldiers killed only a few. . . . At last all horses killed but five. Once in a while some man would break out and run toward the river, but he would fall. At last about a hundred men and five horsemen stood on the hill all bunched together. All along the buglers kept blowing his commands. He was very brave, too. Then a chief was killed. I hear it was Long Hair. I don't know; and then the five horsemen and the bunch of men, maybe forty, started toward the river. The man on the sorrel horse led them, shouting all the time. (This man's identity is in dispute. He was apparently a scout.) He wore a buckskin shirt, and had long black hair and mustache. He fought hard with a big knife. His men were all covered with white dust. I couldn't tell whether they were officers or not. One man all alone ran far down toward the river, then round up over the hill, I thought he was going to escape, but a Sioux fired and hit him in the heart. He was the last man. He wore braid on his arms. (Sergeant Butler?)

"All the soldiers were now killed, and the bodies were stripped . . . We had no dance that night. We were sorrowful. [No mention of fighting Reno's troops at Weir Point or the fighting which ensued on Reno Hill.]

"New day four Sioux chiefs and two Cheyenne and I, Two Moon, went upon the battlefield to count the dead. There were 388. There were 39 Sioux and seven Cheyenne killed, and about a hundred wounded . . . Most of them were left just where they fell. We came to a man with big mustache; he lay down the hill toward the river . . . The Indians did not take his buckskin shirt. The Sioux said, That is a big chief. That is Long Hair," I don't know, I had never seen him. The man on the white faced horse was the bravest man. . . ."[1]

Any account that suggests the Indians at the time of the battle believed Long Hair was the chief, and that they killed him or saw him killed, should be at least partly discredited. It was natural to believe that someone they saw or shot may have been Custer, but usually the reference appears to be thrown in by the Indian or the interpreter to make the story more newsworthy – imagine a story without inferring or mentioning Custer. Although Crow King distorted his account slightly, I think he reflects the true picture when he says, "No warrior knew Custer in the fight. We did not know him dead or alive."[2] If one person's version of Custer fighting to the last is to be accepted, which should it be: Two Moon's, Gall's, White Bull's, Dewey Beard's or others?

Two Moon implies two different accounts of Custer being killed: one on the ridge and another when leading the 40 men toward the river. Two Moon only credits Vic with two white forelegs, but considering how everything was caked with dust, that in itself isn't bad. Since Two Moon was able to make out the mustache and long hair, it would have been nice if he'd told what happened to the supposed 40 troopers. How far did they get? Did they set up a defense? Did they fight to the last man? Did they go into Deep Ravine? Since the implication is that Custer led them, how did he die and how did his body get back up the hill? Garland indicated that the man was probably a scout, and if so, it must have been Mitch Bouyer, especially since the evidence supports his being killed near Deep Ravine. Kanipe thought he recognized Bouyer's body in the gulch with the 28 soldiers, and the archaeologists believe they uncovered his body just above Deep Ravine. Two Moon's reference to a person fighting with a big knife probably means a saber, which none of the troops or Mitch Bouyer were said to have had. If the body was Custer's, when was his buckskin shirt taken off?

Two Moon's story agrees with most Indian accounts that those fighting Major Reno would have heard of General Custer moving on the village when Reno's troops were reaching the bluffs. Two Moon's actual sighting of Custer's men would be off from a timing standpoint, unless they had already moved to the ford and had retreated to Battleridge; otherwise he has to account for a time lapse in the events which psychologically cannot be attributed to Custer.

The story of the last man to die – the one Two Moon thought might escape and who Garland said might have been Sergeant Butler — seems far-fetched. Although the timing differs, it was more likely Foley, as He Dog suggested.

Two Moon's account includes the man on the sorrel horse with the blaze and the white forelegs. Garland believes the man to be a scout since he knew Custer did not have long black hair and his stripped body was found on the ridge. If the man was indeed a scout, it would have been Mitch Bouyer. If there is any truth to Two Moon's story, conjecturally, it could support Custer being shot at the ford. Mitch Bouyer is said to have left the Crow scouts and gone down from the bluff where he joined Custer. White Cow Bull's report implied that Bouyer was by Custer's side when he was shot. It could be expected that after being shot, when Custer was lifted from the water, whether dead or wounded, he was placed on his horse. Undoubtedly someone had to ride with him, and this could have been Bouyer. When they moved to Last Stand Hill they would have placed Custer on the ground (if wounded), shot a couple of horses for protection, and made sure several soldiers were watching him. Mitch Bouyer could have continued to ride Vic.

However, one should also consider Henry Weibert's view of the battle. Weibert wrote the book, *Sixty Six Years in Custer's Shadow,* and spent years examining the terrain, often with a metal detector, as well as studying the various accounts of the battle. It is his contention that General Custer never went down Medicine Tail Coulee to Ford B. Weibert believes Custer viewed the Indian encampment from a point marked M on his map, which is some distance back from the edge of the bluffs. Custer and his troops then crossed upper South Medicine Tail to Blummer Ridge (Nye Cartwright), where they began firing on the Indians. In one of these locations (C on his map), Weibert found brass casings which he says only General Custer would have had. This is the main support for his belief that Custer never went to Ford B. I am in no position to disagree with his contention that the cartridge casings belonged to General Custer, but since I disagree with his conclusion that this finding means that Custer didn't go to the ford, I should describe what other explanations may account for his findings.

Weibert also found brass casings at an Indian firing location which led him to believe that Custer was killed early in the battle while he was leading his command toward the Cheyenne Ford. In explaining his reasoning, Weibert says:

> . . . Remember, I think he was killed right at the start. Therefore, he would have fired very few rounds. [After point C.] and they would have been in only one location, down toward the Cheyenne Ford and, by the odds, be very hard to find. Therefore, no brass cartridges will be found anywhere other than where I have found them, at the Blummer's Ridge position and at the Indian's position. The one at the Indian position most likely came off of Custer's horse or possibly from the rounds that he could have dropped when killed. . . . There was just no way for them to have ended up at the Indians' position, and they had to be in the Indians' hands fairly early in the Battle."[3]

I have no reason to contest Weibert's findings, so I must question his reasoning. There are various reports concerning Vic, Custer's horse, some saying Vic was found on the battlefield and others that he had been captured by Indians. I do not accept or reject either report. However, it is entirely possible that Vic – after Custer was shot at the ford – bolted into the Indian camp where he was captured, and Custer's ammunition could have been taken by an Indian or Indians. Various other possibilities can also be imagined. Custer's gun may have been picked up; he could have dropped cartridges as he moved to the ford; cartridges may also have fallen or a cartridge belt may have been left behind as Custer was dragged from the river or as he was examined.

Both location C and W would have been natural Indian locations – the first after the troopers left and were moving to Battleridge, and the second once they had reached Battleridge. I do not believe Weibert should base his major premise on brass casings found at point C, although I do agree the casings support the early shooting of Custer. In my opinion they certainly do not refute his moving to the ford and getting shot there. I reject Weibert's other reasons for believing Custer didn't move to Miniconjou Ford.

The only valuable details to be derived from Two Moon's story of the battle are the substantiation of the surprise element and that the Indians attacking Reno were not aware of Custer until Reno's troops were retreating to the bluffs.

SOURCES

1. Graham, *The Custer Myth,* McClure's Magazine, Sept. 1898 by Hamlin Garland, pp. 101-103.
2. Ibid., p. 77.
3. Weibert, Henry and Don, *Sixty Years in Custer's Shadow,* p. 144.

Two Moon
Wooden Leg's comments on Two Moon

All Cheyennes who had fought in the battle were asked to come and join the other Indians and the white people in a peace feast. The place is only two short days of wagon traveling from our Lame Deer Agency. But only a few Cheyennes would go there for the gathering. Among us there was much talk as: "Soldiers will be there. Seeing us might anger them so much as to make them want to kill us." (A few old Cheyennes still talked this way in 1926. Fear kept them from attending the fiftieth anniversary of the battle. TBM) Seven of us decided to go (included were Bobtail Horse and Two Moons).

In a big council lodge of the Crows, a white man doctor asked different ones to tell something of the great battle. (Doctor Dixon – TBM) He said he had heard the white people say that Two Moon was a great warrior there, and he asked Two Moon to make a speech. This Cheyenne stood up and talked a long time. He said he had been the big chief of all the Cheyennes during the fight. He filled the ears of his hearers with lots of other lies, while the rest of us laughed among ourselves about what he was saying. Other Cheyennes and Sioux were asked to get up and talk, but none of them would do so.

. . . In questioning Wooden Leg's cousin, the younger Chief Little Wolf, was asked.

"Did you see Custer, either before or after he was killed?

"I do not know. Nobody knew anything about Custer."

. . . "Tell me all about what you saw and what you did at the battle?"

But Little Wolf would not tell. I said to him: "Go on, tell the truth, but do not talk like Two Moon's did." He was afraid, though. There were many white people and soldiers all around us, and he feared they might become angry.

. . . But none of them except Two Moon would say anything further about the fight. Bobtail Horse was either nervous or scared, so he got tangled a little. . . . The doctor did not ask him any further question.

. . . I (Wooden Leg) went to Washington when I was fifty-five years old. Little Wolf, Two Moon and Black Wolf were two old men with me as delegates to speak for our tribe. Three younger men who could talk the white man language went with us. At a meeting with white men, there were some speeches made. Two Moon did most of the talking for us. Two Moon told these people he was a big chief leading all the Cheyenne at the Custer battle. None of us said anything in dispute of him at the meeting, but when we got away to ourselves Black Wolf said to him: "You are the biggest liar in the whole Cheyenne tribe." Two Moons laughed and replied: "I think it is not wrong to tell lies to white people."[1]

One important element in this testimony is the view that no one among the Indians knew Custer at the time of the battle. It is regrettable that Bobtail Horse was too scared or nervous to respond to questions, because his answers might have been very enlightening. The fear some Indians felt should always be considered in their testimony, particularly in the years immediately following the battle. Two Moon's lying and his belief that it was all right to fabricate for the whites would reflect an attitude that a good many Indians must have shared.

SOURCES

1. Marquis, *Wooden Leg*, p. 348.

Kate Bighead
Cheyenne

The next morning (June 25, 1876) I went with an Ogalala woman to visit some friends among the Minneconjou Sioux, up the valley toward where the Uncpapa camp circle was at the upper end or south end of the camps. We found our women friends bathing in the river, and we joined them. Other groups, men, women and children, were playing in the water at many places along the stream. Some boys were fishing. All of us were having a good time. It was somewhere past the middle of the forenoon. Nobody was thinking of any battle coming. A few women were taking down their lodges getting ready for the move on down the valley that day. After a while two Sioux boys came running toward us. They were shouting: "Soldiers are coming!"

We hear shooting. We hid in the brush. . . . Old men were calling the young warriors to battle. . . . We peeped out. Throngs of Sioux men on horses were racing toward the skirt of timber just south of the Uncpapa camp circle. . . . The horsemen warriors were dodging through a mass of women, children and old people hurrying afoot to the benchland hills west of the camps.

From our hiding place in the brush we heard the sounds of battle change from place to place. It seemed the white men were going away, with the Indians following them. Soon afterward we got glimpses of the sol-

KATE BIGHEAD

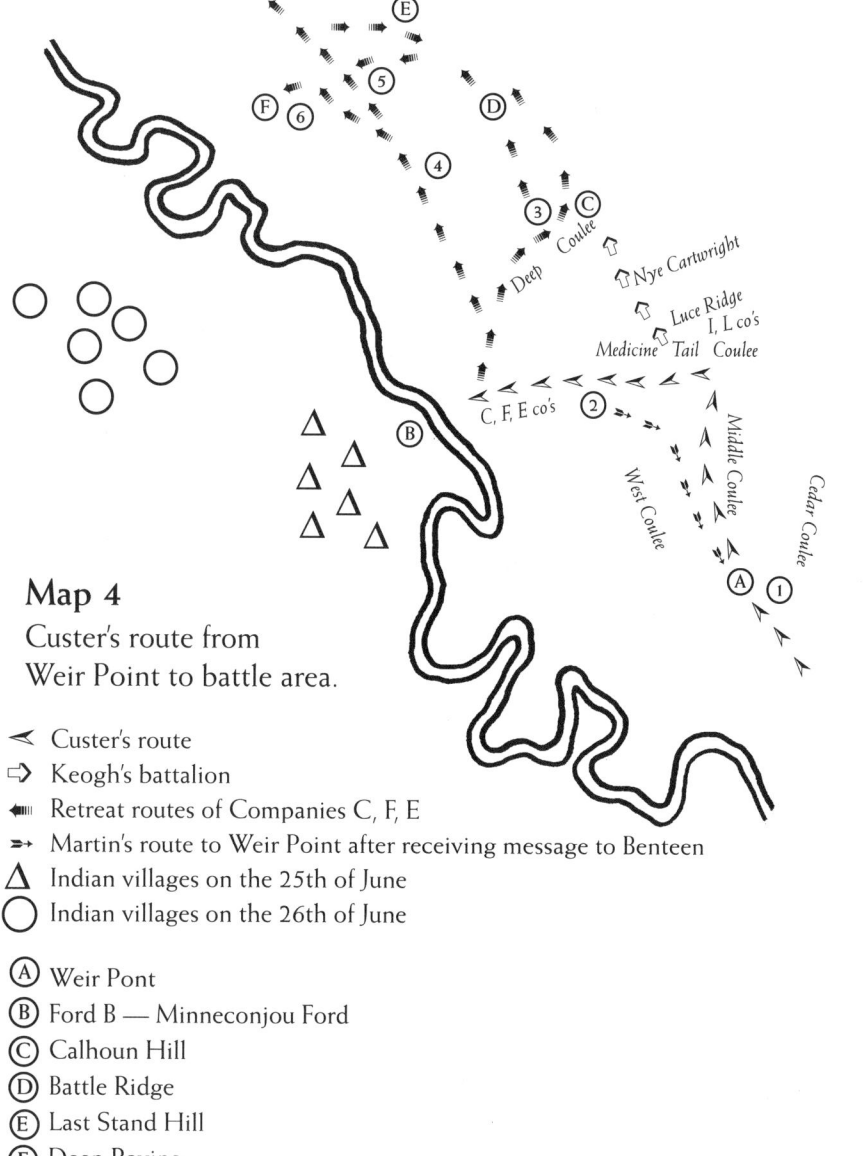

Map 4
Custer's route from
Weir Point to battle area.

- ◁ Custer's route
- ⇨ Keogh's battalion
- ⬅ Retreat routes of Companies C, F, E
- ➤ Martin's route to Weir Point after receiving message to Benteen
- △ Indian villages on the 25th of June
- ○ Indian villages on the 26th of June

- Ⓐ Weir Pont
- Ⓑ Ford B — Minneconjou Ford
- Ⓒ Calhoun Hill
- Ⓓ Battle Ridge
- Ⓔ Last Stand Hill
- Ⓕ Deep Ravine

- ① Location from where Kanipe could have been sent, with his message to the packs
- ② Martin's route to Weir Point with his message to Benteen
- ③ Retreat of other elements of Yates' battalion
- ④ Yates' "main element" retreat
- ⑤ Escape attempt by troops primarily from E company
- ⑥ Kate Bighead's description of where many of those troops committed suicide

diers crossing the river below us. Many of them were afoot. Then we saw that the Indians were after all of them, shooting and beating them.

I came out and set off running toward our Cheyenne camp circle, the last one, at the north end down the river, more than a mile from where I had been hiding. In all of the camps, as I went through them, there was great excitement. Old men were helping the young warriors in dressing and painting themselves for battle. Some women were bringing war horses from the herds. Other women were working fast at taking down there tepees. . . .

Clouds of dust were kicked up by the horse herds rushed into the camp circles, as well as by the horses that had been picketed near at hand by the Indian camp policemen and had been mounted and ridden to the fight when came the first alarm. The mounted Indians were still going to the place where had been the fighting, south of the Uncapapa camp. But before I got to my home lodge, all of them were riding wildly back down through the camp. It appeared they had been beaten and were running away. but I soon learned what had happened. I hear a Cheyenne old man calling out: "Other soldiers are coming!" . . .

On a high ridge far out eastward from the Cheyenne camp circle I saw those other soldiers. A few Indians were out there, and shots were being exchanged at long distance. Great throngs of other Indians, many more Sioux than Cheyennes, were lashing their ponies through the waters of the river or had crossed it and were on their way up the coulee valley toward the high ridge. It appeared there would be no end to the rushing procession of warriors. They kept going, going, going. I wanted to go too.[1]

The testimony of Kate Bighead confirms the sense of panic that both Custer and Reno created in the village, as well as the earlier time when Reno's attack took place. Reno's men had retreated to the river and most of them would have reached the hill before there was an alarm telling them Custer was attacking. She indicates the confusion in the camps, with warriors moving one way, women and children another, people yelling and taking down tepees. With all this chaos added to the gunfire and noise surrounding the Reno engagement, it stands to reason that Custer could have moved down Medicine Tail Coulee and fired at the few Sioux and Cheyenne east of the river without the camp being aware of him. Then Custer neared the ford, and was seen by a few Cheyenne and Sioux who raced to the ford. The Crow scouts fired a few rounds at the village, and shots were exchanged between the Indians at the ford and Custer's troops. The village gradually become aware of the new danger. Even then, for most of the Indians, the view of the ford was blocked by tepees, trees, dust and the bluffs on both sides of the ford.

The shots fired by Custer's troops and scouts would have taken place while Kate Bighead and the rest of the camp were still concerned with the firing and action taking place in connection with the Reno engagement.

Kate Bighead, in her account, refers to Indians coming back from attacking Reno. One should recognize that there were warriors in the village who had already moved against Custer. It took time for the warriors fighting Reno to have returned in the number she remembered. Too often we picture a simultaneous response by the Indians after the first few became aware of Custer's troops. It is as if the Indians had a siren that went off, as well as an unobstructed view of Medicine Tail Coulee. It would be more useful to picture a town of twelve thousand people who are all distressed because of the danger posed by what is happening on one side of town. Men are moving toward the menace, while women, children and older people are running away from it. Some of the women are looking for their children and others are trying to remove valuables from their homes. Then something happens on the other end of town. By word of mouth, how long does it take for the people to know about the new danger and move to meet it? How long for those three miles away? To accept the number of warriors referred to by Kate Bighead would mean that the first recognition of danger had to have taken place some time earlier. Custer would have had time to move to the ford, get shot, and the troops had time to retreat around the cutbank. Some Indians would be aware of what happened and would move immediately to the ford to aid the few Indians there. The retreat from the ford and around the cutbank – caused by Custer being shot and the sight of the Indians – would have placed a large segment of Yates' battalion out of sight of the villages. This retreat would have taken place in a relatively short time with comparatively few Indians involved. The troops seen by Kate Bighead would have been Keogh's troops as well as some of Yates' men who were attempting to join Keogh's battalion as they moved along Nye Cartwright Ridge to Battleridge.

If one accepts Kate Bighead's and Marquis' view of what happened, we would have to assume that Custer spent close to an hour and a quarter from the time Reno became engaged to the time Kate Bighead saw his troops, and he was still a mile away from the village with no sign of an attack or a defensive position having been established. What had Custer been doing during that time? I certainly don't know, nor do I accept the scenarios which attempt to account for it. Apart from this question, the testimony which shows Custer reaching the river has been disregarded.

> ...I crossed the river and followed up the broad coulee where the warriors had gone and were still going. The soldiers had lined themselves out on a long ridge nearer to the river and a little lower then the ridge far out where we first had seen them. [Those troopers had now moved from Nye Cartwright Ridge to Calhoun Hill and Battleridge- Keogh's battalion. Yates' battalion had moved around the cutbank, crossed Greasy Grass Knoll, possibly to the cemetery area, had already established rear guard positions along the South Retreat Line. They then would have moved to Battleridge by the time Kate Bighead, moving up Medicine Tail Coulee would have been in a position to see them.] By the time I got close enough to see well, the Indians were all around the soldiers, I think...
>
> I rode to the right, keeping far from the soldiers and going on to the north side of them.... The Indians mostly were in warrior society bands at different places. ...But all of them I could see on that side were Sioux, no Cheyennes. I kept on going around, searching the north side, then the west side. At the south side, in the deep gulches and behind the ridges between the soldiers and the river, I found none but Cheyenne and Oglala Sioux...
>
> ...On the southern side, where I stopped to watch the fight, almost all of the Cheyenne and Oglala Sioux had crawled across a deep gulch at the bottom of a broad coulee south of the ridge where the soldiers were and about half way between them and the river.[2]

By that time, those soldiers who had retreated along what I call the South Retreat Line would have reached Battleridge. Artifacts show concerted action along that line, but Indian accounts do not support such activity, which I believe corroborates my theory of a retreat rather than an attack or a late defensive maneuver. The absence of bodies would also support this judgement. The Indians refer to escape attempts at the end of the battle but there is no mention of any defensive action along this line on the part of the troops.

> There was a long time – the old men now say they think it must have been about an hour and a half – of this fighting slowly with not much harm to either side. Then a band of the soldiers on the ridge mounted their horses and came riding in a gallop down the broad coulee toward the river, toward where the Cheyennes and Oglalas were. The Indians hidden there got back quickly into the deepest parts of the gulch or kept on going away from it until they got over the ridge just south of it, the ridge where I was watching. The soldiers who had come galloping stopped and got off their horses along another ridge, a low one just north of the deep gulch.[3]

One runs again into a timing problem here. There is no way everyone would have the same time, particularly the Indians, but there shouldn't be the kind of difference in estimates where some say the battle took twenty minutes and others claim an hour and a half or longer. The old men were most likely thinking of the time from when they were aware of the initial "attack" by Custer's troops until the last attack by the Indians or the end of the battle. This would have been close to an hour and a half. The last Indian attacks on the troops at Battleridge could roughly have lasted from twenty minutes in Indian accounts, to possibly forty or forty-five minutes. Any such estimate is speculative but overall would support an hour and a half to two hour figure.

The difference in Kate Bighead's testimony and that of others would be if the twenty eight troopers that left the ridge, in an attempt to escape, rode or ran down the hill. It is somewhat hard to imagine this many troopers running in their boots four or five hundred yards if they have horses to ride, but it is just as difficult to imagine many troopers still having control of their horses. Their reaction could depend on just when it occurred, and would also be influenced by the fact that they were said to be mainly E Company troopers. If they were at the rear end of Yates' battalion as they moved to the ford (which I believe they were), then it is more likely that they stayed mounted rather than C Company which, I believe, was the lead company. Lieutenant DeRudio reported dead E Company horses near Deep Ravine. He Dog's account was probably closest to reality.

> Lame White Man, the bravest Cheyenne warrior chief, stayed in hiding close to where the small band of soldiers got off their horses.
>
> ...I saw one of the white men there kill himself, with his own gun, just after they got off their horses. Soon afterward I saw another one do the same act. From where I was I had a clear view of the soldiers and their saddled horses standing near them showed all of the warriors where the white men were. I think that only a few soldiers, maybe not any of them, were killed by the Indians during the few minutes of fighting there...
>
> On all sides of this band of soldiers the Indians jumped up. There were hundreds of warriors,.... I think there were about twenty Indians to every soldier there. ...The soldiers horses got scared, and all of them broke loose and ran away toward the river. Just then I saw a soldier shoot himself by holding his revolver to his head. Then another one did the same and another. I saw sev-

eral different pairs of them fire their guns at the same time and shoot one another in the breast. For a short time the Indians just stayed where they were and looked.... With these (guns) they went crawling toward the different parts of the ridge where were yet the main body of soldiers...[4]

Kate Bighead must have been watching from along Greasy Grass Ridge. The number of artifacts, both army and Indian, found in this area would signify an earlier movement of troops and Indians. Such movement supports my belief and Indian testimony that Custer's troops reached the ford and then retreated; their rear guard action would account for the artifacts found in those locations.

The suicide angle Kate Bighead and Wooden Leg reported seems to be the hardest for most people to accept. One can understand why this would have been true right after the battle. Writers have attempted to disprove and discredit Bighead's and Wooden Leg's accounts by citing timing differences, and by pointing out that other Indians have claimed the soldiers leaving the ridge did so on foot, except for a few. I believe that part of the battle is confusing for Indians. Many of their reports represent hearsay. Testimony seems to support the view that some troopers attempted to escape on foot and horseback. The ten or so at the last would have been on foot while those Kate Bighead referred to, having left earlier, may have been on horseback. It would seem natural that over a period of time the memories and stories would become interwoven. He Dog believed the soldiers (seemingly the ones Kate Bighead referred to) were both on horseback and afoot. The escaping horses he referred to could be the same ones Kate Bighead mentions.

The falling away by the Indians, whether the soldiers had been on foot or horseback, explains why I believe General Custer did not launch an attack, and if he had organized a proper retreat they would either have been able to reach Major Reno's troops or set up a sound and recognizable defensive position.

The question most difficult to answer is why Kate Bighead and Wooden Leg would testify in this way if they didn't believe it. If they were lying it would appear to have been because of psychological reasons. They could have had such enmity toward the whites that they thought this was a way they could get back at them. They may have thought they would "pull Marquis leg," which doesn't seem plausible, as it appears they had a genuine respect for him. Their testimony doesn't appear to be fabricated in a way meant to inspire animosity, shock the public, or gain them notoriety. I think it would be understandable for these soldiers to have committed suicide, for by that time they could not have questioned the outcome. As I have said before, if the one soldier that the Indians thought would escape shot himself, the soldiers knowing there was no escape could have done so as well. The suicide theory also fits in with the evidence from artifacts or the lack thereof. Kate Bighead doesn't speak of the soldiers going into Deep Ravine and more than likely she would not have been in a position to have seen them shoot each other if they had. Her account appears to have the soldiers leaving Battleridge just north of Calhoun Hill and moving down a "broad coulee." This would coincide with reports of gray horses in the area south of Last Stand Hill. Then, according to Bighead, they would have dismounted on a ridge just to the north of the coulee or gulch they came down. This would appear to be the ridge bordering Deep Ravine on the south.

If the above scenario is true, it makes one wonder why most of the bodies were said to have been found in the ravine. It is possible – since Kate Bighead said they used the soldiers' guns against those on the ridge, and because they would have been exposed to rifle fire – that the Indians, in order to obtain the guns and ammunition, would have pulled the bodies into Deep Ravine. This might account for the marks on the side of the ravine some of Reno's troops reported. Also, soldiers burying the dead may have found it easier to place them in Deep Ravine than burying them outside of it.

It is also odd that other Indians, when speaking of those making a run to escape down the hill, didn't say how they were killed. It's possible that at least the officers who were responsible for burying these soldiers realized they had committed suicide. In different accounts the troopers were reported to have been shot in the head, in the side, and in the back. Supposedly the Indians below Last Stand Hill had bows and arrows. The stigma could have been enough to have prevented any reports of suicide from leaking out.

> I started to go around the east end of the soldier ridge. Just then I saw lots of Indians running toward that end of the ridge, and the soldier horses there were running away. Pretty soon I saw that all of the white men were dead... I did not see how they were killed, but I think they must have killed themselves. The Indians crowded on westward along the ridge and along its two sides. I followed.... I stopped to look over a little hill and watch a band of soldiers on the ground at the north slope of the ridge. Warriors were all around those men, creeping closer and closer. The white men's horses were all gone from there. After I had been looking but a few minutes at those men I saw them go at shooting each other and

shooting themselves, the same as I had seen it done by the soldiers down by the river.

The remaining white fighters collected in a group at the west end of the ridge, where our men say there now is a big stone having an iron fence around it.... The remaining soldiers were keeping themselves behind their dead horses.

The shots quit coming from the place where the soldiers were lying behind their dead horses. All of the Indians jumped up and ran toward them, supposing all of them were dead. But there were seven of the white men who sprang to their feet and went running toward the river.... I did not see what happened to the seven men who ran down the hillside ... the talk I heard afterward was that all of them, and all of the others who had hidden behind the horses, killed themselves.

All of the lodges in the six camp circles were taken down as soon as the dead warriors were taken there. New camp spots were chosen, all of them back from the river and down the valley from the first location. The Indian regular custom was to move camp right away when any death occurred among the people in the camp. Not many of the big tepee lodges were set up at the new spots. Instead, the poles and skins for them were packed for moving away quickly if necessary. the women gathered willow wands and built little dome shelters, or the people slept that night without any shelter except robe bedding.

Some months afterward, when we learned that Long Hair was chief of the white men soldiers killed at Little Bighorn ...[5]

Again Bighead refers to suicides. She doesn't mention anything of White Bull, Crazy Horse or others. There are a number of reasons why most Indians would not mention suicides, if they took place. Henry Weibert debunked Kate Bighead's suicide stories for several reasons. Kate Bighead said she saw several different pairs of soldiers shoot each other by firing simultaneously, and Weibert believed this to be impossible.[6] I would tend to agree with him. However, I wouldn't debunk troops committing suicide because of it. Most of the suicides reported were troopers killing themselves. From Kate Bighead's position I doubt if she could have made that sort of a distinction. She probably saw soldiers shooting each other. The word "simultaneously" just happened to be the word Marquis used. Weibert's main reason for believing the suicide stories were "bunk," appears to be his conviction that soldiers would not have done it simply because they were soldiers and seasoned veterans. His main supporting argument would seem to be that none of Reno's men committed suicide under similar circumstances.[7]

Weibert, along with almost everyone else, has brought attention to the panic exhibited by Reno and a large number of his troops in fleeing to the bluffs. For him to believe that if they had been followed and encircled by the Indians (without Benteen and the packs arriving) many of them would not have committed suicide, is naive. People commit and have committed suicide under much less trying circumstances. To believe that Reno's troops faced anything comparable to Custer's command is absurd. Many were not seasoned veterans, and even the veterans would not all have reacted as Butler did. Reno would be a prime example of such behavior. Benteen used his recruits as justification for his inaction. Kate Bighead and Wooden Leg would not, at the time, and especially in talking to Dr. Marquis, have needed to rationalize the Indian killing of Custer's command. There is more reason to believe the Indian psychology as expressed by Wooden Leg than that of Weibert. Wooden Leg said the anger from the whites brought on by such statements prevented them from saying the soldiers committed suicide. The whites' reaction to Marquis' book and Weibert's own comments at such a late date represents strong supporting evidence.

As I have indicated, the location of the camp on the 25th is of major importance. Kate Bighead's description of the preparation for moving, and the new sites combined with the lack of any understandable ulterior motive, would support the idea that such a move did indeed take place.

Kate Bighead's admittance that she learned it was Custer only several months later makes hers, I believe, a more truthful account than those of the Indians who said they saw or knew it was Custer during the battle or right after. This would be doubly true since she was one of the few who would have known or been able to recognize Custer. It gives her other statements more credence.

But I learned something more about him from our people in Oklahoma. Two of those Southern Cheyenne women who had been in our camp at the Little Bighorn told of having been on the battlefield soon after the fighting ended. They saw Custer lying dead there. They had known him in the South. While they were looking at him some Sioux men came and were about to cut up his body. The Cheyenne women, thinking of Me-o-tzi, made signs. "He is a relative of ours," but telling nothing more about him. The women then pushed the point of a sewing awl into each of his ears, into his head. This was done to improve his hearing, as it seemed he had not heard what our chiefs in the South said when he smoked the pipe with them. They told him then that if ever afterward he should break that peace promise and should fight the Cheyennes the Every-Where-Spirit surely would cause him to be killed.[8]

This part of her testimony corroborates White Cow Bull's story, whereas one doesn't find Indian accounts substantiating those of the various Indians who referred to their special deeds or even to Custer's at Last Stand Hill. It would also account for why Custer's body, supposedly, was not mutilated.

SOURCES

1. Marquis, *She Watched Custer's Last Battle*. Her story interpreted in 1927.
2. Marquis, *Custer on the Little Bighorn*, pp. 37, 38.
3. Ibid., p. 38.
4. Ibid., p 39.
5. Ibid., p. 39, 40.
6. Henry & Don Weibert, *Sixty-Six Years in Custer's Shadow*, p. 128.
7. Ibid., p. 68.
8. Op. Cit., p. 43.

Joseph White Cow Bull
D. H. Miller, Interview

The old man sat cross-legged in the Montana sun, posing for me with his gaunt shoulders draped in an ancient trade-cloth blanket, gnarled fingers clutching a cottonwood cane. It was hard to imagine that his scraggy hands had once been dexterous with firearms, or that his watery eyes, with bluish, washed-out irises, had been among the keenest of any warrior's who had fought in the Battle of the Little Bighorn.

We were camped that August day in 1938 at the Crow Fair.... An Oglala Sioux from Pine Ridge Indian Reservation in South Dakota, he had come to have a last look at the battlefield before he died.

... I loaded the old man in my car and headed south out of camp on U.S. Highway 87, by-passing the entrance to Custer Battlefield and National Cemetery so he could first see the site of the great Indian village where he had camped sixty-two years earlier.... none the less (he) soon managed to point out where the wide camp circles each a half mile in diameter, had sprawled along the Little Bighorn River.

... The Shahiyela (Cheyenne) camp was farthest north. We Oglala were camped just southeast of them, with the Brule in a smaller circle next to us. Next were the Sans Arc, then the Miniconjou, the Blackfoot Sioux, and farthest south next to the river were the Hunkpapa. I was twenty-eight years old that summer.

... I had never taken a wife, ...One woman I wanted was a pretty young Shahiyela named Monahseetah, or Meotzi as I called her.... she was from the southern branch of their tribe, just visiting up north, and they said no Shahiyela could marry her because she had a seven-year old son born out of wedlock and that tribal law forbade her getting married. They said the boy's father had been a white soldier chief named Long Hair; he had killed her father, Chief Black Kettle, in a battle in the south (Battle of the Washita) eight winters before, they said, and captured her. He told her he wanted to make her his second wife, and so he had her....

"Was this boy still with her here?" I asked him.

Yes, I saw him often around the Shahiyela camp.... He was named Yellow Bird

... Later interviews corroborated the old Oglala's statement that Monahseetah and Yellow Bird had been in the Little Bighorn camp at the time of the fight, many of my Cheyenne informants insisting that their strict moral code, more rigid then that of the Sioux, imposed restriction on their relations with a fallen woman....

"Tell me about the battle with Long Hair," I said.

That morning many of the Oglalas were sleeping late. The night before, we had a scalp dance to celebrate the victory over Gray Fox (General Crook) ... I woke up hungry.... After I finished eating I caught my best pony, an iron-gray gelding, and rode over to the Cheyenne camp circle. I looked all over for Meotzi ... I rode on to visit with my Shahiyela friend Roan Bear. He was a Fox warrior, belonging to one of that tribe's soldier societies, and was on guard duty that morning. He was stationed by the Shahiyela medicine tepee in which the tribe kept their Sacred Buffalo Head ... We settled down to telling each other some of the brave deeds of the past. [Many talks like this would have taken place among the Indians after the battle, and some of the stories must have grown.] The morning went by quickly, for an Elk warrior named Bobtail Horse joined us to tell us stories about his chief, Dull Knife, who was not there that day.

The first we knew of any attack was after midday, when we saw dust and heard shooting way to the south near the Hunkpapa camp circle.

Just then an Oglala came riding into the circle at a gallop.

"Soldiers are coming!" ...

I put this into a shout of Shahiyela words so they would know. I saw the Shahiyela Chief, Two Moon, run into camp from the river, leading three or four horses ...

... Two Moon led them out at a gallop ...

After Two Moon's band left to fight Major Reno, a new threat developed from Custer's detachment advancing down Medicine Tail Coulee toward the river and the Cheyenne camp. [Indicates the camp was close to the ford.]

"They're coming this way!" Bobtail Horse shouted, "Across the ford! We must stop them!"

We saw the soldiers in the coulee were getting closer and closer to the ford, so we trotted out to meet them. An old Shahiyela name Mad Wolf, riding a rack-of-bones horse, tried to stop us, saying:

"My sons, do not charge the soldiers. There are too many. Wait until our brothers come back to help!"

He rode along with us a ways whining about how such a small war party would have no chance against a whole army. Finally Bobtail Horse told him: "Uncle, only Earth and Heavens last long. If we four can stop the soldiers from capturing our camp, our lives will be well spent."

At this point I interrupted White Cow Bull, suggesting that we try to get closer to the crossing known as the Miniconjou Ford. He agreed it would refresh his memory on a few details to go, so I eased the car down a dusty lane between cultivated fields until we reached the river. He was in silence a long moment before resuming his narrative. Then he spoke in low tones, the Sioux words resonant in the morning quite:

The Sans Arc and Miniconjou camp circles were back from the ford. We found a low ridge along here and slid off our ponies to take whatever cover we could find. For the first time I saw five Sioux warriors racing down the coulee ahead of the soldiers. They were coming fast and dodging bullets the soldiers were firing at them. Then Bobtail Horse pointed to that bluff beside the ford. On top were three Indians that looked like Crows from their hair style and dress. [It should be noted White Cow Bull mentions three and not four.] Bobtail Horse said"

"They are our enemies, guiding the soldiers here." [Bobtail Horse seemed to have been saying a lot – it's too bad he didn't say more in later interviews.] He fired his muzzleloader at them, . . . I fired at them too, for I saw they were shooting at the five Sioux warriors, who were now splashing across the ford at a dead run. My rifle was a repeater, so I kept firing at the Crows until these Sioux were safely on our side of the river. They had no guns, just lances and bows and arrows. But they got off their ponies and joined us behind the ridge. Just then I saw a Shahiyela named White Shield, armed with bow and arrows, come riding down river. He was alone, but we were glad to have another fighting man with us. That made ten of us to defend the ford. [This is becoming an elaborate story and yet correlates with others if it was being made up.]

I looked across the ford and saw that the soldiers had stopped at the edge of the river. I had never seen white soldiers before, so I remember thinking how pink and hairy they looked. One white man had little hairs on his face (a moustache) and was wearing a big hat and a buckskin jacket. He was riding a fine-looking big horse, a sorrel with a blazed face and four white stockings. On one side of him was a soldier carrying a flag and riding a gray horse, and on the other was a small man on a dark horse. This small man didn't look much like a white man to me so I gave the man in the buckskin jacket my attention. He was looking straight at us across the river. Bobtail Horse told us all to stay hidden so this man couldn't see how few of us there really were.

The man in the buckskin jacket seemed to be the leader of these soldiers, for he shouted something and they all came charging at us across the ford. Bobtail Horse fired first, and I saw a soldier on a gray horse (not the flag carrier) fall out of his saddle into the water.* The other soldier chief was firing his heavy rifle fast. I aimed my repeater at him and fired. I saw him fall out of his saddle and hit the water.

Shooting that man stopped the soldiers from charging on. They all reined up their horses and gathered around where he had fallen. I fired again, aiming this time at the soldier with the flag. I saw him go down as another soldier grabbed the flag out of his hands. By this time the air was getting thick with gun smoke and it was hard to see just what was happened. The soldiers were firing again and again, so we were kept busy dodging bullets that kicked up dust all around. When it cleared a little, I saw the soldiers do a strange thing. Some of them got off their horses in the ford and seemed to be dragging something out of the water, while other soldiers still on horseback kept shooting at us.

Suddenly we heard war cries behind us, I looked back and saw hundreds of Lakota and Shahiyela warriors charging toward us. They must have driven those other soldiers who had attacked the Hunkpapa camp circle and now were racing to help us drive off these attackers. The soldiers must have seen them too, for they fell back to the far bank of the river and those still on horseback got off to fight on foot.** As warriors rode up to join us at the river a big cry went up.

---

*White Cow Bull's description of two gray horses having entered the stream would give credence to those believing E Company was first in line. Lieutenant Roe, in his book *Custer's Last Battle*, p.10, mentioned a Sergeant of E Company who rode into the stream before the Indians opened fire.

**Why I believe the lead company was C Company is primarily based on my assumption that once the command had stopped, the lead company in order to fire more effectively would have dismounted. (White Cow Bull indicates this.) The difficulty of controlling their horses would have caused many to either break away or be turned loose. The lack of C Company horses found on the battlefield, the number of Indian reports citing gray horses, the location of C Company soldiers, as well as the late escape of E Company members found in Deep Ravine with reports of their being on horses, have led to my conclusions. White Cow Bull's statement the troops were running infers moving on foot as they left the ford rather than riding and would tend to back my view. One should also note the running by both White Cow Bull and White Man Runs Him denotes a disorganized retreat.

"Hoka hey!" the Lakotas were shouting. "They are going!"

I saw this was true. The soldiers were running back up the coulee and swarming out over the higher ground to the north.1

I would support the essence of White Cow Bull's account for several reasons, primarily as it corroborates my basic theory. His is the only logical explanation of the events that I have found. It fits in with other Indian testimony as well as the general assumptions made after the battle by the whites in suggesting Custer went to the ford. Martin saw some Indians who could have been the five Sioux White Cow Bull mentions. The specific names White Cow Bull uses for the Indians who supported him at the ford are the same ones mentioned by others, and though some of the Indians describe them crossing the ford to meet the troops, the names remain the same. This agreement indicates that they were there at the time. We know most Indians were concerned with relating their own exploits, which was their natural tendency. How many Indians indicated what Gall, White Bull, Crazy Horse, Two Moons, Dewey Beard, and others were doing?

Upon examination of Indian testimony, there are a number of general conclusions that can be reached and accepted: (1) There was a surprise factor – with both Reno and Custer. (2) Those Indians attacking Reno learned of Custer's threat to the village during Reno's move to the bluffs. (3) There was no ambush of Custer's troops. (4) Initially there were few Indians at Ford B when Custer reached Medicine Tail Coulee. (5) There was movement of some of Custer's troops along Nye Cartwright Ridge. (6) There was action around Last Stand Hill. (8) Troopers made several attempts to escape in groups of varying numbers. (9) Once the troops were along Battleridge, and the Indians engaging Reno arrived, the fighting didn't last long.

The narratives of the specific action at the end of the battle between certain Indians and General Custer are so conflicting they all need to be questioned. They reflect the Indians' attempts to either satisfy or deceive the whites, or to gain notoriety for themselves. Some accounts were also enhanced by the whites for their own ends.

Analysis of Indian testimony forces one to factor in the surprise by Custer's troops. Initially, Custer was not faced with a large number of Indians as the command moved down Medicine Tail Coulee to Ford B. These facts correlate with White Cow Bull's account, and help answer the basic questions I have raised: Why there was no evidence of a major attack by General Custer's five companies, or an attempt to retreat to join with Captain Benteen's forces, which they assumed would be moving toward them. White Cow Bull also addresses the issue of why there wasn't a sound defensive position established, and implies a division of Custer's five companies.

There are two events most Indians would not have wanted to reveal, particularly those Indians who saw them happen. The first is Custer being shot at the ford. The Crows who knew what happened wouldn't have testified to that effect for understandable reasons. By the time those Sioux and Cheyenne who were at the ford found out it was Custer they had been fighting, and were interviewed, they would have known the whites' perspective on what happened: namely, that Custer was bravely fighting until the last, going down with his guns blazing. They could also have been concerned with what might happen to them. One should note Bobtail Horse's nervousness when questioned, as brought out by Wooden Leg. Both these considerations would have been enough to keep the Indians quiet. The second event Indian witnesses would be reluctant to disclose is the issue of the troops committing suicide.

What I question about White Cow Bull's story is whether Custer was indeed wearing a buckskin jacket. The evidence is divided but I believe he took his jacket off. Those who said he did were close to General Custer at the time. It was a hot day so it might be expected, although I have not seen any references to others taking theirs off. If Custer did, there is a possibility that he may have put it back on before moving to the ford and the attack he would be leading, particularly if in his mind there was any charm connected with it, or if he believed it might help in his being recognized by his command. It would be natural for White Cow Bull, thinking he had shot Custer, to use such a definition. Custer was portrayed as wearing a buckskin jacket.

Vic didn't have four white socks and I would question if White Cow Bull had been sure of seeing four, even though he may have realized the horse had white stockings. This point, like the question of the jacket, would reflect an acceptance of the stories which maintained Vic had four white socks. The dust, confusion, excitement, and, in White Cow Bull's case, even the water, would have made such descriptive sightings improbable.

. . . (Bobtail Horse) He and I led the massed warriors across the ford, . . .

Another warrior named Yellow Nose, a Sapawicasa (Ute) who had been captured as a boy by the Shahiyela and had grown up with them, was very brave that day. After we chased the soldiers back from the ford, he galloped out in front of us and got very close to them then raced back to safety.

I kept riding with the Cheyennes, still hoping that some of them might tell Meotzi later about my courage. We massed for another charge. The Shahiyela Chief, Comes-in-Sight, and a warrior named Contrary Belly led us that time. The soldiers horses were so frightened by all the noise we made that they began to bolt in all directions. The soldiers held their fire while they tried to catch their horses. Just then Yellow Nose rushed in again and grabbed a small flag (guidon) . . . he carried it off and counted coup on a soldier with its sharp end. He was proving his courage more by counting that coup than if he had killed the soldiers.

Now I saw the soldiers were split into two bands, most of them on foot and shooting as they fell back to higher ground, so we made no more mounted charges. I found cover and began shooting at the soldiers. I was a good shot and had one of the few repeating rifles carried by many of our warriors. I kept firing at the two bands of soldiers – first at one, then at the other. It was hard to see through the smoke and dust, but I saw five soldiers go down when I shot at them.

White Cow Bull summarized a general view of what took place. He would have been in the forefront of those who followed the retreating Custer companies, whereas the other Indians interviewed would have arrived later. The most difficult part to visualize and understand is why the soldiers moved as quickly to the north as White Cow Bull and other evidence suggests. Why didn't they go back on their own trail where they knew help would be coming? The only answer would seemingly be a completely disorganized retreat such as the one Reno made from the timber. Most of the Indians were, at first, crossing to the south of the troops which must have caused them to move around the cutbank and to the north. This is why, I think, the three company commanders went to Custer and were with him from the time right after he was shot at the ford until they were killed close to him on Last Stand Hill. The companies retreated hurriedly. Mounted and unmounted soldiers mixed together, and the officers were never able to separate and regain control of their companies as individual fighting units.

The two groups White Cow Bull fired on would have been Keogh's and Yates' battalions. White Cow Bull would have became aware of Keogh's battalion when they were fired on by them as they moved from Nye Cartwright across Deep Coulee. When Keogh's troops were shooting from Luce Ridge, it may have been at Wolf Tooth's band. It is regrettable D.H. Miller didn't establish with certainty where White Cow Bull was and where the two bands of soldiers were at the time he fired on them. I would assume White Cow Bull would have been on the south side of Deep Coulee and then fired on both battalions. He then would have followed the main element of Yates' battalion as they moved toward the area below Last Stand Hill. By that time Indians would have been on the west side of the Little Bighorn and also firing on these troops. If John Stands In Timber was correct (although he was not aware of the action at the ford), the troops moved to the area where the cemetery is today. The troops, particularly elements of C Company who were more likely to have been on foot, would have used rear guard action from West Calhoun Ridge to where the archaeologists place the South Skirmish Line. Francis B. Taunton, in his pamphlet, contains a reference to a letter by Goldin, in which Goldin says, "The faint trail leading along the edge of the bluff to the point where we found the men and horses of Smith's troop . . ."[3] This description supports my belief that the "main element" of Yates' battalion in their retreat from the ford would have moved around the bluff to the north, and then to the area below and to the north of Custer Hill. The rear guard action at that time resulted in the artifacts the archaeologists associate with a South Skirmish Line, which I refer to as the South Retreat Line. This could be why Joseph White Bull says he saw three companies below Battleridge. (Although he undoubtedly heard this from someone else, since he would not yet have returned from fighting Reno.)

White Cow Bull then remarks that in the latter stage of the battle he fought between troopers on Last Stand Hill and the river. This contention supports my hypothesis that these troops were there during an earlier period. The fact that the horses around Battleridge were to a large extent bays and grays according to Benteen and most Indian reports, would indicate that the soldiers on foot were mainly from C Company. This view is supported by the location of the bodies of identified C Company soldiers. If Yates' battalion did hold for a time in the area north and west of Last Stand Hill, it means that under the prevailing battle conditions there was no chance for the company commanders to have separated the men back into company formations. The bugle calls reported by Indians may have signified an attempt to do so. The troop movement to Battleridge may have been brought about by the sighting of Keogh's battalion approaching the southern end of the ridge and the hope to unite with them.

. . . It was a day of bravery – even for our soldier enemies. They all fought well and died in courage, except for one soldier on a sorrel horse. Two Shatiyelas and a

Lakota chased after him shooting at him as they rode. But the soldier's horse was fast and they couldn't catch him. I saw him yank out his revolver and thought he was going to shoot back at these warriors. Instead he put the revolver to his head, pulled the trigger, and fell dead.[4]

I would question the bravery statement. It appears to be the typical Indian response used to placate the whites.

Turtle Rib not only refers to the chase and the soldier shooting himself but indicates he was the third Indian to give chase. Correlating statements add veracity to both Indian accounts. If this was Corporal Foley, as He Dog's report would indicate, there are several circumstances one might speculate took place. Corporal Foley's body was found not too far from Ford B. Consequently, to have seen the soldier shoot himself, White Cow Bull would have to be near Greasy Grass Knoll and Deep Coulee. Furthermore, Corporal Foley may have been distancing his pursuers, but he would certainly have noticed the large number of Indians still crossing or gathering in the ford vicinity, so his chances of getting through would have been nil. Since he couldn't go back, he shot himself. The stories of Foley – if he was the lone soldier – give the appearance of being enhanced through campfire telling, or possibly being a way of pointing out but limiting to an acceptable level the subject of suicide by troopers.

> In a little while all my bullets were gone. But by that time the soldiers lay still. We had killed them all . . . When the women and children heard us, they came out on the ridge to strip the bodies and catch some of the big horses. . . .
>
> I began looking for bullets and weapons in the piles of dead bodies. Near the top of the ridge I saw a naked body and turned it over. The face had little hairs on it and looked like the white man who had worn the buckskin jacket and had fired at me across ford - the same one I had shot off his horse. . . . I remembered how close some of his bullets had come, so I thought I would take the medicine of his trigger finger to make me and even better shot. Taking out my knife, I began to cut off that finger.
>
> Just then I heard a woman's voice behind me. I turned to see Meotzi and Yellow Bird and an older Shahiyela woman standing there. The older woman pointed to the white man's body, saying:
>
> "He is our relative."
>
> Then she signed for me to go away. I looked at Meotzi then and smiled, but she didn't smile back at me, so I wondered if she thought it was wrong for a warrior to be cutting on an enemy's body. I decided she wouldn't be proud of me if I cut the white man's finger, and I moved away. Pretending to be busy looking for bullets, I glanced back. Meotzi was looking down at the body while the older woman poked her bone sewing awl deep into each of the white man's ears. I heard her say:
>
> "So Long Hair will hear better in the Spirit Land."
>
> That was the first I knew that Long Hair was the soldier chief we had been fighting and the white man I had shot at the ford. . . .[5]

This story corresponds to the one told by Kate Bighead, who learned of it from Southern Cheyenne in Oklahoma. When two Indians offer supporting details of an event but are not otherwise connected, as Kate Bighead and White Cow Bull, the story gains additional credence.

Wooden Leg also mentions Bobtail Horse, Roan Bear and Buffalo Calf and four Sioux crossing the ford and going to meet the soldiers. This fact also lends integrity to White Cow Bull's story, as do the testimonies of Curley, White Man Runs Him, and Goes Ahead by way of his wife Pretty Shield.

SOURCES

1. Miller, *American Heritage,* Echoes of the Little Bighorn, June, 1971.
2. Ibid., p. 34.
3. Taunton, *Custer's Field,* p. 15.
4. Ibid., p. 34.
5. Ibid., p. 34.

Cedar Coulee

Most writers today claim General Custer and his five companies went down Cedar Coulee to Medicine Tail Coulee, and then, depending on the author, a number of different scenarios take place. As pointed out in the examination of Martin's and Curley's testimony, I don't believe Custer went down Cedar Coulee. As with many other incidents concerning the battle, writers were prone to accept pivotal views without questioning or at least giving supporting evidence. The insistence that Custer went down Cedar Coulee is a good example of such attitude. I kept looking for testimony which would substantiate this move by Custer and I couldn't find any. People would simply state it as a fact and even base their theory of what happened later on this unwarranted supposition. When I first went to the battlefield this was one of the things I thought odd, as I couldn't see, in my mind, Custer doing this. I finally found Jerome Greene, who did make several references to support his opinion. The footnotes are found in his book, *Evidence and the Custer Enigma*.

> Page 17 – Custer then directed his five companies forward again and pressed to the right down a narrow cedar-lined coulee leading away from the river. [Footnote 18] Martin and the Crow scouts, Curley and Goes Ahead, indicated this as Custer's route down to Medicine Tail Coulee. Graham, *The Custer Myth*, p. 11, 13, 19, 20, 290.

If these references are the basis for writers to claim that Custer went down Cedar Coulee, I want to give them special attention. I have indicated before that with all the testimony supporting Custer's bravery, impetuousness, ambition, and his desire for victory, it should have been imperative for him to take action against the Indians as quickly as possible after separating from Reno and moving to the ridge. He should have done two things: First, Custer should have gone to Weir Point in order to get a better view so that he could determine the quickest and best way to reach the village. It would take overwhelming evidence for me to believe that he didn't. Secondly, it would also take such evidence to convince me that Custer went down Cedar Coulee (Note map). Greene's footnotes appear to be the reasoning used to support Custer's move down Cedar Coulee; therefore they will have to be examined with this movement specifically in mind.

The first footnote is found on page 11 of *The Custer Myth*. This is from an early Curley story that I have previously examined – one that appeared in the Helena Herald, 15 July 1876:

> ...Custer, with his five companies, after separating from Reno and his seven companies moved to the right around the base of a high hill overlooking the valley of the Little Horn through a ravine just wide enough to admit his column of fours. There were no signs of the presence of Indians in the hills on that side (the right bank) of the Little Horn. [This would appear to dispute Kanipe's observation of seeing Indians on the ridge. Those scouts would have been ahead of Custer and should have been aware of any sizeable group of Indians.] and the column moved steadily on until it rounded the hill and came in sight of the village lying in the valley below them.... Custer appeared very much elated and ordered the bugles to sound a charge, and moved on at the head of the column, waving his hat to encourage the men. When they neared the river, the Indians concealed in the undergrowth, on the opposite side of the river, opened fire on the troops which checked the advance. Here a portion of the command were dismounted and thrown forward to the river and returned the fire of the Indians.

Even this portion of Curley's account shows the influence of a reporter; as for what I am attempting to determine, there is nothing here to support the contention that Custer went down Cedar Coulee. In fact, in my view, just the opposite is true.

Digressing somewhat from this examination, I find that the Helena description poses the general problem found in the accounts of Curley, Martin, Kanipe and the other Crow scouts. The problem is the question of just where Custer reached the ridge and his subsequent action until Martin was sent back and the Crows left. What is particularly disturbing is the fact that the answer should have been determined at a time when the major participants could have been brought together to discuss their differences and decide on exact locations. Considering the importance in ascertaining what Custer did, coupled with the interest and writings of the period, it becomes nothing short of incredible that such basic factors are left unsubstantiated. Now they are a matter of conjecture.

Curley's remarks, as well as others made by Curley, Reno, Martin, Kanipe, the Rees, the other Crows, along with sightings by troopers, lead one to believe that Custer first arrived on the ridge somewhat north of Reno's entrenchment, which most likely would have been Sharpshooter Hill. I have come to believe Custer was ahead of his command when he first reached the ridge where he talked to his scouts and then met his troops near Sharpshooter Hill. They proceeded down the ridge with Custer again in advance of the main column which would have been strung out behind for some distance. I believe the reporter taking down Curley's interpreter's account, misunderstood Curley when he said, "the column moved steadily on until it rounded the hill and came in sight of the village lying in the valley below." Curley is not indicating a move around Sharpshooter Hill but the move down the ridge and around Weir Point where Custer could see the village "lying below." This viewing caused Custer's elation, suggested by Curley and also indicated by Martin. My reason for believing this version, besides later statements made by Martin in which he said Custer viewed the village from Weir Point, is the fact that from Sharpshooter Hill or other high points near there, Custer would not have been able to see enough of the village to have become "elated" and he certainly would not have seen dogs and children playing as Martin repeatedly stated, nor would the village be "lying below." Although I doubt if Custer ordered his buglers to sound a charge, whether near Sharpshooter Hill or Weir Point, I certainly cannot see Custer charging down Cedar Coulee from its head near Sharpshooter Hill, moving in a direction away from the village and not knowing the terrain or the way to reach the Indian encampment.

Two other points should be noted. Curley makes a reference to column of 4's and as in other early accounts he claims Custer moved to Ford B.

In this reference I can not see any evidence that would verify Custer's having gone down Cedar Coulee.

The second reference Greene uses is Curley's interview with General Scott. Curley said:

> ... Custer kept going on the ridge and the men followed him. Custer's men were about 100 yards ahead of us. We scouts followed Custer. We galloped our horses and moved fast after Custer and his men. Custer went to a point on the ridge and then turned to the right and followed a coulee in a northerly direction. When Custer left, Mitch Boyer and we scouts remained on the point. When we looked down to the camp we noticed there were not many around and Mitch Boyer said he thought the Indians were out campaigning somewhere and suggested we hurry down and fight them. There were five of us altogether. We went further north on the high bluffs and came near the Indian camp just below the bluffs. Each of us fired 2 or 3 shots at the camp. Custer had reached the river when we were at this point on the bluffs. The Indians commenced moving as soon as Custer reached the river.[1]

I believe Curley is saying that the scouts watched from the area of Reno Hill as Custer's troops moved to the ridge; when the troops moved down the ridge, they followed. (We need to recognize that according to Curley, Martin and Kanipe, the troops moved down the ridge, not back from it or along Cedar Coulee.) Martin didn't see the scouts or know if they were around, since the scouts were behind the troops and the five companies moved in a column of fours or twos – a formation I believe they assumed before or when they moved on to the ridge. The high point Custer went to must have been Weir Point. He then moved to the right in a northerly direction down a coulee, but there is no indication it was Cedar Coulee. In fact, as I pointed out when examining Curley's accounts, of the three coulees that Custer may have taken, Cedar Coulee lies in the least northerly direction. After Custer and his command started down the coulee, Bouyer, Curley and possibly all four Crows moved to that high point. They still did not see many warriors in the camp, just as Martin said Custer had not. This would mean Reno still had not engaged the Indians; there wouldn't have been any question where the braves were if Reno had attacked. All of Custer's troops would not necessarily have left the ridge by that time. Curley then says that the Crows and Mitch Bouyer went farther north on the high ridge and came out on the bluff just above the ford where they fired several shots at the camp. However, to Curley, north could have meant any of the three coulees, for he said Bouyer and the Crows were moving north as they followed the bluffs along the river. More than likely the Crows moved along the west ridge of Western Coulee. Curley says nothing about Indians lying in ambush, waiting for Custer. It isn't until Custer reaches the ford that Curley indicates the Indians are moving – some toward Reno and some toward Custer. At that time the braves would be on their way to meet Reno, going after their horses, or preparing for battle. The women would be looking for their children, taking down tepees, and finding places of safety. Warriors, as they became aware of Custer's troops or received word of the new danger, turned and moved toward the ford. Indian camps didn't have alarm systems. There was noise, dust and confusion, and it took time for all of the Indians to become aware of the new threat and reach the scene or gain a position from which to view the situation.

Curley said Custer had reached the river when the Crows fired from the bluffs above the ford. White Cow Bull suggested a similar picture. It should be recognized that if Custer had gone down Cedar Coulee, he would have traveled roughly 2 1/2 miles to reach the ford while the Crows had only half of that distance to cover. Although this fact does not constitute conclusive evidence, it does offer a challenge to those assuming Custer went down Cedar Coulee.

One of the main reasons for the premise that Custer did go down Cedar Coulee is the order Martin reportedly was given: a column right and then a column left. The effect would depend on when and where the troops were when the orders were delivered. Since early reports usually assumed Custer went down the "gorge," the change appears to have come after interviews with the Sioux and Cheyenne brought to light the sighting of troops on Nye Cartwright; along with the need to have Custer failing to move against the village until Reno had retreated.

Writers then assumed all five companies moved down Cedar Coulee to Nye Cartwright. You then have Custer sending only one or two companies to the ford while moving with the others to Battleridge. What's important to remember is that Reno's companies moved through Weir Point and established positions along the west ridge, in front and to the northeast of Weir Point. Benteen's remarks that only when reaching Weir Point could the Indian villages be seen should be factored in to any analysis.

There is no direct reference in the General Scott interview to Cedar Coulee, nor are there facts to support such a move by Custer.

The third reference refers to a letter sent from Russell White Bear to Fred Dustin, postmarked 1938, and said to be Curley's last comments on what happened, given shortly before his death:

> . . . when we reached the ridge the soldiers kept marching on the east side of Reno Hill and going down on the west side of the ridge – down a ravine running northward. At this point Custer and two other soldiers besides Bouyer and I rode over to a high point that overlooks the Big Horn Valley to see what was going on – we could see dust rising everywhere down the valley. Reno's men were riding toward the Indians – Custer nor any of us dismounted. Custer made a brief survey of the situation and turned and rode to his command. He did not ask Bouyer or me about the country – we rode following the creek as you know – we were all the time going away from the valley. We finally came out at the creek – Medicine Tail Creek – and seeing we were a long ways away from the valley – Custer turning left, rode down Medicine Tail. After riding a while, he halted the command – then the gray horse troops left us and started down the creek – when we turned north crossing Medicine Tail Creek going on the hills north of the creek – here the command halted again.[2]

The first sentence could be construed in different ways, one that they did go down Cedar Coulee and another that they didn't. Curley appears to suggest that as Custer's troops passed Reno's entrenchment area, they were to the east of it, but as they reached Weir Point, they went to the west and then moved down the ravine northward. As I have indicated before, Curley used the term "north" in such a way that it could apply to any of the coulees. Curley says that Custer was on the high point before Reno engaged the Indians. This statement appears in many of the Curley accounts, and it is odd that writers who use his testimony to support their views often ignore this part completely.

To believe that Curley and Bouyer rode to that high point with Custer not only refutes Martin's claim and those of the other Crow scouts, but also Curley's previous accounts. In this story Curley is now with Custer all the way. He is not going to the bluff above the ford with the other Crows and Bouyer, or firing on the Indian camp, nor are Curley and Bouyer going from the bluff down to join Custer.

This is one reference that could be used to support Cedar Coulee as the route Custer followed. According to Curley they were all the time going away from the valley and when Custer came out on Medicine Tail the valley was a long way off. I do believe White Bear is indicating such movement, although he uses a relative term since Middle Coulee also goes away from the valley and is farther than one might think when starting down it.

To believe that Custer would have moved down Cedar Coulee away from the valley, went part way down Medicine Tail Coulee, and then sent the Gray Horse Troop toward the ford, stretches the imagination too far. I wouldn't want to have been riding at Custer's elbow at any time, anywhere, if that is the way he planned an attack.

I don't see how one can assume that all the Indians waited for Custer, as most writers using this scenario have suggested, and that Custer further divided his command. If the Gray Horse Troop moved near the ford, then dismounted to inspect it, I don't think they would have had time to rejoin the command unless their dismounting and mounting were quicker than even Reno was credited with.

This testimony reflects a phenomenon I saw in many of Curley's stories, as he spun them over the years: as interpretations evolved in regard to what Custer did, so did Curley's recollection of the events. At first Custer went to the ford, but as that changed and the writers began to say that Custer didn't go, so did Curley. Because it was hard to disavow all such references, Curley then claimed that one company went to the ford or at least toward it. Since the Indians remembered seeing the Gray Horse Troop, it then became the company in question.

In his early statements Curley never said or implied that he or Bouyer were with Custer when the troops were moving along the ridge or toward Medicine Tail Coulee – all the available evidence would negate such a view. Martin would not have denied seeing the scouts if this story was true. I also believe that any account of Curley's that suggests he was with Custer when the General engaged the Indians is pure and simple fabrication, either by Curley or the interpreter, or is proof of poor analyzing and conjecturing on the part of the writer.

Goes Ahead, from the *Arikara Narrative*:

> . . . As Custer swung off the trail, after Reno left him to cross the upper ford, there was an Arikara scout and four Crow scouts with him. Custer rode to the edge of the high bank and looked over to the place where Reno's men were, as though planning the next move. When they had arrived at about the point where Lieutenant Hodgson's headstone was placed later, the three Crows scouts saw the soldiers under Reno dismounting in front of the Dakota camp and thought that the enemy were "too many." Close to where Reno and Benteen later in the day were attacked by the Dakotas, on the ridge of hills above the river, the three Crow scouts were left behind and Custer's command went down the draw toward the lower ford on the run. Custer had told the Crow scouts

1. A view from high point south of Weir Peak, near where Lt. Varnum saw the Gray Horse Troop. Cedar Coulee is on the right. The photograph suggests why it is unlikely that Custer went down Cedar Coulee.

2. A view from the west side of Weir Peak. Cedar Coulee below.

3. A view from the east side of Weir Peak. Photographs 2 and 3 are taken looking back toward Sharpshooter and Reno Hill. The terrain supports the hypothesis that Custer did not go down Cedar Coulee, but rather moved to Weir Peak to view the Indian village.

to stay out of the fight and they went to the left along the ridge overlooking the river while he took his command to the right (Goes Ahead is sure Curley the Crow scout was not with him.) At this point Curley and Black Fox, Arikara scout, disappeared. Black Fox rode a bay horse and Curley rode a bald-faced pony. The three Crow scouts rode along the high ridge, keeping from the view of the Dakotas till they came to the end of the ridge and to the bluff just above the lower ford. They then dismounted and fired across into the Dakota camp . . .[3]

Hairy Moccasin, one of the Crow scouts, claims that Custer was ahead of his command, and the scouts seem to agree that Custer went to the edge of the bluffs near the area where the Hodgson marker was later placed. This view could support my contention that Custer was far enough ahead of his troops when he arrived on the ridge that he spoke to Bouyer and then moved back to meet the command as they came onto the ridge. This scenario could also explain why Martin was not aware of seeing Bouyer or the scouts while on the ridge: by then the troops had moved ahead of the three scouts to Weir Point from where Custer viewed the village.

The three Crows indicate they saw Reno go into action. Goes Ahead claims they were near the later location of the Hodgson marker when that happened. According to Hairy Moccasin, Custer's command saw Reno go into action. White Man Runs Him told Walter Camp that Custer sat on the bluffs and saw all of the Reno fight in the valley. Walter Camp's comment to that statement was that it was preposterous, which I think it was. I believe what one sees in these narratives, and what one should keep in mind, is that the Crows, having been condemned for leaving Reno and Custer, were attempting to justify their actions. If Custer could watch Reno in action and not go to his aid, retreating instead, then why should they be criticized for leaving, especially since they had orders to do so, and as scouts they were not expected to take part in the actual fighting? I believe these are good examples of witnesses trying to vindicate themselves as well as make their story fit into what the whites thought took place. We should also remember that Curley said Custer did not see Reno go into action, and Goes Ahead told Walter Camp that Custer had gone out of sight behind the bluff quite some time before the Reno fight began.[4]

There's no doubt the Crows saw Reno go into action. The question is where that happened, where the four Crows separated, and whether they got back together before they separated again.

I think we can assume that the Crows stayed close to the edge where they may have met Custer, then as Custer and the command moved down the ridge, they – or at least three of them – continued to hold in that area. Custer's command would have been strung out for some distance as they moved along the ridge. Custer, in advance of the troops, went to where he could view the village. He came down about the time the command moved up or, if Kanipe was right, dashed up. They proceed toward Medicine Tail Coulee. At least three of the Crows held back (as reported by Curley in his 1908 interview with Walter Camp[5]), and as they began to move on down the ridge, they saw Reno dismount and go into action. This version of the events would not coincide with Curley's accounts if the four Crows and Bouyer were still together.

The implication is that Bouyer and Curley moved along with Custer's command and then climbed up to the high point as Custer and the lead elements moved out.

Bouyer and Curley could still have seen a peaceful village. Bouyer may then have told Curley to go back, which might account for some of the stories of the Crows separating at that time. Bouyer could have gone with the three older Crows who were now coming up, and they moved to the bluff overlooking the ford. Recall that White Cow Bull spoke of firing at three Crows on the bluff, not four. It is possible that Curley, as he said in his interview with General Scott, also went to the bluff and fired on the village. Deciding which of the above versions is true would be conjectural, but I believe that my descriptions give a fairly accurate general picture of what happened.

Goes Ahead said that Custer went down toward the lower ford on the run. If the troops were going down Cedar Coulee, they would not be going toward the lower ford and it is not likely they would go on the run away from the village. Goes Ahead's phrase, "Close to where Reno and Benteen later in the day were attacked by the Dakotas...", is usually interpreted to mean the position where Reno entrenched, but it could have referred to Weir Point where Reno's troops were first attacked before retreating. The three scouts then went along the ridge to Bouyer's Bluff with Custer's command to the right of them. Since the term "parallel" has also been used, it's more apt to indicate Middle Coulee than Cedar Coulee. The interesting aspect of Goes Ahead's statement is again the inclusion of Black Fox with Curley while on the ridge.

Here again, I don't see any confirmation that Custer went down Cedar Coulee. When the testimony is examined in its entirety, it would contradict Custer having done so.

The following is the last statement Greene used to support a Custer move down Cedar Coulee. Trumpeter Martin:

> ... Then the General and I rode back down to where the troops were, and he talked a minute with the Adjutant, telling him what he had seen. We rode on, pretty fast, until we came to a big ravine, that led in the direction of the river, the General pointed down there and then called me. This was about a mile down the river from where we went up on the hill, and we had been going at a trot and gallop all the way ... The last I saw of the command they were going down into the ravine.[6]

Since the Adjutant wasn't with Custer when he viewed the village, one should apply it to DeRudio's supposed sighting. Greene and others think that Martin is referring here to going down Cedar Coulee, and believe such interpretation is supported by Martin's statement that they moved to the right and to the north. I believe one has to conclude that the ravine leading to the river which Martin had reached while with Custer was Medicine Tail Coulee. The fact that he said it was a mile down river from where he and Custer went up on the hill suggests that they were following the river, and though to an extent Cedar Coulee would also have taken them down river, it wouldn't be as apparent or as pronounced as the other coulees. It is extremely doubtful whether Martin could have gone down Cedar Coulee to Medicine Tail Coulee and then come as close to the ford as he had maintained, returning to reach Benteen when he did. Many of the same writers who allege that Custer went down Cedar Coulee, claim that Martin had left before they reached Medicine Tail. If that was true, there would have been no need for him to tell Boston Custer where the General was, for the end of the column would not have passed out of sight. Nor, when returning, would he have seen troops in Medicine Tail – either Yates' battalion retreating or possibly Keogh's battalion moving to Nye Cartwright Ridge.[7]

These references seem to be the testimony used to support the idea that Custer moved down Cedar Coulee. Since they are all circumstantial and speculative, contradicting not only our knowledge of Custer's psyche but also his ability as a commander, I would certainly disagree with anyone's conclusion based on the above, which suggests Custer moved his troops away from the valley and the Indian encampment and went down Cedar Coulee.

I would add in support of my position the following by Henry Weibert and Fred Dustin.

Henry Weibert examined the terrain with metal detectors. Although he doesn't believe Custer moved along the ridge near the edge of the bluff – a view which I think evidence supports – neither does he believe that Custer went down Cedar Coulee, since he has not found any artifacts to support such a contention. His statement and certainly Fred Dustin's must be noted.

Henry Weibert:

> Now back to Custer and his route into the battle. If you remember, we had left Custer overlooking the valley below. Up to this point, he had followed the long low ridge coming up from North Fork of Reno. As I have said, very little evidence was found on this ridge that definitely put Custer on this route. Part of the reason is that this was later to become one of the Indian positions used to fire at Reno and Benteen. The presence of this many Indians has removed any possibility of finding many articles that could be definitely placed with Custer and his men. There were several items found along the upper end of the ridge that could have been lost by Custer but were most likely taken off their dead bodies and returned by the Indians when fighting Reno and Benteen. From here Custer will go down the ridge, southeast of Cedar Coulee, not down the bottom of Cedar Coulee. Therefore I feel that Custer used this ridge instead of the bottom of Cedar Coulee. And besides, it's the easy way to go.[8]

Fred Dustin:

> Another point in doubt with some has been Weir's Peak. Again, our common–sense when on the ground leads us directly to it. Following Custer's trail down the slope which gradually narrows into a valley, we come to a high eminence on our left with two separate peaks near each other. Ascending the nearest to its top, we find we have a dominating view . . . Descending to the trail at the foot of the peak, we see that it turns sharply to the north, becoming a narrow valley, the "gorge" mentioned by Benteen as being "filled with Indians." On our last day on the field, I followed down this gorge alone to Medicine Tail Coulee, expecting to come out within a few hundred yards from the river [no way could one expect to by going down Cedar Coulee], to my surprise, I found myself about a mile from it. As I came out of the gorge I saw a solitary horseman riding at a lope along the side of a ridge a half-mile or so distant, but he quickly disappeared...but presently rode toward me, and as he came near I saw he was an Indian. He introduced himself as Frank Bethune, a brother-in-law of the Crow scout, Goes Ahead, who was with Custer. Said he, "you came down the same coulee that Custer did. I have talked over the fight with Goes Ahead many times, and he told me what happened as he saw it. Bouyer and the three scouts, Goes Ahead, Hairy Moccasin and White Man Runs Him were on the bluffs, but Custer came this way." Here once more was a revelation: like myself, Custer had expected to come out near the river.[9]

SOURCES

1. Graham, *The Custer Myth*, p. 13.
2. Ibid., p. 19.
3. Ibid., p. 20.
4. Camp, Hammer, *Custer in 76*, p. 178.
5. Ibid., p. 157.
6. Graham, *The Custer Myth*, p. 290.
7. Camp, Hammer, *Custer in 76*, p. 101.
8. Henry and Don Weibert, *Sixty-Six Years in Custer's Shadow*, pp. 112, 113.
9. Dustin, *The Custer Tragedy*, "A Prelude," p. xiv.

13
Analysis of Writers' Scenarios

Curse Not His Curls
by Robert J. Ege

> With a friend like Benteen, Custer didn't need enemies. Later in life, Benteen turned on nearly all his comrades . . .
>
> Some critics have claimed that Custer's fall was due or at least partially due, to his failure to heed the advice of his scouts. However on this expedition his scouts failed him miserably. Chief white scout, Charlie Reynolds, was almost unfamiliar with this area. The usually dependable Arikara Bloody Knife, shared Reynolds lack of knowledge. The word "Sioux" struck terror in the hearts of the Crows. Mitch Bouyer, the half Sioux, had little rapport with the Crows . . . at the Crow's Nest, Custer was totally unaware of the strength of his enemy's fighting force as well as their intent; . . . He had no definite knowledge of the terrain surrounding the village.[1]

I believe this passage represents a bias that is present throughout Ege's book. I don't know how anyone could read through most of the evidence and not realize that Custer, who was an experienced Indian fighter, was aware that he was facing an exceptionally large encampment.

The Crows were undoubtedly fearful of the Sioux, but this should have been all the more reason why Custer would have listened to them, which I believe he did. I have never read a claim that Mitch Bouyer was not respected by the Crows, but even if it were so, it does not mean that this would have made any difference.

> General George A. Custer, following his tragic death, became the target of many critics for dividing his command into three battalions. . . .
>
> Reconnaissance . . . If there was one thing that the General lacked and was sorely in need of, it was precise information. The stalwarts who scouted for the expedition did not provide sufficient information and details upon which a definite battle commitment of entire regiment should be based. . . . He chose to conduct a "reconnaissance-in-force." It was his plan to advance cautiously, gathering information as he went. . . .
>
> This is clear by the messages he sent to Benteen ordering the captain to bring up the ammunition packs and reinforce him. Custer didn't detail a platoon to search for Benteen; on two separate occasions, he sent one man. The orderlies had no difficulty in locating Benteen, for he was within cooperating distance but not in a cooperative mood.[2]

Although I do blame Benteen for a "cover-up," this last statement is a general criticism which doesn't appear to recognize the many factors Benteen was faced with, and consequently lacks objectivity. Writers such as Ege often speculate on what was in Custer's mind, when certainly no one, even at the time, could possibly know. I think one can guess Custer's reason for splitting his command, as most writers have, and make a judgment on whether he should have done so or not. However, Ege has no grounds to assume that Custer knew Benteen wouldn't have continued on in the direction he was sent, especially since the writer has just brought out the lack of knowledge of the terrain. One of the couriers Custer sent was not to Benteen – the Kanipe message was for the packs and Captain McDougall, and it certainly didn't indicate Custer knew Benteen had returned to the main trail. As I have indicated, I believe that after Kanipe left, Sergeant Major Sharrow or a third courier rejoined the command and told Custer that Benteen was back on the main trail, which prompted Custer to send Martin.

> . . . The Crows informed Gerard, who promptly related this information to Reno. Gerard then rode after Cooke and Keogh, who were then returning to Custer. He overtook them about 100 yards from the river, explained the turn of events, [Indians not running but moving against Reno.] and returned to the Reno formation. . . .
>
> . . . The appearance of several mounted warriors, in his immediate front . . . [Reno] . . . Reno's men, if faced by 500 Indians, would have held a strong advantage in fire power. Reno's enemy was by no means 500 in number . . . His men had been on the skirmish line less than 15 minutes and had suffered but one fatality. That occurred when Sergeant Miles F. O'Hara's horse was struck by a spent bullet. The mount bolted and carried the "M" Company non-com directly toward the Indian line.[3]

I believe Girard, according to his story, was warned by Rees, but it seems more writers should have wondered where all these Indians disappeared to in such a short time, and why there is no record of that maneuver in Indian accounts. There are different versions of O'Hara's death and the number of troopers killed on the skirmish line.

> Unknown to Reno, Custer, from a vantage point on the bluffs, with fearful apprehension, witnessed the charge down the valley. Custer could see, and for the first time was aware of the immense size of the village. . . . The General's tension was relieved when the charge broke

into a skirmish line. He was pleased with this maneuver and expressed his appreciation with a cheer and a wave of his hat. Lt. Charles DeRudio claims to have witnessed this gesture and most historians have accepted it as a fact. It might have been true, but the distance between Custer and the point where DeRudio was fighting in the valley is roughly one mile.[4]

Ege's manipulation of time is obvious in this passage. He believes Custer saw Reno go into a skirmish formation, and so waved his hat to indicate his approval. Ege questioned DeRudio's sighting of Custer, but he does so because of distance; whereas, if DeRudio's own accounts are correct, it is impossible for him to have seen Custer because of the time factor. DeRudio claims he saw Custer waving his hat less than six minutes before Reno fled the timber, not when he was setting up a skirmish line. I don't think Custer waved his hat for some thirty minutes. I would agree with Ege that DeRudio would not have been able to distinguish Custer from that distance, and certainly not Adjutant Cooke's whiskers. Troopers also said they saw Custer waving his hat. The sighting took place, according to their testimony, on the way down the valley. This would be some ten to fifteen minutes before they set up a skirmish line. I doubt if Custer spent that much time on the ridge waving his hat. I don't think there is any real evidence to support the claim that Custer saw Reno set up his skirmish line.

> There is no accurate time check on any of the troop movements after the command departed from the "Crow's Nest" at noon. [They departed from the Crow's Nest before noon. Ege undoubtedly means the divide.]
>
> After first viewing the village, Custer moved northward for about 3/4 of a mile. Here, along with his brother Tom, Lt. W. W. Cooke, Trumpeter Giovanni Martini, and probably some others, he separated from the column and rode to the highest elevation on the field, Weir Point, for another view of the village. [This would be his first real look at the village.] The column must have been 2/4 – 1 mile east of Weir Point at this time. Most historians place it much closer.[5]

According to Ege, with the column on the ridge above the valley, the command, including Custer, went down Cedar Coulee for some distance; this after seeing Major Reno deploy in a skirmish position. Ege indicates that even though by this time Custer had an idea of the size of the village, apparently he wasn't too worried about Reno and his troops: General Crook was expected and Colonel Gibbon would be there in another day. One might believe that if Custer was thinking that way, he would have deemed it better to have gone back and united with the packs and Benteen, or at least waited for them along the bluffs or in Cedar Coulee. It is difficult for me to conceive of the command moving down Cedar Coulee when the terrain beyond was blocked from view by Weir Point, only to have Custer move back to Weir Point for another view.

> After viewing the village again, the general and his group returned to the main body of the command. His battle plan included Benteen and the reserve ammunition.[6]

I agree with Ege that Custer's "battle plan" included Benteen, but not in the way Ege does. I believe Custer realized it could become necessary to have additional aid and decided it would be better to have the packs on his side of the river. I also believe that until Custer received a message that Benteen was back on the trail, his prior plan was to have Benteen support Major Reno from across the Little Bighorn; otherwise his message via Kanipe would have been to Benteen (as was his later message), and would have included orders for McDougall and the packs. I think one could infer that his battle plan was still to attack. Custer knew the importance of aiding Reno as quickly as possible; he would have realized that such a move was necessary if he was to defeat the Indians. Custer's statements on viewing the village support such a position. To assume that he looked for a defensive area to the north or planned to draw Indians off, is not compatible with sound reasoning: it contradicts both Custer's psyche and the existing evidence, and has to be labeled speculation based on selective use of few facts.

> There was little chance of the Indians ever making a charge or assaulting Reno's position in force. [In the timber] Singularly, Indians often exhibited great courage and daring in the "war game." However, fighting in a group, their philosophy of battle was to avoid any possible risk. One warrior believing in his own "strong medicine," might believe himself impregnable. . . . military men were resigned to figure a certain percentage, depending upon the situation, as expected casualties in Indian fighting. Indians were not endowed with this philosophy. They preferred to fight at extremely long range or to ambush a foe. This weak spot in their battle strategy no doubt saved the men at the Hayfield Battle, the Wagon Box Fight and at Beecher's Island. The defenders in these fights faced far greater odds than Reno did on June 25, 1876, and the majority lived to tell the tale . . .
>
> For reasons that have never been explained, after the command had been in the woods for 20 to 25 minutes, Reno decided to vacate the area.[7]

In general the above paragraph is correct in reviewing Indian fighting patterns. Numerous reasons have been given and accepted by some writers and opposed or not recognized by others in discussing the question of whether Reno should or could have remained in the timber. It would be more useful, however, to use the inverse reasoning: If Major Reno and Captain Benteen should have remained in their position, what about Custer? Why didn't Custer establish a defensive position he was able to hold? Some, of course, say that he did and then blame the fact that he didn't maintain it on the sighting of Company D on Weir Point – a weak excuse which again shifts culpability from Custer to Reno and Benteen. When Reno retreats, his maneuver becomes a rout, but a retreat by Custer which shows few signs of organized resistance is usually not considered a rout. Again, many do not concede that Custer retreats: his actions, even when they don't end in an attack, constitute an offensive maneuver. And historians stress objectivity.

The following refers to when Reno's forces moved to Weir Point:

> . . . They were really watching the final phases of Custer's last fight. If the troops under Reno and Benteen had made a menacing gesture, such as a charge or rapid advance in their direction, they would have undoubtedly fled to the village.[8]

Here is another instance where inverse reasoning could be applied. For one thing, Ege is not talking about a charge of two or three hundred yards or a quarter of a mile, but of two and a half to three miles. To believe that warriors would all flee to the village and let them unite is fanciful thinking. The movement of packs and the wounded would have been slow. The force would either be divided or, if unified, would move very slowly. Most writers think the Indians numbered from three to six thousand warriors. By that time they were fairly well armed; though they might have fallen back from a frontal assault, to assume that the troops could have moved that far seems unrealistic. I don't think they would have found any of Custer's troops alive to have joined up with.

Getting back to the inverse reasoning, one should ask why Custer didn't make such a charge back to unite with them. Certainly at first he would not have been faced with the number of Indians that were there later. Why didn't Custer make "a charge" back to join Benteen at a time when he was supposedly looking for and setting up a defensive position? If he knew so much of what was happening to Reno, he could have suspected that the two would be together. This was Custer's command – he was to support them and support was particularly needed in the conditions that developed. Instead, writers suggest that when Custer saw Major Reno's forces on Weir Point, some three miles away, he deployed his companies to help them. This maneuver supposedly caused his defeat. That is to ignore Indian evidence suggesting that Custer was defeated some time before Weir's company appeared, and that any movement by Custer's troops was in the opposite direction.

If Ege's scenario describes what actually happened, Custer deserved to have been defeated and one should not blame the outcome on Benteen and Reno.

> The importance of the General's orders to Benteen cannot be over-stressed. At the time the order was issued, Custer was aware that Reno was engaged in the valley. From his high vantage point on the bluffs; it was obvious to Custer that Benteen would find few, if any, Indians in the area where his mission would take him, and he knew absolutely no reason to believe his order would not be obeyed. His actions were predicated on the assumption that his subordinates would act in accord with his direction.
>
> In considering Custer's action, and keeping in mind that he was awaiting the arrival of Benteen it must be assumed, for lack of contradictory evidence, that at no time did Custer attempt to charge across the ford into the Indian camp.[9]

Here Ege appears to know as a fact not only what Custer saw, but what he was thinking, and he bases his explanation of Custer's actions on these very questionable and speculative premises. Apparently Custer knew that Benteen would only go a certain distance and then would turn back to the main trail, just as he knew by then that there were no Indians in that vicinity. Prior to this speculation, Ege has referred to Custer's lack of knowledge of the terrain, and one might assume that Custer could have seen, or had brought to his attention, the tracks of the Indians who had gone in that direction to fight General Crook. There was also the possibility of Benteen running into war parties or agency Indians moving to join the Sioux. If, as Ege implies, Custer knew by then that there were no Indians in front of Benteen, and he was aware of the size of the Indian encampment, he must have assumed that the Indians would not cross the Little Bighorn and move to oppose Benteen. Since Martin's horse was shot, it was conceivable that he might not have been able to return to Benteen with Custer's message.

I don't think Custer, at this stage, had given up the thought of attacking the Indians as soon as possible, and certainly had no plans to move further north to establish a defensive position to wait for Benteen.

ANALYSIS OF WRITERS' SCENARIOS

There are two other points to be made to set the stage for what probably occurred on Custer's field.

It was still necessary for Custer to keep his column concealed from the Indians. By doing so, he prevented the enemy from anticipating his movements and thus avoided a defensive maneuver prior to complete formulation of his battle plan. While his advance was progressing, Custer constantly kept high ground between himself and the Indians. At the point Custer sent Martin on his way to Benteen, his command was just below or east of the summit of the 3,400 foot elevation denoting Weir Point ridges on the U.S. Geological Survey map of the area.

Lastly, while Custer was awaiting the arrival of Benteen and the ammunition packs, he was searching out and trying to select a place that would lend itself to the type of defense Custer and his five troops could provide. Ground higher then that occupied by his adversaries, in conjunction with terrain suitable to protecting his horses, was desirable. Cavalry, primarily an offensive weapon, was greatly reduced in battle efficiency when placed in a stationary position. The General was gambling on Benteen's prompt appearance, and the terrain he selected would be the rallying point for reunification of part of his command. Reinforced and well-supplied, he could then resume the offensive with eight troops instead of five.[10]

It is difficult for me to understand how Ege and other writers who have similar suppositional views as to what Custer thought and did, can come up with their theories. According to Ege, Custer went some two or three miles from where he separated from Major Reno and still hadn't completed a plan of attack. Ege does point out that a cavalry is primarily an offensive weapon; he might have added that this cavalry was led by the man considered one of our most offensive-minded commanders. According to writers like Ege, Custer believed that Reno was confronted by a large number of Indians; so large, in fact, that Custer supposedly was afraid to attack with his five companies, and that at a time (and the only time) when a small number of soldiers could have expected to launch a successful attack. In this scenario Custer had seen a peaceful village, just awakening, and yet he is already planning a defensive strategy rather than an offensive one. He is not going to worry about Reno who has established a skirmish line, nor is he worried that Benteen might go to Reno's aid (although I believe this was part of his original plan). Many of these writers who blame Benteen for not going to assist Custer say that it was because of his enmity toward the General; yet Custer is said to be so naive as to predicate his whole success on Benteen moving rapidly to aid him. One might point out that while Custer was searching for a high point and going further north to find it, Weir Point, Luce or Nye Cartwright Ridges would have sufficed. Some officers under Reno thought that Weir Point was a good defensive position and they were surprised when the troops pulled back from the Weir Peaks. Other officers differed in their opinions. Certainly there was no higher point in the area and Custer's aid would not have had to cross North and South Medicine Tail Coulee. They would have been in a position to have control over the Indian movement along these coulees. In other words, besides moving farther away from Benteen's relief, you also provide the Indians with better movement to cut off this aid and to surround you. Even if Benteen and the packs had moved as quickly as possible to support Custer, it would have taken a long time – when speed was essential for success. I credit Custer with realizing the nature of these circumstances.

Ege appears to support Marquis' placement of the Cheyenne camp site just north of Ford B. Such a location would be another reason for Custer to believe that he could accomplish what most writers suggest was his battle plan: to flank the Indians and attack them from both sides.

Custer's messages sent by way of Kanipe and Martin reflect his conviction that a battle was imminent and he would need all of his troops. I don't think we should accept the supposition that Custer thought it necessary for them to unite before he could launch an attack. Time was of the essence. Custer knew the Indians were there and he would want Benteen and McDougall moving as quickly as possible to be in a position to support his attack. A hundred and twenty additional men was not going to offset the importance of a synchronized assault.

> ... After Martin departed, Custer turned his column slightly to the right, in a direction away from the river. He rode for about 1000 yards. This brought him to a large defile of ravine known as Medicine Tail Coulee.[11]

According to Ege, Custer left his column 3/4 of a mile east of Weir Point, went to Weir Point and then returned. To do that he would have to leave the column very close to Medicine Tail Coulee, go to Weir Point, spend 5 to 10 minutes observing the valley, return to his column, talk to them, and then move out. Custer, at that time, sent Martin with his message, and after going another thousand yards he reached Medicine Tail Coulee. That would have taken over half an hour from the time he was on the ridge and first viewed the valley. At that point he could and should have launched an attack on the village.

In describing these events Ege appears to have forgotten what he said earlier, and he goes back to the view shared by most writers: namely, that Custer left his column at the foot of the hill when he went to view the valley. This inconsistency makes one think that Ege is piecing together various bits of information without really coordinating them to fit the view he is trying to establish.

Ege supports Curley's account of Custer holding for some 15 to 20 minutes and of Custer talking to Bouyer.

> ... The column was in good concealment. The discussion between Custer and Bouyer was probably relative to the topography that lay ahead ...
>
> Medicine Tail Coulee, if followed down from the heights to the river level, leads to the Little Bighorn ... any gathering of troopers, approaching the village in this defile, would have caught the immediate attention of the Indians, [This is an over-statement – most of the view of Medicine Tail would have been cut off, the Indians were preoccupied, especially at first – when the troops should have been moving down the defile.] When the march was resumed, Custer again moved away from the village. There is no certain explanation for this maneuver, ... according to Curley, who was still observing from a higher elevation. The Gray Horse Troop, under Lt. Algernon E. Smith, or possibly a platoon of the Gray Horse under Lt. James G. Sturgis, was sent toward the village. Dr. Charles Kuhlman advanced a plausible theory that Custer may have been "playing a bluff" and was attempting to lead the Indians into believing he was launching an attack upon their village ...[12]

I can't see anything plausible in this account: one minute Custer is trying to conceal his troops, the next he sends a company or platoon for the Indians to see; one minute he doesn't think he is in a good offensive position, the next he is trying to draw an attack. Such behavior might be plausible if the troops had moved to the ridges and cutbanks to lead the Indians into a trap, but not when they merely went farther north so they could be seen. One minute the troops seem intent on establishing a defensive position as part of the strategy to give Benteen time to arrive, and the next they are drawing an attack by the Indians.

> The general led the four remaining troops eastward to the high ridges that lie one mile east of the battlefield. Custer selected the place he was able to make his stand from his evaluation of the topography between his column and the river. His observations were made from the lofty heights of the East Ridge. Subsequently, he moved to this site. He arrived at what is now known as Custer Ridge, or the Battle Ridge, about 4:40 P.M. It was about 40 minutes after Benteen had received the message, via Martini, to join the general with all speed.
>
> After taking positions on the ridge, "I" Company, under Keogh, was on the north end. "C" and "F" were in the center and "E" and "L" were held temporarily in reserve on the opposite end. Almost immediately, the command was surrounded by the well-concealed enemies. Arrows began to rain down on the troopers. In a matter of minutes each of the countless cuts and ravines, every sizeable clump of sagebrush, and every hillock of turf concealed an armed warrior ... the one-sided battle continued for an hour ...[13]

It's really hard for me to recognize this account as a "logical" portrayal of Custer's moves. Here Custer seems to have forgotten Reno: he is attempting to conceal his troops from the Indians; he is waiting for Benteen; he is looking for a defensive position; he sends a company or platoon to the ford; and he isn't worried about this company being attacked by the Indians who will "immediately" see them as they descend down the defile. He now moves his four companies farther to the heights of East Ridge and then he moves to Battleridge. However, during the time he is looking for a good defensive position, he doesn't see all the Indians sneaking up the cuts and ravines, concealing themselves to such an extent that when he finally gets to Battleridge, they are all around him. I am amazed Company E was able to get through all these Indians, go to the ford and still make it back in time to establish a defensive position.

> ... The Seventh was engaged in a hold-off campaign, but losses were heavy. Despite Custer's losses in casualties his plan was to hold his position until additional men and supplies arrived which to press and assault.
>
> There is an historical notation upon which to base this appraisal. That note is contained in the field notes of W. M. Camp, who compiled much of this valuable data through lengthy interviews with Curley. Shortly before departing from Custer's column, Curley had a brief talk with "Mitch" Bouyer who explained to him that, "Custer was seeking a high place to make a stand and await the arrival of other soldiers." This bit of historical fact transforms logical assumption into concrete analysis, fortified by Custer's position on the ridge and the original copy of the "last order," which is preserved in the library at West Point.
>
> All through the first hour of the one-sided conflict, the general anxiously awaited and constantly watched the Weir Point elevation for reinforcements he had every reason to expect. At about 5:30 P.M., he spotted the men on the point. Although Custer probably used field

glasses, any change in the surface of that point he had kept so long under scrutiny, would have been visible to his naked eye. The sun, bright over the western horizon, shone on reflective surfaces and there were the unmistakable colors of the red and white guidons. The laggardly Benteen was finally on his way.

This knowledge resulted in Custer's one and only defined troop maneuver since taking his stand. In order to clear the way for the approaching column and to provide a protective corridor for its advance, the general ordered troops "C" and "E" under his brother, Tom, and Lt. Smith, to form a skirmish line toward the river. To complete the maneuver, he put the fighting Irishman, Capt. Myles Keogh, in temporary command of troops "L" and part of "F" in addition to his own "I" troop, and had him form a similar line along Custer ridge toward Weir Point. The balance of the command remained with the General... It was hoped that skirmishers could drive and keep Indian infiltrators away from the reinforcers line of advance. It was a sensible strategy. Had the relief column proceeded according to expectation, it may have met with success.

... The Indians, wary of this change in tactics watched for threatening developments. When nothing happened, the Cheyenne, Lame White Man shouted to his ...

... Custer's position on the ridge was completely surrounded by countless and unseen Indians. Sioux and Cheyenne, following the experienced leads of Crazy Horse and Two Moon respectively, had circled Custer's position and were coming in from the north and west. Chief Gall and those who had selected his "medicine" to lead them crawled up through the depressions that marked the field from the south ...[14]

Without trying to establish why Custer wouldn't have sent E and C Troops toward Weir Point, considering their location, it should be recognized that this thrilling episode is proven historically true by none other than Curley, in his interview with Camp. If you accept that fact, you will probably accept the rest of Ege's account as well. Camp's interview with Curley will of course have to be accepted, because Curley was Camp's friend and Camp was a better interviewer than others. The fact that Curley had told numerous different and conflicting stories is not important because they were not true, even though those accounts in which he claimed he was not with Custer coincide with the testimony of the other Crow scouts and the Arikaras, and they conform to a more plausible timing sequence.

When Ege states that, "this bit of historical fact transforms logical assumption into concrete analysis...", I have to confess I don't comprehend the meaning of the terms "historical facts," "logical assumption," or "concrete analysis," as he understands them.

After fighting for fifty minutes of the hour that Ege felt the battle lasted on Custer's Hill, Custer – who has not only been watching the Indians through the dust and gun smoke but also has kept his eyes glued on the ridges to the south – at last sees Benteen coming. Even though he is surrounded by thousands of Indians, his troops have already suffered heavy casualties, and Benteen is still several miles away, he sends out all but one of his companies to the south and west. Now, if Benteen had just galloped those two miles to his aid (I don't know what he would have done with the packs), he probably would have defeated the Indians. Is this logic?

If Custer's troops were able to do what Ege claims they did at that particular time, they still must have been fairly well intact. The tremendous number of arrows that had been raining down on them, which Ege says did so much damage, must not have been very effective. Custer was still not worried about Reno. According to Curley, Bouyer told Custer about Reno's retreat, back in Medicine Tail Coulee, and it had no effect on his thinking concerning what might have happened to Benteen or the Indians in regard to their relative positions, the condition of the wounded, and the need for Custer to unite with them.

Possibly Custer thought Reno was still in the timber, and he knew, as Ege and others have pointed out, that a small number of troops can hold out against overwhelming odds if they keep their defensive formation.

I think there has been a lot of unjust criticism of Custer and the moves he made. To me, those writers who are supposedly supporting Custer and blaming Reno and Benteen, when analyzed, are actually portraying Custer as not only cowardly but also lacking intelligence and certainly military expertise. I believe my view is more realistic. Custer went to the ford and was the first to fall. (This often happens to officers leading troops.) His getting shot resulted in a retreat that for the most part was disorganized, except for certain rear guard action, and for I and L Companies when they first moved to Battleridge from their reserve position.

My hypothesis casts no negative reflection on General Custer; in fact, it suggests just the opposite. There are those who criticize his leadership of troops and have compared it to General Crook in the Battle of the Rosebud. General Crook stayed behind and directed his troops so that he then knew their whereabouts and the conditions they faced; consequently he lost very few men and was able to withdraw in good order. However, one should recognize the difference between a general controlling infantry and cavalry, and a commander of cavalry. The general controlling both infantry and calvary, as witnessed in any Civil War battle, would be expected to stay behind and direct their troops, not be out leading his infantry. The cavalry commander would be required to lead his troops so that he could control their movement.

Custer would have attempted to do the only thing he could from his position, to aid Reno and defeat the Indians. Considering the state of the village, Custer would have created more havoc when his troops swept into it. His attack would probably have caused the Indians to retreat and attempt to scatter. The need for Custer to place a battalion in reserve was imperative: to give instructions to Benteen and the packs when they arrived, and put them in a position to prevent an effective scattering of the Indians or to come to Custer's aid. Custer would realize the need to attack quickly while Reno was still fighting in the valley. This was the only way he could expect to defeat the Indians. Captain McDougall, moving on the scene with his enlarged company, would have put additional pressure on the Indians. However, even if Custer had failed, one would not criticize his plan or his actions. They would fit into the image of Custer as a courageous and dashing cavalry leader. The only criticism would be that he should have recognized the strength of the Indians and remained near the ridge above the valley. This would not only have allowed Benteen and McDougall to join him but would have aided Reno as well. They then would have been in a position to either threaten the Indians, attack them, or support an orderly retreat by Reno. Custer's actions were justified as I envision them.

SOURCES

1. Ege, Robert, *Curse Not His Curls,* Publisher Fort Collin's, Col. – The Old Army Press, 1975. p. 70.
2. Ibid., p. 73.
3. Ibid., p. 79.
4. Ibid., p. 82.
5. Ibid., p. 83.
6. Ibid., p. 83.
7. Ibid., pp. 84, 85.
8. Ibid., p. 91.
9. Ibid., pp. 97, 98.
10. Ibid. p. 98.
11. Ibid., p. 100.
12. Ibid., p. 100.
13. Ibid., p. 101.
14. Ibid., pp. 105 – 106.

Legend into History by Dr. Charles Kuhlman

(JP – Dr. Kuhlman's general view of what happened was presented in his orientation summary starting on page xix.)

This plan was abandoned when, a little before noon, he (Custer) received information which convinced him that his command had been discovered by Indians.

Good tactics now demanded an immediate advance. So the command was halted as it reached the divide and organized for reconnaissance in force in order to pick up as much information as possible as they went along . . .

. . . Here they flushed a small band of warriors who fled down the trail. [Near Lone Tepee.] At the same time a heavy dust was seen in the valley, which was taken to mean that the Indians were in wild flight. Custer at once ordered Reno to go in pursuit.

Reno went down Ash Creek at a fast gait, crossed the river and galloped down the valley about two and a half miles. After about 15 to 20 minutes he moved into the edge of some timber along the sides of a basin some fifteen feet below the plain: fought here for another 15 to 20 minutes, . . . Not having men enough to cover this defensive position, he remounted his command and retreated to the bluffs east of the river, where, in about 10 or 15 minutes he was joined by Benteen, and by the pack train about an hour later.

Meanwhile Custer, after Reno had left, proceeded slowly down the trail for some distance, turned to the right diagonally toward the river, and then rushed up the slope northward and with his staff rode forward to the edge of the bluffs, arriving there a few minutes before Reno went into dismounted action in the valley about a mile and a half to the west. He remained there for perhaps five minutes and then resumed his march downstream. As the column neared the high ridges now officially designated as Weir Point, he sent Sergeant Kanipe with an order to the packtrain to hurry forward.

Dr. Kuhlman, like many other writers, makes a third cardinal mistake in his analysis. The first was believing that Custer did not know the general location of the Indian encampment, nor had any plans to attack it at the time he divided his command. The second was believing that the orders Custer gave to Captain Benteen and Major Reno were not more extensive than they reported. The third is contained in the above comments. Kuhlman does not analyze the testimony to establish where Custer and Reno separated, nor does he examine the time it would have taken Reno to reach Ford A, cross, reform his troops and begin his move down the valley. He believes the separation took place at the Lone Tepee. In my view, he is wrong. To me an analysis of testimony suggests that the event took place within two miles of Ford A. This location is not extremely important in itself. However, the fact that the only two actual witnesses, Sergeant Kanipe and Trumpeter Martin, claim that Custer moved to the ridge shortly after the separation, is important. It would appear that Custer watered his horses at or near the junction of the North Fork Tributary and then moved rapidly to the ridge. I would assume Custer did not spend 15 minutes along Reno Creek after the separation. Again, Kanipe and Martin's statements, as well as the statements of the three Rees in Soldier's testimony, would not support a longer period of time. At a gallop, Custer should have reached the ridge in ten minutes, but I will add another five for good measure. Custer would then have been on the ridge thirty minutes after the separation. If the separation took place two miles from Ford A, Reno should have taken forty minutes to reach it, cross, move through the timber, reform and be ready to move down the valley. Custer's troops should have reached the ridge in thirty minutes and Custer himself, more than likely, even sooner. I would then support Martin's contention that they did not see Reno when Custer's troops first appeared. Most likely, as the troops formed into a column from a line formation while they moved onto the ridge, Custer again preceded his troops down the ridge. He, Martin and some officers and staff then moved to Weir Point. Here they saw a peaceful village. Reno's troops would have been descending down the valley as Custer's five companies were moving along the ridge. Both troops sight each other. This would not mean that Custer saw Reno's troops – and Martin definitely did not – which could happen for a variety of reasons.

> At Weir Point Custer once more halted the command and from the top of one of the ridges surveyed the Indian camps and the terrain downstream. Then on again northeastward down a deep ravine leading into the head of South Medicine Tail about two miles straight east of the Middle Ford. After going about 300 yards he sent Trumpeter Martin with the now famous order to Benteen to come on, be quick and bring the packs.
>
> Coming to the head of South Medicine Tail he followed it down for about a mile, then halted for 15 or 20 minutes. At the end of this period he sent the Gray Horse Troop down the coulee and with the remaining four troops turned northeastward toward the head of a high ridge about a mile east of the battlefield, and followed its curving crest past the head of Deep Coulee.
>
> While Custer was making this detour, the Gray Horse Troop moved down South Medicine Tail to within about a half mile of the Ford, and then left it to go to a fairly high ridge about a half mile to the north, . . . At the ridge they dismounted, deployed as skirmishers, and slowly moved toward North Medicine Tail down which Custer was now coming to pick them up. As the two detachments neared the point where they were about to meet, Custer fired several volleys down the coulee, scattering and driving back the warriors who had come up from the Ford. Then the Gray Horse Troop rejoined Custer and the whole command rode northwestward to Custer Hill and halted. Here they stood for an hour or more, strictly on the defensive, with only two troops engaged in a light and almost harmless skirmish.
>
> Meanwhile, on Reno Hill, there was divided command, doubt, indecision, hesitation and delay. But most disastrous of all, a premature move by Captain Weir and his troop that deceived Custer and led him to a responsive action which, unsupported, sealed his doom.[1]

This is Kuhlman's general scenario which Hardorff, Ege, and Ellison have followed with some variations. My objections to it are based on several considerations. I don't believe Reno had gone into action when Custer viewed the village from Weir Point. However, if we accept Kuhlman's view that Reno had engaged the Indians, Custer would have seen a village in turmoil with the appearance of preparing to flee. One might assume that this situation would prompt Custer to hurry and attack the villages. Did it? Not according to Dr. Kuhlman, who suggests that Custer moved down Cedar Coulee rather than Middle or Western Coulee. Once Custer reached Medicine Tail Coulee, did he hurry to attack the village? No, he waited 15 to 20 minutes. Why? Custer had sent messages to McDougall and Benteen, so he wanted to give them time to move closer to his command. Was Custer worried about not fulfilling his commitment to support Reno? No, because Reno should be able to hold his position even against an overwhelming number of Indians, and Custer would still support him even if it was by drawing the Indians away from him. Was Custer going to take any action at that time? Yes, he was going to send the Gray Horse Troop down South Medicine Tail Coulee while he himself moved northwestward over Nye Cartwright Ridge. Shouldn't he have worried that Martin might not be able to reach Benteen or that Benteen might go to the aid of Reno? No, Martin should have been able to join Benteen because they had passed through that same area not over ten or fifteen minutes earlier and they had encountered no trouble. Benteen's orders were to come to the aid of Custer, not Reno, so naturally he would do so no matter what Reno's situation might have been. Shouldn't Custer have waited in South Medicine Tail Coulee until Benteen arrived? No, Custer wanted to find a good defensive position and since he didn't know the terrain, he did not want to wait too long. Besides, waiting would cause the Indians to see Custer's troops and they would launch an attack. Wouldn't this make it more difficult for Benteen to reach and unite with Custer? No, Benteen would have at least 120 men and Custer would send out about the same number from his defensive position and with such a force the two or three thousand Indians should not create any major problem. Since Custer was supposedly informed by Bouyer that Reno had retreated to the bluffs, should he have been worried that there might be wounded who, along with the packs, might create a problem for Benteen in coming to his aid? No, they should have been able to set up a defensive position with Reno's troops and possibly some of McDougall's. What would Custer have done after his troops and Benteen's united? With the additional 120 men – minus those that got killed or wounded on the way and the few that he had lost earlier – Custer would have been in a position to launch an attack on the 3,000 or so Indians now surrounding them, or he could have held his defensive position until Gibbon arrived. Couldn't the same thing have been accomplished if Custer had stayed near Weir Point? No, because Custer was an attack-minded leader – that second option would have resembled a retreat and Custer never retreated. Also, Custer didn't like the location as a defensive position and he was sure somewhere to the north there would be a more desirable one.

I cannot accept such answers as sound or logical and I give Custer more credit than his actions in this scenario indicate.

Dr. Kuhlman, on Indian testimony:

> . . . That is still regarded by many students as a mystery beyond the stark fact that every man in the battalion was killed. But how? Only the Indians knew the answer to that question, and they have told a thousand tales, many of them lurid, some of them fantastic, and all of them disjoined and "spotty!"[2]

In the next few pages Kuhlman accepts certain portions of the Indian testimony about the fight and rejects others. For example, he accepts Cheyenne testimony that they fought on foot but discredits those Indians who speak of fighting mounted. I think Indian testimony is fairly clear in supporting both, and it is a valid way of looking at the battle that ensued. The Cheyenne crossed the river below Battleridge and dismounted, moving up through the ravines and gullies while those Indians encircling Custer to the north were more apt to be mounted, although many of them fought on foot as well.

Benteen's remarks that only two Indian ponies were found on the field could be questioned; if so, it should be related to the time period and the condition of the troopers. If the firing from a defensive position on the ridge had lasted several hours, as Kuhlman contends, the number of ponies killed would have been much higher, even though most of the Indians were dismounted. There are too many Indian accounts of moving on horseback from one area of the battlefield to another, and also the reports of driving trooper horses to the villages. I believe these accounts depict a disorganized retreat to Battleridge, during which the Indians on horseback stayed out of effective range, closing in only when the retreat was moving and disorganized. If there had been the long skirmish time portrayed by Kuhlman and others, it is difficult to imagine individual Indians, as well as groups, not making sweeps fairly close to the soldiers, if for no other reason than to show the Indians watching the battle their bravado. Such acts, undoubtedly, should have resulted in more ponies being killed.

If my version of events is correct, the Sioux and Cheyenne who crossed Ford B forced Custer's three companies to move northeast from the ford. Keogh's two companies held in reserve, which had moved to Nye Cartwright ridge, then went to support Custer's three companies. By the time Keogh's battalion reached the vicinity of Calhoun Ridge, they were forced to form skirmish positions. By now the Indians that had been engaging Reno's troops were arriving. The dismounted Indians fired upon Keogh's and Calhoun's companies from what is now called Henryville, while the mounted Indians stayed out of range but remained threatening. The number of Indians kept increasing, both from the village and from Reno's engagement. To the north, Crazy Horse's followers, along with Wolf Tooth's band and others, were now in position, again with some mounted and some on foot. Particularly at the end, as recounted by Joseph White Bull and others, there were charges through the dwindling soldier lines where the soldier fire would have been mainly ineffectual. Overall, the lack of dead Indian ponies was a result of an unorganized defense.

[Dr. Kuhlman emphasizes the location of the camps, which I think has too often been ignored. It's a fundamental detail that has led to many misconceptions.]

> [Referring to the work of Dr. Marquis.] A good example of how carefully the work was done, is the fixing of the location of the various camps during the battle. This

seems to have occupied them several years, a number of Cheyennes at different times going over the grounds with Dr Marquis; and there is little doubt that on the resulting map these camps are correctly located . . .The Cheyennes corrected this misconception by explaining that all the camps were moved downstream after the close of the Custer fight because it was the custom to abandon a camp as soon as possible after a death had occurred in it. . . . Their own camp was farthest downstream a trifle below the mouth of Medicine Tail Coulee before the removal. This is a very important fact. No end of mistakes have been made in an attempt to reconstruct the Custer action because of this misconception.[3]

Dr. Kuhlman points out the Indian using bows and arrows and why they desired to do so and why they were effective.

> . . . This method could have been used with deadly effect against the Custer group crowded together on the exposed slope with the knoll behind them, betraying their position to warriors who could find shelter by the hundreds behind the ridge only a little over 60 yards to the west and southwest . . .[4]

Dr. Kuhlman should have realized that the above statement doesn't say much for General Custer, nor does it support Kuhlman's own contention that Custer held out without any difficulty until he saw Company D come over Weir Point. Kuhlman should have remembered that according to him, Custer moved around for some time looking for a defensive position. Custer would have done better if he had stayed at Weir Point or even Luce Ridge.

One should also recognize what effect the attack with bows and arrows would have had on the horses. It certainly would have created difficulty controlling them during the period Dr. Kuhlman believes the troops were subjected to the attack.

Dr. Kuhlman then takes up the background and the movement of Custer's troops to where they reach the divide and the division of troops take place.

> . . . None of the dispositions made at this time had any reference to a plan of battle. No data for the formulation of battle tactics were as yet at hand. What was being done now was for the purpose of securing such data and at the same time move as rapidly as possible to deprive the enemy, as far as might be, of the initiative. For whether the Indians were in one village or in several it was important to move against them. If they fled, the sooner the troops moved to pursue or intercept them the greater chance of success. If the warrior force was dangerously large, as there was considerable reason for thinking it might be, Custer risked destruction if he waited to be attacked.[5]

This statement is similar to statements made by other writers; and apart from the fact that I believe Custer did have a plan of attack at the time of the division, I otherwise agree with it. One could add that the statement would be especially true when the commander in question was General Custer, known for courage and daring. Yet these same writers, including Dr. Kuhlman, suggest that while facing a large Indian force in a situation where attacking is imperative, Custer waited instead, taking his time, going the long way and literally self destructing. Kuhlman believes that Custer moved away from the Indians after leaving Weir Point, then waited another fifteen or twenty minutes, and finally sent one company toward the Indians while he moved with his other four companies farther away before moving back toward the Indians. Dr. Kuhlman, and most of the other writers who apparently support and attempt to defend Custer, don't seem to recognize the dichotomy in their remarks.

Reno crossing Ford A:

> . . . Scouts . . . called to Gerard who was just east of the ford, that the Indians were coming up the valley in great numbers. Gerard shouted the information to Major Reno, who made no reply, but continued forming the troops in three parallel columns as the men straggled out of the river to the open ground in the loop. Being aware that Custer believed the Indians were fleeing . . . Gerard looked for Cooke, met, or overtook him 75 to 80 yards from the river and told him what the scouts had said. Cooke promised to report it to Custer and left. When Gerard got back to the river the command was about 500 yards down the valley. He hastened after it with several of the scouts who had waited for him at the ford.[6]

In the Girard testimony Kuhlman is using, Girard was east of the ford when informed by the scouts of the Indians moving up the valley. Without explaining why he was east of the river when Reno had already crossed, or why, with troops crossing, he yelled the information to Reno, Girard states that he went back some 80 yards where he met Cooke and gave him the message the Indians were not running. By the time Girard returned, Reno's troops had not only finished crossing the river and realigning, but they had also passed through 50 to 200 yards of timber without any effect on their formation and were 500 yards down the valley. This sequence should require an explanation, particularly with Girard's different versions of where events took place. Dr. Kuhlman is very meticulous in examining the terrain around Reno's skirmish line and timber position, and analyzing the accounts relating to them. From my knowledge it would be hard to refute his view of what happened, as it pertained to Reno's valley operation and the fighting that took place; but I don't understand why he didn't show as much interest in Reno's crossing of Ford A and the terrain surrounding it. The timing, in relationship to Reno's crossing the ford, Custer arriving on the ridge, the sightings of Custer, and Custer's supposed sighting of Reno, are important ingredients that Dr. Kuhlman should have attempted to include in his analysis.

Kuhlman believes that Benteen, outside of acting as if he didn't know Custer wanted him to go to the valley of the Little Bighorn, would have followed orders. Benteen's only mistake was not sending a messenger to Custer to inform him that there were no Indians upstream.

I have discussed elsewhere my view of the orders Benteen may have received. Sending a message to Custer would have been an obvious duty of Benteen's. If it was not just the oversight Kuhlman believes it was, what else might have caused it? Since I believe Benteen should have also sent a message that he was returning to the main trail, it could lead one to think Sergeant Major Sharrow or a third courier may have realized that Benteen was back on or moving to the main trail, and so Benteen didn't think there was any need to send a message. In my mind, there is no question that Custer was aware of where the main body of Indians would be found. In expressing his view of his orders at the Court of Inquiry, Benteen went beyond a concern that he should have sent a messenger to Custer. As I have suggested in my analysis of the Reno Court of Inquiry, the interrogations were attempting to place Reno in a position where it would appear he had not received any other orders and a simplified version of those he had. Reno expected support from the rear but did not have any idea where Benteen was or what his orders were, so he had no reason to expect aid from him. Consequently, there was no reason for Reno to remain in the timber, and he made a decision which he felt was in the best interest of his troops: they left the timber in order to obtain a stronger defensive position on the bluffs.

Kuhlman's comments on the Reno Court are noteworthy and, in general, I agree with his analysis:

> ...Although only Reno's conduct was under investigation, the rest would have been less than human had they not felt themselves more or less under attack, or at least under suspicion. This natural feeling caused them to assume an attitude of extreme caution which was reflected in their testimony, to the complete mystification of the unwary student who accepted their stories at face value. Their self-protective reaction took the form of evasion, misplaced emphasis, and statements so general or indefinite that they blurred or concealed certain details which, had they been revealed at this time, might have served hostile critics as a basis for charges of both incompetence and cowardice...This did not mislead the court in any matter pertinent to the inquiry, and was not intended to do so. It was intended for the general public against whose criticism Reno was seeking protection. Indeed, the failure of Recorder Lee to press his questions at the right junctures leads to the inference that a tacit understanding existed that an opportunity should be given for this kind of backfiring provided that the necessary facts for a just decision should be furnished at the same time...[7]

At this time Dr. Kuhlman makes some of his deprecating remarks about Trumpeter Martin, which appear to justify his ignoring Martin's testimony.

To Dr. Kuhlman, the movement to Weir Point by Reno's troops and its timing are instrumental to the position he took, the effect of this sighting on Custer's actions, and the length of the fighting on Last Stand Hill.

> Thirteen years later, in his article in the Century, Godfrey gives us the missing link, as it were, between Custer's firing his last shots and the puzzled troops on Weir Point. He said that toward the last he heard shots that seemed to be a great distance off. Immediately after these shots a great dust cloud arose on Custer field out of which finally rode the crush of warriors from which the troops fled back to Reno Hill.
>
> Into this, like a hand in a glove, fit the stories of the Cheyennes about the non-combatants, old men and boys, dashing onto the field on their ponies when the shout went up that all the soldiers had been killed, raising a dust that "nearly choked me," as Kate Bighead put it.
>
> ...The last shot, as mentioned by Godfrey, may have been a spurt of firing when the last survivors on the top of Custer Hill ran away toward the river, ...
>
> It will be seen, from the detailed account of the troop movements, that the last shots were fired as late as 6:30, and probably somewhat later then that....For Reno did not reach Weir Point before 6:10 to 6:15, ...and Godfrey did not hear these last shots until Reno was well on his way back to Reno Hill or already there.
>
> ...both Reno and Benteen were especially emphatic in their opinion that Custer and his command had been wiped out long before they started downstream...
>
> But this was not the impression they had left on the mind of Lt. Maquire right after the battle. Maquire, reporting to the Chief of Engineers for the fiscal year ending June 30, 1876, said of the action on Custer field; "This part of the fight did not from all reports, last over two or three hours."[8]

Dr. Kuhlman may be right in his analysis. However, several things should be pointed out. Remember that Lieutenant Maquire and others believed, at the time of his report, that Custer had moved to Ford B, and then was forced to retreat. It seems natural that a retreat covering close to two miles would have lasted that long.

The other major point I would make is that Captain Godfrey's statement found in the *Century* article, which Kuhlman quotes in footnote #40, does not read as he stated it on page 108. On page 108 Kuhlman reports Godfrey as saying: ". . . that toward the last he heard some shots that seemed to be a great distance off. Immediately after these shots a great dust cloud arose on Custer field out of which **finally** [my emphasis] rode the crush of warriors from which the troops fled back to Reno Hill." In his footnote, however, Godfrey says: "The firing ceased, the groups dispersed, clouds of dust arose from all parts of the field, and the horsemen converged toward our position." Godfrey also said that these shots seemed to have come from farther away than the large group on the hill, and he never used the word "finally." My impression is that the clouds of dust arose from the horsemen beginning their major move toward the troops they had seen or heard moving toward them. Since many of the warriors, following the defeat of Custer, moved over the battlefield collecting guns and ammunition, firing into the bodies of wounded or dead troopers, many just trying their new weapons, others looking for their own dead or wounded, the desultory firing that was heard more likely came from them rather than the last of the fighting on Custer Hill.

It's also interesting that Dr. Kuhlman uses Kate Bighead's account of the non-combatants rushing to the scene of the battle as an explanation for the dust cloud which Godfrey noticed from Weir Point, indicating the battle lasted until that time. What Dr. Kuhlman fails to mention is another of her statements in which Kate Bighead says that, "after the big battle on and around the ridge had ended, most of the warriors went to fight against the first soldiers up the valley."[9] She also gives the impression that the warriors collected guns, bullets, and other articles from the soldiers, including their clothing, and one could surmise that this was done before the Indians were aware of the troops on Weir Point. She recounts the story of the villagers being frightened when Indians on cavalry horses and dressed in dead soldier's clothing dashed back to the village, and points out that non-combatants watched the battle from the western hills across the valley. She states that the Cheyenne buried their dead that afternoon.[10] All in all, it is difficult to establish the exact time when the Custer battle ended, but my impression would be that it took place before the troops reached Weir Point, and this I would gather from Kate Bighead's story.

One might also mention that Dr. Kuhlman does not use Kate Bighead's testimony that she saw some of these troops commit suicide and heard of many others, including those on Custer Hill. These reports would also throw his view of events off. It is odd, though natural, that we tend to accept the statements that support our opinion, but disregard those that don't, even if they come from the same person.

> Although Benteen's conduct was not under investigation he actually out-did even Major Reno in distorting facts. [I believe Benteen realized he had more to cover-up than did Reno.][11]*
>
> The impatience (not to give it a harsher name) on the part of Weir, laudable as it was in intent, led Custer to make a premature move that turned a safe holding action into a series of ambuscades for his troops which resulted in destruction.[12] . . . It was Custer's response to Weir's appearance on the high ridge that led to the disaster . . . Custer was perfectly safe as long as he remained in his position on the Hill.
>
> On the other hand, had Reno made no move at all, nothing serious would have happened to either command, for it cannot be too often repeated that the Indians did not want a fight here – or anywhere else.[13]
>
> The subject of the present chapter sets an exacting task for the historian; for, after Custer had passed the high ridges we have called Weir Point, no white man except his orderly trumpeter, John Martin, saw him or any of his men alive except those who rode with him. From this point on the history of the five troops must be reconstructed from the numerous, conflicting Indian stories, Custer's two orders, the route he followed, the firing heard, the nature of the terrain and the distribution of the dead men and horses on the battlefield, the whole checked carefully against time and distance.[14]
>
> Martin's testimony was so confused, contradictory, and in many cases so at variance with known facts and the testimony of more coherent witnesses, that both Recorder Lee and Mr. Gilbert, Reno's counsel, soon threw up their hands and dismissed him; and Colonel W. A. Graham nearly fifty years later, had no better luck with him.[15]**

I don't understand this dismissal of Martin's testimony without any explanation as to where he was wrong. Dr. Kuhlman's attitude toward Martin is shared by other writers. As I have explained in my analysis of Martin's testimony at the Court of Inquiry and in his interviews with Camp and Graham, I do not see this inconsistency. Certainly questions that should have been asked were not,

---

* Note Appendix 2, Part A.
**Note Appendix 2, Part B.

and historians, at the time, should have taken Martin back to the battlefield and had him point out definite places and recollect the events. That this was not done has made me question the writers, and since there were definitely cover-ups at the trial, I can't help wondering if both sides were afraid of how he might testify. (After reading the full transcript of the trial, there is no doubt in my mind that the questions directed at him were for the purpose of confounding him. Basic questions concerning orders, distinct places and individuals were not asked. He was the one person who could have destroyed Reno and Benteen and the military's case to absolve Reno.) Apparently it was simpler to merely accuse him of being a dumb Italian and dismiss him. Kuhlman already went through an elaborate analysis of witness testimony and revealed their duplicity; yet he can speak of more coherent witnesses. Martin admitted he was mixed up as to time and distance, but so were the others and they were not as honest about their confusion. It is also true that in looking at Martin's testimony one should recognize his difficulty in understanding questions. His answers often reflect this difficulty; but his honesty, especially in comparison to others at the trial, can not be disputed. I believe this is the reason for Kuhlman's deprecating remarks. It appears to me that Kuhlman did what he accused the unwary student of doing – he accepted statements at face value.

> . . . Adjutant Cooke and Captain Keogh who had gone down to the river with Reno at a fast gait and had started back when Reno had nearly completed reforming his column after crossing . . . the message brought by Cooke . . . alarmed Custer . . . and caused him to rush up to the top of the bluffs . . .[16]

It is unfortunate that Dr. Kuhlman, who is quick to dismiss Martin's general testimony, is perfectly willing to accept that of Girard, in spite of all its inconsistencies.

> The instant Custer came to the edge of the bluff and looked upon the Indian village he knew that the order to Reno was a serious blunder.
> . . . There were three or four minutes of dreadful suspense for the little group on the bluffs as they watched Reno approach the river loop beyond which lay the great village. . . . The suspense ended as the line of horsemen suddenly slithered to a halt, dismounted and went into action. . . . Custer looking down on the scene from an elevation of 300 feet, expressed his appreciation with a cheer and a wave of his hat, and act of approval which neither Major Reno nor anyone else in his command except DeRudio saw, as far as is known, though parts of Custer's command were seen in motion near this point by Varnum and Gerard a few minutes later.[17]

Kuhlman's contention that Custer was watching Reno form his skirmish line and then waved and cheered his approval, contradicts the testimony of both Martin and Reno's troopers. Martin doesn't claim seeing Reno's command, and the troopers saw them either, as they regrouped or as they rode down the valley. One has to consider these accounts and not merely dismiss them "out of hand," because they don't agree with your scenario. I particularly believe this is true when one cannot account for the spatial dichotomy which comes into play. You should not reject or ignore Martin's claim that Custer viewed a peaceful village, when the spot you are using is so distant that it is extremely doubtful whether they could have seen much of the village, let alone recognize dogs and children. Since Kuhlman uses Curley's remarks to support his view, he should explain why he refutes Curley's account which indicates that he and Bouyer saw a peaceful village. If Custer is watching Reno set up his skirmish line, he should also see the awakening of the village. Troopers' statements of seeing Custer's command on the ridge, when moving down the valley, would discount a sighting at this later time. Kuhlman credits DeRudio with seeing Custer and his waving, but he ignores the time period in which DeRudio places the event (in fact he places it before the Girard and Varnum sighting). Custer certainly didn't sit on the ridge viewing Reno and the Indians for some 45 minutes – as all the supposed sightings would suggest.

One other point should be made. In my estimation it is extremely doubtful that at the time Custer was viewing the valley and what he could first see of the village, he believed he had made a serious blunder. He would certainly hope for the packs to hurry, but his exclamation, heard by Martin, certainly did not indicate apprehension, nor would the troops' reaction, mentioned by Kanipe and Martin.

> But what was to be done now? The cautious, routine soldier would, in all probability, have recalled Reno instantly by trumpet, sent a company or two to the river and lined up the rest at the brink of the bluff to protect his crossing, and then fallen back on Benteen and the packs. Such a move would have betrayed his weakness and relieved the warriors of all fear of flank and rear attacks. They outnumbered the whole regiment five or six times and would have swarmed after the retreating detachment from the very beginning . . .[18]

Dr. Kuhlman should have avoided using paradoxical statements. He pointed out emphatically; "On the other hand, had Reno made no move at all (after moving to Reno Hill) nothing serious would have happened to either command; for it cannot be too often repeated that the Indians did not want a fight here – or anywhere else."[19]

I don't think one would have expected Custer to move back to Reno Creek to meet the packs, but we can assume he would have immediately sent a messenger to both Benteen and the packs. (We know he did send a messenger to the packs.) He could even have sent a company to better advantage at that time, rather than later, when Dr. Kuhlman has Custer sending the Gray Horse Troop into the midst of the Indians. There are several places where he could have established a defensive position, one of them being the place where Reno later set up his.

I think the point should be made that since Custer's first message was to the packs he must not have thought Benteen was back on the trail. I believe Custer expected Benteen to be moving toward and then down the valley of the Little Bighorn in support of Major Reno. Custer realized Benteen could be moving on the east side of the Little Bighorn and Kanipe might see him, but it wasn't until Kanipe had departed that he learned Benteen was back on the main trail and not far ahead of the packs.

It's difficult to accept Dr. Kuhlman's contention that in spite of being concerned about the size of the Indian village, Custer moved four miles farther away from Benteen, McDougall and Reno without launching an attack on the Indians, and then all he did was something he could have accomplished back where he was in the first place. There is no way a commander of Custer's ability would move over unfamiliar terrain in order to launch an attack sometime in the future when his command was united.

Apparently Dr. Kuhlman also recognized this problem and tried to provide an answer:

> But what could have been worse then what Custer did, the critic may ask? Here he was with a fourth of his regiment down in the valley, unsupported, with hundreds of warriors fast encircling them. Benteen was an hour's march back on the trail, and the packtrain about twice that distance. And what does Custer do? He deliberately leaves Reno in the lurch and rushes four miles downstream, evidently with the wild idea of attacking the village in the flank or rear . . .
>
> So it would have been, had he made such an attack. But he did not attack when he had the opportunity to do so, and hence there is no basis for the assumption other than the fact that he continued his march downstream. On the other hand, all that he did, or had ordered done, from this time on is wholly inconsistent with such an assumption.
>
> Since the surface indications here do not make sense, we must look deeper to discover Custer's plan of action as he was now hammering it out., If we start with the assumption, or working thesis, that he realized the enemy was too strong to risk a definitive action, and that it was necessary to play for time until Gibbon came up, everything he did and ordered done after seeing the village, becomes clear and consistent. Having reached this conclusion he worked out the details as he rode along.[20]

To me, Kuhlman's answer is unsatisfactory. Neither surface indications nor underlying explanations make sense. If Custer wanted to wait for Gibbon, he would not have separated even further from the support he so desperately needed. He would have realized that time was necessary to establish a defensive position. He would not have gone wandering around unfamiliar terrain looking for one. A defensive position on the ridge would have been more likely to cause the Indians to move toward Gibbon or where Custer thought Crook was coming from. Even using Kuhlman's criteria, and no matter where the defensive position was established, the Indians could have been expected to scatter – something Custer would not have wanted. ***Custer didn't plan to attack?!***

> After leaving his lookout on the bluff, he rode on for perhaps a quarter of a mile, thinking over the situation, and then sent Sergeant Kanipe to the packtrain with an order for it to come on "straight across country." A little farther on he came to the high ridge, now officially designated as Weir Point. The ravine down which the column was marching turns to the right at this point. Here he halted again and with his orderly, Martin and several others, rode to the top of one of these ridges, . . . and made another observation of the village. From this point he could see all or very nearly all the camps he had not been able to see from his first observation point. Since he was in search of a good defensive position in which to reassemble the regiment and await the arrival of Gibbon, we must assume that while on this high point he scanned the ground downstream near the valley. If he did so, he could hardly have failed to note the relatively high mass of land jutting into the valley about a mile below the lowest camp. This would be the ideal place of his purpose, provided it contained a good defensive position, . . .
>
> Up to this point we have depended solely on analysis and constructive reasoning to discover Custer's plan of action. There is, however, one piece of oral evidence completely confirming our major thesis. This is in the field notes of the late W. M. Camp and reads as follows: "The remark of Bouyer to Curley, that Custer was seeking a high point to await the arrival of the other troops; and Bouyer's remark that he did not think they would come, having probably been 'scared out,' shows that Custer had probably been waiting for Benteen, and watching for the result of Reno's battle."[21]

One shouldn't be sarcastic, but reading Kuhlman's

account it's very difficult not to be. Custer had been watching for the results of Major Reno's battle against a village – a village he is afraid to attack even though it means disobeying his own instructions given to Reno. Of course, he didn't say just when or how he would support Reno.

According to Kuhlman, after seeing Reno form his skirmish line Custer moved to Weir Point. I assume it's fair to say that Custer watched Reno for a few minutes during which time he would have seen Reno move a few hundred yards or so before he attempted to establish his skirmish line, as Kuhlman states in his discussion of Reno's action in the valley. Custer then moved down the ridge. However, according to Kuhlman the troops moved down the ravine just east of the ridge (Cedar Coulee). This contention contradicts both Martin's and Kanipe's testimony as well as what we can construe from Reno's troopers' accounts. One way or the other, Custer then reached Weir Point and went up one of the peaks to observe the village and the terrain. At that time, by all Indian reports, the village was in a state of near panic, but this condition must not have impressed General Custer enough to suggest that if he attacked it would create even more consternation; nor was he concerned that the Indians might scatter if he didn't do something immediately. Anyway, "not like a cautious, routine soldier might do," the courageous, daring Custer announced to his men that they were going to look for a defensive position. This news caused the troops to break out cheering and they dashed ahead looking for this ideal location. Custer had seen one some distance away, but he was not too sure of it, so he decided to move even farther away from the support he had sent for, in order to examine it. He didn't believe there was any particular hurry (as the Indians were intent on wiping out Reno's troops) unless he went back to unite the rest of his command – and then the Indians would have swarmed all over them and there would have been no hope of maintaining a position until Gibbon arrived.

If any part of this scenario might cause you to question if Custer would have thought or acted in that way, you can suppress your objections. Kuhlman has the proof that this was, in fact, what Custer was planning: The interpreter for the Crow scout Curley said that Curley said to Walter Camp that Bouyer said that Custer said that he was looking for a defensive position. This proves Kuhlman's thesis.

As I have stated numerous times before, I can't believe how a person can condemn Indian testimony and then accept one statement in support of a thesis but ignore any others. Kuhlman uses his interpretation of Goes Ahead's account to determine where Custer reached the ridge and where the Crows turned back, but he ignored the testimony where Goes Ahead states that Curley was not with them. Kuhlman accepts Curley's remarks that he was with Custer during the early stages of his last battle, but ignores Curley when he claims that Custer did not see Reno establish a skirmish line, or that Curley went back to Reno Creek, or that he saw Custer reach the ford. Curley's testimony as to what he did before Bouyer joined Custer can be partially substantiated by the other Crows as well as Arikara statements, and the only major question concerning Curley should be where he and the other Crows separated. I don't think there is any doubt that Curley did not go with Bouyer when Bouyer joined Custer, as one then finds too many discrepancies in Curley's stories. Since many of the accounts told by Indians and whites came years after the battle, it is only natural that certain differences occur even in one person's account, but there should not be inconsistencies on certain major personal points. Curley's testimony includes such contradictions. Whether they should be blamed on Curley or an interpreter makes no difference in how they should influence one's analysis.

> . . . from their position on the bluffs Bouyer and Curley saw Reno retreat, and Bouyer signalled the fact to Custer, after which they rode down and joined him . . .
>
> . . . From this, as well as from the time Custer's presence north of the coulee was discovered by some of the warriors who had followed Reno to the bluffs, it would seem that he halted on this flat for fifteen to twenty minutes . . . Now that he knew that Reno had fled to the bluffs where he would soon receive reinforcements, there was less need of haste in creating a diversion. He knew that as soon as he, Custer, mounted the high ground north of the coulee he would be discovered and that then the warriors would swarm against him.[22]

Since Custer knew by then that Reno had retreated to the bluffs, his main objective was still to find a defensive position so the command could unite. To say that he would move farther north to obtain that position without knowing if it existed, is tantamount to suggesting that Custer lacked both intelligence and common sense.

Apparently Custer is not worried about Major Reno, so he now takes fifteen to twenty minutes to rest before continuing to search for a position to defend. He still expects the remainder of the command to reach this defensive position even though he knows the Indians will see him when he mounts the high ground north of the coulee and will 'swarm' against him.

One would think, from the picture Kuhlman has drawn, that Custer recognized the following aspects of

ANALYSIS OF WRITERS' SCENARIOS

the situation: the village was so large it caused Custer to change his plans from attacking it to finding a defensive position. Reno was forced to retreat to the bluffs, so he must have encountered a large number of Indians which would still be attacking him. Custer knew Benteen was back on the main trail but unsure of how close to Reno he would be. When Custer had been on the ridge, he was afraid to move back to set up a defensive position because the Indians could easily defeat them. One might then assume that Custer would believe it was imperative to create a diversionary move immediately: that had been his main objective in moving farther north, since he could have set up a defensive position where he was. We might suppose that Custer was also afraid Reno could be overrun quickly, and even Benteen and the packs could be in danger. A move farther north and east would then not even have a diversionary effect. But no; apparently Custer wasn't worried that any of these things might happen, so he rested for 15 to 20 minutes. Not knowing where Benteen or McDougall were, but realizing that Reno could be in extreme danger, might lead one to believe that Custer would have gone to his aid; but that didn't happen either. Instead, Custer moved farther away, looking for a defensive position, expecting the rest of the command to follow him there. This scenario in my view, is the height of fantasy.

A working thesis is an absolute necessity for the historian. It is to him what the probe is to the surgeon. But he must not become so enamored of it that he cannot modify it altogether when the evidence demands it.

The field notes of Mr. Camp, some of which we are using here, illustrate perfectly. It is quite evident that Camp came to his researches in the field already convinced that Custer had attacked at the ford, that the Indians he questioned detected this and answered his questions accordingly.[23]

All the Cheyennes consulted by Dr. Marquis over a period of years, stated positively and without hesitation, that Custer was not at any time in Medicine Tail Coulee or nearer the ford than where the bodies of his men were found. When they first saw him he was on a ridge about two miles east of the river.

This is, in part, born out by Mrs. Spotted Horn Bull and her husband who told Godfrey that Custer was never near the ford...

Recorder Lee said in his summation: "Leaving out mere matter of opinion, it appears to me, from all the testimony, that General Custer never attempted a crossing at Ford "B." He must have gone around the head of the ravine, and evidently sought to attack the village lower down."[24]

I find Kuhlman's conception objectionable. His premise as to Indian testimony would apply to the Cheyenne and Marquis interviews as well as Walter Camp's. I don't believe the Cheyenne, considering the turmoil taking place in the Indian villages, were in a better position than anyone else to have viewed Medicine Tail Coulee at the time Custer moved to the ford. I have covered this point elsewhere, including Mrs. Spotted Horn Bull's rambling.

Kuhlman uses Recorder Lee's summation to support his view that Custer never went to the ford. As I indicated in my analysis of the Court of Inquiry, this was the basic contention of those who were intent on accusing Major Reno. It was used within the context of Custer's objective to attack the village and his attempt to come to the aid of Reno. The accusers contended that Reno should have realized Custer's intentions and should not have left the timber. By leaving the timber he disengaged the Indians and prevented Custer from launching the attack. Lee recognized that Custer's plan was not an attempt to find a defensive position but to attack. It's hard to imagine any of the officers and men at the Court of Inquiry accepting Kuhlman's thesis, regardless of their support for Reno or lack thereof. Kuhlman should have also recognized that, according to Lee, Custer was moving downstream, because, in their view, the Indian villages extended below Last Stand Hill and not, as Kuhlman and Marquis claim, just north of the Miniconjou Ford.

> We believe the statement by Benteen to the Court of Inquiry, and the one by Curley to White Bear, tie in and are usually confirmatory; for, when Benteen, with part of his company, went to examine the Custer battlefield on the 27th, he went down what he called the "gorge" up which the warriors had swarmed on the 25th. He then later changed his mind and told the Court of Inquiry that he thought Custer had gone "east of the second divide and not to the river at all;" which is to say he had turned to the right at Weir Point, as Martin and Goes Ahead said. The gorge enters Medicine Tail at the flat about a mile from the ford, on which we believe Custer halted for some time, and where Bouyer and Curley must have rejoined him, unless, in this also Camp's notes are unreliable.[25]

Though I have discussed this form of reasoning before, explaining why I disagree with it, certain points should be mentioned again. The initial beliefs of the officers and men are often more reliable than the later accounts where they begin to speculate. Their feeling that Custer went down the "Gorge" or Middle Coulee and then to the ford was based on what they thought Custer would have done. The view could also have been effected by certain signs that later they may not have remembered noticing. This in itself would not mean that they were right, but neither would a statement by Benteen. Kuhlman goes to some lengths to stress Benteen's unreliability as a witness, pointing out that he was attempting to cover-up not only for Major Reno but for himself as well.

Besides the basic cover-up which took place at the trial, it also benefited Benteen to suggest that Custer was defeated rather quickly. He claimed that Custer did not go to the ford, thus shortening the time of his movement, and he portrayed a panic and rout among Custer's troops to indicate a shorter time span before Custer was overrun. Benteen's other testimony shows that he was attempting to establish the premise that his moving faster would not have saved the General.

Benteen supposedly based his claim that Custer did not go to the ford on the fact that few bodies were found near there. This didn't seem to have bothered him at first, possibly because when his troops first came into contact with the Indians they also had few casualties.

Dr. Kuhlman and others continue to assume that since Martin said that Custer moved to the right as he left the ridge, he went down Cedar Coulee. If he had looked at his own map, Kuhlman could have seen that to go down the "Gorge" after moving between the Weir Peaks, Custer's first command could have been a "column right." Goes Ahead's statement can be interpreted the same way, for he said that he went to the bluff with Mitch Bouyer beyond the point where Custer turned right down a coulee. This statement does not necessarily indicate that Custer went down Cedar Coulee, for it could even refer to Custer's move to the right after they had gone half way down Middle Coulee, or, for that matter, West Coulee. The statement does confirm that Goes Ahead went beyond Weir Point with Bouyer, and since Kuhlman is using Goes Ahead's account he should also have remembered that according to Goes Ahead, Curley was not with them at that time.

> Remembering further that Benteen said he thought Custer might have come to within about 660 yards of the river, he must have had some evidence in mind leading him to this conclusion. What evidence could he have had other then the scratched-up cutbank where the Gray Horse Troop scrambled out to go to the ridge where the evidence of a skirmish was found.[26]

The evidence Benteen could have had is that which he shared with Martin. Martin said he was sent back with the message some 600 yards from Ford B, and Benteen was the one who told him it was approximately that distance from the ford.[27] The "scratched up cutbank" Kuhlman refers to came from the retreat of Yates' "main element" from Ford B.

Parts of the letter Benteen wrote to his wife on July 4, 1876, contains evidence to support my view that Martin showed Benteen where he left, although Kuhlman's interpretation of the letter contradicts my belief.

> Benteen: "From that point (Weir Point, C.K.) Cooke sent the note to me by Martin, which I have quoted on 1st page. I suppose after the five companies had closed up somewhat Custer started down for the village all throats bursting themselves with cheering (so says Martin). He had 3 1/2 to 4 miles to go before he got to the ford – as the village was on the plain on opposite side to Custer's column to cross at all, is a moot question, but I am of the opinion that nearly – if not all of the five companies got into the village – but were driven out immediately – flying in great disorder and crossing by two fords instead of the one by which they entered. "E" Co. going by the left (Note by C.K.; he means the ford at the mouth of the deep ravine running up to the battlefield almost directly north in which 18-20 bodies of E Troop were found) and "F," "I" and "L" by the same one they crossed . What became of "C" Co., no one knows – they must have charged them below the village, gotten away – or have been killed in the bluffs on the village side of the stream – as very few of "C" Co. horses have been found . . . After the Indians had driven them across, it was a regular buffalo hunt for them and not a man escaped. We buried 203 of the bodies of Custer's command the second day after the fight – the bodies were as recognizable as if they were in life.[28]

Benteen's identification of the place Martin was sent back from doesn't correspond to what Martin himself said elsewhere, or to the idea that he was sent back during a move down Cedar Coulee. I would assume that Martin indicated where Custer viewed the village, and he said he received the note after that event. Benteen could have interpreted his words as meaning that both happened at the same time, since Martin, over the years, mentioned running into Boston Custer and several troopers before he returned to the ridge, and he indicated repeatedly that he was with Custer when he reached Medicine Tail Coulee. I think it is safe to assume that Benteen wrote down his comments in the existing form either because he misinterpreted what Martin said, or he did it carelessly, without recognizing the later significance such remarks would have.

Benteen states that, according to Martin, the troops leaving the ridge started out cheering, which would certainly not support Kuhlman's theory. According to

ANALYSIS OF WRITERS' SCENARIOS

Kuhlman, Custer saw that Reno was under attack by a large number of Indians and he was afraid to move against the village. Cheering by Custer's troops would not suggest that they were to charge down Cedar Coulee looking for a place to establish a defense; rather, it would indicate that they were planning to attack the village. Cheering would also support Martin's statement that they viewed a village which was unaware of the threat from either Reno or Custer and which they hoped to strike as quickly as possible with a good chance of defeating the Indians.

Benteen's opinion that Custer even crossed into the Indian encampment shows that he and others figured Custer would attempt such a maneuver. It also points out Benteen's assumption that the location of the bodies and other evidence signified a panicky retreat, and that E Company's troops were killed in Deep Ravine during this retreat. However, we are certain, from Indian accounts, that the Deep Ravine episode didn't take place at that time.

The lack of C Company horses is an interesting point in Benteen's letter. As I have said, the absence of these horses may suggest that they were the first to dismount, which more than likely meant that they were the lead company as they reached the ford. The action of the Indians, the soldiers' difficulty in controlling their horses while firing effectively, and the number of recruits in the company, all could have contributed to losing their horses, at a time when most of the horses would have been uninjured. Their horses were then captured by the Indians.

Benteen's reference to being able to recognize the bodies was probably for the benefit of his wife and the soldiers' relatives. It contradicts most reports on the condition of the bodies. However, it raises the question of suicide since Indians didn't usually mutilate the body of an enemy who had killed himself.

> Dr. Kuhlman continued: It should be stated here definitely that Custer took his whole battalion down to the west end of the ridge while these movements were taking place, and that the action began here, not on the east end of the ridge.[29] . . .The skirmish near Medicine Tail began around 4:15. Custer arrived on the Hill around 4:40, leaving 25 minutes of skirmishing before he got there. . . . this agrees with the testimony of Gerard, . . .[30]

If we use Kuhlman's time schedule, Custer stayed out of action for over an hour from the time Reno became engaged. Girard's testimony as to when he heard the first firing must be approached with caution. There could have been firing during the time Girard was concerned with his own safety, as the gunfire between Reno and the Indians in the valley occupied his attention.

> For about an hour after his arrival, then, everything seemed to go as Custer must have desired . . . His maneuver to bring the warriors downstream . . . as well or better then he could have expected; and as far as he could see he was holding them there while he was resting his horses and incurring small loss.[31]

I don't know how much contact or experience Dr. Kuhlman had with horses, but if he thinks that with Indians all around, firing with guns and bows and arrows at both the horses and men, these animals were resting or even controllable, he is mistaken.

> If the situation up to this time was substantially as we have described it, we are forced to the conclusion that what Custer now did can be explained only on the assumption that he had seen Weir's troop on the high ridge and thought that Benteen was there with his whole battalion. Any other construction makes his actions incomprehensible. For he now sends "C" and "E" to form a skirmish line from near the hill to near Greasy Grass Ridge bordering the south of the field and a half mile from the Hill, "E" in the lead.
>
> The situation in the rear of the line also was anything but satisfactory, from the defensive point of view. But in spite of all this it is improbable that a serious disaster would have occurred here had not Lt. Sturgis who commanded Troop "E" dismounted his men and left them standing holding their horses by the reins, good evidence that no immediate action was expected here. Further evidence for this construction is the fact that neither Tom Custer nor Smith had gone down with their commands, as far as evidence shows. ...Had immediate action been expected it would have been decidedly a point of honor for them to be with their men. . . . for the troops must have been sent down the instant Weir was seen on the high ridge . . .[32]
>
> But the serious mistake made by Lieutenant Sturgis would probably not have mattered had it been really Benteen who was seen on Weir Point ready to hurry forward as soon as he had located Custer; for in that case the dismounted warriors facing the line, and those in the rear also, would almost certainly have rushed to their ponies they had left in the gulch and ravines, instead of attacking. . . .[33]

One should keep in mind that if Reno set up his skirmish line at 3:05, which is roughly Kuhlman's estimate, Custer could have been at the middle ford and the Indian village by 3:20. According to Kuhlman, Custer arrived on Custer Hill at 4:40 and held there for another hour. Thus we have over a two hour span in which Custer initiates no real action.

During his move to the ridge and the time he was there,

Custer should have seen the Indians encircling his position. According to Kuhlman, he knew that Reno had joined Benteen. This contention is derived from Curley's remarks, which Kuhlman accepts. It might also be fair to assume that Custer realized Reno must have taken some casualties – dead and wounded – and this might be the reason for the delay in reaching him. Dr. Kuhlman may have thought that Reno would have left his wounded under the protection of a company or two, and some might say this would have been acceptable. Since Benteen's orders were to bring the "packs," one might surmise that to gain speed they would only bring some of the ammo packs; even so, their movement would have been slow. For Custer to have sent E and C Company into what he had to know was a large number of Indians (as it had prevented him from launching his attack with his five companies), and to do this when Benteen was still three miles away, would have been the height of stupidity.

On top of that, Dr. Kuhlman blames Lieutenant Sturgis because he had his troops dismount. Did Dr. Kuhlman actually believe they could have stayed on their horses while they waited for Benteen's troops? Did Kuhlman really think that with the village and their people only a short distance away, the Indians were all going to rush down to engage Benteen, or that none of them would? Kuhlman gives Godfrey deserved credit for stopping the Indians on the retreat from Weir Point and thus preventing a possible disaster. Could Kuhlman have expected Reno to have moved farther than he did against the Indians? Kuhlman would have undoubtedly said yes, because Custer's troops, being intact, would then have attacked as well. However, although Reno was on his skirmish line or about to engage the Indians, and Custer supposedly knew that Benteen and McDougall were close behind – at a time when he should either have thought he had caught the village asleep or saw they were in a state of confusion and near panic – Custer did not believe it was safe to attack the village. Instead, he moved to set up a defensive position. But now, with the Indians all around him and seeing that Benteen was supposedly three miles away, Custer moves four of his companies from this defensive position. This scenario shows me that Kuhlman has a good imagination but an illogical mind.

> From the analysis of this material a clear picture emerges. Among the Indian accounts that of Kate Bighead is the clearest up to a certain point.
> Finally she saw a body of troops on the ridge mount their horses and come galloping down the coulee almost directly toward her. Though she does not mention the color of the horses, we do know that it was the Gray Horse Troop seen by Mrs. Spotted Horn Bull from across the river . . .
> This is all these two excellent witnesses would tell Dr. Marquis about the few minutes of deadly fighting here. Not a word about the ghastly mess found in the ravine behind the line, or the short exchange of shots where the left of "C" was turned, and where the Indians must have incurred the greater part of their admittedly heavy loss. Instead of going on with the description of the actual fighting, they told him a fairy tale to account for the 50 bodies more or less that were found where the line had stood and to the east of it . . .
> Fortunately the distribution of the markers, . . . the finding of nearly a platoon of the Gray Horse men . . . Lame White Man among them . . . tumbled into the ravine after the troopers and crushed them by sheer weight of numbers.[34]

Dr. Kuhlman continues to use testimony selectively and then proceeds to project his views. I see nothing in his writing except speculation to substantiate these opinions. Many Indians claim that the troops ran from the hill rather than rode. Kuhlman brushes off Wooden Leg's and Kate Bighead's accounts of soldiers committing suicide as fairy tales, but has no explanation for why the two would talk about suicide instead of describing the "crushing attack" and the "deadly fighting" which Kuhlman says took place. He claims that Lame White Man lay with the bodies of the white men in the ravine, yet I have not found any testimony to that effect. Wooden Leg claimed he found the body and he certainly didn't indicate it was in the ravine. Wooden Leg said that the battle lasted until about noon, and according to Marquis this is also the belief of all the Cheyenne. Even if one recognizes a difference in the way they viewed time, it would still be difficult to accept that the fighting lasted as long as Kuhlman thinks it did.

One of the basic difficulties Kuhlman has is finding testimony which fits his hypothesis. I know of no Indian accounts which would corroborate or suggest directly or indirectly a deployment of companies in the manner described by him during this stage of the battle.

> The results, then, of this preparatory move to facilitate Benteen's passage from Weir Point to Custer Hill, was the loss of the Gray Horse Troop and approximately a third of Troop "C," 50 men more or less, and leaving 50 carbines . . .
> What Custer now did shows that he knew he could not hold out indefinitely unless he received reinforcements. . . . The troops he had seen on Weir Point disappeared 15 to 20 minutes before and were presumably on his trail somewhere up Medicine Tail Coulee, and about

this time troops again appeared on Weir Point and in much greater strength then before . . . But again they halted . . . he must somehow show them where he was and do what he could to help them over the three intervening miles. With only 150 men he could not carry off his wounded in the presence of possibly 2000 warriors now exultant over the defeat of Reno and the destruction of the south line. But neither could he abandon the wounded. Some troops must remain to protect them until the rest of the regiment arrived. The only remaining alternative was to use the three troops still intact. "F," "I" and "L," to make contact with those on Weir Point and return with them to the defensive position on the hill.[35]

This might have succeeded had the facts at this stage of the action been such as Custer believed them to be. Though he must have felt that the situation had become extremely grave, the chance of success were still in his favor when calculated on the basis of past experience in Indian warfare. There seemed little question that the three troops he was sending out to make contact with those on Weir Point could do so and return.[36]

This is speculation carried to the extreme. Dr. Kuhlman should start out by not changing the few known facts that we have. D Company, led by Captain Weir and Lieutenant Edgerly, didn't disappear once they reached the place where they could be seen near Weir Point. According to Kuhlman this first sighting compelled Custer to initiate his action by sending Companies E and C to facilitate the movement of these troops who Custer thought was Benteen. How sending these companies or platoons to the area would aid Benteen without resulting in their own destruction is difficult to comprehend. With all the Indians milling around, it is impossible to understand how Custer could have thought that the troops on Weir Point had not seen him, making it necessary to send troops out from his defensive position. They could have blown their bugles, fired volleys, and waved their guidons instead. Nor would it have been possible to mount three companies at that stage of the fighting, from the standpoint of horses or men. If Custer did what he supposedly did, because he knew he couldn't hold out indefinitely, no wonder he was defeated. This would be the time to maintain the defensive position. Past experience in Indian warfare would have suggested remaining in place, rather than dashing across country where the Indians would be most effective. To believe that the troops could have moved to Weir Point and back again is beyond me. However, if, by the greatest stretch of imagination, one can see this happening, it is even more difficult to expect to find any of the fifty or sixty men left behind alive when the troops returned. But Kuhlman believes that the chances of success would have been in Custer's favor if things were the way he perceived them to be, and if Reno and Benteen had continued their move to Custer's aid.

I believe that if Kuhlman's thesis was correct, Custer's only chance would have been to keep his defensive position when he saw troops on Weir Point, and hope they would form a defensive position there. Then, if either side was left with a smaller number of Indians and could see the Indians were attempting to overwhelm the other, they could have executed a threatening maneuver against the village. This type of action would have allowed Custer to follow what Kuhlman believed was part of Custer's plan: to hold out until Gibbon and Terry arrived. It would also have resulted in a situation such as Kuhlman thought existed, if there had been no movement by Reno's troops to Weir Point.

The fact that this was not done helps substantiate the following reasoning: Custer's troops had been wiped out some time before Captain Weir moved to Weir Point. Custer's troops had retreated in a confused disorganized manner for the most part, and no sound defensive position was set up. No troops were sent out to establish skirmish lines. The formation of semi-skirmish lines were attempts by some of Yates' and Keogh's battalions to stem the Indian attack during a retreat launched in the hopes that a defensive front could be made.

Kuhlman uses Two Moon's reference to forty men moving toward the river (p. 192), interpreting it as Captain Keogh's move. He points out that Two Moon was not in a position to see the others. After what Wooden Leg said about Two Moon's fanciful testimony, one should be careful in accepting it, and certainly should not put additional meaning to his words.

> If Calhoun (Troop "L") had waited until the other troops were ready, it is probable that no attack would have been made. . . . Calhoun was ready to march. But troops "F" and "I" on the north wing of the ridge naturally held their ground until all who were to remain were in position for defense. He (Calhoun) was several hundred yards on his way before the men of "F" and "I" could secure their mounts, form in column and follow, Keogh in the lead at the head of his own troop.[37]

It would have been interesting to see the troops form their columns under the barrage of arrows and gunfire they must have received from the Indians. If Lieutenant Edgerly had trouble mounting his horse, imagine the problems these troopers had. Would they have formed columns of twos or fours?

The warriors let Calhoun pass. He headed straight for

the ravine . . . We must see clearly with the mind's eye the three troops ride away eastward from the Hill. Calhoun several hundred yards in advance, Keogh in the center and behind him Troop "F: minus its commissioned officers, Captain Yates and Lt. Reily. We must also clearly visualize the position of the warriors and keep in mind the fact that the troops did not know of their presence here or anything as to their numbers. . . .[38]

As any knowledgeable trooper or historian, Kuhlman knew that the Indians fought in groups and without discipline, yet he claims that they allowed Calhoun's troops to pass them undisturbed. This apparently happened with several thousand warriors encircling Battleridge, warriors of different tribes and with numerous chiefs. In the midst of the battle, Kuhlman's Indians are so well organized that they allow the troops to pass. Can this be construed as logic? Then Kuhlman goes on to indicate that some of the horses were wounded and had arrows dangling from them, and they began to plunge wildly forward. What did Dr. Kuhlman think was happening to them for the hour and a half that he portrayed as the time when the sniping and shooting of arrows took place? What was happening when troops I, L, and F were mounting their horses? How could Custer have not known there were Indians where these troops were being sent? I believe Kuhlman's imagination was working overtime to think that the soldiers would not have been aware of Indians in that area after the Indians had been encircling the troops for over an hour.

There doesn't seem to be any question that the Indians were moving to and nearing Weir Point when Companies M (French's) and D (Weir's) left their position in front of Weir Point and began their retreat to Reno Hill. This would not have taken place in Kuhlman's scenario, and one might add that his hypothesis is not supported by Indian testimony. I have not seen any Indian claim that while they were fighting Calhoun's and Keogh's troops or the remnants of Custer's forces on Last Stand Hill, part of the Indians took off to confront Reno's forces which had appeared on Weir Point. Though I have not read any actual statements given by the Indians, the inference in several of them is that by then the battle had been over for some time. The Indians do not mention any such movement by Custer's troops on Battleridge as portrayed by Kuhlman.

> General Godfrey speaks of this incident and the destruction of the rest of Calhoun's men as Gall had explained it to him during a reunion of participants on the tenth anniversary of the battle, 1886. Either Gall's memory betrayed him or Godfrey misunderstood him. For Gall is represented as having gone up the ravine which runs northeastward from the Middle Ford and passes about a third of a mile east of the Calhoun position opposite which Custer is said to have dismounted Keogh's and Calhoun's troops and sent them on "double time" to take positions on the east end of the battleridge, leaving their horses and horseholders in the ravine where Gall surprised and destroyed them. But no bodies of either men or horses were found on the east wing of the battleridge. We have already quoted Mrs. Spotted Horn Bull showing that Gall rode along the bench near the river, not up the eastern ravine as indicated on Godfrey's map.
>
> If one studies the U.S.G.S. Survey map and notes that the markers for the horseholders are on the east wing of the battleridge, he will require little, if any, oral description to visualize what happened. He will also note that these horseholders were, under Godfrey's conception, between Calhoun's own skirmish line and the warriors coming up from the south – a complete absurdity. He will also note that there is not a single marker on the ridge where Keogh's and Calhoun's lines are said to have stood; that Calhoun's skirmishers were killed in the ravine behind the ridge, and that Keogh's whole troop was destroyed while it stood in column of platoons well down the slope north of the ridge. All this is so absolutely irreconcilable with Godfrey's conception that no further discussion of it would seem to be necessary.[39]

I have examined Mrs. Spotted Horn Bull's testimony elsewhere and have explained why I mistrust it. I generally accept Gall's testimony as to where he had gone, although I would question his interpretation of what the troops were doing or had done. Gall, in one of his interviews, mentioned taking some horses back to the village, and this may be when Mrs. Spotted Horn Bull saw him. I believe Gall's testimony fits my interpretation of what happened, so further discussion seems necessary. The testimony would appear to be correct if the troops that were moving from Nye Cartwright to Battleridge, were indeed Keogh's battalion. They would have tried to provide protective fire against the Indians moving up North Medicine Tail Coulee, and, as the troops crossed the coulee to Battleridge, they would have dismounted, and then moved to Calhoun Ridge, attempting to establish skirmish positions. At that time, if I am correct, Yates' battalion would be near the present cemetery area. I would conjecture that Captain Keogh either hoped a defense could be established along Battleridge or, once united, they could still retreat back the way they had come to join the rest of the command. I don't believe it is unlikely that the horseholders would have let the horses go when surprised by the Indians. They would then retreat to join their companies and would not necessarily have had to leave either dead horses or men.*

If one were to accept Dr. Kuhlman's view of what happened, then naturally the horses would not have been left in the location indicated by Gall. Although many of Gall's statements are contradictory and questionable, I accept his general outline of the events, after he joined the battle. Simply put, what I believe is that Gall took part in the attack on Reno, and during the time Reno moved to the bluffs, Gall heard of the new danger to the camps: the arrival of Custer. By the time he got there, the troops were on Battleridge. He did take part in the attack on Calhoun's and Keogh's forces. I think Dr. Marquis' account was probably true where he suggested that Gall took off with some horses, either before, during or after they overran Calhoun's and Keogh's companies. I would then question if he played any part in the finale on Last Stand Hill.

The above discussion brings out the primary emphasis of Kuhlman's view of what happened to Custer, and I have indicated why I disagree with it. In his book Kuhlman attempts to examine, in minuscule fashion, the events that took place. Dr. Kuhlman certainly deserves credit for his thorough knowledge of the terrain and his attempt to break the action down and analyze the details, but I would also criticize his effort because he tries to achieve the impossible. His method often leads to misconceptions, as he is attempting to support, at all costs, his theory of what happened. Kuhlman relies too much on the testimony of Curley, Mrs. Spotted Horn Bull and Kate Bighead, while at the same time ignoring or disregarding the parts of their testimony which disagree with his viewpoint. He uses very little analysis of other Indian testimony, most of which would not have supported his thesis.

Dr. Kuhlman should be commended for his concern, his knowledge of the terrain, and the time he spent on his project. I agree with many of his statements. But although he attempted to ride at Custer's elbow, I am afraid he was too far in the rear. He realized that at the Reno Court of Inquiry there were cover-ups which made future attempts to analyze what happened more difficult. However, he chose not to address that issue and consequently did not reveal the basic cover-ups, so he fell into the trap he had warned his students about.

Though Kuhlman supports logic, he is not consistent in its use. The essence of any analysis of the battle is the question of why there was no sign of an attack by Custer against the Indians, and Kuhlman's discussion, in my view, does not provide a logical answer.

SOURCES

1. Kuhlman, Charles. *Legend into History: The Custer Mystery.* Harrisburg, Pa, Stackpole Co., 1951, pp. xx, xx1.
2. Ibid., p. 1.
3. Ibid., p. 14.
4. Ibid., p. 18.
5. Ibid., p. 49.
6. Ibid., p. 54.
7. Ibid., p. 97.
8. Ibid., pp. 108, 109.
9. Marquis, *She Watched Custer's Last Battle*, (Next to last page of pamphlet), Copyright, 1953.
10. Ibid., (previous page).
11. Kuhlman, *Legend into History*, p. 111.
12. Ibid., p. 117.
13. Ibid., p. 118.
14. Ibid., p. 152.
15. Ibid., p. 154.
16. Ibid., p. 154.
17. Ibid., pp. 157, 158.
18. Ibid., p. 158.
19. Ibid., p. 117.
20. Ibid., p. 159.
21. Ibid., pp. 159, 160.
22. Ibid., p. 161.
23. Ibid., p. 165.
24. Ibid., p. 167.
25. Ibid., p. 168.
26. Ibid., p. 169.
27. Camp, Hammer, *Custer in 76,* p. 105.
28. Kuhlman, *Legend into History*, p. 169.
29. Ibid., p. 177.
30. Ibid., p. 179.
31. Ibid., p. 180.
32. Ibid., p. 181.
33. Ibid., p. 183.
34. Ibid., pp. 183–185.
35. Ibid., p. 189.
36. Ibid., p. 191.
37. Ibid., pp. 193, 194.
38. Ibid., p. 194.
39. Ibid., pp. 197, 198.

---

*The remains of four horses were found in this area by Blummer and Bethune – *Evidence and the Custer Enigma*, Greene, p. 26.

Keep the Last Bullet for Yourself
by Dr. T. B. Marquis

After years of working with these veteran warriors and transcribing their stories, Marquis reached a simple but shocking conclusion about the Battle of the Little Bighorn: the troopers with Custer panicked and most of them committed suicide. Marquis knew his explanation would not be popular. It was so unpopular, in fact, he could not get it published even though he had written two other solid worthwhile books on the subject: *Memoirs of a White Crow Indian* and *A Warrior Who Fought Custer*.[1]

Introduction by Joseph Medicine Crow

Besides White Man Runs Him, Marquis interviewed nearly all the relatives and close associates of Custer's other Crow scouts (Curly, Goes Ahead, Hairy Moccasin, White Swan, Half Yellow Face). He obtained and recorded perhaps the best account of the special part these scouts played in the events of the Custer march from the Yellowstone to Medicine Tail Coulee, where Custer, the Son of the Morning Star (as the Scouts called him), eventually made his fatal contact with the "hostiles."

Tempted as I am to review all the material in this book, I must nevertheless restrict my observations and remarks to some of those aspects that he touches upon which I consider uniquely revealing. I may give three examples.

First, Thomas Marquis's careful and detailed comparison of the respective mental attitudes and combat styles of the soldier and of the warrior is an approach heretofore lightly treated or else ignored altogether, even though it gives a powerful answer to the question: Why did Custer lose? Two – comparisons with other battles . . . Third, . . . no axe to grind.

I shall not labor to advance my own opinions, but will merely repeat remarks and statements made by General Custer's Crow scouts. These men played a unique and important part in Custer's search for and pursuit of the "hostiles." They were almost constantly at his side, along with their interpreter and advisor, Mitch Bouyer, a half-Sioux married to a Crow woman. The general was quite considerate of them, and the scouts likewise thought kindly of him and regarded him with high esteem, ..But they felt very sorry for him when he made his decision to attack at once, heedless of their advice to wait for No Hip Bone (General Gibbon). [Their desire to wait for Gibbon contradicts Ree statements.] As his last act of consideration to his faithful scouts, General Custer dismissed them just prior to his final charge down Medicine Tail Coulee.[2] [my underlining]

I believe this statement by Joseph Medicine Crow, whose grandfather was White Man Runs Him, is very significant. His remark that he wouldn't advance his own opinions indicates that they would differ, somewhat at least, from Marquis'. He shows a great deal of respect for Marquis, which could mean that if the Indians knew Marquis' view of what happened, they might reflect this in their stories. Since Marquis didn't say that Custer came down Medicine Tail Coulee, either in his maps or his writings, I believe Joseph Medicine Crow is saying indirectly, but succinctly, that he believed the Crow scouts felt Custer and his troops did move down Medicine Tail Coulee. His grandfather, White Man Runs Him, certainly stated in his interview with General Scott that Custer did so, and the other Crows had confirmed that view in their interviews.

Marquis quotes Sergeant Culbertson, Lieutenant Godfrey, and Captain Benteen to suggest that many of the men were recruits who had never been in a battle and were poor horsemen. This lack of experience, according to his sources, was a factor in the defeat of Custer. Marquis' description of the Indian encampment, just before Reno's troops went into action, is notable as it indicates that the Indians were surprised. It is particularly important in attempts to correlate Custer's actions with what he saw when viewing the Indian camp and whether he saw it after Reno was engaged or before. Either way, the best method is to "ride at Custer's elbow."

It is also believable that the Indians were surprised, as they say they were, at the arrival of the soldiers. This is indicated by the circumstances prevailing when the first charge was made by the soldiers. Practically all of the tipis were standing. A great throng of women, children, and old people left the camp and went running away from the soldiers to the hills. The troops were quite close to the camps before they met resistance. The warriors meeting them were only a few when compared with the great numbers who came afterward. The first few were probably mostly the camp policemen, or dog soldiers, which every Indian tribal camp regularly kept ready for immediate action. The many who came afterward were all the other warriors. They were not at first ready...

If the approach of the soldiers had been known a sufficient time beforehand, the situation at the camp would have been quite different from what it actually was. All of the tipis would have been down. All of the household property would have been in packs, and the packs would have been on pack ponies. Everything would have been ready to be taken away with the women, children, and old people, instead of being abandoned as was the actual case. Or, if the warning had been given in time to allow even some part of such preparations to be made, that same extra time would have allowed the warriors - and many more of them – to have prepared themselves and advanced further out from the camps than they did . . .

. . . Some minutes would elapse before word could be spread to all of them. In fact, a large number of people in the camps first got notice of the attack when they heard the shooting of the guns just south of the Hunk camp.

There was a whirlwind of excitement and bewilderment in all the camps. Pony herds were hurried in for warriors to get their mounts. There was a rushing to get ready, and a rushing forth by each warrior as soon as he was prepared. Family non-combatants seized packs, abandoning all property, . . . Children screamed for mothers not in sight . . . A selected campsite and a cunning ambush to entrap Custer? What a ridiculous fancy![3]

This account is important in attempting to establish a timing sequence. It is regrettable that earlier writers didn't determine conclusively where and when Custer viewed the village. I believe it was from Weir Point, but the issue shouldn't have been left to speculation, nor should have the route Custer took to Medicine Tail Coulee.

I also don't know how writers can ignore Martin's numerous and consistent accounts that they saw a peaceful village, nor Curley's claim that Custer had left the ridge when Reno became engaged. This would mean that Custer was within fifteen to twenty minutes of being able to attack a village which by then would be reacting to Reno, as Marquis has indicated. How many of those ten thousand plus Indians, who were excited and milling around, with the noise, dust and gunfire from Reno's troops, were going to notice Custer's men as they moved to the ford?

I think one can speculate and envision a number of things, if my scenario is correct or fairly close. Only a few Indians were aware of Custer's troops as they moved to the ford. After Custer was shot, his men picked him up and with other wounded started to retreat, whether according to orders or not. They were not at the ford over five or ten minutes. If Custer moved from Weir Point, as could be expected, Reno's troops were still in the timber. Within another five minutes Custer's troops that had dismounted and those who were mounted around Custer, moved back out of sight of the village. Custer was with Yates' battalion, and some of Yates' men had dismounted at the ford, particularly those in C Company; others on horseback moved toward Keogh's battalion, which Custer had placed in reserve. There was still a comparatively small number of Indians who had crossed the ford, but enough to have caused the troops to move north rather than back over their trail. This would indicate an unorganized, spontaneous retreat. Most of the Indians were just becoming aware of Custer's troops; those attacking Reno were not. Indians in the village viewed Keogh's battalion on Nye Cartwright Ridge and possibly some of the mounted troops of Yates' battalion, who moved in their direction and perhaps joined them.

Let us carry this hypothesis somewhat further. What if Custer had not been shot at the ford and those troops had smashed into the already panicky village at a time when Reno was still in the timber? Captain Benteen and Captain McDougall would be moving into the area and Captain Keogh's battalion would be seen on the ridge to the east of the village. The Indians and the non-combatants were fleeing to the northwest. Keogh's battalion would move off Nye Cartwright across North Medicine Tail Coulee down Calhoun Coulee to Cheyenne Ford, creating even more panic. By that time Benteen's troops would have crossed the Little Bighorn or would have been seen on the ridge above the valley, and Major Reno's would break out of the timber but not to retreat.

Could Custer have won a victory? I think he could have. The outcome would depend upon several events which I think actually did take place. Custer would have viewed the village from Weir Point and he would have seen a peaceful village just as Martin said he did.

If that indeed happened, only two things would have prevented an exceptionally good chance for a victory: First, the events took place according to the scenarios presented by Marquis, Kuhlman and others; scenarios in which Custer moved down Cedar Coulee and then farther to the north for whatever reason, taking whichever action the various writers have ascribed to Custer. Second, Custer moved to Ford B, but he was shot at the ford, stopping the attack. The shooting and the delay created a situation which brought on a retreat.

If Custer was in any way the talented general he was said to have been, even without any legendary qualities attributed to him, he would have moved to the ford as his officers and troops, at the time, believed he did.

Marquis' view of Custer waiting until the 26th:

Rational and unbiased thought can attribute to Custer in this regard only one incentive . . . a fear that otherwise the Indians would escape and leave him holding an empty bag. This was a prime consideration in all military circles during the campaign. There was no talk of any apparent expectation of defeat in battle. The main problem discussed was rather how to catch the Indians and compel them to fight. All the officers in all the military bodies in the field were in constant trepidation lest the elusive red people should escape.[4]

I agree with Marquis, but I believe he should have continued to use this view as a basic premise for judging Custer's actions. Custer would certainly want to attack the camp as quickly as possible in order to prevent the escape. The only excuse Custer could have had for moving farther to the north would be to prevent the Indians from escaping. But I believe his major motivation was to defeat the Indians by charging their camps as quickly as possible, not only to aid Major Reno and coordinate his attack, but to increase their panic and disorder. I do think his concern for the Indians scattering would be a primary factor in having Keogh's battalion move to Luce or Nye Cartwright Ridge.

> The dividing of Custer's forces at the last moment before proceeding to the attack has been condemned by practically all reviewers of this action. But the condemnations have been based on knowledge gained afterward, whereas judgement should be rendered on the basis of the knowledge available to Custer at that time . . . [Marquis should have remembered this, with respect to a few observations he would soon make.]
>
> Six separate tribal camp circles were arranged in a long group on the west side of the Little Bighorn River . . .
>
> Cottonwood trees in full leaf along the river and high bluffs and hills along its east bank hid all of the five Sioux camps from the view of whoever might be east of the bluffs immediately bordering the river. There is no high point on the divide to the east, nor anywhere else in that direction from which any of the five Sioux campsites could have been seen. Conversely, one who stands on any of those sites and looks toward the distant eastern hills cannot see any of them, not even the highest points. He can see only the bluffs just across the river in front of him. Those who disbelieve this should go and see for themselves.
>
> But the Northern Cheyenne camp was in plain view from the hills for several miles to the east of the river and might have been seen from high points still further away. There were neither trees nor bluffs east of it. On the contrary, just across the river east of it was a broad coulee and a long slope toward the hill country further eastward. The Northern Cheyenne camp was thus the Indian camp Custer and his scouts had seen, and this was the camp - and doubtless the only camp – he had in mind when he parted from Reno and started across the hills toward it.[5]

Marquis suggests several points that should be emphasized. The Cheyenne Camp was located across from Ford B, and not some distance to the north as most maps indicate. Marquis' work with the Cheyenne, and his extensive attempt to determine the exact location of the camp sites, mean that his view has to be respected and, I believe, accepted.

Equally important is his statement that not even the highest points east of the river were visible from the camp sites, except for the funnel vision back up South Medicine Tail Coulee from the area directly back of the ford. I would add that even from there Custer's troops moving down whatever coulee to Medicine Tail could not be seen from even the Cheyenne location; and when the troops moved back up North Medicine Tail Coulee (which I believe the Yates battalion did) they would have soon passed from sight of anyone on the west side of the Little Bighorn. This supports my contention that with the excitement and their concern for the attack by Reno from the south, most of the Indians would not have known about Custer and it would have been some time before they became aware of his troops moving against them. By the time some of them knew and were in a position to see Custer, they noticed Keogh's battalion moving along Nye Cartwright Ridge. Again, this sighting came after Indian attention was drawn by the action that took place at the ford. Then they moved to locations where they could see up Medicine Tail Coulee from opposite the ford, or possibly they moved back along the foothills to the west; either way a fairly lengthy period of time would have elapsed from Reno's attack before the troops on Nye Cartwright would have been noticed.

I believe Marquis' view supports my premise. The attention to Medicine Tail Coulee was drawn by action at the ford, but most Indians first sighted or became aware of Custer's troops when they saw Keogh's battalion. The troops were moving along Nye Cartwright Ridge in support of the retreating Yates' battalion, which by then was out of sight from all but a comparatively small number of Indians that had already crossed the ford. That group had caused most of the main element of Yates' battalion to retreat up North Medicine Tail.

I have not seen any testimony which would suggest that Custer or Reno's forces had sighted any village before they separated. They could have seen smoke from the village and the ponies in the valley to the west of the camps from the Crow's Nest, but not the Cheyenne camp. One camp would not account for all the Indian camp sites they had passed.

The main support for the Cheyenne camp location just to the north of Ford B is the Indian testimony to that effect. There is no reason to suspect, that as regards the location of the camp, the Indians would give a false answer. Dr. Kuhlman also accepts this view; what makes it unusual is that it reinforces the camp site location, yet is antithetical to both of their hypotheses.

ANALYSIS OF WRITERS' SCENARIOS

It may be that Custer was expecting Reno to strike the same camp, the only one that could be seen. He then had no way of knowing that Reno was going to be met by a host of Hunkpapas two or three miles up the river from the camp he had seen. If it really was his intention to strike this invisible camp from below, while Reno would strike it from above, then the bitter accusation that he thrust Reno into a hopeless charge while Custer and his men dallied in the hills is utterly confuted. From the point of separation with Reno going the valley route, the two detachments would have arrived at the Cheyenne camp at about the same time.[6]

Elsewhere in his discussion, Marquis condemns those who accused Custer for splitting his forces, because they were using knowledge available afterward but not in Custer's possession at the time. Here he is making the same mistake in speculating, not only on what Custer saw, but also on his knowledge of the terrain he would have to cross to arrive at the same time as Reno. To me, what makes this even worse, is that Marquis now throws this speculation aside and claims that Custer moved farther to the east and north, which would have prevented Custer from carrying out his plan.

Custer's first view of the great combined encampment came after he and Reno were both well advanced on their separate courses to the attack. Then it was that he sent the hurry-up message to Benteen. Then it was that, instead of 1500 Indians estimated in his conversations with his officers, he found himself plunging into about 12,000 of them. [I believe Custer's estimation was 1500 warriors whereas the Indian Bureau's estimate was less.][7]

The Reno men tell of Custer's waving his big white hat at them. All of the interpretations of that gesture have been that he was cheering them in their charge. It may be, though, that his amazement at the discovery of so many Indians caused him to try to convey to Reno some reversal order. It is not altogether improbable that the supposed encouraging wave of the hat was really a vehement prohibitory gesticulation, and that it was accompanied by a shouted admonition, such as: "Stop! Wait until Benteen comes!"[8]

I would be more inclined to wonder if Reno's troops could have seen him waving his hat from where most of them implied they saw him – when they were reforming or were half way down the valley. I do believe they saw Custer's command. Be that as it may, Martin would have realized what Custer did and said, and since Martin doesn't recall seeing, or anyone mentioning, Reno going into action, I believe Marquis should account for his statement. Martin might have been confused by the questions and his time and distance estimates, but I think he was as honest a man as anyone who testified. To disagree with him, you should offer more factual and logical evidence than I have found any writer using. It is also interesting that Marquis suggests the possibility that Custer told Reno to hold until Benteen arrived, and that shortly afterward Custer sent a message to Benteen to hurry and come to Custer's aid. The suggestion would imply Marquis thought Reno knew that Benteen had orders to support him.

> . . . [visitors at the battlefield] A frequently heard comment is: "He ought to have kept his force together for the attack."
> Good idea, casual visitor. But, go on and tell us more. Where should the attack have been made? . . . Or should he have massed his men and attacked the only camp actually seen, which was four miles north of Reno Creek, and which later proved to be only the Cheyenne camp circle? In other words: Where were the Indians? How many of them were in the region? Were they all in one camp, or in camps at various places? Imagine yourself in Custer's place, with his lack of knowledge of the true case – and decide at once, as he had to do. Also, keep in mind that, if the full regiment goes en masse to the wrong place, its commander renders himself ridiculous.[9]

I agree with Marquis except for Custer's knowledge of the Cheyenne camp site. I think caution can be the better part of valor and Custer could have waited and had his scouts reconnoiter, even though it is understandable why he didn't. His behavior would be compatible with his action-oriented temperament, but it is then hard to imagine Custer doing what Marquis claimed he did. Why are Reno and Benteen accused of not attacking, but Custer is excused for not doing so?

> There has been much debate as to precisely where the Custer detachment moved in the last mile or so to the place of the final stand at the battle ridge. There has been much theorizing about the possibility that it went down a narrow coulee now known as the south prong of Medicine Tail Coulee, just east of, and almost parallel to, the bluffs along the river from the Cheyenne campsite; they were met by the Indians. It is supposed that the fighting began there, and that Custer gradually retreated to the ridge.
> But the Indians are unanimous in their statements that the Custer soldiers were first seen moving at a trot on a high and long ridge running almost parallel with the river, and almost two miles east of the Cheyenne camp. The Cheyenne watched them, and the soldiers had the Cheyenne in full view. A few warriors went out in that direction and exchanged long-distance shots with the sol-

diers. Other warriors—Cheyenne and Sioux—followed. More of them, and yet more of them, lashed their ponies through the waters of the river and went tearing on to meet the white invaders. It was not until after the soldiers had gone a considerable distance beyond that part of the ridge nearest the Cheyenne camp that the column swerved left to a lower ridge nearer the river. By this time there was a vast throng of warriors at their front, while others were beginning to encircle them. They took up their position on this ridge, and there a pitched battle began. There it also ended. The soldiers never got any nearer to the river then they were when they died.

The southern prong of Medicine Tail Coulee afforded much the shorter and easier route of approach for Custer. Its upper beginning is near the bluff where the Reno men saw him as he waved his hat. It was in this vicinity that Trumpeter Martin left to carry the hurry-up message to Benteen This last man to leave the Custer detachment is quoted as having said that they were just then about to start down the coulee. [Actually Medicine Tail Coulee, and Martin said he definitely saw Custer closer than Marquis said they went.] It is quite natural to believe that such was the case. This allows room for speculation as to how it came about that the first view the Indians had of Custer's men was far out on the ridge.

One explanation might be as follows. The troops were actually about to start down the coulee, but when Custer saw the great size of the camp he decided that the approach he contemplated would surely be repulsed. He waved a warning to Reno either to change his charge into a retreat or to make a careful stand. Then he took his own detachment to the high ridge, in full view of the Indians, as a threatening demonstration that would draw them to him or scare them into flight . . . [I don't know how Marquis could even include this as an explanation; it goes against testimony and logic.]

Another explanation, however, and seemingly the best one, is this. The decision not to go down the coulee was based upon thoughts of the great number of untrained men who would thus be brought into a sudden encounter with a force just discovered to be vastly superior in numbers. Perhaps Custer had seen indications of unsteadiness among the Reno men as they went into that initial combat that resulted in their swift and calamitous defeat. It was his special business, at the critical moment of his own contemplated approach, to note the mental state of his own men. Doubtless he did so, and it is highly probable that he saw among them many signs of unsteadiness, trepidation, or distinct perturbation – premonitions of the uncontrollable panic that afterwards did develop among them. He therefore decided that he definitely would not lead his men in that state of mind into a sudden frontal attack on that immense camp. Instead, he would take them along the hills to make a gradual approach that might enable them to achieve some degree of composure. Coupling this, though, with the idea of enticing the Indians out to meet him, he felt that his tactics in this respect had been a thorough success.[10]

I do not question Marquis' sincerity or his knowledge and contacts with the Indians; I do however question his statements and certainly his logic.

I have not found the written testimony of the Indians to be unanimous, and that in itself would make me wonder if they didn't perhaps agree on what they thought Marquis wanted to hear. Marquis questioned White Man Runs Him and relatives of the other Crow scouts, but he fails to account for the statements White Man Runs Him and Curley made to General Scott. Does Pretty Shield tell him a different story than she did to Linderman, and if so why? Some of the Sioux testimony suggests that Custer moved to the ford. It is true that Kate Bighead, Wooden Leg and Mrs. Spotted Horn Bull said that Custer's troops didn't go there, but they should have been asked where they were when Major Reno's troops were still in the valley. I would cite White Man Runs Him's grandson Joseph Medicine Crow's statement in the introduction to Marquis' book. He mentions the troop movement down Medicine Tail Coulee for a reason, even though he doesn't carry through with it. The reason he doesn't, I believe, is his respect for Marquis and his desire for the book to stand as written.

Since Medicine Tail Coulee was the closest and best route to attack the Indians, I don't think Marquis' explanation as to why it wasn't taken is acceptable. He blames it on the number of recruits and their reaction. However, Custer knew the make up of his command before and it hadn't bothered him. The notion that Custer saw Reno's troops' reaction doesn't agree with the account of the troopers or officers while on the skirmish line. Some fast and high firing was mentioned, but there was no indication of panic, and even if there had been, it is extremely doubtful whether Custer could have made it out from that distance. Neither Kanipe nor Martin felt that Custer's troops were worried; in fact, they indicated that the troops were anxious to attack. This was the time when Custer tried to decide which route to follow, and subsequently made the decision Marquis is referring to.

Even if I accepted Marquis' view, I can't envision Custer ignoring Reno's predicament and moving a mile or so farther back in order to calm his troops, at a time when they were able to see the size of the village and they faced the Indian attack. One should point out that the troops would not have seen the size of the village (Marquis should have remembered his previous statements). The number of Indians attacking Reno was not great during that period.

At that time, Custer, according to Marquis, rushed Martin back to Benteen. If Custer was concerned with the makeup of his troops, Major Reno's position, and the size of the village, rather than sending a message to Benteen, he should have moved either to join forces with him or to establish a defense. If he wanted to entice or draw the Indians off from Reno, he should have set up a threatening defensive position around Weir Point or Sharpshooter Hill, rather than moving farther away from both the Indians and the aid he was sending for. Why would he move off from the eastern ridges to Battleridge, when he had already lost any advantage of an attack, and he would only be placing his troops farther away from any aid? By then, he must have been aware of the Indians who were pouring out to meet him, and yet, according to Marquis, he moved to Battleridge instead of moving back the way he came. This movement only benefited the Indians. If Custer actually did this, he certainly should not have been in command.

As I have said, Marquis should have asked all those Indians who were unanimous in stating that Custer never came closer than the eastern ridges and Battleridge, where they were after Major Reno first attacked? Did they go to fight Reno? Were they taking down tepees, or moving to the hills? If there were 12,000 Indians, I wonder if more than 500 would have seen Custer at the ford, or before his troops had retreated around the cutbank. The other Indians would only have became aware of Custer's threat to their village when they saw Keogh's battalion moving along Nye Cartwright Ridge.

If my timing is correct, or nearly so, when Custer moved to the ford practically all of the warrior Indians would have been moving to meet Reno or preparing to fight; non-combatants would be confused and panicky, moving to the benchland, taking down tepees, and looking for their children. The dust, the tepees, the trees and the bluffs would have prevented most of the Indians from sighting Custer while he was at the ford. Most of those, like Kate Bighead, would have thought that the warriors they saw returning from fighting Major Reno were the first Indians to move against General Custer – which was not true.

The timing is also wrong in Marquis' scenario, as in so many others. According to these scenarios', Custer's command would have been moving on the ridge above the valley as well as the eastern ridges while Reno was fighting in the valley; yet the Indians did not become aware of him for at least another 45 minutes. The theory that Custer would have waited on the ridge, or in some ravine, is not logical, considering his goal at the time, and even more illogical when one considers his psyche.

From Marquis' statements, one can see that his conviction that Custer moved down Cedar Coulee is based on the Indians sighting of troops along Nye Cartwright Ridge, coupled with the timing correlation of the ensuing action on Battleridge. I am sure this is also one of the basic reasons why others have accepted the idea that Custer moved down Cedar Coulee.

SOURCES

1. Marquis, Thomas B., *Keep the Last Bullet For Yourself: The True Story of Custer's Last Stand,* Reference Publications, Inc., p. 7.
2. Ibid., pp. 11, 12.
3. Ibid., pp. 81, 82.
4. Ibid., p. 94.
5. Ibid., p. 95, 97.
6. Ibid., pp. 97, 98.
7. Stewart, *Custer's Luck,* pp. 242, 243. *Report of the Secretary of War,* 44th Congress, Vol. 1, 1876, page 77. [General Sheridan, in bringing out his orders to General Crook and General Terry, said: ". . . could not encounter more than the hostiles, estimate by the Indian Bureau at 500 warriors, or by anybody at the time at more than 800 warriors," p. 29.]
8. Marquis, *Keep the Last Bullet For Yourself,* p. 98.
9. Ibid., p. 98.
10. Ibid., p. 99, 100.

The Custer Myth – A Source Book of Custeriana by Colonel W. A. Graham

Colonel Graham's book on Custeriana, *The Custer Myth,* has been the primary source book for persons interested in the Battle of the Little Bighorn. In his work, Colonel Graham summarizes his view of the events that took place. I take issue with his assessment on a number of points.

I will begin with Graham's account of the 7th Cavalry moving toward the Little Bighorn. According to Graham, Major Reno received his attack orders after Captain Benteen had moved to the left, and Major Reno and General Custer had reached the Lone Tepee.

Up to that moment, it is fairly clear that Custer had formed no plan of battle. His information of the enemy was insufficient for him to have done so. He gave Reno no other instructions, and no other word was ever received from him by Reno, who went in apparently expecting Custer to follow and support him from the rear.

It is quite possible, even probable, that this was Custer's intention at that moment, for he did follow Reno for a considerable distance.

The Adjutant, Lieutenant Cook, and Captain Keogh, both of whom were killed with Custer, rode to the river with Reno's command. At the river bank (about 2:30) the scouts saw the Sioux coming up the valley to meet Reno, and Girard who had not yet crossed over, rode back, overtook Cook, then on his way back to Custer (who was still following) and reported to him that the Sioux were coming in large numbers to meet Reno. Cook said he would report the fact at once to Custer. This was about 2:45.[1]

This is the usual version of the events, and one with which I disagree, as I have suggested numerous times in my examination of testimony. In general, I cannot conceive of Custer not having a plan of attack by the time he gave Major Reno his attack orders, and I believe he was reasonably sure of the general location of the Indian village.*

There is no basis for accepting Girard's statements, as they are inconsistent, and I found no indication from whites or Indians that the Sioux or Cheyenne were moving down the valley toward Reno at that time. One should use more than Girard's testimony as verification, especially since such sightings were not brought out by any others, except Herendeen. The same is true about the question of whether Cooke or Keogh went to the ford with Major Reno, although one does find several troopers who felt that at least Cooke did.

I believe Custer didn't begin his flanking movement sooner, not because he wasn't sure of where the Indian village was, but for other reasons. He was concerned about the terrain and he wanted confirmation from Benteen that there was no major Indian threat from the south; he also wanted verification of his orders for Benteen to move to the Little Bighorn Valley, and, if he found no Indians, to then move downstream in support of Reno. Since Custer hadn't heard from Benteen, he waited until the last minute before making his move.

The message which Graham claims Custer received from Cooke should have had the opposite effect, causing him to hurry to support Reno from behind, particularly if that had been his original plan. It seems unlikely that Custer would have moved into unknown terrain to the north after seeing the bluffs without being sure where he could launch an attack, especially since Custer knew time was of the essence. Not having heard from Benteen, he would not have wanted to leave the packs exposed.

> It was at this moment, or very soon after, as it seems to me, that Custer's plan took form. The Indians were moving toward Reno, who would meet them on the plain. By dashing down the river, he could cut in behind them, and hit them from the rear, and he would send for Benteen and put him into action in the center, between Reno and himself.[2]

I agree that this was Custer's plan, but he would have devised it after he knew the general location of the Indian camp – which he did after coming down from the Crow's Nest. I believe Custer was mostly concerned with the time when he could implement his plan. Graham's scenario is curious at this point. He believes that after receiving the message from Cooke, Custer formulated his plan, which included sending a message to Benteen to inform him that he would be expected to attack the Indians in the center between Reno and Custer.

Graham's scenario is interesting for a number of reasons.

First: This, to all purposes, is the exact message that Martin told Graham that Custer gave Reno. However, no one has either believed or accepted Martin's statement.

If Custer planned the above strategy, he wouldn't have expressed it at the time Graham suggests. He certainly would have wanted Major Reno and Captain Benteen to hear the message – not Cooke, Martin or even his own officers. This point supports Martin's contention that it was the message given to Major Reno when he received his attack orders.

Second: The account indicates that Benteen received additional orders. However, they wouldn't have been sent at that time. Custer could and should have sent them a short time before, or possibly just after giving Reno his orders. There is a strong possibility that Custer may have wanted Reno to circle the camp as far west as possible, realizing the Indians might scatter in that direction, as they actually began to. Custer was also expecting Benteen, once he reached the Little Bighorn, to move down the valley. The orders Graham may have surmised could very well have been the orders Custer gave to both Benteen and Reno. Graham's use of the concept of the center is informative, but it raises the question of where the center was. I don't

---

*Note verification in W. Kent King's book, *Massacre: The Custer Cover-Up*.

think one should assume that Custer thought there would be several locations along the east side of the river from which to launch attacks. However, since Trumpeter Martin and Sergeant Davern both claim that Reno received orders similar to those in Graham's supposition, their testimony supports my belief that these were the orders Custer actually gave. If this was so, I would think that the instructions would have allowed for the action on the battlefield to determine whether Benteen should support Reno from the center or to his left, which could account for the difference between Martin's and Davern's recollection. This support by Benteen would come, as he followed orders to move down the valley and aid Reno. I doubt if any of these considerations would have had to do with a message from Girard by way of Adjutant Cooke.

It is impossible to believe, when he rode to the top of the ridge with Martin, as he did shortly after leaving Reno's trail and starting down the river at a gallop, that Custer thought the Indians were "asleep in their tents," for Cook must already have told him that they were streaming up the valley to meet Reno. He probably said, "We've caught them napping: or "asleep" an expression which Martin, then a green Italian unused to American colloquialisms, interpreted literally. But from the ridge, evidently, he did not see either the Indians or Reno's command. I assume that the timber below hid them from view. But he did see the village and this, I think was his first view of it. It was apparently deserted by its fighting men. What more natural, than, that he should cheer and shout to his men, "We've got them this time!" and dash for a ford that he might cross and attack in the rear, and did not know, nor had any suspicion, of what was in store for his own detachment.[3]

Graham again makes the mistake of relying on Girard's account. It is difficult to believe that Custer would have made the statement about having caught the Indians napping in the overall context expressed by Graham. There were a large number of Indian warriors who would have been in the valley confronting or moving to meet Reno, and many in the village still preparing to do so. If there was any consensus in the Indian accounts, whether Sioux or Cheyenne, or for that matter the Arikara scouts, it was that the Indians were surprised. To have Custer make a remark, once Reno had gone into action, even faintly resembling the one in Graham's account, seems absurd. Since it is fairly certain Custer expressed himself in some such manner, if Graham wished to be historically correct, he should have changed his format.

I find it both sad or amusing that Graham can say Martin was not able to distinguish the difference between napping and sleeping, a difference which is essentially irrelevant, but he does not question Benteen's remark or apply this reasoning to Martin's supposed use of the word "skidaddling." If this had been done, it might have provided Graham with an insight into why Benteen used this term in such a derogatory way.

> ... The greater part of the Sioux had not gone to meet Reno, but, before Martin was out of sight or hearing, attacked him (Custer) in the ravine which led to the ford; and, as subsequent events show, in such numbers as to force him further down the river than he intended to go. And there, still driven back by the hordes which cut him off from Reno he was struck again by the crafty Crazy Horse, who crossed the river below him and attacked his rear. In the meantime Reno, finding the odds too great against him, routed, had fled back across the river . . .[4]

I find it baffling how anyone could read the Indian accounts and not realize that they were surprised by both Reno's attack and by General Custer.

A number of other questions come to mind. How can one take a position that Custer didn't know what he was going to do until the last minute, but the Indians did? How can anyone familiar with the history of Indian battles and their problems in ambushing an enemy, believe that the Indians, within some thirty minutes, would have had enough discipline and organization to send some warriors to attack Reno, arrange the camp to look as if it were asleep (or napping), and have most of the warriors in ambush waiting for General Custer? How can one turn Martin's statement about the Indians firing on Custer into an ambush that would have left no testimony of such by the Indians, and neither signs or testimony of a major attack by the troops or an organized retreat?

> ... Hundreds of the Sioux under Gall had already left Reno, and dashing down the valley to the point where Custer, already hemmed in, was fighting for his life, they fell upon him like a thunderbolt, and in a short time the fight was over.[5]

Colonel Graham then proceeds to justify Major Reno and Captain Benteen's slowness in moving downstream.

Graham's thesis is similar to many others with which I cannot agree, as it is based on several questionable premises. He believes that Custer did not accept the reports of his scouts, who pointed out the size and location of the Indian encampment. He accepts Girard's claim that as the Indians were proceeding to attack Reno, he gave the message about this movement to Adjutant Cooke who forwarded it to Custer, thus causing him to change his plans and travel downstream.

He also accepts Major Reno's and Captain Benteen's claim concerning the orders they received. These orders vindicated their actions and supported the view that Reno moved downstream ahead of General Custer.

Graham's acceptance of these positions resulted in a distorted hypothesis, and created many errors in his account of the battle.

SOURCES

1. Colonel W. A. Graham, *The Custer Myth, A Source Book of Custeriana,* University of Nebraska Press, 1953, p. 293.
2. Ibid., p. 293.
3. Ibid., p. 293.
4. Ibid., p. 293.
5. Ibid., p. 293.

Evidence and the Custer Enigma
by Jerome Greene

There was no question about Custer's intentions when he came down from the Crow's Nest and assembled his officers. While personally unable to see any village, he told them he nevertheless believed that one existed nearby. He would move ahead, determine its location, and attack without delay. The advance position went to Captain Frederick W. Benteen . . . The Indian scouts moved ahead with instructions to drive off or capture the Sioux pony herd.[1]

I agree with Greene that Custer possibly didn't see the village. However, I don't think Custer had any doubts about the general location indicated by the scouts. This view contradicts the impression – mainly portrayed by Captain Benteen – that Custer didn't believe there was such a village near there.

. . . Custer shortly called another halt and this time made battalion assignments . . . Significantly, Second Lieutenant Winfield Scott Edgerly, near Custer at the time of the division, maintained for the rest of his life that Custer further assigned battalions presumably of two and three companies each, to Captain Keogh and Captain Yates . . .

. . . Major Reno moved forward with his three companies, . . . After two miles the soldiers reached the Little Bighorn. The river was swollen from melting spring snows, causing Reno to divert briefly to the south before finding a suitable crossing. As the battalion entered the stream, the interpreter, Fred Girard, looked beyond to a village sprawled across the valley floor two miles away. The warriors had stopped running and were being joined by others. Sensing trouble, Girard rode back to inform Adjutant Cooke and Captain Keogh, who had accompanied the soldiers to the ford. The two officers turned back immediately and took the news to Custer.[2]

Since Lieutenant Edgerly was with Benteen's battalion and heard these orders, it is odd that Captain Benteen maintained he never did, insisting that he only heard those which directed him to move to the left.

If Major Reno moved to the Little Bighorn, and didn't at first find a suitable crossing, then moved to the left or south before he finally did, how much time did this search consume? It must have taken several minutes, and the period should be included in estimating the time it took Reno to cross Ford A.

Greene's account of Girard sighting the village several miles away is questionable, since his location as well as the ponies and the dust in the valley would have prevented it. It also contradicts other Girard accounts. I don't understand why more writers are not as perplexed, as I have been, wondering where all these Indians, who were supposedly seen, disappeared to and why. If they had been there, why weren't the Arikaras more concerned as they moved down the valley? Nor, I might add, were Lieutenant Varnum, Lieutenant Hare, Captain Moylan or others particularly concerned. Indian testimony certainly does not support their gathering before Reno made his move down the valley. Girard's testimony was considered unreliable by many, yet everyone appears to accept his story of warning Cooke and consequently Custer, even though Girard's accounts have been remarkably inconsistent.

. . . Reno dismounted his troopers, and during the ensuing hour, made a costly stand in the cottonwood timber . . . The resulting retreat was a panic-stricken rout, . . . The warriors shortly withdrew their attention downstream.[3]

Judgments about the demise of Custer and his five cavalry companies are difficult to make. As with all incidents in history, there exists no perfect witnesses. Only two soldiers and four Crow Indian scouts watched the battalion's march into battle, and they offered just partial descriptions . . . Sioux and Cheyenne were not always reliable witnesses . . .

The human memory is notoriously unreliable . . . the fact that testimony by warrior-participants seem questionable does not prevent approximations of truth, regarding what happened . . . In 1956, National Park Service employees began searching the battle site with metal detectors. By locating cartridge casings and other metallic refuse, they successfully determined various soldier and Indian held positions. This information proved useful in corroborating certain Indian reports...

By using this information, a fairly accurate history of what happened, from the time Custer ordered Reno's assault, can be devised. To begin with, Custer apparently had no particular plan in mind. He sent Reno to prevent the escape of a small party of Indians without knowing anything about the terrain. More then this, he was uncertain a village lay just ahead. When Captain Keogh and Adjutant Cooke returned from Reno's ford with Gerard's report, Custer diverged from the trail. He turned right, as if to intercept Reno somewhere in the Little Bighorn Valley, but he apparently had no idea where.

Custer advanced at a gallop. After a mile or so, his column reached the bluff tops above the river from which he watched Reno go into battle. This was near the spot later occupied by Reno and Benteen, and Reno spoke definitively of Custer's trail.[4]

Here Greene reverses his earlier view that Custer had assumed the scouts were correct, even though he was not able to see the village himself. With all the signs and indications that Custer would have had, I cannot imagine him moving down Ash Creek without at least a provisional plan of action. I would speculate that his slowness in moving his five companies in a flanking movement to the right reflected his desire to hear from Benteen so that he could be sure of the situation to his left or south.

The view that Custer sent Reno to prevent the escape of a small party of Indians is not true. These Indians probably precipitated Custer's attack orders to Reno, but unless everyone who heard the orders misunderstood them, there was no indication that Reno should prevent their escape and in no way would he have been capable of doing so. I think Reno's attack orders definitely imply that Custer knew the Indian village lay downstream, although he might not have known just how far away the location was. Again, note Major Reno's report on 5th of July 1876.[5]

... It should be noted that Trumpeter John Martin, the orderly who accompanied Custer to the ridgetop, said he saw nothing of Reno's battalion from the vantage point. Inasmuch as time sequence placed Reno near the village, and as three of the Crows with Custer at the time saw Reno's men from the same ridge. Martin was either mistaken or Major Reno's command was partially hidden by timber in the bottom. Perhaps Martin, an Italian immigrant who understood little English, simply did not know what to look for from this position.[6]

Greene, at least, didn't ignore Martin's remarks, although I think he should have remembered his previous comments about witnesses and memory. Greene is attempting to fit Custer's movement into a timing sequence, which is understandable and necessary, but I disagree with his conclusions.

The three Crows moved along the ridge until they reached the bluff above the ford from which they supposedly fired on the village. During that time, they saw Reno go into action.

I have discussed the testimony Greene is using, in my analysis of the question of whether Custer went down Cedar Coulee. For Greene to accept statements that should be disputed, and then insinuate that Martin was too ignorant to know what was going on, is inexcusable. Martin's testimony does not imply that he didn't know Major Reno was sent to attack the village – in fact he was the one person who knew what Reno's real attack orders were – nor does his testimony suggest that they were not concerned with where Reno was when Custer viewed the valley. The troops were in a position to see Reno, and would have known if he was moving down the valley or was engaged when they reached the ridge. It is possible that during Custer's move down the ridge from the area near Reno Hill to Weir Point, Martin would not have been in a position to see Reno. A more pertinent question is whether Custer was so far ahead of Reno that they didn't see him starting down the valley before Custer and Martin left the ridge. One should consider the slower Rees account.

Following his observation, Custer descended the point and conferred with Lt. Cooke. [This was brought out by Martin, and would refute DeRudio's sighting.] He then directed his five companies forward again and pressed to the right, down a narrow cedar-lined coulee leading away from the river.

... Company F headed a column of fours as the troopers entered Medicine Tail Coulee; Companies C, E, I, and L followed behind. John Martin remembered "the gray horse company (E) was in the center of the column." This formation further indicates that Custer divided his command into two battalions. Captain Yates commanded Company F, while Keogh commanded Company I. Yates' battalion thus seemingly consisted of three companies – F, C, and E, while Keogh headed the other, composed of I and L.

Entering the broad coulee, Custer now turned left, starting down the gentle slope toward the Little Bighorn River, nearly a mile away and concealed by Medicine Tail's natural bend. He halted briefly by a small creek while the troopers tightened their saddle girths. Trumpeter Martin rode to the rear bearing a message for Benteen.

As Martin started out of Medicine Tail, he glanced back. Warriors already were firing at Custer's men, he later recalled. He turned up the narrow cedar draw and met Boston Custer racing towards him . . .

. . . Reaching the blufftops, Martin viewed Reno's battalion below, at the time it retreated into the woods.[7]

I don't think Martin's impression of warriors firing on Custer's men is any factual substantiation for the view by many that Custer had been attacked by a large number of Indians at that time, except for one of Curley's fabrications.

It is interesting to note that Greene often uses Martin's testimony to support his analysis of events when the statements lend themselves to his interpretation, but he rejects Martin's consistent testimony on simple, basic questions, such as his not sighting Reno in the valley.

The timing sequence is important to Greene. He believes that when Custer had reached the ridge near Reno Hill, he observed Reno going into action – although Greene doesn't mention any move down the ridge, which is prominent in the accounts of the Crows, Kanipe and Martin. One can assume that this is the right scenario: Custer actually went to a high point, usually considered to be Weir Point, from which he viewed the village. Leaving out this second move, Custer had close to a two mile jaunt to Medicine Tail Coulee by way of Cedar Coulee from the time he supposedly saw Reno going into action. This should have taken fifteen minutes. One could point out that Martin didn't mention any stopping and tightening of girths at the time he received his message; but, to use Greene's and others' line of reasoning, he might not have recognized the importance of this detail. One might also mention that the place where Cedar Coulee enters Medicine Tail Coulee is closer to two miles than one from the Little Bighorn. By the time Martin got back to Reno Hill, it would have taken another twenty minutes – his horse was moving slower, he had to climb up a rise, and he stopped for a minute or two to talk with Boston Custer and several troopers. We should add another five minutes for Custer's initial discussion with Cooke and to account for the distance they covered as they moved down Medicine Tail Coulee before reaching the spring, halting and giving the message to Martin. Some forty-five minutes had to elapse, and Reno was just moving into the timber, which means that Reno was on the skirmish line longer than other participants, white or Indian, give him credit for.

Martin's conjecture was fairly accurate. After the orderly had left, Custer continued down Medicine Tail Coulee towards the Little Bighorn, evidently intending to attack the Indian encampment. And he would have done so, had Indians not stopped him when he reached the stream. Warriors hidden in the underbrush across the river now fired on him, and Custer ordered his men to dismount and to defend themselves.

Numerous oral recountings by Indian participants bear out this action, as does diverse material evidence uncovered at the scene with the aid of metal detecting instruments. Some early testimony described soldiers who rode into the water before turning back in the face of hostile gunfire. Horned Horse, a Dakota maintained in an interview that Custer "made a dash to get across, but was met by such tremendous fire . . . that the head of the command reeled back toward the bluffs after losing several men who tumbled into the water . . ." An early account by the Crow scout, Curly, confirmed this. He saw a sergeant and several others enter the stream. When the hostiles fired, two men dropped from their saddles into the water.[8]

I don't believe there is any Indian evidence to confirm that a large number of them waited for Custer, and I don't think Greene offers any of his own. The loss of several men should not have stopped Custer. The three Crows, supposedly on the bluff above the ford, certainly did not mention any large number of Indians, nor would their move to the bluff or their firing indicate such presence. According to the Indian accounts, the camps were still in a state of excitement brought on by Reno's attack, and would have been throughout Reno's fight in the valley. There was no major reason for an attack not to have been, temporarily at least, successful. The need to attack at that time would have been apparent, as I have said many times in analyzing the statements of different participants and writers. If Custer decided to retreat, there is no sign of a well-managed and disciplined maneuver. Greene claims that Custer attempted to do just that, and I don't think there is any evidence to support it. There is some evidence in regard to Keogh's battalion, and in this I agree with Greene. Parts of the other three companies made some attempts, but the overall signs would be of a disorganized retreat.

It is hard for me to accept the supposition that Reno's men became disorganized in their retreat from the timber,* and the implication that several companies did the same in their retreat from Weir Point, yet Custer's troops would not have done so under much more extreme conditions more conducive to creating a panic than those suffered by Reno's troops.

---

*A "panic-stricken rout," to use Greene's term. p. 13.

The tremendous gunfire should have been coming from the troops and not the Indians, and the loss of several men should not have stopped an attack under the leadership of the courageous Custer. Greene mentions, but doesn't consider fully, that the only event which would have caused the command to react the way they did was for Custer himself to have been shot.

> The Indians sudden shooting was too much. The soldiers' return fire had little impact on the tribesmen concealed along the opposite bank, so Custer drew back. Sitting Bull later corroborated this [I don't believe Sitting Bull was in any position to corroborate any particular point once Reno's firing commenced.] . . . Simultaneously, warriors filed across the Little Bighorn downstream from Reno's hilltop position and moved into the ravines along Custer's flank.
> . . . This sudden action forced Companies I and L, under Keogh and Custer's brother-in-law, First Lieutenant James Calhoun, to fall back in Medicine Tail Coulee, a maneuver that cut them off from the rest of the command.[9]

I agree, in essence, with Greene's comments about Keogh's battalion. Although he may be correct, I would think that Custer, considering his concern for Benteen, the packs and scattering Indians, was resorting to the common cavalry practice of placing some units in reserve. I also agree that the commanders in Keogh's battalion, which was in the rear, were able to maintain greater control over their troops. However, the timing and the Indians sighting of troops on Nye Cartwright Ridge favor the view that they were sent there by Custer before he moved to the ford.

> . . . Custer, meantime, received heavy frontal attacks, forcing him to draw his skirmishers back further from the river. Indian eyewitnesses said that the soldiers, dismounted, pulled back slowly, leading their animals.[10]
> To be sure, some Indian accounts seemingly deny Custer's approach to the ford . . . Wooden Leg . . . saw soldiers "on distant hills down the river" from his position near Reno's Hill. He crossed the Little Bighorn and rode north, where he observed "lots of Indians out on the hills across on the east side . . . fighting the other soldiers there." But he likewise told of Indians crossing to meet the troopers, reminiscent of what other Cheyennes told Grinnell. Wooden Leg, in fact, named the same individual as given in Grinnell's book *The Fighting Cheyenne.*[11]

Greene should have noted that there is no reference to a large number of Indians meeting the troops when they reached the ford; and more importantly, he should have referred to White Cow Bull's account in which he (a Lakota) mentions the same Indian names.

> . . . Kate Bighead, another Cheyenne, noticed soldiers on a high ridge east of the Cheyenne camp, . . . "A few Indians were out there," she recalled, "and shots were being exchanged at long distance." . . . Doubtless some witnesses arrived late upstream – as Wooden Leg admittedly did – and simply missed seeing action at Medicine Tail ford.
> Other testimony in support of the ford theory came from army personnel who examined the site two days later. Most surviving Seventh Cavalry officers agreed that Custer tried to cross at the mouth of Medicine Tail Coulee, . . .
> On the other hand, First Lieutenant Edward Maquire, General Terry's staff engineer, recalled signs of fighting in the form of expended cartridges at the ford, though he made no distinction between military and Indians shells. In addition to the dead cavalry mounts found there . . . Fred Gerard saw others on the west side of the stream within the village limits, a point lending credence to those Indians accounts of soldiers reaching the camp.[12]

The footnotes indicate that those authors who oppose the theory that Custer reached the ford, believe that the horses were driven to the village by the Indians, where some later died. I am sure the authors would use shell casings in the same manner. These observations are not enough to refute either Greene's hypothesis that Custer went to the ford, or the sighting reported by White Man Runs Him, Pretty Shield's statements credited to Goes Ahead, Curley's accounts, White Cow Bull and other Sioux and Cheyenne testimony, nor Martin's implied references.

> There were even some reports of bodies being recovered at the ford. A corporal named Ryan said that several lay strewn in the general area. Another witness saw some dead soldiers in the water, a fact that might account for several bodies which were never located. Years later a Sioux told Gibbon scout Thomas LaForge that Minton (Mitch) Bouyer, Custer's mixed blood Crow interpreter, had died near the stream. The Indians took Bouyer's calfskin vest and threw the body into the water. . . . On balance, it seems certain that Custer's soldiers battled warriors at the river's edge, various accounts to the contrary notwithstanding.
> At the same time, related action occurred on the high ridge one mile east of the ford. In the 1920's, a local rancher, Joseph A. Blummer, picked up . . . Subsequently, R. G. Cartwright, a school teacher from Lead, South Dakota and Army Lieutenant Colonel Elwood L. Nye found the following items in the same area . . .
> Additional 45/70 cartridge shells were found along

Nye Cartwright Ridge in 1968, 1969, and 1971, until the total numbered well over two hundred casings. Former battlefield superintendent Edward S. Luce discovered still more on a ridge running at right angles to Nye Cartwright and forming the north rim of Medicine Tail Coulee.

Obviously, at least part of Custer's command passed over Nye-Cartwright Ridge. Companies I and L, lagging behind in reserve, evidently became separated from C, E, and F, as they engaged the Indians at the ford. Seemingly, the warriors who struck Custer's left flank drove I and L a short distance back up Medicine Tail Coulee. Then, in a dash to rejoin the command, the two companies rode left, out of the draw, and moved up to the present Nye Cartwright Ridge. Along the top they dismounted. Some fired back at warriors behind in Medicine Tail Coulee, while those on the Nye Cartwright slope fired at least three volleys to distract the Indians menacing Custer's skirmishers, who now retreated diagonally north from the ford. . . . A few expended cases from Indian weapons have been found scattered at a point about 600 yards southwest from, and below, . . . They suggest a certain amount of sniping activity directed against the passing column.

Supporting this belief, Blummer and another local resident, Frank Bethune, found the skeletons of four fully equipped cavalry horses on a route extending from the present battlefield fence to Deep Coulee, about four hundred yards south. . . . The respective position of the two battalions, . . . at the river and the other composed . . . on the ridge, present a plausible answer to the mysterious end of First Sergeant Butler of Company L. Butler's body was found on a direct line between the commands, denoting his possible route as a liaison between the battalions. . . . this assessment of the concurrent actions at Nye–Cartwright and Medicine Tail Ford is in substantial agreement with that of Don Rickey, Jr., a former historian at Custer Battlefield Monument.[13]

I believe Greene, and those mentioned in his text, are correct. The account is supported by existing artifacts, testimony and logic. Though I am not exactly sure where the 7th Cavalry horses were found, it appears likely they were in the location Gall referred to.

The suddenness of the relic discoveries on Nye Cartwright Ridge caused an instant distraction away from the proponents of the ford theory and created a catalyzing effect on subsequent consideration about Custer's movements. Nobody thought much about two concurrent actions, despite the fact that Lieutenant Edgerly's narratives, from the beginning, strongly intimated that very probability. The initial Nye-Cartwright finds occurred years later, leading a few early students of the episode to conclude that the entire Custer command passed over the ridge and that it never approached the river. Indeed, there exists substantive testimony for this view. The Hunkpapa war chief, Gall, interviewed at the tenth anniversary of the battle, somewhat supported the conjecture that Custer's soldiers never came within one-half to three-quarters of a mile of the ford. . . . He probably arrived late and saw only Companies I and L as they moved over Nye Cartwright Ridge . . .[14]

Gall could not have participated in the attack on Reno, done the various things he reported doing, and then have seen the action that took place at the ford. I don't think there is any question that Greene's explanation of what happened is correct, as so many pieces of the puzzle fall into place. Testimony, timing, logic and artifacts come together in a way no other scenario can claim.

Unsolicited support for Godfrey's theory came from the Crow scout Curly, shortly before his death in 1923. In a radical departure from his earlier statements of Custer reaching the Little Bighorn, Curly told Russell White Bear that the Colonel ordered just the gray horse company to the ford while he and others "continued going northward – his trail was about 1 1/2 miles from the river."[15]

Greene makes the point, I have brought out a number of times in examining testimony by Curley: as views changed, so did Curley's story. Although I have no way to assess the integrity of Russell White Bear, he is an example of an interpreter giving an account without any corroboration, and although this, in itself, certainly does not make it false, it should raise question marks for the historian.

The extreme extension of Godfrey's idea, Charles Kuhlman's *Legend into History,* appeared in 1951. . . . Other then the shell finds on Nye Cartwright ridge, Kuhlman offered no physical evidence to support his contentions. He necessarily relied on Indians' testimony favoring his ideas, although his means of employing verbal evidence betrayed faulty historical method. For, example, Kuhlman ignored Curley's earliest statements about fighting at the river, but accepted Russell White Bear's account of Curley's Godfrey orientated story . . .

There are practical objections to Kuhlman's hypothesis, to be sure, as noted by the late Edgar I. Stewart:

First, the country back from the river is badly cut up and not at all suitable for cavalry . . . Secondly, to ride away from a fight was not in keeping with the Custer character or disposition. It is almost inconceivable that he, believing as he did, that attack and victory were practically synonymous terms, would execute such a maneuver. Furthermore, he was seeking a ford by which he could cross the river and attack the Indian village, and this was the first opportunity that presented itself.

Perhaps the Custer personality best dispels Kuhlman's argument. As Second Lieutenant Charles A.. Varnum stated: "Anyone who knew George A. Custer would find it hard to believe that he could keep still for five minutes under the circumstances.[16]

I strongly agree with Greene and his method of substantiating his judgements, particularly as it pertains to Custer's personality. His discussion, however, does raise a question: Why does Greene maintain that after losing a few men, Custer did not continue his crossing of the ford to attack the village? The fact that shell casings and other artifacts were found at the location supports the idea that Custer went to the ford, but it does not contradict the view that no major attack took place at the crossing. There is no testimony, either, to indicate that Custer faced a large number of Indians there. Custer had to realize that if there was any hope of defeating the Indians, it had to happen then. He could not wait for the arrival of the packs, or Benteen. Custer would not have been stopped by the loss of only a few men.

The basic question remains: If the troops indeed reached the ford, why was there no sign of a major attack? I maintain that there is only one answer to the question: Custer had to be one of those shot at the ford. This was the only event which could have prevented the attack. A similar situation has happened in many other cases in military history: after a leader had fallen, his troops met with a defeat. By the time Custer's body was recovered, dead or severely wounded, and placed on a horse, the sight and actions of the Indians caused a retreat . Under such conditions, and with our knowledge of Reno's similar situation, it is unrealistic to assume that Custer's troops did not also panic and enter into a disorganized retreat, particularly when there is testimony to support the fact that it did take place.

> Thus the debate has continued. Certainly, the relic finds on Nye Cartwright Ridge provide important clues of the progress of Custer's battle. If anything, similar discoveries at the mouth of Medicine Tail Coulee, taken with corroborative participant experiences, point up the existence of a disconcerted effort by two very surprised and separate battalions to deal effectively with an overwhelming and fiercely determined foe. . . .
>
> No wild dash took place among the troopers. They managed an orderly, somewhat hesitant retreat, for Custer must now have been apprehensive about the state of Companies I and L. In this respect, Hump, a Dakota, remarked that the men were "confused and they retreated slowly . . ." Horned Horse said that the soldiers were afoot "firing whenever they could over the backs of their horses . . .[17]

Again, I believe Greene becomes inconsistent. He claims that Custer was apprehensive about Keogh's battalion, when I think it would be the reverse. Yates' battalion was the one under fire and retreating. Keogh's battalion could have moved back on the trail they came over and joined the rest of the command without difficulty. This could also have been accomplished by Yates' battalion if they had been retreating from the ford in the orderly fashion expressed by Greene.

A few other examples can help clarify the discussion: Godfrey's company held back the Indians on the retreat from Weir Point. The Indians retreated into Deep Ravine when a few troops attempted to escape from Battleridge. Wooden Leg indicated that the initial reaction of the Indians was to give way when Major Reno's troops left the timber. In these cases the Indians were superior in number compared to the troops – yet they gave way. Wouldn't they have done the same when faced with an organized withdrawal by Yates' battalion?

Testimony doesn't indicate a large number of Indians in Medicine Tail Coulee at the time when both Greene and I assume the retreat would have been initiated. Can one possibly accept scenarios of an organized retreat moving to the north rather than back to a place where Custer knew most of the rest of his command would be, and where he could expect they would be moving to meet him? The question then becomes; why such a move wasn't accomplished? The only plausible explanation is the possibility of a disorganized retreat. This doesn't mean that some groups would not have attempted to form and prevent a rout, and would have been partially successful, particularly those surrounding Custer, including the company commanders of Yates' battalion. The evidence, supported by artifacts and testimony, suggests attempts to hold back the Indians by dismounted troopers, mainly of C Company, as Yates' "main element" retreated across the western part of Calhoun Ridge and Greasy Grass Knoll. Keogh's battalion could have rejoined Reno, Benteen and the rest of the command, but their duty was with Custer. Both the artifacts found on Nye–Cartwright Ridge and some testimony support their attempt at such a move, which was meant to both protect and join the retreating Yates' battalion, with the hope of setting up a unified defense.

Metal detectors have exposed evidence indicating the

route of the retreat. In the area around Deep Coulee there were unearthed . . .

As the troopers retreated north, Sioux and Cheyenne warriors occupied Deep Coulee and the surrounding ground. Detector research revealed many Indian shells scattered along Deep Coulee for half a mile.

Those items demonstrated that warriors occupied the west end of a small ridge, shot at the soldiers retreating past them, then shifted around to the south side continuing their fire . . .

In this area, the Indians successfully stampeded some of the cavalry animals. Bob Tail Horse, a Cheyenne, told of gray horses breaking away from their holders. . . . Low Dog, a prominent Oglala, said that the troopers "held their horses reins on one arm while they were shooting, but their horses were so frightened that they pulled the men all around, and a great many of their shots went up in the air and did us no harm." Accounts by Flying Hawk, Feather Earring, and Sitting Bull uphold this contention.[18]

One would have to assume that soldiers would let their horses go under such conditions, because an excited horse is not easy to control. I also think that most of the companies would have been dismounted and the horses in control of horse-holders, if an organized retreat was taking place, similar to Godfrey's action with K Company in the retreat from Weir Point. This testimony gives supportive evidence to the hypothesis of a disorganized retreat.

Not all of the Indians followed Custer up the rise. Some rode with Crazy Horse downstream, planning to cross the river, to strike the soldiers from the north, and to stop the retreat. . . . of immediate concern to Custer, however, was a broad deep ravine . . . Through which many warriors converged on the troops. Hundreds of Sioux and Cheyenne moved into this gulch . . .

On gaining the battle ridge, the soldiers deployed as skirmishers. Thus engaged, they quickly became targets for hostile sharpshooters hidden in . . . Only daredevil braves, . . . rode close to the skirmishers . . .

Constant pressure by the hostiles forced Custer to drift towards the northwest end of the ridge. Companies C and F now rode down the hillside, hopeful they could establish lines to check those Indians approaching up the great ravine from the river. Company E, many of its horses gone, remained on the hill with Custer. Kate Bighead referred to C and F in her account . . .

Companies I and L, meantime, tried to rejoin Custer. As they continued up the southeastern rise towards his position, the troopers engaged the Indians occupying Deep Coulee who successfully stampeded their animals . . . W. Vaughn, moreover, found many Indian shells at a point southwest of this particular location, now called Calhoun Hill.[19]

I don't believe there is any evidence to sustain the contention that the troopers deployed in skirmish fashion on Battleridge; in fact, practically all of Major Reno's officers and men believed they hadn't. The only skirmish lines generally thought to have existed were on Calhoun Hill and Last Stand Hill, not along the ridge. Indian testimony does not convey the impression that the troops Greene refers to as Companies C and F were trying to establish skirmish lines. Any movement of soldiers from the ridge were attempts to escape. Kate Bighead and other witnesses who referred to a number of troopers leaving the ridge are speaking of only one group, not two. They appear to have been mainly E Company troopers, and their bodies were found either in Deep Ravine or just outside of it. I have not been able to determine where Kate Bighead indicated that the soldiers were F and C Company troops, and I would certainly question her ability to make such a determination. According to her account, they were all killed or committed suicide on a ridge overlooking Deep Ravine.

"One Company [L?] that had lost its horses was near where the road goes now, and the men, all on foot, were trying to work their way toward the gray-horse company on the hill [near the present monument?] half a mile from them. About half the men were without guns. They fought with six shooters,". . .[20]

. . . Crazy Horse and his followers . . . unleashed a furious assault from the north and east.

. . . difficulty with their own carbines . . . this trouble might account for certain Cheyenne stories that the men appeared "panic-stricken" while some informants claimed that the soldiers, all drunk shot each other. Such reports were perhaps rationalizations by people fearing retribution for John Stands In Timber said that Wooden Leg later retracted statements describing drunkenness and mass suicide among the soldiers.[21]

We often criticize others for adopting certain statements which support their theory, even when they are questionable, such as Kate Bighead's account concerning F and C troops leaving the ridge, and then rejecting others which at times are more reliable in essence. I think Greene should have excluded Dr. Kuhlman's rationalizing, and questioned John Stands in Timber's statement referring to Wooden Leg's change of heart. What needs to be challenged is not whether John Stands In Timber made the allegation, but within what framework it was made, and what Wooden Leg actually said.

ANALYSIS OF WRITERS' SCENARIOS

Although I have covered this point before, I believe the subject is important enough to warrant its reiteration.

First, the question of Kuhlman's rationalization. In accepting Kuhlman's view that the Indians who said the troops shot each other feared retribution, Greene, like Kuhlman before, has reversed the situation. Wooden Leg, Kate Bighead and others at first feared retribution, for it was clear to them what the white man felt about such claims. Only after a number of years did some Indians feel free to tell the truth to a friend, Dr. Marquis. Even today it is often taboo to admit someone committed suicide. Admitting it must have been even more difficult then, especially in regard to the troops under General Custer. Everyone preferred to think that those men went down fighting with their guns blazing.

John Stands In Timber said:

> I went with two army men to see him (Wooden Leg) one time. They wanted to find out about it. (suicide) I interpreted. They took him some tobacco and cash and other things, and we asked him if it were true that the Indians said the soldiers did that. He laughed and said there was just too many Indians. The soldier did their best. He said if they had been drunk they would not have killed as many as they did. But it was in the book.

A few details require comment here. First of all, John Stands In Timber was with two army men, which, considering the subject, would be intimidating. Secondly, it certainly seems they were attempting to bribe Wooden Leg and imply that if he retracted what he said, everything would be okay. Whether that was their express intent or not, it's quite understandable that Wooden Leg would have taken it that way. Third, Wooden Leg did not deny that the troops committed suicide. He merely said that there were too many Indians, which was true, and the soldiers did their best, which they undoubtedly did. But this bravery wouldn't keep them from committing suicide. He probably realized that the troopers were not drunk, and this is the only comment Wooden Leg actually retracted.

> ... On Custer's hill, disorganization constituted a major problem... Because narratives agree that Company E was there, for Two Moon noted that "those who were on the hill where the monument now stands... had gray horses and they were all in the open."[23]

I would question what Two Moon said, but there isn't any doubt that members of E Company were on the ridge. What I gather from Indian testimony is that the Gray Horse Troop did stand out. One can see their prominence in the testimony of Benteen, Godfrey and Varnum, as well as that of Indians.

Since the Gray Horse Troop was near the ford and Indians remember seeing them, it's easy to see why those who didn't believe Custer went near the ford claim that the Gray Horse Company was sent in that direction. It was only natural that the Indians recalled seeing gray horses when attacking those on Battleridge. Since they were supposedly the last company in Yates' battalion, as they moved to the ford, they were apt to have remained mounted and so retained their horses for a longer period of time than the other two companies. If my evaluation is correct, they would then be the ones who attempted to retreat back the way they came and join Keogh's battalion. Their actions would account for Indian sighting as well as the troops location along Battleridge.

> Evidence relating to the fate of Company E appeared in testimony describing the unit's complete destruction towards the end of the battle. As Iron Hawk recalled, "We saw soldiers start running down hill right toward us. Nearly all of them were afoot, and I think they were so scared that they didn't know what they were doing."[24]

It is unrealistic to accept this statement and then assume that when the troops were forced to stop, some of them would not have committed suicide.

Again, I question whether there were two groups of soldiers, making up close to thirty or forty men, that moved down from the ridge: the one, supposedly mounted, and leaving shortly after the troops reached the ridge, and the other which left on foot toward the end of the battle. The first is usually considered by writers to be soldiers engaged in an offensive move, and the second as troops attempting to escape. Greene supports this interpretation. He also accepts the view that the battle on the ridge was brief. I believe his reasoning shows several weaknesses: Like many other accounts, Kate Bighead's testimony, when analyzed, only indicates one movement involving a large number of troops – namely an escape attempt. I associate body locations of C and F Troops below Battleridge with their retreat to the ridge. It would be somewhat of a miracle if their company commanders led a charge and were still able to return to Last Stand Hill; yet if a charge was made at that time, it should have been led by the company commanders.

Those attempting to escape at the end undoubtedly did not have horses to mount, or very few. The number of E Company soldiers found in or close to Deep Ravine would suggest they were Company E troopers. This assumption poses another problem: Where were the bodies of the 40 men that moved off the ridge earlier? Reno's troops who testified on the subject seem to believe that there were 28 soldiers primarily from E Company in or around the Deep Ravine, and only about 12 others between there and the ridge.

This is my analysis of what happened: I agree with Greene that the fighting on the ridge did not last long after the troops reached it. If there was anywhere near the number of Indians, as most testimony suggests, it was certainly apparent to Custer's troops, and they would have realized the hopelessness of their situation. Any of Yates' troops that were still mounted would have been intertwined, but the Gray Horse Troop was more likely to be still intact. Some of those members seeing the river and the trees may have thought that their only chance to escape was to reach them, and would have made the attempt only to be thwarted by the Indians and the ravine itself. As Iron Hawk said, the troops were in a state of panic at the time. Those on horseback dismounted and, as Kate Bighead and Wooden Leg reported, most of them committed suicide. I don't think any of them returned to the hill. Then, a short time later, at the end of the battle, some seven to twelve men attempted to escape on foot. With the dust, confusion, and little effort to recall these specific details for several years after the battle, the differences in Indian testimony arose. This is where writers should apply the statements they have made referring to why Indian testimony needs to be scrutinized.

The suicide scenario is speculation, but one must recognize and understand why Indians would not have reported that soldiers committed suicide. We should also realize that the soldiers burying the bodies afterward would not have placed the stigma of suicide on their former comrades, although they may have suspected that the wounds and evidence showed that many took their own lives. The problems Marquis experienced when he tried to publish his book, *Keep the Last Bullet for Yourself,* which presents the testimony suggesting suicide, is evidence enough.

> As the gray horse company was being wiped out, the troopers remaining on Custer's hill faced dangerous odds, too. The warriors edged closer . . . Near the end, several soldiers broke from the hilltop and ran down a draw towards the river. They were abruptly cut down by the hostiles.
> . . . Within two hours of his march down Medicine Tail Coulee more then 220 soldiers lay dead or dying on the field. . . . Most Indian accounts were virtually non-existent for at least another year.[25]

Green added a postscript to his book in which he incorporated and discussed the 1985 archaeological findings.

Greene's book comes the closest to portraying the events as I think they happened. However, I don't believe his thesis offers logical answers to my three basic questions. Still, I would consider it required reading for any student or person concerned with determining for themselves what happened to General Custer.

SOURCES

1. Greene, Jerome, A. *Evidence and the Custer Enigma,* Golden, CO.: Outbooks, Inc. 1973, p. 10.
2. Ibid., pp. 11–13.
3. Ibid., p. 13.
4. Ibid., pp. 15, 16.
5. *Report of the Secretary of War,* 44th Congress, Vol. l, 1876, 1877. Page 32 ". . . at 9:25 P. M. [24th] Custer called the officers together and informed us that, beyond a doubt, the village was in the valley of the Little Big Horn."
6. Greene, *Evidence and the Custer Enigma,* pp. 16, 17.
7. Ibid. pp. 17, 18.
8. Ibid., p. 20.
9. Ibid., p. 21.
10. Ibid., pp. 21, 22.
11. Ibid., pp. 24, 25.
12. Ibid., pp. 25, 26.
13. Ibid., pp. 26, 27, 28.
14. Ibid. p. 29.
15. Ibid., p. 30.
16. Ibid., pp. 30, 31.
17. Ibid., pp. 32, 33.
18. Ibid., pp. 33, 34.
19. Ibid., pp. 35, 36, 37.
20. Ibid., pp. 37–39.
21. Ibid., pp. 39, 40.
22. Stands In Timber, *Cheyenne Memories,* p. 4.
23. Op, Cit., p. 41.
24. Ibid., p. 42.
25. Ibid., p. 42.

Markers, Artifacts and Indian Testimony
by Richard G. Hardorff

Any attempt to reconstruct the Custer battle should naturally begin with the route followed by his troops. We know that his command traveled over the site now known as Reno's entrenchments because it was observed by members of Major Marcus A. Reno's battalion. Lt. Charles A. Varnum later testified that he had seen the Gray Horse Troop moving along the bluffs, which meant that E troop was on the left flank of Custer's moving column. This is corroborated by Sergeant Daniel A. Kanipe who recalled that Custer's command advanced with the five troops abreast, each troop in column of twos, its formation from left to right being E, F, L, I, and C.[1]

I have dealt with this subject in analyzing Kanipe's testimony – the only testimony I have read that describes the troops in a line formation after separating from Reno. I oppose Hardorff's conclusions on several matters. The fact that Varnum saw E Company doesn't mean that it was on the left flank of a line formation, since they could have been seen while in a column formation. Choosing Kanipe's account over those of Martin and Curley also requires justification. It is possible that the troops could have been five companies abreast as they moved toward the bluffs after watering their horses, but I question if they would have continued in such a formation as they traveled along the bluffs. Other writers, such as Graham, have said that the command was last seen in a column of twos with the Gray Horse Troop in the center. This, and the fact that a C Company sergeant, Kanipe, was Custer's first messenger, led to the assumption that this company, under the General's brother Tom, was the first in the column, followed by F, E, I and L. Though it is possible that they were in a line formation, Hardorff is making something very questionable sound like a certainty, opening himself up for criticism.

Half a mile north of Reno's entrenchments, Custer halted his command while he went to a hillock to reconnoiter. He was seen at this point by Lt. Charles DeRudio from the valley below.

Trumpeter John Martin and the Crow scouts corroborated the location of Custer's observation point.

...This reconnaissance took place a few minutes after 3 P.M., and coincided with Major Reno's deployment in the valley...

After watching the deployment of Major Reno's battalion, Custer descended into Cedar Coulee which curves in a northerly direction for one half mile, its location being east of the line of bluffs which terminate at Weir Point. Since the head of Cedar Coulee did not permit abreast descent, troops formation was changed.... The Crow scouts, however, remained on the bluffs near the river and went at least as far as Weir Point, although Custer himself never ascended this vantage point.[2]

Hardorff points out that any attempt to reconstruct the Custer battle should naturally begin with the route followed by his troops; in this I agree with him. However, that reconstruction should include a fairly accurate determination of the time relation between events. Hardorff mentions Reno's troops seeing Custer near the place where Reno entrenched. That event took place either as they reassembled after crossing the ford or, as some troopers claimed, when they were part way down the valley where they established their skirmish line; or more than likely, at both times. Lieutenant DeRudio said he saw Custer during Reno's fight in the valley some six minutes before they left the timber. Hardorff seems to assume that Reno was on his skirmish line and in the timber for at least 30 minutes. To that time we can add another 5 to 10 minutes, since Reno's troops saw Custer while regrouping, and later while moving down the valley. One should also consider Martin's inference that Custer reached the ridge several minutes before Reno started his regrouping. Given these considerations, Custer would have been on the ridge for at least 34 minutes: 10-15 minutes, for the time when Reno's troops sighted him during their move down the valley; 30 minutes on the skirmish line and in the timber; minus the 6 minutes before Reno left the timber, at which time DeRudio said he saw Custer. Custer would have, by all accounts, come down and talked to his men and the other officers who had not been with him (according to Martin, this would have included Adjutant Cooke, who DeRudio claimed to have been on the point with Custer). We should then add another 5 minutes. What we have then is Custer staying on the ridge for some 39 minutes, during which time he could have moved to Last Stand Hill and back again. Remember that General Miles said that he was able to ride at a controlled hand gallop from Reno Hill to Last Stand Hill in 10 to 15 minutes. This also means that Custer would have had plenty of time to move down any coulee and attack the Indian camps at Ford B while Reno was still in the timber. In fact, he could have reached the bluffs when Reno was skirmishing and still have done so. We should factor in to such an examination the realization (which can certainly be attributed to Custer) that, for a flanking movement to be successful, the attack should be synchronized with other elements of the attacking force as closely as possible. The testimony of the three trailing Rees must also be considered, for they should have caught Custer while he was still on the ridge, instead of seeing the other Ree scouts out ahead of Reno's troops as they moved down the valley. Even if there was not testimony to the contrary, the probability of Custer remaining on the ridge for nearly thirty minutes would be nearly nonexistent.

In examining statements, we should keep in mind that Martin and the Indians would not have considered that the bluffs terminated at Weir Point.

> Trumpeter John Martin later recalled that Custer's command had traveled in the shadow of towering bluffs, and that half way down Cedar Coulee he was dispatched with a message for Captain Frederick W. Benteen. Martin, retracing his steps and reaching the bluffs at the head of Cedar Coulee, gained his last glimpse of Custer's column, which seemed to have fallen back from the river and was just then ascending the rise of land north of Cedar Coulee's mouth.
>
> It seems unlikely that Trumpeter Martin had seen Custer's command at the river, due to time limitations. Moreover, the line of bluffs, west of Cedar Coulee prevented any such observation from Martin's location. Therefore, Martin probably reported what he thought he had seen rather than what he actually saw, which is a subconscious distortion quite common to the human mind. We may conclude therefore, Custer had followed Cedar Coulee to its junction with Medicine Tail Coulee and crossed the dry stream bead in order to gain the vantage ground to the north.[3]

Hardorff's estimate of Cedar Coulee's length would make little difference if Martin was given his message half way down the coulee and then met Boston Custer half way back to the ridge.[4] The rear of Custer's column should have been in sight, and Boston Custer would not have needed to ask any questions as to where the command was, or whether Custer had been attacked. Even if we say that the last company could have made the left hand turn down Medicine Tail Coulee and been out of sight, it certainly wouldn't have happened by the time Boston Custer started down Cedar Coulee. Since Hardorff doesn't have Custer making this left hand turn, it should have been even more apparent to Boston Custer where the General was.

> ... From the foregoing letter, we also learn that Camp doubted Custer would have seen Major Reno's valley fight. However, the next year, Camp was told the same by Hairy Moccasin, the validity of this statement being substantiated by Lt. C. A. Varnum and others who saw Custer's column advancing along the bluffs. Unfortunately, Walter Camp passed away in 1925, at a time when the relics on the heights north of Medicine Tail Coulee were as yet to be discovered. Had he known about these finds, Camp's opinion of Curley, and conclusions of the action in Medicine Tail Coulee, might well have been different.[5]

As I have stated, in examining the Crow's testimony, Hairy Moccasin's statements are not particularly conclusive. Curley is more consistent in his assertions that Custer did not see Reno become engaged. Furthermore, there are statements made by Martin which Hardorff ignores. The artifactual evidence, though important in obtaining an accurate view of what took place, has to be balanced against other possibilities.

> The statements of the three Crows are nearly uniform in that they saw Major Reno's retreat from the timber, below, which in turn motivated their own hasty departure, but not until after firing several rounds into the tepees from the bluffs above.... Thus, the three Crows could have seen the opening stages of Custer's deployment in Medicine Tail Coulee, the observation of which synchronized with the time and scope of Trumpeter Martin's observations. Moreover, from the statement of independent sources we can trace the whereabouts of the three Crows which is more then can be said of Curley.[6]

I don't believe that the three Crows saw Reno's retreat from the timber and that this motivated their withdrawal. Their withdrawal was precipitated by what happened to Custer, not Reno.

White Man Runs Him, in his General Scott interview, gave several different accounts of their witnessing Major Reno's retreat.[7] As I have explained elsewhere, many of White Man Runs Him's answers were given in an attempt to justify the actions of the three Crows, particularly pertaining to Custer seeing Reno's predicament, and they reflected the Crows' resentment toward Curley. The scouts may have seen Reno's retreat during their own fall back, although this is questionable. White Man Runs Him's answer to the specific question asked by General Scott whether or not he saw Reno retreat was that he saw him fighting in the valley but didn't know he had retreated back to the bluffs. Yet the scouts would have left Bouyer's Bluff by that period, which would mean that from a time and viewing standpoint, the scouts retreated back from the ridge or had already gone past Reno Hill.

Hardorff uses the three Crows' testimony about firing from the bluff above the ford, but ignores their accounts of seeing Custer there. Hardorff states that the scouts may have seen Custer's opening development in Medicine Tail

ANALYSIS OF WRITERS' SCENARIOS

Coulee, but he fails to explain why he thinks their statements about Custer reaching the ford are incorrect.

Hardorff's reasoning is refuted by what I consider to be the most important "event-time-event" consideration. A careful analysis negates the time schedule which Hardorff uses to support his hypothesis. Hardorff believes that the Crows fired from the bluff, and then left upon seeing Reno retreat. If that is what happened, they must have gone back some three miles along the bluffs, now occupied by warriors pursuing Reno, moved to where they met Captain Benteen, then turned back and went with Benteen to Reno Hill, and arrived shortly after Reno. This would have been impossible.

Hardorff's scenario contradicts other testimony and raises questions of timing. From the perspective of common sense, it is hard to believe that the three Crows, with Custer's troops nearly two miles away, would have fired on the village with the Indians so close and in large numbers.

My main criticism of Hardorff is that he presents certain conjectural statements as if they were facts.

> The reasons for Custer's ascent to the heights north of Medicine Tail Coulee becomes clear from the following. From the location where Custer entered Medicine Tail Coulee, only a limited view can be obtained of the flats west of the Little Bighorn. The view to the southwest was obstructed by high bluffs which terminated in a cutbank near the river, while the river itself could not be seen. The view to the right was similarly blocked and anyone who takes time to visit Medicine Tail Coulee will affirm the "tunnel" vision which confronted General Custer. The distance to the Little Bighorn from the point where Custer's command entered Medicine Tail Coulee is about one and a half miles. Since this later deep, winding stream bed was strategically disadvantageous, it became imperative to gain a better view of the lay of the land and the Indian encampment before committing his troops to any technical engagement. For this reason, Custer ascended the rise of the land and halted on the elevation now known as Luce Ridge.
>
> The view from this position was not at all reassuring to Custer. The Indian encampment seemed to have stretched past the mouth of Medicine Tail Coulee and farther to the north than was anticipated. Clusters of tepees were also seen on the flats well beyond to the west, giving credibility to the scouts reports of an enormous Indian village. . . . their numerous dust clouds giving the impression that a formidable force was approaching Custer's front . . .
>
> The observations from Luce Ridge seemed to have altered Custer's strategy; instead of charging ahead, he decided on a posture of waiting. How long he remained here is not certain, but inferential evidence suggests that he might have occupied the heights for at least a half an hour. Trumpeter Martin stated that on his way to Captain Benteen he saw Major Reno's skirmish line fall back to the timber, the movement concurring with Custer's reaching Luce Ridge about 3:30 P.M. We also know from Lt. Edward S. Godfrey that at about 4:20 volley firing was heard, its refuse being found half a century later.[8]

Hardorff should remember what Martin said about coming in sight of the village, for as Hardorff himself states, one has to be a comparatively short distance from the river in order to see the village.

Hardorff's reasoning, which he shares with several other writers, is interesting. He claims that Custer moved his troops down Cedar Coulee away from the river and the village, and reached Medicine Tail Coulee. Then Custer realized he couldn't see the village and the river. It became imperative to gain a view of the lay of the land before he committed his troops. He then moved up the north embankment of Luce Ridge. Yet, when he realized that his view of the village, and the terrain beyond Weir Point less than a half mile ahead, was blocked, was he concerned enough to move to this high point? No. Instead Custer charged down Cedar Coulee in a direction away from the village, not knowing where it would lead. According to Hardorff, Custer had seen Reno form his skirmish line which, one might think, would mean that he wanted to reach the village as quickly as possible. Not so. In Hardorff's scenario Custer sees no reason to hurry, presumably because he knows Reno can and will hold out indefinitely.

Since there is evidence suggesting that Custer went to Weir Point, Hardorff should explain why he believes Custer didn't do so. Hardorff uses the Crows' testimony when it supports his own view, but when the Crows indicate that Custer went to the ford, he ignores their statements. I don't think the Crows ever indicated they camped out on the bluffs until Custer decided to move. One should not suggest a theory unless contradictory accounts can be satisfactorily dealt with. While Custer was supposedly sitting around, he would have heard the firing taking place where he knew Reno was, and, no matter what the size of the village, he should have known that if he wanted to succeed that was the time to attack. If the risk was too great, Custer should have moved to link up with the packs and hopefully Benteen. This, we should keep in mind, is Custer, not Reno; this is the courageous attack-minded leader, one who would not want Benteen or Reno to get credit if the Indians were defeated and whose main fear was that the Indians might scatter.

In Hardorff's next paragraph we find out that the command entered Medicine Tail Coulee at a point about one and a half miles from the ford. This could be a good guess, but to Hardorff this is a known fact, which I don't believe it is, nor does Hardorff prove or even attempt to prove it as such. I think it's more likely that Custer entered Medicine Tail Coulee a mile or less from the ford. Martin indicated to Camp that when he was with Custer they were closer to the ford than most writers suggest, and that when he showed Benteen where he turned back, Benteen said it was only 600 yards from the ford. This estimate not only supports my judgement but also fits into a logical timing sequence. Hardorff, in support of his view, turns to Camp and, like him, ignores Martin's account. Camp uses Curley's supposed statement from Bouyer to confirm his idea, which Hardorff appears to approve. Interestingly, he disclaims most of Curley's other accounts. Why he accepts this particular one, he doesn't say.

According to Hardorff, Custer saw that the encampment was of greater size than he had realized, and extended to the north and west farther than he had thought. Here is another instance where a writer disregards, without explanation, some Indian remarks and the opinions of established writers such as Dr. Marquis and Dr. Kuhlman, who claim that the Cheyenne village was on the north end, and on the 25th was located just north of the ford.

As Lieutenant Varnum said, to imagine Custer sitting around for five minutes is incredulous; but Hardorff has him do so on Luce Ridge for half an hour – and this on top of the half hour on the bluffs above the valley. Apparently, the firing around Reno must not have bothered Custer. At that time the village, by all Indian testimony, was in an uproar: tepees were being taken down and the non-combatants were moving out of the village, but Custer was not concerned that the Indians might scatter. Custer had promised to support Reno and, of course, he planned to eventually, so that justified his inaction at that time. Most writers have condemned Major Reno and Captain Benteen for not rushing to the sound of gunfire in an attempt to aid Custer, but the two officers at least had a somewhat tenable excuse given their need to wait for the packs and prepare the wounded before they could move. Still, according to Hardorff, Custer was justified in his inaction: things didn't look too good down by the river, the village was larger than he had thought, and there was a large dust cloud. One might think that if Custer was so concerned, he might have gone back to meet Benteen. Not so: that would be retreating and Custer didn't do that.

To some extent, Custer's position on Luce Ridge dominated the surrounding area. His troops were deployed in skirmish order along the crest, the location of which controlled Cedar Coulee, Medicine Tail Coulee and the sloping front to the west. However, his firing range did not include the river itself, which was one and a half miles away . . .

Control of the river at Medicine Tail Coulee was imperative to Custer's strategy, it being one of the fording places not only for his own command, but also for the Indians who would eventually confront him. Therefore, a troop movement toward the river would serve a dual purpose: it would control the river while securing an open front over which his troops could maneuver, and this show of military force might inhibit Indian aggression allowing Custer time to wait for Captain Benteen's arrival.

We know from Indian testimony that a troop movement toward the river did occur, but which troops is in question. It is certain that Custer by now had divided his command into battalions. This division might have occurred on Reno Creek, because Sergeant Daniel Kanipe spoke of Captain Myles Keogh commanding three troops, among them C Troop, while Captain George Yates thus commanded only two troops. This troop assignment is supported by formation in which Custer's command traveled over Reno's entrenchment position, consisting of the right battalion with I Troop flanked by L and C, while the left battalion consisted of E and F, F being on the inner flank, Captain Myles Moylan also referred to Custer's battalion division, with Captain Keogh's commanding three troops and Captain Yates two. Since Captain Keogh's commission antedated that of Yates,' it would naturally follow that Captain Keogh would have command of the odd troop.[9]*

Although I believe a division was made, it's debatable whether it took place in the way described by Hardorff. I wonder why Martin didn't note it and why writers such as Graham and Greene suggest a division with the three companies under Yates. Since I believe Custer did move to the ford in order to complete his plan of attacking the Indians, I assume that he moved with three companies and held two in reserve. Because I also believe that Custer led the attack, I would use inverse reasoning. Custer placed the commander with the lesser qualifications in charge of the three companies because he himself would actually be there in the lead, whereas the two companies that

---

*Even though the initial division (if at Reno Creek) may have given Captain Keogh 3 companies, due to the reasoning presented by Hardorff, this could easily have changed as the command moved down Medicine Tail Coulee. The defile, the messages to Benteen and the packs, could have caused Custer to have reversed his order for the reason I presented.

ANALYSIS OF WRITERS' SCENARIOS

would be operating on their own would be led by the ranking officer. I also think that when Varnum saw E Company on the ridge, they were in the process of leaving and were moving out in companies and in a column of fours, with E Company in the middle as Martin indicated. This would mean that F and C Companies were ahead, in the middle was E, followed by I Company and then L in the rear. I think the position of the companies when found on Battleridge, along with the three company commanders that were with Custer on Last Stand Hill, support this reasoning.

> The Cheyenne statements to anthropologist George Grinnell, shortly after 1900, suggest that two troops of Custer's command had descended Medicine Tail Coulee and advanced as far as the flat near its mouth. One of the troops seen here was mounted on Gray Horses, which, therefore, confirms that the battalion of Captain Yates, consisted of E and F Troops. Curley, too, claimed to have seen E Troop near the river, and since the Cheyennes corroborated this statement, we may accept it as true.[10]

I would challenge any Indian statement regarding the units and the number of the troops. Even if they were aware of what was meant by "companies," which I doubt, I don't think that with the shooting, dust, and confusion they would have paid any attention. They might note the gray horses, but that would be all I would credit them with. One should also realize that most Indians would not have seen the troops that moved to the ford. The Curley testimony which Hardorff uses suggests that one company not two—Company E—moved toward the ford. I assume that Yates' battalion consisted of E and F Companies, but I would not exclude C Company on the evidence Hardorff presents. If E Company was the lead company, or the only one sent to the ford, they should have been the first riderless horses, not the last.

> Since some Indian accounts refute Captain Yates' position near the river, we may infer that either Captain Yates spent very little time at this location, or the Indian observations were made after Captain Yates had withdrawn . . . because the early Cheyenne accounts speak of a lengthy skirmish near the river . . . This is within the realm of possibility because a detachment of Captain Yates' troops would have searched for a ford by which Custer's entire command could later cross.
>
> The initial force opposing Captain Yates' command consisted of some 20 warriors, their sniping fire being delivered from the east back of the river. This force was constantly augmented by warriors . . . the primary concern of the Indians was to block the anticipated advance of Captain Yates' troops across the river . . .

> When the expected military aggression did not materialize, small parties of Indians began to infiltrate the bottom land east of the river . . . Probably by Custer's directive, Captain Yates flushed the warriors out of Deep Coulee and proceeded to climb the gradual slope to Calhoun Ridge.[11]

Hardorff then quotes from interviews with He Dog, Good Voiced Elk and Two Moon. Hardorff believes that their testimony corroborates his view of the events.

On the basis of hearsay evidence, these Indians stated that as Custer's troops (this would be Yates' command according to Hardorff) approached Ford B, there was sporadic firing and possibly some troopers were killed. Only a small number of Indians were at the ford; one account saying that they were on the east side and another on the west. The troops fell back and a line was set up from Foley marker to around where Butler's marker is.

The main questions I have in regard to this account are the same ones I have asked before. Hardorff indicates there wasn't much activity when Custer reached Medicine Tail Coulee, and since Reno was under attack, if Custer had a plan that would befit an offense-minded, courageous cavalry leader, wouldn't it be logical that it would entail launching an attack as quickly as possible? If so, wouldn't he have moved along the quickest route to attack the village, which must have been in chaos at this time? No! Custer wants a better view of the village and there is lots of dust, so now Custer believes he should reconnoiter. He does this by splitting his command again and sending two companies to see if he can attack across the ford, at some later time, after Benteen has joined him. Shouldn't Custer be worried about Reno and the need to go to his support? No, he knows Reno will be all right because he had established a skirmish line, or possibly Bouyer and Curley have now joined him, and he's aware that Reno had to retreat. Yates' battalion still doesn't meet any considerable resistance. There are some twenty Indians, but their number is increasing, so Custer retreats (or rather attacks) as they fire down and clear out Deep Coulee. Wouldn't Custer now think that it would be better to try to unite with the rest of the command and wait for General Terry and General Crook, especially if he knew that Reno had retreated to the bluffs, and he would be in a good position to prevent the Indians from scattering to the south and east? No, that would look like he was retreating, and Custer never retreats. Then shouldn't Custer establish a strong defensive position around Luce Ridge, so that he could hold out until Benteen was able to reach him? No, Custer believes there must be some better defensive area to the north where he could establish a defense and wait for Benteen. Wouldn't Benteen be apt to assist Reno, and, because of the attacking Indians, not be able to get to the aid of Custer? No, Custer would know that Martin had reached Benteen and his orders were to come to Custer's aid and not Reno's.

If one accepts the above scenario of events, there's no right to claim, or even imply, that Custer was a capable, courageous, attack-orientated cavalry leader.

> The distribution of artifacts on both ridges provides a clue not only to Custer's route, but also to his strategy. The position which controlled two interior lines: The first was up Cedar Coulee, from which direction Captain Benteen was expected to arrive, while the second line was toward the river established by Captain Yates' command. The establishment of these interior lines allowed Custer time to wait for Captain Benteen. With Benteen's arrival, both commands could swiftly traverse the ground to Yates' battalion near the ford and commence the attack.
>
> Unfortunately this strategy did not materialize. Increasing pressure on the flanks of Captain Yates' line forced his battalion onto Calhoun Ridge. Probably at the same time, Custer's command engaged in random skirmish fire with warriors returning from Major Reno's valley fight. Of nervous energy, and with his patience taxed to the utmost, Custer must have now decided to abandon Luce Ridge for the following reasons: Captain Benteen's battalion was nowhere in sight, and since Captain Yates was forced from the river bottom, Custer's holding position and further delay would only impair his chances of a vigorous attack. Accordingly, he assumed the offensive. [?]
>
> After circumventing the north branch of Medicine Tail Coulee, Custer's column reached the summit of Nye Cartwright Ridge. The view obtained of Captain Yates' position was not reassuring to Custer. The river bottom was probably filled with warriors, . . . Immediate action was imperative, and upon descent from Nye Cartwright, Custer halted his column behind the slopes crest and delivered three volleys which scattered the Indians in Deep Coulee. His front cleared, Custer crossed Deep Coulee and reunited with Captain Yates' battalion on Calhoun Ridge . . .
>
> On arrival at Calhoun Ridge, Custer must have called a hurried conference with other officers. Most scholars concluded that a defensive strategy was developed during this consultation, and that Troops I and L were assigned to cover the withdrawal of the balance of the troops. However, such theories ignore Custer's personality which accepted victory as being synonymous with attack. [my underlining] It should be clearly understood that Custer had delayed action as long as possible until forced to take the initiative. Further delay would only impair his chances of success, and, after vacating Nye Cartwright Ridge, the first opportunity for a bold front came near Calhoun Ridge. He most aggressively pursued this, probably with the second battalion commanded by Captain Keogh.
>
> To initiate his offensive, [?] Custer ordered Captain Keogh's battalion to take possession of Calhoun Ridge, the western terminus controlling the river and Deep Coulee. [Hardorff must now have Keogh's battalion switching position with Yates, who had been located along Calhoun Ridge.] The purpose of this move was to find another river crossing farther down. Apparently, a part of Captain Keogh's command had attempted to gain control of Deep Ravine, the southern branch of which borders Calhoun Ridge on the north . . .[12]

It is not clear if Hardorff suggests that Custer left Keogh's battalion on Calhoun Ridge and was planning to attack at Cheyenne Ford with Yates' two companies, or if he took C Company with Yates' battalion. I assume that Custer went with Yates' battalion. Did they get as far as the ford, or just to Deep Ravine, on this offensive move? Did Custer think that the Indians blocking his move to Ford B would not do the same at any other crossing? I have not read any Indian accounts of their stopping an attack aimed at crossing the Cheyenne Ford. There are the escape accounts which mention 40 men, and, even if the Indian chronology was wrong, I hope Custer would not have attempted his offensive with just one company.

> Evidence to support this theory comes in part from the Indian accounts which state that when Custer descended from the high eastern ridge, his troops moved as if to reach the river lower down. The western position of slain bodies also refutes the premise that Custer was acting defensively. Moreover the bluff top at the extreme western end of Calhoun Ridge contained a quantity of expended military casings, denoting a position held by Captain Keogh's battalion. Although it has been theorized by some that this firing refuse came from carbines taken from Major Reno's slain troopers, the position and concentration of this large a number of cartridge cases seem to contradict this. However, this same location also contained a quantity of shells from various other weapons, which suggests that this position was overrun by Indians, some of the soldiers having been shot down and the balance driven back towards the "Last Stand" area.[13]

Hardorff's statement supports my theory better than his. The Indians must have seen the westerly movement from Luce Ridge to Nye Cartwright to Calhoun Hill and Battleridge. There was also movement by some of Yates' battalion toward Keogh's; but the main element of Yates' battalion moved around the north cutbank, ridge or hillock, along the western end of Calhoun Ridge, across Greasy Grass and then either they were forced, or decided to move, in the direction of the present cemetery. If I am correct, they had three company commanders and a wounded Custer with them. Although they were confused and disorganized, they probably established some rear guard formations along the west end of Calhoun Ridge and along Greasy Grass knoll. When they retreated to the current cemetery area and halted they established some rear defense line. They then fired at the Indians crossing the river below them and at those that had followed them around the cutbank. Most of the Indians crossing at Ford B were only aware of Keogh's battalion and concentrated on them until the main element of Yates' battalion moved to Battleridge, which took place at approximately the same time the Indians returning from the Reno battle arrived. The military artifacts found along this line do not suggest an attack or even a tactical defensive line (South Skirmish Line) but rather rear-guard skirmish lines inside a retreat line (South Retreat Line).

> Although only three markers had been placed on the west end of Calhoun Ridge in 1890, new evidence reveals that as many as eight troopers might have been slain near this bluff top.... It seems quite plausible, therefore, a squad of Captain Keogh's troopers might have been stationed on the bluff to clear the opposition from Deep Ravine and to gain a passage to the river below.
>
> Careful examination of the Indian accounts reveal very little testimony regarding the actions on Calhoun Ridge. Indeed, some of the accounts convey the impression that none of Custer's troops halted there; but instead, this evidence suggest a disorderly troop movement from Nye Cartwright to Custer Hill. Such statements of course, contradict the reality of slain bodies and firing refuse. Since most of the Indian accounts lack the chronological connections of incidents, it is very tempting to the researcher to arbitrarily extract any segment which supports the hypothesis. However, in order to pursue the historical truth, the researcher of Indian testimony should not stop at what happened, but he should strive to learn when and where did "what happened" happen, because it is here that Indian accounts show their greatest weakness.[14]

Hardorff continues with Indian testimony to suggest that there was fighting on Calhoun Hill. I don't believe there is any question about that point. What I don't see is how he is connecting the evidence with an offense. I don't think you can determine by the artifacts that were found whether the troops were attacking or retreating. The testimony and evidence indicates to me that there was resistance along a line of retreat, and then the soldiers were surrounded before they could establish an adequate defense. They were then killed in a confused fight along Battleridge, except for those troops attempting to escape. Hardorff makes an issue of whether troops leaving the ridge were mounted or not and when the effort took place, but he does so in order to refute certain testimony, particularly that of Wooden Leg. He accepts some chronological accounts while rejecting others, without making a strong case for either.

Hardorff also addresses the testimony concerning the bodies found in Deep Ravine. Captain Myles Moylan thinks that the soldiers found there were fighting and retreating – attempting to scramble up the other side. Captain McDougall says they were found half in and half outside of the ravine. Lieutenant Hare refers to 28 men of Company E and claims that they were shot in the back. McDougall maintains they were shot in the side. William Hardy points out that the bodies were lying on top of each other. All of these comments lead to interesting analysis and speculation.

Hardorff summarizes his findings, beginning on page 64. Most of his views I have already dealt with. Both battalions, after uniting, were blocked from going to the river where part of Troop C was overpowered. The rest fell back to Calhoun Hill. Hardorff claims that Troops I, L, and C deployed for a holding action while Custer took E and F and moved along the eastern slope of Custer Ridge. This, according to Hardorff, might still be considered an offensive move; but then, they were forced on the defensive. Calhoun Hill was overrun and some of the survivors of L Company fell back on Troop I. I don't know what happened to the rest of C Company but they must have been killed on Calhoun Ridge, and I am not sure how Tom Custer ended up with George Custer. Hardorff does mention the final charge of troopers from the ridge and he refers to them fleeing. While I realize the dangers of conjecturing from shell casings, it would seem to me there were enough of them located in the area below Last Stand Hill to indicate extensive resistance. However, the lack of bodies would mean that it was not a final skirmish or defensive position, but rather one of troops retreating to (as John Stands In Timber brought out) the Cemetery area and then to Custer Hill.

The last part of Hardorff's summary, which I dispute, suggests a reason why Custer would have waited for Benteen. Hardorff thinks that Boston Custer saw Benteen's battalion back on the trail. It is true that Boston Custer did pass Benteen and he also saw Martin. Along with that, we can assume that he saw Reno engaged and got a fair, or at least a general, picture of the number of Indians involved. It is extremely questionable whether Boston Custer would have given General Custer a message that Benteen should be along shortly. If he was able to give Custer such a message I don't think it would have taken place before Custer had already made his plans and committed himself and his troops to those plans. It seems that Hardorff is using Boston Custer as justification and even proof that Custer waited for some time, and he must have waited because he expected Benteen to soon join him.

In contrast, I believe sending Martin to contact Benteen and Kanipe to McDougall would indicate the period of time when Custer became aware that Benteen was back on the main trail. Custer's plans would not have been affected by any such news from Boston Custer. By the time Boston Custer reached the General's command, Custer was already shot and his troops were retreating.

SOURCES

1. Hardorff, Richard G. *Markers, Artifacts & Indian Testimony,* Short Hills, Don Horn Publications, 1985, p. 9.
2. Ibid., p. 9.
3. Ibid., p. 10.
4. Camp, Hammer, *Custer in 76,* p. 104.
5. Hardorff, *Markers, Artifacts & Indian Testimony,* p. 20.
6. Ibid., p. 21.
7. Graham, *The Custer Myth,* pp. 15, 17, 18.
8. Op. Cit., pp. 22, 23.
9. Ibid., pp. 23, 24.
10. Ibid., p. 24.
11. Ibid., p. 25.
12. Ibid., pp. 38, 39, 40, 41.
13. Ibid., p. 41.
14. Ibid., p;. 42.

Sole Survivor
by Douglas Ellison

Introduction: Of Curley's legitimate interviews, the most in-depth were admittedly those done by Walter M. Camp, who interviewed him four times, in 1908, 1909, 1910, and 1913. On the other hand, probably the clearest and most straightforward of Curley's accounts is that which he gave to his intimate friend and fellow tribesman, Russell White Bear, a few days before his own death on May 21, 1923.

Although Walter Camp was a stickler for details, he was under the mistaken, though popular, impression that Custer had attempted to cross the Little Bighorn with his entire battalion, and therefore asked his questions with this in mind, consequently taking Curley's answers out of context. In the Camp interviews, therefore, it appears that Custer's entire command, including Curley, rode down to the river and then retreated under heavy fire to the present battlefield area.

In his account, as given to Russell White Bear, however, Curley told a different story, saying that he had left the command on what has since become known as Nye Cartwright Ridge. Since White Bear had not interviewed Curley, but had asked him to tell his own story of the battle, there was little danger that his story had been taken out of context, and there was obviously little chance of it having been administered.[1]

Early in his book, Ellison starts making simplistic statements and basing opinions on very little evidence. He condemns Camp for taking a biased position and placing Curley's answers out of context, although he gives him credit for the most in-depth interviews. All of us take positions which can be biased; what matters and should be considered is what evidence we are basing these opinions on. Have we attempted to analyze opposing views objectively, even though we may differ and the position we take may be wrong? Camp interviewed Curley and others on the scene. His view of what happened is therefore derived from these interviews. Once he had established his premise, it was natural for his questions to be predicated on that basis. I believe that Camp was misled by Curley or his interpreter's stories of being with Custer: I think the only part of Curley's accounts one can accept are those before the Crows left Custer, and even parts of these are suspect.

Ellison accepts White Bear's story at face value, not because of any historical verification. Did White Bear write it down as Curley told it to him, or did he wait until he wrote the letters – one, three, and another eighteen years after Curley's death? Did White Bear have an ulterior motive? Did Curley even tell him this story? Why did Curley give so many different accounts? Since White Bear acted as one of the interpreters for General Scott, why didn't White Bear explain why Curley lied to General Scott? The General Scott interview is the only version of Curley's narrative which has any corroboration.

Ellison uses Curley's story of Custer having a conversation with a young man riding a sorrel-roan horse and then writing out a message which he subsequently sent with him. He treats this account as verification for Frank Finkel's role and any comments he made that would support Ellison's theory. In his first letter, White Bear says that the messenger rode off to the north, but in the second, he doesn't mention the direction the messenger took. Though Finkel was supposedly wounded and dazed when he left the battlefield, the fact that in one letter it says he rode off to the north is sufficient for Ellison to support the credibility of both Finkel and Curley.

Reno's fight in the valley:

> Company G was then pulled off the skirmish line and moved into the timber, but this so weakened the line that Companies A and M were also ordered to fall back to the timber about 15 minutes after the battle had begun.
>
> ... About half an hour after Reno ordered his command into the timber, he led them out across the valley and to the high bluffs across the river..
>
> ... Reno's demoralized command collected on what would become known as Reno Hill, where they were joined about 10 minutes later, at 4:20, by Benteen's three company battalion and about an hour later by the pack train and its escort.
>
> Custer kept well informed of the condition of Reno's battalion in the valley, as any competent commander would have, and knew within moments of his retreat, planning his subsequent actions with this in mind.[2]

Ellison's timing sequence is rather vague. Using Ellison's chronology, an hour has gone by from the time Reno started down the valley until he left the timber. Custer made his move to the ridge overlooking the valley, and Ellison claims he left before Reno established his skirmish line. What was Custer doing after he left the ridge? He had 45 minutes, at a time when you would think he'd be concerned with synchronizing an attack on a village, which, by Indian testimony was going through a chaotic stage verging on panic. Did Custer do it? No, not according to Ellison, and, one might add, a number of other writers.

> Custer, after ordering Major Reno's battalion ahead to engage the Indians, led his battalion on their trail for a short distance, halted briefly at a branch of Reno Creek to water his horses, and then, probably after hearing the Gerard-Cooke report that the Indians were not running as expected, he turned his battalion sharply to the right and moved downstream at a fast trot and gallop.
>
> Passing just to the east of the bluff where Reno would later be besieged, Custer's command soon mounted the ridge just north of there at a gallop, where for the first time, they came in sight of the Indian villages, although the lay of the land prevented them from seeing the north end.
>
> Very soon after this, Knipe received Custer's order, delivered verbally by his brother, Thomas Custer, Knipe's captain, to go back and tell Captain McDougall to leave the trail he was following and bring the pack train straight across country to Custer's battalion as quickly as possible ...
>
> Following Knipe's departure, Custer halted his command at the base of a high hill at the north end of the ridge. With an orderly, Trumpeter John Martin of Company H, and probably several others, Custer then rode to the top of the hill to gain a clearer view of the valley.
>
> The party then returned to the command, which continued downstream going again at a trot and gallop.
>
> Mitch Bouyer and four of the Crow scouts rode along the high bluffs between the command and the river, undoubtedly with orders to watch for any new developments in the valley. At some point, three of the Crows turned back, and only Mitch Bouyer and Curley, the youngest of the Crows loaned to Custer, rode on.
>
> Although some historians maintain that Custer. from the overlooking bluff, saw Reno halt and form his skirmish line, the evidence indicates that he had rejoined his battalion by that time, and was informed of Reno's action by Mitch Bouyer from his position on the high bluffs.[3]

This is the point where I believe Ellison, and others who share his views, go from comparatively sound speculation to unsound guesses. They take two positions which I reject. The first is their acceptance of only one version of Curley's story – the one which fits their theory. The second is their failure to explain why they accept that particular version of events and not his others, nor the statements that apply, made by the other three Crows, the Rees and Martin. One might also ask why Bouyer, if he felt that joining Custer was like going to his death, would send the other Crows back, but would take Curley with him, and then later tell Curley to escape because he was too young to die?

I agree with Ellison that Custer didn't see Reno form his skirmish line, although it would have happened soon after Custer rejoined his command.

Several other aspects of Ellison's evaluation should be highlighted. Ellison believes that Custer knew within moments about Reno's retreat. He claims that Bouyer went along the bluffs parallel with the river, which by all accounts is what he did; but he also suggests that Custer went down Cedar Coulee and then along Nye-Cartwright

Ridge. I don't think Bouyer was in any position to have signaled Custer of Reno's retreat, considering their location, as well as the timing sequence, I don't think it could have happened in that way.

> ... This is evident by the following statement taken from Curley's 1908 interview with Walter Camp: "When they (Bouyer and Curley, DE) got to the top of the first of these peaks, they looked across and observed that Reno's command was fighting. At the sight of this Bouyer could hardly restrain himself and waved his hat excitedly for some little time."
>
> At this time the command was following a large ravine, now known as Cedar Coulee, which turns away from the river near Weir Point and enters much larger Medicine Tail Coulee almost two miles back from the river.
>
> At some point in Cedar Coulee, probably just after having been informed of Reno's halt by Bouyer, Custer called Trumpeter Martin to him and said, "Orderly, I want you to take a message to Colonel Benteen . . ."
>
> Martin recalled that after receiving his message: "My horse was pretty tired, but I started back as fast as I could go." He added: "The last I saw of the command they were going into the ravine." The ravine he referred to could only have been Medicine Tail Coulee.
>
> In a few minutes Martin was back on the hill from which he and Custer had overlooked the valley, but, before getting there, he heard firing from the direction he had just come, and assumed the Indians had been waiting in ambush. When he arrived on the hill he saw Reno's battalion fighting in the valley, just as the skirmish line was being withdrawn into the timber.[4]

At times we get tied up with wording and often one word can change the essence of meaning. In the above statement to Graham, as it is recorded, Martin said that the last he saw of the command they were going down into the ravine. The statement would imply that he was not with the command since he saw them turn and start down Medicine Tail Coulee. However, if we leave out the word "into", the meaning changes and actually suggests what Martin alludes to in his other statements.

In Martin's various remarks, there are several points concerning terrain, distance and timing which should have influenced Ellison's thinking. Ellison believes that Custer had left Weir Point before Reno set up his skirmish line. Custer then charged down Cedar Coulee, turning left when he reached Medicine Tail Coulee. Martin was sent back when the troops were part way down Cedar Coulee. According to this view, on his way back to Weir Point, Martin heard firing and looked back in that direction from which he had just come, namely to the east down Cedar Coulee. In other words, Indians began firing on Custer when he was a mile and a half southeast of the ford. If the report is true, this could have been Wolf Tooth's band. However, Martin could have looked down Middle Coulee, after leaving Custer in Medicine Tail Coulee, and could have heard firing and seen Indians. This possibility would be substantiated by Indian testimony. Commenting on his interview with Martin in 1908, Camp said that Martin thought the firing came from Ford B at his right. Camp thought it may possibly have came from the Reno engagement. The length of Cedar Coulee below Weir Point to its juncture with Medicine Tail Coulee is roughly about a thousand yards. Since Martin had not yet reached Weir Point, he shouldn't have traveled over 500 yards before he heard the firing. In no way should Martin have thought that it was coming from Ford B, nor should Camp have surmised that it may have come from Reno's fighting in the valley. However, the firing could have been from either source, if Martin was moving up Middle Coulee.

> As the command continued down the coulee, while no doubt being harassed by ineffectual long distance fire, Mitch Bouyer and Curley still remained on the high bluffs east of the river watching Reno's fight in the valley. Curley later said that from Weir Point, he and Bouyer saw Reno retreat from the valley and that Bouyer signalled the fact to Custer, after which they rode down toward the command.

Ellison should have remembered his earlier remark that Curley's account to Russell White Bear was the most accurate of his statements. In that account, Curley implied that he and Bouyer went down Cedar Coulee with Custer, and before that, he and Bouyer went to the hill (Weir Point) with Custer when the General viewed the valley. Ellison should have explained why he is now assuming that Bouyer and Curley remained on Weir Point. He might also have clarified why he rejects Martin's statement in which he said that he didn't recall seeing Bouyer "at that time," referring to Custer's presence at Weir Point.

Supposing that Mitch Bouyer and Curley remained on Weir Point and saw Reno retreat, it is not clear why Curley did not mention that he or Bouyer saw Martin on his way back, especially since they should have seen the Indians fire on him, or why he did not comment on Martin's meeting Boston Custer. Since Curley and Bouyer would still have been on Weir Point, when Martin was viewing Reno, it is odd that Martin didn't recall or refer to seeing them. Certainly, he should have remembered their being with Custer, when Custer went to the high point.

Curley and Bouyer must have waited on Weir Point a long time, if they were there with Custer before Reno set up his skirmish line, and until his retreat from the timber.

ANALYSIS OF WRITERS' SCENARIOS

I believe Martin's timing, in his report of seeing Reno still on his skirmish line but starting to move into the timber, appears approximately correct, when one considers the amount of time Martin needed to reach Benteen and the location of their meeting, and Benteen's arrival shortly after Reno had retreated to the bluffs.

Continuing to support Curley's story, Ellison claims that Bouyer signalled Custer who was about a mile away, telling him that Reno was retreating. Curley and Bouyer then moved down Middle Coulee to meet Custer. Ellison says nothing of the Crows and Bouyer moving to Bouyer's Bluff overlooking the ford and the village, where they supposedly fired several rounds before turning back. Curley and the other three Crow scouts recall that event, and many writers have accepted it in one form or another. Since Ellison approves of this particular Curley version of what happened, he should explain why he rejects the others. Historical objectivity should not be based on accepting one view over others without explanation.

It should also be remembered that somewhere along Martin's return route, he was shot at by Indians and his horse was wounded. This is usually assumed to have happened between the time he was given his message and when he reached Weir Point, as Boston Custer noticed his horse was limping. Considering the short distance he had to travel in Cedar Coulee, it is doubtful if it would have taken place there. On the other hand, as I suggested earlier, if Martin did not leave Custer until he reached Medicine Tail Coulee and he was moving back along Middle Coulee, this could easily have happened. Custer's command should have been at or near the ford so Indians would have been firing on them. We know there were Indians moving to attack Reno on both sides of the river, and they would have been in a position to fire on Martin.

I will reiterate the basic point which prevents me from accepting the notion that Martin received Custer's message while moving down Cedar Coulee. Martin met Boston Custer between the time he received the message for Benteen and the time he reached the hill. Since Ellison, Kuhlman and others who share this opinion, assume that Martin received the message from a few hundred yards to half way down Cedar Coulee, there would not have been any need for Boston Custer to ask where the command was since it would still be in sight. However, this would not be true if Martin received the message some 600 yards from the ford and was returning to the hill by crossing the ridge between West and Middle Coulee. He then would have met Boston Custer while moving up Middle Coulee to Weir Point. The Custer command would have been hidden by the Middle and West Coulee ridge behind Martin.

Keogh's battalion moving to Luce or Nye Cartwright Ridges would also have been out of sight. In other words, in this version of the events, Martin's testimony, as well as timing, terrain, and Indian firing, correlate. On the other hand, timing, events, testimony and terrain appear too varied and too often at odds for me to accept the scenario used by Ellison and others.

> Probably as a result of Bouyer's signal, the command halted on a flat about a mile east of the river, at the foot of the gulch down which Bouyer and Curley were coming.
>
> It is quite possible that Custer rode out to meet Bouyer as he and Curley were advancing toward the command, for Curley later told Walter Camp: "Bouyer probably told Custer Reno had been defeated, for Bouyer did a whole lot of talking to Custer when he joined him and kept talking when they were riding side by side." . . .
>
> Curley recalled that during this halt in Medicine Tail Coulee, Custer's men dismounted and readjusted their saddles. [It is a good thing the Indians Ellison has been referring to didn't attack Curley and Bouyer as they came down the coulee since they should have been in that area, and at this time must not have been firing on Custer's command.]
>
> Another significant fact given by Curley is that at some point before he left the command: "There was a hurried conference of officers, and Bouyer told Curley that the subject of conversation was to the effect that if the command could make a stand somewhere, the remainder of the regiment would probably soon come up and relieve them. Personally, Bouyer did not expect that relief would come as he thought the other commands had been scared out."[6]

The reference to being "scared out" appears to be an addition intended to corroborate the accusations made against Benteen and Reno. One tries to refrain from sarcasm, but in no way does this account make sense. Somewhere in his analysis, Ellison should have stopped relying on Curley's questionable chronicles. The author talks about Custer's troops dismounting and readjusting their saddles. According to Curley's account, accepted by Ellison, by then, Custer knew that Reno had retreated and would be attempting to reach the bluffs. From Custer's message we know that he was concerned about receiving Benteen's support. We also recognize that he was one of our great cavalry leaders, courageous to a fault, still at least a mile from the village, and not under any real fire from the Indians; we also know that he had seen what he believed was a peaceful village. What is now his main concern? According to Ellison, he was not going to attack; instead he realized that he had to make a stand. Assuming that this was the situation, what would one expect any competent commander to do? Would he move farther to the north over unknown terrain, or would he move back in order to join the rest of his command which he expects to be coming together on the bluffs he just left a short time before? There can only be one answer that makes any sense, but it is not the one Ellison chooses. That's not all. As he continues, his scenario becomes even more incredulous:

> Beyond doubt, his conference of officers occurred in Medicine Tail Coulee immediately after Bouyer and Curley rejoined the command. This assumption is supported by another statement Curley gave to Walter Camp: "We (DE – Bouyer and Curley) joined Custer on Medicine Tail Coulee as he was advancing toward the village. He did not halt after we joined him (DE – the command was already halted at that point). He had all the bugles blowing for some time, the purpose of which I did not understand."
>
> The bugles were undoubtedly blowing Officer's Call, supporting the belief that his conference of officers was held in Medicine Tail Coulee. The conference would have resulted, of course, from Bouyer's report that Reno had retreated from the valley, necessitating an immediate change of plan.
>
> It appears that the halt in Medicine Tail allowed the fifty or so warriors who had been harassing the command a chance to move in closer, putting the stationary troopers at a decided disadvantage. Based on information obtained from Curley, Walter Camp declared: "The hot fire then impressed Curley with the idea that it would be necessary for Custer to retreat, and he did so, going in a direction downstream (north) and quartering back upon the high ridge. (DE – undoubtedly Nye Cartwright Ridge.)[7]

Custer, who knows of Reno's retreat to the bluffs, and is this far back from the ford, apparently still doesn't believe in the need to aid Reno, or to join up with Benteen; instead he moves farther north.

It's hard to understand how, after the conference in Medicine Tail Coulee, Custer moved downstream, and in quartering back, moved onto Nye Cartwright Ridge. Did they then go to Luce Ridge before deciding to move to Battleridge?

I would have to assume from Ellison's account that Custer's move to the north was undertaken in order to find a place to make a stand, because he had been subject to overwhelming fire from these fifty Indians. It apparently didn't bother Custer to the point where he might continue to quarter back and attempt to link up with the rest of his command, because he decided to split his command even more by sending E Company down Medicine Tail to check out the ford.

There is little doubt that the details given by Curley to Walter Camp, which Camp represented as happening on the retreat back from the river, actually occurred on the move from Medicine Tail Coulee to Nye Cartwright Ridge. This can be seen in the following quotation made by Curley, with only one justifiable correction: ". . . we had not proceeded one-third of the way to the ridge before the Sioux were thick upon both our right and left flanks firing into us heavily. [I can't help wondering what happened to E Company.] I do not know whether or not any one was killed on the way to the ridge, but the firing was so heavy that I do not see how the command made the ride without some loss. Going up from the river (DE – Medicine Tail Coulee) Sioux on all sides except front. Mitch Bouyer told me to keep out of the skirmish as much as possible; they might wish to send me with a dispatch to the other troops." Hammer, p. 162-163.

The long line of several hundred empty cartridge cases along Nye Cartwright Ridge, first discovered in the 1920's, seemed to indicate volley firing. In 1909 Curley had told Walter Camp: "After we made the ridge just west of where Calhoun's marker is placed, we were twice ordered to load and fire together. It occurred to me at the time that this must be some signal." In 1910 he told Camp the volleys were fired at the Sioux who were closing in."[8]

By analyzing the little firsthand information, however, and by employing simple logic, a clear and believable picture emerges of what Custer's thoughts and actions were in his last battle.

First of all, when Custer had first ordered Reno ahead to attack the Indians who were believed to be running away, he would naturally have intended to support Reno's attack from the rear, which would, supposedly, have thrown the disorganized Indians into a panic when hit by five companies of cavalry at full charge.

But, upon hearing that the warriors were in fact massing to meet Reno's attack. Custer settled on a new objective, and he raced downstream toward the opposite end of the village.[9]

Custer would have expected Reno to make contact with the Indians; however, knowing Reno had only three companies, and realizing that he didn't know where Benteen was, how soon he would arrive or what the terrain was like downstream, Custer's reaction to such news would have been to support Reno from the rear even if he hadn't been planning to.

It is interesting to read all the plans Custer devised once he arrived at the Little Bighorn, but Ellison, like other writers, claims that he moved all morning without any.

> Gaining his first view of the village from towering bluffs east of the river, Custer decided to push ahead with his plan to hit the Indians in their rear, as Reno battled at their front. Sgt. Knipe was thus ordered back with his

> message to bring on the pack train with the reserve ammunition as quickly as possible . . .
>
> Continuing to press downstream, Custer was soon informed by Mitch Bouyer . . . Reno had halted his charge . . . in skirmish order, this was not a catastrophe, but it did mean that Custer could not waste time in getting into action, for Reno's three companies, with one fourth of the men out of action and holding the horses, would now be in far greater danger of being surrounded and ripped to pieces by the Indians.
>
> He thus dispatched Trumpeter Martin to find Benteen . . .[10]

I agree with Ellison that Custer would realize the need to aid Reno quickly, whether he knew he had formed a skirmish line or not. However, I question his other statement, for if Custer was using the reasoning here presented, he would not have given an order for Benteen to come to his aid, but rather would order him to assist Reno.

> That Custer was indeed planning to push on as fast as prudently possible down Medicine Tail Coulee and hit the village, the north end of which was just opposite the mouth of the coulee, is supported by several statements given by Curley to Walter Camp . . .
>
> Custer would of, course, have abandoned this intention when he received word from Bouyer that Reno had retreated from the valley. This changed everything, and Custer ordered a halt. . . . a conference of officers was held . . .[11]

I have already pointed out that Ellison's timing is off by 30 to 40 minutes. Custer could have reached the ford and attacked the Indians some 30 minutes earlier. What Ellison doesn't explain is why Custer, who admittedly was in a hurry, went down Cedar Coulee when the quickest route would be going down either of the other two coulees. This is an important question to which I haven't found a logical explanation. We know that Custer was not familiar with the terrain; he had questions as to the size and exact location of the village, and he would certainly want to find the quickest route to attack the village. The place where Custer first came onto the ridge would not provide satisfactory answers; the one location that stood out and where he could find these answers was Weir Point. One would assume that this is where Custer would have gone, and there is evidence to indicate that he did. Once he was there, he would have been able to determine the quickest route to attack a peaceful village that he knew would soon erupt. Any claim that he took the longest route to accomplish this task must be accompanied by a logical explanation which goes beyond accepting a particular story told by Curley or Frank Finkel.

> . . . For Custer to march back toward the other battalions, which Frank Finkel believed could easily have been done, would have forsaken all hopes of victory, which would have been unthinkable to Custer, especially since three fourths of the regiment had not yet for all practical purposes, entered the fight.
>
> Custer's decision, therefore, as Mitch Bouyer told Curley at the conclusion of the conference, was "that if the command could make a stand somewhere, the remainder of the regiment would probably soon come up and relieve them."[12]

I certainly don't see this account as a clear, logical and reasonable interpretation of what happened. Custer's move to the north, away from the rest of the command and into basically unknown terrain is possible, in Ellison's view, but a move to the south, where Custer knows his command is located, is unthinkable. This type of reasoning hardly deserves to be called logic. Custer might even have thought that by moving to the south, and making a stand, he would have been in a position to prevent the Indians from escaping in that direction and actually force them to move in a way that would correspond to his original orders.

> Although it was necessary for Custer to assume a defensive position for the time being, it is very clear he was not resigned to merely fighting a defensive action until Terry and Gibbon arrived. There is no question but that at this time Custer was still planning to destroy the largest Indian village ever seen in the West. . . .
>
> . . . As the command was moving over Nye Cartwright Ridge at this time, the attack on the village could only have referred to a later intention on Custer's part; obviously after the regiment was reunited.
>
> Custer's attitude at this time was entirely in keeping with his known personality, and he would have known that if he kept the regiment on the bluffs that night, the village would be gone in the morning. Should that happen, he knew he would be severely censured, to say nothing of facing a possible court-martial charge.
>
> But, until the rest of the regiment arrived, Custer could do nothing but find a suitable defensive position and wait . . .
>
> But first the command must stay on Nye Cartwright Ridge and await the return of the gray horse company which had been sent to the river following the halt and conference in Medicine Tail Coulee. From Nye Cartwright Ridge, the command could hold the Indians in check more by show than by force, . . .
>
> Why had Company E been sent to the river? Was it, as Charles Kuhlman theorized, to draw some of the warrior force away from Reno's beaten command by creating the impression among the Indians that the north end of their village was being attacked? This would have

been unnecessary, as Custer's command had been under fire almost from the moment it entered Medicine Tail Coulee . . .

There is one obvious explanation for Company E having been sent to the river. Custer had of course been told by Mitch Bouyer, . . . ford at the foot of the coulee . . . But as riverbeds change from year to year, it was vital that the ford be suitable at this time for an orderly crossing under fire . . . Reno's retreat at least gave Custer an opportunity to reconnoiter the ford . . . before approaching it under fire in a fast offensive movement . . .[13]

This passage calls for some analysis: the command is halted; Bouyer and Curley have joined them and a conference is being held. Custer has sent one messenger, another goes to the north. The fifty Indians are presenting such heavy fire that Custer temporarily abandons his plan of attack. First, there aren't any Indians there; then the Indians are thick on all sides but the north. Custer doesn't need to attack by the ford, even if he had planned to, because Reno has retreated; he plans to attack later when the command is united; but first he splits his command by sending E Company to scout the ford for this later assault. Even though the Indians are thick, except in front, Custer isn't worried that E Company won't be able to go down to the very doorstep of the village and reconnoiter the ford (the ford must be reconnoitered for this later attack and it wouldn't be enough to know that the Indians have been coming across it). Custer needs to unite his command. Even though the Indians are heavy around him, he is not worried that Benteen, Reno and the packs won't be able to make it through – he knows that Reno has retreated to the bluffs. Reno may have had some wounded and the packs would be moving fairly slow, but this doesn't worry Custer, nor does he think about the problems they might present when they arrive. This is peculiar logic, and it is unacceptable, in my view, as a basis for a true scenario of the events.

According to White Cow Bull, only 10 Sioux and Cheyenne warriors including himself . . .

Ellison repeats White Cow Bull's story and then said:

. . . According to this incredible and positively debunked theory . . . This account and several others like it are the basis for the theory presented by some writers, including David Humphreys Miller, that Custer led his entire battalion to the ford with the sole intention of charging across to the village.

When, so the theory goes, the man wearing the buckskin jacket, who was Custer himself, fell from his horse into the water, the entire command halted in the midst of their hell bent charge and then, panic stricken at the loss of their commander, retreated in complete disorientation to the present battlefield site as hundreds of warriors came charging across the ford ready to meet the new threat after having just routed Reno's command. Finally the last few survivors, still carrying Custer's body, struggled to what would become known as Custer Hill where they were quickly killed. According to this incredible and positively debunked theory, the entire running fight from the ford to Custer Hill lasted no more than half an hour until all the soldiers were dead.[14]

If White Cow Bull's story is incredible, I don't know what adjective could be used to explain Ellison's. I don't know who has debunked it, certainly not Ellison. Interestingly, his wording implies that Custer had other intentions than charging the village, when most writers, including Ellison, practically agree that attacking the village was Custer's original intent and even his later one. Of course it was not Custer's sole intention to charge a village, but rather to charge the village in order to defeat the Indians and to aid Reno: his actions reflect all of his other motives as well.

It is certainly Ellison's prerogative not to agree with White Cow Bull's account and any theory derived from it. When one considers a particular theory incredible (as I do Ellison's), it is hard not to be cynical, but one should try to present it as accurately as possible. White Cow Bull doesn't say that the entire command was in a hellbent charge. They started the attack after they hesitated; this was more of a movement forward than a charge. Custer, and the three or four with him, were not rushing across the ford. The timing of the struggle against Custer differs in Indian testimony. Most of those referring to a half hour, arrived after the troops reached Battleridge. White Cow Bull himself doesn't give a time estimate. He also says nothing about Custer having led his whole battalion; in fact, he speaks of firing on two different groups and he doesn't say that they retreated completely disorganized.

It is hard for me to imagine why White Cow Bull's story would be considered incredulous, after Ellison and other writers have come up with various concoctions in which one of the most daring cavalry leaders in our history is either moving to a defensive position, without even instituting a major move against the enemy, or is retreating because of a few Indians in front of him. These scenarios are particularly amazing, since attack is the recognized forte of a cavalry unit, and many of these same writers levied criticism at Reno for not continuing to attack a force known to be much larger than would have initially faced Custer. Indians usually fell back in front of a charge by troopers, as they had with Reno in the valley, and on the hill, and according to Indian accounts, that's what they did when elements of E Company attempted to escape toward the end of the battle.

It is difficult, in fact, impossible, for me to believe that Custer wouldn't launch an attack as quickly as he could reach the Indians – which would be at Ford B – whether he knew Reno was retreating or not. Such knowledge could be considered even more of a reason to attack.

Custer's turning to the north and following Cedar Coulee seems unlikely, when he must have realized that, to have any chance of success, he had to reach the river and the Indian village, while they were still preoccupied with Reno. Time was of the essence, and though Custer might have started down Cedar Coulee, which is more of a move to the east than to the north, his movement from column right to column left would soon have taken place. If, during that period, he ran into the number of Indians that some writers think he did, it seems that his maneuver would be to fall back and hopefully reach Benteen, McDougall and – even though he would not have known at the time – Reno. The claim that Custer waited until the other troopers arrived and then planned to launch an offensive is, in my view, unacceptable. Waiting wouldn't have enabled Custer to launch an offense, for, by the time these writers claim Custer changed his other plans and decided to wait for Benteen, he was already aware of the number of Indians he was facing. Custer undoubtedly suffered losses, and certainly, the battalions moving to meet him would have also by the time they united. If Custer thought Reno was still in the valley, he shouldn't have been waiting for Benteen, but attacking, and if he was aware that Reno had moved to the bluffs, he would know that Reno must have some wounded. If the battalions had united, some companies would have had to stay with the wounded when he launched his belated offense. The only benefit from uniting would be to establish a better defense and this would not have been accomplished by a move farther north.

Since there is no evidence that Custer attempted to fall back – which he certainly could have accomplished – then the question becomes: what would stop an attack, and why is there lack of evidence of any major battle ensuing where that attack should have taken place? The only answer I see, or have been able to find, is that something happened to Custer. It is hard to imagine the shooting of any other officer which would have stopped Custer from mounting such an attack, even if it was his own brother Tom. On the other hand, it's just as hard to believe that Custer's troops would not have stopped after he was shot.

Then, circumstances used to justify the defeat of Custer would have taken over. The size and sight of the village, the number of Indians, the number of recruits, and panicky horses, would have caused a retreat that was disorganized and prevented a sound defensive position from being established. This caused their defeat. This is only a theory, but it is logical and does have testimony to support it.

Besides the positive statements of Curley, and the implication by Frank Finkle, that Custer was personally never at the ford, there are other strong objections to the belief that he was the officer who fell there.

First of all, at least seven officers in Custer's battalion, besides Custer, were known to wear buckskin jackets . . . In addition, both Peter Thompson and the Arikara scout Soldier later declared that Custer had tied his buckskin jacket to the back of his saddle before the battle began.

White Cow Bull did state later in the interview that as he walked among the naked dead on Custer Hill after the battle he thought he recognized the man who had worn the buckskin jacket whom he had shot at the ford, and heard that it was Custer. He had admitted, however, that he had never seen a white man at close range until the fight at the ford, and due to the heavy coating of dust that many accounts said made it difficult for even friends to recognize each other, such an identification would have been extraordinary.

Nor does White Cow Bull's description of the officer's horse match that of Vic, the thoroughbred sorrel mare that Custer rode into battle, for instead of four white stockings, Vic had only three.

Taking everything into consideration, there seems to be no doubt that the officer who was wounded and perhaps killed at the ford was actually Lt. Algernon Smith of Company E, who was then pulled from the water and carried back to his command by his company.[15]

It's perplexing how one can base a theory on statements made by Curley or Finkle. Curley's testimony contains so many variations on what he did after leaving the ridge that if a writer accepts one version and not another there should be a very good explanation why.

It is natural to question White Cow Bull's account of shooting the man wearing buckskin, since there were other officers wearing buckskins, and it's doubtful Custer was wearing his buckskin jacket when he went into battle. I do not think that claim, however, discredits White Cow Bull's story. I would imagine that if one had questioned White Cow Bull after the battle as to how the man at the ford was dressed, he would probably have said he didn't remember. He might recall that the man rode a sorrel horse, had a mustache and his gun, but he would have been too preoccupied to have noticed much else. Because the man was leading the troops and because of what may have happened on the battlefield afterwards, White Cow Bull could have thought it was Custer whom he had shot. Hearing the reports of what Custer wore and seeing the pictures, he probably came to associate them with the man he shot. In interviewing Indians after a period of years, many writers seem to make the error of disassociating their knowledge from the white man's accounts of the battle. Indian testimony, particularly at first, would have been affected by fear of penalties that might be inflicted upon them, and by a desire to satisfy the interrogator. The accounts show very little concern about lying to the white man, which I think is understandable. One should keep in mind that many of the men who were with Reno said that Custer was wearing a buckskin jacket. This group included Lieutenant Godfrey. It is possible that Custer might have donned it before going into battle, when he was moving down Medicine Tail Coulee and the battle was imminent. Indians aren't the only ones that believed what you wore, or did, might bring you good luck. Jackets might also have became so dust-coated that in the heat of battle someone could have assumed that person was wearing buckskin. I do think more solid evidence than just this one reference is necessary to discredit White Cow Bull's story.

In attempting to discredit White Cow Bull's identification of the man he had shot at the ford as Custer, Ellison fails to mention that it was the Cheyenne women who knew Custer and identified him while White Cow Bull was there. The story of the Cheyenne women sticking the awl in Custer's ears and preventing a Sioux from mutilating him was told by other Indians as well, and gives credence to White Cow Bull's story. Since this white man was the first that White Cow Bull had seen up close and he was concentrating on him, his face could have been indelibly printed on his mind.

White Cow Bull's reference to Vic having four white socks illustrates my earlier remark that the Indians became familiar with what the whites said about the battle. This phenomenon is exemplified by the different stories of a man on a sorrel with white stockings who was braver than all the others. It is true that Vic had three white socks and not four, but even Lieutenant Godfrey referred to Vic as having four white socks and he had seen the horse numerous times. It is possible that White Cow Bull realized the sorrel horse had white stockings, but it is extremely doubtful he would remember the exact number, and his account would reflect the influence of later stories. Still, I wouldn't challenge his testimony because of it.

Ellison amazes me in what he considers debunking testimony and then accepts the declarations of someone like Curley whose stories are so varied and, in many instances, preposterous. The assumption that Custer sent E Company to the ford to scout it for a future attack, to me, is incredible. Ellison states that E Company was fired on by the Indians at the ford, so he is giving White Cow Bull's story some credit.

Ellison goes even further by crediting Indians with shooting an officer, but it cannot be Custer because Curley and Finkle say he didn't go to the ford in the account which Ellison is using. It is odd that the supporting evidence to discount White Cow Bull's shooting of Custer is White Cow Bull's recollection of four white socks instead of three. According to Ellison there is no doubt that the officer shot at the ford was Lieutenant Smith. Was Smith riding a sorrel with four white stockings? Since he was commander of the Gray Horse Troop you would expect him to ride a gray horse. If White Cow Bull had stated he thought he shot Custer and said that the man he shot was riding a gray horse there would have been reason to debunk his story, but it should not be done on the basis of one white stocking.

> The "small man" mentioned by White Cow Bull has been supposed by some to have been the half breed guide Mitch Bouyer. Since Bouyer had accompanied the main portion of the command over Nye Cartwright Ridge, however, the man at the ford could not have been him.
>
> The assumption that Company E had been sent to the ford on a reconnaissance is supported by White Cow Bull's statement that "the soldiers had stopped at the edge of the river." For what purpose, if not to survey the bank for its abruptness and softness? And when the troops rode over the bank into the water, no doubt to determine its depth and the solidness of its bed, and perhaps also to water the horses, the hidden handful of warriors naturally supposed they were "charging" and unleashed a ragged volley that caused two or three casualties among the soldiers.[16]

Ellison persists in making categorical statements based on Curley's unverified remarks. The other Crow scouts, and even Curley himself, claim that Bouyer went down from Bouyer's Bluff right next to the ford and met Custer, rather than going from Weir Point down Middle Coulee or having been with Custer in a move down Cedar Coulee.

Ellison continues to astonish me with his lack of logic and inconsistency. To back his assumption that it was Company E, he uses White Cow Bull's statement that they stopped at the edge of the river and White Cow Bull "supposed" they were charging. I don't know what happened to the "hell-bent" charge Ellison referred to before. His belief that this reference verifies his view that this was a reconnaissance mission is certainly a hasty conclusion. It is hard to believe that if Custer approached the ford he would not be interested in the solidness of the bed and the depth of the water, particularly since Ellison points out that he was so concerned he split his command and sent Company E to the ford for that purpose. However, I would question Custer's concern at that time.

It would be nice to know what happened to the fifty Indians who apparently were engaged for over an hour. They would have expected some help and, according to most of Curley's accounts, they received it. You'd think that these Indians might have been able to defeat Company E with their forty or so troopers. Still, Ellison thinks that Company E might have watered their horses at the ford. This would have taken exceptionally controlled horses and men.

> While Custer's five companies remained together on Battleridge, they were in little danger of being overwhelmed, for as Charles Kuhlman aptly expressed it in his superb work, *Legend into History*, "... 210 men, more or less armed with breech-loading carbines and colt revolvers are not as easily bowled over as ninepins."
>
> This phase of the fighting was suddenly brought to a close as a group of soldiers, later identified as Company E, galloped off Battle Ridge to a lower ridge about a half mile closer to the river. As the troops approached this ridge, scores of warriors, mostly Cheyenne and Oglala Sioux, who were hidden on this portion of the field rushed back to a safer distance and watched as the troops dismounted and formed a skirmish line, with each man holding his horse individually.
>
> The only logical [?] explanation of Custer's sudden dispersal of troops from Battle Ridge is the first appearance of troops on Weir Point, which Custer would naturally and justifiably supposed was the rest of the regiment coming as ordered, prompting him to open an avenue of approach by holding the Indians in check on the lower ridge. Unknown to Custer's command, of course, was that the troops on Weir Point at the time were only those of Company D, while the other companies and the pack train were still a mile or more back on the trail.[17]

Dr. Kuhlman's remarks, referring to five companies being able to defend themselves, is well taken, but seemingly forgotten, assuming that Custer did move this far north, searching for and establishing a defensive position. That they would break it up for the reason Ellison and others adopting this scenario suggest, is inconceivable to me.

Ellison claims that Company E galloped off Battleridge and established a skirmish line on a lower ridge. It is amazing that they even got back from Ford B, and it would be interesting to see what sort of a skirmish line they could have set up – let alone maintain – while holding their horses. Indian testimony suggests that they fell back when these troopers, either on horseback, on foot, or both, moved down the slope to where they were killed or committed suicide. It shows that a comparatively small number of troopers could cause the Indians to fall back in front of them.

Although one can see Weir Point from Battleridge and Last Stand Hill, it is questionable considering the dust, distance, Indians and shooting, if someone would have noticed Weir's company (if Custer or any of his men had been still alive at that time). Assuming that the events happened the way Ellison describes them, we then have another terrific move on the part of Custer. He sends 28 or 40 men to hold and help protect a movement of troops three miles away against what most writers thought were thousands of Indians. Then he continues to disperse his command by moving out Companies I and L. It's odd that with all of the Indians surrounding him, Custer would think that he could move a company against them, the Indians would fall back and the company could hold out for another fifteen minutes, but he couldn't attack with his five companies when there were far fewer Indians. Ellison should also realize and consider that there is no Indian testimony to support his view except for the Indian reports of escape attempts by 28 or 40 men.

> After Company E had been sent to the lower ridge, and probably just after it had established its skirmish line, it is apparent that Custer ordered the Keogh battalion, Companies I and L, to march back along Battle Ridge to meet and return with the troops believed to be advancing from Weir Point.
>
> First Sergeant James Butler of Company L was later found on the rise between Medicine Tail and North Medicine Tail Coulees. His body lay on a direct line between Companies L's final position and Weir Point, indicating without doubt [?] that he attempted to break through the mass of Indians alone and reach the troops who had been seen on Weir Point. Numerous empty cartridge cases found under his body bore mute testimony of his courageous one man stand after having been unhorsed and left afoot.[18]

It is understandable that Butler would have made a run in that direction, if the opportunity arose, but this doesn't mean that it happened after he saw the troops on Weir Point; in fact, this would have been an unwise move, for he couldn't have thought that the troops had not seen them fighting thousand of Indians. I believe he was left behind by Captain Keogh when his reserve battalion moved through Deep Coulee to Battleridge. He was to take a message to Captain Benteen, when the opportunity presented itself; however, he was seen by the Sioux, followed and killed, as inferred by Wooden Leg.

> A number of horses, apparently from Company C and F, in addition to any which had been seriously wounded in the course of the battle, had been shot and killed by the troops to form a barricade around the field hospital at some point during the battle. It is quite obvious that only the dismounted men of C and F, together with any men from the other companies who had lost their horses, were left to guard the position while those still mounted had gone out as part of Keogh battalion, for there are reports that men of other companies were found among those of I and L.[19]

I have not seen any Indian testimony indicating such a movement of mounted troops at that stage of the battle, when practically all of the Indians were surrounding the troops and certainly such a move would have been noted. I believe this lack of testimony supports my theory that I and L Troops were in reserve and then moved to Battleridge when Yates' battalion, which had gone to the ford, were forced to retreat around the cutbank toward the Cemetery and move to Last Stand Hill. A number of the mounted troops from Yates' battalion, having been cut off from retreating back the way they had come, then moved toward Keogh's battalion, which would explain the men of other companies being found among those of Companies I and L. This could also account for the confused appearance that Gall mentions when first observing the troops moving along Nye Cartwright Ridge and that Godfrey attributes to unmanageable horses.

> A very significant fact is that of the officers who could be identified, every one in Yates' battalion was found on Custer Hill, while every one in Keogh's battalion was found with the remains of their men far south along Battle Ridge. This provides strong evidence for the belief, as expressed above, that at the end of the battle the battalions were operating as separate combat units, and that the Keogh battalion was marching away from the other battalion in an attempt to bring on the reinforcement.[20]

Ellison's evidence does not indicate such a move, but I do believe it supports my theory as I have outlined it above. I think the distance and dust around Battleridge enabled the troops on Weir Point to be in a better position to note what was going on in the area of Last Stand Hill. Yet, there is no evidence that any of those soldiers observed troop movement on Last Stand Hill or Battleridge. Such a troop movement, for the purpose and at the time Ellison and others have stated, would be made with what flags they could muster flying and bugles blaring. And though I believe there were cover-ups in connection with the battle, in no way would all of the troops or officers have ignored and covered up such sightings.

If he was a competent and courageous general, Custer would have moved quickly to the ford. With the Indian village in a state of turmoil, he would have launched a major attack, which would then be evident through bodies, artifacts and Indian testimony. There is no sign of such an attack. If Custer had believed the odds were too great to strike, then an orderly retreat to unite his command or to establish a strong defensive position could be expected. Since there is no evidence of either, I think we have two choices: We either condemn Custer for a lack of competency or we assume that he was shot at the ford, and then attempt to visualize the impact this shooting would have had on his troops. I don't think this is an incredible or debunked theory.

The quote used in comparing Major Reno, who had an outstanding Civil War record*, and General Custer would be appropriate: "... he (Reno) demonstrated that the courage to follow is one thing, while the courage to lead is something very different."

SOURCES

1. Ellison, Douglas W., *Sole Survivor: An Examination of the Frank Finkel Narratives,* Pub. North Plains Press, Aberdeen, S.D., 1983, p 10.
2. Ibid., p. 49.
3. Ibid., pp. 49, 50.
4. Ibid., pp. 50, 51.
5. Ibid., p. 52.
6. Ibid., p. 52, 53.
7. Ibid., p. 53.
8. Ibid., p. 54.
9. Ibid., p. 57.
10. Ibid., p. 57, 58.
11. Ibid., p. 58.
12. Ibid., pp. 58, 59.
13. Ibid., pp. 59, 60.
14. Ibid., pp. 60, 61.
15. Ibid., p. 62.
16. Ibid., p. 62.
17. Ibid., p. 63.
18. Ibid., p. 65.
19. Ibid., p. 66.
20. Ibid., p. 66.

---

*Reno's army record as published has been considered a cover-up by many. Note W. Kent King's, *Massacre: The Custer Cover-Up*, pp. 42-43.

ANALYSIS OF WRITERS' SCENARIOS

The Custer Tragedy
by Fred Dustin

Fred Dustin wrote one of the more enlightening books on the Battle of the Little Bighorn. He spent much of the time on the Reno phase of the battle, in which he defends Major Reno's actions and gives him more credit than he deserves. However, with all the criticism of the Major, it is important to see the side of those who defend him. Dustin is critical of General Custer, and, in my view, goes too far in this direction, but he reserves his main censuring for Lieutenant Godfrey, or actually the writings of the later Captain or General Godfrey. Though I disagree with many points Dustin attempts to make, his book should be required reading for anyone interested in formulating a view of the battle.

> During the day, three of these deserted camp-grounds (23rd) were passed and halts made at each, says Godfrey, "while everybody was busy studying the signs and trying to figure out how old the trail was etc."
> ... The day's march had been thirty-three miles ... on the 24th, 28 miles.[1]

> The reader's attention is called again to Terry's orders: "should it (the trail) be found to turn toward the Little Bighorn ... he (Terry) thinks that you should proceed southward, perhaps as far as the headwaters of the Tongue, and then to turn toward the Little Horn, feeling constantly, however, to your left, so as to preclude the possibilities of the escape of the Indians to the south or southeast by passing around your left flank."
> ... There was no lack of competent scouts: Bouyer and the Crows were the best guides and keenest observers in that whole region. It was their own hunting grounds, and here they had made and received foray after foray, and were at home on every mile of territory. Neither the Rees nor Crows were in the least deluded as to the number of the Dakota, for after their examinations of the abandoned campgrounds, they well knew that not far ahead were probably two thousand warriors with their families, who, while they were simply wishing to be left alone, were not at all unready for another fight.[2]

General Terry's orders could be expected to have had some impact on Custer's thinking and actions. They also portray a primary concern that the Indians would not scatter before effective action could be taken against them.

I agree with Dustin that the Crows were competent scouts and familiar with the area; but I differ with him on his two primary inferences. One is that these Indians knew every foot of ground like the back of their hand. Dustin isn't alone in presenting this viewpoint, which I believe is exaggerated and creates a false impression. These Indians roamed over thousand of miles of bluffs, ravines, hills, streams, timber, rivers and mountains; and though they would be generally familiar with the land, to assume that they knew every ford, ravine, or hillock is giving them too much credit. It may be true that Bouyer had participated in foray after foray over this area, but Dustin's blunt statement still distorts the picture.

The second point which I have made numerous times is, in my view, responsible for some of the most consequential errors made when attempting to determine what happened to General Custer: giving the impression that Custer was not aware of any of the signs suggesting the size of the Indian encampment, or the number of Indians, he might have to face, and that he completely disregarded the warnings from his scouts. It is probably true that Custer wasn't the great Indian fighter as many have portrayed him; on the other hand, he had been in Indian territory for a comparatively long period of time, had fought them and must have acquired a certain knowledge of Indians, their trails, signs, and fighting methods. The early commendations he received from his commanding officers during the Civil War had to do with his ability to note and report pertinent signs of the enemy. The comments of the Rees and Crows suggest that he was generally liked and respected. It is not evident that he rejected, or even that he didn't see, the signs his scouts were attempting to point out at the Crow's Nest, such as smoke from tepees or Indian ponies. The fact that he didn't insist on going to the top might imply an acceptance of their sightings. Lieutenant Varnum couldn't see the signs, but it didn't mean he disbelieved his scouts. What Custer didn't agree with was the presumption that he shouldn't move against the Indians, or wouldn't be able to defeat them. Custer was not one to divulge information to his officers, although I believe the two principal ones, Major Reno and Captain Benteen, received more information than they reported. Custer seemed to have been receiving messages regularly, according to Trumpeter Martin, and he requested them, if he didn't, from what Lieutenant Hare reported. The sending of four messages that we know of to Captain Benteen and McDougall (and, either, one message was more explicit than Benteen let on, or another was probably sent), would lend credence to both a desire for and consideration of information. It should be recognized that by sending these messages, Custer showed a concern and understanding, and a application of an overall strategy. Although I may be giving Custer too much credit, I do believe Benteen was the key to undermining

Custer's plan of attack, although not after Custer reached Battleridge. If Benteen had followed what I think Custer originally expected, I cannot help wondering if the troops might not have been successful (if Custer wasn't shot), although it is possible that, as Dustin claims, the whole command would have been wiped out.

> Bouyer, and the Crow and Ree scouts, who had ascended the Crow's Nest, knew that there was an immense aggregation exactly where they pointed out to Custer, and Bouyer and the Crows knew the country; they knew the valley of the Little Big Horn and its topography: they knew that an attack on that Indian community was an invitation to disaster for so small a force as Custer commanded.
>
> When Custer arrived at Davis Creek, he was at the parting of the ways, for it was at this point that under his orders, he should have proceeded farther south, to give Gibbon time to get within striking distance of the Sioux. Nothing ever developed during or since the campaign that justified Colonel Custer in departing, not only from the spirit of his orders, but from the letter itself.[3]

This is an example of a passage in which those opposing Custer's move against the Indian encampment become too rigid in their analysis. For one thing, it exhibits "Monday morning quarterbacking"; we know what happened, it didn't pan out, so we should have realized it wouldn't. Keep in mind that though the scouts may have felt it was foolish to attack the Indians, it doesn't appear the officers did, nor that they thought they would be defeated if they did attack. Their main consideration, expressed in Custer's orders, was concern over whether the Indians might escape. To condemn Custer when the fear they had been discovered seems to have been the primary motive for his not waiting – and as Godfrey would have pointed out, a large camp can scatter as quickly as a smaller one – appears to be an unfair judgment. One might also recognize that the inferences and evidence suggest that Custer did understand and accept the scouts' reports of the general location and size of the Indian camp.

I am not too bothered about the strict application of prior orders, since they don't bear on what my primary focus in examining the battle has been, but I do think it is interesting to see the different viewpoints applied by various writers. Dustin condemns Custer for not following orders, but not Major Reno or Captain Benteen; others have reversed this position by their condemnation of Reno and Benteen, but not Custer. Actually, all three of the major officers didn't follow their orders strictly, which to a degree is understandable.

The central question, in reference to this subject, is the assumption that Custer was so naive that he didn't issue more definitive orders than he is credited with doing; orders that could have been expected from any non-commissioned officer, let alone an officer, and certainly one with the commendable ratings that Custer had.

> If the reader has followed this narration closely, it will not be hard for him to understand JUST WHY Custer divided his force. When he was at the summit of the Crow's Nest he repeatedly expressed his opinion that the Indian scouts, Ree and Crow, did not see any village in the valley of the Little Big Horn; that he did not believe they were there. He had his field glasses but he could not make out anything whatever. That the hostiles were <u>somewhere</u> ahead of him he well knew, but he did not believe the trained senses of his own Indians were as good as his own surmises. Again we note that strange self-sufficiency, egotism, and conceit that on that fatal Sunday brought their legitimate fruitage.
>
> His orders to Benteen were; "to move to the left . . . to a line of bluffs five miles to the left and front – to hunt for Indians . . . Bouyer and the Crows were familiar with the country; time and again some of them had traversed it. They knew the lay of the land; Custer did not, nor did he trouble himself to find out from those who knew. Bouyer could have told him all about those bluffs "to the front and left," and save Benteen a weary, wasted ride. Half-Yellow Face or Hairy Moccasin could have shown him how futile his divided attack would be . . .[4]

This passage is illustrative of a tendency I have pointed out repeatedly. In my reading of testimony I have not encountered any statements by Custer to suggest that he thought the scouts did not see a village. The statements I have read indicated that Custer had not seen what the scouts were reporting, and though he might have been skeptical, he was not saying they were wrong. Red Star even said that Custer nodded twice to confirm that he saw what the scouts and Charlie Reynolds were pointing out. I believe the evidence supports the view that Custer accepted the scouts' reports, and, to me, his actions also indicate that he did.

Dustin is using Custer's orders to Benteen to bolster his contention that the General did not accept the scouts' opinion of where the encampment was, and sent Benteen to look for it, since he did know it was somewhere ahead. This contention supports the idea which Benteen tried to convey – with success, I might add – that Custer didn't believe his scouts, that he had no plans and that he sent Benteen on a wild goose chase. I am not a military man, but I believe Custer understood the situation, and he must have known what he had to do. If one

ANALYSIS OF WRITERS' SCENARIOS

assumes that Custer had a certain degree of intelligence, then I think one could credit him with the following attitudes and decisions: First, I am intrigued by what I would call the dichotomous views of writers. Many point out the Indians' ability to set up ambushes, and even to do so with Custer, as he moved down Medicine Tail Coulee. However, they say that Custer didn't believe his scouts, and he didn't have any plan of battle. Their proof is his division of command, complimented by his sending Benteen off to the left to look for Indians. They suggest that if he had asked, or followed his scouts' advice, he would have known Indians were not there. Were these scouts perfectly sure there weren't Indians in that direction? I doubt it. Shouldn't Custer have been concerned that the Indians might be setting up an ambush, and shouldn't he have made sure they didn't? Custer must have learned something from the Battle of the Washita; he must have known, for example, that the Indians often separated their camps.

I will point out again that I am not a military man, but if I thought there was a large force of Indians ahead of me, even though I accepted my scout's opinion of where the Indian encampment was located, I would want to make sure there were not Indians waiting for me as my main command moved down Ash Creek. Remember that Custer was informed through Bouyer via White Man Runs Him about the route to follow to reach the Little Bighorn, and he took their advice. We don't know what other things Bouyer may have told Custer as to the terrain ahead, and what actions the Indians might take.

Getting back to my earlier statement, I believe Custer first planned to send Benteen to the bluff to look for Indians and then return; but later, possibly because of advice from Bouyer, other scouting reports, his view of the landscape, or further development of his plans as he moved down Ash Creek, Custer wanted Benteen to continue on to the valley of the Little Bighorn. By doing this, Benteen would be in a position to protect Custer's left flank, and, on reaching the valley he could make sure there were no camps or Indians that could move against him. To assume that Custer was not concerned there might be Indians in that direction unjustly discredits Custer as a commander.

Two major actions affected the events at that point. First, Benteen did not send any message to Custer at a time when Custer expected to receive one. Custer moved fairly slowly down Ash Creek; he was not aware of where Benteen and his battalion were. Custer came to the Lone Tepee and Girard reported that a small group of Indians were fleeing in the direction of where Custer believed the main camp to be located. Custer knew then he could not wait much longer before putting his plan into action, but he was still concerned as to the whereabouts of Benteen and he also thought of the packs. This is what a good commander would have been doing and I can't believe Custer wasn't one of them.

It seems to me that this situation led to a second prerequisite, which would have been to send another message to Captain Benteen. Whether this was a third messenger, or whether it was Sergeant Major Sharrow, I don't know, but the later messages Custer sent suggest that he did send one at that point. Benteen had already received the message to move to the valley, so Custer would have expected this new courier to reach Benteen by the time he entered the valley. Custer still delayed as long as he thought practical before he gave Reno his attack orders. Custer then knew he had to make his move to flank the Indians, if he expected to defeat them and prevent them from scattering. He hoped Benteen would be moving to the valley, as ordered, and would be able to support Reno in the center, or on the left, depending upon the situation. I think, because of Lieutenant Edgerly's, Private Corcoran's and civilian packer John Frett's reports, that the messenger, a sergeant, didn't find Benteen entering the valley of the Little Bighorn, but instead found him back on the trail near the morass. In returning to General Custer, the Sergeant passed and spoke to some Ree scouts and reached Custer before he sent the message to Benteen by way of Trumpeter Martin, but after the message he sent to Captain McDougall by way of Sergeant Kanipe.

By then, Custer realized that his original plan had to be changed, and it would be better for Benteen to angle across and support him. Custer had already ordered the packs to cut across country. I don't think it takes too much imagination to realize that after Custer saw the valley and the Indian encampment, he did not want the packs to attempt a crossing of the Little Bighorn for various reasons, not least of which would be the distance factor and the difficulty of fording the river. Nor would he want them to remain along Ash Creek as their initial instructions may have directed. There would have been no question by that time where the battle would be taking place. When the returning messenger reported Benteen some distance back on the main trail and not far ahead of the packs, he would also have reported on Major Reno's situation at that time: he was on the skirmish line and in no immediate danger. There would have been little question that Benteen should angle across toward the area where Custer expected both he and Reno would be engaged, and to make sure he brought the packs. Custer then sent Martin with the message.

The impression given by many writers is that Custer's decision to divide his command, as a result of which the troops ended up too far apart to be effective, reflects Custer's lack of planning. I think that perception was created by Benteen's statements to justify his actions. Benteen had orders to move to the valley, and if he believed the information about the location of the Indian camp, as he said he did, he should not have taken his oblique move back to the main trail. His slowness in reacting to the messages he received after reaching the main trail is inexcusable and cannot be justified by any concern for his horses.

As for those who point out that Benteen never said he received such orders, they need to ask themselves the following questions: If you were in his place and were questioned after the battle, knowing what happened to Custer, would you have said you received orders indicating Reno was being sent to attack the Indian encampment and that when you reached the Little Bighorn valley you should move to support him? Later, with the accusations being levied at Major Reno and Captain Benteen, would you expect either of them to have admitted receiving such orders? The lack of said orders is the basis for their defense at the Reno Court of Inquiry. How many others, apart from themselves, knew the extent of their orders? Lieutenant Wallace had to be involved in the cover-ups, and the only other person who had direct knowledge was Trumpeter Martin. This is the reason for the questions used to discredit him, and for the lack of direct examination as to the orders given by General Custer. Yet, as I previously stated, considering the messages we know Custer conveyed, can one really believe that he would have sent Reno into action without notifying Benteen? Most agree that Adjutant Cooke gave Reno his orders, although some say that Custer and Reno rode together and Reno received his orders directly from Custer. In most accounts Adjutant Cooke is even said to have gone to the river with Major Reno, and though I don't believe he did, I do think something would have been said concerning Captain Benteen and the part he had been assigned to play in the attack.

Dustin then, as Dr. Kuhlman did, spends a lot of time and study on Reno's skirmish position and the action that took place. Part of it is due to Dustin's attempt to justify Major Reno's actions, and though his discussion is interesting and important from that standpoint, I would have preferred it if he had spent the same amount of effort on analyzing the time it would have taken Major Reno to traverse the mile and a half to Ford A, cross, reform and be ready for his move down the valley. This is the significant time relation which is of the essence in determining what took place afterward, and even five minutes could have made a great deal of difference. There is an acceptance of the period from 5 to 15 minutes for the crossing which I think is much too short. Even by a conservative estimate, the crossing would have taken 20 to 25 minutes.

It is also important whether Girard reported to Adjutant Cooke that the Indians weren't running. Girard's statement is accepted without analysis, although most writers, including Dustin, have nothing good to say about Girard's veracity.

> . . . There seems to be a very substantial agreement that this position [Reno's skirmish line] was held about fifteen minutes . . . Varnum said that about the time Reno ordered the battalion to dismount, he saw the gray horse troop (Smith's) moving down the bluffs on the opposite side of the river, distant about three quarters of a mile.
>
> . . . Also, at the Court of Inquiry, DeRudio testified that he saw Custer, Cooke, and a soldier, or other person on a high point about opposite where the line halted not long before Reno's retreat. He recognized the Colonel and Cooke "by their dress and the immense beard of the latter" and stated they were "about a thousand yards distant."
>
> There are apparent discrepancies in DeRudio's statements that require analysis. He says that the point where he saw Custer was just a little below where Dr. DeWolfe was killed. If so, the distance was at least a mile and a half, but he also testified that "it was nearly opposite his position in the bottom, . . . It was not on Weir's Point, but one nearer the river . . . It was on "the highest point on the right bank." If Custer was on "the highest point", he was actually about opposite DeRudio, but at least a mile distant. While we must make allowances for excitement and confusion, it would seem that he was mixed up, both as to his estimate of distances and positions . . . we find a solution. From the accounts of Trumpeter Martin and those Crows who accompanied Custer, it seems that officer twice came out on the bluffs for a look at the valley below. Some of Reno's command saw a portion of Custer's battalion as it passed along back of the front range of bluffs where they were parted by a ravine. As Reno had advanced at a trot and gallop, while Custer moved more slowly, their commands were nearly opposite each other, and there is little doubt that DeRudio saw Custer twice, first near the Hodgson marker, where he first rode to a viewpoint, about the time Reno halted to fight on foot, and later, when Custer was seen to wave his hat from the "high point." DeRudio was quite flurried, and his confusion was not unnatural under the exciting circumstances of the fight.

> The men remained on the skirmish line fifteen or twenty minutes under hot fire . . .[5]

The sighting of Custer on the ridge was a critical part of the cover-ups during the Reno Court of Inquiry. Dustin's explanation of the discrepancies in DeRudio's testimony is that DeRudio saw Custer twice. It is entirely possible that DeRudio saw Custer or his troops on the ridge, as I believe other officers did when Reno moved down the valley. This was when enlisted men reported seeing them – seemingly while regrouping and moving down the valley. These sightings would fit into what I consider a proper timing sequence. They would also indicate a movement along the ridge and not back from it.

Two points, in my view, refute DeRudio's sighting when in the timber. First of all, he would not have been able to recognize Custer by his blouse and Adjutant Cooke by his beard at the distance that separated them. His second error was that he couldn't have seen Custer at that time from the timber. There is no way Dustin and other writers can accept Varnum's sighting of the Gray Horse Troop, no matter where on the ridge it was observed, and still accept DeRudio's sighting from the timber. The same would apply to the sightings by the troops. Between Varnum's sighting and DeRudio's, at least twenty minutes would have elapsed; another ten minutes would have to be added to include the troopers' viewing Custer. As a result, we would have roughly a half hour during which time Custer had not moved a mile. The two major witnesses, Kanipe and Martin, said that Custer was moving at a rapid gait during that time (the collapse of several horses would indicate that). These considerations, along with the Ree accounts of Custer's movements, and Martin spotting Reno's troops moving into the timber when he reached the ridge after Custer left, make DeRudio's sighting from the timber impossible.

Dustin, like other writers, claims that Custer came to the edge or high points twice to view the valley. It is possible that he may have done it three times, if I am right in assuming that Custer reached the ridge before his troops and met Bouyer there. At that time, Custer may have been seen by the Rees, who said they saw Custer with Curley and Black Fox. Custer then met the troops on the south side of Sharpshooter Hill, as Curley and Martin seem to imply, and he may have gone either to the high point opposite Sharpshooter Hill or up the hill. Then, not being able to see all he needed, Custer moved on down to Weir Point.

This point is not as important, however, as the relative position of Major Reno and General Custer. I believe Custer did reach the ridge ahead of Reno's move down the valley, which is why Martin didn't believe they saw Reno. As they were regrouping, Reno's troopers may have seen Custer at the high point near Sharpshooter Hill, and when halfway down the valley, they saw Custer's troops moving along the ridge on their way to Weir Point. I assume that Custer was already at Weir Point when this sighting took place. This would have been approximately the same time Kanipe and Custer's troops saw Reno's.

Dustin spends some time justifying Major Reno's move from the timber, and in so doing uses officers' testimony at the Reno Court. He uses the same approach he employed in his attempt to establish that Reno did not lead a panicky retreat from the timber. Dustin said of the officers' testimony that they were all made at the Court of Inquiry. The fact that the officers were under oath supposedly settles the matter. Colonel Graham used this same reasoning in his discussion.

As I have suggested before, anybody who uses this rationale to substantiate their views is extremely naive, for they should be aware of officials, including our highest officials in government and business, who have lied and distorted the truth even on the witness stand. The trial centered around this action on the part of Major Reno, and certainly the officers were not going to discredit him, particularly when it would also be a reflection on themselves.

I am not attempting to be too harsh in judging Reno's actions, but I do consider Dustin too lenient. The retreat showed disorganization, confusion and could not be called a disciplined military retreat. I don't know how the military manual described the way a retreat should be conducted, but I'd imagine several things. First, I accept General Stonewall Jackson's statement that if the enemy is retreating, you want to pursue them, for they will become panic stricken. Second, it didn't appear that the Indians posed an immediate threat – they were not about to overwhelm the soldiers – and the lines of Reno's troops were not being penetrated, nor were they in a situation where they had no other choices; consequently, I think the manual would say that the commander should make sure all company commanders were aware of his decision, and I assume they would be expected to establish flankers and a rear guard. This did not happen, and I would condemn Major Reno for not having done so. Third, unlike Reno himself, I would not consider this a charge in the military sense of the word, although one might call it that in the generic sense. Dustin commends Wooden Leg's account, and he should have recognized that Wooden Leg, who was near the area where the troops broke from the timber, said that they at first fell back, so Reno wasn't really charging the Indians, nor was he forced from retreating back to Ford A. This may have been a good development, since Jackson's theory would have had even more of a chance to affect the troops. The last point is that if this "charge" up the bluff with the Indians in hot pursuit continued, I believe it would have disintegrated into a panic, and undoubtedly, many were in such a state during the flight. I find it impossible to label this "charge" as a well organized retreat.

I don't know if Major Reno should have been particularly condemned – possibly his company commanders were more at fault. However, Captain Thomas French, leader of M Company, in a letter to Adjutant Cooke's mother, claimed he thought of shooting Reno during their wild dash to the bluffs. Be that as it may, I do think one should use Reno's retreat in an objective comparison to the situation faced by Custer's command, which definitely encountered more extreme conditions. Outside of Benteen's remarks, and those of a few other soldiers, I have not read any comments to suggest that Custer's troops showed any signs of being disorganized until the final moments.

I agree with Benteen and others who believe that there were actually few signs of a military defense. There is some evidence suggesting that Keogh's battalion, and particularly Calhoun's company, did set up a skirmish line, and there was certain rear guard action by members of Yates' battalion on Greasy Grass knoll or the western part of Calhoun Hill, as well as some artifactual evidence along the so called South Skirmish Line and on Last Stand Hill. These, in the main, seem to have been pockets of resistance and not skirmish lines within a defense perimeter.

In his discussion, Dustin offers his view of Girard, who was the most vociferous critic of Reno among the men who were with him. Dustin defends Reno against Girard's charges, but doesn't mention Girard's message to Custer by way of Cooke. Girard was the interpreter of the Rees.

> There was one witness, however, whose testimony was not only contradicted by the officers but by himself, Fred Gerard. His testimony was not only rambling but incoherent and disconnected. . . .
>
> Another sample of his testimony: "From the ford (Reno's first crossing) the march was in a column skirting the edge of the timber, making a circuit and the skirmish line was drawn up, out from the outward edge of the bend of the timber. There were no Indians then within one thousand yards." This one statement alone is sufficient to demonstrate the utter unreliability of Gerard's testimony as a whole. The command <u>did not make</u> a circuit from the ford; it <u>did not</u> skirt the timber along the river, and <u>did not</u> touch the stream until <u>after</u> the skirmish line was formed, and instead of there being no Indians within a thousand yards, they were close up on the left and front. Further on he says: "When I first came to the ford . . . the bottom was alive with Indians, at least fifteen hundred of them," and further, "I think Reno could have held out if he were determined and resolute."[6]

Dustin also examines the duties and actions taken by the scouts, and he does a commendable job of supporting their conduct.

Dustin points out that "Stabbed had been detailed to follow a trail to the left and was behind the rest." He doesn't mention the statement of a Ree scout named Soldier who claimed that Stabbed had taken a message to someone on the left; in fact, Dustin ignores the question of the message altogether. I wonder if anyone attempted to follow up this lead to determine whom he may have taken a message to and what it may have consisted of. Camp feels the message was to Benteen, but he doesn't give any supporting evidence. Statements of this type should have solicited more curiosity and someone should have tried to find out their meaning.

After discussing the action of the Arikaras, Dustin continues:

> Red Star saw Varnum, with his orderly who was wounded in the ankle. He also saw the pack mules in a depression, and while looking down at them, there came over a ridge from the northward the three Crow scouts: "Goes Ahead, Hairy Moccasin and White Man Runs Him." Red Star says: "They came to the Arikara scouts and told them to go back because the army was beaten; 'the Dakota kill the soldiers easy,' that Curly, White Swan and Half-Yellow Face were killed. They, the Crows, intended to circle to the west and go home where they lived."
>
> . . . If the reader has kept track of the individual scouts, he will see that they are all accounted for. [Except Dustin didn't mention Black Fox; this was at the time the scouts decided to leave Major Reno on the bluffs.][7]

Benteen's march, when approaching the Little Bighorn and sighting the action in the valley.

> . . . "I thought the whole command was thrashed, and that was not a good place to cross." . . . Off to the right observing the battle were several Indians on higher ground, whom he took for hostiles, "but on riding toward them found they were Crows." Godfrey and one or two others make the same mistake; they were not Crows but Rees, whose movements have already been related. They motioned the command to go to the right . . .[8]

ANALYSIS OF WRITERS' SCENARIOS

I believe Dustin is mistaken in his observation that these were not Crows. From my analysis of Arikara accounts, I believe there were several groups of scouts who attempted to drive off some of the Sioux ponies. Kanipe passed some of these men when he moved to join Benteen. Dustin uses the following statement by Godfrey to justify his view that they were Rees and not Crows:

> It was near this time that Benteen appeared, having followed Reno's trail nearly to his first ford, thence turning to the right up the ridge where, as he relates in his report; "I then moved up to the bluffs and reported my command to Major M. A. Reno." It was during this change of direction from the ford that Godfrey says: "There was a short time of uncertainty as to the direction in which we should go, but, some Crow scouts came by driving a small herd of ponies, one of whom said "Soldiers' and motioned the command to the right." This was correct except as to their being Crows. They were Rees as we have seen. They had stripped for battle, and Godfrey's mistake was not unnatural, for to undiscriminating eyes, they all looked alike, . . . just Indians, but of course Godfrey had not time to observe that they wore their hair in braids on each side, and that it was parted on one side, while the Crows wore their hair cut off in front and reached up (pompadour) with braids on the sides. This is an example of the error of a supposed authority, for other writers, since Godfrey's story appeared in the Century over forty years ago, have naturally repeated it . . .[9]

I would conjecture that Godfrey remembered passing Indians with ponies. These would have been Rees, probably the same group Kanipe mentioned. However, he forgot the circumstances and connected this event with meeting the Crows. Though Dustin may be right that Godfrey was not able to distinguish between the two for the reason he mentioned, it remains doubtful in my opinion. Godfrey had been with these scouts for some time and he mentioned sitting and talking with them. Besides, these Crows then went with Benteen to the ridge. I think Godfrey may have made the mistake of mentioning the captured ponies in his account of meeting the Crows. However, the Crows may have picked up several Sioux ponies since there were probably a number of them loose in the area. They are said to have given one to Black Fox, albeit after leaving Reno Hill. It is questionable if both Benteen and Godfrey were mistaken. Additional proof for such a view is found in a Walter Camp letter to General Charles A. Woodruff in February, 1910, quoted in Hammer's book of Walter Camp's notes:

> White Man (White Man Runs Him) . . . In regard to Benteen's statement about meeting the Crows, he is very clear as to time and place, and is corroborated by Godfrey and several of the enlisted men – and by Goes Ahead and White Man Runs Him, himself. Benteen met the three Crows on the first rise of the bluffs north of the mouth of Sundance Creek. This is 1600 or 1800 feet north of Ford A and about 1 1/8 miles, in an airline south of Reno Hill. Godfrey stated to me personally that they (Godfrey being with Benteen) met the Crows here and that he, personally, rode up to one of the Crows and tried to talk to him. He says there could be no mistake about these men meeting Benteen's command on the bluff at this place: in fact, White Man goes into details about it. He could not be mistaken about the identity of the command, because there was no other command then Benteen's in the vicinity.[10]

I have referred to Dustin's mention of Red Star, the Arikara scout who met the three Crow scouts near Reno Hill and was told that Curley, White Swan and Half-Yellow Face were killed. I have not encountered Red Star's statement in any of the sources, but it could very well be true, and have no reason to doubt it except for the inclusion of Curley among the dead. The three Crows might have noticed the other Rees, and failing to see the two Crows, they might have thought they were dead. It's possible an interpreter or recorder added Curley, or the Crows may have stated the other Crows were gone or missing and the interpreter thought they meant they were dead. Since Curley had just left the three Crows, they would have known he was not dead, but they had warned him of the danger when he separated and moved toward Ford A; so again, semantics could have entered in. Keep in mind Red Bear mentioned talking to *four* Crow scouts. Then the four Crow scouts left. The split with Curley and the meeting of the three with Red Star, and then with Benteen, took place shortly afterwards.

I consider these sightings and meetings significant, not only because they shed light on Curley's various stories, but, more importantly, they serve as an indication that Custer had reached Ford B before Reno left the timber. I believe one can accept the Crow accounts that they fired on the Indian village as Custer moved within a few hundred yards of the ford, before Bouyer left them to join Custer. According to their testimony, which is consistent with their natural inclinations, the Crows stayed until they realized the troops were not going to be successful, and then left. They had over three miles to go on tired horses to the place where they met Red Bear, Red Star and Benteen. When they met Benteen, Reno's troops were just retreating across the Little Bighorn to the bluffs. Even by a conservative estimate, 30 minutes had gone by since the Crows had fired on the Indian village. If one went back half an hour before the Crows met Benteen, Major Reno would still have been in the timber.

There isn't any timing sequence that would contradict this scenario unless one assumes Custer is somewhere between Reno Creek and the place where he first engaged the Indians, and he does nothing offensively or defensively for 45 minutes to over an hour.

Dustin defends Major Reno's actions after the troops reached the bluffs and Reno Hill by contending that the soldiers were short of ammunition, although this is contrary to Godfrey's statement and various others. Dustin also defends Reno's and Benteen's assertions that they didn't hear any amount of firing downstream.

> Previous to Benteen's arrival, firing had been heard down the river by the men still in the bottom, and perhaps as distinctly by at least many of those on the hill, but any person who had experience in a hilly country knows how sounds are reflected and deflected, and that frequently a change of position of a few rods may entirely eliminate sounds that are very distinct to others near at hand.[11]

> ... there can be no doubt that Custer's battalion became engaged about the time Reno retreated to the bluff, and he only had about a mile to ride after he was seen by DeRudio on the spur, to the middle ford, which he unquestionably approached near the mouth of Medicine Tail Creek, and it was here that the first firing was heard while the later heavy firing was on and around the present Battlefield Reservation.[12]

Dustin proceeds to justify the delay in moving downstream, and when the troops finally move, he supports Major Reno's assertion that he himself controlled the advance. I question this claim, but it is of no major importance today. What is odd in this account is that there is no mention of the retreat from Weir Point and nothing is said concerning Godfrey's and Troop K's action during the retreat.

> From where Custer diverged from the great trail to Reno's final stand, it is about a mile and a half, but his trail on the Battlefield sheet is not correctly platted... There can be no question that he was looking for a place to cross the river, and instead of "supporting" Reno, he was getting away from any support that he himself might need. Once more we have a picture of an infatuated egotism; with him, the best guide in that whole country and four Crows who were, so to speak, right at home. Bouyer had warned him, Bloody Knife had warned him, Stabbed had warned him. Bouyer and the Crows could have told him of every feasible ford; they could have told him that those bluffs continued downstream for three miles with little or no chance of crossing, even if unopposed by warriors fighting for their families and herds. Then why his inordinate self-sufficiency and conceit? In an opening chapter we have said that to explain some acts of men, we must know something about the men themselves, and we now recall some of the WHYS, . . . his court-martial in 1867; his trouble with Sully in 1868; the Stanley affair; the Belknap testimony; the "swing clear" statement, and last but not least, Terry's written orders.[13]

Again, I have to take issue with Dustin for I don't think we know just what Bouyer and the others told Custer or how he applied the information, nor do I think we know the extent of the orders he gave to either Reno or Benteen. The orders Custer issued could very easily have been based on the information he had received from his scouts. I cannot help concluding that Custer had a plan, and it centered around Benteen moving to the valley of the Little Bighorn, and then proceeding down it in support of Reno. In such a plan, six companies would be attacking the village from one direction while Custer and his five companies would approach it from the other end. When Custer viewed the valley from the ridge, Reno had not yet attacked and the Indian village was basically peaceful. At that point, Custer knew the exact location and the approximate size of the village, and he determined the route he would take to attack the encampment. Custer could ascertain it would be foolish to have the packs attempt to cross the ford or to hold in the valley of Ash Creek. (An assumption that his first plan might have been to hold in the valley, could answer some of my earlier questions concerning the packs.) Custer would have sent Kanipe with his message to McDougall for the packs to cut across country.

Custer's actions suggest that he didn't know Benteen was back on the trail; otherwise the message would have been sent to Benteen and would have been similar to the one Martin would soon take. We know that Benteen's orders were to move to the valley of the Little Bighorn, making sure there were no Indians to the south, and I am quite certain (though probably alone in this conviction) that Benteen was expected to move down the valley and support Major Reno from the left or center depending on the situation.

Custer then went from the ridge to Medicine Tail Coulee, during which time a courier (I believe Sergeant Major Sharrow) joined Custer, informing him that Benteen was far back on the main trail and the packs were close behind him. Custer, now within sight of the north end of the village, must have realized several things. From the gunfire and the messenger's report he would have known that Reno was now engaged. The courier undoubtedly told him the Indians were attacking Reno; however, Reno had established a skirmish line and seemed to be comparatively well off, but he had not entered the village. Knowing that Benteen was back on the trail, Custer preferred that he move in his direction rather than moving to and crossing the Little Bighorn at Ford A. Custer knew that the main attack would take place on his end and he would need support. Custer then sent Martin with his message to Benteen to hurry and to bring the packs. After sending Martin back, Custer probably moved closer to the village. Knowing that his attack would have to be in a column formation, and still fearing that the Indians would scatter (which, considering what was happening in the village, he had every right to believe), he placed Keogh's battalion in reserve. (Since Curley was apt to still be on the ridge, his accounts of the command stopping, and a conference taking place, more than likely stemmed from this action.) Custer must have realized the topography was ideal for Keogh's battalion to move to the ridge – now known as Nye Cartwright Ridge – and from there to observe the course of the battle. If the Indians scattered to the north and west, Keogh could move to cut them off, and if Custer should need help he would be in a position to render that aid. I don't think there is any question that Custer still contemplated an attack and predicted a victory at that stage.

Although Custer wanted Benteen to move to the area, he would not have delayed his attack in order to wait for him. Keogh was probably given orders for Benteen when he arrived. Benteen was an additional back up, and if a retreat became necessary, they would be in a position to unite and establish a strong defense. I suspect Custer considered the possibility of a retreat. Contrary to the impression given by some writers, Custer had retreated at different times during the Civil War.

I think a commander with the stature of Custer would have been concerned – and his message indicates that he was concerned – with all of his troops, and the ways in which they could best be brought to bear on defeating the Indians. I do not believe that such speculation is "Monday morning quarterbacking," and though I may be giving Custer too much credit – I am sure someone like Fred Dustin would think so – testimony and Custer's known actions would support such a hypothesis.

The following statement refers to when Custer was at the Crow's Nest, at a time when Dustin and others say he rejected and wouldn't accept the scouts sightings. I have used this before, but it applies here as well:

Red Star: In the party were Custer, his bugler, Tom, Red Star, Gerard, Bloody Knife, Bob-tailed Bull and Little Brave. They rode hard toward the hill . . . When they got to the foot of the hill, and came to the scouts. Charley Reynolds came up and he and Custer went ahead leaving the others behind. Charley Reynolds pointed where Custer was to look, and they looked for some time and then Gerard joined them.

Gerard called back to the scouts: "Custer thinks it is no Sioux camp." Custer thought that Charley Reynolds had merely seen the white buttes of the ridge that concealed the lone tepee. Charley Reynolds then pointed again, explaining Custer's mistake, then after another look Custer nodded that he had seen the signs of a camp. Next Charley Reynolds pulled out his field glasses and Custer looked through them at the Dakota camp and nodded his head again. Crooked Horn told Gerard to ask Custer how he would have felt if he had found two dead Dakotas at the hill. The scouts had seen six Dakota Indians after Red Star and Bull left them. . . . and they wished to kill them first. They did not do so because they were afraid Custer might not like it. Custer replied that it would have been all right . . . Then the scouts sat down and one of the Crow scouts, Big Belly, got up and asked Custer through the Crow interpreter what he thought of the Dakota Camp he had seen. Custer said: "This camp had not seen our army, none of their scouts have seen us." Big Belly replied: "You say we have not been seen. These Sioux we have seen at the foot of the hill, two going one way, and four the other, are good scouts, they have seen the smoke of our camp." Custer said, speaking angrily: "I say again we have not been seen. That camp has not seen us. I am going ahead to carry out what I think. I want to wait until it is dark and then we will march, we will place our army around the Sioux camp." Big Belly replied: "That plan is bad, it should not be carried out." Custer said: "I have said what I propose to do, I want to wait until it is dark and then go ahead with my plan."

Red Star, as he sat listening, first thought that Custer's plan was good. The Crow scouts insisted that the Dakota scouts had already seen the army and would report its coming and that they would attack Custer's army. They wanted him to attack at once, that day, and capture the horses of the Dakotas and leave them unable to move rapidly. Custer replied: "Yes, it shall be done as you say."[14]

I have no reason to believe that Red Star would have any ulterior motive for lying. Consequently, I think his statement is generally true. It refutes numerous points that have been made and validates others. For one thing it indicates that Custer planned to wait another day. The statement that Custer planned to encircle the camp should make one recognize that this or another similar maneuver, would most likely become part of his ultimate strategy. A third basic point is that we see Custer not only talking to but listening to his scouts, showing that Dustin's criticism is not accurate. In fact, Custer goes so far as to change his plan because of the scouts' advice. It is absurd, in my view, to suggest that Custer had moved by all these camps, hearing and seeing various signs the scouts supposedly were aware of, but he did not accept them simply because he would not pay attention to the scouts.

Possibly the main point Red Star makes is that Custer accepted and even saw the signs the scouts were pointing out as to where the camp was. Custer's words and his plans imply a recognition of the general location of the camp. He would not have plotted to wait until dark and then encircle the camp if he hadn't known anything about it.

White Man Runs Him's later statements reflects a desire not to be subjected to additional blame for Custer's attacking when he did.

Discussing Custer's move once he reached the ridge, Dustin takes issue with Godfrey's later views of the route Custer followed. He relates the following remarks by Sergeant Kanipe.

> "When we reached the top of the bluffs, the Indians had disappeared, but we were in plain view of the Indian camps, which appeared to cover a space . . . four miles long . . . Reno and his troops were again seen to our left moving at full speed down the valley. . . . Kanipe continues: "Custer and his troops were within about one half mile of the east side of the Indian camps when I received the following message from Captain Thomas Custer, (his troop commander) . . . 'Go to Captain McDougall. Tell him to bring pack train straight across the country. If any packs come loose, cut them and come on quick – a big Indian camp. If you see Captain Benteen tell him to come quick – a big Indian camp!'"[15]

When reading Kanipe's or Martin's statements, or, for that matter, any others, one should remember that they were made some time after the battle and are likely to be jumbled in their chronology and locations. Unless the speaker brings out a particular point and indicates where a particular event took place, one has to view things in a general way. The most important point to determine concerns the relative positions between Custer's troops and those of Major Reno. In other testimony, Kanipe said that they saw Reno's troops in action, but in the above remarks he claims that they were moving at a gallop down the valley. He doesn't say where C Troop was, in relationship to General Custer, and is not clear on how Tom Custer received his orders. I assume that Kanipe got his message somewhere beyond the Lookout Point where Dustin thought he did. The location could have been anywhere between the highest point along the edge of the bluffs to just beyond Weir Point. Kanipe said that Custer didn't stop when he moved along the ridge, and though I think this was due to Kanipe's location behind Custer, with the troops strung out, Kanipe could have been moving up, to the time he received the message. Kanipe was on the ridge with Walter Camp, and it is regrettable that this point wasn't pursued further. My opinion is based on the reasoning that Custer's troops came onto the ridge north of Reno's entrenchment area and Kanipe would not have been able to see the valley until then. Since this would be the approximate location of Lookout Point and Kanipe referred to moving down the ridge, I do not think he received the message at that time.

This location is not within one half mile of the east side of the Indian camps. It is possible that Custer may have decided to send word to Captain McDougall just before or, I am more apt to think, right after he viewed the valley from Weir Point. Kanipe's report of seeing Major Reno's troops moving down the valley correlates with Reno's troops viewing Custer on the ridge. After Kanipe received the message and was moving off the ridge, Reno was establishing his skirmish line. All of these events would be somewhat twisted together in Kanipe's memory, which is why I think that if Custer's troops were in a line formation, as Kanipe remembered, it was not as they moved down the ridge but on their way to the ridge.

Dustin in a footnote concerning this:

> After visiting the battlefield . . . a number of things that before were obscure, or in doubt, were cleared up. Standing on the ground, I could see the same topography and landscape that Custer did. The Crow scouts said: "Custer first went to the top of the ridge and waved his hat." It is not very clear just where this occurred, and if read carefully, the stories of the Crows, Kanipe and Martin, are not only in agreement, but give a picture of Custer's movements and observations up to the time Curley left him . . .[16]

At Custer's Lookout, he could probably see the signs of Reno's engagement in the valley and part of the Indian camp. Here he sent back his messenger, Sergeant Kanipe. The troops continued down the gentle slope to Weir's Peak; this Custer ascended with Martin and others and saw the whole Indian camp, but now Reno's command was hidden by the fringe of trees, but he could still see signs of battle in plenty, and that Reno was very near the upper end of the camp. The topography is deceitful, and he thought that the rapidly deepening and descending coulee at the right of the peak would bring him out near the river; it was an easy trail while to lead his five troops over the steep bluffs would be not only illogical but very difficult.[17]

It will be apparent to the reader that, in brief, the story of Custer's movements from the lone tepee to the middle ford are not in any fog of obscurity, and if we say that he moved to Reno Hill near where his column was seen by Varnum, that he himself rode out to the edge of the bluff above the DeWolfe marker and was seen by DeRudio and others waving his hat; that he rode on, halted his command, and rode with Martin to the high point, rode back, waved the battalion down the draw, sending Martin back with his last message: and continued on to the middle ford, looking for a crossing, but found that place defended by hundreds of warriors, and was pushed to the right by a heavy fire from across the river from Indians concealed in the undergrowth, we have surely approximated the truth.[18]

Dustin seems to have ignored Kanipe's statement that he saw Reno's troops moving down the valley. Instead, he suggests that they are engaging the enemy, which not only twists Kanipe's remarks but contradicts any acceptable timing sequence. Varnum said that he saw the Gray Horse Troop across from Reno's skirmish line, which in no way would be Reno Hill, and DeRudio could not have seen Custer from the timber in this location nor could he have done it from a timing standpoint. I would say that Dustin approximated the truth except for the basic ingredients: timing, sightings, the location from which Martin was sent back and the estimate of the number of warriors waiting for Custer.

In his testimony before the Court, Martin said: "We looked on the bottom and saw the Indian villages; at the same time we could see only children and dogs and ponies – no Indians at all. General Custer appeared to be glad and supposed the Indians were asleep in their tepees." We revert back to what the Crow scouts said, "there were not many around," and Bouyer suggested they were out campaigning somewhere," and so they were. It will be remembered that when the command was riding down Reno's Creek, before Custer left Reno, and long before reaching the lone tepee, Indians had been seen ahead, and later forty or fifty were fleeing before Reno's battalion. The lone tepee not only marked the place of the general great camp of a few days before, but at that time, it was near the camp of a small body of Dakota who were on their way to joining the great camp down the river.

They had been alarmed by the young men that the scouts had seen at the Crow's Nest, and had hastily pulled down their tepees. Those seen by the troops were the warriors, acting as rear guard to the women and children . . .

It seems impossible that Custer should have believed the Indians asleep in their tepees, but he seems to have been in a strange condition of infatuation. When he rode out on the bluff, above the DeWolfe marker and downstream from it, it would have been impossible for him not to have seen the fight that Reno was in, to hear the barking of the carbines and crack of the rifles, to say nothing of the whoops and yells of the Indians.[19]

Dustin doesn't explain why Bouyer thought they were out campaigning, and with all the ability Dustin has credited him with (and that I assume he had), it seems strange that Bouyer would make such a statement. Since he had moved closer to the valley than Custer himself, it's rather curious that he would not have heard the same things or possibly even more than Custer. Dustin has no trouble condemning Custer, saying that it was impossible for him not to have been aware of all this, but he fails to explain why Curley said that Bouyer felt much the same way, or explain why, in Curley's narratives, Custer left the ridge before Reno became engaged.

What I really think is striking in Dustin's writing is that there is no analysis of these statements, except for an indirect accusation of Martin for not knowing what was happening. Like other writers, Dustin suggests that Martin couldn't see Reno's forces because they were hidden by the trees. (Martin's ability has been disparaged, but I didn't realize it included being deaf.) The statement, which is no excuse, actually constitutes an indictment of Custer, Martin, Bouyer and Curley. In Dustin's final analysis, he concludes that the Indians had already left the villages.

Dustin goes on to say:

The largest tribe were the Oglalas, at the upper end of the camp, with which Reno was almost in touch, and they numbered probably three thousand persons, . . . [Dustin then quotes Wooden Leg] "We find that at the alarm and firing up the river, there was a rush of young men from the Cheyenne village at the extreme lower end of the camp, nearly three miles away.[20]

The tribe nearest to Reno's attack, and the largest, were the Hunkpapa, not the Oglalas. Since Dustin was quoting Wooden Leg, he could have mentioned that Wooden Leg said they were completely surprised. He went to a social dance the night before and was sleeping late that morning. When they realized they were being attacked, he ran to where the herdsmen were grazing their ponies, which had to be some distance away. There, the herdsmen ran off, so he had to walk back to camp where his father had caught his pony, which had been driven in by other herdsmen. It doesn't take a great deal of thinking to realize the Cheyenne would have been the last to know what the firing meant, and it would have taken Wooden Leg some time to have run to where the herdsmen were, walk back to camp, get prepared and move to meet Reno. Custer would have to have been well on his way to the ford by the time Wooden Leg left to go to meet Reno's troops.

> What accounted for the "quietness" of the great camp? As soon as the alarm came, there was a rush of women, old men, and children away from the camp to the low hills or bench land westward. They had no intimation of the numbers of white soldiers, and were surprised by the attack. This must not be understood as "a surprise attack," for it was not. It was neither a Washita nor a Sand Creek. The Indians supposed it was Crook's forces . . .[21]

Dustin, and other writers whose thesis revolves around the concept of Reno attacking before Custer viewed the village, and who claim that the report by Martin that the village was asleep, reflect either ignorance or the fact that the Indians had already left, should look a little closer at their reasoning to see what they are actually saying.

The essence of their thesis is that the Indians had already left, when Custer viewed the village: Reno's attack had taken place; the Indians were excited and left the camps. One then has what looks like a peaceful village. Custer and Martin went to the high point and Custer thought he had caught the Indians napping. One officer thought they were out on a buffalo hunt and Bouyer suggested they had to be out campaigning somewhere. Martin couldn't see Reno in action because of the trees.

The spectators must also have been deaf and all the Indians must have reached the low hills and been hiding. The warriors were either fighting Reno or were already waiting in ambush for Custer, who they somehow knew would be coming down a coulee to Medicine Tail and then on to the Miniconjou Ford. This scenario is debatable and additional questions easily come to mind.

This was a camp which most writers say stretched some three miles and contained ten or twelve thousand Indians. I have not read any Indian testimony to suggest that they were aware of being attacked, until there was some firing by the Indian scouts, or until Reno established his skirmish line. One should keep in mind what Wooden Leg said he was doing before he went to attack Reno. Gall and others gave similar impressions. How long after Reno went into action would it take for all the camps to realize what was happening and have women find their children, gather some belongings, take down tepees, and then leave, so in viewing the village it would give the appearance of being peaceful? However, we must remember that this is not all: the Indians left some children playing in the villages, along with some dogs and even ponies. According to this scenario, they really must have been intent on misleading the troops so that Custer would move against them and at Ford B. Curley's statement that he saw Indians moving to meet Reno, and others going to meet Custer, must have been another one of his errors, or it must have taken place much earlier than he said it did. Some of the Indians went to meet Reno, and the others, knowing that Reno and Custer would separate, were going to establish their ambush. They must have accomplished this task before Custer looked down at the village. One might assume that they had planned and rehearsed this maneuver for several days.

This scenario is extremely fanciful. It even seems enigmatic that Dustin and others have accepted it. I would think they might have questioned their hypothesis. If they ever did, they might have asked: What if Martin or Curley were correct and the village was peaceful? What would this mean? The first answer would seemingly be apparent: Major Reno must not have gone into action when Custer viewed the village. What about Lieutenant Varnum's sighting of the Gray Horse Troop? How would this fit in? What about Lieutenant DeRudio's sightings? If Custer viewed the village from Weir Point, as Martin and Curley have indicated, what state would the village have been in some twenty minutes later when Custer arrived at Ford B? How many Indians would have been in a position to see Custer's troops before they arrived at the Ford? Was Custer planning to attack the village? What could have stopped such an attack?

I want to briefly look at the situation again, since I think this is extremely important. Most writers believe that there were some ten thousand or more Indians in the camp. Indian testimony suggests that very few of the Indians had their ponies available. They were surprised by Reno's attack and were not aware of it until firing broke out. Women were running after their children, taking down their tepees, getting together their belongings. Warriors were preparing themselves for battle. Indians from all the camps were going, as soon as they were ready, to meet Reno. The village may not have been in a panic but there was utter confusion. There is no way Martin or Curley could have reported sighting a peaceful village or one with no activity anytime after Major Reno went into action.

ANALYSIS OF WRITERS' SCENARIOS

Although I have no faith in most of Curley's accounts, he was consistent in saying that Custer had left the ridge by the time Reno became engaged. The Indians say that the camp was quiet; in fact, many stress the peacefulness of the morning until Reno's troops began firing and the village erupted. (One should keep in mind when assessing timing, the Indian accounts of when the action began.) Can there be any doubt that when Custer viewed the village Reno had not gone into action? I think the timing was so close that not all of Custer's troops had left the ridge by the time Reno established, or was setting up, his skirmish line. But I see no way that testimony, timing or logic would have Reno engaged before Custer began his move off the ridge.

> At the time that Reno left the timber, Custer was at the middle ford; Benteen, five or six miles away; McDougall, behind Benteen with the packs; no individual fighting unit within supporting distance of another. Had Reno not retreated to the bluffs, his finish would have been only a matter of minutes. Had Benteen, instead of turning back from the upper Reno ford and joining Reno, charged down the valley, he too would have shared the same fate, and as to McDougall with his troops, what could have been done?[22]

This passage is pure unfounded speculation on Dustin's part. At the time Reno left the timber, Benteen wasn't five or six miles behind. Custer's troops had already retreated from the middle ford. As I have previously stated, Benteen is the questionable cog in what Dustin is portraying, and behind that lies Dustin's and others' acceptance of the orders Major Reno and Captain Benteen said they received. I think Custer gave orders to Benteen to move to the valley – that being the Little Bighorn – and then to move down that valley. Custer expected him to attempt to encircle the Indians, depending on Reno's position. Custer would be flanking the village. The General himself moved fairly slowly until after he gave Reno the order to attack, mainly because he was waiting to hear from Benteen. Custer realized that Benteen needed time to move into position. The scouts undoubtedly informed him that Benteen's initial going would be slow, or Custer would have known from merely looking in the direction Benteen had gone. Benteen's slowness is apparent and the only question is how slow he was and why. Benteen should have known, even without orders, that an attack was imminent, and at such a time you cannot spare your horses. I know of none, as there were with Custer's command, that dropped or even were straggling way behind. I don't believe Benteen revealed all of his orders – after the battle he was smart enough to realize that they would have incriminated him. Rationalization set in. I assume that Custer hoped and believed Benteen would be close behind; and by all reports, he could have been if he had not taken his oblique back to the main trail but instead had crossed one more ridge to the South Fork and then angled to the river or back to the main trail.* Initially, Custer expected Benteen to be moving to help Reno, but after hearing, possibly from Sergeant Major Sharrow, that he was back on the trail and close to the packs, Custer wanted them to move quickly toward him and not cross the Little Bighorn. Here, again, Custer's orders were not followed in the manner he expected. Benteen didn't accept the urgency of his orders. The packs were to cut across country, but instead they moved beyond the Lone Tepee, and according to Lieutenant Mathey, rested for 15 minutes.[23]

It appears that nobody attempted to examine this issue; but another Benteen scenario seems to have been in operation with regards to the packs. According to Lieutenant Mathey and Captain McDougall, they didn't receive any message from Custer by way of Kanipe, so they too were not moving in the way Custer expected them to. By the time Custer heard that Benteen was back on the main trail and sent Martin to order him to hurry and to bring the packs, Custer could only hope they were not far behind. This uncertainty didn't diminish Custer's need to continue with his plan to attack the Indians. Time-wise, Custer should have reached the ford some fifteen to twenty minutes after Reno had gone into action – possibly prior to that – which would mean that Reno was still engaging the Indians in the valley and the Indian village was in a state of confusion. The question should then be: Why didn't a Custer attack take place? This is the basis of my original curiosity about the battle; but my specific question now is whether Dustin's scenario is correct. If Benteen had crossed the ford with the conditions being as Dustin portrayed them, more than likely he would be correct. On the other hand, if Custer's plan had gone into operation the way I believe he planned it, possibly a major victory would have taken place. If Benteen's three companies had moved against the Indians while Reno was still engaged (and shortly after they became engaged), and if Custer's troops struck a village as disrupted as it has been portrayed, with Keogh's battalion on the ridge east of their camp and McDougall arriving soon after, it is possible and even probable that Custer would have won. This is a speculative scenario, but I believe it has testimony, logic, psychology and artifacts which support it.

---

*See *Benteen's Scout,* by Roger Darling, pp. 29, 30, 31.

It is very doubtful if Custer's fight lasted an hour after he approached the ford at Medicine Tail Creek. DeRudio saw Custer a few minutes before Reno's command started to leave the bottom. Kanipe, Martin and the Crow scouts say that the Custer battalion went on a gallop. As the distance from where DeRudio saw Custer to the middle ford is about two miles, if we allow ten minutes for Custer's ride to Weir Point while the troops were halted, it could not have taken over half an hour at the longest to reach the ford where the firing began, making the time around 3:30. From the ford to where the first thick group of bodies lay was about a mile, and certainly the charge over this space, or rather the forcing of the command to the right to that point by the Indians, could have taken but a few minutes. According to the Indians, there was but one charge made by a single troop, evidently Smith's, and whether that was similar to Reno's, to escape, we can never know.[24]

Dustin doesn't examine Lieutenant Varnum's sighting, particularly as it would relate to DeRudio's sighting, which is something that must be done, whether to correlate the two or deny the possibility of one or the other. Also, you shouldn't ignore or even refer to the two sightings by DeRudio without justifying his last sighting. Dustin says that this came but a few minutes before Reno left the timber, and this is also what DeRudio testified. If that is so, then Custer must have viewed Reno's action some twenty-five or more minutes after he first became engaged. By the time Custer came down and talked to the troops and they left for Medicine Tail Coulee, Reno would already have been retreating. It is then necessary to explain how the Crows' could fire on the village with Custer coming down Medicine Tail and still get back to meet the Rees and Benteen. One must also explain Martin's statement that when he arrived on the point from which he and Custer viewed the village, Reno was engaged and still on the bottom. Martin then would not be able to continue several miles and meet Benteen where he did, and move with him to a place near Ford A with Reno's troops still retreating to the bluffs.

Dustin should have also clarified why he suggests in his map and his statement that Custer's troops traveled some distance back from the ridge, then halted and Custer moved to Weir Point. In this scenario Custer's troops would have been moving from the southern end of Cedar Coulee to below Weir Point. What Dustin should have demonstrated is how they were able to see what was going on in the valley and how those in the valley could have sighted them. This would apply to Varnum's sighting of the Gray Horse Troop and Kanipe's remarks of having moved along the ridge in sight of the valley below. Martin also said that they moved along the ridge.

I agree with Dustin that a consensus of Indian accounts suggests that there was only one "charge" made by the troops, but I disagree with his contention that we will never know if it was an attempt to escape or not. In the strict sense, Dustin is probably right, but Indian testimony and common sense suggest to me that without question the "charge" was a desperate attempt to escape.

> Since the lips of some of the Cheyenne and Dakota warriors have been unsealed, there have been some deeply interesting stories told, which bear the earmarks of truth, and of these there are more in the relation of Wooden Leg, then a young Cheyenne, who took part in the fight, both with Reno and Custer, than in all the others together. They are told so naively and recorded so well that the whole book may be commended to the reader who wishes to get the Indian viewpoint.[25]

I agree with Dustin's remarks, but find it peculiar that while he is quoting Wooden Leg, he does not accept his view that the Indians were completely surprised by the troops' attack on the 25th. Wooden Leg also reported the troops committing suicide and Dustin doesn't mention whether he supports this assertion or not.

> If we consider that thirty-six years had elapsed; that the Ree narrative was given in the Ree language and was interpreted from that into English, it is not hard to understand these apparent discrepancies. When Red Star states Curly and Black Fox were with Custer when that officer "stood on the bank where Hodgson's monument now stands," he may have either meant Reno instead of Custer, or have been misinterpreted. Curly and Black Fox were surely with Reno on the bluff, and Black Fox was surely with Reno in the fight in the valley, and came on the hill with the other Ree scouts, as before related, meeting Curly there, and retreating soon after as noted in the text.[26]

Dustin attempts to explain the remarks by Red Star, which is commendable, but I believe Red Star knew what he saw. If he was indeed mistaken or misinterpreted, it would have been more likely in regard to Curley or Black Fox. Dustin indicates that this sighting took place after Reno retreated to the bluffs, whereas I don't think there is any question that Red Star was referring to sighting Custer when he first reached the ridge. I think Red Star saw Custer on the ridge near the Hodgson marker. He may have been misconstrued by stating that he also saw Curley and Black Fox, but meant he saw them when they got together at the ford, at the time Reno had retreated. Goes Ahead then agreed with him. The interpreter could have thought he was indicating that he saw them with Custer on the ridge. Red Star had met the three Crows just after Curley left to go to the river to get a drink, which is supposedly where he met Black Fox. The misrepresentation of Red Star's remarks would be a natural mistake for the interpreter. Red Star's statement of seeing Custer on the ridge is part of the reason I think Custer came onto the ridge ahead of his troops. Custer met with Bouyer, and went to the edge of the bluffs with him and the Crows to view the valley. Some of the Rees had crossed the Little Bighorn and some had not. Reno hadn't cleared the timber at that time. Red Star, after seeing Custer on the ridge, moved down the valley ahead of Reno's troops. This scenario corroborates my view that Custer reached the ridge before Reno cleared the timber after his crossing at Ford A.

In their accounts, the Rees do not mention Black Fox being with them on the ridge after they left the valley. I also don't believe that Curley ever said that he was on the ridge with Reno after leaving Bouyer. As he suggested in his General Scott interview, Curley passed the entrenchment area, joined the other Crows, and moved off the ridge when he rode toward Ford A, leaving the other three. I assume that the four first met Red Bear and White Cloud before Curley departed. The three Crows saw Red Star and then Benteen, and they went back to Reno Hill with Benteen's troops. Curley and Black Fox might have met Lieutenant Mathey and the packs and then moved northeast along the bluffs. They probably saw Sioux chasing the Rees with their captured ponies and believed it was safer to circle around that area. If this indeed happened, Curley and Black Fox could have seen, from a distance, the last of the Custer battle. Since Last Stand Hill can be seen from Ridge B (a ridge referred to in tracing Benteen's scout to the left), there should be several locations where Curley could have seen the last of the fighting on Battleridge after leaving the Reno Creek area. This is where I think Curley's hill viewing statement was used by different interviewers to fit their particular scenario.

> From the flat below Busby, where they had found some food, Curly crossed the narrow divide to Tullock's Creek down which he rode, and arrived opposite Gibbon's wagon train camp and its guard. We will let Thomas H. LeForge, the interpreter relate what occurred.
> (Thomas LeForge) ". . . I saw an Indian come on horseback to the opposite bank. He dismounted and set himself at building a fire,... By sign-talk I learned he was one of my scouts, Curley, the seventeen year old Crow. He signed an inquiry as to the whereabouts of Gray Beard, their name for General Gibbon . . . Curley mounted his horse and rode away in that direction. I suppose he had a dispatch. He gave me no intimation of there having been a fight. He told me afterward that he was so sleepy he was thinking everybody knew about it. . . . From these escaping scouts, the column of soldiers learned of the calamity . . . I interpreted for Lieutenant Bradley when he interviewed Curley, several days after the Custer battle occurred. He was spoken then as the "sole survivor" of the disaster. But he himself did not lay claim to that kind of distinction. On the contrary, again and again during the long examination of him by Bradley, the young scout said, "I was not in the fight." When gazed upon and congratulated by visitors he declared, "I did nothing wonderful; I was not in it." He told us that when the engagement opened he was behind with the other Crows. He hurried away to a distance of about a mile, paused there, and looked for a brief time on the conflict. Soon he got still further away, stopping on a hill to take another look. He saw some horses running away loose over the hills. He turned back far enough to capture two of the animals . . . but later released them. He told me that he directed his course toward Tullock's Fork . . .
> Romantic writers seized upon Curly as a subject suited to their fanciful literary purposes. In spite of himself, he was treated as a hero. He took no special pains to deny the written stories of his unique cunning. He could not read, he could speak only a little English, and it is likely he knew of no reason why he should make any special denial. The persistent claim put forward for him by others, but as though it came directly from him, brought upon him the Sioux accusation. "Curly is a liar' nobody with Custer escaped us." But he was not a liar. All through his subsequent life he modestly avowed from time to time what he did to Bradley. "I did nothing wonderful; I was not in the fight." I knew him from early boyhood until his death in early old age. He was a good boy, an unassuming and quiet young man, a reliable scout, and at all times of his life he was held in high regard by his people.[27]

I believe this is one of the more honest and informative explanations of Curley's actions. I wish certain points would have been investigated further and brought out, because they could have clarified many puzzling matters. There is no question in my mind that Curley was never with Custer, once Custer left the ridge to move to Medicine Tail Coulee. Dustin appears to adopt a similar position.

Because of the vagueness of the wording and descriptive locations, I cannot say that this account substantiates my assertions, but I must point out that it doesn't refute them either, as it does the claims of many other writers.

In my analysis of Curley's various interviews, I maintained that the General Scott interview is his most accurate, perhaps due to General Scott's expertise in the use of the Indian sign language. Here, LeForge stresses Curley's knowledge of the sign language, which would mean that the interpreters would not have attempted to color or distort Curley's remarks.

There are several important statements and implications in Curley's account. LeForge claims that Curley said he was behind with the other Crows when Custer's engagement started. This doesn't necessarily mean that he was with them: he could have been, or he may have been near them when they were on the bluff overlooking the Miniconjou Ford. Curley would still have been in a position to see them fire on the village and possibly have done so himself. He more than likely moved back to Weir Point, which would be roughly a mile depending on just where he departed.

Curley then makes a relative statement, saying that soon he got farther away and stopped on another hill. "Soon" could mean anything within the next hour, which approximates the time he would have been in the immediate vicinity. I don't believe there are any hills between Weir Point and Reno Hill, or along the ridge from which one could have seen Custer fighting. The hill was probably to the east or northeast of Weir Point. It may be the one the Crows refer to as "Custer's Last Sighting."

I believe Curley did go toward Ford A, and, in the area, he met Black Fox; they then moved toward the northeast rather than continuing along Reno Creek. It was there that they went onto a hill and observed Custer's fighting. Then they moved toward Busby. Afterward, Curley separated from Black Fox, and moved, as he said, toward Tullock's Fork and then the junction of the Little Bighorn and the Bighorn River.

You would think that, at some time, Curley would have been questioned as to whether or not he was with Black Fox; if he was, I have not read of it.

These general statements by Curley help one to see how they were expanded upon by interpreters more intent on making a good story or supporting what they knew the interviewer may have wished to hear. The capture of the two horses could be made to appear as if it took place after Curley lost his own horse, possibly from Sioux who were killed as Curley was attempting to escape the fighting. Depending on the interpreter, viewing the fighting from the hills could be used to signify different locations and times during the battle where Curley left Custer and Bouyer. This could be molded, as it was, to fit into various dramatic escapes. As LeForge states, Curley could have been unaware of all of the modifications of his testimony.

Most of Smith's troops were lying in a ravine, as indicated on the map. Perhaps they had rushed into the supposed protection of the cover it afforded only to be picked off rapidly by Indians who fired from right and left, up and down the gully, for it has been stated that most of these men were shot in the side which would be logical from the situation. [I don't believe this is logical.]

The stories told and written about "the soldiers being in perfect military position, with skirmishers advanced and the officers in their places behind the lines is fiction. There were no "lines:" there was no "behind the lines," . . . It would be difficult to state, in view of all the known facts, that there was any organized resistance. Custer had led his five troops into a trap, and its jaws were sprung the moment he tried the ford at Medicine Tail Creek. . .

Colonel Gibbon did not visit Custer's field until after the dead were buried. . . . Arriving at the ravine where Smith's men were found, he noticed that its lower course was filled with brush, and thinking that perhaps some soldiers might have taken refuge there, he and those who accompanied him looked carefully but found nothing until they had proceeded some distance up the little open valley toward Custer's last position, when they suddenly came on a body in the tall grass, which was in an advance stage of disposition, . . .

The party continued onward toward the site of the monument; Gibbon says: ". . .along its southwestern slope and as we ride up towards it, we come across another body lying in a depression just as if killed whilst using the rifle there. We follow the sloping ground bearing a little to the left or westward until we reach the top, and then look around us. On the very top are four or five dead horses, swollen, putrid and offensive, their stiffened limbs sticking straight out from their bodies. On the slope beyond, others are thickly lying in all conceivable positions, and dotted about on the ground in all directions are little mounds of freshly turned earth, showing where each brave soldier sleeps his last sleep. Close under the brow of the knoll several horses are lying nearer together then the rest, and by the side of one of these we are told the body of Custer was found. The top of the knoll is only a few feet higher than the general surface of the long straight ridge, which runs off obliquely towards the river, in the direction of the ford at which it is supposed Custer made the attempt to cross.[28]

I believe that Colonel Gibbon's remarks help substantiate the view that the men, following the battle, thought that the bodies in the Deep Ravine were mainly Smith's men, and that they were found toward the front of the ravine. What is even more important is that in Gibbon's account of his move from Deep Ravine to Last Stand Hill, there is no reference to any large number of graves,

ANALYSIS OF WRITERS' SCENARIOS

and I think he would have referred to them if there was; nor is there any mention of a "south skirmish line" or an appearance of such.

Gibbon mentions the ridge running obliquely toward the ford, which he felt Custer attempted to cross. I think his statement helps support the belief that Custer did move to Ford B. It corroborates such a contention because it reflects the troops' view of what they thought Custer would have done. This perspective could have been strengthened by signs registered subconsciously, as well as possible statements made by Trumpeter Martin. Martin would have talked to others and supposedly showed Benteen the place from which he left, explaining or pointing out to General Terry where various incidents that he was aware of took place.

There are also two comments which contribute to a general and speculative picture of the events. The first has to do with the soldiers' bravery. Although I am not attempting to degrade the soldiers, I think the statement represents the aura surrounding Custer's phase of the battle until today. It's not hard to understand why comments such as those made by Benteen, Wooden Leg, Kate Bighead, and Marquis would have been disregarded and censored.

The other is Gibbon's comment concerning the two horses lying closer together than the others in the place where Custer's body was found. It could be that the horses were shot to provide protection for Custer, who may have been seriously wounded.

Dustin then gives his view of what happened as Custer moved down Medicine Tail Coulee toward Ford B:

> One, a boy in years, halts, hesitates, and slowly rides back to an elevation. It is Curly. The others halt, fire a few shots at the village not far across the stream, but the one wearing the vest of hides speaks to them saying:
>
> Go back; your duty is done . . . I SAID I WOULD GO WHEREVER HE WOULD GO: I AM GOING, and he and I and all his soldiers are Going TO THEIR DEATHS. Go back and live to tell the story!
>
> Thus speaks Bouyer, and we see those three red warriors riding back, but they pause from time to time, and so have brought the tale now told.
>
> Bouyer rides forward and overtakes the head of the column, which moved down the long slope approaching a ford and a ravine, but as it turns toward the stream, a host of red riders are crossing, and the troopers fall back repulsed and ride up the long slope toward the ridge whose apex we are on. We see a horde of whooping savages rising from behind hill and mound, from gully and sagebrush. They are in front, behind, to the right and to the left. The crack of rifle and carbine and the whizzing of arrows fill the air with dread sound. Soldiers fall; they run together, and finally, in a last rally, they gather near the very spot where we stand. Then comes a wild, circling charge of red warriors, and how soon it is all over! That Indian with the hide vest lies among the dead; so does the blonde soldier.[29]

This is a melodramatic account and is not written for its factual content. It still depicts Custer facing enough Indians to prevent him from attacking the village; but, even in this portrayal, the estimate doesn't ring true. If there were so many Indians crossing the ford as to have prevented Custer from attacking, there would be several things that I have not found in Indian testimony. First, the account contradicts the element of surprise and the general condition one could have expected the camp to have been in at the time Custer moved toward the ford. Indian accounts suggest that either a few Indians first crossed the ford to go and meet the troops, or that they fired from their side of the ford, partially hidden by a ridge or gully. Most Indians do not even mention seeing Custer's troops except back along Nye Cartwright Ridge. This makes it very doubtful that there were many Indians in the vicinity of the ford. If there were, it is questionable if the Crows would have moved to the bluff overlooking the ford and the village, let alone have fired into the camp. If they did, it seems like they would have been chased by some of these hundreds of Indians. This consideration also suggests that if Dustin and others were correct in their claim that Reno was retreating to the bluffs about the time Custer moved to the ford—since we know a number of Sioux crossed to the ridge—it is practically impossible that the Crows would have ever gone back and joined Benteen.

In his closing pages, Dustin continues to defend Major Reno's actions, and, to a lesser extent, Benteen's. Here, Dustin is condemning Whittaker, the writer who was an avid supporter of Custer and whom many consider the man responsible for pointing the finger at Major Reno and causing him to ask for a Court of Inquiry.

> Quoting from Whittaker's "Life," which was published subsequent to the "Galaxy" article, we find that he therein summarized the "causes" of Custer's defeat in the following underscored words: l. <u>Had Reno fought as Custer fought, and had Benteen obeyed Custer's orders, the battle of the Little Big Horn might have proved Custer's last and greatest Indian victory.</u>" 2. <u>Had not President Grant, moved by private revenge, displaced Custer from command of the Fort Lincoln column, Custer would be alive today and the Indian war settled.</u>". . .
>
> What happened at this court? Every officer in the fight

then living, except two, French and Gibson, testified, and answered affirmatively, with the exception of a remark or two by Godfrey, in reply to a question as to whether Reno did all he could and did it well, which he answered in the negative, and expressed the opinion that Reno did not exhibit cowardice, but "rather, nervous timidity," a statement directly opposite to that of every other officer who testified.[30]

Whittaker's statement that if Reno's troops had fought the way Custer's had, the battle might have been won, is illuminating in several ways. Whether Whittaker used it first, or not, I don't know; but the statement keeps appearing in writing and verbal accounts of various individuals, and it is especially significant as it appears in Indian testimony. This occurrence doesn't substantiate it, but it indicates to what extent the Indians were aware of what the white man was saying and synchronized their testimony to support and ingratiate themselves with the interviewer by offering what they thought he wanted to hear. There is no evidence that Custer's troops fought so bravely; in fact, the consensus would be the opposite. In Indian accounts of the battle, except for the statements suggested above, it's difficult to find any evidence either testimonial, or artifactual, that a determined resistance developed. As I have indicated earlier, Reno's troops, on their retreat from the timber, and even from Weir Point, showed signs of panic and certainly confusion, but because of the situation, they were able to regroup, and once they were organized, their conduct and basic courage became evident. Custer's troops were never able to accomplish this task and, except for pockets of resistance, were never able to establish a cohesive front.

What bothers me in this case (as well as in many other examples in history) is the judgmental attitude taken by those who were never involved in a battle, and at times by those that were in situations where they were able to exhibit courage. Such individuals consider themselves justified in condemning others. The officers and troops in the Battle of the Little Bighorn were human and their reactions were determined by the situation. As I have already mentioned, Reno's troops are good examples of people showing both courage and panic. I realize that a leader can make a difference, and certainly a strong point of Custer was his leadership quality, which Major Reno appeared not to have. This quality was what set Custer off from other officers. I could even say it is the essence of why I believe my scenario is correct. What strikes me as odd is how Whittaker's and others' assumption about Custer can be reconciled with the absence of any sign of a substantial attack taking place. Where is there any sign of a strong organized defense? The only evidence is in some Indian testimony which appears to fit the description I have already explained. It is impossible that the Indians didn't know what the whites were saying against Reno. Whittaker should have been asked which force held out for two hours and which for two days. It isn't enough just to blame Reno and Benteen.

Even though I believe their orders were more extensive than Reno and Benteen let on, I agree with Whittaker's conclusion that Custer was very close to a victory over the Indians. If Benteen had moved faster and Reno had held out longer, victory may have been accomplished with one essential ingredient: a major attack by General Custer. We should not condemn Major Reno for not holding out in the timber, if we can't, conversely, show substantiating testimonial evidence that Custer found 500 or more Indians waiting for him at the ford.

Did Major Reno know that Custer was moving along the ridge and would be attempting to strike the Indian village, and did he know that Benteen was expected to support him? Yes, I believe Reno did. He must have known that Custer and his men were sighted on the ridge, and I suspect that he himself saw them. Why then didn't Reno stay in the timber? In the strict sense he should have; however, after the battle, Reno must have realized that if he admitted to such orders, or having seen Custer's troops on the ridge, considering what the outcome had been, it would have placed him in an untenable position. In this connection, I would mention two things: Although Reno would not have known it, and so it would not have affected his decision (nor should it taint one's analysis), General Custer's troops were already retreating before he left the timber. Reno could tell that his situation was getting worse, yet he didn't see any signs of Benteen or Custer. He had to make a decision based on concern for his troops, and this is what he supposedly did.

After the Indians left Reno and Benteen's troops on Reno Hill to move downstream, I would certainly question some of Reno's actions. But again, this is on the basis of hindsight, and my misgivings do not extend to believing that the outcome would have been changed.

Dustin uses officer testimony at the Court of Inquiry to support his contentions. I do believe, in examining testimony, that officers were not altogether supportive of Reno's actions and may have thought that he was overly confused or should have taken more time to organize the retreat from the timber, or to have gone sooner to check on the firing they heard downstream after reaching the bluffs. They, however, would have realized that any condemnation of Major Reno's actions would indirectly be condemning their own. They would also want to present a united army front against outside accusations. My criticism of Dustin mostly concerns his belief that just because a statement was made by an officer at the inquiry, it proves that the statement was true. There is also room to question why the two officers, French and Gibson, were not brought in to testify. Lieutenant Varnum's account in the book, *Custer's Chief of Scouts*, and Captain French's letter to the mother of Adjutant Cooke, as quoted in King's, *Massacre: The Custer Cover-Up*, should be considered.

Dustin also goes too far in his criticism of General Custer. I am certainly not a Custer supporter and I recognize he was egotistical and not necessarily superior in basic courage or knowledge. It is easy to understand why his age, his personality and his notoriety would have irked an officer such as Benteen. Though many of the qualities which brought Custer recognition and promotion did not necessarily mean that he was that much superior to others, I do think they signify that he was a highly competent officer. He would not have been so thoughtless or vain as to ignore evidence that he could not only see but also had been told to him by his scouts. From testimony, it is evident to me that he was not only receiving reports from his scouts, but was seeking them. He sent a number of messages to his officers, which is one reason I believe Benteen's and Reno's orders were more extensive than they admitted. I cannot accept testimony, primarily Benteen's, that Custer didn't believe the reports that he was going up against a large Indian village and what its general location was. I don't think any of the whites or scouts knew it was quite as large as it turned out to be. That Custer had general plans for an attack is borne out by testimony, particularly by his scouts. When Custer gave his attack orders to Reno – whether riding by his side or through Adjutant Cooke – I believe he outlined them more in the manner suggested by Sergeant Davern and Trumpeter Martin. I cannot imagine Custer not sending a message to Benteen, either shortly before, or just after, he gave the attack orders to Major Reno.

There is no question in my mind that there were coverups to protect Reno, Benteen, and in general, other officers and the army's reputation. General Custer moved to the ford and was shot, and there was no organized resistance by his five companies that followed.

SOURCES

1. Dustin, Fred, *The Custer Tragedy*, Ann Harbor: Edwards Brothers, 1939, p. 95.
2. Ibid., p. 98.
3. Ibid., p. 102.
4. Ibid., p. 109.
5. Ibid., p. 114.
6. Ibid., p. 127.
7. Ibid., p. 132.
8. Ibid., p. 136.
9. Ibid., fn. 5, p. 131.
10. Camp, Hammer, *Custer in 76*, p. 178.
11. Dustin, *The Custer Tragedy*, p. 139.
12. Ibid., p. 141.
13. Ibid., p. 152.
14. Graham, *The Custer Myth*, p. 33.
15. Dustin, *The Custer Tragedy*, p. 152.
16. Ibid., fn. p. 154.
17. Ibid., p. 154.
18. Ibid., p. 155.
19. Ibid., p. 155.
20. Ibid., pp. 155, 156.
21. Ibid., p. 157.
22. Ibid., p. 157.
23. Nichols, *Reno Court of Inquiry*, p. 513.
24. Ibid., p. 159.
25. Ibid., p. 160.
26. Ibid., p. 163.
27. Ibid., p. 164.
28. Ibid., p. 186.
29. Ibid., p.189.
30. Ibid., pp. 206, 207.

Custer's Fall
by David Humphreys Miller

. . . One Bull, Sitting Bull's twenty-three year old nephew and body guard, had arisen early to take the family horses to graze at the nearby river . . . As the morning wore on the village gradually came awake and stirred into its usual activity. . . . many women moved out to the surrounding hills to dig for wild turnips . . . others remained in camp . . . Some of the young men went fishing. It was a lazy day, and the pace was leisurely. . . Few people expected to encounter enemies, in spite of the warnings . . .[1]

Iron Hail (Dewey Beard), aged seventeen, was also a Minneconjou. That morning he slept late like most of the other young people . . .

. . . Their father, whose name was also Elk Head, was custodian of the sacred Buffalo Calf Pipe of the Sioux Nation. . .[2]

. . . Long Hair's manner betrayed no lack of confidence. His earlier mood of introspection and doubt seemed to have vanished . . . He had even discarded the shirt of blue-gray flannel in favor of his old campaign jacket of fringed buckskin with brass buttons . . .[3]

. . . After saluting, the Adjutant cantered across to Reno and promptly relayed the orders:

"The General directs you to go after the hostiles, Major. Take your battalion and bring them to battle. Charge the Indians wherever you find them. The General will support you with the whole outfit." Then he added "He further directs you take the scouts with you.". . .[4]

. . . "The Sioux are running away," he said.

Advised of this, Long Hair ordered Half Yellow Face and White Swan to go up on the next ridge for a looksee. The two Crows were confused by Custer's attempt at sign talk. Misunderstanding his orders, they turned sharply off to the left and rode after Reno's battalion. Bouyer shrugged, then led the four remaining Crows up the ridge.

Custer turned his full attention now to his own battalion of five troops. Following Reno's course, but taking a more leisurely pace, he moved out at the head of his immediate command. Soon Reno's battalion was so far ahead it was no longer in sight. As the tail end of Custer's command passed the lone tepee, a four-man detail swung out of the column long enough to set it afire.[5]

. . . Reno's command crossed the Little Big Horn shortly after 2:30 P.M., as white men tell time. Custer was a full three-quarters of a mile behind as Reno re-formed his battalion in thick timber across from the mouth of Ash Creek. Stragglers looking back caught a last glimpse of Custer as he came up the stream at the head of his troops. With boyish exuberance the General waved his hat in his old beloved gesture of confidence, and no one doubted he and his battalion would be close behind Reno in the charge down the valley.[6]

This is a reversal of the usual statements concerning Custer's buckskin jacket. I have not read any account where stragglers looked back and saw Custer, let alone estimated that he was three quarters of a mile from the ford. The most authenticated accounts of where Major Reno received his orders or separated from General Custer were those given to General Scott by White Man Runs Him and Curley. Both claimed that the event took place on a flat about a mile and a quarter from the mouth of Ash Creek. Martin said that they travelled several hundred yards along Reno's trail before moving to the ridge, and though this would approximate what Miller is saying, I would question the implication that Reno had already crossed the ford and was reforming in the timber. He could have been crossing the ford, possibly, but could not have been reforming. I believe McIlhargy would have returned, if this timing and distance were true.

Reno led his detachment out into the valley at a brisk trot. . . . In a spurt of speed the battalion took the gallop, G Company moving up into line with the other troops. . .[7]

One Bull was at the river, tending the family horses after the midday watering, when he heard shooting at the Hunkpapa camp. . .

The camp was in a uproar. Everything was confusion and noise. While warriors dashed away to catch their ponies, older men shouted advice at the top of their lungs. In head-long flight, women and children were rushing away on foot or on horseback toward the north end of the village. All too often, stumbling children and scurrying dogs got in the way of the warriors and their plunging mounts. The women had not time to strike their lodges. Grabbing up babies and clutching young children to their sides they hurried off to safety.[8]

. . . One Bull led his warriors out in a counter charge. To his right Chief Black Moon rode up with a large body of camp police, bent on saving a large part of the pony herd now threatened by the Arikaras.

Camp by camp, the alarm spread through the village. . . . The first thought was to get away . . .[9]

It was the voice of Gall, . . . Around him the warriors began to rally. The soldiers were close now, but coming on more slowly as the Sioux resistance built up.[10]

ANALYSIS OF WRITERS' SCENARIOS

> ... By the time White Bull rode up, the warriors had rallied under his brother, One Bull, and Gall.[11]

> Four miles north, in the Cheyenne camp circle, the people milled about uncertainly ... While the warriors hurriedly prepared for battle, the women stirred into activity, beginning a mass exodus from the camp ... Fewer then a handful remained to guard the Cheyenne circle.[12]

One should note the surprise and the uproar in the camps. It takes time for news to spread; it isn't automatic.

The whole camp would not have extended for four miles, especially since Miller agreed with Marquis and Kuhlman's view that the Cheyenne circle was just to the north of what became known as the Miniconjou Ford, which would be approximately two miles from where Reno's troops moved into the timber from their skirmish line and only a little over a mile from the south end of the Hunkpapa camp circle.

> Reno's position in the timber was fast becoming untenable ... Although he was not close enough to report the fact to Reno, Lt. DeRudio of A Company now saw mounted troops moving along the bluffs across the Little Big Horn. Even at that distance he could recognize Custer's buckskin clothing and Adjutant Cooke's immense whiskers. Lt. Varnum also caught a glimpse of the gray-horse troop marching along the bluffs, but away from Reno's position. It was not until later that Varnum remembered the gray-horse troop had been assigned to Custer's battalion.[13]

The above passage does not do credit to David H. Miller's account, but it does indicate a condensing of time factors which he and others have done. I realize that Miller is writing a story and not a historical treatise, but his treatment of time does little to lend credence to the positions he takes on other controversial issues.

Lieutenant Varnum saw the Gray Horse Troops when the skirmish line was being established, and Lieutenant DeRudio claimed he saw Custer six minutes before he left the timber. If one accepts DeRudio's sighting, it becomes necessary to explain what Custer was doing for at least twenty five minutes. Miller should know it was impossible for DeRudio to recognize Custer's buckskin jacket or Adjutant Cooke's whiskers; furthermore, he should have remembered that DeRudio said it was a blue jacket. If DeRudio had said he saw Cooke's white horse, his statement would have been more believable.

> ... Reno's retreat had come off with such alacrity ... By sheer weight of numbers, the hostiles turned the ragged column toward the river. With the ford hopelessly out of reach upstream, Reno had no choice but to cross the river and make for the bluffs on the opposite side.[14]

This may have been true, but according to Wooden Leg, the Indians at first pulled back when Reno broke from the timber. This behavior is compatible with what the Indians generally did, and it would seem that an organized retreat back to the the ford may have been successful. On the other-hand, it would have been disastrous if it had not been better organized than the retreat which took place.

> A great cry went up among the warriors; "Crazy Horse is coming! Crazy Horse is coming!"[15]

> Downstream, near the timber, Indians were setting the brush afire to drive out the soldiers hiding there.[16]

> Most of the village was deserted. The women and children and old people had gathered along the benches west of the village, ...[17]

> Many of the warriors also seemed willing to let the soldiers go now that they had been beaten. Only a few bothered to cross the river and harass Reno's men as they climbed the bluffs... the warriors continued to loot and strip the bodies of their enemies and recount their deeds of honor.[18]

> Shortly after the last of Reno's battalion disappeared from view in the thick timber on the Little Big Horn's far shore. Long Hair Custer dismounted and knelt a minute or so in prayer. Mitch Bouyer and the four Crow scouts were respectfully solemn as they grouped around him... Finally Custer stood up and turning, shook hands with each of the Crows ...[19]

> Mounting again Custer let the scouts lead out to the top of the ridge. From there they could see that the village was farther away than any of them had thought.[20]

Miller strays from all historical evidence that I am aware of by suggesting that Custer prayed and talked to the Crows. Neither Martin nor Kanipe mentioned it, nor did the Crows according to my knowledge. The Crows do say they went to the ridge after the first two Crows who were supposed to go went with Reno instead. I know of no account suggesting that they then returned with any information for Custer. I would think that if such a ceremony took place, it would have happened – if Custer was far enough ahead of his troops – when he arrived on the ridge, where, I would assume, he talked to Bouyer and the Crows.

> ... By that time, they all saw that Reno's attack on the south end of the village was well under way. The fir-

ing of the soldiers' guns was so continuous that it sounded like a taut blanket being torn.[21]

... Spurred by the din of the battle across the river, Custer speeded up the column, leading it out at a gallop along the ridge. It was all the small ponies of the Crows could do to keep ahead of the soldiers... Then they came to a break in the ridge, where the column halted. While the Crows rested their mounts, Custer and his brother, Tom, rode on past and drew up on a nearby knoll. From this point, Reno's command was out of sight beyond the timber, although firing could still be heard up the valley. Looking across the other way, several hundred tepees were in plain sight, but most of the village lay hidden behind the dense cottonwood growth along the river. Custer studied the camp awhile with field glasses. The village seemed deserted. A few old people hobbled about on sticks, dogs slunk here and there – the usual lazy activity of a hot summer afternoon.

"We've got them!" Custer exclaimed "We've caught them napping! etc. . . . ."[22]

Miller again contradicts the known testimony, without any verification. This type of reporting casts doubt on many of the findings that could help shed light on what took place that memorable day. Miller contends that Reno had gone into action in the valley as Custer was moving along the ridge. The gunfire, along with the dust stirred up by the troops, the Indians moving against them, as well as the Arikaras who were trying to run off Lakota ponies, could leave no doubt that there was action taking place. Custer speeded up, then came to a knoll where Reno's command was out of sight beyond the timber. Reno was on his skirmish line at that time and I don't believe there is any high point from Reno Hill to Weir Point where Reno's troops would not have been seen. I don't know where Tom Custer comes into the picture or, I should probably say, where Adjutant Cooke does. On page 88, Miller described how Reno's attack turned the camps into an uproar, with braves going after their ponies, those that had them rushing toward Reno, others preparing themselves for battle. Reno was supposedly on his skirmish line 15 to 20 minutes. According to Miller, the four Crow scouts and Bouyer found it difficult to keep ahead of Custer. How was it then that Martin continued to maintain through the years that Custer did not see Reno go into action, and even Curley said he didn't? Martin also didn't see Bouyer and the Crow scouts. Curley said they were following Custer's troops along the ridge. What now takes place, according to Miller? Custer goes to the high spot and studies the part of the camp he can see. It seems deserted, with a few old men wandering around, just a lazy summer day. Come on now, Mr. Miller, there

is a battle raging close by; there still have to be braves coming back with their war ponies and getting prepared and moving toward the fighting. All of the women and children couldn't have disappeared. This camp should still be in a state of bedlam, and you have Custer saying he had caught them napping? Did he think there were no warriors facing Reno?

... The soldiers' strategy was suddenly plain. Having divided into comparatively small forces, the soldiers had obviously planned to strike simultaneously at both ends of the great encampment. Though their timing was somewhat off. [The timing would be off a great deal if the picture DHM is bringing out was true.] ... this new band of soldiers stood poised at the head of Medicine Tail Coulee, which gave on a shallow ford directly across from the north end of the village. By moving fast down the coulee and across the ford, the soldiers could drive like a hunting arrow into the heart of the camp – with time to spare before the warriors could reach the endangered area.[23]

Miller is now saying that the ford lay directly across from the north end of the village. This fits Marquis and Kuhlman's version, but there is no way the Indian encampment would have extended four miles; nor can his metaphor of striking the heart of the village be in any sense true.

On the near side of Medicine Tail Coulee, the Crow scouts found a hilltop from which the whole valley was visible. From its head the coulee sloped down almost a mile to the ford across the Little Bighorn. Halting the command at the base of the hill, Custer galloped up to the crest with Trumpeter John Martin at his side. From here the General got his first look at the entire sprawl of the hostile village. With the scouts and trumpeter he went back down the hill and led his column on to the head of the coulee, riding rim-mouthed and silent. From where he left Reno's trail, the command had trotted or galloped a full three miles. With drawn carbines and cocked pistols, the troopers waited for the long charge down Medicine Tail Coulee. Custer turned to his trumpeter . . .[24]

Again I realize that Miller is not writing a factual historical account, but even a factual historical story should not reflect these differences. The command's movement, distances, and heads of coulees are hard to follow. It would appear that the scouts were on top of the hill and signaled Custer and Martin to come up so as to view the valley, which they did. The seven of them then went back down the hill and would have gone to the head of Medicine Tail Coulee, which implies a move down Cedar Coulee. There Custer decided to send Martin with his message to Benteen. Miller doesn't explain why Martin would not remember seeing Bouyer or the Crow Scouts if he had gone up the hill to them and then they rode back down a coulee together. It is also odd that the three Crows never mentioned it in any of their recorded interviews.

> Trumpeter Martin was the last white man to see Custer and his command alive. As he rode away at a gallop; the Crow scouts flushed out five horsemen hidden near the head of the coulee. [The Crow scouts must not have gone to the bluff overlooking Ford B or fired at the village from there.] Lookouts posted along the bluffs, these hostiles banded together to see what the soldiers would do. Once discovered, they whooped and fired their rifles and waved buffalo robes to frighten the cavalry horses. Then they whirled into the coulee and scurried off down toward the river. [These five according to Miller's interview with White Cow Bull didn't have rifles.] Custer shouted the column into rapid pursuit, the gray-horse troop, E Company, leading.[25]

I believe Miller would be basing his statement on Indian accounts, which, rather than expressing an actual fact that the Gray Horse Troop was leading, would reflect a recognition and recollection of seeing gray horses. All three companies of Yates' battalion were said to have led the column.

> Off to one side Mitch Bouyer was talking to Curley, . . . He'll take us right into that village, . . . He handed Curley a pair of field glasses, "Ride back over the bluffs a ways, then head east for one of the high points yonder. Watch a while, and if it looks like the Sioux are besting us, go to No-Hip-Bone (General Terry) and tell him we are all killed. Now go!"

> . . . The others raced down the coulee to catch up with Custer. It was hard going down to the ford . . . With the battalion moving at a fast trot, the scouts were hard put to get ahead of the troopers and come up with Custer. . . . (Custer) called out to them above the clatter of the troops . . ." You are not to fight this battle. Go back and save your lives." . . . Bouyer left Custer's side and rode over to them . . . Without added leave taking, Mitch Bouyer swung his horse around and galloped off down the coulee with Custer.[26]

This was one of Curley's numerous stories. In this one, he was supposedly told by Bouyer to go to a high point and observe, and if it looked like the Sioux were winning to go to General Terry. The story shows how an interpreter could manipulate one of Curley's accounts, as illustrated by LeForge: Curley mentions going to a high point and looking back; the interpreter then adds details to create the version portrayed here. This particular story, I believe, was generated for several reasons. It justified Curley's going to Colonel Gibbon and General Terry, and not being with Major Reno as the courageous Indian hero of the battle might otherwise have been expected to do. It also excused his leaving Custer, while being able to account for various events which took place during the fighting.

The other Crows do not mention going down and being with Custer, but they do mention going to the bluff above the ford and firing several rounds at the village, probably right after Bouyer left to join Custer.

> The Cheyenne camp was all but deserted. . . . Only four other fighting men who were able-bodied remained out of nearly seven hundred. The others had raced off to join the Sioux in defending the Hunkpapa camp. . . .[27]

The fact that aid for the few Indians at the ford arrived as quickly as it did would mean that there were still many Indians getting prepared, along with those who had just obtained their ponies or were leaving camp to join in the attack on Reno.

Miller then recounts the White Cow Bull story.

> . . . With troopers clattering almost at their heels, the Sioux plunged into the ford [the five the troops had just flushed out] and splashed across the river at a dead run. The soldiers reined up at the water's edge, giving the Sioux time to join the embattled Cheyennes on the far shore. . .

> Goes Ahead looked down and saw the soldiers halted in a straggling column [somehow the three scouts must have led the troops down the coulee and were able to reach the bluff above the ford] all the way back up the coulee, although there seemed little to stop them on either side of the river. The battalion could easily ride over the ten hostiles defending the camp. Then he realized that Custer was uncertain as to how many hostiles lay hidden behind the ridge, and while it seemed unlikely a mere handful would have the audacity to oppose him, ambushes were routine hazards in fighting the Sioux. And so Custer waited before finally giving the order to charge.

> At last he turned to shout an order, and the command was echoed by his officers back up the coulee. Custer led out. Even in shallow water his horse Vic had a mincing, prancing gait . . . Mitch Bouyer rode on one side of Custer, an orderly carrying the General's battle flag on the other. For a moment there was a lull in the firing from the hostiles behind the ridge. As the foremost ranks of troopers took to the water, the Crows heard a frenzied yelping upstream. Looking up sharply, Goes Ahead saw hundreds of mounted hostiles coming on fast, streaking through the cottonwoods that fringed the river. Having

whipped Reno, the warriors were taking a short cut to the ford, racing to meet the new danger.[28]

Those Indians attacking Reno would not have had time to learn of Custer and return. These would have been Indians on their way to fight Reno. Here Miller should have quoted Curley from one of his more rational remarks. Curley said that looking down he saw thousands of Indians on the move, some racing toward Reno and some turning to move against Custer. One might also note that this would mean Curley was on the bluffs above the valley and not moving to some eastern hill. Though one can dispute my time reference, I don't believe Reno would have left the timber at that moment, and those Indians attacking Reno continued to until after he reached the bluff and many took time to examine the retreat area for wounded and weapons. This, of course doesn't mean that some Indians moving against Reno would not have turned back sooner.

. . . (Custer) fell, a hostile bullet through his left breast. No Indian, Crow, Sioux or Cheyenne, could say whether he died at once or later, after his men carried him up the ridge from the river. The wound, in any case, was mortal.

As the troopers splashed to a halt around their fallen commander, Mitch Bouyer quickly jumped off his horse into knee-deep water to keep Custer from going under. A moment later, the orderly with the flag crumpled from his saddle. A trooper grabbed at the flag and kept it from falling.

The three Crow scouts on the bluff did not wait to see more. With Son-of-the-Morning Star down, the fight was already over. Jumping on their ponies White Man Runs Him and Goes Ahead joined Harry Moccasin, now well out in front, in a pell mell dash for safety back the way they had came.[29]

There is no doubt that the three Crows met Benteen close to 4 miles away. It would have taken the Crows some 25 minutes to cover that distance after Custer was shot. Considering their meeting with Red Bear and Red Star, the time lapse would have been closer to 35 or 40 minutes. They were able to make this move without running into any large number of Sioux. This consideration contradicts Miller's timing as well as that of most other accounts, and supports my contention that Reno was still in the timber when Custer reached the ford. I agree with Miller that Custer was shot at the ford either by White Cow Bull, Big Nose or some other Indian. If there wasn't any testimony to prove it, I would still maintain that this is what must have happened. It is understandable why the Crows never told anyone, nor did the few Sioux and Cheyenne that would have known about it. The existence of Crow as well as Sioux and Cheyenne testimony that someone was shot at the ford, with similar numbers and Indian names, is stronger corroborating evidence than one finds for any other action involving Custer and his five companies. The Crows were right above the ford and Goes Ahead certainly knew who Custer was. Two stories in Indian accounts have not been accepted to this day: one is Custer being shot at the ford, and the other has to do with trooper suicide.

. . . White Cow Bull could not see all that happened then for he was kept busy dodging bullets . . . But it seemed as though some of the soldiers dismounted there in the river and were dragging something from the water, while others still mounted kept shooting. With gunsmoke hanging thick in the still air, with no letup in the firing, they fell back to the far bank where the entire troop dismounted. By this time the first of the Sioux and Cheyenne from upstream were riding up to help out the ten warriors behind the ridge. As more and more of them reached the ford a great cry went up.

"Hoka Hey! They are going!"

It was true - White Cow Bull saw the soldiers falling back as though seized with sudden panic. The number of warriors was increasing every minute, and they were massing for a counterattack across the ford. But it was something else that seemed completely to demoralize the soldiers just then – something that occurred within their own ranks.

. . . As the steadily increasing horde of hostiles swarmed across the river to surround the dismounted soldiers, the troopers frantically climbed out of Medicine Tail Coulee and ran on foot toward the higher ground back from the bank. Leading their mounts and firing at the Indians all the way, the soldiers reached a little knoll where they tried to make a stand. With troopers dropping all along the route, it was plain the fight could end in only one way.[30]

Those troopers retreating and holding their own horses could not have been firing effectively, and many would have let their horses go or the horses would have broken away. I don't believe it would have been possible for them to have remounted, which is why the Gray Horse Company would not have led the command. Since it's unlikely they could have continued to control their horses and there were few Indian reports of sorrels during the fighting, or dead sorrels on the field after the battle, it's logical to conclude that C Company was in the lead. Their sorrels would have broken away during this time and been captured by the Indians.

If the retreating soldiers had been organized and under

ANALYSIS OF WRITERS' SCENARIOS

officer control they would have placed their horses in the charge of every fourth man, and retreated in an orderly fashion, as Lieutenant Godfrey did with Company K in the retreat from Weir Point. They then would have retreated back the way they had come in an attempt to join the rest of the command. I think the three company commanders would have gone to Custer when he was shot at the ford, a disorganized retreat would have begun, and they were never able to return or regain control of their companies. As a result, they ended up on Last Stand Hill together while their troops were scattered in different locations.

I believe I and L Companies had already been placed in reserve and had moved to Nye Cartwright Ridge. They had been placed in reserve by General Custer. My belief is based on a number of elements: the sightings made by Indians while back on the ridge fighting Reno, those made from the Indian village, Wolf Tooth's account as told by John Stands In Timber, a common cavalry practice and, finally, common sense. Custer would have been concerned about the possibility of Indians scattering or setting ambushes, and being in a position to receive aid if needed. He must have realized that the troops would be more effective there than by following in a column formation, and he probably recognized a need to direct Benteen when he appeared. I believe Curley's accounts recognized this separation; but again, it was made to fit the prevalent version.

Because many of Yates' battalion were dismounted and disorganized, they were forced to the knoll to the north which, depending on ones' interpretation, would have been Greasy Grass or West Calhoun Ridge. As Miller said, "where they tried to make a stand." This rear guard action was where the casualties occurred.

"Come on!" shouted Bobtail Horse, running to his pony. They're running! Hurry!"

He led the way across the ford, the camp defenders now foremost in the countercharge . . .

As the warriors charged the knoll, the troopers opened such a heavy fire that the Indians had to fall back. . . .

In getting out of Medicine Tail Coulee, Custer's command split into two battalions. Last to go down the coulee, I and L Companies – both mounted on bay horses – were now farthest back from the river in a solid formation of a column of fours.

[As previously stated, I believe they were placed in reserve, which would account for their being seen on the ridges to the east of the ford.] They scrambled up a ravine toward the main hogback ridge, a continuation to the north of the bluffs and hills that edged the river. As senior captain of the detachment, Captain Myles Keogh was in command.[31]

Since Miller had talked to White Cow Bull and Bobtail Horse, this account is further support for my hypothesis in that the Indians refer to firing on two battalions. I don't believe these Indians were aware of Keogh's battalion until they had moved up Deep Coulee and were being fired on by them. However, I don't believe the battalions separated at that time. Keogh's battalion had been placed in reserve earlier and was now moving to aid the retreating Yates' battalion. As more Indians arrived from upstream, they saw Keogh's battalion and became concerned with it. Yates' "main element" had retreated north and was out of sight. By the time most of these Indians were aware of this "main element," they had moved to Battleridge, so it was only natural that many Indians would have thought all five companies had been together.

Under attack since the fallback at the ford, the other battalion – consisting of F Company mounted on bays, C Company on sorrels, E Company on grays – moved dismounted and in echelon formation north along the hogback's western slope; F as the spearhead of the advance, C as the right contact wing with the other battalion, E the left, holding the position nearest the river. Captain George Yates of F Company commanded the maneuver.

The two battalions made a co-ordinated attempt to reach a high knob on the north end of the hogback ridge (present location of the monument), where they could take up the strongest available defensive position and make a stand until help came.[32]

I could go along with this part of the scenario, but I would question how coordinated the attempt was. A coordinated effort would involve retreating the way the troops came. Since they didn't do that, and the Yates' battalion company commanders were all together, I can only conclude that what took place was a disorganized retreat in which, due to Indian pressure, the troops moved to the north. I also don't think one can discount John Stands In Timber's account of troops moving to the cemetery area. However, rather than the whole command, they were probably just the "main element" of Yates' battalion, and they would not have moved there in the way described by Miller.

By this time the principal Indian fighting leaders were coming up, bringing their contingent of warriors into the fray. Crow King led a big party of Hunkpapas and Blackfeet Sioux up Medicine Tail Coulee to envelop the smaller battalion from the east. Gall and a huge horde of Hunkpapas, Minneconjous, and Sansarcs also used the coulee as an avenue of attack, keeping a relentless pressure on the soldiers from the rear. Comes-in-Sight and Brave Wolf led a main Cheyenne attack along the left flank..

Once on the field of battle, warriors began to fight independently of their band and leaders . . .[33]

Up on the ridge the gray cavalry horses were stampeding . . . Now a strange thing happened. A whole group of soldiers started running on foot down the hill toward the Indians. It was obvious they were so terrified that they did not know what they were doing. They fired guns into the air and made meaningless motions with their arms. At first, the Indians around Iron Hawk fell back, so weird was the performance of the soldiers . . . It was a signal to charge and the warriors rushed in. In no time at all the soldiers were all down. Most of them put up no fight at all but let themselves be killed without a struggle . . .

Hemmed in on three sides, with E Company chewed to pieces, Custer's command was forced along the ridge. What had begun as an orderly advance under fire was rapidly disintegrating into a complete rout . . .

So far, the leading troops F and C had suffered the least casualties and maintained almost intact formations . . .[34]

Miller is correct that it was at that time that the leading warrior chiefs were arriving from attacking Reno. However, this contention contradicts his earlier remarks and timing.

I dispute some of Miller's general statements in the above passage. I think the way the commanders ended up would indicate a lack of organization rather than suggesting an orderly retreat. One might also remember Benteen's remarks concerning the lack of dead Company C horses on the battlefield. This is emphasized by the lack of Indians referring to sorrels in comparison to bays and grays. Such a situation could not have occurred if their company had an almost intact formation at that stage of the battle.

. . . Approaching the knob at the north end of the hogback, the two companies had almost reached it when a full thousand Oglalas and Brules under Crazy Horse charged up out of a deep ravine that encircled the end of the ridge . . .

Another powerful force of Indians – Cheyennes under Two Moon – circling the end of the ridge by way of the ravine swarmed up over the crest of the ridge to strike the soldiers from their exposed flank on the uphill side, the envelopment of Custer's command was now complete . . . The Indians held back from further massed mounted charges . . . settled down to long-range sniping at the contained foe . . .[35]

. . . Halfway down the slope of the hogback toward the river, about forty soldiers of C Company mounted their sorrel horses and broke out of encirclement. Charging west, they came galloping toward the deep gulch held by most of the Cheyennes and Oglalas and Brules. The Indians fell back, drawing them on. When the troopers reached a low ridge just vacated by the Indian, they halted and dismounted . . . Suddenly the soldiers went crazy. Instead of firing at the attacking Indians . . . all but four were dead.

These four remounted and tried to escape back the way they had came. Three of them were easily overtaken and killed by the pursuing warriors. The fourth broke away and galloped up the river.[36]

The differences in the accounts makes it hard to determine just which of them is correct or comes closer to describing what actually takes place. Some witnesses claim that the troopers were riding, and others that they were running. There are also problems with numbers. The Indians may have been reasonably sure when there were seven or eight men, but not when they say there were forty. Someone, for whatever reason, used that number and other Indians and writers perpetuated it. I think there was only one main group attempting to escape from the hogback. If we accept the account of the early group of soldiers running down the hill that Miller mentions without specifying the number, and then add the forty C Company troopers and seven to ten that are mentioned by the Indians at the very end, the result is some seventy troopers who would have been killed. However, most descriptions of the dead below Battleridge refer to forty troopers altogether, which one might suspect is why the number forty appeared. Some reports refer to this larger number leaving the ridge *before* I and L Companies were wiped out, and others, as in this writing, *after* they were. It is difficult to imagine troopers still having control of their horses at that stage of the battle, or envisioning the forty remounting.

Part of the difficulty, in piecing together Indian accounts into a time sequence, is the fact that they never attempted to do so after the battle. They merely recounted those particular events in which they took part and stood out in their memories, regardless of whether they involved fighting against Reno or against Custer. It wasn't until the whites started to try and piece these statements together that the Indians attempted to reconstruct the events of the battle in a time framework.

Miller claims that most of the troops committed suicide. This is another reason why I believe that there was only one main group of troopers who attempted to

ANALYSIS OF WRITERS' SCENARIOS

escape Battleridge. Most of the men found either in Deep Ravine or outside of it were E Company troopers. They were also the ones that Kate Bighead and Wooden Leg claimed committed suicide. As I have already stated, it is hard to envision forty horses available at that stage of the battle, or to imagine troopers mounting them under the hail of arrows and gunfire that was taking place. One would also wonder, if that was the case, why a number of these horses were not killed at that time, and if they were why Benteen wanted to know what happened to C Company, as so few of their horses were found on the battlefield; he certainly wouldn't be wondering what happened to the men.

Miller points out in his discussion that those describing the mass suicide of C Company were Black Wolf, Pine, Limpy, Bobtail Horse, Rising Sun, Red Fox, and Dives Backward – all Northern Cheyenne.

> It was slightly past afternoon. Less than a half-hour had passed since Custer's fall at the ford. During that brief interim, the two hundred fifteen members of his command had been wiped out to a man.[37]

The time period indicated by Miller is too short. The retreat from the ford to Last Stand Hill would be close to two miles. The number of troops on foot, resistance offered at different locations, and the gunfire heard by Reno's troops suggest that the retreat required an hour or possibly two. Even such a period of time indicates a poorly established defense, reflecting an unorganized retreat.

To me, Miller's difficulty is his attempt to weave testimony he has received from the Indians with that of prevalent writers' scenarios. Since they do not correlate, his portrayal lacks the authenticity it could have had.

> It was after five o'clock before Captain McDougall and the pack train reached Reno Hill.... Benteen actually led the advance with ...
>
> Not far from Reno Hill they were joined by the three Crow scouts who had been with Custer at Medicine Tail Coulee. Goes Ahead, White Man Runs Him, and Hairy Moccasin had circled wide to avoid hostiles, had seen Weir and D company only in the distance. Now they intended to cross over to the Rosebud and go back up the Yellowstone, but Benteen ordered them to stay with the command.[38]

If the three scouts circled as widely as Miller suggests, the time it took them to reach Benteen must be extended several hours. It is too well substantiated by the Crows themselves, as well as Godfrey, Benteen, Martin and Red Bear, that they met the three Crows down in the valley, before Benteen moved to Reno Hill, not when moving to or back from Weir Point. If the scouts were planning on leaving (which they were), they should have been long gone by that time.

> ... the Sioux designated certain lodges as burial tepees and left them standing in the Hunkpapa circle when the move was made to the new camp site in the bottoms.[39]

This comment supports Wooden Leg's account as well as Marquis' and Kuhlman's opinions. D. H. Miller suggests that the Indians sang kill-songs referring to "Long Hair." This would indicate a widespread knowledge that they had fought Custer – a knowledge which I doubt they possessed.

> The other three Crow scouts who had ridden with Custer could have refuted Curley's story, for they had been far closer to the action, had seen Custer fall, and had stayed a while longer near the doomed command. Now ... (three scouts) were in disfavor with Seventh Cavalry survivors for having "deserted" Reno Hill the evening of June 25, although their duty to the soldiers had ended with their location of the enemy village that morning. They were a long time getting back in the Army's good graces. Hero of the hour, Curley, was whisked off to Washington to be wined and dined and feted as the "sole survivor of Custer's Last Stand.". . .[40]
>
> ... For ten years an intense controversy had raged within the Crow tribe over the stories newspapermen had put into Curley's mouth when the Army had taken him to far-off Washington. Upon his return, the other scouts – knowing how untrue his stories were – called him a liar and made him a laughing stock in the tribe. Yet to the whites, Curley was still a hero. Few outside the Crow tribe dared refute the statements attributed to him. It was years later, after the turn of the century, before historians decided to consult Goes Ahead, White Man Runs Him and Hairy Moccasin. By that time they had drifted into outspoken feuding with Curley and his faction, a rift that never healed until Curley and White Man Runs Him, last of the scouts, died in the 1920's.
>
> At the Little Bighorn reunion Gall did his best not to disappoint his audience, although no competent interpreter was on hand to translate his words ...
>
> Further significant inaccuracies grew out of Gall's statements. He claimed that Custer had never brought his troops down Medicine Tail Coulee to attack the village by the ford ... Completely misled, Benteen, Godfrey, and other Seventh Cavalry officers present assumed that earlier and more accurate ideas of Custer's movements had been entirely wrong ...
>
> ... Among the Sioux and Cheyennes, White Cow Bull, Bobtail Horse, and other defenders of the ford agreed in later years that the soldiers halted in midcharge,

halfway across the river, when a white leader in buckskin was shot from a sorrel horse. Had this been any officer other then Custer he would have been left behind in the ford. Only Custer's body would have been carried by the troops as they fell back.[41]

I don't believe any other officer would have been left behind at the ford or, for that matter, any wounded trooper. Nor do I think that a shooting of any other officer would have stopped the troops from crossing the ford and attacking the village, and there certainly would have been more signs and testimony if they had crossed and been repulsed after entering the village.

> The fact that they fell back at that point was in itself conclusive. The sharp switch from offensive to defensive tactics indicated something had gone drastically wrong. Indians at the ford insisted that the soldiers' charge down Medicine Tail Coulee could have swept into the village and might have won the battle for the whites. Only one solution is clear: when the troops halted in midstream, Custer was no longer in command![42]

I agree wholeheartedly with Miller's summation. As I have said earlier, this is the only answer where all the necessary ingredients come together: timing, testimony, psychology and logic.

> . . . early attempts to get accurate stories on the battle from the Sioux and Cheyennes were beset with numerous difficulties. . . . A few like Gall went out of their way to deceive the whites. Claiming to have been head chief of all Cheyennes at Little Bighorn, Two Moon later made light of the fact that he had not told the truth . . .
>
> The disparity among various Indian versions of battle made it all the easier for the hero-worshippers to perpetuate the Custer legend.
>
> . . . various warriors claimed credit for having killed Long Hair . . .
>
> For by fear . . . Strangely enough, none of the five warriors who faced Custer at the ford – one of whom almost certainly fired the fatal shot – ever came forward to say he was the slayer of Long Hair.[43]

David Humphreys Miller then goes over the sources for his information. They include two of the warriors who fought at the ford – White Cow Bull and Bobtail Horse.

SOURCES

1. Miller, *Custer's Fall*, p. 55.
2. Ibid., p. 57.
3. Ibid., p. 69.
4. Ibid., p. 82.
5. Ibid., p. 82.
6. Ibid., p. 83.
7. Ibid., pp. 84, 85.
8. Ibid., pp. 88, 89.
9. Ibid., p. 91.
10. Ibid., p. 94.
11. Ibid., p. 97.
12. Ibid., p. 98.
13. Ibid., p. 100.
14. Ibid., p. 105.
15. Ibid., p. 107.
16. Ibid., p. 110.
17. Ibid., p. 113.
18. Ibid., p. 114.
19. Ibid., p. 117.
20. Ibid., p. 118.
21. Ibid., p. 118.
22. Ibid., p. 119.
23. Ibid., p. 120.
24. Ibid., p. 120.
25. Ibid., p. 121.
26. Ibid., pp. 121, 122, 123.
27. Ibid., p. 123.
28. Ibid., pp. 126, 127.
29. Ibid., p. 128.
30. Ibid., pp. 129, 130.
31. Ibid., pp. 131, 132.
32. Ibid., p. 132.
33. Ibid., p. 132.
34. Ibid., pp. 136, 137.
35. Ibid., p. 138.
36. Ibid., p. 144.
37. Ibid., p. 158.
38. Ibid., p. 164.
39. Ibid., p. 178.
40. Ibid., p. 199.
41. Ibid., pp. 206, 207, 208.
42. Ibid., p. 208.
43. Ibid., pp. 208, 210, 211.

Custer's Luck
by Edgar I. Stewart

The Indian camp was poorly situated for defense... The fact that there were so many women and children present has been cited as proof that an attack was not expected. While under ordinary conditions this would be good circumstantial evidence, it is not in this case for the simple reason that there was no place of safety to which the noncombatants could be sent. (fn. – Deland, *The Sioux Wars*, p. 458; Albert Britt, *Great Indian Chiefs*, p. 218; McLaughlin, *My Friend the Indians*, p. 131.)

... There can be no doubt, however, that by ten o'clock on the morning of the twenty-fifth – two hours before the troops crossed the divide – the Indians knew where Custer was, his approximate strength and also that his force was the only one within striking distance of their camp.[1]

Stewart uses five footnotes to support the above statement. This illustrates what I consider a major problem in Stewart's book. He is a prime example of an historian who uses footnotes extensively and often in a contradictory and conflicting manner. I assume he equated such a procedure with being objective; but instead, his writing presents a melange from which the reader is forced to choose. Does Stewart support the above premise that the Indians were not surprised? At this point one would certainly believe that he does. However, later, he presents arguments to suggest that the Indians were surprised. This type of writing may make for interesting reading but it contributes little towards understanding or clarification.

I do not know of any Indian testimony or actions indicating they were not surprised, except in the general sense of knowing that troops were in the area. According to Indian statements, they planned to move that evening toward the Bighorn mountains – certainly any place in that direction, or away from the forces moving against them, would be safer than where they were. The main reason why I discredit such reports is the Indian reaction, once they realized Reno was attacking: they began to take down their tepees, mothers started looking for their children, and many fled to the foothills to the west. Some chiefs were even out picking turnips or were engaged in activities from the village, and other Indians report that they were swimming or sleeping. Dr. Marquis's account, which I addressed in analyzing his book, *Keep the Last Bullet for Yourself*, offers the best evidence I have found to refute the views of those who believe that the Indian camps were aware of the nearness of Custer's troops.

On the night of the twenty-fourth, ... the Indians, as usual held social dances in all of the circles; and, as one of the leading Cheyenne participants in the next day's fighting expressed it, "It seemed that peace and happiness were prevailing all over the world and nowhere was any man planning to lift his hand against his fellowman."[2]

I don't think one can have it both ways. That the Indians realized soldiers were in the area is probably true, but it is also true that they were not prepared for an attack that morning. After the battle many of the Indians thought they had been fighting Crook's troops, which they would not have believed if they had been following Custer's command the way it is described. I don't know what sort of communications network the Indians used, but one mistake made by several writers and other commentators is to assume that if a few Indians realized something, all of the Indians knew about it, and almost immediately. The Indian encampment was not only large, but it was made up of a number of separate tribal villages. What happened in one area wasn't necessarily recognized in another, nor would gunfire or dust necessarily signal an attack by troops.

Stewart appears to have accepted Benteen's and Reno's interpretation of the orders they received. Stewart points out that while Benteen was still in sight, he received two supplementary directives, from Trumpeter Henry Voss and Sergeant Major Sharrow. I question both the need to have sent two orders so closely together, and the notion that Custer did so.

We should recognize that the orders received by Major Reno and Captain Benteen had to be the center of their attempt to off-set the accusations levied at them for causing Custer's defeat. These charges were primarily aimed at Reno; however, he was more justified in his actions than Benteen.

According to Benteen, at the division of the command he was given orders to go to a line of bluffs about two miles away and to "pitch in" to anything he came across, notifying Custer at once. Chief Trumpeter Voss' orders, which soon followed, were for Benteen to go to the second line of bluffs; supposedly Sergeant Major Sharrow's instructions, some fifteen to twenty minutes later, were to go on to the valley if nothing was seen from the second line of bluffs.

Major Reno would have been subject to a court martial for not remaining in the timber, and blamed for General Custer's defeat, if he had received orders which indicated Custer's strategy, which included a flanking attack by Custer and his five companies; and Captain Benteen was expected to advance to the valley in support of Reno (if he had found no Indians). The same would have applied to Captain Benteen if he had acknowledged that the orders he received from Trumpeter Voss and Sergeant Major Sharrow not only indicated that he was to proceed to the valley of the Little Bighorn, but also that Major Reno would soon be given orders to cross the Little Bighorn and move against the Indian camp; and Benteen, once he reached the valley, if he found no Indians, was to move in support of Major Reno. Benteen would have been indicted for not complying with those orders. Again, these orders were the quintessential element in vindicating or indicting Reno's and Benteen's actions.

What seems odd to me in this scenario is the need for three orders that are practically the same: those given to Benteen at the division, and those delivered separately by Voss and by Sharrow. Yet, it has generally been accepted that Custer did not send any message to Benteen when he issued his attack orders to Major Reno. Using this same line of reasoning, it is also difficult to imagine Custer not informing Reno of his plans for Benteen. I wonder what Adjutant Cooke and Reno talked about as Reno moved to the river? Trumpeter Martin and Sergeant Davern were the only two living men, besides officers, that may have been aware of the contents of Custer's orders, and they both testified to such extension of the orders. This led to my assumption that Custer's orders were not as simplistic as the officers made them out to be.

In this context I will outline my hypothesis again. I believe the following took place:

Custer's original orders, at the division of the command, were for Benteen to go to the bluffs that they could see from their position, and to make sure there were no Indians to the left of Ash Creek where Custer knew the command would be moving. As Custer started down Ash Creek, he realized that the bluffs extended even farther, parallel to Ash Creek, and would reach the valley of the Little Bighorn. He then sent Trumpeter Voss with the message which not only ordered Benteen to go to the next line of bluffs, but to continue to the valley of the Little Bighorn, and if there were any Indians, to "pitch in" to them. When Custer made the decision to wait until the next morning to attack, he remarked to the scouts that he would encircle or, in other words, flank the Indians. When Girard, at the Lone Tepee, indicated that he saw Indians fleeing in the direction of where Custer assumed the Indian camp was, Custer knew he couldn't wait much longer before launching his attack. He was still hoping to hear from Captain Benteen; he didn't realize that Benteen had already begun his oblique and was moving back to the main trail. At that time, I believe, Custer sent Sharrow with his message to Benteen. Since Custer was not aware of just where Benteen was, although assuming he was moving on a somewhat parallel course toward the Little Bighorn, he sent the Ree scout, Stabbed, with Sharrow. Custer, in his message, would have informed Benteen that he was, or would soon be, issuing his attack orders to Reno and ordering Benteen to support Reno by quickly moving down the valley. Keep in mind that Custer, when nearing the Lone Tepee, would have desired a report from Lieutenant Hare as to what his scouts had observed. At that time, Custer sent Sharrow to obtain the report from Hare. Lieutenant Hare was not that far ahead of Custer. I think Hare, in his message, would have said his scouts had not seen any sign of Indians to the south. This enabled Custer to go ahead with his attack plans; however, he would still have to move comparatively slow with his five companies in order to give both Benteen and Reno time to move into position.

Why do I believe Sharrow would have been sent at this time? My reasoning would be as follows: The evidence indicates he was sent to Captain Benteen at some point. If he had been sent earlier, I don't believe he could have met Benteen near Plateau A or Ridge B and still have made it back to Custer as he was approaching the Lone Tepee. We know Custer was concerned with receiving reports and one would have been from Hare who was not too far ahead. He sent Sharrow to obtain that report. As I stated, I think Hare's report would have indicated Custer had nothing to fear from Indians to the south. This, coupled with Girard's indication that Indians were fleeing in the direction of the main Indian camp, would mean Custer could not wait much longer before launching his attack. The Sergeant Major would not have been sent to Hare if he had just got back from taking a message to Benteen—his horse would have needed a breather. However, if he had just returned the short distance, after obtaining Hare's report, he would have been available, and then sent with his message to Captain Benteen. Sharrow and Stabbed would have gone to a high point along the bluffs bordering Valley 3 where they would have seen Benteen moving back to the main trail. Sharrow then sent Stabbed back to inform Custer. Stabbed caught up with Soldier, White Eagle, and Bull and they proceeded to the ridge. Stabbed moved on ahead of the other three and delivered his message to the rear guard near Weir Point. The Sergeant Major met Benteen along Valley 3 or near the morass, as stated by Lieutenant Edgerly and Private Corcoran, although later they were under the natural impression that it was Sergeant Kanipe. At the morass the packs came up and the civilian packer John Frett remembered a Sergeant saying that Custer was attacking. After watering his horse, Sharrow left to return to General Custer. He spoke to the Rees on the ridge and then continued on and joined Custer's command. Whether he, or the soldiers Stabbed met, delivered the message to General Custer that Benteen was back on the main trail and not far ahead of the packs, wouldn't matter. What is important is that the message was delivered between the time Sergeant Kanipe was sent back and the time Trumpeter Martin was. Custer sent Martin to order Benteen to move to support him rather than crossing the Little Bighorn to aid Reno in the valley. Custer didn't send two non-essential messages (if they indeed contained what Benteen claimed), and two later important messages as carried by Kanipe and Martin, but failed to send one at the time he was about to begin his attack on the Indians.

> In the years following the battle, the orders to Benteen suffered not a little from conscious and unconscious distortion, from rationalization and from faulty memories. What the actual orders were we do not know . . .
>
> The command could have been seen at any time coming down the rough country from the divide, and it was at some time during this stage of the march that the Indians in the village first became aware of the proximity of the troops.
>
> . . . The ground throughout the entire battle area was so dry that it sent up enormous clouds of dust from any movement of horses and mules . . . the soldiers were then about eight miles from the village.[3]

According to different accounts, there were several groups of Indians and a tremendous number of Indian ponies grazing or being herded. The command must have kicked up a certain amount of dust, but they would not necessarily have been noticed. The location of the Indian villages, along with Indian testimony, would suggest that they were not. Since this is not the type of information the Indians would have felt reluctant to divulge, I don't think one could say that they were aware of Custer's command before Reno engaged them. This doesn't mean that a certain number of Indians may not have been aware and either their system of communication was not effective or they were, for whatever reason, not sufficiently concerned to warn others.

> Custer now ordered the scouts to pursue the fleeing hostiles but they refused to go, . . . Custer decided to send Reno's battalion ahead to attack the enemy.[4]

Stewart mentions the orders given to Reno and he presents the differing view by Sergeant Davern and Trumpeter Martin. He discredits them because he believes Custer did not yet know of the existence of the village. I have already explained why I disagree with Stewart on this point.

Stewart believes that it was Varnum's or Kanipe's sighting, or Cooke's message from Girard, that caused Custer to abandon his plan to support Reno from the rear and instead launch a flanking attack. Again, I disagree and elsewhere explained why.

> How far it was from the Lone Warrior Tepee to the place where Reno crossed the river is a matter of dispute. The estimates of the officers who rode behind the Major varied greatly, ranging all the way from three-quarters of a mile to five miles. Since the three troops rode at a trot or gallop and apparently covered the distance in about fifteen minutes (although three officers say from twenty minutes to a half hour) the gait at which the battalion rode is also disputed, the officers differing over whether it was a trot or a gallop. Similarly the time consumed in reaching the ford varied, according to the officers from ten to thirty minutes. The fairest guess would seem to be that it was from three to four miles.[5]

One should note that the officers differ in their estimates of time and distances; yet there is no condemnation of these officers or an attempt to discredit them as is done with Trumpeter Martin. Martin's supposed "stupidity" is usually substantiated by Benteen's remarks or other generalizations. I don't think the variance in Martin's statements is different from those in the statements of the officers referred to above. This difference in treatment made me suspicious of the reasons behind the accusations. I can understand that because of his accent and his difficulty understanding what was said, Martin could have been made fun of by the troops, but he certainly had enough intelligence for the questions and matter at hand. What I find puzzling is why he wasn't asked more direct and discerning questions. Could the investigators have been afraid of the answers he might have given?

> [Reno crossing Ford A] . . . There was a delay of some ten or fifteen minutes in crossing. The horses . . . watering . . . men filling canteens. There was much confusion on the farthest bank . . . somewhat disorganized . . . Reno halted briefly to close up the column. It was now a little after two-thirty.[6]

The crossing, and the time it would have taken, is more important than most have considered, and little analysis seems to have been made. It appears that often a period of ten or fifteen minutes was suggested by someone and then seemingly accepted without much thought.

Stewart says, "it was now a little after two thirty," and

he claimed that Reno received his orders at approximately 2:15 P.M., shortly after passing the Lone Tepee. This would make it close to 4 miles to the ford.* If one accepts even a 10 minute crossing, it is impossible to arrive at such a time estimate. Reno, according to him, probably trotted most of the way, although some in the rear may have believed he galloped part of the distance. Thus, it must have taken Reno close to 30 minutes to reach the ford, and with the 10 minutes to cross, it should have been at least 2:55 P.M. Twenty-five minutes could make the difference between winning and losing and it is certainly crucial in determining what the troops saw and what action they took.

Stewart then presents the messages and sightings that have been described in order to explain what compelled Custer to move to the ridge rather than supporting Reno from the rear. The writer does a commendable job but his discussion lacks clarification or analysis.

> ...A short distance after turning to the right, Custer halted at a small stream to water his horses...this stream was probably the north fork of Reno Creek. (According to what Martin later told the Reno Court Custer may have watered his horses in the main stream of Reno Creek before he turned to the north.) Here both Lt. Cooke and Private McIlhargy reached him with the report that the Sioux were swarming upstream to meet Reno, which report, supplementing that of Lt. Varnum, probably reinforced his earlier belief that the village was running away and that the rear guard was coming up to cover the retreat by fighting a delaying action as far as possible. Since it is always easier to flank an advancing enemy then a retreating one. Custer apparently decided...[7]

I don't think Cooke or McIlhargy could have met Custer at that time, or before he made his move to the bluffs. The most reliable reports of where Major Reno and General Custer separated suggest a place near the North Fork of Reno Creek, some 1 1/4 miles from the mouth of Reno Creek. The North Fork is also the location where Custer is believed to have watered his horses. Visiting the place with General Scott, White Man Runs Him and Curley pointed out a flat about a mile and a quarter from the river, which they both agreed was the location where Half Yellow Face and White Swan were sent to the ridge, and when Reno moved out they crossed over and joined him rather then continuing. Bouyer and the four Crows then went to the ridge. The distance from Ford A coincides with Varnum's report as to where he saw Reno's troops moving past Custer's. John Gray, who did extensive work in attempting to establish a chronological time table based on distance and motion, also thinks that this is where Reno received his attack orders. I believe Custer had been hoping to hear from or see Benteen's battalion and had delayed giving Reno his orders for that reason. Once he gave them, he knew he couldn't delay his flanking move any longer.

Custer sent a message to Benteen, either at the time he called Reno over to his side of Reno Creek or when he gave Reno his attack orders. Time-wise, I would say it was when he called for Major Reno. Once Reno received his attack orders, it took him 10 to 15 minutes to reach the ford. Custer moved to North Fork, which could have been only a few yards from where he issued the orders, and allowed his command to water their horses, as Martin indicated. It seems improbable that Custer would then delay an additional 20 to 30 minutes, which would have been the minimal time it would have taken either Cooke or McIlhargy to have reached him. Neither Kanipe or Martin suggest that Custer delayed for that period of time. The slow Rees should have caught up to Custer.

According to Martin, Custer watered his horses. Kanipe doesn't mention this fact, but I think one can assume that Custer did. If McIlhargy had met Custer at that location, he would have returned to Major Reno since Reno said he expected a reply.

It is hard to imagine Custer waiting when faced with the prospect of the Indians scattering. This was his major concern from the time he first gave Reno his attack orders. If he thought Reno would reach the Indians first, wouldn't Custer have been afraid that the glory might have gone to Reno if he delayed? Was Custer known to have ever followed his command into battle? Kanipe doesn't mention waiting, or taking their time, after Reno left. He says, "Custer, with his five companies, followed Reno's trail, on after him, some distance down Benteen Creek; seeing about fifty or a hundred Indians up on the bluff to the right of the Little Bighorn he turned square to the right, increasing our speed...The command never halted."[8] Martin claims that the command halted to water the horses for about 5 minutes: "We were there about ten minutes altogether..." Before this statement Martin said, "...we remained on the right side of the river and went on the jump all the way."[9]

I am in no position to answer the question of how Custer watered his horses and compare it to how it was done by Major Reno. I would guess that as Custer came to the North Fork, the companies pulled up in line and

---

*The location of the Lone Tepee from the ford differs. Here I am using the generally accepted location and the one portrayed by Stewart.

watered, then checked their gear and re-cinched. I would think Reno's troops would have watered as they crossed the ford in a column formation. Lieutenant Wallace said that they crossed in column of twos.[10] If Custer could take 10 minutes, I would think it would take Reno a much longer time to water and cross a ford which was belly-deep.

One should recall Colonel Graham's letter to Captain Carter, and the reference to Reno's time on the skirmish line. Graham wrote, "You know how long military movements take. Figure it out. Could it have taken less then fifteen or twenty minutes to do the things he did?"[11]

That is my question, when it comes to a troop made up of three companies moving to the river in a column formation. They must have extended for some distance. They halt, check the river, and not being satisfied, move farther south to where they cross in a column of twos with the horses watering. They are not chasing Indians at this stage, nor are they retreating. Would they have charged across? Would the officers have conversed? Wouldn't it have taken a minute or two for each horse to cross the belly-deep, fast moving stream while drinking as well? Some horses were excited; some probably had difficulty while crossing. One trooper even suggested that there was quicksand. There was some milling around on the other side; some riders refer to checking their gear and most of them probably did. Reno had sent a message to Custer and we can assume that he expected an answer; consequently he would not have been in too big a hurry. The terrain near the ford is rough and broken, and the tributary crossing would have added to the time. There was also timber to pass through, before and after crossing – 50 yards according to one report and 200 according to another. Then the troops reformed. The consideration of all these circumstances gets back to Graham's question: Could all of this activity have been completed in the 10 or 15 minutes that most writers and participants accepted?

Another factor needs to be analyzed as well. Custer, at first, gave orders for the two Crow scouts to go to the ridge, but they misinterpreted the orders and went with Major Reno when he moved out. Then Bouyer and the other four Crow scouts moved to the ridge. This behavior indicates that Custer was anxious to know what the Indians were doing in the valley – a view which would have augmented Varnum's report. Even without Kanipe's sighting, which is questionable, there is enough evidence to indicate that Custer was concerned about the situation and wanted to move to the ridge. In fact, I cannot imagine Custer not moving to the ridge while his troops were watering or immediately afterwards. I believe any competent commander would have felt the necessity of going to the ridge and making his own observation of the situation. One should also remember Custer's earlier remark at the Crow's Nest (as reported by Red Star), which suggested that he planned to encircle the Indian camp. I doubt if Custer abandoned the idea.

Stewart's description of Custer's reasoning, when he heard that the Indians were moving against Reno, is fairly sound. Yet, I still disagree with him. This issue has been addressed before, but I will re-state my reasoning:

If this event was the impetus behind Custer's move to the ridge, it could have proved dangerous since Custer didn't know the terrain and wouldn't know if he would be able to find a location quickly enough to provide the opportunity to cut the Indians off. Since most writers believe his plan was to support Reno from the rear, I think such a warning would accentuate the need for him to carry out this plan, and would have caused him to implement it immediately. Applying the reverse reasoning, if Custer didn't think Reno was in any immediate danger, he would have been more apt to move to the ridge, thinking that he would be able to find some place to flank and attack the Indians and synchronize the attack of all his troops, something any commander would know was important.

This point is brought out by S.L.A. Marshall, considered by some as our foremost military historian, in his book, *The Indian Wars*. Referring to Captain Keogh's and Lieutenant Cooke's move to the ford with Reno, Marshall says:

> . . . but they must have stayed long enough to encounter the weak and unorganized fire from the fringes of the enemy camp. It might have been better all around had they not gone at all. The quick, the superficial glance, convinced them. They spurred back to Custer to report that all was going well, which was the truth as they knew it . . .[12]

According to Marshall, this report persuaded Custer to believe that he could instigate a flanking attack. Although I have never read anyone else suggesting that this is what Keogh and Cooke reported to Custer, Marshall's reasoning is the same as mine.

Chapters XV, XVI, and XVII of Stewart's work focus on Reno's fight in the valley, his retreat to the hill, Benteen's coming to his aid, their move toward Custer after the packs arrived, and finally their retreat and the battle that ensued on Reno Hill. Chapter XVIII brings out the conjectural view of the events which ended in the defeat of General Custer's five companies on Last Stand Hill.

This is the period of time which aroused my curiosity in the Battle of the Little Bighorn and I will pay close attention to Stewart's account of the events that transpired.

Stewart had done a tremendous amount of research, which resulted in an immensely interesting and informative chronicle of what happened during this eventful period. He continues to accept conflicting testimony and weaves the accounts into an absorbing story of what happened on that fateful day. My major criticism of Stewart, as I have already mentioned, is his failure to take a critical view of the testimony he uses. However, for anyone interested in the Battle of the Little Bighorn and the events surrounding it, his book is a must.

> The question asked by Reno's officers and men, "What has happened to Custer?" is one that has echoed ever since and which still waits for a reply. And it has never been answered, for, of the members of that command who followed the Lt. Colonel of the 7th Cavalry after Trumpeter Martin was sent back, not one returned, so that of the details relating to the complete destruction of the five companies with Custer we know almost nothing.
>
> Not only do we have no adequate evidence upon which to base any definite conclusions, but the entire subject had been overlaid with such a mass of supposition and theory that it is often difficult, if not impossible, to separate the few facts that there are from the much greater mass of conjecture.
>
> . . . All the information we have, and it is little enough, is based on the testimony of four Crow scouts who escaped, and who apparently witnessed at least part of the battle, even if they did not participate in it; or the accounts of the Indians in the hostile camp, who alone know anything resembling a complete story of the disaster, and on the mute evidence of the "remains": the trails, tracks, position of the bodies, and the general topography of the land. . . . Of the human testimony, much is contradictory and unreliable. The Crow scouts told different stories at different times, and not one of them was in a position to give more than a general description of the opening phases of the battle. The army officers, and others who examined the field at various times afterward in many cases tailored their testimony to suit their prejudices, and told stories on one occasion, which were quite at variance with the accounts given at another time.
>
> The stories of the Indians who were in the hostile camp suffer from several drawbacks. Recorded at various times after the events which they described, their accounts are marked by forgetfulness, both real and assumed, and by pronounced rationalization. For the Indian had learned early and from bitter experience that it was much better for him to tell what he knew his auditors wanted to hear, and if he didn't know, to keep still. Moreover, many of the Indians were afraid of being punished should they admit taking part in the battle which Long Hair lost his life. Also we must not forget that the Indian in battle is an individualist, and not being bound to any particular group is free to come and go as he pleases . . .
>
> Given these limitations, it is obvious that the Indian sees a battle from the point of view of an individual, and is not much interested in group activities. He will relate that action of one warrior or soldier in detail without being able to tell what the other members of the group were doing at any particular time. The Indian also suffers from the all too human tendency to magnify his own part in the proceedings, unless he deems it expedient for reasons of personal safety to deny participation altogether. . . . some refer to the Indians as being infernal liars . . .[13]

Stewart explains that the account that follows is based upon the few facts we have, some possibilities and a large dose of speculation. He then proceeds in a manner which illustrates the source of my main criticism of his work: he uses inane and conflicting reports and mixes them with seminal remarks with equal impunity.

> The Indians were not at all surprised at the appearance of Custer's command. They had known for some time – perhaps for days – the approximate location of the regiment. In fact, Flat Iron, one of the Cheyenne Chiefs, later went so far as to declare that plans for the entrapment of Custer and his men had been worked out at a council the night before the battle. . . . They also knew of the division of the command which had sent Benteen to the left, but apparently did not know of the existence of the pack train and its escort until Captain McDougall joined the other troops on the bluff. The hostiles were probably aware of the second division of the command and had watched the troops until they came down into the valley. They saw Custer's five companies riding along the bluffs toward the lower end of the camp and knew that they were not on dress parade . . . They also knew just how far Custer would have to go before reaching the ravine which would take him down to the ford opposite the Minneconjou circle, and they would calculate almost to the moment just how long it would take him to reach it. Thus plans to meet the attack could be made with deliberation and without undue haste.[14]

This is a good example of the basis for my criticism of Stewart. The above text is highly questionable and Stewart must realize it, but the reader might accept it as true. Stewart has spent the first part of the chapter discussing problems the Indians had as fighters: they acted as individuals, they had several chiefs, they were of different tribes and camps, they couldn't control their own warriors. Then Stewart appears to accept these claims that the Indians received information gathered from miles away and that they sat down to plan how to meet the moves the troops would make. Like many other writers, Stewart believes that Custer did not know what he was going to do until after he reached the Little Bighorn. Though I undoubtedly have not read all Indian testimony, that with which I am familiar has not given any accounts of such planning – just the opposite in fact. To my knowledge, the Fetterman Massacre is the only documented instance of such prior planning on the part of the Indians who, in that case, were initiating the action. Planning against known responses enabled them to not only prepare the action well in advance but also to rehearse it. As for the battle in question, I cannot see how even a white army could receive such information and then coordinate the troop and civilian movement necessary to carry it out in the way suggested by Stewart's remarks.

> The sight of Custer's column had either distracted their attention from Reno – which was possibly what Custer intended – or else the hostiles expected a synchronized attack by the two detachments, for it was not until they saw the dust cloud raised by Reno's advance that they became aware of their danger. Thus, before Custer's attack could develop, the battalion under Major Reno provided a temporary diversion, the camp was thrown into confusion, and Gall led a small force of warriors, mostly Uncpapas and Blackfeet upstream to meet the new danger. . . . for despite the Major's belief that he had the entire fighting force of the Sioux and Cheyenne in front of him, such was not the case, and little attention was paid to his detachment until after the force under Custer had been disposed of. As far as the Indians were concerned, the fight against Reno was a holding action, pure and simple, and the main fighting force of the hostiles – probably at least three-fourths of the warriors – was held in readiness to meet the attack which they knew was coming from across the river.[15]

Did Stewart actually believe this scenario? Outside of the fact that it portrays Custer advancing along the ridge and making his move before Reno had established his skirmish line, I don't see any rational, realistic perspective in the account. Indian testimony suggests that Reno surprised them and they were not waiting for Custer at that time. What percentage of warriors went to fight Reno is not clear, but I don't think there is any doubt that those who were prepared went to meet Reno whether they were Hunkpapa, Oglala, Cheyenne or members of other tribes. The Indian testimony indicates that they were not ready for a number of reasons, but none of them suggested that they were waiting for Custer's troops to attack.

> Soon after Custer's command was seen on the bluffs, Crow King led several hundred of his fellow Sioux across the river and up the gully to the south. The main body of Oglalas and Cheyennes moved down the stream until they reached the ford a short distance below the Cheyenne circle.[16]

Stewart never mentions why he didn't accept Marquis's, Kuhlman's and others' estimation of the location of the Indian camp circles on the 25th.

The above account gives the impression that Crow King was waiting for Custer and then moved across the Little Bighorn to South Medicine Tail Coulee. Crow King, according to his own testimony, participated in the attack on Reno and was partly responsible for preventing the Indians from chasing Reno up the bluffs.

> . . . Other smaller parties of warriors crossed the Little Bighorn and moved up various ravines and gullies toward the benchland above the river, resembling nothing so much as "ants rushing out of a hill." The terrain was admirable for concealment, . . . but making the terrain little suited to the formations necessary for the successful maneuvering of cavalry.
>
> Many warriors were concealed behind the ridge along which the Custer command was riding, so that when the time came to spring the trap the soldiers would be attacked from all directions. A number of the warriors, especially those at the heads of the two ravines, were very close to the soldiers, but the latter were apparently unaware of the close proximity of the enemy. At the same time a goodly number of hostiles seem to have gathered on the west bank opposite the ford to resist any attempt of the soldiers to cross. Here apparently, the Sioux had first decided to make their stand . . .
>
> While nearly all of the officers, from General Terry down, had taken it for granted that the Indians would begin to scatter as soon as they caught sight of the troops, and Reno had been committed to action in the belief that such scatteration was already taking place, Custer from the bluffs, . . . It was only too obvious that the Indians were not running . . .[17]

It is interesting that Custer sent Reno after the Indians, anticipating that they would scatter, and still planned to follow with his troops.

There are numerous Indian accounts indicating that they were ready to flee, at least temporarily, and several times they fell back from attacks or charges by Reno, both in the valley and on the hill, plus their retreat from the panic "charge" of E Troops near the end of the struggle.

But he [Custer] was probably not at all disheartened and little disturbed. He had superb faith in this regiment and welcomed great odds against him since the greater the odds, the greater the credit for successfully overcoming them... He knew that Reno was outnumbered and that he was dismounting and deploying instead of charging the village as he had specifically ordered.... however, Custer certainly had no reason to believe that Reno's battalion was in any danger or that it would not hold its position long enough to create the diversion so necessary to the success of his plan of battle,...

Martin was probably sent back about three o'clock or shortly thereafter. [It is hard to believe that Martin would be three hours off as to the time he was sent back.][18]

At approximately the same time the Indian attack on Reno was beginning to develop.... Just as Martin left, the column, with Troop F in the lead and followed in order by C, E, I, and L, rode down a swale that led into Medicine Tail Coulee and within a few minutes was under attack by a few Sioux warriors who were waving blankets and buffalo robes in an attempt to stampede the horses. We know little of the strength of this attacking party, but it certainly was not formidable and possibly did not consist of more than a dozen warriors. In fact Cheyenne accounts say that the troops were following five Sioux who were running towards camp... a circumstance that might indicate that it was part of the old decoy and ambush trick which Custer should have recognized and possibly did.[19]

Here again we have the recognized military concern that the Indians may be attempting an ambush; yet many of these same writers condemn Custer for initially sending Benteen to check the bluffs to the left of his intended march. The implication, at this time, is clearly misleading. One cannot discredit the four Crows' accounts and actions, nor would the Indians have been able to accomplish an ambush following Custer's observation from Weir Point or any high point.

Whether Custer rode down Medicine Tail Coulee towards the river or whether he led his command across the ridges toward the hogback, where they were to perish to a man, is a subject still hotly disputed. Custer's troops were never in Medicine Tail Coulee at all and were not at anytime near the ford... and several of their warriors rode out to meet the soldiers and exchanged a few long distance shots with them. When the column reached the lower ridge and it was found, so these Cheyenne say, further progress was blocked by the large number of Indians in their front, the troops halted and deployed along the ridge. This account is contradicted by one of their own fighting chiefs, Brave Wolf, who insisted that Custer's men came down close to the stream but did not succeed in crossing.[20]

The fact that only a few warriors rode out to meet the soldiers and engaged in long distance fire brings out two essential points. First, in conjunction with other testimony, it suggests that few Indians were initially aware of Custer's command. Second, no matter what coulee Custer used to reach Medicine Tail Coulee, he should have moved quickly to the ford. There would have been no rational reason for *both* Yates' and Keogh's battalions to have moved to Luce or Nye Cartwright ridge.

Since there is evidence that Custer did move to the ford, but retreated soon afterwards, the fact that only a minority of Indians did report this event certainly doesn't refute it but actually corroborates their story, particularly since there was little reason for them to mention it if it wasn't true and it is understandable why the majority differed.

Another theory assumes that Custer, on reaching Medicine Tail Coulee, and realizing that his command was badly outnumbered, turned to the right and led his command away from the river rather than toward it. A short distance on, he turned to the left and again rode parallel with the stream. This maneuver was designed apparently to serve several purposes: to draw the Indians away from their village and to gain time in which to allow Benteen to come up and attack in the center while Reno and Custer were pushing their attacks from the ends. Then Custer turned again to the left and rode in the direction of the Little Bighorn and the ridge where he met his death.

Against this theory there are several arguments, first, the country back from the river is badly cut up and not suitable for cavalry, and no competent... commander. ... Secondly, to ride away from a fight was not in keeping with the Custer character or disposition. It is almost inconceivable that he, believing as he did, that attack and victory were practically synonymous terms, would execute such a maneuver. Furthermore, he was seeking a ford by which he could cross the river and attack the Indian village, and this was the first opportunity that presented itself.

Two of the Crow scouts who were with him say that Custer led his two battalions down the coulee toward the camp as though expecting to cross the river there, and all of the contemporary evidence indicated that he did just that...

... Whether Custer ever reached the ford is one of the most perplexing of all the questions concerning this much-argued-about battle. It might be that if we had the answer, the solution of some of the other questions would be easier. Several Indian accounts insist that the troops never reached the river at all, but were driven back by the large number of Indians in the ravine. Flying Hawk said that Custer started down the coulee but stopped because the Indians were all around him, while Gall maintained that Custer did not reach the river, but stopped about half a mile up the ravine and was then gradually forced back and to the right, away from the direction from which the command had come.[21]

I think this account can be dismissed for several reasons. It contradicts too much other testimony, whether by Martin, the Crows, or the Sioux and Cheyenne. If most Indians were confronting Custer, there were not enough of them to prevent his five companies from making an organized, tactical withdrawal back over the trail and uniting with the aid Custer had sent for. As Stewart points out, the terrain was not conducive, either for cavalry maneuvers or a defensive stand.

Custer, being faced by Indians on all sides, would not have moved further north; instead, he would have either led a charge through the Indians into their village or moved back over the trail by which he had just come.

> Earlier reports contradict this account of so early a retreat and insist that there was some sharp fighting at the ford. Brave Wolf, a Cheyenne stated emphatically that they fought there for quite a long time and that the soldiers were right down close to the stream but none of them were on the side of the village. George Bird Grinnell, who got his information from the Cheyenne, was of the opinion that a part of Custer's command did come down nearly to the ford, and that two companies – one being the gray horse troop – reached that point. Here they apparently halted and dismounted, an example which was followed by the companies behind them and which apparently constituted a tragic blunder, for the Indians state that had Custer kept on and crossed the river the Indians would have fled and a great victory would have followed. Dr. Eastman, whose informants were Sioux, supports this conclusion by saying that Custer, having found it was impossible to cross the river, dismounted his men. Some of them began to fire into the camp at fairly long range, while others examined the banks. Other historians believe that Custer reached the ford only to find several hundred Indians in his front, threw out dismounted skirmishers, and when they were unable to advance, remounted and began to retreat; . . . Granville Stuart, who examined the field not long after the battle, speaks of the place where Custer tried to cross the river and was driven back.[22]

In essence, these reports are, I believe, true. Brave Wolf's phrase "a long time" is a relative one. A few points are important to note in this passage. These writers agree that the troops or several companies reached the ford. These are early writers, all of whom were close to and respected by the Indians. They speak of the troops reaching the ford and dismounting. They do not indicate any great number of Indians which stopped the troops. To say that Custer found it impossible to cross, so he dismounted his troops, is not realistic. This is not the action that a Custer, as described by practically every writer, would have taken. (Stewart's own characterization of Custer is similar.) The comment is made that the Indians would have fled if the troops entered the village, and we should remember the state of the village at that time as described by Indians (taking down tepees, the flight of the non-combatants, the general commotion). What would have stopped these troops and caused them to dismount? The only logical answer is that something happened to General Custer.

> White Man Runs Him, who, with the other Crow scouts, remained on the high point of the bluffs, said that he knew for sure that Custer went to the ford, for he saw him go that far. He added that there were thousands of Sioux on the opposite bank who began moving as soon as Custer reached the river, some going down stream and others up the valley to where the Crows could see Reno, who in full retreat had already reached the foot of the bluff.[23]

White Man Runs Him did say that he saw Custer go to the ford. However, he never said that there were a thousand Sioux on the opposite bank and that as soon as Custer reached the river some started moving downstream and the others up the valley; nor did he suggest that the Crows could see Reno, who, in full retreat, had already reached the foot of the bluffs. This account is erroneous and it presents a distorted picture. First, it was not White Man Runs Him who referred to the thousands of Sioux, but Curley, and what he portrayed was the movement of Indians toward Reno, fighting in the valley. When Custer reached the ford, some of those Indians turned back towards him.[24] In answering a direct question by General Scott as to whether White Man Runs Him saw Reno retreat, the Indian said, "No, I saw him fighting across the river but didn't know he had retreated back to the bluffs."[25]

> Of the army officers who examined the field after the battle, Lt. McClernand could recall no dissenting opinion concerning Custer having descended from the bluffs by following the coulee which led to the river. He conceded that Custer might never have reached the stream,

but insisted that the command did enter the coulee and turned toward the river, apparently with the intentions of crossing . . . That no bodies were later found near the ford, a fact for which Benteen said he never could account, in itself means nothing since the highly mutilated bodies of several soldiers were later found on the site of the village, and those which were nearest to it would be the ones which the Indians would be most apt to drag into their camp.

. . . Corporal Ryan, who was one of the first white men to visit the scene, states that several bodies were found at the ford while another contemporary observer declares that there were several bodies in the river although no evidence that any of the soldiers had reached the opposite bank.

. . . An account by Pretty Shield, a wife of the scout Goes Ahead, says that Custer, with Bouyer on one side and his flag on the other, rode into the water of the Little Bighorn river and was killed by a bullet fired by a Sioux named Big Nose who was on the opposite bank, Custer's body falling into the stream and being swept away.[26]

According to Pretty Shield, Goes Ahead said that Custer was shot at the ford, but Pretty Shield didn't say that Custer's body was swept away. Nor was it Pretty Shield who said that the Lakota Big Nose shot the man at the ford who fell into the water; an Indian at the trading store reported that Big Nose had told him he shot the General. One should also realize that it is not possible for Custer's body to have been allowed to be swept away by the current; the troops would have carried him with them whether wounded or dead. I have speculated that the troops probably put him back on Vic, and Bouyer or possibly Tom Custer, mounted Vic in order to support Custer.

I do believe that a consensus of the evidence presented by Stewart definitely supports the contention that Custer went to the ford and several soldiers were killed there.

The death of their leader is said to have resulted in confusion and demoralization throughout the command, making their complete annihilation comparatively easy. While this story is generally disbelieved, it at least has the merit of opening up some interesting possibilities.

[The following is from footnote 67, Linderman, *Red Mother*, pp. 236-238, 247.]

Marquis expressed his belief that this story was in error, that it was some other soldier, not Custer, who was killed at the river. "Custer is said to have been killed in the story of Goes Ahead to his wife, from her to the interpreter and from the interpreter to Linderman. There must have been a mix-up in persons. It was some other soldier, not Custer, who was killed in the river." This is on a typed note attached to the frontispiece of the copy of Red Mother in the Big Horn County Branch Library, Crow Agency, Montana.[27]

Marquis was undoubtedly not aware of White Cow Bull's story, which describes the event the same as in Pretty Shield's report of Goes Ahead's testimony. You then have corroboration of the incident by Indians on both sides of the fighting. Marquis's note appears to reverse his earlier opinion that Custer's troops never reached the ford.

In his telegram of June 27, sent via Fort Ellis, General Terry reported: "Custer's trail from the point where Reno crossed the stream passed along and in the rear of the crest of bluffs on the right bank for nearly or quite three miles. Then it comes down to the bank of the river, but at once diverges from it as if he had unsuccessfully attempted to cross; then turned upon itself, almost completes a circle and ceases. It is marked; by the remains of officers and men and the bodies of his horses, some of them dotted along the path, others heaped in ravines and upon knolls, where halts appear to have been made."

Sheridan also spoke of "the point where Custer reached the river," and a dispatch in the New York Herald reported that Custer had apparently tried to ford the stream but had been repulsed and driven back, his trail leading back to the bluffs and northward.[28]

Although I realize words can be twisted to substantiate any theory, I would say that General Terry suggests several essential points. They are made doubly important because we know that he spoke with Martin, and Martin explained to him where particular events happened. My interpretation of General Terry's account is that Custer moved near the crest of the bluffs until he moved off the ridge down one of the three coulees leading to Medicine Tail Coulee. The phrase "to the rear of the crest of bluffs" I think refers to West Coulee or Middle Coulee, and that for several reasons. I think Captain Weir would have followed Custer's trail from Reno Hill to Weir Point. Lt. Edgerly, going along Cedar Coulee until near Weir Point, did not recall seeing any tracks of General Custer. Sergeant Kanipe and Trumpeter Martin indicate or imply moving along the ridge in plain sight of the valley. Reno's troops sighted Custer's command and according to Kanipe, Custer's command sighted Reno's moving down the valley. I believe the general consensus of the troops and officers is that when Custer left the ridge, he moved down one of these two coulees and it appears to have been taken for granted. I think they could have noticed and followed the trail of the command without necessarily making special note of it. Those companies following D Company moved through and established positions beyond Weir Point.

With my attempt to "ride at Custer's elbow" it has been inconceivable for me to see him going down Cedar Coulee with time being of the essence. Terry's remark that "then it comes down to the bank of the river," doesn't imply any mile and a half to go to reach the river. This statement supports most of Martin's testimony and those of the officers and enlisted men.

Terry says about the trail that it "at once diverges from [the ford] as if [Custer] had unsuccessfully attempted to cross; then turned upon itself, almost completes a circle and ceases." Again I must stress several points which I believe support my theory. If Custer had made a determined effort to cross at Ford B, there would have been more signs and testimony, both white and Indian, to suggest that such an attempt took place. There is no evidence of this having happened. Benteen assumed that they entered the camp and then some troops retreated by moving downstream. They then crossed the Cheyenne ford, which would account for the bodies in Deep Ravine and toward Last Stand Hill. I think that when General Terry said that the trail "turned upon itself," he meant that it moved to the rear. He then recorded the fact that bodies were found along Greasy Grass and West Calhoun Ridge, from Deep Ravine to Last Stand Hill, along Battleridge to Calhoun Hill – roughly a complete circle. The important point is that both Terry and Sheridan thought Custer moved to the ford.

> ... he [Girard] was almost alone in his estimate, practically everyone else agreeing with Captain J. S. Payne that, while the ford was not good, it was a practicable one such as cavalry on the plains was accustomed to use, and the officers of the regiment also agree there were plenty of places where the command could have crossed ...
>
> Several other possibilities deserve consideration. If Custer's command was attacked in the coulee a short distance before reaching the ford, the attacking force may have been in such numbers as to force him to the right and down the river. Or it may have been that the sight of the belligerent and overeager Sioux riding to meet him convinced him that a major battle was in the making, and since a country broken into narrow and choppy ravines with deep sides is not a good place in which to maneuver cavalry, he simply ordered his command to the right in an attempt to secure more room to fight.29

I will ignore the aspect of the attacking force, which I have dealt with numerous times. As for direction of movement, it is difficult to imagine that without knowing the terrain to his right or north, Custer, who had already sent a messenger to both McDougall and Benteen, would move in that direction. With his companies intact, if he was faced with a force of Indians so large that he wouldn't attack, there's no reason for Custer to move farther away from the rest of his command.

> Cavalry is very weak on defense. Almost entirely an offensive arm, it can defend itself best only by attacking; thus room in which to maneuver is essential. Or Custer may have moved downstream in search of an unprotected crossing since the ground on the other side of the stream was broad level prairie, ideally suited for one of those dashing cavalry charges which had given both commander and regiment their reputation. Or he may have realized the inability of his small command to handle successfully the forces opposed to it and have sought defensive position which could be held until Benteen could "come on." Furthermore, by moving downstream he was drawing the great mass of Sioux after him and away from the ford, getting them between his own command and the expected reinforcement, this making possible a later attack from both directions.30

I have dealt with these scenarios elsewhere. I might stress again that the concept of Custer moving to the north, whether to find a ford or a defensive position for a later attack, seem preposterous. These suggestions – that Custer was afraid to move down South Medicine Tail Coulee because there were too many Indians, and he expected to find a ford farther north which wouldn't be defended by a like number of Indians; or that he was going to move to the north and establish a defensive position at which several hundred troopers were going to join him, and even if they arrived intact, that this number of additional men were going to change the situation so that he could launch an attack – are, in my judgement, flights of fantasy.

> Or, the sight of the dust cloud moving down the river on the opposite bank may have made Custer aware of the movement of Crazy Horse and his followers. Obsessed as he was with the idea that the Indians would not stand and fight but would run away if given even half a chance, it was only reasonable for him to assume that the village, or at least a large part of it, was in flight. As a result he would quite naturally have turned downstream in the hope of being able to intercept and destroy it. Or Custer may have sensed the movement for what it really was, and attempt to flank and destroy his command, and in order to forestall such a maneuver, turned at about forty-five degree angle to the right and begun

the movement downstream. [The timing would be off, for this to be a reasonable move on Custer's part. By accounts, Crazy Horse's appearance north of Last Stand Hill indicated his late move from the village, and occurred after Custer's troops had already moved to the north.]

. . . It may be, as it has been argued, that the command was in full retreat, since they did not go back over the trail by which they had advanced. There may have been disorder in the retirement, although we do not know.

The command was apparently in two battalions, the one farthest back from the river consisting of Troops I and L in solid formation, probably in column of fours. . . . The other three troops F, C, and E – probably in that order, and, apparently in echelon formation – moved north along the western slope of the ridge, and were probably under attack from the very beginning. . . . It was possible as the change in direction was made, and the soldiers began to move downstream that Sergeant Butler of Troop L was killed.[31]

In general, I agree with the latter part of the above scenario; however, I do believe Keogh's battalion was placed in reserve and sent to Nye-Cartwright Ridge, or moved there to attack Wolf Tooth's band. They then moved along Nye Cartwright across Deep Coulee to Battleridge, as Yates' battalion was forced to the north.

> By this time Custer had probably decided that all he could do was to take up the strongest defensive position available and wait for assistance, so the troops head for the north end of the ridge, a position which offered some possibilities, however slight, for a defensive stand. It was here that Reno's flight from the valley contributed most disastrously to Custer's defeat. Gall and a large number of his warriors had crossed the river below the place of Reno's second crossing and had made their way up the bluffs, intending to cut off the fleeing troopers before they reached the top. But Gall was hailed by one of his warriors, Iron Cedar, and told of Custer's increasingly close approach to the village. So, almost immediately, most of the warriors were called from the attack on Reno's demoralized detachment, and began to hurry downstream toward the new battle, . . . riding north along the ridge and following Custer's trail.[32]

Unless Custer took a nap, he would have reached the ford at least thirty minutes before Reno reached the bluffs, and his retreat would long since have taken place. The action indicated above would have had no effect on his decisions or the outcome. Martin had to have passed this point some time before and would either be back on Reno Hill with Benteen or close to arriving there. This would indicate why Boston Custer was able to reach Custer's command, and why Gall may have thought that Custer never reached the ford. When Gall arrived in the vicinity of Custer's troops, they had already reached Battleridge.

> . . . Custer was now threatened by an attack from the South, and to meet the new danger he ordered Lt. Calhoun's troop dismounted and deployed as skirmishers, their task being to hold the oncoming enemy in check until the rest of the command could get into position. A short distance farther on, Troop I was also dismounted, not so much because Troop L had failed to stem the savage onslaught as to cover the retirement of Calhoun's men when that would become necessary or feasible. That there was an appreciable interval of time between the order to Calhoun and the similar order to Keogh is apparent from the fact that the dead horses of the two companies were found some distance apart. Had the orders to the two troops been given at approximately the same time, the horses would have been much closer together.
>
> In the meantime, the three troops closer to the river were being forced by Indian pressure up the side of the ridge. Troop F, being in advance, probably suffered the fewest casualties, but Troop E was being slowly but surely cut to pieces by the Indians who had previously hidden in the ravines. Lt. Smith may have dismounted some of his men and deployed them as skirmishers, and some of them may even have killed their horses and fought behind them in order to cover the retreat of the remainder of the battalion. Many of the men of this company were later found in and near a ravine – about half of them in the ravine and the rest on a line outside. While there is the distinct possibility that they had gone into the gully in an attempt to hide or to escape, it is more probable that they tried to make a stand; and since most of them had been shot in the side of the head, it is altogether likely that they had been attacked from both sides almost simultaneously. By this time the command was surrounded on at least three sides, if not completely encircled, and there were probably so many Indians that there was little unoccupied ground in the vicinity.[33]

As mentioned previously, I believe it is more likely that Keogh's battalion was placed in reserve and then moved from Nye Cartwright Ridge to Battleridge. They became the primary target for most of the Indians crossing the ford and those coming from Reno's battlefield. It would have been necessary for Captain Keogh to have established a skirmish position as they moved to Battleridge, which I believe would have been done by his orders and not from anyone in Yates' battalion.

The main element of Yates' battalion had also established temporary skirmish positions as they were forced to the north across Greasy Grass Ridge and to Deep

ANALYSIS OF WRITERS' SCENARIOS

Ravine. These semi-skirmish positions were on Greasy Grass and West Calhoun Ridge. Yates' main element moved toward the now cemetery area and again certain troopers instigated rear guard action along what many call the South Skirmish Line and I refer to as the South Retreat Line. Whether they became aware of Crazy Horse's move or the sighting of Keogh's battalion as they proceeded from Nye Cartwright Ridge, or only because of defensive reasons, they moved to Battleridge. By that time the Indians had encircled them and the troopers realized that there was little or no hope. The rest of the command was too far off and there were too many Indians between them. Now there wasn't time to establish a strong defensive position to hold off the Indians.

Stewart is trying to present an orderly situation which at that time was not present. There is no mention in his text of those Indian accounts in which possibly as many as 40 troopers attempted an escape. The claim that they set up a skirmish line, or even made a stand at that time, contradicts Indian testimony. I believe the most significant factor in examining Indian accounts of the move by the 28 or 40 troopers, is that the Indians mention the move but not the manner of their death. Indians do indicate that they fell away from these men, and Lame White Man called them back, but if these troops were sent by orders to establish a skirmish line and then put up any sort of resistance, this fact would have been noted and brought out by numerous Indian reports. If most of these troopers were shot through the head, wouldn't this action have been mentioned, especially if, as this account states, they were fired on simultaneously from both sides? How many Indians might have been shot by those on the other side of the troops? If Wooden Leg was right, most of the Cheyenne who were the main group fighting in this area only had bows and arrows. One might wonder why their skulls weren't crushed as it appears that many of the soldiers' skulls were reported to have been. There is one account according to which more Indians were killed in this area than any other, but it is not backed up by specific testimony. If it was true, the casualties would most likely have come from their attack and the resulting fire from Last Stand Hill. It could support John Stands In Timber's account of the Indian "suicide boys." The only accounts of trooper action near Deep Ravine are those by Kate Bighead and Wooden Leg in which they talk about the troops committing suicide.

> Just how long the action lasted is another of those matters of conjecture. Two years after the battle some of the Sioux participants insisted that the contest was quite even, lasting for about two hours before a massed charge turned the left of the line and the command was rolled up.... All of the evidence indicates that they did not break, but died to the last man in the position where they had been placed.[34]

In determining the time while using Indian accounts, one must remember that they had a personal way of looking at a battle. Since they arrived on the scene at different times, their statements vary. I am sure some of the Indians who alluded to the duration of the battle being only fifteen to twenty minutes are referring to the last stage, while others are gauging it from the time Custer reached the ford.

All of the evidence does not indicate that troopers fought bravely to the last. In fact, from what I have read, there is no question that many didn't. Those Indians portraying the troopers fighting bravely to the last are the ones usually quoted. There are many writers who advise caution in evaluating Indian testimony, and then accept such statements without question.

There seems to be little acceptance or recognition of the destabilizing psychological pressure these troops were subjected to. The length of the retreat, the condition of horses and men, the fear of torture, and any realistic vision of what the scene must have presented to these men would not rule out suicide on the part of many.

I think that from the first firing at the ford, the battle would have lasted over an hour, but not over two.

> Lt. Hare believed that it did not take the Indians more then forty-five minutes to wipe out Custer's command, and thought that the initial attack on Custer occurred about the time Reno left the timber or a little before. Lt. Wallace agreed with him, being of the opinion that Custer was heavily engaged by the time Reno reached the bluffs, and Lt. Varnum believed that Custer was in action before Benteen joined Reno. Other members of Reno's command had other ideas. Edgerly thought that the fight did not last more than fifteen or twenty minutes, or half an hour at the most, while Mike Sheridan put it at not more than an hour, or, on a guess about an hour. Herendeen, who heard volleys and scattering shots from the direction of the battlefield, stated that the fight began after he had been in the timber about thirty minutes and lasted for an hour, while Girard, who also heard the firing from the woods, estimated the duration as twice as long, and declared that the single scattering shots lasted until dark. [It is interesting how estimates were apt to correspond to the position a person took on Reno's and Benteen's action in going to Custer's aid. Girard had the firing lasting the longest and was the main accuser of Reno.]
>
> ... the accepted theory has been that, owing to the

suddenness and ferocity of the Indian attack, Custer did not have the opportunity to form a regular line of battle as each unit of the command found itself with a separate fight on its hands. Captain Benteen, who was one of the first to make a detailed examination of the field, was impressed by the lack of battle lines, which he described by saying that one could scatter a handful of corn on the floor and get as close a resemblance to lines as were to be found. He also believed that the troops had been as much the victims of panic as of the Indians, and was positive in his declaration that the only evidence of a stand to be found was on Custer Hill. With his opinion Lt. Hare agreed, stating that there was no evidence of the command's having made a stand; and the fact that the bodies were scattered over some ten acres of ground – here, there and everywhere – he indicated to some observers that the officers had completely lost control of their men and that there was little organized resistance.

With this theory, there has been considerable disagreement. Calhoun's men were admittedly on a skirmish line, and Edgerly thought that Keogh's men were. . . . Flying Hawk claimed that Custer's men made at least four separate stands, while other hostile accounts put the number at five.[35]

There is bound to be a difference of opinion regarding this phase of the battle. I believe there were pockets of resistance at different stages. I have to take issue with the claim that the suddenness and ferocity of the Indian attack prevented Custer from establishing a defensive line. I think the behavior of Yates' battalion, as described by Benteen, proves that an organized retreat did not take place. As I stated above, I realize that Benteen's and Reno's position is aided by a short, disorganized resistance by Custer's command; however, I believe Indian testimony and the results would support Benteen's claim. As I have repeatedly brought out, if there had not been a breakdown in discipline and organization, the troops would have had time to retreat back over their trail or set up a defensive position. But, as the situation developed, there were mounted and dismounted troops; there were troops staying with the main element and those attempting to reach Keogh's battalion; there were horses turned loose or breaking loose; there were also pockets of resistance set up in the retreat by the main element, whether one would call them skirmish lines or not. Keogh's battalion maintained a semblance of order until it was overrun in the late stages of the battle and this, coupled with the attack on Last Stand Hill, is when one finds the suddenness and ferocity of the Indian attack. This is theorizing on my part, but it represents a consensus of the views I have gathered from reading Indian testimony and, I believe, it is logically sound.

Just why Custer had moved his command downstream we do not know, but it was undoubtedly for perfectly valid reasons. He made his last stand where he did, in a position that was not too favorable for defense, for reasons which are equally unknown, although the probability is that the Indians, having surrounded the command, forced him to halt and fight where he was.

The Indians who fought mounted indulged in the usual wild charges, warriors intoxicated by excitement rushing in on individual soldiers and fighting hand-to-hand combats. Many of the hostiles rode around and around the little group of soldiers, "swirling like water around a stone." . . . but both Sioux and Cheyenne insist that most of the soldiers were not killed by riding over them, but rather by shooting them from behind the hills, since every ravine and every bit of brush hid one or more Indians who kept up an almost incessant fire. Many of the soldiers were later found to have been shot in the back. "The soldiers toward the river backed away and after that the fight did not last long enough to light a pipe."

Most of the Indians bear witness to the courage of Custer's men. Gall speaks of the extreme bravery of the soldiers, who were right down on their knees loading and firing until the last man was killed and Sitting Bull later declared: "I tell no lies about dead men. Those men who came with the 'Long Hair' were as good men as ever fought." Brave Wolf concurred in saying "it was hard fighting; very hard all the time. I have been in many hard fights, but I never saw such brave men." According to the Sioux, none of the soldiers offered to surrender and they do not mention any suicide, thus following the code of the frontiersmen – in fighting Indians, save the last bullet for yourself.[36]

As has been discussed, it was natural for the Indians to speak of the bravery of the soldiers. It is interesting that Mrs. Spotted Horn Bull criticized the bravery of Reno's men but applauded that of Custer's in a way that suggests an Indian awareness of the white man's condemnation of Reno and treatment of Custer as a martyr. If my view of Gall's participation in the battle is correct, he was near Calhoun Hill at a time when Calhoun's company had established a skirmish line and were heavily engaged. Gall shortly left with some horses which he took to the village, and by the time he returned the battle was over. Sitting Bull did not take part in the battle and his statement was made for effect. I think it is transparent where Indian testimony was meant to placate the whites. There are too many contradicting stories by Sioux of attempts to surrender, suicide and panicky behavior, besides those related by the Northern Cheyenne. Stewart only mentions Marquis's account of several suicides and he ignores those accounts in which the Cheyenne told Marquis that a large percentage of Custer's troops committed suicide. These claims are not refuted by a few Indian remarks of the bravery of the troops, particularly after Stewart brought out how Indian testimony has to be questioned because, "the Indian had learned early and from bitter experience that it was much better for him to tell what he knew his auditors wanted to hear . . . ."

> Two Moon, the Cheyenne Chief, told of one member of the detachment, apparently an officer, riding a sorrel horse with a white face and white forelegs, who led a group of about forty men in a sortie toward the river in an apparent attempt to escape. About four or five others are said to have been mounted while the remainder were on foot. Two Moon described him as wearing a buckskin shirt and having long black hair and a black mustache . . . but that description. . . .It is possible that the individual was Bouyer. The description is not too far off, and his body was found near the river. But it seems hardly probable since he was well known to the Indians and they should have recognized him.[37]

It is difficult not to speculate on some of these occurrences. As I mentioned before, I think that after Custer was shot at the ford, the person who may have held him on his horse Vic, was Bouyer. He could have brought Custer to Last Stand Hill and placed him on the ground with as much protection as possible, and may have remounted Vic. Kanipe mentioned that he thought he saw Bouyer's body in Deep Ravine, although Colonel Gibbon, by one account, thought the body was near the river. The skeletal remains of what was claimed to have been Bouyer's body were found down the slope from Last Stand Hill before it reaches Deep Ravine. If the dust was as bad as reported, it would be entirely possible that Bouyer would not have been recognized. I also find it possible that instead of Bouyer, Custer's brother Tom rode with the General after he was shot.

> Red Horse, who describes what was probably the same incident, gives some indication the officer may have been Custer . . . Red Horse, who says that he saw the man several times during the battle, described him as being the bravest man the Indians had ever fought. [This was really playing on the whites and the known image of Custer. However, if there was such an individual at the end it could very well have been Tom Custer.] but said he did not know whether or not it was General Custer . . . Kate Bighead says that when the shots quit coming from Custer Ridge, the Indians got up and ran towards it, at which time seven of the soldiers sprang to their feet and went running for the river. Another version relates that there were ten men, . . . and that they, the last of Custer's men, were killed before reaching the river. The Indians also tell that some of the men on gray horses attempted to escape and that the dismounted soldiers on the hill fired into them to try to make them come back, . . .the bodies of these troopers, mostly of C and E, were found scattered between the ridge and the river. The conclusion is fairly obvious that with their officers dead they sought to escape by seeking refuge in the trees and brush along the river, but were met and killed by the Indians. Looking at the marking which today designate the places where the bodies of these men were found, it seems apparent that they died in a desperate effort to escape.[38]

Several characteristics of Indian testimony are important to consider. I think the Indians often got a chuckle out of the gullible white man who believed anything they were told if it didn't discredit the white man's image of himself or the image he had of the battle. This attitude is evident in Two Moon's statement suggesting that it is all right to lie to the white man. Of interest is a more recent report of an Indian whose grandmother told him about Wounded Knee and the killing of his grandfather and the other Indians which took place there. Although the Indian works with the white man and has left the reservation, he says he still has a hatred for the whites. Could the Indians whose testimony we use to determine what happened at the Little Bighorn, who lost loved ones as well as their freedom and way of life to the white man, not have had similar thoughts?

SOURCES

1. *Custer's Luck,* Stewart, Edgar I., University of Oklahoma Press, Norman and London, Copyright 1955, pp. 314, 315.
2. Ibid., p. 315.
3. Ibid., pp. 318, 322.
4. Ibid., p. 325.
5. Ibid., pp. 330, 332.
6. Ibid., p. 331.
7. Ibid., p. 333.
8. Hammer, Camp, *Custer in 76,* p. 92.
9. Graham, *The Reno Court Abstract,* p. 129.
10. Ibid., p. 129.
11. Graham, *The Custer Myth,* p. 307.
12. Marshall, *The Indian Wars,* p. 141.
13. Stewart, *Custer's Luck,* pp. 431, 432, 433.
14. Ibid., p. 434.
15. Ibid., pp. 434, 435.
16. Ibid., p. 435.

17. Ibid., pp. 436, 437.
18. Nichols, *Reno Court of Inquiry,* p. 394.
19. Stewart, *Custer's Luck,* pp. 437, 438.
20. Ibid., p. 439.
21. Ibid., pp. 439, 440, 441.
22. Ibid., p. 441.
23. Ibid., p. 442.
24. Graham, *The Custer Myth,* p. 14.
25. Ibid., p. 18.
26. Stewart, *Custer's Luck,* pp. 442, 443, 444.
27. Ibid., p. 444.
28. Ibid., p. 445.
29. Ibid., pp. 446, 447.
30. Ibid., p. 447.
31. Ibid., p. 448.
32. Ibid., p. 449.
33. Ibid., pp. 449, 450.
34. Ibid., p. 451.
35. Ibid., pp. 452, 453.
36. Ibid., 459.
37. Ibid., 460.
38. Ibid., 461.

Archaeological Insights into The Custer Battle
by Douglas D. Scott and Richard A. Fox Jr.

Archaeological Perspectives on The Battle of the Little Bighorn
by Douglas D. Scott, Richard A. Fox Jr., Melissa A. Connor and Dick Harmon

I will first quote the archaeologists' remarks which have a bearing on my theory, and then follow with an analysis and comments. From the book, *Archaeological Insights into The Custer Battle*:

Custer left the ridge near the point where he had seen Reno's battalion. He proceeded in columns down a short draw (Cedar Coulee) leading to Medicine Tail Coulee. . . There he apparently bore left down Medicine Tail Coulee, intent on fording the river to press the attack. It is at this point in the sequence of events that the consuming mystery of the Custer fight begins.

Custer must have finally realized the gravity of the situation as he swung into Medicine Tail Coulee. There the northern half of the village came into full view, [They would have had to have moved within a few hundred yards of the ford for that much of the village to have come into view.] and resistance began. Lt. William W. Cooke, . . . dispatched Trumpeter John Martin with a written order for Benteen . . .

The progress of Custer's advance down Medicine Tail Coulee is a source of debate. Some argue that the cavalry attack was repulsed a considerable distance from the ford at the mouth of the coulee; others maintain that the column reached a point near the river where elements crossed into the camp. The historical data are contradictory, and on these data alone a case can be made for either argument. However, artifactual evidence (e.g., cartridge cases and bullets) found over the years at the ford indicates that some elements of the command may have progressed to the river intent on crossing . . . Clearly the battalion was turned back there.

. . . At least a portion, if not the entire battalion, redeployed, retreated or was driven eastward to Nye-Cartwright ridge.[1]

. . . Some students have concluded that Custer ordered two companies immediately northward while the remaining companies proceeded eastward to the ridge. There is presently little direct evidence for the separation of the companies but various Indian and government cartridges and bullets (the Indians used a variety of weapons and ammunition; the troopers carried Colt pistols and Springfield carbines) found in past years on the Nye Cartwright Ridge indicates action there. In any case, Custer's battalion ultimately moved to the point where memorial markers now stand.[2]

The shallow graves hastily prepared in 1876 were susceptible to disturbances by erosion and scavengers. Wolves and coyotes were no doubt frequent culprits, but so also were two-legged scavengers.[3]

The first of two reburial details arrived in the summer of 1877. It was under the command of Captain Michael Sheridan, the younger brother of General Phil Sheridan . . . Captain Sheridan reported that he had reinterred exposed bones and remounded all the graves he could find. Sheridan drove cedar stakes at each grave so that they could be found in the future if necessary.

. . . an accurate record of burial locations were never kept.

In 1879 the army sent another detail to the Little Bighorn, this time not only to inspect the graves but to erect a memorial monument. Captain C. K. Sanderson commanded . . .[4]

. . . upon completion of his task Sanderson noted that the field appeared to be clear of bones and speculated that the many horses bones had led to reports that Custer's dead were scattered about. . . . In 1881 these graves were opened, and the remains were reinterred in a common grave, where they lie today.[5]

The last 1881 detail razed the cordwood marker but in its place erected an imposing granite memorial with the names of the Seventh Cavalry dead, including scouts and enlisted men. That monument stands today . . . the graves from which remains were removed were marked with stakes. According to the official report, all remains were collected and reburied, but over the years numerous finds of burials and incomplete remains have demonstrated the contrary. Indeed, human remains were frequently encountered in the 1983-84 archaeological investigations. In any case, the haste in 1876 led to problems in finding grave sites in 1877, 1879, and 1881. All these efforts were carried out without an official program to preserve grave locations. That was not to occur until 1889 . . . to replace deteriorated stakes with permanent markers.[6]

. . . The markers were placed at locations that exhibited stakes, fragments of bone, depressions, or luxuriant stands of grass. Many of the stakes driven in 1881 were missing, and much of the decision making was apparently guesswork. . . . To complicate matters further, 249 markers were placed on a field where only about 214 men had originally been buried. The extra markers either represented men officially listed as missing from Custer's command and unaccounted for, or were intended to memorialize Reno's dead. In either case they were randomly placed on the Custer battlefield.[7]

In later years, a few more markers were randomly placed on the Custer battlefield, mostly without documentation.

. . . Shovel and auger tests were conducted in Deep Ravine in an attempt to locate the remains of the missing men of Company E, who were supposedly buried there after the battle . . . state that the dead of Company E were left where they were found, huddled in a mass in Deep Ravine. The reburial party in 1881 (King 1980) was unable to find where there were remains for reinterment in the mass grave . . .

. . . Six excavation units (A1 through F) of various sizes were dug in Deep Ravine,

. . . Since we were unsuccessful in finding the missing men's remains, with traditional excavation procedures, we implemented a power auger survey. . . . all with negative results.[8]

In the book, *Archaeological Perspectives on the Battle of the Little Bighorn*, the authors discuss the markers found on the field and particularly Markers 33 and 34 which, they are certain, indicate where the remains of Mitch Bouyer were found.

We began this work knowing that at least forty-two of the markers were incorrectly placed, mainly those extra markers set in 1890. We guessed that another twenty-eight might be spurious-markers set for the dead in Deep Ravine but not placed in Deep Ravine. This would mean that as many as seventy markers on the field could be erroneous. Our projections suggest that about thirty-seven markers are the second marker in a pair or the rare occasion when the pair represents no fallen soldier. Another projected thirty-five markers are single markers that are spurious. . . . we suspect the marker population on the field could include seventy-two spurious markers.

. . . However, the identification of Mitch Boyer on the South Skirmish Line has added a new dimension. As discussed above, Boyer was one of the twenty-eight men supposed to be buried in Deep Ravine. Four explanations were presented: Mitch Boyer was misidentified, the South Skirmish Line was referred to as the ravine, the memories of the participants had dimmed by the time the account was taken by historians, or Gibbon's account is accurate. . . . If the lower end of the South Skirmish Line was referred to as the ravine, then some of the twenty-eight men could be buried along that portion of the line and may be correctly marked. This still means that the number of incorrectly placed markers is between forty-two and seventy. Our statistical projection of seventy-two incorrect markers on the field . . . remain the same . . . but there are locations of fallen soldiers which are not marked – that is those in Deep Ravine.[9]

The question of the bodies which were said to have been buried in Deep Ravine but which were never found, constitutes one of the unsolved mysteries associated with the battle. In Chapter 8, the archaeologists discuss their findings and projections related to that mystery.

. . . A major unanswered question regarding the battle that took place . . . is what happened to twenty-eight men, presumably from Company E, Seventh Cavalry. The remains of these men have never been adequately accounted for, in spite of four official attempts to do so; one immediately after the battle, another in 1877, another in 1879, and still another in 1881. Personal accounts on these occasions claim that an unknown number of men, mostly from E Company, were annihilated in a gully heading on the southwest side of Last Stand Hill . . .[10]

On the basis of contemporary accounts, it is likely that the troopers who were annihilated in Deep Ravine were trapped in a headcut with nearly vertical walls more than six feet high. . . . The bodies in Deep Ravine were said to be so putrid that members of the burial detail became nauseated. An effort to remove the bodies from the gully was abandoned, and a mass burial was made instead by simply caving off the gully sides. . . . Several accounts claim that many exposed bones were observed the following years during reburial efforts, but there are conflicting statements as to just where the presumed concentration of bodies was located in Deep Ravine. . . . So we are left with uncertainty as to where the soldiers fell, whether their bodies were removed and reburied, and whether some may have been flushed down the ravine by a "gully washer."[11]

. . . While the area between trenches 1 and 11 remain untested, all of our circumstantial evidence gathered to date points to the area between 30 and 60 meters (98 to 197 feet) below the present headcut as the most likely area for the burial of the missing troopers. This allows for 10 meters, more or less, or headward migration of the 1876 headcut. This is the reach that shows the most evidence of slumping, which is probably caused by the shallow water table's fluidizing the base of the banks. Such action at the burial site after the 1876 battle would likely aid burial and allow the denser metal items to sink farther in the muck of unit x.[12]

I will now quote and discuss the essence of the archaeologists' views regarding the events that took place on the Custer battlefield.

. . . The following interpretation of the chronology and sequence of the battle is derived from the study of the spatial distribution of artifacts taken in combination with firearm-identification analysis and historical documentation.

. . . First, it is clear that at least the final Seventh Cavalry position is in a V-shaped formation. . . . This formation stretched along the east side of Custer Ridge and along the South Skirmish Line, . . . artifacts around Custer ridge corresponds to Calhoun Hill, the Keogh position, and Last Stand Hill. The cluster is also evident at the northernmost extent of the South Skirmish Line. These troop positions are further corroborated by the presence of impacted bullets from Indian-associated weapons.

At least seven discrete Indian positions . . . Two positions are on Greasy Grass Ridge, . . . Henryville Ridge . . . Knoll 200 meters northeast of Last Stand Hill. . . .

The three additional Indian positions are on the lower end of Greasy Grass Ridge and on the flanks of the upper portion of Deep Ravine . . .

. . . On the other hand, the scattered findings of the army bullets within the western area of the battlefield suggest that soldiers, perhaps those on the South Skirmish Line, laid down fire at the Indians advancing from the encampment on the west side of the Little Bighorn River. In like manner, the virtual absence of battle-related artifacts from some areas suggest that the combatants found some topography inadequate and did not utilize those areas.[13]

From the archaeologists' maps, I assume that the particular area referred to as having few battle related artifacts is that which lies to the west of the middle portion of Custer Ridge between Calhoun Ridge and what the archaeologists refer to as the South Skirmish Line. The topography should have been used if the companies had been operating together in a disciplined manner, as this should have been within a perimeter established by an effective defensive maneuver. That it wasn't, I believe, supports my theory of what happened. Since no offensive action or sound defense is indicated by artifacts or suggested by testimony, one should suspect a confused mixed movement on the part of the troops. When crossing this upper tract, Yates's "main element" showed some rear guard action around Greasy Grass and West Calhoun Ridge, and then moved to below what is now the cemetery. They established semi-skirmish positions along what the archaeologists call the South Skirmish Line. During this time Keogh's battalion crossed Deep Coulee to Calhoun Hill, and then the exposure to gunfire and the location of the troops prevented the Indians from penetrating this area until the final minutes.

. . . We offer some clarification regarding the historical reality of the South Skirmish Line. This concept was introduced by Kuhlman (1951), who concluded, from the numerous marble markers along the line, that troopers skirmished there at near regular intervals. Taunton and Hardorff have rejected Kuhlman's thesis on two grounds: (1) historical accounts (McDougall in Hammer 1976:12; Thompson in Hammer 1976:248) suggest that no more then twelve bodies were found there, and (2) a mere dozen men could not have formed regular skirmish intervals over an area 500 meters long . . .[14]

The thesis does not hold up when compared with the archaeological data. Indeed, the archaeological data demonstrates the contrary. Clearly the number and nature of the finds in this area support the idea that a fight took place here. Whether or not a line at skirmish intervals existed is yet open to debate; gross artifact patterning might suggest the South Defensive Area is a more appropriate appellation. Nevertheless, a distribution of combat-related artifacts is clearly discernible from just short of Last Stand Hill to Deep Ravine.

. . . The evidence at hand supports the concept that the South Skirmish Line was an integral part of the Seventh Cavalry defensive effort and formed one projection of the overall V-shaped formation.

. . . King has argued that roughly the southern half of the line was abandoned as the soldiers fled into Deep Ravine and were killed.

. . . By whatever route Custer and his men reached Custer Ridge, the last segment of the battle ensued. This is the segment that the current archaeological data can elucidate. The following interpretation of event is, we believe, logical and defensible. It is based on a careful study, of the artifact patterns. . .

Upon gaining the ridge, Custer, or someone else in command, deployed a group of men on a line facing in a southerly direction. Traditionally, the men deployed are assumed to have been from Company L and possibly some from Company C, owing to the presence of identifiable remains of men of these two companies in this location after the battle . . .[15]

. . . the rest of the command moved along the ridge to the north. The commander may have noticed another group of Indians moving on his position from the west and north, traditionally identified as Crazy Horse and Lame White Man with more Sioux and Cheyennes. To respond to this new threat another deployment was made from below Last Stand Hill south to the head of Deep Ravine. Historians generally identify this groups as the officers and men of Company E and F and sometimes Company C. This is the South Skirmish Line.[16]

In the meantime, a third element of the command historically identified as Captain Myles Keogh and the men of Company I, deployed below the ridgetop on the east side of Custer Ridge. Perhaps they were being held in reserve, perhaps they were on their way to aid Calhoun, or perhaps they had been covering Calhoun's withdrawal. It is even conceivable that Keogh and his men were one group attempting a breakout during the last segment of the battle. In any event, they were not sent along the ridgetop. The archaeological data do not support the theory that Keogh and his men were pushed from the ridgetop to the base of the ridge, where they were killed . . .[17]

. . . The fight may have been a running one until this final deployment, but after that the units stood their ground . . .

. . . The cartridge-case evidence suggests that as the Calhoun position fell, some Indians broke off and moved northwest toward Deep Ravine and the South Skirmish Line . . .[18]

. . . The Indian attackers coming from the north and west met the men deployed from Last Stand Hill to the head of Deep Ravine. . . . The relatively small number of Indian cartridge cases found to the north and west of the South Skirmish Line suggest that the Indians attacking from this quarter were not as well armed as those attacking Calhoun. . . . this area is somewhat biased. This area now contains the national cemetery, the Visitors Center, and a road. The construction of these facilities probably destroyed some information, but how much will never be known. . . .[19]

Perhaps the Indians joining the fray from the south after the Calhoun fight added the right combination of firepower and numbers to overwhelm the South Skirmish Line. There is very little evidence of fighting in or around Deep Ravine, with the exception of that immediately adjacent to the head of the ravine. The head of the ravine defined the south end of the South Skirmish Line. Most of the archaeologically recovered battle-related items found in or along the ravine suggest that the Indian positions received only light fire from the soldiers.

Cartridge cases fired from some of the same Indian weapons that had been used at Calhoun Hill and near Deep Ravine are also found near Last Stand Hill . . .[20]

In summary, the cartridge cases data suggest Indian movements along two broad lines. One was from south to north, from Calhoun Hill to Last Stand Hill through the Keogh position; the second was from Calhoun Hill and Greasy Grass Ridge to the South Skirmish Line, joining with the Indian group attacking from the north and west. These two broad and probably opportunistic movements converged at Last Stand Hill, indicating that the hill was the last position occupied by the remnants of the five companies . . .[21]

There are also army carbine round which were fired in .45/55 carbines in two of the other Indian positions on Greasy Grass Ridge and at Henryville, southeast of Calhoun Hill. Since these positions were utilized early in the battle, these data can be interpreted two ways. One is that some army carbines and ammunition fell into Indian hands in the valley fight and at the Rosebud fight . . . this is a credible interpretation, but there is an alternative. The finding of army cases in these areas may suggest that these artifacts mark a segment of Custer's line of retreat to the final battle scene. This alternative would suggest that Custer did not retire without some intermittent fighting. In fact, given the all too general but provocative patterning of relic finds at Nye Cartwright Ridge, where at least some elements of Custer's command were engaged, the troop movement to Custer Ridge was probably under pressure.

. . . The Indians noted that near the end, the soldiers began using their Colt pistols . . . The archaeological findings support the statements in general. Relatively few Colt bullets . . . were found . . . These were associated with the South Skirmish Line and the Keogh area.

. . . not many soldiers had an opportunity to fire their revolvers . . . It suggests that many of the soldiers were already dead or wounded and out of action by the time the Colt came into play. . . . Perhaps these rounds were fired by Indians into the bodies of the soldiers after the troop positions had been overrun. Indeed, many Colt bullets, as well as some .45/55 carbine bullets in troop positions, were found vertically impacted, or nearly so, into the ground. This could occur as Indians fired downward into the bodies.

The archaeological evidence suggests that the Indian

battle accounts, taken as a whole, are more accurate than those of the soldiers who buried the dead.

There are those who will dispute one point or another in our interpretation. <u>We invite such criticism, as scholarly debate is the most effective means to achieve a better understanding of past events.</u>[22] [my underlining]

I agree whole-heartedly with the above comment. I think this has been one of the main problems in determining what took place at the Battle of the Little Bighorn. Each writer or commentator has presented his view of what happened and used what substantiation they could find to support their thesis without actually analyzing the validity of evidence and indicating why they agreed or disagreed with particular views. In other words, to arrive at a better conception of what happened, you should be critical of others' viewpoints, just as they should be objectively critical of yours.

Although I believe the work of the archaeologists has been invaluable, I definitely do not agree with their analysis of the chronology of events as they pertain to the Custer part of the battle which lies within the National Park boundary. I will divide my analysis into two main parts: one will be concerned with Mitch Bouyer and Deep Ravine, the other will focus on the general movement of the troops.

Although Mitch Bouyer's body was reported in several different locations, the archaeologists feel certain that it was Bouyer whose partial remains they found at marker 33 and 34. Sergeant Kanipe had reported seeing what he thought was Mitch Bouyer's body with the 28 troops in Deep Ravine. If this was true, the archaeologists give several reasons why his body might have been found where they claim it was. These reasons have been included in their remarks.

My basic disagreement with the archaeologists' view on Deep Ravine, and the movement of troops, stem from what I consider a major fault not only of the archaeologists but other writers, and that is their failure to recognize the panic or near panic that took place, and the overall disorganization of Custer's troops. I have pointed out elsewhere that while it seems to be acceptable to criticize Reno's movement from the timber, and the retreat of D and M Companies from Weir Point (although this retreat is usually glossed over), one only finds references to an organized and disciplined movement on the part of Custer's five companies until it finally breaks down at the end. This attitude is even reflected in Indian testimony – Reno's troops could be criticized, but not Custer's. One might recall General Stonewall Jackson's advice to John Imboden:

> There are two things never to be lost sight of by a military commander, always mystify, mislead, and surprise the enemy if possible; and when you strike and overcome him, never let up in your pursuit as long as your men have strength to follow; for an army routed, if hotly pursued, becomes panic stricken, and can then be destroyed by half their number.[23]

To expect this admonishment not to apply to Custer's five companies that were retreating from a much larger force than their own, and with the realization that the Indians didn't take prisoners – or if they did it was only to subject them to indescribable torture – and to imagine that the soldiers would be reacting as if they were on the parade ground, can only be described as fanciful thinking.

This brings me to the additional point which, I believe, should be contemplated along with the four reasons the archaeologists give to explain why they haven't found the bodies in Deep Ravine, and Mitch Bouyer's body was found above Deep Ravine in graves marked 33 and 34.

This fifth reason is based on the assumption that Kate Bighead was correct in suggesting that most of these troops committed suicide. If that indeed happened, what reaction would the rest of the troops have had when they came on the scene after the battle? Would they have been able to recognize that many had committed suicide? What would the army's reaction have been? What would have been done with the bodies?

Dennis Lynch indicated seeing members of the 7th Infantry carrying some of the bodies out of the gully and he thought they buried them on the ground above Deep Ravine. This contention was refuted quite strongly by W. R. Logan who said that the bodies were buried where found in the gully. There are several possible reasons for the differences, although I am sure that if there was a cover-up, the army's position would have been strongly asserted. However, one should consider that the time when the bodies were viewed could have made a difference. Sergeant Kanipe may have seen them before anyone was assigned to bury them. Then, the 7th Infantry could have started the burial process by bringing the bodies out of the gully, and had done so with the seven Lynch referred to. We know that Captain McDougall was then assigned to bury them and took over from the 7th Infantry. (The detail change to the 7th Cavalry might raise questions.) Bouyer could have been one of those whose bodies were taken out and buried where the archaeologists found him. The others were left in the gully and were buried there; Logan may not have been aware that any had been removed from the gully.

However, overall evidence and implications are extremely suspicious given the obfuscation of the reports of burial parties after the battle and later. It is one thing not to be able to find the bodies one hundred years after the battle, but it is another not to find definitive reports of the bodies during the five year period following it. One must also consider that there doesn't appear to be artifactual evidence of any intense fighting taking place near Deep Ravine. The often repeated explanation is that weather, "gully washers," and erosion have caused this phenomenon.

Several reports should be considered in connection with this issue. Some claim that the men found in the gully were shot in the head; one suggests wounds in the side, and one in the back. Captain McDougall, who made the charge that many were shot in the side, said that they may have been attacked from both sides of Deep Ravine. He was in charge of their burial and was a former commander of Company E.

Whether a good many were shot in the head, side, or back, one would have to envision a hot exchange taking place between the troops and the Indians, particularly if the firing took place on both sides of these troops. If the troops were in the gully, it is hard to visualize a large number of Indians positioned on both sides of the troopers and able to kill the number of men involved by firing into their bodies, even if they were part of an extension of a skirmish line from near Last Stand Hill. According to Wooden Leg and Kate Bighead, most of the Indians in that area were Cheyenne and Oglalas. Wooden Leg indicated that these Indians had fewer guns than the Sioux in other parts of the battlefield. This contention is also supported by the archeologists who mention, "the relatively small number of cartridge cases found to the north and west of the South Skirmish Line, which suggests that the Indians attacking from this quarter were not as well armed as those attacking Calhoun."[24]

The archaeologists also point out; "There is very little evidence of fighting in or around Deep Ravine, with the exception of that immediately adjacent to the head of the ravine."[25] As I have indicated earlier, if these troopers had formed a skirmish line in the gully or moved into the gully and were conducting disciplined firing against the Indians, there should have been a heated exchange. If the troops in the ravine indeed exchanged fire with the enemy, there should have been impacted bullets representing army and Indian firing and, one would assume, other artifacts in and near the ravine.

If there was one thing the troops would have kept to themselves, it would have been their knowledge that many of Custer's troops committed suicide. Whether the evidence of suicide was apparent during the burials in '76, I don't know, but I assume it should have been fairly clear if the suicides were as wide-spread as Kate Bighead and Wooden Leg contended.

If what I surmise is correct, I would be very surprised if any bodies turned up anywhere in Deep Ravine, no matter how deep or in what direction the area is searched. Even if my scenario is wrong, I think that Captain Sheridan in '77 must have taken the bodies out of the gully and reburied them along the line which leads to Last Stand Hill. Sheridan could have been expected to realize that the gully was not the best place to leave the bodies. However, the transfer should have then been recorded.

If my scenario is right, Sheridan must have recognized that the number of gunshot wounds in the head or side could have only meant one thing: suicides. I believe he was already aware of this when he went to the field, but one way or the other he could have decided, or had orders to bury, the troopers among others, knowing that only one interpretation would be made if the bodies were uncovered together in the ravine. This could also be the reason why there was no official record concerning the bodies.

The question that bothers me, if my scenario is correct, is how the bodies got in the gully. If they ran in there and then committed suicide, why didn't Kate Bighead refer to it in that way? How could she have been in a position to have seen or described it the way she did? In other words, the men would have been outside of the gully as she portrayed it. I realize that Lt. Bradley, who first saw and counted the dead, did not mention seeing any number in a gully, but this omission does not constitute substantial evidence that there weren't. Could the troops or the 7th Infantry have been placing them in the gully rather than taking them out when Lynch observed them? Some accounts refer to them as being heaped up, which would indicate that they were placed in the ravine and not that they died there. Could the Indians coming back through the gully and desiring the weapons and ammo, have dragged the bodies in, and could that have been the reason for the marks on the side of the gully that some thought were caused by troopers' attempts to escape?

Though this conjecturing is not instrumental to finding an answer to my main questions, it does bear on them, and it does make for compelling speculation which continues to be one reason why this battle provokes the interest it does.

The second area of my disagreement with the archaeologists concerns their hypothesis regarding the general movement of the troops. I believe they are using archaeological evidence without proper historical backing, and for a proper conclusion to be reached artifacts must relate to both testimony and logic.

First, the archaeologists reject Taunton's and Hardorff's scenario, for they say it disagrees with the archaeological evidence. They support their evidence by a conjectural historical view of Dr. Kuhlman. Actually, the archaeological evidence, as I see it, does nothing more than prove that in certain locations there was Indian and army firing, movement and lives lost. Dr. Kuhlman's theory has been fairly well discredited on several grounds by Greene, Stewart and others who have pointed out what I consider to be sound and logical objections to his major premises.

Second, the historical evidence doesn't support the view that skirmish lines were established during the latter phase of the fighting, or by a deployment of troops from Battleridge. The trooper testimony, as portrayed by Taunton and Hardorff and questioned by the archaeologists, is supported by Indian testimony or analysis of their testimony, and by Colonel Gibbon's portrayal of the battlefield on the 27th. If skirmish lines had been established from Battleridge to the southwest, in what the archaeologists call the South Skirmish Line, or if there had been a southernly movement of troops along Battleridge, this action would have been noted by the Indians. When reading Indian testimony, one should consider that the number of Indians taking part early in the Custer area of the battle was a proportionately small number, and certain actions could have taken place with many Indians unaware of them. However, the action associated with Battleridge – which included Calhoun's and Keogh's companies, as well as any formation of a South Skirmish Line or defensive line that Scott and other writers think happened – and the fighting on Last Stand Hill, would have taken place during the last phase of the battle. This would be a time when most Indians were either watching or were personally involved. Consequently, it would seem reasonable to assume that fighting and deployment along Battleridge and the South Skirmish Line would have appeared in numerous accounts – but it didn't.

In the scenario presented by Scott and Fox, one would expect several things to occur. Primarily, this South Skirmish Line or Defensive Line would have been overrun, or a large number of troopers would have had to return to Last Stand Hill. Either of these situations would have been reflected in the testimony of those Indians interviewed, and therefore would lend support to such a thesis. In the case where the skirmish line had been established and finally overrun by Indians, there would have been more bodies, and those bodies, plus the presence of a skirmish line would have been indicated by the troopers following the battle. The Indian testimony does not support either of these scenarios. Officers and soldiers have indicated only four locations where a number of bodies were found: Calhoun Hill, the area east of Battleridge where Keogh's body was found, Last Stand Hill and Deep Ravine. In view of all the testimony, I feel safe in claiming there was no attempt to establish or maintain a South Skirmish Line toward the end of the battle.

The point which needs clarification is why so many battle related artifacts were found in this area? I have no reason to deny the validity of the archaeological evidence, so the probability is that the fighting along this line had occurred earlier, before too many Indians were aware of it happening. Are there any Indian accounts substantiating such a movement or action by the troops? I believe the movement to and retreat from the ford portrayed by the Crow scouts, Martin, White Cow Bull and numerous other Indians as well as John Stands In Timber's story, either imply or indicate such action.

John Stands In Timber relates that his friends, who were members of Wolf Tooth's band and the first to arrive on the ridge where the monument now stands, saw troops moving close to what is now Highway 87. These troops turned back and held below Last Stand Hill. During that time it could be expected that they established some rear guard action against the Indians. The location of the South Skirmish Line fulfills this requirement. There were Indians on Greasy Grass Ridge, across the river, and Wolf Tooth's band, and they both fired and were fired upon. By the time most of the Indians arrived, these troops had moved to Battleridge.

I suspect that few, if any, bodies found below Custer Hill were soldiers killed at that time; instead, they were part of the later attempt to escape, which is mentioned numerous times by the Indians. (I am not referring to bodies found on West Calhoun Ridge, and from there to the South Skirmish [Retreat] Line. These were troopers killed in the retreat from the ford as mentioned by White Cow Bull.)

The escape attempts, as well as most of the events of this latter stage of the battle, were clouded in the Indian memories, due to the excitement, confusion, dust, attempts at self-glorification, the effect of time, and a tendency to mold their stories into what they perceived the white man wanted to hear. There are numerous variations in the accounts of the fighting which took place at the end: false claims of recognizing Custer, varied estimates of the time the battle took and of the level of the troopers' courage, the number of troopers trying to escape and the troopers on horseback or on foot. Still there is a general consensus which I believe one can accept: most of the Indians fighting in the area below Last Stand Hill report the attempts to escape. They differ as to time, number and the use of horses. What should be stressed is that none of them, except for Kate Bighead, Wooden Leg and some of the others that D. H. Miller and Marquis talked to, indicate in any direct way what happened to those troops.

Several Indians refer to 40 some troopers trying to escape from Battleridge; yet we can be sure that, at the time, they were not counting these soldiers. Most likely this number reflects the white man's account of seeing some 28 in Deep Ravine plus the 12 bodies found between Battleridge and Deep Ravine. I think we can be confident that there were not 68 troopers who left the ridge along with the 7 or 10 who left at the very end of the battle. This possibility would not coordinate with either testimony or body counts. Therefore, I see no reason to discredit on the basis of archaeological artifacts and an historical hypothesis, the testimony of members of the 7th Cavalry who saw the bodies after the battle and said that there were around 28 in Deep Ravine and about 12 other bodies between Deep Ravine and Last Stand Hill.

The archaeologists hypothesis assumes that whoever was in command after the troops reached Battleridge deployed Company L, and possibly a part of Company C along the hogback in a southerly direction while the others moved to the north. It appears that during that move, the commander sent E, F and possibly a part of C Company to set up the South Skirmish Line, while Captain Keogh and the men of Company I deployed on the eastern side of the ridge. As previously stated, I don't think a consensus of Sioux and Cheyenne testimony supports such a movement.

Scott and Fox say that up until this deployment, it may have been a running fight. Again, I disagree, mainly because of the generality of the statement, for it implies that the two battalions moved together in reaching Battleridge. To do this, they would have to cross Nye Cartwright Ridge and Deep Coulee, moving to Battleridge together, and never to the ford. There is no logical way to correlate such movement with Indian testimony, or that of Trumpeter Martin.

One other interesting factor brought out by the archaeologists regards their findings pertaining to Colt pistol bullets. They point out that the Indians refer to the troops using their pistols at the end of the battle, but that relatively few Colt bullets were found and these were primarily along the South Skirmish Line and the Keogh area. They mention that many of the Colt bullets, as well as some .45/55 carbine bullets, were found in troop positions and were vertically impacted or nearly so. They say this could have happened after the Indians had picked up the pistols and fired downward into the bodies. They fail to mention that it could possibly have resulted from the troopers firing their pistols into their own or their buddies' heads.

I will reiterate my general view of the archaeologists' speculation: They are creating a scene which reflects too much organization and discipline, which I don't believe existed by the time the troops reached Battleridge, except for some individual and small group action.

Captain Benteen was certainly the most outspoken officer, vitriolic and with a biting, caustic tongue. This characteristic, plus his need to cover-up, has to be considered in viewing his testimony. On the other hand, he was probably the best officer on the field and his observations on what happened should not be dismissed without some thoughtful consideration.

My scenario of the events while conjectural, is more realistic and logical, and accommodates both archaeological and historical evidence.

SOURCES

Scott, Douglas D. & Fox, Jr., Richard A. *Archaeological Insights into the Custer Battle.* Norman, University of Oklahoma Press, 1989.

1. Ibid., p. 13.
2. Ibid., p. 14.
3. Ibid., p. 15.
4. Ibid., p. 16.
5. Ibid., pp. 16, 17.
6. Ibid., p. 17.
7. Ibid., pp. 17, 18.
8. Ibid., p. 33.

Scott, Douglas D., Fox, Jr. Richard A., Connor, Melissa A., Harmon, Dick. *Archaeological Perspectives on the Battle of The Little Bighorn.* Norman: University of Oklahoma Press, 1989.

9. Ibid., p. 88.
10. Ibid., p. 224.
11. Ibid., pp. 224, 226.
12. Ibid., pp. 224, 225, 241.
13. Ibid., pp. 121, 123.
14. Ibid., p. 123.
15. Ibid., p. 124.
16. Ibid., p. 125.
17. Ibid., p. 125.
18. Ibid., p. 126.
19. Ibid., p. 127.
20. Ibid., p. 128.
21. Ibid., p. 129.
22. Ibid., pp. 123, 124, 125, 126, 127, 130.
23. Bowers, *The Stonewall Enigma,* MHQ, The Quarterly Journal of Military History, Spring, 1990, Volume 2, Number 3, p. 119.
24. Scott, Fox, Jr., *Archaeological Perspectives on the Battle of The Little Bighorn,* p. 127.
25. Ibid., p. 128.

Custer's Last Campaign
by John Gray

After extensive research to determine why Custer didn't make a recognizable attack with his five companies, I read John Gray's book, *Custer's Last Campaign*. The reviews it received made it required reading. Robert Utley referred to it as, "The most important book ever written about the Battle of the Little Bighorn." It is certainly a very informative book and I agree with much of it. However, I would not recommend his overall method, which Gray refers to as a "time-motion" analysis, and I cannot support his major conclusions.

The "time-motion" analysis is similar to what I have described as a "time-event-time" attempt to arrive at conclusions which I believe have, previously, and in Gray's book, led to incorrect deductions. The primary weakness of the method is the necessity to place events and actions of the participants in an obdurate mold. I do not question the need to develop a time sequence; however, it should be flexible enough – and will be more accurate – if events are correlated and a general time is accepted. I refer to this more flexible system as an "event-time-event" determination. There are too many interpolating factors when attempting to analyze the movement of troops and the actions that they took, on the basis of a time-motion analysis. One finds this particularly true in establishing exact time, distance, and speed criteria; yet these determinations are of the essence in constructing a time-motion theory.

I commend Gray for using Ree accounts which have too often been ignored, but in the same vein, one cannot overlook Sioux and Cheyenne testimony, or the conflicting Crow accounts, as Gray has done. One of my major criticisms concerns Gray's acceptance of certain aspects of Curley's differing accounts, while ignoring that of others, particularly General Scott's interview.

In attempting to find an answer to my questions as to why Custer failed to attack an encampment verging on a state of panic, it was apparent that I needed to examine the testimony of participants and the scenarios presented by both them and other writers. This was especially true once I arrived at a general hypothesis of what had prevented Custer from attacking. To develop a theory, I cannot ignore testimony and scenarios which oppose my ideas, but must confront them as objectively as possible, even if my arguments become redundant. This means that I must add Gray to the list, and explain why I agree with parts of his scenario but disagree with the usefulness of his time-motion method and with his conclusions.

I begin my analysis with Chapter 17, "**To The Crow's Nest And The Divide.**" I agree with the prior chapters pertaining to the battle, and I have not attempted to analyze any of the command's actions before they arrived at Halt 1 near the divide.

I believe, at the time of the Reno Court hearings, there was a change in the "official" time when General Custer, on the 25th of June, 1876, divided the 7th Cavalry into battalions, and that this was one of three major cover-ups at the Reno Court. The "official" time given at the Court has been accepted by everyone that I am aware of, and little examination of timing for that morning has been made. John Gray gives the most extensive breakdown of events from the Crow's Nest sighting of the Indian encampment to the division of the command. I will try to show why I don't accept his version.

Gray states the difficulty of reconstructing time, which is certainly true of any given time concerning the Battle of the Little Bighorn. Estimating time would be particularly difficult for the officers when one considers that the command was moving during the night from near the present town of Busby to where they established what is called Halt 1 around 3:15 A.M. Lt. Varnum, the officer in charge of the scouts, whom Custer sent to the Crow's Nest, had been up practically all night, and one can assume he was not checking his watch. It is doubtful that officers back at Halt 1 would have been aware of any more than the orders Custer gave for the command to move out at 8:00 A.M. Then, to attempt to recall time long after the battle was over, would be extremely difficult. We know Lt. Wallace, the itinerist who was the official time taker, was inconsistent in both the times taken and in their correlation. If I am correct and there was the changing of the "official" time when Custer divided his command into battalions, from around 10 A.M. to 12:05 P.M., and that it was one of the major cover-ups at the Reno Court, then this must have made it extremely difficult for officers to present time estimates. I assume this is why there were so many unaccountable timing distortions. There were times given before the change, and it would have been difficult to adjust the two hour "official" time change with their recollections.

Gray brings out the local sun times which are important considerations. Those I would be concerned with are: the nautical, civil twilight, sun rise, and meridian. Nautical time would be when you have the first break from darkness. Civil twilight ends the darkness and is when the two Crows first made out the smoke from the Indian campfires. This would have been when they woke Varnum, and he said: "I crawled up and watched the valley till the sun rose,"[1] during which time he was attempting to see the Indian village being pointed out by the Indian scouts.

ANALYSIS OF WRITERS' SCENARIOS

The Local Sun Times:
Nautical twilight   2:44 A.M.
Civil twilight   3:34 A.M.
Sun rises   4:13 A.M.
Meridian   12:00 A.M.

Distances:

Halt 1 to Halt 2 was 3 3/4 miles. The Crow's Nest 1 mile from Halt 2. Halt 3, 1 mile from Halt 2.

Gray brings out that General Custer, at the Busby campsite, after sending Varnum, Reynolds and some of the Crow and Ree scouts to the Crow's Nest, moved the command during the night to what is referred to as Halt 1. The morning of the 25th, when Custer received the message of the hostile Indian camp sighting from the Ree scout, Red Star, he and a small party went to the Crow's Nest. The command followed Custer to what is referred to as Halt 2, which was about a mile from the Crow's Nest. There, Custer rejoined his command, crossed the divide and about a mile northwest from Halt 2, would have divided the command at Halt 3. Leaving out some of Gray's listed events, which I do not believe necessary in forming my time considerations, I will present the events and time as Gray believed they took place. I will give my time estimate for major moves, and then will explain my reasons.

Varnum at the Crow's Nest	Gray's time		My time
2 Crows first sight Sioux village at Little Bighorn	3:40 A.M.		
Varnum and the scouts study he Sioux village	4:00		
Varnum sends two Rees to Custer at Halt 1	5:20		4:45.
Ree Couriers			
Leave Crow's Nest with note to Custer	5:20		4:45
Arrive scouts' camp at Halt 1	7:20	4 3/4 miles	6:00
Custer's Party to Crow's Nest			
Custer's party leaves for Crow's Nest	8:00		7:10
Custer's party arrives at Crow's Nest	9:00	4 3/4 miles	7:45
Custer-Varnum party leaves Crow's Nest	10:20		
Custer-Varnum party arrive at Halt 2	10:35	1 mile	9:00
The Command			
Leave Halt 1	8:45		8:00
Arrive at Halt 2	10:07	3 3/4 miles	8:45
Custer-Varnum party arrive	10:35		9:00
Leave Halt 2 under Custer	11:45		9:30
Crosses Divide	12:00		
Halt 3, Custer assigns battalions	12:05 P.M.	1 mile	10:00 A.M.

My criticism of Gray is the same as I have made before. Gray established an overall timing sequence, in this case a 12:05 P.M. "official" division of the command, and then fits events within this structured framework. This he refers to as his time-motion analysis. I realize, in the one sense, this is what I am doing, but I have tried to make an objective progressive time analysis of events as I envisioned them to have taken place. In my first estimate I had the division of the command before 9:30 in the morning. I then extended it to come closer to the 10 o'clock time, which I assume is what Gray had to do in order to arrive at his "official" 12:05 P.M. division. My extension then corresponded to the earlier time indicated by Major Reno;[2] or to Colonel Graham's reference that,

"According to first interviews and accounts, Custer went to the Crow's Nest at daylight, the command crossed the divide and was separated into battalions about ten o'clock;"[3] and General Edgerly, in his letter to Colonel Graham in 1923, gave 10 o'clock as the time of the division.[4] I have wondered why Edgerly, who would certainly have known that the "official" time as presented to the Reno Court was two hours later, would have stated such a time, and why more historians have not been concerned.

I will go over the reasons for my differences, as presented on the above chart. Overall, a major question I would have is why Gray uses much slower times for movement by Custer, Red Star and the command than in estimating later movements. For example: he has Reno, after receiving his attack orders, move a mile and a quarter to Ford A, check it out, cross and be ready to move down the valley in twenty minutes; yet it takes Red Star, who said he was moving fairly fast, two hours to go 4 3/4 miles.

In estimating timing movements that morning, we should keep several points in mind. The topography between Halt 1 and Halt 2 is primarily a gradual incline, and certainly not difficult for the horses. One might remember General Miles said he rode at a walk from Reno's entrenchment area to Last Stand Hill (roughly four miles) in 30 minutes.[5] Edgerly said the 7th was a fast walking outfit and should have covered a mile in 16 minutes.[6]

Gray has Trumpeter Martin leaving Custer with his message to CaptainBenteen on a tired and wounded horse, and going over more difficult terrain traveling at 7 1/2 miles per hour.[7] These are statements which should raise questions and explanations.

Gray has Lt. Varnum sending Red Star back at 5:10 A.M. while I have the time as 4:45 A.M. We know that Varnum was trying to see what the scouts were pointing out to him during the period the sun was rising, 4:13 A.M.. Varnum was not able to see the smoke from the village or the specks

302

representing horses, but he did accept the scouts' sighting, as his message would have indicated. I cannot see where Varnum would have studied the Indian village for a hour and twenty minutes, at which time he writes out a message, gives it to Crooked Horn, who then sent Red Star with the message, accompanied by Bull. I would think 4:45 A.M. would be the latest acceptable figure. Red Star said "he urged his horse on for he had the note."[8] This would indicate he was moving fairly fast. I find one of my major criticism of Gray, and others, is that they bracket certain statements and give their version of what the person meant or they disregard pertinent remarks. Gray, in contrast to what Red Star said, stated: "Red Star then rode slowly, in order to keep Bull's slow horse in sight."[9]

Considering the above, should it have taken Red Star 2 hours to travel 4 3/4 miles to a recognizable camp site. I would certainly say an hour was long enough; but I will extend my estimate to 6:00 A.M. Red Star said the sun was just rising - I would assume over the hills around Halt 1.

Red Star does not note any length of time before Custer came, and received the message, nor any appreciable time before they took off for the Crow's Nest. Custer, supposedly, rode bareback around the camp informing others of the sighting, and I would assume giving his orders for an 8 A.M. command departure. Godfrey said he saw Custer sitting with the scouts, so some time would have been taken before Custer and his smaller party would have left for the Crow's Nest. However, Custer should have been ready to move out around 7 A.M. I would say Custer would have left the command by 7:10 A.M., and since I am sure he didn't walk his horse the 4 3/4 miles, by 7:45 A.M. he would have met Lt. Varnum and moved to his observation site at the Crow's Nest. I might add that, in all of my timing figures, I am giving what I consider to be a conservative estimate.

I cannot see Custer observing for an hour before he returned to his command, which had reached Halt 2; however, I will extend it to 9 A.M. Gray and I now have an hour and 35 minute difference.

Contrary to Gray's time-motion analysis of the command's movement, I can see no reason to dispute their leaving Halt 1 by 8 A.M. as Custer had ordered. According to General Godfrey, the command left promptly at 8:00 A.M.[10] They then moved to Halt 2 passing over what could be considered good terrain. They should have arrived at Halt 2 by 8:45 A.M.

Custer should have arrived back from the Crow's Nest by 9 A.M. I then cannot see Custer spending an hour and ten minutes at Halt 2 before moving. I would have him leaving by 9:30 A.M. They then cross the divide and Custer halts the command, roughly 1 mile from Halt 2, at Halt 3. He then divides the command into battalions and gives assignments. This should have been done by 10 A.M., not 12:05 P.M.

I think General Godfrey, in his narrative as found in Graham's, *The Custer Myth,* on page 136, gives an illuminating account which brings out the distortions associated with timing and the difficulty officers had with coordinating their views with the "official" timing change. Godfrey states the command moved out promptly at 8 A.M. and "marched uninterruptedly until 10:30 A.M., when we halted in a ravine and were ordered to preserve quiet, . . . We had marched about ten miles." Godfrey must have realized that to coordinate timing with the "official" time, he had to say they went ten miles instead of the distance of 3 3/4 miles, in order to arrive at a acceptable 10:30 A.M. time figure. This brings out the difficulty I mentioned before, that officers would have in realizing and adjusting their remembrance with the change that took place in the "official" time.

I realize these times I use in my analysis are merely estimates, but I cannot see Custer or his command taking the time Gray credits them with. The sighting of the Indian encampment had to be of extreme importance. After Custer realized and accepted his scouts' statements that his command had been noticed by the Sioux and he could not expect to surprise them by waiting until the 26th, there is no way that he would have delayed as long as Gray has him doing after returning from the Crow's Nest. Gray had to extend time periods from the sighting of the Indian village by the Crow scouts to Custer's division of the command in order to be able to fit the events into the "official" time division of 12:05 P.M.

Chapter 18, The Descent to the Lone Tepee

Gray indicates several things: Custer's rapport with his scouts; the fear of the Indians scattering; his concern with the terrain to his left; and Custer's recognition of the general location of the Indian encampment. I agree with all of these points and consider them essential.

In discussing Custer's reasons for calling Reno to his side of Reno Creek, Gray writes,

". . . the possibility that these were signs of hostile presence or action would prompt him to unite his force.[11] In other words, Gray suggests the realization, on Custer's part, that they would be going into action fairly soon. I reiterate a major premise that I have pointed out repeatedly: either at that time, or when Custer gave Reno his attack orders, Custer would have sent Benteen a message as well. Gray suggests that before reaching the Lone Tepee, Custer sent Sergeant Major Sharrow ahead to Lieutenant Hare.[12] The Sergeant Major should have just reported back from Hare as Custer approached the Lone Tepee; it is then, I believe, that he was sent to Captain Benteen with a message. That message instructed Benteen to continue on to the Little Bighorn, and indicated that Custer would soon be giving Major Reno attack orders. It directed him to move down the valley in support of Reno, if Benteen had seen no Indians. (Both Sergeant Davern and Trumpeter Martin inferred that this was the content of his orders.)

Gray is undoubtedly correct that Reno's first order, after being called to Custer's side of Ash Creek, was to lead out rather than attack.

Gray claims that at the Lone Tepee, Girard was with Custer, busy smoothing out Custer's differences with the Rees; consequently, he was in no position to climb a high bluff and sight the Indians "running like devils."[13] However, one should note that Girard's calming of the Rees came after his supposed sighting of the Indians.

Again, Gray emphasizes Custer's desire to hear from Benteen. I fully support such an interest by Custer, but this concern should have been reflected in two main considerations: Custer's knowledge that he could not delay much longer from issuing attack orders to Major Reno, and his need to notify Captain Benteen of such an action. It is difficult to assume that a competent commander, who realized the general location of a large Indian encampment, would (fail to) send someone out to check for any Indians on his left, in order to prevent possible scattering or an attack from this direction; or, that realizing he would be sending Reno's battalion to attack the camp from the south, he would not have expected Benteen (if there were no Indians to the left), not to move down the Little Bighorn valley in support of Reno while he tried to encircle or flank them with his five companies.

> Benteen's off-trail scout presents a problem, for his officer's account are vague and faulty and Benteen himself resorted to flagrant falsehoods. Under cross-examination at the Reno Inquiry, he turned utterly irrational regarding the orders Custer gave him . . .[14]

Gray still accepts the contents of Custer's orders to Benteen, as expressed by Benteen himself. The initial order was to move to the nearby bluff, check for Indians, and if there were none, to return. Custer soon realized the need to proceed to the next ridge, and sent his first courier. Since the second ridge was no better, Custer sent a second courier. I doubt if Custer sent the second courier at that time, because it was Sergeant Major Sharrow, with practically the same message as the first courier, who, during that period, was sent to Lieutenant Hare. However, if Custer did dispatch someone, he must have sent three messengers to Benteen, for I cannot believe that Custer would have failed to convey a message that he would soon be ordering (or had ordered) Reno to attack the Indian camp.

Gray makes the following noteworthy remarks which illustrate his recognition that Custer was concerned with Benteen's mission and obfuscation of his orders:

> These follow-up orders reveal how anxious Custer was to know about Indians in the upper valley, for this information would affect his mode of approach to the village.
>
> Benteen's official report resumes with an incoherent account of his off-trail scout, with no hint of these follow-up orders: . . .
>
> Benteen testified (p. 320 [Reno Court]) that the couriers came separately, but he remained evasive about the orders they brought . . . That these follow-up orders permitted Benteen to go beyond the first and second ridges seem certain. It is equally certain that they did not countermand the initial order to hurry and rejoin the main command as quickly as possible. If he was to be absent longer than originally expected, it was appropriate for Custer to urge him to report by courier and caution him to use discretion, so as not to be left behind. But Benteen's claim that he was given discretion to return, only if he found no Indians, seems absurd.
>
> As it turned out, Benteen was, in fact, left behind. He ignored repeated orders to hurry and never reported by courier, two omissions that add up to indiscretion. When it later developed that Custer's battalion was wiped out, Benteen must have realized that his indiscretion had spared his battalion the same fate as Custer's. This recognition apparently drove him to an indefensible cover-up, so simplistic as to be transparent, and which scarred his conscience for the rest of his life. Such painful prying into Benteen's psyche offers a speculative explanation of his deceptive accounts of his off-trail scout.
>
> Gibson had thus secured the intelligence that Custer was anxiously awaiting, negative in that no Indians were seen, but positive in that it would allay Custer's concern about Indians escaping or attacking from that direction. It is incredible that Benteen never revealed that he had accomplished his mission . . .[15]

I believe the major reason for Benteen's reticence was that he knew he had not accomplished his mission. My basic criticism of Gray emerges as he becomes absorbed with mileage and estimating time, rather than an analysis of why Benteen was evasive and irrational when it came to his orders. Although Benteen's slowness in reacting to his known orders and his failure to send a message to Custer are contributing factors, Gray should have looked deeper into the issue and correlated Benteen's behavior with Reno's paradoxical accounts and vagueness on his orders.

Gray raises the issue of whether Benteen could have overtaken Custer at the Lone Tepee. This is a legitimate question, but I believe a more important one would be why Benteen didn't cross the ridge to the valley of South Fork and then complete his mission to the Little Bighorn valley. It is hard to imagine that Lieutenant Gibson, in reporting to Benteen his sighting of the Little Bighorn, would not have indicated that once they crossed the ridge they could have very easily reached the Little Bighorn. Benteen would then have been in a position to fulfill his mission. I agree with Lieutenant Godfrey that at least two basic objectives would have been part of Custer's orders: once Custer realized that the bluffs extended beyond the first bluff and to the Little Bighorn, then, as Godfrey points out in his *Narrative*, "There is no doubt that Custer was possessed with the idea that the Indians would not 'stand' for a daylight attack, that some of them would try to escape up the valley of the Little Big Horn . . . This idea and another that the village might be strung out along the valley for several miles were probably the ones that influenced him to send Benteen's battalion to the left."[16]

However, I believe that the hidden, and not even the inferred part of his orders, brought either by the second or a third courier, added: Once Benteen reached the Little Bighorn, if he had not contacted any Indians or seen any camps, he was to proceed down the valley and support Major Reno, either to his left or between Reno and Custer, who would try to encircle (flank) the Indian camp. The inferential nature of such orders was suggested by Reno's orderly, Davern, and Custer's orderly, Martin. It may explain why any mention of orders was so upsetting to Benteen: he realized that he had not completed his mission; if he had hurried, he could have supported Reno at a time when it may have not only prevented Custer's command from being wiped out, but it could have brought about a victory.

Chapter 19 – The Approach to the Little Bighorn

Gray believes that the orders to Reno were given at the "flat" about one and a half miles above the river. He uses as evidence the Crows' reports, which I also believe are the most authentic. Reno followed the Indian trail crossing Reno Creek to the left side, then proceeded to the Little Bighorn. Gray believes that Girard made his statement about the Indians fleeing at that time, rather than at the Lone Tepee, and he gives several reasons to support his belief. Gray's reasoning appears to be sound. Most significant is his substantiation of the location where the separation of the command took place and where the attack orders were given.

Gray contends that Adjutant Cooke then went to the ford with Reno, and he uses statements by Lieutenant Wallace, Sergeant Davern, Sergeant Culbertson, and Girard as confirmation of this view. I am not aware of Davern's confirmation, although Girard certainly did support this idea. According to my knowledge, Culbertson only indicated that Cooke accompanied Reno until he recrossed Reno Creek, and this I believe he did. Dr. Porter and Private Morris said that Cooke didn't go to the ford.

Gray accepts Girard's statements in which he said that the Indians were not fleeing, and that he gave the message to Adjutant Cooke. Gray also suggests that Davern and Culbertson met McIlhargey before they crossed the ford. I reiterate that if Custer's troops were following Reno, and if all these events took place as quickly as Gray proclaims they did, McIlhargey should have returned and reported back to Reno, and Girard would not have had to follow Reno down the valley. Gray, as others, does not explain why he ignores the testimony of Culbertson, Lieutenant Hare, Dr. Porter, and Captain Moylan, all of whom indicated that there was no significant number of Indians in the valley. One should also explain, in this context, the actions of Hare, Lieutenant Varnum, Major Reno, the troops, the Rees as well as the Sioux and Cheyenne accounts that do not refer to any large number of Indians in the valley during that time. Reno's attack orders, the Rees' battle preparation, the sighting of Indians and the awareness of the general location of the Indian encampment, all suggest a prior knowledge on the part of the command, they would soon face the Indians.

Gray stresses Custer's concern for Benteen's whereabouts after giving Reno his attack orders. I agree, and again point out that during that period, not having heard from Benteen, Custer would have believed it imperative to inform Benteen of the action he was taking, or about to take. At the time, he must still have expected Benteen to be moving to the Little Bighorn, and his message would have included orders for Benteen to move down the valley in support of Major Reno. I believe he sent these orders at the time he called Reno over to his side of Ash Creek, and his messenger met Benteen either at the morass, or, there is the distinct possibility that the messenger met Captain Benteen as he returned to the main trail down Valley 3. (Valley 3 – as designated by Roger Darling in his book, *Benteen's Scout*.)

Gray maintains that Cooke had reached Custer at 3:01. After the General heard that the Indians were not running, he attempted to flank the Indians. Gray states:

> By following [Bouyer and the Crow scouts to the ridge], he could see the terrain and action for himself,

and find a route from which to make a flank attack that might support Reno sooner and more effectively than by following around in Reno's rear.[17]

In discussing the reasons why Custer went to the ridge, Gray should have realized that Custer would have recognized those motives at the time he gave Reno his attack orders, and he should have considered the following points: Custer had in mind the "encircling" of the camp – he had expressed this intention to his scouts. Secondly, Custer had used such methods before and they were a common practice. Finally, Custer would be concerned with the need to synchronize the attacks, and to prevent the Indians from scattering.

It is for these reasons that I believe Custer had already made his move to the ridge, preceding his five companies. Since he did not know the terrain to the north nor the location of Benteen, if he was still in the valley, only a mile or less from the ford, and then heard (as Gray and others believe) the news that the Indians were moving to attack Reno, he would have moved quickly to implement his support from the rear, particularly if, as Gray claimed, that was his initial plan.

Gray continues his narrative with Benteen's march, his meeting Kanipe, Martin and the sighting of Reno's retreating troops. He then contemplates the relative positions of Benteen and the pack train. I believe there is more to the pack train story than Gray and others suggest, but the issue deals more with personal cover-ups than the effect on Custer's actions.

Gray then reverts to his timing sequence and continues to make categorical assumptions based on distance, gaits and a timing estimate by Godfrey. His analysis involves creating a perimeter around events which necessitates his placing known events within this framework. The major estimates are as follows: Reno leaves the Lone Tepee at 2:15 and receives his charge orders at 2:43. Reno then travels a mile and a quarter in 10 minutes; he crosses Ford A in 10 minutes and is ready to move down the valley at 3:03. The scenario then jumps to 4:20, within which time frame one has to accommodate Reno's charge down the valley, his fighting, and his retreat to the bluffs, and to relate these events to the movement of Custer, Benteen and the packs.[18] Although such procedure is necessary to an extent, creating an obdurate mold, as Gray does, requires fitting all of the known action into this inflexible structure.

Even before becoming familiar with Gray's book, I rejected a time-event-time analysis, the main reason being that there are too many interpolating factors which can affect the gaits and time–two factors which, in turn, can affect the perceived action. I believe the most contorted period is the one after Reno received his orders. The troops were intermingling. Did Reno move out immediately? Did his troops have any problems recrossing Reno Creek, as they did, according to Reno, when they first crossed it to join Custer on the right side? It is hard to imagine a group of 120 men in a column formation coming to an unknown crossing, moving a short distance to the south, crossing a belly-high ford in columns of two, watering their horses, recinching and checking their gear, passing through timber, reforming, and being ready to move down the valley in a total of twenty minutes from the time of separation. This is the most important timing sequence in determining Custer's actions, and any errors here are apt to profoundly influence the view of other events. I don't believe it is possible for Reno to have accomplished these tasks in less than 40 minutes.

Chapter 20 – Reno's Fight and Retreat

Gray presents his itinerary distances and timing for these events and states that they are simple to compute: "A 2-mile charge down the valley, a 1-mile retreat to the crossing, and a 1/2-mile climb to Reno Hill." He claims that the charge took 15 minutes, the retreat 7 minutes, and the 1/2-mile climb 10 minutes. The van troops arrived on the hill at 4:10, which means that the fighting in the valley took 35 minutes.[19] He accepts Godfrey's 4:20 as Benteen's arrival time. I question both this estimate and the placing of the events in such a rigid time framework.

Gray then proceeds to address the valley sightings of Custer's troops and attempts to fit them into this mold and action, which I believe creates and expands his previous time errors. Rather than clarifying things, his attempt contributes to further muddy-up the already murky waters, as there are too many chances and reasons for errors. Time and distance as well as gaits are the major source of conflicting statements– both honest mistakes and deliberate distortions. This is why I believe that an "event-time-event" determination leads to more logical conclusions. Instead of categorically stating that Reno started down the valley at 3:03 and Custer began his move to the ridge at 3:01, one can arrive at a truer picture by accepting that there were valley sightings of Custer's troops, and various testimony supports that Custer came on the ridge north of Reno's entrenchment area. These sightings indicate that Custer was on the ridge, moving down it, at the time Reno's men were part way down the valley. The exact time or relative locations become speculative; O'Neil's and Varnum's sighting suggests that

Custer's troops were leaving the ridge when Reno's were establishing their skirmish line. Gray's assumption that this placed Custer 1/2 mile below Reno Hill and disappearing into the head of Cedar Coulee is only his opinion; but now Gray has to fit other sightings and testimony into this strict temporal and topographical frame.

Gray's use of Girard's Reno Court testimony as to his sightings of Custer is misleading. Gray says that Girard, "... verbally testified (p. 133, [Reno Court]) to '1 1/2 or 2 miles from Ford A.'" He also points out that Girard's later interviews specified Reno Hill, but this reference is "eliminated by timing."[20] Although Gray is correct in stating that Girard's timing is incorrect, he should have examined why Girard was attempting to indict Reno; consequently, his sightings at the time Reno was setting up his skirmish line had to place Custer back close to or even before Reno Hill. Otherwise Custer had plenty of time – at least 35 minutes – to attack the Indian village before Reno left the timber and, using Gray's timing, a minimum of an hour before the Indians were released from attacking Reno. Girard must have realized this requirement at the Court when he indicated on the map where his sightings took place: the first on Reno Hill, and the second at Weir Point, where he believed the command would have been when Reno reached the bluff.

Gray accepts DeRudio's sighting of Custer, but establishes his own time reference: "I estimate his sighting came about 3:30 or 3 minutes before the command entered the timber."[21] Gray fails to explain why he doesn't accept DeRudio's own estimate that his sighting took place only 6 minutes before Reno left the timber.[22] It is interesting that Gray then observes: "It is significant that this sighting was 12 minutes after the preceding sighting at 3:18 during which time Custer's column could have trotted another 1.2 miles down Cedar Coulee, far beyond its bend at the eastern base of Weir Ridge, unless it had halted."[23] How far could Custer have gone if one accepted DeRudio's timing of 6 minutes before Reno left the timber? According to Gray's timing, this would mean that Custer was sighted not 12 minutes after, but 29 minutes (3:18 to 3:47; 6 minutes before 3:53 when, according to Gray, Reno left the timber). Gray seems to accept DeRudio's recognition of Custer and Cooke by the former's clothes and the latter's beard, which I believe was impossible. Gray believes that DeRudio saw Custer at Weir Peak, and the troops halted below it in Cedar Coulee. I agree that the troops halted at Weir Point, but just where and at what exact time could be questioned. I certainly wouldn't accept DeRudio's erroneous time and descriptive sighting. As I have explained elsewhere, if he indeed sighted Custer, it must have happened as he moved down the valley along with Reno's troops.

Gray attempts to dissociate Black Fox from Curley, which is necessary to support his hypothesis. He claims that Red Bear and White Cloud left Reno Hill around 4:10 and went to where they met "four" Crows. Gray estimates they met them at 4:15. Red Bear said that he and White Cloud met four Crows; however, Gray believes that they met three Crows and Black Fox. He explains that, "Red Bear probably failed to recognize Black Fox because he was now riding a strange pony, and, perhaps at a distance, was holding the extra mounts."[24] This, to me, is too speculative. Red Bear certainly knew Black Fox, and as Pretty Face said, Black Fox was the only Arikara who wore a white cloth about his head. One might recall Dustin's belief that Godfrey and Benteen mistook the Rees for Crows because they weren't aware of the difference in the way they fixed their hair. Curley, in his interview with General Scott, indicated that he was with the other three Crows during this period. All in all, I believe Red Bear and White Cloud met "four" Crows.

Gray also attempts to correlate Girard's, Herendeen's and DeRudio's hearing of firing from the Custer part of the battlefield into a time frame. They certainly heard firing, but to determine the action or the time when Custer's battle commenced is entirely too conjectural.

Chapter 21 – Disorder on Reno Hill

Gray tries to establish the time of the events which took place on Reno Hill, leading to Captain Weir's downriver jaunt; and to determine when the rest of the command followed. I have no quarrel with many of his estimates. However, his time determinations again become too fixed.

Gray, I believe, makes another erroneous interpretation of Black Fox's activities in order to disassociate him from Curley, thereby allowing Curley to be with Custer.

Gray realized that Black Fox was not included on any list of Ree scouts, once they retreated from the valley, so he surmised the following scenario:

> After a three-day ride the horse herders and rear guard [Gray divided the Rees into two main groups—the horse herders and rear guard.] arrived at Major Moore's Powder River base camp, as recorded there by a sergeant of 6th Infantry: 'Billy Cross, with Custer's Indian scouts, came to this camp in two different parties. Cross and one party (G–eleven rear guard) came at about 2 p.m., June 28, and another party of ten more (G–horse herders), leading surplus ponies, about 5 hours later (7 p.m.).' Note that the horse herders had started back first but arrived second, and thus they had been overtaken and passed by the rear guard.

ANALYSIS OF WRITERS' SCENARIOS

Note also that the rear guard numbered eleven, for it included Black Fox, as will be shown. [fn. 1]*

When these scouts brought the first news of the Custer battle to Major Moore on June 28, Billy Cross, as the only one fluent in English, was subjected to a lengthy debriefing, . . . The debriefing also solves a long-standing puzzle about Black Fox, to whom we now turn.

Despite their usual confusion regarding Black Fox, Ree accounts agree that he overtook and joined the rear guard, . . . at the mouth of the Rosebud on the morning of June 27. [Gray then gives Little Sioux's account of the meeting.] Note first that Black Fox had two horses, one his own and the other a Sioux pony (given him earlier by the three Crows). Note also that no other scout is left unaccounted for, so that Black Fox was the sole scout who could have joined the others on the back trail.

This fact positively identifies Black Fox as the unnamed scout whom Billy Cross referred to in his debriefing as an overtaking Ree: 'One of the Ree scouts overtook us yesterday (June 27) and told me the fight (at Reno Hill) was going on yet . . . . This other scout told me that . . . (more men) had been killed on Monday (June 26).' Cross was thus saying that this other scout, who could only have been Black Fox, did not leave Reno Hill until June 26 but overtook the rear guard on June 27. An addendum to the debriefing confirms this:

'Another scout (G–Black Fox), just arrived, was interpreted to say: "I left Monday (June 26) about 10 (a.m.). They were fighting Sunday night and early Monday morning. They commenced about sunrise; the Indians began the attack. I 'skinned out' because it was getting too hot. The troops were out of water and didn't try to get down to water (G–but did after he left). Bloody Knife was killed in the first day's fight."'

Not only is every detail given by Black Fox correct, but his overtaking ride is reasonable and feasible . . .

This revelation of Black Fox's late departure yields a bonus, for the misinformation about this Ree scout has entangled the three Crows and Curley. Red Star provides a last glaring example; although a horse herder, he ventured to tell Libby (p. 120) what Black Fox told the rear guard on overtaking them: 'In answer to their queries, Black Fox said he and Curley got together near Reno ford. Curley told Black Fox he would take him back to show him where the soldiers left some hardtack. So Curley took Black Fox to the flat below the hills overlooking the present Busby, north side. Curley told Black Fox that for his part he was going home.'

---

*The footnote refers to a letter printed in the *The New York Herald*, August 1, 1876. This letter is reprinted in Graham's, *The Custer Myth*, pp. 356-357. The letter conveys a condemnation of Billy Cross, and it didn't specify any number of Rees in the first party, and suggested that there were nine in the second.

This nonsense apparently gave birth to the fable that Curley went home by way of Busby and the mouth of the Rosebud. To begin with, Curley headed for Gibbon's base camp at the mouth of the Bighorn and insisted he met no one. Since he knew the country intimately, it is absurd to think he would take so roundabout a route, every inch over enemy Sioux country. That Black Fox would be seeking hardtack, when it was freely available at Reno Hill, is equally absurd. What makes the tale impossible is that when Black Fox left Reno Hill at 10 a.m., June 26, Curley was far down Tullock's Fork, and when Black Fox met the three Crows on the bluff before 4 p.m. on June 25, Curley was still with Custer.[25]

According to Gray, this account positively proves that Black Fox was not with Curley, and consequently, that Curley's stories of being with Custer are true. I don't agree with Gray for the following reasons:

Even if I accept Gray's interpretation of Billy Cross's testimony, it is difficult, in fact impossible, for me to envision Black Fox at around 10 A.M. on the 26th leaving Reno's entrenchment area with two horses, one given to him by the Crows the day before. Black Fox said the Indians began the attack at sunrise–they must have left around 10 for coffee. It would have been interesting to see how Black Fox sneaked out with his two horses. Did the Sioux chase him? One might expect that this escape would have been mentioned not only by Young Hawk and the other Rees, but also by the soldiers on the hill, for it should have been quite an achievement.

Black Fox's remarks, I believe, support Red Star's account. Black Fox and Curley met near Ford A. They left the area and since neither had been on Reno Hill, they were hungry; so they went back to where Curley knew there was some hardtack. They had left before the other Rees; this would account for Black Fox being missing from their reports. After Curley decided to leave, it was natural for Black Fox to have returned. He probably arrived toward nightfall,* then moved closer early the next morning (the 26th), and from some vantage point saw Reno's command encircled, and the Indians attacking. Faced with this scene, he turned and left.

I am in no position to judge Curley's route, but am sure he was capable of moving through Sioux territory, especially since he knew where the Sioux were. White Man Runs Him claims that Curley was with the Rees. It is difficult to understand why the Rees created the story of Black Fox and Curley being together, or of their earlier

---

*This would support the Crow's story and time element. Black Fox met the three Crows, who gave him the Sioux pony, and from whom he received information concerning the situation on Reno Hill.

sighting of Curley and Black Fox with Custer near the present location of the Hodgson marker. However, as previously explained, I believe Red Star's account of seeing Black Fox with Curley and Custer near the Hodgson marker was an interpreter error. What I think Red Star actually said was that he saw Curley and the scouts with Custer at the time Custer first came on the ridge and talked with Bouyer. Then Red Star said he saw Curley and Black Fox get together near Ford A. Goes Ahead would have agreed to this and not that Black Fox was with them on the ridge. One should remember that the Crow scouts, after having fired on the Indians at Ford B, would have returned and gone past Reno Hill, where they met Red Bear and White Cloud. After leaving the other three, Curley went toward Ford A to get a drink. The three Crows subsequently met Red Star and then Benteen. It is probable that Red Star, in his later interrogation, not only mentioned seeing Custer and the scouts on the ridge, but also, that he saw Black Fox and Curley near Ford A.

I could never explain to my satisfaction the Ree's early sighting of Black Fox with Curley, This was also true with statements by the other Crow scouts that Curley left them on Reno Creek, with the inference being that it was before they were sent to the ridge. One knew this had to be an error, for Curley was certainly with them as they moved down the ridge. Since we know how hard it was for interpreters to correlate Indian statements, this explanation sounds reasonable and would account for both errors.

As I have indicated in my analysis of Curley's testimony, there is only one interview that I accept as being comparatively accurate, and that is the one with General Scott. Although Curley does not say he met Black Fox by the ford, he does indicate that he separated from the three Crows and went toward the ford in his desire to get some water. Lieutenant Mathey's meeting with two scouts should be considered.

Chapter 22 – Custer Moves Down the Right Bank

Gray uses Reno's troops' sightings of Custer's troops, along with Sergeant Kanipe's and Private Peter Thompson's sighting of Reno's troops, to establish the relative positions of Custer and Reno. This is necessary. However, Gray attempts to mold general statements into exact literal translations in order to fit sightings into his time-motion analysis. He places Reno's troops' early sightings before Custer's move onto the bluffs, which is usually considered to have taken place several hundred yards north of Reno's entrenchment area. Custer, according to Gray, moved in sight of the valley until they reached the bluffs. I do not believe the terrain would have been conducive to such a move; but if Gray is correct, it would constitute a further indictment of Major Reno for not realizing that Custer was using a flanking movement. One should keep in mind that these sightings happened in a comparatively close time frame, especially as these men thought back on what had taken place. Gray believes that Reno's troops were moving down the valley before Custer's reached the top of the bluffs, and that Reno engaged the Indians before Custer left the ridge. My view is the reverse: I think Custer reached the ridge before Reno cleared the timber, and Custer's troops were moving along the ridge at the time Reno's began his charge down the valley. I have presented my view and the evidence to support it a number of times; now I will only attempt to refute major points of Gray's hypothesis. I must, however, reiterate that the question concerning the time it took Reno to reach the ford, cross it, reform and be ready to move down the valley after he had separated from Custer, is the most important element of timing analysis–one's whole scenario centers around it.

I must also restate my view that the most honest man to testify was Trumpeter Martin, although that doesn't mean his estimates were correct all of the time. Gray writes-off Martin's claim that he hadn't seen Reno's troops, by saying that he either didn't look or couldn't see over the bluff's edge.[26] Gray stresses Custer's desire to see what was happening to Reno, which, after all, is supposedly what caused him to go to the bluffs, for otherwise he would have followed Reno. In this context, it is difficult to believe that when Custer and Martin reached the bluffs, looked into the valley, and Custer saw Reno moving safely down the valley rather than being attacked by the Indians, he would not have made some gesture and statement to Cooke and others which would have caused Martin to realize that Reno was on his way down the valley. Reno's troops are said to have charged down the valley some distance from the river; and the Rees were leading so they wouldn't have been hidden by the bluff's edge. If Reno's troops were ahead of Custer, one would expect Martin to have become aware of them. However, if Custer, Cooke, Martin and several others had been moving some distance ahead of the command, and Custer's troops saw Reno's, as they began their dash down the valley, it would be possible and even probable for Martin not to have seen them.

> [Kanipe] (1903, p. 280) Custer . . . charged up the bluffs on the bank of the Little Big Horn. . . When we reached the top . . . we were in plain view of the Indian camp, . . . we were charging at full speed. Reno and his troops were seen to our left, moving at full speed down the valley. At sight of the camp, the boys began to cheer.

ANALYSIS OF WRITERS' SCENARIOS

Some horses . . . last words . . . Custer and troops were within half a mile (G – sic) of the Indian camp, when I received the message from Capt. Custer . . . , [Gray quotes message to McDougall and Benteen] (G – then on my return,) the packtain went directly to the bluff, where I had left Custer. When we reached there we found Reno . . . and Benteen (G – thus Reno Hill).[27]

Gray takes this statement literally and bases his interpretation on it. This is his prerogative, and should be respected, but I believe Kanipe is merely saying that they reached the bluff, and while moving down the bluffs at full speed, they saw the Indian village and Reno's troops as they charged down the valley. This is a general statement of what took place. However, Gray disavows Kanipe's statement that they were within 1/2 mile of the Indian village when he received his message, and considers it an error (which, in the strict sense, it is). I assume that Kanipe is giving his impression of the spatial distance, which certainly places him beyond Reno Hill. One should note that in his interview with Camp, Kanipe referred to a "high point,"[28] and in 1910 Martin specified Weir Point.[29] At the Reno Court, Martin said that they went 300 yards past this high point when Custer sent a message which Gray said was taken by Kanipe.[30] These remarks should be correlated, refuted or explained - not just brushed off by ignoring them, or using time-motion analysis based on speculative projections.

Gray uses Camp's 1908 interview with Kanipe to further support his premise. In it, Kanipe says that, ". . . When the command got up on the bluff . . . we could see across the valley . . . see Reno, his three companies and about 35 Indian scouts going right to the Indian camp, which we could plainly see . . ."[31]

Gray interprets the "bluff" as Reno Hill; I believe it is a general reference to the whole ridge. There is no question that Custer's troops saw Reno's in the valley, as Reno's would have seen Custer's on the ridge, but Gray and I differ as to where and when the sighting took place.

Gray next addresses Kanipe's letter to Camp, in which Kanipe makes a definite reference to leaving at Reno Hill.[32] I don't accept Reno Hill as the location where Kanipe received his message, since it contradicts too many other accounts. I think since Kanipe was not answering a specific question, he used the reference in the sense that Custer's command moved onto the bluff or ridge near Reno Hill. Kanipe probably vaguely associated his leaving the command with Reno Hill. One should keep in mind that there were five companies along with stragglers, and since Kanipe was given the message, his company must have been in the lead, with the others strung out some distance behind. If he received the message on Reno Hill, and had last seen the Indian scouts going to the Indian camp, he would not have passed them where he said he did. Walter Camp must also have been under the impression that Kanipe meant he received his message near Reno Hill, since he wasn't able to reconcile this location with Kanipe's sighting of the Rees.[33]

The third Kanipe interview Gray uses is an article from a newspaper reprinted in Graham's book, *The Custer Myth*. There are numerous errors in the letter, but one can accept the statement that the sighting of the Indian camp had brought on yells from the troops. Thompson and Martin also indicate such a reaction. Kanipe says: "We galloped to the far end of the bluffs."[34] This statement clearly suggests that "bluff" or "bluffs" could mean the whole ridge, and it implies that Kanipe went farther than just beyond Reno Hill.

Thompson's statement, as quoted by Gray, is also ambiguous in its references to the exact time and location. Thompson agrees with Kanipe that in seeing the camp, the troops cheered and began to gallop their horses. To take his statement literally, I would have to assume that they had not seen Reno's troops at that time. When the troops broke into a gallop, Thompson was left behind and Reno's troops were still a mile distant from the Indian camp. Thompson also says: "We soon gained the top of the bluffs and viewed the surrounding country. We came in sight of the village . . ."[35] This statement indicates movement before they viewed the camps. I believe more than these accounts is needed to prove that Reno's troops were ahead of Custer's, or that Kanipe received his message at or close to Reno Hill.

Gray then quotes a part of Martin's Court testimony which I believe is very illuminating, and of which I hadn't been aware. (I used Graham's *Reno Court Abstract* in my original research; it wasn't until my book was published that I read the full transcript of the trial.):

Martin, "From the watering place (North Fork) to the top of the ridge was about an hour and a half (G – *sic*, he was asked the distance, and 1 1/2 miles is correct for Reno Hill). We went down the right bank of the river. We did not travel very fast, but at a regular trot up (G – climbing). The horses began galloping again on the level. [When the village was seen, if the other accounts are correct. It does indicate movement along the ridge.] From on top of the ridge we could see the river below (G – downstream); the river was right at the foot of the bluff (G – true at Reno Hill). [Basically would have been true until they neared Weir Point.] There we looked down (G–downstream) [Would be considered down if from

Weir Point.] on the bottom and saw the Indian village and the ponies, dogs and children around the village. We did not see any warrior Indians at all. Custer thought they were sleeping in their tepees. We could see nothing of Reno's column at all (G – see below). We could not hear any firing (G – Reno was still charging). After seeing the village and no Indians around, Custer pulled off his hat and waved it: Courage, boys, we have got them. As soon as we get through we will go back to our station." Some fast horses wanted to go ahead and it was hard to hold them back . . . (G – ellipsis postponed). We went about 300 yards farther and Custer called his adjutant (G – sic, Tom Custer) and sent an orderly (G – Kanipe) back to Benteen (G – and McDougall).[36]

As I have pointed out, the river was under the bluffs as the troops went along, and although it broke away as they neared Weir Point, this configuration could easily lead to an error in recollection. One should realize that, at the time, Martin wasn't mainly concerned with where the river lay. He later recalled, either from their reaching the ridge near Reno Hill, or from having fought on Reno Hill, that the river was below the bluff. One also has to consider the other references Martin made to highest point and Weir Point, as these are as close to being specific locations as one is able to gather. The galloping, after the village was sighted, could be accepted, but it took place along the ridge in both Thompson's and Martin's accounts. This appears to have happened before a sighting of Reno's troops. In Thompson's case, the sighting seems to have occurred after he was left behind. Kanipe's accounts could be taken either way. Since the Hunkpapa village should have been close to 2 1/4 miles from Reno Hill, I doubt if one could distinguish warriors and children from such a distance.* Gray dismisses Martin's claim that he hadn't seen Reno's troops by saying that he must not have looked; and of course, he would not have heard Custer or the troops commenting on seeing them (if they did) when they first reached the ridge. Gray claims that Martin may not have been able to see over the bluff's edge. When Reno's troops moved down the valley and neared the place where they set up their skirmish line, they were not under the bluffs and Indians must have been starting to go to meet them. This development would have created more activity in the village than Custer purported and Martin indicated.

Gray's reference to Martin's Reno Court testimony, of which I was not previously aware, is illuminating because it supports the essence of the premise I have made, namely that the main aspect of the cover-up at the inquiry involved the orders Benteen and Reno received, and that the Court attempted to discredit Martin for fear of what he might reveal. Martin couldn't be ignored, and had to be called as a witness. However, the interrogators believed they could manipulate him and his testimony, and that is what they did. They asked questions which could be used to discredit Martin and thus have him dismissed. Gray points out that "Because Martin's testimony (pp. 312-313 [Reno Court]) was elicited in such disorderly fashion, [he places] his answers in more coherent sequence."[37] This is fairly substantial proof that the officials were attempting to cast doubt on his reliability as a witness and thereby justifying dismissing him. Martin was the one person who could have known that Benteen's and Reno's orders were more extensive than the two officers admitted. Gray goes on:

> In the postponed ellipsis, Martin told of events that followed Kanipe's departure (to be quoted later). He apparently realized this mistake and tried to correct himself in the last quoted sentence by speaking of an orderly (not a trumpeter) in the third person (not as himself) being sent back, as we know Kanipe was. But before Martin, a recent Italian immigrant with poor English, could make that clear, the interrogator interrupted with a bombshell order: "Tell about the order you got there." Martin, of course, had got no order there but, as an obedient witness, jumped far ahead of his story. The ellipsis only partially filled the gap, but the witness later gave a red-flag clue to the hiatus, by saying that on his ride back to Benteen he went 3/4 mile before reaching the point where "Custer saw the village the first time." This phrase also implies that he knew Custer saw the village more than once.[38]

Gray refers to a "bombshell order" by the interrogator in the postponed ellipsis. What was the reason for this behavior? Why did the interrogator want Martin to jump from this order to an order that everyone was aware of? Was it because the interrogator and Benteen were prepared to discuss the familiar order, even though it was somewhat damaging to Benteen? When the interrogator heard Martin refer to Benteen, he could not have been sure what else Martin may have heard (or probably he was). Reno's defense (actually the Courts) undoubtedly didn't want other orders brought up, hence the "bombshell." Along with previous attempts to discredit the witness, this scare led to the dismissing of Martin. The official dismissal, along with Benteen's degrading remarks, have caused Martin to be ignored as a creditable witness ever since.*

---

*Note again Benteen's remarks when Reno's troops moved to Weir Point: "On arriving at the elevation I then had my first glimpse of the Indian Village . . ." (Graham, *The Custer Myth*, p. 195).

* Note Appendix 2, Part B.

ANALYSIS OF WRITERS' SCENARIOS

Although Gray believes that Martin's accounts support his view that Kanipe received his orders just beyond Reno Hill,[39] I claim that it corroborates my view that Kanipe received his orders just beyond Weir Point, and that Martin was given his some 600 yards from Ford B. The three quarters of a mile would approximate the distance to Weir Point. Martin says that they viewed the village just before he was sent back from Medicine Tail Coulee.* (Camp, p. 103) I don't think one can or should ignore or disregard Martin's statement to Camp (pp. 104, 105). Martin says that although "it has been asserted by some writers of late years that Custer's command never got nearer the river than is the point where he was found dead, [he saw] him and his command right down on the flat within a few hundred yards of the river, retreating from it." Camp points out, in his field notes (p. 103, fn. 6), that Martin "Thinks he left Custer 2 miles north of Reno Hill. After he left Custer he traveled up hill for some distance." Two miles north of Reno Hill would place him in Medicine Tail Coulee, close to 600 yards from Ford B. Going "up hill" would involve a move back to Weir Point, especially along the route I believe he took, as I discussed it in my analysis of Martin's testimony. Camp: (p. 101) "At the same time he saw Custer retreating up the open country in the direction of the battlefield. (He did not tell this at the Reno Court of Inquiry because it was not desired that he should tell all he knew, and said that afterward he never was invited by officers to discuss what he knew of the battle, and never volunteered to do so.)" Camp (p.103), Martin, ". . . followed Dry Creek straight for village. About half way down to Little Bighorn we came into full view of the village . . ." Camp (p. 105), Martin: "I showed (on June 27) Benteen where I left with note from Custer, and Benteen estimated the distance to be 600 yards to Ford B." This is clear and definite testimony by the one person who should know that both he and Custer were closer to the river than Gray and others maintain. One should not accept some of Martin's reports and ignore or write-off others, particularly on the basis of the degrading and uncalled-for remarks by Benteen. One has to consider what the effect would have been if Martin had managed to bring attention to the orders that Custer gave to Benteen and Reno if these orders were similar to what I assume they were. Nor should we dismiss Sergeant Davern's view of the nature of Reno's orders or Martin's remarks to Colonel Graham. Martin:

Then the General motioned to Colonel Reno, and when he rode up the General told the Adjutant to order him to go down and cross the river and attack the Indian village, and that he would support him with the whole regiment. He said he would go down to the other end and drive them, and that he would have Benteen hurry up and attack them in the center.[40]

Again, the question is why Martin was ignored and discredited. As I have stated, in examining Martin's remarks, I believe there was no more honest witness in the Custer drama. Why was he never brought back or asked the pertinent questions during the trial? Why did Benteen denigrate him? Why, if not because the Army and the Court, plus Reno and Benteen, knew that he was the one person who would have been in a position to have known the extent of Custer's orders, and it would be hard to refute any statement he made about them. These orders, if revealed, would have led to both Reno and Benteen being blamed for not following them, thereby causing the demise of Custer and his five companies.

What further increases my wonderment, is the credulity Gray and others give to the statements made by either Curley or his interrogators in order to justify the inane actions they credit to Custer, while rejecting out-of-hand, without examination, Martin's accounts.

I disagree with Gray's categorical interpretation of time, movement and sighting locations. I have covered the differences in analyzing individual testimony of Indians (Rees, Crows, Sioux and Cheyenne), officers, troopers and writers' scenarios. Rather than attempting to describe them again, I, at this point, reject Gray's interpretation on the basis of simple logic.

Gray places the separation of Reno and Custer at 2:43, a mile and a quarter from the Little Bighorn and about a mile and a half from Reno Hill. Reno Hill is a little over a mile and a half from the place where Cedar Coulee reaches Medicine Tail Coulee, and Gray records that Custer halted close to the head of the coulee at 3:49. This is over an hour from the time of separation. According to Gray, Reno had engaged a large Indian force when Custer saw him. Under these circumstances the following points should have been apparent to Custer: At the time of Reno's attack the Indian village had erupted and was in a state of confusion. A cavalry needs to attack to be successful. If the commander is dividing his forces and attempting to flank an enemy, he should synchronize his attack. One of his main fears is the scattering of the Indians. Furthermore, Custer is considered one of the most courageous, attack-minded cavalry leaders in our history. But what is Custer doing during this critical period, according to Gray? Why, he has halted, of

---

*The quotes found in this paragraph are from Camp, Hammer, *Custer in 76*.

course. Even if we assume that Gray was correct in his time-motion analysis of Reno's action, and Custer had waited until 3:01 to move to the ridge, and then moved at a fast gait until Martin left him (trotting or galloping as all reports suggest); if Custer then traveled directly to Weir Point to verify the information Gray realizes he would be after, and then gone down Middle Coulee (or "Weir Coulee," as Gray refers to it), he would have reached the ford after traveling 3 3/4 miles from where they separated. If, as Gray maintains, Martin could have travelled at a speed of 7.5 miles per hour with his tired and wounded horse after leaving Custer, Custer's command should have been able to do that as well. Custer then should have reached the ford in approximately 30 minutes. If we add 15 minutes for viewing (although I can't pinpoint timing and events the way Gray is apparently able to), that would mean that Custer could have reached ford B by 3:46. Reno should have still been in the timber, as Gray places the beginning of Reno's retreat at 3:53. What is important is that if testimony and events do not coincide with Custer's psyche, then one had better re-examine the premise and conclusions. Custer would not have halted once Reno went into action!

Therefore, it is completely illogical to believe that Custer would not have moved and acted as quickly as possible to take the following steps after reaching the ridge: (1) Going to the highest point (Weir Point) in order to view the Indian village. (2) Determining the quickest way to attack the village, which at that time was already in or about to enter a condition verging on panic. This would mean going down Middle Coulee – certainly not Cedar Coulee. (3) Attempting to attack the village at Ford B.

Gray and other writers claim that Custer must have halted and engaged in all kinds of inane actions because there were no signs of a major attack being launched at the ford by his five companies. Since their answers contradict our knowledge of Custer's psyche, they should have formulated a different premise which could also be supported by testimony. This, I believe, is what I have done. My analysis includes the testimony of the Crows and Rees, as well as the Cheyenne and Sioux, along with that of the last white man to see Custer alive: Martin. Although speculation cannot be avoided, mine is within Custer's psychological makeup, and I have fewer unresolved contradictions in supportive testimony than other writers.

As we have seen, Gray, in his analysis of the Crow accounts, places Black Fox with the three Crows, and Curley with Custer. He completely ignores both the testimony of White Man Runs Him and Curley's interview with General Scott. I cannot accept Gray's belief in what he considers evidence to support Curley's notion that he was with Custer. I have covered these reports extensively and stated the reasons why I reject them.*

Gray uses Goes Ahead's interview with Libby (p. 160), where Goes Ahead said that the scouts "rode back along the bluff and met the Arikara Scouts."[41] Gray believes that the plural was a slip, whereas I assume that the Crow scouts did meet the Arikara scouts. If the Crows did fire from the bluff above the ford, as they stated (and their statement is supported by the testimony of White Cow Bull and Bobtail Horse – a Sioux and a Cheyenne); and if Reno's forces were still fighting in the valley, as I believe they were, then the Crows should have met the scouts rather than just one scout. This hypothesis is further supported by the fact of their meeting with Red Bear, White Cloud and Red Star.

Gray's insistence that the use of the word "scouts" instead of "scout" was a slip, illustrates not only a tendency to bend the testimony in support of his view of the events, but also suggests an over reliance on words as expressed by interpreters. Gray attempts to tie the scout in question with Black Fox, and uses a Hairy Moccasin statement to support it. He claims that Goes Ahead told Young Hawk – an Arikara who had fought in the valley and stayed with Reno on the hill – that "The Ree who wore the rabbit ears (Black Fox) was the one whom we three Crows picked up. . . . We saw a man going away off and we chased him and found out he was a Ree. I told the Ree that I had captured five head of horses and I gave a black one to Black Fox." Gray then comments: "This statement does not locate the meeting, and the ellipsis in the middle times it as 'after the Custer fight' and 'when we left the Little Big Horn,' but it had to be before the battle."[42]

The version of the statement that Young Hawk conveyed to Camp is different. In this version, Young Hawk said, ". . . a Crow Indian" [Goes Ahead] said, "we picked up [Black Fox] after the Custer fight. When we left Little Bighorn we saw a man going away off and we chased him and found out he was a Ree."[43] This is an explicit statement. In it, Goes Ahead suggests that the meeting took place when the Crows left the Little Bighorn – which they did late in the day. Earlier, they had gone to the ridge with Benteen. The indication that they met Black Fox after the battle certainly implies that Black Fox was not with them when they met Red Bear, White Cloud and Red Star, or Benteen, or when they moved to Reno Hill with Benteen. This implication supports my version of the events in that it precludes the possibility of their meeting "before

---

*Also refer to General Roe's account as brought out by Private Taylor in his book, *With Custer On The Little Big Horn*, p. 108.

the battle." Goes Ahead's statement to Young Hawk actually reinforces the view that Curley and Black Fox met after Curley had left the three Crows and went toward Reno Ford, much as Curley related these events to General Scott.[44] In this same context, the statement by Young Hawk does not support Gray's contention that Black Fox was with Reno on the Hill until the morning of the 26th.

I would speculate that the following may have been the actual sequence of events: Curley met Black Fox near Ford A. Having quenched their thirst, they were hungry and so went to retrieve the hardtack, after which Curley departed (as Red Star reported Black Fox had indicated). Black Fox returned to where he hoped to meet the other Rees that he had left. He was seen by the Crows and chased (whom I can't imagine chasing anyone at the time Reno retreated, but I find it possible they would after leaving). The Crows informed him of the situation, gave him a horse and went on their way. If Billy Cross's report is correct, Black Fox may have stayed in the vicinity overnight and saw the early attack on Reno, after which he left. If Black Fox also made the statement concerning water to Billy Cross, it probably had to do with Curley going to obtain a drink and meeting him. Black Fox mentioned this meeting to the Crows, who may have said that this was one of the reasons they left Reno Hill, and may have indicated that the soldiers were also thirsty and without water.

As I have pointed out, there are two significant events in my scenario which makes it incompatible with Gray's. I believe Custer went to the ford and was shot; this event caused a disorganized retreat. The three, or possibly all four, Crows fired on the Indian village from a bluff above the ford as Custer's command approached. When Custer was shot and his troops retreated, the Crows fled back to where they met Benteen, and Curley met Black Fox. Gray, on the other hand, doesn't believe Custer went to the ford, primarily because there was no sign of an attack. The refusal to accept this hypothesis has forced Gray and others to resort to incorporating several inane actions. First, they must claim that Custer went down Cedar Coulee and then halted. Then they must find an excuse for some troops to go to the ford or at least toward it. Martin should have left before reaching Medicine Tail Coulee. It is hard to explain Custer's failure to attack, and some writers use the word egregiously in reference to a move to the north. They claim also that a defense was set up in order to wait for Benteen, and they use the sighting of Weir's company to justify the breaking up of the defense and their being overrun by the Indians.

Chapter 23 - Custer's Maneuvering and Skirmishing

Gray questions the traditional view that Custer made a wild dash to the ford and was met by a thousand warriors who forced him to retreat. He calls his own perspective the "separation halt." Gray believes that the traditional view can be refuted because "it violates the evidence gathered two days after the battle, that nearly all of the bodies of Custer's dead were found on the distant Custer field, with no trail of carnage from Ford B. This finding has also been the basic reason for my curiosity about the battle, but the fact that no attack was levied, whether at the ford or elsewhere; nor a strong defense established (although many writers attempt to create one); all led me to believe that something must have happened to Custer at the ford. With plentiful testimony to back my hypothesis and contradict Gray's view, and with timing sequences as well as psychology and logic on my side, I would have to find better reasoning and evidence than Curley's interpreters' fanciful stories to be able to accept the hypothesis Gray and others have presented.

Gray gives one of Curley's accounts to support his view:

> [Curley] Custer, turning left, rode down Medicine Tail Coulee. After riding awhile he halted the command (G-to hear Boyer's report). Then the gray horse troop (Co. E) left us and started down the creek, when we turned north, crossing Medicine Tail Creek, going on the hills north of the creek. Here the command halted again: Custer wrote a message and handed it to a young man on a sorrel-roan horse, who galloped away.
>
> [Gray] Curley thus confirmed the second halt (4:04) in upper Medicine Tail Coulee, which may now be called the separation halt, for Custer here divided his command, sending a part on down the coulee and leading the remainder up and out of the coulee to its north rim, where he halted again and sent off a courier.[46]

I can accept the notion of separation, but not the timing, the list of companies sent, and the purpose Gray and others have outlined. Gray rests his case on Curley's (or what I believe is his interpreters') attempts to obtain news footage by fitting Curley's accounts into new conjecturing by writers. "Separation" was a basic cavalry maneuver to place a part of an attack force in reserve. Custer must have thought that this was essential when he moved to Medicine Tail Coulee from Middle Coulee, just after sending Martin back, for the following reasons: (1) It was a basic cavalry tactic. (2) Considering the terrain, all five companies could not contribute to the attack. (3) By moving Keogh's battalion to Nye Cartwright Ridge, he put them in a position to aid the attack if necessary, to prevent "scatteration" by the Indians, and to provide Benteen and the packs with further instructions when they arrived.

It was now 4:04, according to Gray, when Custer made his second halt. This great, attack-minded commander had now gone an hour and 21 minutes from when he separated from Reno, and an hour and 3 minutes since he began his move to Reno Hill, and he still hadn't launched an attack. It had been 46 minutes since Reno set up his skirmish line, but Custer had not felt the need to "support" Reno yet. Apparently some analysts can accept these reasons and the time-motion analysis – I can't.

Chapter 24 – Curley's Escape

I have dealt specifically with Curley's various remarks, or his interpreters' accounts of his escape. Because of the direction Curley and Black Fox took in leaving Reno Creek, it is more than likely that he saw the last of Custer's fight, and interpreters filled in the gaps necessary to obtain news coverage which centered on the need for him to have been involved with General Custer, only leaving him under orders, at the last minute.

Chapter 25 – The Final Minutes

Gray explains why he does not examine Lakota or Cheyenne testimony:

> It is not possible to reconstruct the fighting action on the Custer field, for no participant with Custer survived to describe it, and accounts from Indian participants reveal little more than their attitudes and fighting tactics. A proper reconstruction requires evidence on who did what, when, and where, on both sides, and all tied properly together, but such evidence is lacking. Pure speculation needs no evidence, but since it merely fills a vacuum with vacuity, it yields no progress. On the other hand, a search for evidence that imposes constraints may at least reduce the possibilities to a finite number. Since there is more evidence on where the killing action occurred than on any other aspect, I am prompted to focus on this dimension and see what may be inferred from it.[47]

This is a verbal way of dismissing a primary source of information, not only for the Custer field of operation, but the Reno one as well. I believe the evidence the Indians present is as good as any other testimony. However, one has to recognize the problems they had in remembering time and distance (problems which Gray should have realized were no different than those of the others whose testimony he does consider), as well as certain fears and a natural tendency to enhance their own exploits. In interpreting Indian testimony, therefore, one has to establish a general consensus tempered with logic. There is no reason they should be excluded from any endeavor to recreate what happened to Custer's command. The position of bodies and artifacts should be assimilated with Sioux and Cheyenne testimony.

Gray continues:

> If the counterclockwise hypothesis is true, it follows that men equivalent to more than one company left Custer Hill before the final slaughter there began, and proceeded to the South Skirmish Line. Furthermore, they apparently crossed a conspicuous gap before their own heavy losses began.[48]

I do not agree with Gray that a South Skirmish Line was attempted or established at this stage of the battle. Sioux and Cheyenne accounts (ignored by Gray) do not support such a premise. They do reveal, however, that there were escape attempts. If a South Skirmish Line was established, numerous Indians should have mentioned that the line was overrun, stressing their personal prowess in accomplishing it. One should also expect a major officer to have been with any company sent to establish such a line.

> [Gray] The next gap, though tiny, is of special significance for through it runs Deep Ravine, here steep-sided, formidable to cross, and dangerous to be trapped in. The 14 widely scattered soldiers markers beyond on w' perimeter are probably all legitimate and are equivalent to about one-third of a company. Again, if the counter-clockwise hypothesis is true, these 14 men came from the South Skirmish Line and so must have crossed Deep Ravine, an act of desperation forced by an overwhelming Indian attack on the South Skirmish Line. Though in a flight for life, all fell before reaching Calhoun Ridge.[49]

W' perimeter extends along Greasy Grass Knoll toward the South Skirmish Line. This is the line I believe the "main element" of Yates' battalion retreated over to the cemetery area, setting up rear guard action at what I call the South Retreat Line.

Again, there is no Indian reference to such fighting on the South Skirmish Line or an attempt by some to reach Calhoun Hill, although there are numerous accounts of troops leaving Calhoun Hill and moving toward the area where Keogh's body was found or on to Last Stand Hill. It is odd that the troops would flee toward the Indians and not back to Last Stand Hill. White Cow Bull reports that he and other Sioux and Cheyenne fired on troops retreating from the ford along what one could consider w' perimeter. They also fired on other troops, which I assume was Keogh's battalion attempting to support the retreating Yates' battalion.

Gray reports what Lt. Bourke recorded in his diary. He was with General Sheridan's burial party in 1877. "[From Custer Hill] a frightened party of 30 or 40 men, still running, strove to gain the bank of the river. They were killed like wolves . . ."[50]

Gray is using the account to verify Bouyer's location, which I agree with. However, I believe that the account suggests recognition after the battle that there was not a South Skirmish Line but merely an attempt to flee the field. I believe these people were better able to judge, and their views should not be dismissed lightly. It is true that some officers at the Reno Court said that they thought there was evidence of a skirmish line, but this seemed more of an attempt to sustain the image that all these men fought courageously to the end.

Although Gray's book is required reading for any Custer buff, I don't agree with his conclusions. Gray, in my view, places too much emphasis on trying to create an exact time itinerary. This insistence has caused him to enact his own interpretation on testimony because of the need to place it within his rigid time frame. He was forced to invent Custer's reaction after Kanipe and Martin left, with only Curley's comments to use for verification. Curley's early remarks indicated that Custer went to the ford; his later ones don't (except for General Scott's interview). In examining Curley's statements, I have explained why I believe the General Scott interrogation is Curley's only overall true account. To surround Curley with a newsworthy aura became the objective of too many, and to do so meant that it was necessary to place him with Custer; otherwise he would have done less than the other Crows. As writers scenarios changed, Curley's accounts changed with them.

I commend Gray for attempting to analyze testimony which has been sadly neglected. However, Gray should not have attempted to explain Custer's action following Martin's departure without including the accounts of the Sioux and Cheyenne. To reiterate: Once you try to center your whole hypothesis on a time-motion analysis, or as I have referred to it, a time-event-time analysis, any error continues to magnify itself. Since such a premise rests on the most widely variant and intangible components – time (affected by speed, fatigue and terrain) and distance (affected by memory, and an ambivalence often of ephemeral reference points) – chances of not miscalculating become minuscule.

SOURCES

1. Camp, ed. Hammer, *Custer in 76*, p. 60.
2. Overfield, *The Little Big Horn, 1876*, pp. 43-44. Nichols, *Reno Court of Inquiry*, p. 360.
3. Graham, *The Custer Myth*, p. 216.
4. Ibid., p. 215.
5. Ibid., p. 311.
6. Ibid., p. 216.
7. Gray, *Custer's Last Campaign*, p. 339.
8. Graham, *The Custer Myth*, p. 32.
9. Gray, *Custer's Last Campaign*, p. 236.
10. Graham, *The Custer Myth*, p. 136.
11. Gray, *Custer's Last Campaign*, p. 249.
12. Ibid., p. 253.
13. Ibid., p. 257.
14. Ibid., p. 258.
15. Ibid. pp. 260, 261, 262.
16. Graham, *The Custer Myth*, p. 138.
17. Gray, *Custer's Last Campaign*, p. 279.
18. Ibid., Note time itineraries – pp. 272-273.
19. Ibid., p. 288.
20. Ibid., p. 293.
21. Ibid., p. 294.
22. Graham, *Reno Court Abstract*, p. 115.
23. Gray, *Custer's Last Campaign*, p. 294.
24. Ibid., p. 303.
25. Ibid., pp. 329-332.
26. Ibid., p. 336.
27. Ibid., p. 334.
28. Camp, ed. Hammer, *Custer in 76*, p. 100.
29. Ibid., p. 103.
30. Gray, *Custer's Last Campaign*, p. 336.
31. Op. Cit., p. 92.
32. Ibid., p. 137.
33. Ibid. p. 93.
34. Graham, *The Custer Myth*, p. 249.
35. Gray, *Custer's Last Campaign*. p. 335.
36. Ibid., p. 336.
37. Ibid., p. 336.
38. Ibid., pp. 336, 337.
39. Ibid., p. 337.
40. Graham, *The Custer Myth*, p. 289.
41. Gray, *Custer's Last Campaign*, 350.
42. Ibid., p. 350.
43. Camp, ed. Hammer, *Custer in 76*, p. 192.
44. Graham, *The Custer Myth*, p. 14.
45. Gray, *Custer's Last Campaign*, p. 358.
46. Ibid., p. 358.
47. Ibid., p. 384.
48. Ibid., p. 393.
49. Ibid., p. 393.
50. Ibid., p. 397.

Little Big Horn Diary Chronicle of the 1876 Indian War
By James Willert

In a continuing attempt to examine other viewpoints as to why Lt. Colonel George Armstrong Custer didn't launch a full scale attack on the Indian camp with his five companies, and because the book was so highly recommended, I read James Willert's, *Little Big Horn Diary, A Chronicle of the 1876 Indian Wars*. My critique only covers the Battle of the Little Bighorn portion of the book. I thought the book was an exceptionally fine general account of the battle. I was particularly impressed with the extent of the research done by Willert, and his ability to weave participants testimony into a tremendously interesting portrayal of what went on at the time. He did this by including the participants of the various components involved in the battle: the Seventh Cavalry, the Indians, along with General Terry and Colonel Gibbon's commands. However, I consider it a general account of the campaign in contrast to an investigative study. A major criticism is that Willert accepts too many of the statements that were made, especially by officers at the Reno Court. He appears to take a Fred Dustin or a Colonel Graham approach to officer testimony, assuming that they wouldn't lie or distort the truth because they were officers and under oath.

I think Willert is overly sympathetic with Major Reno with respect to his retreat from the valley. However, Willert does recognize there were cover-ups of officers' testimony concerning the action of Major Reno on the 25th after reaching the bluffs. Reno's conduct at the time of the trial was a major issue, but I consider it a minor one today. This is why I wish Willert had recognized and examined the need for Major Reno, Captain Benteen, the military and the defense to cover-up what I look at as the major issues. I believe most writers today realize the officers, whether through military pressure to exonerate Major Reno or because they recognized the traumatic experiences Reno and they had been through, would have had no real desire to see him court-martialed. As S. L. A. Marshall said, "Only rest, with preferably a few winks of sleep, will initiate recovery,"[1] and it appears Reno did regain his composure by the 26th.

I consider there are three major issues that I think any historian should analyze for cover-ups, even if they end up accepting the testimony as given. The acceptance of conflicting evidence would have brought court martial charges against Major Reno and an indictment of Captain Benteen. The three issues would be: (1) the orders Custer gave, (2) timing, and (3) the sighting of Custer on the ridge as Reno's troops moved down the valley. The third could be called a sub-heading of number two, but I think it is important enough that it should be looked at on its own. Any examination of the Reno defense's summation should make it apparent how they attempted to ignore or discredit statements made by those non-military witnesses who would not have been subject to military pressure. My criticism, as I will attempt to show, is that Willert doesn't question, examine, or even seem to realize the importance of the three issues. In each, an analysis should be made as to whether Custer gave more extensive orders than portrayed by Major Reno and Captain Benteen; whether there was an "official" time change; and whether there were early sightings of Custer's battalion on the ridge as Reno's troops moved down the valley, and if so, what effect this should have on one's scenario of the events that transpired. These questions should be asked, examined and their ramifications accepted or rejected.

My interest and research has concentrated on the happenings and testimony of participants, both Indian and white, concerning the events that transpired primarily on the 25th of June, 1876. My critique of James Willert's work will begin on page 254 of his book.

Seventh Cavalry – Page 254

Willert writes that it was early in the morning on the 25th. The sun was just rising over the eastern ridges when Red Star rode into camp with a message from Lt. Varnum that the scouts had seen the Indian encampment. Custer received the message, then rode around the camp telling the officers of the sighting and what their orders were. He informed them that the command should move out by 8:00 A.M. Custer then held a brief conversation with Red Star, Bloody Knife and some of the officers in which he indicated his desire for the command to remain where it was. They would then move during the night and surround the Indian village, attacking it the morning of the 26th. Custer and a small party then proceeded to the Crow's Nest. As Willert points out, the command was still under the assumption that they would move out at 8:00 A.M., which according to Lt. Godfrey,[2] was when they did.

Willert has Custer arriving at the Crow's Nest at 9:30 A.M.; I disagree. One can refer back to my more complete analysis of timing found in my examination of Chapter 17 of John Gray's book, *Custer's Last Campaign*. Keep in mind that the Crow's Nest would have been approximately 4-1/2 miles from Halt 1, which was the command's camp the morning of the 25th. The Crow scouts, from the

ANALYSIS OF WRITERS' SCENARIOS

Crow's Nest, would have spotted the smoke rising from the Indian camp shortly after dawn. Dawn would have been at 3:34 A.M., so by 3:45 A.M. they should have noticed the smoke coming from the Indian campfires. The Crows would have notified Lt. Varnum who would have went up to their observation post, and though he could not see the smoke, he accepted the scouts' sighting. He then sent his message to Custer via Red Star, who was accompanied by Bull. Red Star should have left by 4:45 A.M. and arrived by 6:00 A.M. at the army camp (a conservative estimate). Sunrise would have been at 4:13 A.M.[3] The sun would certainly have risen over the eastern hills by 6:00 A.M. Custer would have been anxious to verify for himself the sighting and placement of the Indian camp; therefore, I can't see Custer receiving the message around 6:00 A.M. and then waiting for close to three hours before leaving for the Crow's Nest. The terrain would not have created any particular problems, and, according to Red Star, they "rode hard" to the Crow's Nest.[4] They should have covered the 4-1/2 miles in less than 30 minutes, and arrived at the Crow's Nest closer to 7:30 A.M. than 9:30 A.M., as Willert maintained.[5]

Willert then has Custer asking Lt. Varnum if he had verified the sightings, and when Varnum said he had not, Custer was displeased.[6] This is typical of Willert in that he surmises what Custer or others are thinking or have said. This makes for interesting reading, but is not necessarily accurate or objective analysis. I am not aware of Custer being disgruntled with, or even having asked, Varnum such a question. I don't know just how he would have expected Varnum to have verified the sightings. Early dawn is the best time to have seen the smoke rising from the Indian encampment.

Willert states that Custer did not see the signs of the Indian camp, but accepts or believes he cannot reject the sightings. Willert does not acknowledge Red Star's statement that Custer, after Charlie Reynolds explained his viewing mistake and pointed to where he should look, nodded, and then did so again when he looked through glasses.[7] Willert does indicate how Custer initially did not believe the command had been sighted by the Sioux, that they should wait, and then encircle the camp at night and attack the next morning. The scouts persuaded him that the command had been observed and they should attack that day. This is important to those who believe that Custer did not listen to his scouts, and that his plans were to support Reno by following him into battle.

I believe that, more than likely, the only officer besides Major Reno and Captain Benteen that was involved in the decisions and stratagems of the inner circle at the Reno Court was Lt. Wallace. I have stated this throughout my manuscript. Willert indicates Wallace's agreement with positions taken by Major Reno and Captain Benteen without seeming to associate it with any cover-ups or recognizing the need (considering he was the official itinerast) for his support.

Willert refers to Lt. Godfrey's 8 o'clock time for when the command moved that morning, but states that Wallace, the official itinerast, recorded the time as 8:45 A.M.[8] I see no reason that the troops would not have been ready to move out by 8:00 A.M., and since I think the later time is necessary for the Reno Court timing defense of Major Reno and Captain Benteen, I would go with 8:00 A.M. Willert goes along with the command reaching what is known as Halt 2 by 10:00 A.M.; but since this is only 3-1/2 miles from their campsite at Halt 1, I believe they would have reached there by 8:45 A.M.

I will emphasize again that timing, to me, was a major cover-up, and without changes in the "official" time Major Reno would have faced a court martial and Captain Benteen an indictment at the Reno Court of Inquiry. The variations associated with timing statements by officers and enlisted men, as well as packers, scouts, and the Sioux and Cheyenne have to be analyzed and a reasonable explanation given. In an analysis you must understand that if the "official" time was 10:00 A.M. for the division of the command, and not 12:05 P.M., this would have an effect on the charges at the Reno Court.

Willert states that, "Shortly before noon, this June 25th, Custer raised his gauntleted right arm, gave the signal to move forward,"[9] and they would have left Halt 2 and crossed the divide. I disagree with this timing. As previously stated, I believe Custer would have arrived at the Crow's Nest around 7:30 A.M. He would have gone to an observation point and probably spent no more than fifteen or twenty minutes before nodding that he had been able to make out the smoke coming from the Indian village or the specks representing the Indian ponies. He then met with the scouts who persuaded him to attack that day since they believed the Sioux were aware of his command and would undoubtedly attack or scatter. Custer then agrees. I am sure he didn't change his mind about attempting to encircle or flank the Indian villages. According to Red Star, ". . . the army now came up to the foot of the hill and Custer's party rode down and joined the troop."[10] I think that by 9:30 A.M. Custer would have moved from Halt 2, crossed the divide, and arrived at Halt 3 – a distance of 1 mile – where the division of the command would have taken place. This should have been no later than 10:00 A.M.

Willert describes the division of the command, and I would agree with his account, except for the fact that he did not wonder why Lt. Edgerly of Benteen's battalion appeared to hear the complete division, whereas Benteen professed to not having known because he had left. I have covered this and my reasoning elsewhere.

Lt. Wallace's "official" time was 12:05 P.M.; Willert gives Captain Myles Moylan's opinion as stated at the Reno Court as "about 12:30" [P.M.].[11]

In addition to the time outline above, I have given my reasons for not accepting the "official" time of the division, presented at the Reno Court as 12:05 P.M., so I will not go into any extensive review of my reasoning. However, many of the numerous distortions in the various accounts concerning timing are, I believe, due to this change. I continue to wonder why more people have not been as perplexed as I have with the differing time accounts. Colonel Graham poses this question in his book, *The Custer Myth,* on page 215, to General Edgerly:

> It puzzles me greatly that nearly all the early accounts of the fight put its occurrence several hours earlier than do the later ones. According to the first interviews and accounts, Custer went to the Crow's Nest at daylight; the command crossed the divide and was separated into battalions about ten o'clock; Reno's fight commenced about noon; Custer's about 12:30, and Benteen joined Reno about 2:30. But Wallace's itinerary and most of the later accounts, and in particular General Godfrey's story, show that Custer did not go to the Crow's Nest until *after* 10 A.M.; that he stayed there *over an hour* and that the command did not cross the divide until noon; that it was 2 P.M. when the lone tepee was sighted; about 2:15 when Reno got his orders to cross the river and charge; . . .[12]

Colonel Graham then accepts the changes, apparently because they were given by officers at the Reno Court.

If there was a deliberate change in the "official" time the division of the command took place, the question that should be asked is why? I don't think the answer is hard to find. The one time that was difficult to change was when Major Reno and Captain Benteen went to investigate gunfire from downriver. There were too many people who knew and had said it was after 5:00 P.M. If Benteen met Reno by 2:30 P.M. (more than likely earlier), and they heard gunfire at that time, but didn't go to investigate until after 5 o'clock, then this could not be justified, even by an extension of the time when the packs arrived, or the necessity of taking care of the wounded. The sound of gunfire could not be denied, even though Reno, Benteen and Wallace said they had not heard any, or enough to be concerned about. Benteen had orders to hurry to Custer's aid, and certainly Sgt. Kanipe and Trumpeter Martin – even though enlisted men – could have informed them of Custer's actions if they had been concerned enough to ask. From a human standpoint we might excuse the time taken, due to the experiences Reno and his troops had suffered and the general conditions they had faced, but, certainly, it could not be excused from a military point of view. However, no matter how long the defense tried to extend the arrival time of the packs, the necessity to wait for them, and the need to take care of the wounded before moving – it would not have been enough. The time had to be changed.

Willert, after the separation of the command, accepts Major Reno's statement that he had no knowledge of Custer's plan of action. There is no reason that Major Reno would not have known the general plan of action. He certainly knew the Indian camp had been located and that there would be an attack. Even if he didn't know for sure why Benteen was sent to the left, the natural assumption should have been for what it was: to determine if there were any Indians or Indian camps that could have spoiled Custer's plans to attack the known Indian encampment. If there were no Indians, he would be expected to aid in the attack.

Willert also accepts Benteen's account of the two messages Custer sent, and places the reason for their incongruity on Custer. Benteen may have been correct, but again, historians should question these statements by Benteen. Practically all writers realize and have brought out certain fabrications, distortions, and outright lies made by Benteen, but on basic critical matters, such as his lack of knowledge of Custer's plans, they are willing to accept Captain Benteen's and Major Reno's accounts, even if the messages that any competent commander would have been expected to send are not the ones they reported. One should also realize that if the messages you might have expected Custer to send were the actual ones he did, then both Major Reno and Captain Benteen would have been subject to court-martials. One should keep in mind Edgar I. Stewart's comments in his book, *Custer's Luck*:

> In the years following the battle, the orders to Benteen suffered not a little from conscious and unconscious distortion, from rationalizations, and from faulty memories. What the actual orders were we do not know. We have only Benteen's word for them since all of the others – Voss, Sharrow and Cooke – died on the heights with Custer, and it would have been comparatively easy for the orders to have been misunderstood or misrepresented, either deliberately or otherwise.

ANALYSIS OF WRITERS' SCENARIOS

Custer's initial orders to Benteen would have been to go to the bluffs to the left and look for any signs of Indians and to "pitch into" any that he came across. Before reaching the ridge, Trumpeter Voss arrived with the message that he should continue on to the second line of bluffs.

Willert then brings out that Benteen "pressed on. But once more, he was overtaken with further instructions from Custer – this time by Custer's Sgt. Major William H. Sharrow. The orders were that if Benteen's explorations discovered nothing ". . . from the second line of bluffs . . . to go on to the next valley . . . ."[13]

Willert, in referring to these orders, said:

> "Why Custer employed such an irregular, and almost 'slapdash' method to emphasize his instructions to Benteen, we do not know, save that these were *afterthoughts* when Benteen had departed, and Custer wanted the latter's probe to take a broad sweep into the adjacent valleys."[14]

Willert gives Private Windolph's view that it was a foolish maneuver. Besides the fact that I do not believe it was a foolish move but a necessary one, for anyone to not question whether Custer was responsible for a senseless second courier message, or that it might not have been the complete message carried by the Sgt. Major, or it might not have arrived at the time portrayed by Captain Benteen, to me, does not show any attempt to analyze events but merely to report them. We have a "senseless" message sent to Benteen by Custer, but supposedly no message when he sends Reno to attack. This would indicate he would have had no particular plan for Benteen to take part in the forthcoming battle. I do not believe this. One should also remember that the Sgt. Major was sent by Custer to Lt. Hare, as they neared the Lone Tepee, at a time when it was unlikely that the Sgt. Major would have been able to have returned from taking his message to Captain Benteen. This is especially true if one accepts the time Benteen said he received the message, and if one considers the probable route the Sgt. Major would have taken. We know that Benteen said his orders were to go to the Little Bighorn, and he then professed to not knowing where or how far he would have to go in order to reach the river. However, one should remember that he believed the scouts' report on the location of the Indian village. Any of the officers should have been roughly aware of where and how far the Little Bighorn was. In other words, shouldn't one question Benteen rather than Custer?

Willert's acceptance of Benteen's description of his move to the left bears out my criticism of Willert. I believe it was a sound military move on the part of General Custer to have Benteen move to the left. Benteen's description of it being a "wild goose chase," and that he went up and down those hills for ten miles, reflects Benteen's attempt to rationalize his actions. Willert, in his acceptance, said:

> As Captain Benteen and his battalion drew near the ". . . very high bluffs . . .", whose summits Custer had assigned them to cross in search of the enemy, Benteen must have wondered at the difficulties of the task before him, and to the advisability of the orders. Considering the enormous hostile aggregation in the valley of the Little Horn, *dividing* the strength of the regiment seemed itself a risky and foolish tactic; [Benteen's movement didn't reflect this concern] moreover, sending 125 men [Benteen's battalion] over a rugged terrain to stem the Indians' projected withdrawal appeared a vain and ill-considered move – that is, if the battalion ever managed through the valley at all. Benteen described the ground: ". . . To say the country terrain was rough is but putting it mildly – expletives could be worked in front of 'rough' that would be more truly descriptival, and by no means exaggerative of the lay of the land . . ."[15]

The bluffs were not what I would describe as very high bluffs. As I have stated many times, for Custer not to be concerned, since he was acting on the assumption that the Sioux were aware of his presence, and for him to have risked an attack as his troops moved down the valley, seems foolhardy. He would certainly have wanted to make sure there were no Indian camps to the south of where the known Indian village was. I have ridden over Benteen's route to where he returned to the main trail, and though his statement, ". . . We had to go by files through defiles and circuit round rugged hills which were too steep to ascend . . ."[16] is true to an extent, it still is an exaggeration. Willert should question such statements and be aware of Benteen's need to rationalize his behavior.

Willert states:

> As nothing was observed by Gibson [Lt. Gibson was sent to the top of the ridges to observe and report back to Benteen] from the crest of the first ridge, nor from any of the succeeding elevations along this line, there was no effort made to proceed to the second ridge. Visibility of the terrain beyond was as clear from the first elevation as it would have been from the second, so there seemed little value to be gained by struggling with the battalion to the further ridge.
>
> As the command advanced over and around the rugged defiles of the first ridge – without result of any kind – Captain Benteen became ever more restive and impatient with the situation.[17] [my brackets]

I am not sure of what Willert refers to as the first ridge

and the second ridge. I have used Roger Darling's maps and references, both in my accounts, and when I rode over the terrain with the rancher, Chip Watts. After ascending the first line of bluffs, Benteen would have moved along Plateau A. He would have sent Gibson to what is referred to as the overlook on Ridge B. Benteen would have passed by and crossed a defile into Valley 3. Gibson was sent to what is known as Gibson's Lookout, which would be along Ridge C. From the prior elevations, contrary to Willert's account, Gibson would not have been able to see the Little Bighorn, but he was able to from the overlook on Ridge C (Gibson's Lookout). Gibson admitted being able to see the Little Bighorn, and though he doesn't say that he informed Benteen that once they crossed Ridge C and into South Fork the terrain leading to the Little Bighorn would be comparatively easy, he should have told him, and probably did.

I have previously given my scenario of the events that followed, so will only give an abbreviated summary. Benteen would have already made up his mind and started down Valley 3 when he received the report from Gibson. At this time Custer should have been at the Lone Tepee or not too far beyond. Custer, after Girard said the Indians were running, would realize that he was soon to launch his attack and would want Benteen to be aware of this. Lt. Hare should have reported that his scouts had seen no signs of Indians to the south. Custer would assume Benteen would be continuing to the Little Bighorn, and would've wanted him, once he reached the river, to move in support of Reno. I believe, at this time, he would have sent orders to Captain Benteen by the Sergeant Major – or a third courier – along with the Ree scout, Stabbed. They would have gone to the ridge northwest of Gibson's Lookout and seen Benteen returning to the main trail. The courier would have sent Stabbed back with a message to General Custer that Benteen was back on the main trail, and then joined Benteen as he moved down Valley 3. After presenting Custer's orders to Benteen, he would have watered his horse and then returned to General Custer.

Willert then appears to accept the following remarks made by Benteen: "... I went up and down those hills for 10 miles ... the horses were fast giving out from steady climbing ... and *as my orders had been fulfilled, I struck diagonally for the trail the command had marched on* ..."[18]

Willert might remember that Benteen said he "... circuit round rugged hills which were too steep to ascend ..."[19] As Stewart said, "... examination of the region discloses that the terrain was not nearly as bad as he represented it."[20] The question one needs to try to answer is why Benteen believes he needs to represent the trail the way he does. Is it because he realized his slowness possibly caused the defeat and death of so many? Does he realize the need to extend and justify the time it took him to reach the rest of the command, so that once he had reached the ridge and joined Reno the attempt to go to the aid of Custer would not appear too long? Or, might at different stages and times it had been for both reasons?

When analyzing the time cover-up, one should remember Benteen, shortly after the battle, said:

> ... then "Right Oblique" was the word until we got out of the hills to the trail; my command getting to it just ahead of the train of Packs, the horses not having been watered since evening before, and this being along about *one o'clock* P.M. of a hot June day, ...[21] [my italics]

Custer's Battalion – Page 270

Willert takes up Custer's move to the Lone Tepee; his calling Major Reno and his battalion forward; Gerard reporting that the Indians were "running like devils"; the Ree scouts' reluctance to move after the fleeing Indians. All of this is well documented and Willert provides an interesting account of the events. However, he does accept Lt. Wallace's statement of the time and that he was riding with Reno.

Lt. Wallace's riding with Reno should raise questions. One should recognize these remarks were made at the Reno Court, at a time Major Reno needed verification from an officer for the orders he said he received. One must consider Varnum's reference to Wallace being by Custer's side when Reno was moving to the attack, and Varnum calling back to Wallace not to stay with the "coffee coolers". Custer then "laughed and waved his hat and told Wallace he could go & Wallace joined me."[22] They then proceeded toward Ford A. Such a statement by Varnum supports my contention that Wallace was part of the Reno-Benteen defense inner circle at the Reno Court.

Willert:

> Wallace, riding with Reno, recorded the hour as 2:00 P.M., and recalled: "that was when I pulled out my watch and looked at it, and it is my impression that an orderly came about the same time with General Custer's compliments and asked him [Reno] to go over to the other bank. He [Reno] moved over with his battalion and the two moved along from 10 to 15 yards apart, the heads of the two columns opposite each other."[23]

I believe the 1:00 P.M. time for Benteen to have

returned to the main trail, and the 2:30 P.M. time as expressed by both Godfrey and Reno as to when Benteen's troops met with Reno's, makes the most sense logically, and from a timing standpoint. If I were to question the 2:30 meeting time, I would place it earlier rather than later. Major Reno, in his official communique following the battle, referred to being at the Lone Tepee around 11:00 A.M. With these times, one finds a correlation, which is not seen in the distorted analysis of overall timing statements made after the battle with those made at the Reno Court.

Willert appears to believe Major Reno would have received his attack orders near the Lone Tepee. I do not.

> . . . Cooke spurred swiftly to Major Reno's position, and delivered the orders, verbally. The hostiles he said, were ". . . about two and half miles ahead: and "on the jump." Custer's order to Reno were to charge after them [in the recall of Lt. George Wallace]: '[to] go forward as fast as you think proper and charge them wherever you find them!" Custer would bring his column in support behind him. Major Reno's recollection of the orders given by Cooke placed more emphasis upon the village: "General Custer directs you to take as rapid a gait as you think prudent and charge the village afterward and you will be supported by the whole outfit."[24] [Willert's brackets]

Willert then does what I referred to before as a general criticism of his work: he puts words in peoples' mouths that I am not aware they spoke, which at times gives what I consider to be a false picture of events.

> . . . Reno pressed Lieutenant Cooke: "Was Custer going to follow directly behind the forward battalion?" Cooke, of course, had no more insight into what was in Custer's mind than anyone else, so could only echo Custer's imprecise instructions: 'Yes – the General would support him.' This was no answer to satisfy, but it was all Reno could get. He would have to assume that Custer would support him by bringing his column in a second wave behind the forward battalion's attack. As a commanding officer, he sighed to himself in regret, Custer was one hell of a poor superior to have to serve under.[25]

I take issue with Willert's assumption that these are the thoughts and words that passed between them at that time. There is no analysis of these orders, merely an acceptance of Major Reno's charges that were levied at Custer at the Reno Court in order to avoid a court-martial. At the Court, there was no way Reno could have said the orders Cooke gave him were that 'Custer will support you by flanking the Indians, and Benteen will support you from the left, since he should be moving to the Little Bighorn and his orders will be the same as you are receiving.' To believe that Cooke, or any of the officers, didn't have a good idea of what Custer had in mind, is falling into the trap the Defense desired to set at the Reno Court.

Willert appears to believe the orders were given at or near the Lone Tepee. I believe the Lone Tepee was at least three miles from the Little Bighorn, and that Reno did not receive his orders until roughly a mile and a quarter from the river.

There is no investigation, or analysis of the time, that it would have taken to go to the river, cross, water, and move through the timber. Adjutant Cooke and Captain Keogh were said to have gone to the ford in order to "learn what the situation forward was to be."[26] I have explained my reasons for questioning their going to the ford or receiving a message from Girard. Willert accepts that Custer received the message Girard gave to Cooke, and this changed his strategy of supporting Reno by following him into battle. As I have brought out, Custer's strategy, prior to his decision to attack on the 25th, was to surround the Indian encampment; in other words, to flank the Indians. Flanking an opponent was a common practice, and certainly one that Custer had employed during both the Civil War and in fighting Indians. I don't believe he changed his plans. As I have said many times, if he thought the Indians were attacking Major Reno, and still did not know where Benteen was, he would have supported Reno from behind. I don't think he would have left the packs unprotected, and, as Reno stated, he didn't expect Custer to flank him because of the bluffs to the north.[27]

Again, I think that Custer would have moved to flank the Indian village sooner but for the fact that he hadn't heard from Benteen. Contrary to what is the predominant thought, Custer would not have left Benteen out of his plans for attacking the Indian village. He was concerned about the situation to the south, and he also would have wanted to hold off his attack until he knew the whereabouts of Benteen. He knew Benteen was to move to the Little Bighorn. Benteen admitted this. I don't think Custer would have expected Major Reno to attack a village of 1,500 warriors without being supported, and the support from behind was not to come from him but from Captain Benteen. After the battle Major Reno could rationalize his actions in the valley; however, Benteen had to distort his movements. At the Reno Court, both had to distort their orders and actions.

The Crossing of Ford A: The crossing of Major Reno's battalion to the wooded west bank took but a short time – considering the water delays and temporary disorganization of the command, probably fifteen minutes – and was entirely... "unopposed", a factor which belies Gerard's apprehensions....

Where Custer and his five companies were at this moment, Reno had no idea. What was causing the delay of Custer's battalion of promised support, he had no notion. He anxiously watched the trail at the ford for some sign of Custer's command, but he saw none.

... He would have to make some move soon.... Reno dispatched his striker, Pvt. Archibald McIlargy [Co. I], to ride back, locate Custer, and give him the message "... that the Indians were in front... in strong force..."

... McIlargy's message would bring the column more speedily.

Reno once more waited for "... some minutes...", and he and his men continued to observe the activity of the hostiles in the distance....

No word appeared to be coming from McIlargy, so, shortly, Reno sent Pvt. John Mitchell [Co. I] a cook by assignment, with the same message to Custer. As the trooper rode back over the same track as his predecessor, Reno made up his mind that – support or no support – he was going to have to begin his charge into the hostiles' encampment, or lose any advantage of surprise which the sudden appearance of his troops had apparently wrought. He had his orders. He would carry them out.[28]

I have explained many times why the Crossing of Ford A would have taken more than fifteen minutes. After crossing the ford, moving through the timber; and while reforming, the enlisted men said they saw Custer's troops on the ridge. Some of the Rees had seen Custer there before they moved down the valley ahead of Reno's troops. It is hard for me to discount the testimony of enlisted men, along with Captain Moylan's concurrence,[29] that enlisted men had reported seeing Custer's column on the ridge. This sighting – as they reformed, and when moving down the valley – along with the lack of testimony of such a sighting at the Reno Court, is what I consider a major cover-up. It is hard for me not to envision the troops making quite a demonstration, yelling, pointing to the ridge so others could see, and not having the officers, including Major Reno, aware of it. Why is it a major cover-up? If this sighting had come out at the Reno Court, what military excuse could Major Reno have used for not continuing to fight in the valley? He may have been excused for not attacking the village, but not for leaving the timber.

Custer's Command – Page 275

Custer had firm intent to follow Major Reno's battalion into the valley with his supporting command, and was actually effecting this when Lieutenant Cooke and Captain Keogh spurred their lathering mounts back to him with Gerard's message that the hostiles were not running, but, indeed, were riding up the valley to attack the approaching soldiers....

What Major Reno was going to do about the 'charging' Indians, Custer had no idea, but if the battalion engaged the hostiles – which appeared to be the only choice under the circumstances – the Indian village would be left open, undefended and vulnerable. This would provide excellent opportunity for a flank assault upon the camp by his own column.... his best tactic now would be to shift rapidly his own command downriver, cross the stream into the valley and come upon the unsuspecting hostiles from their rear. This flank attack would so confuse and undermine the warriors' confidence that their spirit of opposition would disintegrate... The hostiles would have sealed their own fate.

However, before the victory had to come the fighting, and Reno's battalion, Custer reasoned, should be involved in action with the hostiles very soon. The sound of gunfire in the valley would alert him to commence his own ride downriver to come in behind the hostiles. In the meantime he would rest his men, and scout the ridges overlooking the valley....[30]

For Custer to have decided to flank the Indians only after he had received word that the Indians were going to attack Reno's battalion doesn't make sense to me. I agree that Custer would have considered the effect of a flanking attack, as portrayed by Willert, but he would have done this long before receiving any word that Reno was being attacked by the Indians. Custer sent Reno to launch an attack on the Indians, so for him to hear that Reno would be engaged shortly should have made little difference in his plan. However, that the attack might take place so close to Reno's fording of the river, should only have increased Custer's concern for where Benteen was, and also for the need to protect the packs if Reno's troops should be overrun or encircled. After receiving such a message, I can't imagine Custer changing his mind and deciding to then initiate a flanking attack by moving downstream. Custer's two main concerns at the time should have been: (1) where was Captain Benteen? and, (2) to be able to synchronize his flanking attack with Major Reno's.

The idea that Custer waited to hear gunfire in the valley before he launched his flanking movement is difficult for me to fathom. His scouts were either with Reno or already on the bluffs, so it is questionable, if he would have had any idea how far downstream the village was, or a ford which he could cross in order to accomplish his flanking maneuver. As I stated, his primary concern, when he decided to flank the Indians, would be to synchronize his attack with that of Major Reno, while hoping Captain Benteen was close enough to the Little Bighorn so as to enter the attack in support of Major Reno. Willert then has Custer resting his troops waiting to hear the sound of gunfire. This, to me, is a way to compensate for the time interval that would have to have taken place if Willert's scenario – and I might say most others – was correct, since they have Major Reno retreating before Custer can move against the Indian village.

Using Willert's (and others) timing, one would have Custer waiting along Reno Creek for close to an hour after sending Reno to attack the Indian village. It should have taken Reno fifteen to twenty minutes to get his battalion together (according to Wallace they were mingling with Custer's), then to reach Ford A, search for a ford, and be ready to cross the river. (This is using my view that Reno received his orders about a mile and a quarter from the river instead of three miles back near the Lone Tepee.) According to Willert, it then takes Reno fifteen minutes to cross a belly high, fast moving stream while most horses watered, and then pass through fifty to two hundred yards of timber and reform his battalion. Reno sends McIlhargy with a message to Custer and waits for a reply. This should have taken another ten to fifteen minutes. Reno hasn't heard from McIlhargy, so he sends another messenger. He becomes dissatisfied, and knows he must follow his orders to attack the village; however, one could assume he waited another five minutes. To say Custer waited for nearly an hour before initiating his flanking movement does not strike me as sound reasoning. Such a period of waiting is not reported by either Sgt. Kanipe or Trumpeter Martin, and the slow Rees would certainly have caught the command before Custer had moved to the ridge.

Reno's Attack In The Valley – Page 277

Reno, after not hearing from Custer, moves on down the valley, and as he nears the Indian village they come out to attack his battalion. Reno has his men establish a skirmish line. Willert reconstructs the situation and the fighting in the valley. His ability to incorporate various testimony by the men as well as the Indians into a realistic account of the action and the suspense makes for interesting reading.

Willert disagrees with Grinnell who thought if Reno and Custer had "charged through the village from opposite ends, the Indians would have scattered and there would have been no disaster."[31] Willert believes there were just too many Indians for this to have happened. He may be right, but I would think there would have been a reasonable chance of success if the attacks had been synchronized. This would have depended on Custer launching an attack into the village – which I believe he would have, if he had not been shot at Ford B.

Custer's Battalion – Page 285

According to Willert, approximately half an hour had passed since Reno left the command, and so now, Custer believes it is imperative that he determine for himself what is going on in the valley. There is no way, as I have pointed out before, that I can see this being just half an hour since Reno was given his attack orders and had left the command. Custer had been concerned with what was going on in the valley before he gave Reno his orders, as indicated by his sending the two Crows to the bluffs; and after they turned and went with Reno, Bouyer and the other four Crows went to the ridge. I cannot picture Custer, who was known for his own reconnaissance ability, remaining in the valley for thirty minutes doing practically nothing. One should remember Varnum's words that he couldn't imagine Custer sitting still for five minutes.[32] Many times throughout my manuscript I have explained why I could not possibly support the scenario now being created.

Custer, when he reaches the ridge and sees Reno moving down the valley, blames Reno for not having already launched an attack. Even though I don't agree that is what happened, for Custer to now blame Reno, when, from a military standpoint, the need for a simultaneous attack is what was necessary, and to have Custer in a position where he doesn't even know where he can launch an attack and yet still accuses Reno, is unrealistic.

Custer supposedly now realizes he should have led the attack himself. Was Custer ever known not to have led an attack? This is another reason I have never been able to accept the idea that he was going to support Reno from the rear.

Willert:

> But now what? With Reno's usefulness nullified, all that could be undertaken now would be a strike into the village at some point *downriver* – and with all the force he could muster. McDougall's command and the ammunition packs! Benteen and his battalion! Time would be precious and critical now if any victory was to be had. *Damn Reno's blunder!*[33]

I don't understand the reasoning. Custer had waited along Reno Creek, for supposedly half an hour, waiting for the sound of gunfire which would indicate Reno had been attacked. At the time, Custer had changed his mind from supporting Reno from the rear to flanking the Indian village. He doesn't ride to the ridge to observe the situation; instead, he waits, expecting to hear gunfire, at which time he will attempt to flank the Indians. Did Custer expect to ride down the bluffs behind the attacking Indians? If so, wouldn't he have gone to the bluffs during the time they were resting along North Fork to observe what was happening in the valley as well as the terrain, in order to know where such an attack could be made? Wouldn't he then have seen Reno was in no immediate danger so he could go back to his troops and continue in support of Reno from the rear? Custer only now plans to move downriver, and <u>time now becomes precious</u>? I would have thought Custer would have realized <u>time was precious</u> not only now, but even before he gave Reno his orders to move against the Indian village.

Willert has Trumpeter John Martin saying that "when Custer – after viewing the approach of the Reno battalion in the valley – had resumed the advance of his own column, . . ."[34] Martin never made such a statement: at no time did Martin ever say that Custer saw Reno in the valley. Custer may and actually should have seen Reno advancing down the valley when at Weir Point; however, Martin never saw Reno in the valley until he carried his message to Benteen.

Reno's Valley Fight – Page 287

Willert believes Custer's troops moved along just east of the bluffs. I don't agree, because of the sightings by Reno's troops as they reformed and as they were moving down the valley. One can look to the bluffs from the valley, and it is impossible to see movement beyond the present roadway.

Custer is moving to Weir Point, during which time Reno's men are setting up their skirmish line, and "had come to grips in severe fighting with the massing hostiles."[35] Since I cannot agree that Custer sat around for even thirty minutes after Reno separated to move to Ford A, I believe Custer was observing from Weir Point, about the time Reno was reforming his troops after passing through the timber, and before he made his jaunt down the valley. Custer's troops, some yards behind Custer, would have seen Reno's troops, as reported by Sgt. Kanipe, just as Reno's men saw Custer's on the ridge.

> Where Custer was with his support now crossed nearly every trooper's mind. Some had spotted the 'Gray Horse' troop moving northward behind the distant bluffs east of the river, but those who had not, presumed that Custer would shortly be bringing his battalion of *five* companies down the valley upon Reno's track, and they puzzled at the seemingly *unreasonable* delay.[36]

I would agree that many of the troopers may have wondered where Custer was, but I believe that they knew Custer was attempting a flanking movement, and they were wondering why he hadn't attacked the Indian village. Willert should have examined when those troopers reported spotting (only?) the 'Gray Horse' troop. If Custer's troops were moving down the ridge, when Reno's men were reforming and before they started down the valley, where would they have thought Custer's command should have been by the time they established their skirmish line? These are essential questions that must be answered.

I certainly can understand why Major Reno – whom I believe realized, from both orders and also having seen Custer's men on the ridge – would wonder why Custer hadn't attacked the village. By the time of the Reno Court, Reno was facing the dilemma I have described in my examination of the Reno Court proceedings: he would like to have said that he saw Custer on the ridge while reforming his troops, for this would, in one sense, justify his leaving the timber. Custer would have had plenty of time to attack the Indian village, but Reno knew by the actions of the Indians that this had not occurred. However, if he had admitted to seeing them at that time, he would have had no excuse for leaving the timber. His lack of knowledge of a flanking attack by Custer was absolutely imperative for his defense. The defense was able to use the sighting by Varnum of the Gray Horse troop, as well as DeRudio's, because as long as Reno was not aware of the sightings, they could be used to indicate Custer had time to have attacked the village. Since there were no signs that had taken place, Reno's duty as an officer was to save his own men. For the defense to have brought out the early sightings – but only by enlisted men – would not have been feasible. Some of the officers should have known, and if they did, Major Reno would have been informed. Reno could get by with the officers concurrence of not knowing of the late sightings, but not the earlier ones.

Custer's Advance – Page 290

About the time that G Company was engaged in the fire fight in the woods, Custer and his column halted below the high bluff today called Weir Point. Trumpeter John Martini recalled: ". . . We rode around the base of it and halted. Then the general took me with him and we rode to the top of the hill, where we could see the village in the valley on the other side of the river . . ."

Lieutenant Cooke accompanied the two to the crest. . . . could be seen hundreds upon hundreds of Indian lodges . . .

Custer swept his glass up the valley toward the point where Reno's men were *clearly,* hotly engaged with the hostiles. The sound of firing was heavy, and the dust was thick, but nothing of the battle's situation could be determined for woods veiled the action. Martini observed: ". . . I am sure the General did not see them at all, because he looked all around with his glasses. . . ."

. . . The camp was enormous. But as his eye studied the scene, something of a grim smile crossed his sun-bronzed, bewhiskered features: *the camp had been caught unprepared.* ". . .We've got them this time! . . ." Martini overheard him remark.

. . . However, so crowded were the lodges that only occasionally could movement be observed – and, curiously, [my underlining] this appeared *passive*. Martini said that ". . .children and some dogs . . ." were visible. squaws were moving about, and ponies were ". . . scattered around." The firing from up the valley was heavy so sounds from the village, downriver were almost nil. . . . The young Crow, Curley, recalled: ". . . When we looked down to the camp, we noticed there were not many around and Mitch Bouyer said he thought the Indians were out campaigning somewhere . . ."

. . . If Reno's battalion could keep the warriors of the village *occupied* at the upper end of the camp, his own larger command could *initiate* a strike into the village at some ford downriver, . . . The column could then press through the village toward Reno's position, catch the warriors from the rear, and, in brief time, claim the victory.

. . . But *time* was precious now. [my underlining] . . . They had been fighting the hostiles in the valley at least fifteen or twenty minutes already. Unless support came to their assistance *within the next half an hour,* . . . It was imperative that the *second,* or *supporting attack* be launched into the village as quickly as possible.[37]

It seems to me that Martin's statement that they moved around the base of it (Weir Point) and halted, would mean a movement around eastern Weir Peak. According to Martin, Lt. Cooke did not accompany them up Weir Point, for Custer reported to him when they returned. That the village lay nearly a half mile away would be the same spatial distance described, by Kanipe, and is one reason I think he received his message to take to Captain McDougall at or just beyond Weir Point.

I cannot believe how Willert can use the remarks he does and come up with his conclusions. Custer sees a large Indian village. Reno is "clearly hotly engaged." Martin, in the quote used, states that Custer did not see anything of Reno's column – Martin was not referring to Custer's not seeing Reno's men fighting because of the trees. Although I believe he may have seen Reno's column as they were forming or starting their move down the valley, undoubtedly Martin did not. I don't know how you can read such statements, take only part of them, bring out the firing and noise being created, and have Custer saying, "We've got them this time!" You have Bouyer, according to Curley, after Custer had left, and from the same point, saying, "he thought the Indians were out campaigning somewhere." Reno is hotly engaged and Bouyer could make such a statement? From Indian accounts, after Reno's attack the village went into a state of turmoil and near panic, and yet "curiously this appeared passive." And Willert's answer as to why, is that the tepees were so close together. If Reno was heavily engaged, the Indians would have been taking down tepees, many fleeing to the foothills, and Indian warriors racing toward Reno.

Custer then wonders if Reno can just keep the Indians occupied until he can find a ford downriver, but time is precious now. Custer should have realized that when he was waiting around back on North Fork. However, keep this "precious" need to hurry in mind when it comes to what Willert will soon have Custer doing.

The fact that the Indian village appeared "passive" suggests only one logical connotation, and that is that Reno had not yet fired on the village. Martin said the officers thought the warriors might be out buffalo hunting.[38] I don't think you can disclaim Martin's continual insistence through the years as to how peaceful the village looked, and that is what Custer saw. This means Custer did not wait along North Fork, that he did plan all along to flank the Indians, and that Custer reached the ridge before Reno began his move down the valley.

> Custer's effort to alert Reno and his men to his present position atop the bluffs . . . Lt. Charles DeRudio was one of these: ". . . I did not see General Custer's column at all; but while I was in the woods, Gen. Custer, Lt. Cooke and another man I could not recognize came to the highest point on the bluff and waved their hats and made motions like they were cheering . . . I recognized Gen. Custer, Lt. Cooke and another man I could not recognize came to the highest point on the bluff and waved their hats . . ."[39]

I cannot accept DeRudio's statement. Martin never indicated waving from Weir Point nor that Cooke was with them. The distance was too far for DeRudio to make out Custer's shirt and certainly Cooke's whiskers. If DeRudio saw any of Custer's men it was most likely a rear guard or possibly stragglers. He may have seen Custer waving at the same time Reno's men did – when reforming before moving down the valley.

> . . . <u>Time was critical now</u> [my underlining] – the command would have to move fast. Thirty minutes was all too small a margin to prepare for the assault, . .
>
> Where Captain Benteen and his battalion were at this time, Custer had no idea; he had sent them on a reconnaissance trek which he probably now saw as a foolish judgment on his part. . . .
>
> . . . Custer wished to locate a good crossing place along the river, but he also wished to establish a position upon higher ground where the pack train battalion – and, hopefully, Benteen's battalion of 125 guns – could unite with his command prior to the launching of the attack. He *needed firepower!*[40]

Custer sent Sergeant Kanipe to tell Captain McDougall to bring the packs across country. Custer may have desired a higher ground location for the pack train, which is a reasonable assumption. I might also go along with Captain Keogh and his battalion made up of I and L Companies being sent down Cedar Coulee at this time, but not that Custer would have taken all five companies to do this instead of moving down the gorge and launching an attack as quickly as possible against the Indian village. As Willert keeps bringing up, time was of the essence. This must have been Custer's primary consideration.

I will skip over any in-depth analysis of Willert's account of Reno's fighting in the valley and his retreat to the bluffs. Willert gives a very interesting and enlightening account of what took place. I believe he gives too much credit to Major Reno and his actions in the bottom. It would be well to remember what Captain Moylan said (who was one of Reno's most avid supporters at the Reno Court) in a letter to then Captain Godfrey.

Moylan:

> "I desire to be understood that my defense of Reno is entirely confined *to his act of taking his three troops out of the bottom* [italics by Moylan]. Of his personal conduct in the bottom or subsequently on the hill the least said the better. If what Col. Benteen told me at Meade in 1883 was true, and I know of no reason to doubt it, then Reno ought to have been shot."[41]

Moylan appears to be saying that the only thing he will give Reno credit for, even in the valley, is his decision to leave. I believe Reno was only able to justify his move to the ridge because Custer had not launched an attack against the village in the time one could have expected it to have taken place.

I will not dwell on Benteen's actions as he moved down Reno Creek as represented by Willert. Here again he does a remarkable work in bringing together various testimony. My criticism is that he will accept one side of conflicting testimony without giving his reasons why. As I have stated numerous times, my major interest in examining testimony and writer's scenarios is an attempt to determine why Custer didn't launch an attack against a semi-panic stricken Indian village. I will continue to concentrate on this aspect of Willert's book.

Custer's Battalion – Page 298

> Following Kanipe's departure, Custer led his five companies . . . in the direction of the lower end of the hostiles' camp. . . . He had indeed caught the Indians offguard – or – "napping" as Martini had put it, but what an aggregation! . . . he was going to have to strike into their camp with all the force he could muster – and *soon!* Reno was having a very hot fight . . . , but Benteen's battalion was not yet engaged. Benteen would have to be *located* and his battalion brought forward. Without his fire power – and the pack train's reserve ammunition supply – gaining the victory would be slim . . .
>
> Halting briefly at the entrance to a " . . . big ravine . . ." expressed his mind in a swift instruction to his orderly, Trumpeter John Martini, to ride back over the trail, *locate Benteen and his battalion, and bring them, as swiftly as their mounts could travel* . . . 'Where was Benteen to be found?' he may well have wished to ask Custer had he the nerve. 'I haven't any idea!' Custer may have shouted in reply, 'but find him! Find him! Find him! . . . But he needed the *support* of Benteen and his battalion so Martini would just have to *hunt him out!*[42]

Willert keeps emphasizing Custer's recognition that he must strike the Indian village *soon*, but then has him continuing to delay. Custer, as he neared the village, certainly wanted Benteen to come to his aid, but he would not have hesitated to attack the Indian encampment. I assume he was near the village at the time Reno engaged the Indians, in contrast to Willert's view, but, even under his scenario, I cannot see Custer failing to realize the importance of striking the village while the Indians were in a disorganized state, and attempting to coordinate his attack with that of Reno's. After all, he had sent Reno to attack an Indian camp of what he assumed was fifteen hundred warriors, so I can't understand why he'd be unwilling to attack a camp with his five companies at a time when the Indians appeared to be escaping.

ANALYSIS OF WRITERS' SCENARIOS

I also believe Custer expected Benteen to have reached the Little Bighorn and then to have moved in support of Major Reno. I think what caused him to send the message when he did was the information given him either by members of the rear guard – who received the news from the Ree scout, Stabbed – or from the return of Sgt. Major Sharrow (or possibly a third courier) that Custer had sent to inform Benteen they were about to begin the attack on the Indian village.

As Willert brings out, when Martin reached Weir Point, he saw Reno's withdrawal into the timber. Then one should consider, *if Martin could have made it back to the ridge from South Medicine Tail Coulee, having already heard gunfire from Custer's location and having seen troops retreating, this must have meant that Custer was on the ridge before Reno started his move down the valley, that he saw a peaceful village, and he would have been at Ford B while Reno was still on his skirmish line.*

Martin's statement that he did not know just where Benteen was when he started back would have been a natural one, because he didn't. This doesn't mean he didn't realize Benteen was somewhere back along the main trail.

Willert, in recounting how Benteen received the message from Martin, accepts Benteen's account and includes his derogatory remarks about Martin as he gave them at the Reno Court. Willert's footnotes abound with Reno Court statements given by officers which support the military and the Defense's position. I would question Edgerly's account of Martin saying "... and the soldiers under Major Reno were charging it and killing everybody – men, women and children."[43] I believe Edgerly mixed up Martin with Sgt. Kanipe, who, as he rode down the line of troopers, called out, "We've got them boys,"[44] and probably added a few other choice remarks. Kanipe having left the ridge when he did, and most likely seeing the initial attack by Major Reno, and also realizing that Custer should have attacked the village by then, would have expected that they were successful. Martin doesn't appear to be either that type of person, or in that condition; plus he had seen the Indians attacking and forcing Reno into the timber, and also saw what he claimed were Custer's troops retreating.

Willert accepts Benteen's weak excuse for not sending someone back to hurry or bring up some ammo packs.

Custer's Battalion – page 305

The propitious arrival of "Boston" Custer with the affirmation that Captain Benteen and his battalion were approaching along the main track of the Indians much relieved Custer's personal anxieties concerning the whereabouts of that command, and his mind reasoned that if Martini kept to the backtrail, he should experience no difficulty in locating the battalion and delivering the urgent message. . . . Benteen, of course – . . . would respond immediately and bring his battalion on the gallop, and with the ammunition packs in tow.[45]

I believe Boston Custer would have met a retreating command, with Custer either wounded or dead. Be that as it may, if Custer hadn't known Benteen was on the back trail, when he sent Martin, wouldn't he have sent more than one messenger? It is hard for me to see Benteen and the ammo packs traveling at a gallop.

The now *strong probability* that Benteen's force, with the pack mules carrying the ammunition reserves, would be joining his command in the next fifteen minutes or so, prompted Custer to halt for a brief time within the ravine. He wanted to give Benteen's battalion an opportunity to catch up to him – and this time would be as good a time as any to release the Crow scouts. . . .[46]

We should remember the numerous statements made to the effect that Reno's situation must be relieved, and quickly. But is Custer doing this? No, he is halting briefly with the idea that Benteen, in fifteen minutes or so, will be arriving on the gallop with the ammunition packs in tow. This I can't quite envision. We're not sure just where Benteen would be along the back trail nor how far the packs would be behind him. After all, they might have been as far as Benteen maintained. I'm just not able to see those packs galloping to where, in fifteen minutes or so, they would be arriving to give Custer the fire-power and ammo he needs to launch this urgent attack.

Another criticism of Willert is how he uses the Crows accounts that fit into his scenario, but offers no analysis of their over-all statements, or makes an attempt to correlate them. Curley, though dismissed by Custer, would have been aware of the number of Indian warriors facing him, but would not leave his command because:

. . . Custer's battalion was not in action yet – he was merely coursing down the ravine at <u>moderate pace</u>; (my underlining) the safest place – in Curley's view – was still Custer's battalion! – and to this force, Curley returned.[47]

I can't accept this either. The Crows, once they were dismissed and having recognized the situation, were bent on leaving the whole fighting scene. How could Curley believe the *safest place* was Custer's command? Curley is now with Custer, but Bouyer and the other three Crows go to the bluffs above the village, or have they already been on Bouyer's Bluff? Although Bouyer and the Crows know where all the ravines lead, and that there is a ford, Custer – even though this is his main concern – must not have asked, and they must not have told him. I cannot go along with this supposition.

Willert then relates Major Reno's decision to move to the bluffs, and the problems they faced. Here, though I believe he gives too much credit to Reno, he paints a fascinating account of the action that took place by weaving in the testimony of the participants.

Custer's Last Ride – page 325

The Crow scouts' uncertainties as to Reno's battle situation ... worried Custer, and he spurred Vic forward to lead the battalion down the coulee at a swifter pace. If Reno's troops were having a hard fight against the hostiles in the valley, a second attack would have to be initiated soon [my underlining] to relieve that pressure, or both commands would be in danger of defeat. ... but if such [an attack] were conducted efficiently, and timed well, the disadvantage could be offset and disaster turned into victory.

This was Custer's thinking as the battalion proceeded down the ravine. But – he reasoned – if he did not locate a crossing place into the lower village within the next several minutes, he knew that his strategy would be in serious trouble. ...

The ravine down which the 225 officers and men were riding was long. ... but where did this ravine emerge? Did it come out at the river? – at a suitable fording place? Custer hoped fervently that it did.[48]

It is hard for me to understand Willert's reasoning, or correlation of events. The Crow scouts had been released, but Curley came back to be in a safer place with Custer. Bouyer stayed; the Crows had, by most accounts, fired on the Indian village from Bouyer's bluff just above Ford B. By other Curley accounts that are accepted by Willert, Bouyer talked for some time with Custer. However, Custer is not sure South Medicine Tail Coulee leads to the river and a crossing. Bouyer certainly could have told him, and actually Custer should have realized that from Weir Point.

I assume Willert has Custer moving down Cedar Coulee to South Medicine Tail Coulee. Since Custer has been on Weir Point and had seen the Indian village and the river, he should have realized that the ravine would lead to South Medicine Tail Coulee, which leads to the river and a ford. However, what I have never been able to understand, having been on Weir Point myself, is how anyone in a hurry to attack the Indian village would go down a ravine leading away from it, when there was a perfectly good ravine for a column of fours to go down, which one couldn't help but know, came out closer to the river. Custer then assumes Benteen and the packs are still coming, so he wants to move a portion of his company to the ridges north of South Medicine Tail Coulee. This is understandable, and I believe it is what he did, but not from Willert's location. Custer still realizes a second attack must be initiated soon if he is to be successful.

And yet – Custer puzzled – what if that renewed heavy firing up the valley was *not* Benteen's force committed, but Reno's men still holding on? Perhaps Benteen and the packs were still coming. Perhaps Kanipe and Martini *had* delivered their messages! Would it not be a point of wisdom to give Benteen and the packs opportunity to join him? Certainly, the addition of these troops would provide him a stronger arm for his assault.

Abruptly, Custer raised his gauntleted right arm, reined Vic about, and signalled his officers forward for quick conference to his change of plans.[48]

I cannot see where the renewed heavy firing being associated with Reno's men would change the need for an immediate attack, which had been uppermost in Custer's mind since Weir Point. He is not sure how long he might have to wait for Benteen, but Willert thinks this might be a point of wisdom. Does this really sound logical? After having just discussed how Custer thought if he attacked immediately the "disadvantage" might be offset, would Custer have actually believed that the addition of three more companies, along with the problem of caring for the packs, would make his attack down a comparatively narrow defile more effective? For Custer to recognize the main attack on the Indians would come from this area, and that he would want Captain Benteen to move in this direction rather than crossing the Little Bighorn and supporting Reno, is understandable. For Custer to have held up his attack for an indefinite time in order to wait for Benteen, is not. Considering the terrain and the problems associated with crashing into the Indian encampment, I think he just took three companies, sending Keogh's battalion of two companies to the ridge north of South Medicine Tail Coulee where they would be in both a supporting position, and with orders for Benteen and the packs when they arrived.

Willert has Custer changing his plans:

... Half of the command, Custer advised, would continue forward, follow the ravine down to where it emerged – hopefully at the river. The other half would angle to the right, move behind the hills east of the river and take position on high ground where they could be spotted by Benteen and the pack train. Lt. Algernon E. Smith and the 'Gray Horse' Company E would take the lead toward the river. Capt. Tom Custer's Company C and half of Capt. George Yates' Company F would accompany Smith in support. Lt. James Calhoun's Company L, Capt. Myles Keogh's Company I, and the other half of Company F would circle behind the hills to the higher ground to the north.

Custer did not know whether the ravine would lead to the river or not, but *time* was fleeting, and he knew that his battalion would have to be committed shortly, or his advantage would be lost. Smith's Company E would be his *probe* toward the river. If the ravine emerged at the river, a fording place would have to be located; this was Smith's objective. The remainder of Custer's command would stand as a *guide marker* for Benteen and the packs, and as a *supporting reserve* in the event Smith's command encountered trouble and was forced to withdraw for any reason.[49]

This gets harder for me to follow. Custer is going to send not two or three companies to "probe" toward the river, but two and a half. Smith's objective was to find a ford. Was Smith, if he found a ford, to attack, or wait and send a message back to Custer and the rest of the command? Was Custer then going to take the rest of the command to the ford and all five companies would then attack the Indian camps, or must he still wait for Benteen? His movement further east behind the hills is hard for me to locate. Custer, I would assume, is in South Medicine Tail Coulee. Does he then pass behind Luce and Nye Cartwright Ridges and to the east of Battleridge, and then come up to Last Stand Hill? Willert says this is done so Custer's command could "stand as a guide marker" for Benteen. Wouldn't Luce or Nye Cartwright have been a better position to have established this "guide marker"?

I might have thought Custer would want to lead such an important maneuver by his two and a half companies to the ford, but I guess he thought it was more important to find a place to the north and to wait for Benteen and the packs.

Although we cannot be certain of what immediately followed, the scout Curley says that Custer (through Cooke) wrote another message, handed it to one of the troopers, "... and after a brief conversation, the trooper rode away, heading *north*. This trooper rode a sorrel-roan horse..." ... and that the third message was, without doubt, intended for the hand of *General Terry*.[50]

I think anybody attempting to present a scenario of what took place at the Battle of the Little Bighorn should not use certain testimony from an individual – white or Indian –without examining other conflicting testimony, especially from that same individual. To be truthful, I cannot see how anybody who has analyzed Curley's varying accounts would believe he was still with Custer at this time. However, if one does, they should explain why Curley never reported the message being sent in his early stories. This one supposedly took place only a few days before Curley died in 1923. This was after the Frank Finkle story had came out.

Mitch Bouyer had rejoined the column – apparently at some time during this halt to divide the command – and as the troops prepared to advance again, ... advised the youthful Crow scout, Curley, to get away while he yet had the opportunity. [He advises Curley to watch from a high hill, and if the Sioux are beating them to take a message to General Terry and tell him that they are all killed.]

The troops started forward once more, but had not traversed far when, abruptly rounding a bend in the ravine, they spotted a number of hostiles quirting in their direction. However, the moment the troopers came into view, the Indians whipped their little ponies about and raced pell-mell back the way they had come – down the ravine. The river was not yet visible, but portions of the village could be seen at some distance beyond – perhaps half to three – quarters of a mile away. Custer quickly ordered Lt. A. E. Smith and his 'Gray Horse' Company E detachment to pursue the retreating warriors, and then angled Vic abruptly to the right to leave the ravine to head north up behind the hills.

Custer's action here finds verification from at least three sources: (1) Curley's testimony to Russell White Bear, (2) the *field notes* of Walter Mason Camp, who interviewed Curley and a number of the Indian participants of the battle, in 1910; and (3) in the curiously unexplained *trail of shod horses* discovered by Lt. Edward Godfrey behind the hills of the battle ridge on June 28th, three days following Custer's fight.

Russell White Bear related Curley's recollection: "... 'Custer proceeded down Medicine Tail ... then sent the Gray Horse Troop down the creek and he took the rest of the command to where the fighting occurred.' ..." [Did Custer just send the Gray Horse Troop or two and a half companies?]

Was Custer's move to the right predicated upon the anticipated arrival of Benteen's battalion and the ammunition packs? This would seem highly probable. Curley's testimony to Walter Camp ...[51]

Willert needs to correlate the movement of the scouts and Bouyer with a reason why their knowledge of where the ravines and the fords were did not get presented to Custer. He should also analyze the various accounts given by Curley, and why he accepts the ones he does. Why did the earlier Curley versions of events differ from his later ones? Did Curley fire into the village? Were the three Crows and Bouyer on the bluff above the ford, and if so, where was Curley? If Curley was back with Custer, how was he able to see what happened at the ford? Why is Custer, who has recognized, for the last half hour, that the village had to be attacked <u>soon</u>, still not willing to? I don't consider waiting for Benteen and the packs a reasonable answer. Maybe it would have been for Major Reno, but not General Custer.

I don't believe the verification used by Willert is historically sound. Russell White Bear's account has no confirmation except his word, which any historian should at least question. Walter Camp, who deserves a great deal of credit for his interviews with participants, also doesn't analyze or explain why he accepts some testimony and not others. I consider his questioning poor and paradoxical. I do not look at Godfrey's report as verification of anything but that shod horses, which could be escaping or ridden by Indians, traversed certain ground east of Battleridge.

If Custer's move to the north was predicated on the arrival of Benteen and the packs, meaning that Custer was willing to wait even longer and lose any chance of surprise, then he is certainly not the Custer history has portrayed him to be. We again run into this dichotomous position taken by not only Willert but others, who criticize Custer for being overly courageous and impetuous, but then have him moving away from the Indian camps, and hesitating as he moves down the ravine toward the village. He then sends only part of his command down South Medicine Tail Coulee toward this "immense" Indian encampment, not to attack, but to act as a "probe", with the objective being to find a ford. This is Custer? One should try at least to be consistent.

The Fight At The Ford – page 328

The actual engagement began when the troops of Lt. A. E. Smith and half of the command left the mouth of the Medicine Tail Coulee to pursue the small party of warriors toward the river. These troops had no idea what they would encounter there, but assumed that . . . the north end would be comparatively *undefended*, save for a handful of warriors and non-combatants, who would present no serious opposition.

To some degree, this condition – as hypothesized – was true. However, as soon as the troops crossed the open ground at the mouth of the coulee, and headed for the river ford, shots . . . numerous enough to halt the troopers' rush, if only to determine the *extent* of the hostiles opposition.[52]

If the assumption was that the ford would be comparatively undefended, I can see no reason why Custer would not have attempted to attack the ford, led by himself, and with at least three companies. Certainly Indian accounts would agree that there were few defenders.

Willert now brings out that the Crow scouts – White Man Runs Him, Goes Ahead and Hairy Moccasin – went to the bluffs above the ford. They would have fired into the village if all (four) Crow scouts reports can be believed. Bouyer, by most accounts, would have gone to join Custer at this time. Willert would have him back with Custer moving to Battleridge. Curley would have already left and moved to some lookout position. Willert disagrees with David Humphrey Miller's report, given by White Cow Bull and Bobtail Horse, that Custer was shot at the ford. He mentions Curley saying that he saw two of Custer's men killed at the ford. I question if Curley would have been able to see this if he was now moving back to some lookout area east of Battleridge. He could have, if he was back on the ridge, as stated by White Man Runs Him.

> . . . Charles Eastman, a full-blood Sioux descendant of the warriors at this battle, spent many years interviewing the Indian participants of the action and gathered the impression that ". . . Custer appeared upon the riverbank. Having discovered that it was impossible to cross, he began to fire into the camp, while some of his men dismounted and were apparently examining the banks . . ." And White Man Runs Him . . . recounted: ". . . Custer tried to cross the river at the mouth of Medicine Tail Creek, but was unable to do so . . ." – and, moreover, ". . . I know for sure that Custer went right to the river bank. I saw him go that far. The Sioux were right across the river. Then Custer fired. That was the first firing Custer did."
>
> . . . White Man Runs Him, ". . . I saw him go that far . . .", he related; and yet, Custer's body was found more than half a mile northeast, upon the battle ridge. Pretty Shield, wife of the Crow scout, Goes Ahead, claimed that her husband had told her that *he saw Custer killed at the river* – and yet he makes *no mention* of this in his own *narrative*. Why not? Because he was *not* certain?
>
> . . . But that he was the *buckskin-clad figure*, who allegedly fell at the ford is quite impossible, for Custer never got *near* the river, as shall be shown.[53]

It is odd how one can accept the accounts given by Curley, which were mainly for their newsworthy effect, and yet the statements by White Man Runs Him given to General Scott, who was knowledgeable of the Indian sign language, and whose testimony, along with Curley's, was witnessed and signed by two interpreters (including Russell White Bear), can be so easily brushed aside. White Man Runs Him would have been near enough (in contrast to DeRudio's sighting) to have known it was Custer. Curley's report, recorded by Scott, is ignored. Goes Ahead's account given to his wife, where she states emphatically her acceptance of it plus his taking her to the very place, can be disregarded because "he was not certain"?

We know that the three Crows were excoriated, because of their actions while Curley received the accolades. Is it so hard to understand that they would not have told the whites a story that would have gone against the white man's belief that Custer had gone down fighting on Last Stand Hill? Whites still won't accept his being shot at the ford, or even engage in any serious analysis or examination of the statements used to support it.

<u>I was not able to find where Willert actually shows that Custer never got to the ford.</u>

> . . . Custer may well have realized by this time that he had led his small command into a most critical and dangerous situation, extrication from which could now only be attempted with a <u>bold attack</u> [my underlining] on the village, for the warriors were, indeed, crowding rapidly about the command. Where Benteen's battalion and the packs of the ammunition reserves were, he had no notion – but he could delay no longer – his measure of advantage had run out — he would have to make his move.[54] [His advantage would have run out a long time back, when he remained at North Fork for over thirty minutes and wasn't willing to take three companies – at least – and charge the Indian village.]

The Pack Train – page 334

> . . . Though Kanipe *claims* that he delivered the orders to Captain McDougall, this he probably never did, for neither McDougall nor Lt. Edward Mathey recall any such contact with him.
>
> . . . Though Edgar Stewart accepts the word of Kanipe that he delivered Tom Custer's verbal instructions to Captain McDougall, the apparent truth of the matter is that he did *not*, in fear of encountering hostile warriors in the open country between Benteen's column and the pack train . . . he lost his nerve at sight of figures on horseback whom he mistook for hostiles, . . .[55]

The packers' reports would substantiate Sgt. Kanipe's claim of delivering his message to Captain McDougall. I must again criticize Willert for being too willing to accept statements given by officers at the Reno Court of Inquiry, without any analysis. One should recognize that if Captain McDougall or Lt. Mathey admitted to receiving such orders, they too could have been accused of violating orders from their commanding officer. Their not having received any orders could also help in the Defense's need to extend the packs arrival time in order to cover the late move to investigate gunfire.

The arrival time of Captain Benteen, and then Captain McDougall with the packs; the hearing of gunfire downriver; the Indians leaving; Captain Weir going to investigate the gunfire; Lt. Edgerly leaving with D Company; and the time the rest of the command followed, results in one of the three major cover-ups that took place at the Reno Court. It necessitated the changing of the official time from around 10:00 A.M. to after 12:00 P.M.

Major Reno's time, given in his official report of meeting Benteen on the ridge, was about 2:30 P.M., coupled with Lt. Godfrey's recollection that it was about 2:30 P.M. when "we (Benteen's battalion) joined Reno," is compelling evidence that both Reno and Benteen were together on the ridge by 2:30 P.M. I don't know the order Benteen's companies arrived on the ridge; however, Captain Weir's company had been in the lead at the time Trumpeter Martin would have met them. Benteen could have arrived by 2:15 P.M. How far back the packs were was an important part of the cover-up since the Defense made this the main reason Major Reno didn't move sooner to aid Custer. Lt. Godfrey also jotted down a time of 4:20 P.M., but was never sure just what it represented. He thought it was about 5:00 P.M. when the command moved down toward where the firing had been heard. Colonel Graham believed he had convinced Godfrey that the 4:20 P.M. referred to when Benteen arrived on the hill.[56] This would justify the Defense's position that Major Reno, once the packs arrived, would have moved his command downriver. I think this timing is inaccurate. I can accept earlier timing accounts, but not those arrived at in order to protect the actions of Major Reno and Captain Benteen.

My estimate of events would be: Benteen returned to the main trail around 1:00 P.M. as he first reported. 2:30 P.M. would give him plenty of time to have reached the bluffs. By 3:00 P.M. the packs were up. I think 4:20 would be when Captain Weir started to search for Custer. It would have been after 5 o'clock when the command started downriver, and around 7:00 P.M. when they arrived back at what became Reno's entrenchment site. The Indians may have attacked for two hours before ceasing fire for the night.

I will give some of my supporting evidence, but first I will present Willert's view of events, which supports the position the Defense would have taken at the Reno Court.

Reno's Hill Position – page 333

Entirely unmindful at what was occurring down-river, Major Marcus Reno was having his hands full in establishing some form of defense line against the hostiles pressing his command. . . .

Where was Custer? Where was the support that he was supposed to have provided? . . . Was Custer pulling another one of his damnable tricks, . . . Had he run off to Terry's column when he saw the hell of Indians that Reno's battalion had come up against? Lt. George Wallace summed up the tenor of the attitude of the men at this time: ". . . After we occupied the hill there was no uneasiness or solicitude about Custer; but there was a great deal of swearing about General Custer running off and leaving us!"[57]*

Here one sees Willert's bias against Custer, which is evident throughout, while accepting and painting a favorable picture of Reno. Reno was in a panicky mood when he arrived on the hill and was certainly not setting up any defense. Captain McDougall acted like he had to establish skirmish lines when he arrived.[58] One might say he wouldn't need to, if the packs arrived, as portrayed at the Reno Court, because the Indians would have already left. I am sure the men must have wondered where Custer was: but I am also sure that most, if not all of them, realized he had attempted to flank the Indians and that the gunshots they heard meant Custer was fighting the Indians downriver. It is important to realize that Lt. Wallace gave this testimony at the Reno Court and it indicates his continual support of the Defense's stratagems. Other officer testimony from the Reno Court is used to justify their leaving the timber and that the men, though somewhat "demoralized", were in comparatively "remarkable good spirits."

Willert, however, does state:

> The timely arrival of Benteen's command had given Reno's depleted and demoralized troopers *practical* as well as *moral* support, but it hadn't solved the problem of the situation Custer had led them into. . . . the troops could only hold them off so long as ammunition lasted. When that supply was exhausted – unless assistance arrived from somewhere – they would be entirely at the mercy of the savages. As far as anyone knew the pack train was still some distance back along the main track . . .
>
> As Major Reno and the detail mounted the ridge, [from going after Lt. Hodgson's body] Reno made the inquiry whether anyone had yet spotted the *pack train*? About twenty minutes had passed since Hare's departure. But no one had seen any indication of it, or of the lieutenant. . . .
>
> In any event, the move after the hostiles' departure down the valley was *not* made, and the critical *time interval* during which Custer may have been assisted to some extent, had drained away *in the wait for the packs to be brought forward.*[59]

Both the critical need for the packs and the ammo they carried, as well as the distance behind Benteen, has been overplayed. The necessity for this, considering their otherwise late move to go to Custer's aid, should be apparent. Most of these statements, as can be seen by footnotes, were made at the Reno Court. Both Sgt. Kanipe and Trumpeter Martin have the packs close behind Benteen's column. Martin said Captain McDougall was only about "150 yds. behind."[60] Although Martin later denied going back with a message from Captain Benteen "to bring up the pack train and keep it well up,"[61] for him to have made the statements he did pertaining to the packs, it is hard for me to believe that he hadn't delivered a message to Captain McDougall. It is much easier for me to believe that he was warned of the effect this had on Captain Benteen and the Seventh Cavalry, so he said the court misinterpreted what he said.

> One should recall what Martin told Walter Camp, "He did not tell this at the Reno Court of Inquiry because he was not asked the question. He thinks that in Reno Court of Inquiry it was not desired that he should tell all he knew and said that afterward he never was invited by officers to discuss what he knew of the battle and never volunteered to do so."[62]
>
> John Gray brought out how "Because Martin's testimony was elicited in such disorderly fashion, I place his answers in more coherent sequence."[63]*

In reviewing the questions asked Martin at the Reno Court, it is apparent to me they asked timing and distance questions in a way that was bound to confuse Martin and so justify a dismissal of him as a witness. This is the most important witness in determining the orders Custer gave, and his route and timing, as it would have related to Reno and Custer, both. But if you look at the pages covered by his testimony, compared to other witnesses, they are pitifully short and the questions inadequate.

The Defense's position, which Willert accepts, is that

---

*Note page 499, Hughes-Taylor Critique: Pvt. Taylor's account of "the tenor of the men at this time."

**Note Appendix 2, Part B.

ANALYSIS OF WRITERS' SCENARIOS

Reno's troops were short on ammo, so it was necessary for them to wait for the packs. The packs were some distance behind – so far back that they couldn't even be seen twenty minutes after Lt. Hare had gone to hurry and bring up some of the packs. (Yet Lt. Hare said he was gone only twenty minutes.)[64] Benteen's testimony was that the pack train "was not in sight and therefore more than four and a half miles away."[65]

B.F. Churchill's testimony refutes both the need for ammo and the long period of time before the packs arrived.

> At the Reno Court: Q. Tell where it was the order came about sending the ammunition packs ahead. How far from that tepee? A. I think about half a mile after we passed it.[66]

> When this question was asked to John Frett, also a packer, he said when "near the tepee . . . when a sergeant came from some company of the 7th Cavalry, . . . and said we should hurry up, that General Custer was attacking the Indians."[67]

This would bear out Kanipe's report of taking his message to Captain McDougall and the approximate location. Willert didn't believe Kanipe took the message to McDougall because he saw and was afraid of what he thought were, some hostile Indians..

> As to questions concerning when the packs arrived, Churchill said: Q. Do you know what interval of time intervened between the arrival of Captain Benteen's column and the arrival of those pack mules? A. I think Captain Benteen's column got there a few minutes before we arrived there with the mules. I saw the command coming a little below where we struck the hill going on the bluff. We went right on and came in pretty soon.

As to the urgent need for ammo one should consider what Churchill said:

> Q. Were the boxes of ammunition brought up at that time opened? A. Not at that time.
>
> Q. When were they opened? A. After we moved down the river and back again and the mules were unpacked.[68]

It is hard for me to understand why either packer would lie concerning those questions asked, while it is easy to understand why the Defense of Major Reno would lie in order to emphasize the need for the ammo, and the lateness of the packs arrival time, in order to justify their late move downriver. One should keep in mind that each trooper carried 100 rounds of carbine ammunition as well as twenty-five of pistol. The Springfield carbines were single shot, and many people have brought out the difficulty of extracting the cartridge when they became hot from firing. I cannot believe that most of the men –even firing fast and at random, the way many were reported to have done – would have used up even half of that amount of ammunition. I realize that half of the carbine ammo would be on the backs of the horses, so a certain amount would have been lost. However, with Benteen's battalion carrying their full amount, I don't think the shortage of ammo should be recognized as an excuse.

> Private Davern, Reno's orderly, who was one of the last to reach the ridge in the retreat from the valley, in answer to the question, Q. Did you see his column come up? [Benteen's] A. No, I did not, but I saw the pack train come up soon after I got on the hill.

> Another interesting answer by Davern, which would pertain to when Reno's command went to aid Custer, Q. Do you remember whether Captain Weir moved his command down the stream? A. Not at that time. He did later in the evening.[69]

> Private Martin: Q. How long did you have to wait till the packs came up? A. Probably 10 or 15 minutes, I mean the packs made a long string and in 15 minutes everything was up. Q. Can you tell how long it was after the packs moved up till the command moved down the river? A. I think about an hour and a half. We waited for some men from the bottom, and then moved out together.[70]

There was the attempt by Reno's Defense to discredit non-military and enlisted testimony at the Reno Court. Martin, they stigmatized and dismissed. Davern they referred to as "a private soldier of limited intelligence."[71] They also discredited the packer and other non-officers testimony, which only supports my contention of cover-ups by the officers and the military. Although Martin and the others' testimony would not be completely accurate, at least they were not subject to the military pressure that the officers testifying on key issues undoubtedly would have been.

Custer's Last Battle – page 342

Custer probably had not been on the high ground east of the river many minutes when he became abruptly aware of increasingly heavier gunfire down by the river; this was Lieutenant Smith, Captain Tom Custer and the command ordered earlier down Medicine Tail Coulee after the hostiles. But was happening? . . .

. . . Benteen and the packs of ammunition reserves were not in sight, but *damn,* the situation looked promising!

. . . As Custer took his command position on the knoll at the north end of the ridge, and scanned again the view below, his high confidence abruptly drained. Smith's troopers had come into sight – and they were all hell-bent in *retreat* toward the ridge. Something had gone wrong! . . .

. . . To resume the narrative – when Custer led his three troops – Companies L, I and half of F – over the hills from the east, Smith and Tom Custer had been in action for at least fifteen to twenty minutes, for already, advance numbers of those hostiles who had been *en route* to join the action against Reno upriver, but who had been alerted . . . were arriving to join their brethren at the new attack point.

. . . From this point forward in our exploration of what may have occurred on the Custer field of battle, we have only the somewhat conflicting narratives of the Indians themselves, and the curious positionings of the bodies of the men and the horses who died at their hands. Unfortunately, some of the bodies were *moved* from the places where they fell, . . .[72]

I know I am becoming redundant, but there is no way I can see Custer sending half of his companies to search for a ford that he wasn't sure of and with no definite instructions. If there was a ford should they attack or send a message to Custer? If it appeared there were too many Indians, were they to set up a defense or retreat? Willert has brought out time and time again that Custer recognized the need to attack quickly if a successful offense was to take place, but does Custer lead an attack force down South Medicine Tail Coulee? No, he moves with his two and a half companies further north to Last Stand Hill, where he is in no position to see or support Lt. Smith and the men sent to look for a ford. Whether from Weir Point, Nye Cartwright Ridge, or information gathered from Mitch Bouyer, Custer should have known there was a ford, and where it was.

Willert continues to accept Curley's story that fits into his scenario without analyzing any conflicting Curley accounts. (One might recall that Willert accepted Russell White Bear's statement that Curley said only the Gray Horse troop was sent to the ford.) Curley is not on a hill where he can see the ford, but "concealed in a deep ravine from which but a small part of the field was visible . . ."[73] There is no ravine from which he could see the two soldiers he said were shot at the ford.

However, Custer's command *did make a move* down the ridge slope, but their action had sound intention; it was *initiated* when Custer became *aware* that Smith's force at the ford was having to *withdraw* from the attack [?] point at the river. . . . the sight of the troopers from that vicinity spurring their mounts up the draw to the southwest [North Medicine Tail], . . . that a covering fire could be provided to stem the rush of the hostile pursuers to allow Smith's force to rejoin the command. The hostiles were not as yet a concentrating force between the ridge and the river, and had not yet surrounded the command under Custer, . . . Lt. James Calhoun extended his men on a line parallel to the coulee . . . Capt. George Yates extended the remaining portion of his F Company. Capt. Myles Keogh's I Company occupied the center of the long ridge and remained in readiness to lend their strength to whichever end of the line needed additional support until the command under Smith and Tom Custer could reunite with the main command. Had the hostiles at this time been pressing in on the command on the ridge, there can be little doubt but that Custer would have gathered them into a tight circle of defense, for only by so doing would the command stand any chance of holding the hostiles at bay,' but apparently, the hostiles were yet *at some distance,* gathered only at the ford and environs on either side of this place, so Custer reasoned that there would be *time* to permit Smith's command to rejoin before the situation became such that a defensive quadrant had to be established to save the command. He probably realized that his tenuous line along the ridge was a reckless maneuver under the circumstances, but he was determined to save Smith's command if he possibly could. . . .

Without doubt, Lt. Algernon Smith and Capt. Tom Custer rode directly to where Custer had located his command's flags on the high knoll at the north end of the ridge, but their troops continued to fight their way back until they reached the temporary refuge of the main command on the ridge.[74]

I agree that Lt. Calhoun established a line along what is now known as Calhoun Ridge, but since my timing differs from Willert's, I believe their firing down N. Medicine Tail Coulee came as Keogh's battalion was moving from Nye Cartwright Ridge. The firing, when they were along Calhoun Ridge, though still at Indians coming up from the ford, was mainly at those Indians returning from the Reno engagement. This would be the firing that stopped the Indians momentarily, as Joseph White Bull would have recounted.

It is impossible for me to envision Custer moving to Last Stand Hill and setting up a command from where he was in no position to see Lt. Smith at the ford, or know if he was able to attack the village, or whether he would need aid. All of this could have been accomplished if Custer had set up his command post on the hill by Nye Cartwright Ridge, as well as putting him in a better position to be seen and receive the expected aid from Benteen and the packs.

ANALYSIS OF WRITERS' SCENARIOS

Since Custer, from Last Stand Hill, was in no position to have launched a supporting attack to aid Lt. Smith, if he had advanced into the village, it would appear his main purpose was to wait for Benteen and the packs. We should remember Lt. Smith was sent on a "probe" and to search for a ford (which could have been seen from Nye Cartwright); consequently, I would think Custer was not planning on an attack at this time, so that a much better defense perimeter should have been established.

I also can't see Lt. Smith and Capt. Tom Custer going directly to where Custer was located. Their main concern should have been to conduct a tactical retreat (such as Lt. Godfrey did from Weir Point), so that they could have all reached the rest of the command under control and in good order.

> It is clear that the bulk of Company C and those troopers from F Company, who had been in the assault at the ford, managed to reach the high ridge and command under Custer; but the troopers of Company E – the Gray Horse Troop – were not so fortunate. Executing their withdrawal from the ford action by spurring down along the river bank below the bluffs – probably to elude the major thrust of the hostile warriors up North Medicine Tail coulee in pursuit of Companies' C and the portion of F – and then angling toward the higher ridge by veering into the succession of irregular hills and ravines which characterize the intervening terrain toward the high ridge, . . .
>
> Upon the hill, Custer and his command must have experienced extraordinary anxiety at the delay in the arrival of Company E, . . . warriors were swarming in ever-increasing numbers . . . Companies F and C who had, immediately upon arrival, taken skirmish position down the west slope below the command ridge, to provide the Gray Horse Troop E a protective shield . . . But where were the E troopers? . . .
>
> How long these skirmishers from F and C Companies were able to remain in the forward position down that western slope toward the long ravine, until the encroaching warriors forced them to withdraw, will never be known, . . .
>
> . . . The hostiles were crowding the slopes – there was no way now to save E Company – they would have to fight their way out of their situation as best they could – alone.
>
> Of course, the troopers of E Company now had no chance at all for survival. By the time they had reached the vicinity of the long ravine, the ground intervening to the higher ridge of the command was swarming with warriors – so unable to reach the ridge, the troopers loosed their gray horses, and raced for the protective recess of the ravine. But the effort was a hopeless one, for once within, they found themselves trapped, like fish in a trough, . . . the entire number of twenty-eight men were cut down by the hostiles' fire from both sides of the ravine. Most were shot in the head or back. Deep scratches along the sides of the ravine bore mute witness to their efforts to claw their way to the ground above, . . .[75]

I cannot picture Company E moving along the river bank, for at least two reasons: (1) Unless the river bank has changed a lot from that time, this would be nearly impossible because of the terrain. (2) From all reports that I have read of those troops that reached the ford, there were only a few who actually entered the water; consequently, most of Company E would have been back from the ford. There were not that many Indians who were, or would have been, in a position to have forced them toward the Indian camp and then to the north along the river bank. How did Lt. Smith get separated from the rest of his company?

Assuming Willert's view was correct, even if there were a large number of Indians between them and the ridge, once Troop E came up from the river, and with supporting fire from the ridge, they should have been able to make it with any controlled move in that direction. We know Indians fell back from charges made by the troops. One should realize there are no Indian accounts that portray such a movement by gray horses coming up from the river; however, there are accounts of those fleeing from the ridge during the last stages of the fighting, and even then the Indians gave way until after the men had stopped and got off their horses.

Considering the poor shooting credited to the Indians, plus the difficulty of being able to fire effectively into Deep Ravine, it is amazing that E troopers would not have put up a resistance that Indians would have recounted and bragged about overcoming.

> As Company E was being cut off at the ravine, and F and C companies – under the pressure of hostiles' advance – were falling back to the ridge where Custer's flags stood tall upon the point, Lt. James Calhoun's Company L was becoming hard-pressed by the hostile numbers who had gained tactical advantage by surrounding his troops on three sides. . . . Capt. Myles Keogh and his Company I were in position behind Calhoun's troop at some short distance, dismounted, . . .
>
> From the positioning of the markers on the battleridge, denoting the fallen of Captain Keogh's Company I, it appears clear that his men must have been *running on foot* in the direction of Custer's knoll at the end of the ridge; . . . This strongly suggests that when Custer found

his position gravely threatened by the hordes of warriors who had cut off Company E at the ravine, he ordered his bugler to sound the call that the other companies of his broad-spread command gather swiftly to his position . . .

But the call had been sounded too late; . . . There was naught they could do but fight until they fell, and this they did, as their markers testify upon the field today . . . .

The troopers probably realized that their final minutes had come – that death would be their inevitable measure – and here, as probably at no other time, *suicide* found expression in the furious fighting.

However, suicide was not commonplace here, for the Indians marked the ferocity of the action and of the soldiers' fierce defense until they fell . . . , Crow King said that the troopers ". . . kept in order and fought like brave warriors as long as they had a man left . . . ." Low Dog said the same: ". . . The white warriors stood their ground bravely, and none of them made any attempt to get away . . ."[76]

I am certain there were a number of suicides – just how many I would not even speculate. Willert, at least, recognizes that there would have been some. What I consider odd is how writers will bring out why Indian accounts cannot be trusted, and then turn around and quote them for verification on what should be very questionable statements, but disregard their comments on other often more important matters. Wooden Leg and Kate Bighead are good examples, but their references to suicides and the number of troopers involved are ignored or brushed-off. Low Dog, Crow King, and the other Indians who bring out how the soldiers fought to the last, go against too many other reports of how the troopers fired aimlessly into the air or gave up without fighting back. For example, two pages after stating how the troopers fought to the last, Willert refers to Red Horse recalling:

". . . When we attacked the other party, . . . The soldiers became panic-stricken, many of them throwing down their arms and throwing up their hands . . ."[77]

Another Sioux said: ". . . They did not shoot at us. They seemed so panic-stricken that they shot up in the air."[78]

Willert goes on to say that suicide, as a general behavior of the soldiers upon the Custer battlefield, is hardly possible. This is his opinion, and probably is correct, but it does go against Marquis' findings given to him from statements by Wooden Leg, Kate Bighead, and other Cheyenne.

It strikes me as being naive not to expect Indians, when giving their testimony before white men – and in the case of Low Dog and Crow King, in front of 7th Cavalry officers – to say how brave the men fought. Does one really think they would have said the troops became panicky and many committed suicide?

. . . That Custer fell *early* in this action, or was among the *last* to die, will never be known; and the consideration is probably immaterial, for doubtless, no one survived the contest long . . . The battle action here must have been brief, indeed.[79]

Whether Custer was shot early leading an attack against the Indian village or died later after engaging in the actions as presented by Willert, is not immaterial. Getting shot in an attack, at the time I believe it took place, indicates a courageous Custer with a well-thought out plan of battle that didn't work out because of extenuating circumstances. Custer getting shot and killed at the time Willert proposes, after exhibiting a lack of courage, as well as knowledge of the Indians and obstacles he would be facing, yet still engaging in stupid military tactics, does make a great difference in how history views General Custer.

Willert, in the remaining pages of his book, goes over areas he has previously covered, but supplements them with additional material and insight. This doesn't change his portrayal of the essential actions taken by General Custer, Major Reno, or Captain Benteen, except he does recognize that officers would have supported Reno in certain conduct deception. However, this recognition of cover-ups does not extend to what I consider the three major issues.

Willert brings out:

Major Marcus Reno had lost control of the fighting units of the combined commands. These fighting units of the combined command had departed toward the sound of the gunfire *without him*. . . . But he must never reveal the *facts* of what *really happened*. That would be truly disastrous upon his career with the Army. The story he would report would have to be *supported* by his officers – or, at least, *not denied* by them. Weir and Benteen could possibly be court-martialed for their actions without his authority – they would not counter him. Moylan, Wallace and McDougall pledged support, as did Lieutenant Varnum, and later, Lieutenant Hare . . . ,

Lieutenant Wallace testified, in apparent *full support* to this account by Major Reno: ". . . after the packs and ammunition was distributed, the *whole command* moved in that direction. We were going to find out where Custer had gone to . . . *The movement was by Major Reno's order . . . .*"

He, Luther Hare and others of the Seventh's Command, were Reno's friends, and willing – in his hour of need for supporters – to lend their verbal backing to his name and character, even if this required some slight *revision* of the facts.[80]

What is hard for me to understand is how Willert can recognize that Reno had to <u>cover up</u> the fact that Captain Weir and then Captain Benteen, had left without his permission, because it would be "truly disastrous" to his career, but does not recognize the need for other even more important cover-ups. Willert appears to imply an altruistic motive in Reno's saying he issued the orders for the move downstream, as Captain Benteen and Captain Weir might have been court-martialed if he hadn't taken responsibility for the move, whereas, I believe his main motive was knowing, with the death of Custer and his men, that his troops should have moved sooner than they did. If it was revealed that he not only lost control of his officers but actually opposed the move of Captain Weir and then Captain Benteen, his career would certainly have been in jeopardy. Captain Benteen was in no position to object, for he had to rationalize and attempt to justify his own failure to obey the orders he had received from Custer, as well as his slowness in responding to those messages. This was difficult enough for him to cover-up. He attempted to do this by blaming Custer for sending him to the left, the lack of specific knowledge of Custer's plans, and the difficulty of the terrain. Captain Weir is the only one, from a military standpoint, who may have been subject to disobeying orders: but, with the slowness of Reno's command to investigate the gunfire, the main cover-up was not who issued the orders to move downstream, but when they were ordered. This created timing distortions and the need for an "official" time change. Reno knew that his problem centered around the question of why his command didn't move sooner to where the sound of gunfire indicated Custer's troops were engaged. The issue of whether Reno was in charge and gave the orders for the command to investigate the gunfire is minor compared to the need to cover-up the time lapse before they attempted their move. The exposure of Reno not being in command and actually opposing the move could have hurt his career; the exposure of the lateness (timing) and the cover-ups of the other major issues would have killed it.

Willert, even after recognizing these minor cover-ups, continues to go along with the need for Major Reno to not only wait for the ammo packs to arrive, but accepts the lateness of their arrival. Willert blames Captain Weir for leaving when he did, even though he recognizes the command didn't move immediately after the packs arrived. (Lt. Varnum reported that they used several of the spades brought up by the packs to bury Lt. Hodgson.) However, this doesn't cause him to question if time might be the quintessential cover-up after Reno and Captain Benteen met on the ridge.

Willert supports the necessity to wait for the ammo packs with testimony from the Reno Court which refers to the Reno troops' desperate need for ammunition. Willert uses statements made by officers at the Reno Court in twelve straight footnotes. He knows the officers were willing to support Reno through lying, pretending ignorance, or not remembering, who issued the orders to have the command investigate the gunfire downstream; but, on what I consider the really pertinent issues which reflect on Custer, his decisions, and one's knowledge of what actually transpired on the 25th, Willert accepts the officers' accounts without questioning.

I think one should also put together and recognize the Defense's need for an officer to verify the orders Reno received, to support his claim as to not having heard gunfire from downstream, and also have an officer in a position to extend the "official" time. Lt. Wallace, being the itinerast and thereby the official timer, and the fact that he was not tied up with any company or with the scouts, would make him the ideal officer to bring into the inner circle, helping to create the Defense's strategy. You can see from the preceding quote used by Willert, and the following one, how Wallace fully cooperated with the Defense. Other officers were undoubtedly warned, on certain issues, to confirm, ignore, or not remember what happened. They would have complied because of their concern for Major Reno and Captain Benteen, or how it might have reflected on their own actions and careers. However, in an examination of their testimony, one finds they are not as consistent concerning positions on these basic issues as was Lt. Wallace. Their being a member of Benteen's battalion, or in charge of companies, would mean they could easily deny knowledge of the orders Reno and Benteen received. A general warning by the Defense concerning timing, or the sighting of Custer by Reno's officers as they were still moving down the valley, would have been sufficient. They would then have reacted the way Willert describes in referring to their acceptance of Reno's statement that he issued the orders for the move downstream. This inconsistency could actually support the Defense's case, for too much consistency on major issues could become suspect. At the very least, investigative questioning by writers should take place.

The following testimony, registering the need for additional ammo before they could move downstream to investigate the gunfire heard, reflects how critical it was for the Defense to extend the time before the command even moved.

> Captain Weir's zeal to take the command immediately to the support of Custer . . .[Major Reno's] expressed judgment and determination to wait until the pack train had come up before initiating *any move* at all downriver was sound. . . . Lieutenant Hare departed immediately. [to bring up the ammo packs] The two pack mules, with their packers arrived on the hill, and without delay one box of 1000 rounds . . . of the precious ammunition was broken open for distribution to the troopers. Lt. George Wallace recalled: ". . . the men came up and helped themselves until it was all gone . . ."
>
> The dusty and sweat-begrimned men of the pack contingent were grateful when they found the figures on the hill were *troopers,* and upon arrival, another box of the ammunition was opened for the men; however, curiously, it was left untouched. The packer, B. F. Churchill, was puzzled: ". . . We had unpacked it [note Churchill, as I bring out below, refers to all the boxes being taken off the pack mules – not just one (it).] when we first arrived, supposing they wanted it at once. Why it wasn't used I don't know . . ."81

As I have already stated, it is hard for me to understand why Willert would not have questioned in more depth both the necessity of the ammo and the time the pack train arrived on the hill. Willert describes how officers were willing to, and did, support Major Reno, even when they knew they were lying, or stretching the truth, as it pertained to his conduct and control of the command, in their attempt to aid Custer downriver. However, the need for ammo and the opening of an ammo pack, when they arrived on the ridge, is accepted without question. Note the main testimonial supporting officer is Lt. Wallace.

What I question and dislike is when Willert changes the wording and meaning as expressed by the packer, B.F. Churchill. Churchill didn't say after their arrival <u>another</u> box had been opened. The following is what was said:

> To the question, (Q) "What was done with the ammunition you brought up at the time you brought it up?" Churchill's answer, (A) "The boxes were unpacked at the time and we packed them up again." Then he was asked: "Were the boxes of ammunition brought up at that time opened?" (A) "Not at that time." (Q)"When were they opened?" (A) "After we moved down the river and back again and the mules were unpacked." (Q) "What was the object of unpacking the ammunition when you first came there?" (A) "We supposed they wanted it immediately and we unpacked it for their use."

> (Q) "Why was it not used, if you know?" (A) "I don't know."82

In other words, there was nothing said about one box of ammo opened that the men emptied, as Wallace asserted and Willert accepts, nor another box opened that was not emptied. The question that should be asked is why it was so important to have had a box of ammo opened? Again, the answer is apparent, and not because it was needed before they moved downstream. The waiting for the ammunition packs to arrive was the main reason they were using for the delay in moving to where they knew Custer was engaged. To merely say they had to wait for the ammo packs would not have been enough. The packs were guarded by Captain McDougall's enlarged company, and they knew practically all, if not all, the Indians had left (check Wooden Leg's statement). The packs could have followed the command, and more than likely would have caught the troops that were assisting the wounded. Reno could have left his valley companies behind if he thought they were not emotionally ready. Any fear of Indians luring them into a trap did not stop Captain Weir, nor was his company interfered with, as they moved downstream. Benteen's command could have been sent on ahead, as they were already under orders to come quickly to Custer's aid. The need to bring the ammo packs hadn't bothered Benteen along Reno Creek, so they shouldn't have created an obstacle at this time. However, I believe the packs arrived soon enough, which created the need to extend the period before they arrived. Willert should realize that if the officers were willing to go along with having allowed Reno to issue the orders for the commands downriver move, they would certainly be willing to support his need for ammo before they could have started.

I think if you can accept a minor cover-up, certainly major cover-ups should at least be investigated. You should not discard enlisted men's and Indian testimony because it may differ from that of officers, particularly their testimony at the Reno Court. You should keep in mind what Captain Robert Carter said, in his correspondence with Colonel W. A. Graham. Graham took the view that the officers would not have lied at the Reno Court. Captain Carter, who was a cavalry officer with the Fourth Cavalry, made the following comments: (my underlining)

> <u>I simply discredit, I repeat, the testimony of these officers</u>, after knowing of their daily conversations in the Post Trader's store at Fort Lincoln, the ostracizing of Reno for nearly 3 years, or until he felt compelled to ask for a Court of Inquiry, and then their going as a body before the court

ANALYSIS OF WRITERS' SCENARIOS

and <u>testifying just exactly the reverse</u> of what their talk had been. Even Benteen testifying in Reno's favor.[83]

In reference to time:

> The element of time in this entire riddle, all of which you seem to have worked out with so much precision, is not so conclusive with me, especially after Custer left Reno and until Benteen came up and joined Reno, for no two officers <u>before</u> the Reno Court seemed to give the time alike as to how long Reno was in line, how long in the timber, how long it took them to reach the crossing and up on the bluff, the periods when Benteen came up, or how long the packs were in closing up . . . Here is where my knowledge of some of those officers, and the personal equation makes me discredit their testimony.[84]

Captain Carter's viewpoint should be read, analyzed, and agreed or disagreed with, but it shouldn't be discarded. Carter did accept the prevalent view, following the Reno Court, that General Custer was planning on supporting Reno from the rear, and that he had not informed either Major Reno or Captain Benteen of his plans or why he changed them.

Carter makes the same mistake he blamed others for, in that he believed the officers' statements made at the Reno Court, as they pertained to the orders received from Custer. He accepted what Major Reno and Captain Benteen said concerning their orders were without questioning. Shouldn't he have asked: if they would lie about other issues, might they not have lied about the orders they received? Keep in mind that Benteen, right after the battle, would have understood the need to excuse his slowness in responding to the urgency of the messages, which indicated Reno's and Custer's battalions had or were about to, launch the attack on the Indian villages. He did this by blaming his slowness on having been sent by Custer on a useless mission and the difficulty of the terrain. By the time of the Reno Court, he was blaming Custer for not only his mission to the left, but the lack of orders and for not realizing the size of the Indian encampment. He even said Custer wasn't sure there was an Indian camp. I believe that right after the battle, both he and Reno, as well as the officers and men, realized Custer was planning on flanking the Indians. Orders, which included Custer's plan to flank the Indians, would not have been an issue until it became necessary for Reno to avoid being court martialed and Benteen indicted.

The main topic, following the battle, was Major Reno and his conduct, with timing being used in the accusations. Reno, in his official report, indicated Custer was flanking the Indians, but there was nothing said about not knowing that was Custer's plan, or that he had expected Custer to support him from the rear. Benteen, in a letter to his wife following the battle, reveals how Custer went to the right with the intent of attacking the village.[85] There was no inference that this flanking movement was a surprise to Reno or himself.

Captain Carter should have realized the orders were easier to cover up than either timing or Reno's conduct. How many living people, other than Reno and Benteen, actually knew the orders Custer gave? I can only think of four: Wallace, who, contrary to his statement at the Reno Court, would have been riding near Custer, not Reno. (Either way, he could have known the orders that were given.) Lt. Gibson was apt to know because of being sent to the bluffs by Benteen. (Is this why he wasn't invited to testify at the Reno Court?) Then there was Private Davern, Reno's orderly, and Trumpeter Martin, Custer's orderly, and they both indicated that the orders were more extensive than stated by Major Reno or Captain Benteen. (Is this why they were discredited?)

These issues need more examination than they have been subjected to.

In examining testimony of officers at the Reno Court, one should determine whether they believe the military desired to have Major Reno exonerated, and the issue forgotten, or were they only concerned at getting at the truth? Then, was Lt. Colonel (General) Custer a competent commander, or was he so courageous, arrogant, or overly rash in his actions that he brought about his own demise?

From my study of the General, I believe he was a capable commander and deserved the laurels and accolades he received during the Civil War. I am not able to understand how writers, which includes Willert, can, on the one hand, speak of him as being too courageous, too immersed in his own infallibility, and that his actions were too rash, but then claim he did nothing to aid Reno or to defeat the Indians. Custer should have realized the necessity of synchronizing an attack with Reno, particularly against a camp that, by all Indian reports, was in a near state of panic. It is hard for me to imagine that Custer would not have led an attack on the Indian encampment.

Willert's book provides excellent source material for looking at the entire 1876 campaign. My concern and research has centered around an investigative study of the activities on the 25th of June, 1876. My focus has been on General Custer's actions and decisions which prevented him from launching a recognizable attack on the Indian encampment with his five companies. In my study, I came to conclusions different from those of most writers, including James Willert. I believe that to arrive at logical and objective answers, one must be critical of others' views, and explain why you accept or reject them on issues that directly effect the thoughts and actions you believe took place that fateful day.

I believe any student of the battle should read and analyze as many accounts of the battle as available. They must question Indian and white testimony and try to give logical and objective answers as to why they accept some testimony and not others, often by the same person. Their decisions will then result in the formulation of a theory of what took place. This *modus operandi* can become redundant, but is necessary if a clearer picture is to emerge as to what happened on the 25th of June, 1876, during the Battle of the Little Bighorn.

Although I can't accept James Willert's view on what I consider essential issues, his book is one that should be read and studied by any serious student of the battle, whether you accept or reject his portrayal of events.

SOURCES

1. Marshall, S. L. A., *The Indian Wars*, p. 162.
2. Godfrey, Edward, S., Graham, John, S., *The Custer Myth*, Godfrey Narrative, p. 136.
3. Gray, John, S., *Custer's Last Campaign*, p. 225.
4. Graham, W.A., *The Custer Myth*, p.33.
5. Willert, James, *Little Bighorn Diary*, p. 257.
6. Ibid., p. 258.
7. Graham, W. A., *The Custer Myth*, p. 33.
8. Willert, James, *Little Big Horn Diary*, p. 257.
9. Ibid., p. 263.
10. Graham, W. A.., *The Custer Myth*, p. 33.
11. Willert, James, *Little Big Horn Diary*, p. 266. Nichols, Ron, Ed., *Reno Court of Inquiry*, p. 214.
12. Stewart, Edgar, L., *Custer's Luck*, p. 318.
13. Willert, James, *Little Big Horn Diary*, p. 266.
14. Ibid., p. 266.
15. Ibid., p. 268.
16. Ibid., p. 269.
17. Ibid., p. 269.
18. Ibid., p. 269.
19. Ibid., p. 268.
20. Stewart, Edgar. L. *Custer's Luck*, p. 379.
21. Graham, W. A., *The Custer Myth*, p. 180.
22. Caroll, John M., ed., *Custer's Chief of Scouts, The Reminiscences of Charles A. Varnum*, p. 64.
23. Willert, James, *Little Big Horn Diary*, p. 270.
24. Ibid., p. 271.
25. Ibid., p. 272.
26. Ibid., p. 274.
27. Nichols, Ron, ed., *Reno Court of Inquiry*, pp. 592, 593.
28. Willert, James, *Little Big Horn Diary*, p. 275.
29. Graham, W. A., *The Custer Myth*, p. 141.
30. Willert, James, *Little Big Horn Diary*, p. 276.
31. Ibid., p. 284.
32. Graham, W. A., *The Custer Myth*, p. 323.
33. Ibid., p. 286.
34. Ibid., p. 287.
35. Ibid., p. 287.
36. Ibid., p. 289.
37. Ibid., pp. 290-292.
38. Camp, Walter, Hammer, ed., *Custer in 76*, p. 100.
39. Willert, James, *Little Big Horn Diary*, p. 292.
40. Ibid., p. 292.
41. Graham, W. A., *The Custer Myth*, p. 335.
42. Willert, James, *Little Big Horn Diary*, p. 298.
43. Graham, W. A., *The Custer Myth*, p. 219.
44. Ibid., p. 140.
45. Willert, James, *Little Big Horn Diary*, pp. 305, 306.
46. Ibid., p. 306.
47. Ibid., p. 306.
48. Ibid., p. 325.
49. Ibid., p. 325.
50. Ibid., p. 325.
51. Ibid., p. 325.
52. Ibid., pp. 326, 328.
53. Ibid., p. 328.
54. Ibid., pp. 329, 332.
55. Ibid., p. 333.
56. Ibid., p. 335.
57. Graham, W. A., *The Custer Myth*, p. 143.
58. Op. Cit., p. 333.
59. Camp, Walter, *Custer in 76*, p. 70.
60. Willert, James, *The Little Big Horn Diary*, pp. 338, 340, 341.
61. Nichols, Ron, ed., *Reno Court of Inquiry*, p. 289.
62. Ibid., p. 392.
63. Camp, Walter, *Custer in 76*, p. 101.
64. Gray, John, S., *Custer's Last Campaign*, p. 336.
65. Nichols, Ron, ed., *Reno Court of Inquiry*, p. 289.
66. Ibid., p. 434.
67. Ibid., p. 465.
68. Ibid., p. 503.
69. Ibid., p. 468.
70. Ibid., pp. 352, 353.
71. Ibid., p. 392.
72. Ibid., p. 596.
73. Willert, James, *The Little Big Horn Diary*, pp. 342, 343, 344.
74. Ibid., p. 344.
75. Ibid., p. 345.
76. Ibid., pp. 346, 348.
77. Ibid., pp. 350, 351, 352.
78. Ibid., p. 354.
79. Ibid., p. 354.
80. Ibid., p. 352.
81. Ibid., pp. 368, 369.
82. Ibid., pp. 364, 366.
83. Nichols, Ron, ed., *Reno Court of Inquiry*, p. 468.
84. Graham, W. A.., *The Custer Myth*, p. 315.
85. Ibid., p. 315.
86. Ibid., p. 187.

ANALYSIS OF WRITERS' SCENARIOS

A Critique of Captain Hughes' Letter and William O. Taylor's Book

Captain Robert P. Hughes' letter to his wife, printed in the Little Big Horn Associates Newsletter of Feb. 1999, and also the book by William O. Taylor, who took part in the Battle of the Little Bighorn as a private in Company A under Captain Moylan, give corroborating excerpts or evidence that substantiates my view of what took place at the Battle of the Little Bighorn.

The general view of the battle, as presented by most writers, is brought out in the decisions made at Custer's mock trial that was conducted at Indiana University School of Law on Sept. 18, 1998. The trial was presided over by Supreme Court Justice Ruth Bader Ginsburg. The panel found Custer guilty of violating the 15th and 62nd Articles of War. They said Custer split his forces into four groups that could not communicate or support each other, failed to conduct reconnaissance, ignored the warnings of his scouts, failed to provide for the security of his command, issued incomplete and unclear commands, and refused to accept artillery and rapid fire weapons assigned to him by his senior commanders.

Both in my book, *The Custer Controversy – A Critical Analysis*, and in my full manuscript, I believe I have objectively and rationally refuted these charges. To me these charges made by the mock court and by writers is due to their failure to recognize the mendacious actions of the Reno Court of Inquiry, and the need for officers' duplicity and concurrence with Reno's Defense in order to prevent the court martial of Major Reno and the indictment of Captain Benteen, and more than likely Captain McDougall and Lt. Mathey. The basic premises underlying these guilty charges would portray Custer as not only inept, but lacking the courage to attack the Indian village at a time the success of the battle would have rested in his hands.

In my book, I have brought out that there were three major cover-ups at the Reno Court of Inquiry, and the reasons for them. The three cover-ups were: (1) The orders Custer gave. (2) The sighting of Custer's troops on the ridge by Major Reno and his officers, as Reno's battalion moved down the valley. (3) Changing the "official" time of the division of the regiment from around 10 A.M. to after 12 P.M. These three cover-ups were necessary to protect Major Reno's conduct on the 25th, but their primary significance, from a historical standpoint, is how they have effected the views of Custer's plans and actions.

I will examine some of the statements made by Captain Robert P. Hughes and Private William O. Taylor which help substantiate the decisions, events or action that I think took place that day.

Captain Hughes served as aide-de-camp to General Terry, who was his brother-in-law, and their relationship was close. Hughes's overall point of view would be that Custer was to blame for the failure of the expedition. In his letter, Hughes showed a sketch of the battlefield. The following were the actions and locations as represented by the location numbers that he used: (1) The Lone Tepee (2) Where Reno established his skirmish line. (3) The timber Reno's men moved into before their retreat to the bluffs. (4) The location of their retreat to the bluffs. (5) Ford B where Hughes has Custer moving to. (6) Last Stand Hill. (7) Reno's Ford A crossing.

Captain Hughes, in a letter to his wife, dated June 30, 1876:

> ... on the morning of the 25th, about noon he[Custer] was in sight of the village at the Tepee marked one... After Reno started from 7 General Custer with five companies took the route of figure 4 and his trail led to 5. There he appears to be driven back and his dead horses and his body were lying at figure 6.... (Custer's line) from 7 to 5 over high bluffs and a distance of about three and a half miles would require quite a length of time to traverse -- ... The plan might have worked well enough had Custer seen that Reno had support enough to enable him to hold his position at 2 until he Custer had time to reach and attack with his column at 5 but as that was not done great was the evil done.[1]

Captain Hughes's use of time for that morning is what the "official" time was before the Reno Court. One should realize there is no way Custer could have been at the Lone Tepee "at about noon" and still have the regiment being divided into battalions at 12:05 P.M. – the "official" time used at the Reno Court. It was impossible for the Reno's Defense to justify the length of time before Reno's forces went to investigate the gunfire heard from the Custer battlefield without changing the time of the division from around 10 A.M. to the 12:05 P.M. Even with the "official" change, they still had to not only alter when the packs arrived on the hill, but also say a wait for the packs was necessary by portraying Reno's men as being short on ammunition. This was denied not only by B. F. Churchill, a civilian packer,[2] but also by the shortage of time on the skirmish line as brought out by Private Taylor.

Hughes's account also points out the accepted belief, after the battle, that Custer did go to Ford B. Hughes was most likely with General Terry at the time Trumpeter Martin explained Custer's route to Terry. One should keep in mind that Martin always said he knew Custer went closer to the ford than later writers maintained, and also that Benteen told Martin that it was about 600 yards from Ford B where he received his message from Custer.[3] The Crow Indian reports, as well as some by the Sioux and Cheyenne, should also be considered.

Since I believe the major cover-up at the Reno Court involved the orders Custer gave to Major Reno and Captain Benteen, and that Benteen's initial orders were to move in support of Reno when he reached the Little Bighorn, Custer, by these orders, would have seen, to the extent possible, that Reno was supported. Custer, as he neared the Little Bighorn, would realize from his scouts' reports that they hadn't seen any signs of Indians to the south of the known village. Custer would then have expected Benteen to be approaching the Little Bighorn. His major frustration at the time, I believe, was not having heard from Benteen. Custer had to have recognized that once he gave his orders for Reno to attack, and for his plan to be successful, he would have to begin his flanking move. He then had to gamble that Benteen had received his orders, was nearing the Little Bighorn, and would move in support of Reno.

Hughes also brings out:

> The Crows . . . noted that Custer had gone to attack the Sioux village and that the Sioux had come out and met him and that his men ran and scattered all over the prairies and were killed in all directions. . . . At this time we were only Eight miles from Reno where he was besieged but did not know it at all. . . . I think some of the people escaped. Lt Harrington was not identified and there are about forty men yet to be accounted for and we think or I do at least that some of them will turn up . . . Up to the time Reno abandoned position No. 3 and Custer No 5 there were no killed men, or in plain words, the men were killed for turning their backs to the enemy and letting him ride up in such safety. That is not the way we do, you may rest assured. There are many things in this connection that I can tell you when I come home.[4]

The Crows were certainly in a position to have seen if Custer went to the ford in order to attack the Indian village. That the troops then panicked is also evident. Contrary to the attempts by most writers to prove that there was an organized withdrawal, I think the evidence, when analyzed objectively and without feeling the need to portray the men as fighting to the last, makes clear that, outside of certain rear guard action, and some determined fighting in localized areas, the Crows' report would be justified. However, they would have fled before seeing the complete destruction of the command.

The question is, why was there this panicky withdrawal from the ford? Indian reports indicate there were very few at the ford when this attack should have taken place. I believe it supports the Indian accounts – both Crow and some Sioux and Cheyenne – that Custer was shot at the ford, thereby stopping an attack. Custer being shot, along with other factors, created a non-tactical withdrawal which officers were not able to control.

Hughes's statement that there were many things that he would explain to his wife when he got home certainly suggests that he might not only tell her more details about the withdrawal, but inform her of more egregious actions on the part of some troopers which could raise the specter of suicides. (There remains to this day the interesting question of what happened to some of the men that both Captain Hughes and Major Reno said were not accounted for.)

Since I believe Custer's plan was sound, there were two primary reasons for its lack of success. The main one, that Custer was shot at the ford. The second (although, because of the first, it may not have changed the outcome) was Benteen's failure to have crossed into South Fork, and having realized there was no threat of Indians to the south of the recognized Indian village, and that an attack by Custer was to take place, he would have angled quickly toward Custer's and Reno's known route to the Little Bighorn, and then moved to support Major Reno's attack (which I believe were his initial orders).

William O. Taylor's manuscript, *With Custer on the Little Bighorn – The First – And Only Eyewitness Account Ever Written*, was found by Greg Martin in 1952. This is another enlightening account of the battle.

At the time of the battle, Private Taylor was a member of Captain Moylan's A Company and fought with Major Reno in the valley and on the hill. Taylor retired the following year from the army. He would have collected information from others which he combined with his remembrance of events in writing his story of the battle. For whatever reason, he never published his manuscript. By chance, Greg Martin came across a box containing the writing and was able to have it published. The difficulty of Taylor's memory of timing in contrast to timing statements that came about at the Reno Court of Inquiry is apparent – often without Taylor seeming to recognize their incongruity.

I will begin my analysis of Private Taylor's book on page 31, the night of the 24th:

> Our rest here proved to be but for a few hours only,

ANALYSIS OF WRITERS' SCENARIOS

for about ten o'clock we were awakened and ordered to saddle up for a night march. We were soon in the saddle and, still following the Rosebud, marched some ten miles or more ascending the north fork of the river up the divide separating the Rosebud from the Little Bighorn.

... We halted somewhere about 2 A.M. awaiting news from the scouts who had been sent ahead to locate, if possible, the camp of the Indians. . . .

General Custer, who had gone on ahead to the point on the divide from whence the scouts had seen the smoke rising from the Indian village and the pony herds grazing in the valley near it, some twelve or fifteen miles away, had returned, and a little before eight o'clock came riding bareback, and I think also bareheaded, around to the several troops, giving the officers the information that the Indians had been located, and saying the command would move at once. The men began to saddle up and we were soon in motion travelling up the divide between the Rosebud and Little Bighorn rivers. We did not stop until about 10:30 A.M. When we came to a halt in a ravine, some four or five miles perhaps from the summit of the divide. Here we were ordered to keep concealed, and to preserve quiet. Captain Godfrey says, "It was Custer's declared intention not to attack until the next morning". But in the meantime our presence having been discovered, so the scouts and the others reported, "it was necessary to act at once," and we started again crossing the divide a little before noon.

Soon afterwards the Regiment was divided into Battalions . . .[5]

Here, and in other estimates of time, we will see Taylor go from his own general observations to those later made by Godfrey and others. These lack a logical coherence. For example: Taylor infers Custer was notified that the Indian village had been sighted, as stated by the messenger Red Star when the sun was just rising, and he then went to the Crow's Nest, came back, and the command still moved out by eight o'clock. Godfrey's timing, which Taylor accepts, has them reaching what is considered Halt 2 at 10:30 A.M. Yet Halt 2 is only three miles from Halt 1. The command should have reached Halt 2 by 9 A.M. Whether Custer had already gone to the Crow's Nest, as indicated by Taylor, or, as I believe, first rode around the camp informing his officers of the sighting and that he wanted them to move out at 8 A.M., and then, along with Red Star and a small party, went to the Crow's Nest to observe for himself, is immaterial. The important point is that the command moved at 8 A.M. and would have been at Halt 2 by 9 A.M. Since Custer should have received the message from Red Star by 6 A.M., he should have been on his way to the Crow's Nest to see for himself by 7 A.M. and covered the 4 1/2 miles by 7:30 A.M. Custer would not have taken four and a half hours to observe, rejoin his command, and move the one mile to where he would have divided his regiment into battalions. The division of his command should have taken place by 10 A.M. which coincides with the earlier estimates of when the division occurred. The change in the "official" time took place at the Reno Court of Inquiry, and was necessary for the defense of Major Reno.

[Lone Tepee] It has been stated that "a few Indians were seen near here," and that they kept far enough in advance to be out of danger. As for that, I cannot say; personally, I did not see any of them. [This could have been expected since Reno's battalion was called to cross over Ash Creek and came up after the sighting.] When, within a short distance of the river, Reno received an order that caused us to increase our speed and we soon came to the Little Bighorn, a stream some fifty to seventy feet wide, and from two to four feet deep of clear, icy cold water. [This bears out Curley's and White Man Runs Him's account that Custer's orders to Reno to attack the village would have been given when approximately a mile and a quarter from the river.]

Into it our horses plunged without any urging. . . , While waiting for them to drink I took off my hat and, shaping the brim into a scoop, leaned over, filled it and drank the last drop of water I was to have for over twenty-four long hours. The horses having been watered, we rode out of the river and through the underbrush and then a few yards on the prairie, where we dismounted and tightened our saddle girths, and in about ten minutes were heading down a long but rather narrow valley.[6]

One should keep in mind that Major Reno, after receiving his orders to attack the village, would have recrossed Ash Creek and moved in a column formation to the Little Bighorn. There he would have checked the river for a fording place, and supposedly moved further south to where he found a suitable ford. As Taylor says, the horses drank when they crossed. They then passed through underbrush and timber, which, according to different reports, was both difficult and from fifty to two hundred yards wide. We should keep in mind that Lt. Charles DeRudio and others would have hid there for over a day. The troops then dismount, tighten their horses saddle girths, and reform. From the time Reno received his orders to the time he was ready to move down the valley would have had to have taken forty minutes to an hour to have accomplished. Taylor's halting for ten minutes after passing through the timber reflects the time stated by Major Reno to reform, but has often been used to encompass the time it took to cross the ford, pass through the timber, reform and start to move down the valley. This means that an accurate assessment on the time taken after Custer gave Reno his attack orders, for Reno to have reached and crossed the river, then moved down the valley by the time Custer reached the ridge, Custer would have had to have waited along North Fork for at least forty minutes before he began his move to the bluffs. Neither Trumpeter Martin or Sergeant Kanipe would have had this happening, and as Lt. Varnum said to have Custer sitting still for five minutes would be expecting too much.

> ...On our left were low foothills near which we could see a part of the pony herds, and as we <u>came nearer,</u> [my underlining] could distinguish mounted men riding in every direction, some in circles, others passing back and forth. They were gathering up their ponies and also making signals. We were then at a fast walk. soon the command was given to "trot". Then as little puffs of smoke were seen and the "Ping" of bullets spoke out plainly, we were ordered to charge.
>
> The Major and Lieutenant Hodgson were riding side by side a short distance in the rear of my Company. As I looked back Major Reno was just taking a bottle from his lips. He then passed it to Lieutenant Hodgson. It appeared to be a quart flask . . .[7]

Taylor bears out the fact that there were no large number of Indians coming to attack Major Reno, as Girard said at the Reno Court, so there would be no excuse for him to have ridden back to give this message to Adjutant Cooke. This message is supposedly the one which caused Custer to change his mind from supporting Reno from the rear to his attempt to flank the Indians. Reno's movement down the valley would have been comparatively slow, which should be recognized in estimating time. I assume those Ree scouts, which were in front and to the left of the troops, would have opened the firing which alerted the village.

> But to resume, the river as I have already said, was a very tortuous one, and at this point, it came well out into the prairie, made a sharp turn, and then went back to the bluffs. It was lined on both sides by tall cottonwood trees, and its banks, thick with underbrush, so that it shut off the view of the nearest part of the Indian village which we were fast approaching. . . . [Skirmish line set up.]
>
> The led horses, . . . were then taken into the woods for greater safety, keeping slightly in the rear of the skirmish line. Just how long we remained there I cannot say, but I shall never believe that it was over fifteen or twenty minutes at the most. . . .

> All at once, the skirmishers came rushing into the woods seeking their horses which they could not locate at first owing to the underbrush . . . Then I heard someone say, "We must get out of here, quick!"[8]

I think one has to realize time would be very difficult for anyone to judge. As Colonel Graham and Captain Carter have pointed out, it takes longer to accomplish certain actions then one is apt to think when looking back. Whether the troops moved forward for nearly a hundred yards after dismounting, as some report, or not, I wouldn't know; but just the dismounting, turning the horses over, establishing your skirmish lines, and firing if for only a brief time, is likely to take longer than the fifteen or twenty minutes reported by Taylor. What it does portray is a comparatively short time both on the skirmish line and in the timber. One should take this into account when attempting to determine whether the need to wait for the ammo packs was justified before moving to check on the gunfire downstream from Custer's location, or whether the need was created in order to prevent a court martial of Major Reno and an indictment of Captain Benteen.

> . . . Out of the clouds of dust, anxious to be in at the death, came hundreds of others, shouting and racing toward the soldiers, most of whom were seeing their first battle, and many, of whom I was one, had never fired a shot from a horse's back.
>
> . . .The chances of being wounded or captured were many. One's fate in such a case was easy to imagine, so I reserved one of the six bullets that my revolver contained for the "last resort," . . .
>
> *The fire and* pursuit by the Indians seemed to cease as soon as we reached the top of the bluffs, . . .
> Major Reno was walking around in an excited manner. . . . We had been there but a short time when we were joined by Captain Benteen with the three troops . . . that had been sent off to the left some two hours before.[9]

If Taylor, who had been with the Custer Black Hill's expedition, had never fired a shot from the back of a horse – and this was typical of many of the troops – then this should certainly be taken into consideration in judging the reaction of the men to what we can visualize they saw, along with their realization of what would happen to them if captured by the Indians. One must also consider the difficulty the troopers would have had in controlling horses not accustomed to gunfire, and the yelling and screaming taking place.

> This juncture with all of Reno's command occurred at "2:30 P.M.," so Reno states. <u>A very short time after-</u>

ANALYSIS OF WRITERS' SCENARIOS

<u>wards</u>, [my underlining] Captain McDougall with B Troop, escorting the pack train, came along and joined us. Captain McDougall had also received an order from General Custer to make haste and join him with the pack train. The message to McDougall was delivered to him by Sergeant David C. Kanipe of Captain Tom Custer's Troop C.

For <u>over</u> [my underlining] two hours after the arrival of Captain Benteen's command, we remained there on the bluff, unmolested in any manner.... We had heard firing off in the general direction Custer was supposed to have gone. "Why don't we move?" was the question asked by more than one. The three Troops that had been engaged in the valley were, it is true, somewhat demoralized, but that was no excuse for the whole command to remain inactive. A few of our men had been wounded, but none so seriously that they could not ride with the pack train. All of the officers must have known that Custer was engaged with the Indians, and quite near by, for he had not time to go a great way. The sudden withdrawal of that strong force of Indians who had driven us from the close vicinity of their camp, could indicate but one thing, and that was another attack on their camp, real or threatened, by a force from another direction.[10]

Since both Reno and Godfrey used 2:30 as the juncture time that Reno and Benteen's forces met on Reno Hill, and these reports came right after the battle, and not at the Reno Court, I think one can assume they were nearly correct. One should realize there is no way this could have happened if the division of the command took place after 12 p.m some twelve to fourteen miles from the Little Bighorn.

In considering timing, one should also recognize that enlisted men, or, in other words, those not under control of the military at the Reno Court, have Captain McDougall and the packs arriving fairly soon after Benteen. As Taylor brings out, the question by the men was not where Custer was, as Lt. Wallace stated, but "why don't we move to aid him." The paradox of the accounts made after the battle, compared with those presented at the Reno Court, should be apparent to any objective analysis of the court proceedings. As Taylor said, there was no excuse not to have moved, and that the officers knew the firing came from Custer's battalions. At no time does Taylor indicate that the lack of ammunition was a problem, even before the packs arrived, and from the shortness of the time Reno's troops were fighting in the valley, this should not have been a problem.

> In the latter part of the afternoon, not far from half-past four, a squad of twelve of our comrades were seen coming up the bluffs. [Herendeen and those with him.] . . .

> Soon after the party of twelve rejoined us and somewhere near five o'clock we had orders to "fall in", and mounting out horses we started in the direction Custer was believed to have gone. A very short ride along the side of the bluffs that shut off our view of the Indian village brought us to a ridge that afforded a partial view of what was afterwards found to be Custer's battlefield. . . .

> The whole command was then ordered to retire and we returned to the place we had left a short time before. . . .This was, according to my belief, about six o'clock, and that is the time set by Major Reno in his report. Captain Godfrey seems to think it was a little later but he must be mistaken for it certainly never took us two hours to travel about one mile and return to our starting place, especially when urged on by the advancing Sioux for whose power we were entertaining a greater respect than had formerly prevailed.[11]

Since I agree with Captain Godfrey, I think a restatement from Colonel Graham is appropriate: "You know how long military movements take. Figure it out. Could it have taken less than fifteen minutes or twenty minutes to do the things he did? He did all these things – not one right after another as if on a schedule . . . You have had long experience in handling troops. I have had a little myself. But we both know that situations do not develop, nor are troop movements made, in an instant."[12]

I think we can visualize Reno's troops reaching the hill. Benteen has arrived, followed by the packs. There is the care for the wounded, men milling around and the mixing of companies; the hearing of gunfire from downstream, The questioning by the men. Then Captain Weir, who attempted, but failed to get permission to investigate the firing downstream, starts out on his own. Lieutenant Edgerly calls Troop D together and takes out after the Captain. How long do these actions take? The twelve men are seen coming up the bluff; several are wounded. It takes some time for them to arrive and tell what happened. Captain Benteen then decides the others should follow Weir downstream. The men see to their horses, and get together with their companies. The packs are reloaded on the pack animals and the wounded are prepared for the move. (By some accounts this took place before the twelve arrived.) As Colonel Graham said, such action and movement had to have taken some time. They then move the mile and a half to Weir Point and the leading companies set up defensive positions beyond the high point. They are informed they are to withdraw, but some are still not sure. The Indians, several miles away, start toward them. Godfrey, after taking the time to line his men up in skirmish positions and instructing them on how he wanted them to conduct their firing, is given the message to withdraw. After falling back from Weir Point, he sees Captain Weir's and Captain French's troops tearing back over the peaks. He has his company take skirmish positions in order to hold back the Indians. Godfrey's company then retreats slowly back to Reno Hill. Even using Taylor's time, it would have been later than six o'clock when they returned to Reno Hill. One should remember that Taylor was with Captain Moylan's company, who, at that time, was accompanying the wounded. Just how far they would have moved toward Weir Peaks is questionable. Most likely they were the first ones to have returned. This certainly could have affected Taylor's view of the time taken. All in all, I would say it was 7 o'clock, or after, when all of Reno's forces reached Reno Hill and were attacked by the Indians.

> . . .There is a difference of opinion as to what course Custer took from the point where he saw the village and dispatched his messengers. Some claim that he followed the ridge spoken of until nearly opposite the lower or northern end of the village, when he was furiously attacked by the other warriors who came out to meet him. Others hold that he followed the dry creek down trying to find a crossing place and when near the river was met with such an overwhelming fire that he had to fall back to the ridge which seemed to offer the best chance for a successful defense.
>
> If this last theory is correct, it is the one I have been inclined to believe in, for two reasons. First, General Terry's Report, which says of Custer, . . . "his trail, from the point where Reno crossed the stream, passes along . . .
>
> This description was doubtless due in part to the work of Lieutenant Edward Maguire of the corps of Engineers, who was on General Terry's staff and made a map of the battlefield which was afterwards published by the government.
>
> My second reason is the statement made by the two messengers that Custer dispatched from near the crest of the bluffs, and my inability to believe that he would, after seeing the village close at hand, move his command nearly a mile away from the foe he had so eagerly sought. I am disposed to account for his presence on the ridge by my belief, that after being checked in his attempt to cross the river, and seeing the strength at his front, he believed that by drawing his foes away from the river and village he would render Reno's purpose more successful, and, at the same time, give Benteen, whom he was expecting every moment, a chance to strike the Indians on their flank or cut in between them and their village. This may be merely an idle thought, but it is one that clings closer the more I read and think about the sad affair.[13]

I agree with Taylor in that Custer would not have moved his command away from the "foe", and it is certainly why I don't believe he went down Cedar Coulee. However, by all Indian reports, at first there would have been few Indians at Ford B that would have prevented an attack across the ford into the Indian villages. This was not done, for if it was, the reports of the Indians would have been filled with the account and how they forced them to withdraw. Since Custer knew that Benteen was back on the main trail, and having sent a messenger for him as well as the packs to come to his aid, and if he failed to attack the village because of its size, or the number of Indians facing him or their fire power, he would not have expected that Reno could continue to hold off the Indians while he set up a defense to the north, or by doing so, the Indians would have left Reno so close to their village without continuing to attack him with a large force. I cannot see Custer, in order to wait for Benteen (as so many writers have stated), not attacking at the only time he could possibly have been successful. If Custer had done what Taylor thought he did, and for those reasons he cited, Custer should then have established a better defense than either the evidence or the Indians portray.

> As I stood on this field, which will ever cradle the memory of Custer and his glorious band, . . . I tried to form some idea of the awful sensation which must have come to each of these brave fellows as he realized the horror of the situation; that death awaited every man was evident after the first ten minutes. . . .
>
> . . . Rightfully or otherwise, there was at the time among the enlisted men at least, a deep feeling of resentment against the General. How far this feeling prevailed among the officers, high and low, is not for me to say. Among the men it was felt then that their comrades had been needlessly sacrificed and their own lives put in jeopardy to further ambition. Later on, when more was known in regard to the number of Indians engaged and certain circumstances connected with the affair, the feeling among the men was greatly changed. [Their initial condemnation could be expected, however, the feeling among the officers at Ft. Lincoln appeared to be aimed primarily at Major Reno.]. . .General C. F. Roe [then a Lieutenant] in his story of the Custer Fight, says that Curley, the Crow, was afterwards under his command as a scout, and through an interpreter, gave his account of what occurred with Custer's command. How correct this one, of the many versions that Curley had given is, it is impossible to say, but from his knowledge and experience with the subject, Lieutenant Roe was well fitted to obtain a near approach to the truth.
>
> "Curly says . . . Running down into the Little Bighorn,

to the left on the river, was a high cut bank, some seventy five feet high. Bouyer, Curley, and two or three of the Crows went down, got on that point and looked over into the village. The Cavalry came down the creek by twos. Custer halted his command, went down to the bluff and looked at the village, then went back to the command, which moved down the creek to where it empties into the Little Bighorn.

"After the head of the column reached the river, Curley saw a man on a gray horse, with stripes on his arm, meaning a Sergeant, ride into the river, evidently to see if he could find a ford. At that moment, the Indians opened fire on the column. The head of the column turned back from the river. Custer apparently having made up his mind that they could not cross there, and, as they moved down the river, they motioned to the other troops to break out, so that practically they broke out almost in echelon. Curley ran back and joined the pack train, which was in the rear on Ash Creek. [Greg Martin - No reference has ever been made, that I have seen by anyone connected with the pack train, or the guard (B Troop) accompanying it, of any Crow scouts coming back to them.]

...The gist of the first story told by Curley, as well as that of the three Crows told to Lieutenant Bradley, I believe to be reasonably true. That Mitch Bouyer, the guide and interpreter, Curley and two or three more, of the six Crow scouts rode with Custer's battalion after the division of the Regiment there is no doubt, but that any of them, with the exception of Mitch Bouyer stayed after the first few shots were fired is altogether doubtful, <u>and is not believed by any officer or man who was present on that day</u>. [my underlining][14]

Oscar Wright, who was, for a number of years, the Superintendent at the National Cemetery at Custer's Battlefield, which is quite close to the Crow Indian Reservation, in a letter to the writer, under date of May 1, 1910, speaks of these six Crow scouts.

Mr. Wright continues: "We all believe that Curley, and the three who met General Terry's command, were not in any part of the battle, either with Custer or Reno."[15]

Northeast of the battlefield, and not very far away, lay the foothills of the Little Wolf, or Rosebud Mountains. From their summit there might be obtained by the keen eyed Indians, a fair, and safe view of the ridge where Custer fell. And it was doubtless to these hills that the Crow scouts fled when they saw the overwhelming hordes of Sioux warriors riding out to encircle and destroy Custer's little band. From the shelter of these hills they could work their way northward until they felt it safe to turn to the left and strike for the Bighorn, and then their Agency. This is but a theory, perhaps a mistaken one. But where was Curley for nearly 45 hours after the battle began, and the other three, for, about 16?[16]

The accounts on Curley, by General Roe and Mr. Oscar Wright, are very interesting, enlightening, and supportive. They substantiate, in a general way, what I believe took place with respect to the four Crow scouts that went with Custer. Greg Martin could be wrong that no Crow scout came back and met the pack train. Lt. Mathey indicated, both at the Reno Court and to Walter Camp, that there were several people who met the pack train. In his statement at the Reno Court, he believed the one was a half breed, and, in answer to Lt. Mathey's question whether Custer was whipping them, said that there was just too many Indians.[17] To Walter Camp, Mathey said that he possibly met several.[18] The story Curley told Roe corresponds to the one he told General Scott. In both, he was with the other three Crows when they returned to Ash or Reno Creek. Curley, in the Scott interview, decided to leave the others and go to the Little Bighorn to get water. He also stated that, after leaving, he met the pack train. For Curley to have brought this out in two accounts at different times, to two different officers is more substantiation than one finds in most accepted accounts. Curley also states that the Crows fired into the village, and, in another report, that two men fell into the water. He does mention one trooper crossing into the village, which I assume would have been the Sergeant that Curley mentioned to Roe. White Man Runs Him said Custer's troops fled from the ford, which corresponds to what Captain Hughes revealed in his letter to his wife. Goes Ahead told his wife that Custer was shot at the ford. We know Curley did not join the packs, but said after leaving the packs he moved to the buttes above Reno Creek.

I do believe Curley joined Black Fox near the Little Bighorn and that they met the packs; then, from some point above Reno Creek, saw the last of the fighting on Last Stand Hill. Afterward, the two went toward Busby to find the hardtack that had been left. They then separated. Black Fox returned expecting to meet other Rees, but instead he met the three Crows after they left Reno's troops. The three Crows had met and gone with Benteen to Reno Hill. Either at the time Reno's troops retreated from Weir Point, or possibly as they moved to Weir Point, the three Crows left and saw Black Fox. He told them what had happened with Curley. The Crows, as stated by Goes Ahead, gave him a horse and departed. The following morning, they met Colonel Gibbon's men. Curley, who took a more roundabout route, didn't arrive until later that afternoon. The timing of these arrivals confirms my belief as to what took place; since the steamboat was only eight miles from the Custer battlefield, it shouldn't have taken Curley that long to have arrived if he left Custer at the time and location so many writers have claimed, especially if he was to take a message to Colonel Gibbon.

> That Major Reno should have hesitated to seek out General Custer immediately after his disastrous retreat is not to be wondered at. What acceptable excuse could he offer after such a brief fight in the bottom? No Commander, and General least of all, would be inclined to accept any excuse, for what would have seemed to him, to put it very mildly, as but a half hearted attempt to obey his orders.[19]

Taylor's belief that the fighting in the valley was brief would certainly indicate that the troops should not have been short of ammunition when they reached the hill. This should not be used, as it was, as an excuse for the delay in not going to Custer's aid. It also brings out the feeling that was prevalent concerning the actions of Reno, but was covered-up at the Reno Court.

Accounts written by Indian students at Hampton Indian Institute (Hampton, VA. 1888–1889):

> ... Suddenly, one day about noon, while they were encamped in a long ravine, word was brought that soldiers were marching upon them. The greatest excitement and confusion followed, the women with crying babies on their backs left their tepees and retreated in a very disorderly manner toward a large hill about two miles distant. In the meantime, all the warriors ran for their ponies, and started off to check the advancing enemy... [Reno's men] retreated without order ... Men rode over each other and being frightened themselves, and their horses also, the retreat was made in a very confused unmilitary order...[20]

> [Custer] ... It was early in the afternoon that the attack began. There were four(five) companies of soldiers. They held their ground bravely and fought desperately, knowing that it was the only alternative and resolved to fall fighting to the last. They stood shoulder to shoulder in solid companies and the ranks were broken only by those who were shot. ...The Companies neither made any charge or attempted to fall back. Had General Custer been alive to head his devoted followers, he no doubt would have made fierce charges upon the Indians. I was told last summer by reliable authority that Custer was noted for his fierce and reckless charges during the Civil War.[21]

In the overall accounts written by Hampton Institute Indian students, there is the recognition that Custer's troops were expected to have gone down fighting whereas Reno's left the valley in a panic without having done much fighting. There is no evidence of such determined fighting, and in a consolidated group by Custer's troops. I agree that there would have been a charge noted by the Indians if Custer had been alive; the fact that there wasn't, along with the knowledge that there were few Indians at first near Ford B, certainly supports my belief that Custer was shot at the ford.

Taylor received a letter from John Martini in which he said:

> "When I left General Custer, he was about 200 yards from his command. I could see the Indian village, but not Major Reno's command. I met Boston Custer while I was on my way to join Benteen. He spoke to me, it was about three miles from where I left Custer to where I met Benteen. I was about a half hour, going at a gallop. Mitch Bouyer was at the head of the column when Custer gave me the message. There were also three Crows as I remember."[22]

What I speculate is that this took place when Bouyer left the three Crows to go to Custer. (Bouyer had already told Curley to leave, but he would still have been on the ridge as stated by White Man Runs Him.) Bouyer met Custer some 600 yards from Ford B, just below Bouyer's Bluff. Martin could see the Cheyenne camp from there. Custer would have just received the message that Benteen was back on the main trail. Bouyer would have told Custer about Reno's situation, the size of the Indian encampment, and that the village was breaking up and the Indians scattering to the western foothills. (Reno would still have been fighting in the valley.) Custer realized he wanted Benteen to come to his aid as quickly as possible. He then gave Martin his message to take to Benteen. Custer, with Bouyer by his side, would have moved to the ford. The three Crows on the bluff would have fired on the Indians at the ford or in the village. Curley may also have done so.

If this was true, and I believe it was, then the following needs to be factored into one's analysis of events. If the Crows (three or all four) fired from Bouyer's Bluff at the Indians at the ford or in the village, this would suggest the following took place:

(1) Custer must have continued to Ford B after Bouyer met him, or otherwise the Crows would not have risked firing at the Indians. (2) The Crows would not have left if Custer invaded the village, for they would have wanted to be in on the spoils. In other words, Custer must have retreated before they fled back to Ash Creek. (3) The fact that they were able to flee back to Ash Creek, meet Benteen, go to the ridge, and Reno's troops were still arriving, could only mean that Custer was at Ford B before Reno left the timber. (4) The fact that Trumpeter Mar-

tin saw Reno's troops moving into the timber when he reached the Weir Point location would further substantiate the above. (5) All of this, along with the sighting of Custer on the ridge by Reno's men, would indicate Custer planned on flanking the Indians, and that he was on the ridge before Reno cleared the timber, after crossing Ford A. (6) Custer would not have expected Reno to attack a village, which, in his mind, was apt to hold 1500 warriors, nor leave the packs to be protected by only one company. This suggests that Custer initially expected Benteen, when reaching the Little Bighorn, to back up Major Reno. (7) Overall, it shows that Custer had a sound plan of attack that may have been successful except for the two things I have previously mentioned. First, Benteen failed to cross over to South Fork and move quickly to the Little Bighorn, and down the valley in support of Major Reno. The second, which made the first immaterial even if Benteen would have carried out his orders, was Custer being shot at Ford B. This brought about a disorganized retreat and the destruction of his five companies.

> p. 65: We will now return to General Custer, whose subsequent movements after leaving Reno are but little known. After crossing the divide between the Rosebud and the Little Bighorn, and somewhere about noon, the Regiment had been divided into Battalions....
>
> The two commands, Custer's and Reno's, continued until about 12:30 P.M. when they were within about two miles of the river. Reno was then ordered to "Move forward at as rapid a gait as prudent and charge thereafterwards." Custer soon left the trail and moved squarely to the right, apparently heading for the lower part of the Indian village. His next, and final appearance was on a high point of the bluffs overlooking the river and the Indian camps, a short distance below the point where Reno's command made their hurried and difficult ascent. This occurred while Reno's battalion was charging down the valley and, just before he dismounted, the command to fight on foot. Custer was seen to wave his hat to the charging Battalion, a signal of encouragement and final farewell.
>
> Charging down the valley from the south, and close by, in a line of battle that stretches nearly across the bottom, come a Battalion of Cavalry [G. Martin - three troops] flanked on the left by a number of friendly Indian scouts. On the slope of the bluffs to the right and rear of Custer, perhaps two hundred yards away, and moving in a column of four rapidly to the northward is Custer's own Battalion of cavalry, five troops. [G.M - inexplicably, the author switched, temporarily, to the present tense.]²³

There are several very important points brought out by Taylor. One goes back to the problems of timing. Taylor is going along with the "official" time of the division as presented at the Reno Court; however, he then notes the early time(used after the battle) as indicated by Reno receiving his orders to move against the Indians approximately two miles from Ford A at 12:30 P.M. There is no way the division could have taken place around 12 P.M. and still have the command able to move to within two miles of the Little Bighorn by 12:30 P.M. This should be adequate verification that there was a timing cover-up at the Reno Court.

The sighting of Custer on the ridge as Reno's troops moved down the valley brings out what I consider to be the third major cover-up at the Reno Court. This sighting of Custer would not have taken place if Custer had waited for some message that Reno was being attacked by the Indians. Custer expected Reno to be attacking Indians, so whether they were moving against Reno or Reno was moving against them would have made no difference in Custer's plan of attack. For Reno to have moved down the valley ahead of Custer on the ridge would mean that Custer would have had to have stayed along North Fork for nearly an hour – which in no way correlates with the statements of Trumpeter Martin or Sgt. Kanipe – and the slower Rees would have caught up to the command before they moved to the ridge. The absence of this sighting at the Reno Court illustrates the fact that the Defense realized that admitting to such a sighting would have destroyed Reno's case, for he then would have had no excuse for leaving the timber.

Taylor's last paragraph suggests my belief that Custer went to the ridge ahead of his troops, met Bouyer, observed the valley, met his troops when they came onto the ridge, and then Custer proceeded down the bluffs ahead of his men. These sightings also acknowledge that the troops moved along the bluffs in sight of the valley below and not back from them.

> p. 179: Captain Thomas M. French, Troop M 7th Cavalry was courtmartialed at Fort Lincoln, Dakota in 1879 and sentenced to be dismissed from the service. This was amended to suspension from rank on *half pay, for one year*. ²⁴

p. 183: Roman Rutten Troop M, 7th Cavalry:
> From the ford where we first crossed the river to where we dismounted to "fight on foot" was about 2 1/2 miles. Reno's report says "he did not see Benteen again until about 2:30. At 12:30 (noon) he was 2 miles from the ford, rode fast crossed the river and drove the Indians for 2 1/2 miles . Our rate of speed must have been at least eight miles an hour, and we certainly could not have been fighting dismounted for over 1/2 hour." Sergeant

John Ryan says "about twenty minutes", fifteen minutes was ample time for us to reach the river, and the bluff, no one was disposed to linger on the way. Hence, we should have, and undoubtedly were on the hill at, or very close to 2 o'clock. The Cheyennes say that Reno had been defeated and was on the hill before Custer drew near the river. And they also state that only ten Indians were at the ford, to open (sic) any charge that might have been made.[25]

I believe Rutten's timing is slightly off, if one uses his 12:30 time when Reno received his orders to attack the village. However, the minimum time it would have taken Reno to have reached the ford, crossed, reformed after passing through the timber and be ready to move down the valley would have been forty-five minutes. If Taylor was correct, and they began at a walk, then increased it to a trot and finally, nearing where they set up a skirmish line, they "charged" the Indians, it should have been, at least, 1:30. Whether they moved forward on foot for a hundred yards, as some say, I wouldn't know; but it would have taken some time for them to give their horses to the fourth man, and then set up their skirmish lines. The initial firing which awakened the village was from the Ree scouts. For Wooden Leg to have gone to get his horse, walk back, put on some war paint and then move to where the fighting was – and the troops were still on their skirmish line – then move to the far side before the troops fled from the timber, would have taken a minimum of forty minutes. Reno and the first of his troopers to reach the ridge might have made it there by 2:10.

The important time factor in the above estimates is that Reno was within 2 miles of Ford A by 12:30 P.M. There is no way, as I have said before, that this would be possible if the division of the regiment had taken place at 12:05 P.M. The Cheyenne reported there were only ten Indians at the ford when Custer should have launched an attack. This number of Indians at the ford has been supported by various Indian testimony. We have already brought out enough evidence that Custer reached the ford, so the question is why he didn't attack. There is only one answer that I believe can sustain a comprehensive analysis, and that is Custer was shot at the ford.

SOURCES

1. Hughes, Robert P., Letter to his wife, June 30, 1876. "Captain Robert P. Hughes And The Case Against Custer: An Early Perspective Of The Little Big Horn," – Noyes, C. Lee., *Little Big Horn Newsletter,* p. 6.
2. Nichols, Ronald H., *Reno Court of Inquiry,* p. 468.
3. Camp, Walter, ed. Kenneth Hammer, *Custer in 76,* p. 105.
4. Hughes, Robert P., Letter to his wife, p. 7.
5. Taylor, William O., Forward and published by Greg Martin, Penquin Books, *With Custer On The Little Big Horn–The First – And Only – Eyewitness Account Ever Written,* pp. 31, 32, 33, 34.
6. Ibid., pp. 35, 36.
7. Ibid., p. 36.
8. Ibid., pp. 37, 38.
9. Ibid., pp. 41, 42, p. 47.
10. Ibid., pp. 47, 48.
11. Ibid., pp. 48, 49, 50.
12. Graham, W. A., *The Custer Myth,* p. 307.
13. Taylor, *With Custer On The Little Big Horn,* pp. 70, 71.
14. Ibid., p. 71, p. 77, p. 108.
15. Ibid., p. 109.
16. Ibid., pp. 110, 111.
17. Nichols, Ronald H., *Reno Court of Inquiry,* p. 513.
18. Camp, Walter, *Custer in 76,* p. 78.
19. Taylor, *With Custer On The Little Big Horn,* p. 142.
20. Ibid., pp. 170, 171.
21. Ibid., p. 172.
22. Ibid., p. 177.
23. Ibid., pp. 65, 66.
24. Ibid., p. 179.
25. Ibid., p. 183.

Conclusion

The fundamental unanswered question concerning the Battle of the Little Bighorn is why wasn't there any sign of a major attack by Custer's five companies at Ford B? The absence of an attack has prompted many writers to reject the idea that Custer went to the ford. Consequently, they have been forced to create a number of excuses to explain why Custer did not do so, at a time when any competent commander would have attacked. They have based their conclusions on invalid rationales in which Custer neither attacks, retreats to where he expected aid, or establishes a recognizable defense. If for whatever reason he could not have attacked, and if the five companies were still under the control of General Custer and their company commanders, either a testimonial retreat to where they expected aid from Captain Benteen and the ammunition packs would have taken place, or a defense would have been established and maintained for a longer period of time than the battle actually lasted (according to white and Indian testimony).

From my research, I firmly believe Custer went to Ford B, was shot, and a disorganized retreat ensued. General Custer led Captain Yates's battalion, made up of Companies C, F and E to the ford, after placing Captain Keogh with Companies I and L in reserve. The Indian sighting of Captain Keogh's battalion on Nye Cartwright Ridge, coupled with the quick, disorganized retreat from the ford by Captain Yates' battalion and their eventual attempt to come together on battleridge, caused writers to believe that all five companies had traveled over Nye Cartwright. The fact that there was evidence that some troops had reached or gone toward the ford brought about various scenarios in which Custer sent one or two companies in that direction. There was the natural inclination, which can be seen in accounts from right after the battle, to suggest that Custer established a defense from which he and his five companies bravely fought to the last, until the overwhelming number of Indians finally caused their defeat. The overwhelming number of Indians was certainly responsible at the end; however, the picture of such a defense belies testimony, timing and artifactual evidence. Although I don't pretend that my scenario is correct in every detail, I do believe that my version, if we could go back to that day, would come closer than others to what actually transpired.

A basic conviction that I derived from my study (seemingly not recognized by others) was what I refer to as the three major cover-ups that took place at the Reno Court of Inquiry. Many errors in testimony were distortions due to faulty memory or a desire to protect or discredit certain individuals; but concerning the three major cover-ups, there were outright, deliberate lies which were needed to protect Major Reno, Captain Benteen, the 7th Cavalry, and the desired military image projected by the army hierarchy.

There were other minor cover-ups revolving around questions of varying degrees of importance. One was whether Major Reno should have continued to move against the Indian village as his orders stated. Considering the post-battle knowledge of the size of the village and the number of warriors he would have faced, along with the known decoy practice of the Indians, this violation of his orders did not create any particular problem for the Defense. They stressed the belief that Reno only expected Custer to aid him from the rear, and since he was not in sight, Reno then had to be concerned with his troops' safety. Major Reno felt this safety consideration mandated a move to the ridge above the valley. Even though there were officers who might have disagreed with his decision, it would not be reason enough for court martial charges to be levied against him.

The question of Reno's drinking and its effect on his behavior was another charge which needed officer confirmation or condemnation. Condemnation, the Defense knew would not be forthcoming. The officers, even if they believed that drinking affected Reno's decisions, would not have been expected to support the accusations, for that would have also been an incrimination, even if indirectly, of Captain Benteen and their own actions. Captain Weir and Captain French might have blamed Reno, not only for drinking, but for his unorganized retreat from the timber, his failure to move immediately to aid Custer and an overall lack of courage, but as we know, Weir was dead and French was not summoned to the proceedings. Captain French was undergoing unrelated charges at a distant post, more than likely initiated because of his known views concerning Reno, and the military's desire to prevent him from testifying.

A primary point of contention was: Should Major Reno have stayed in the timber in order to keep pressure on the village? This also would depend on officer's testimony as to their perception of the Indian threat, and if they believed the defensive position could have been maintained under the prevailing conditions and for how long. There were bound to be honest differences of opinion,

CONCLUSION

so the question would not constitute, from this perspective, any insurmountable problems for Major Reno's Defense. However, the issue of whether he should have set up and maintained a defense in the timber was vitally important from other perspectives since it represented the underlying quintessence of the trial, and the basic charges revolved around it. Major Reno's leaving created the necessity for three major cover-ups, the main one being the necessity of obfuscating Custer's orders indicating he would be flanking the Indian villages. The military, represented by Reno's Defense, needed to prevent certain questions from being asked; thus it became necessary for certain participants to lie. As the Prosecution, represented by the recorder, Lieutenant Jesse Lee, later indicated, officers did lie. There would have been certain pertinent, basic and penetrating questions that should have been asked by any prosecutor, but were not. These questions related to Custer's orders, the sighting of his troops on the ridge, and why there were "official" timing differences.

My investigation leaves no doubt in my mind that there were three major cover-ups at the Reno Court of Inquiry which prevented an accurate assessment of the Battle of the Little Bighorn. The desire by the military to avert having court martial charges imposed on Major Reno made it absolutely necessary that Custer's orders, the early sighting of Custer's troops on the ridge, and the time frame be covered up. Since Captain Benteen would also have been charged if Custer's orders were made known, it was easy to gain his support. Lieutenant Wallace, acting itinerast and topographical officer at the time of the battle, would have been the third, and possibly the only other battlefield officer brought into the inner circle for 'behind the scenes' strategy sessions. In my assessment, the Defense must have recognized the need for, and so developed the stratagems which required lying about Custer's orders, ignoring early sightings of Custer on the ridge, and distorting the "official" time of the division of the command. Wallace had to be brought into this inner circle because he would not only have known about the orders Custer issued and the time they were given, but also the early sighting of Custer on the ridge.

Custer's instructions were the focus of the essential cover-up. This deception, combined with Captain Benteen's earlier denunciation of Custer's lack of knowledge concerning the location of the Indian villages as well as the number of Indians he would be facing, portrayed an extremely incompetent Custer. Benteen's charges have too often been accepted by students of the battle. If the contents of the orders were accurately represented by Private Davern, Reno's orderly; and by Trumpeter Martin, Custer's orderly; as well as the statements made by Privates Donahue and O'Neil, they would have revealed a competent Custer (which I believe he was), and necessitated that court martial charges be brought not only against Major Reno but also Captain Benteen. The two orderlies were in a position to have heard the orders, and their testimony basically coincided with the two privates, who said they understood that Benteen was to support Reno when he reached the Little Bighorn, while Custer would flank the Indians. This is substantial proof that these were Custer's directives. Since the privates would have no actual knowledge or involvement with the formulation of the stratagems devised by the Defense, it further corroborates that these were Custer's initial orders. The fact that Lieutenant Gibson was not invited to the hearings would also signify a cover-up, for Gibson was the one person who would have known what Captain Benteen's instructions were. Then basic logic takes over: If these were the orders and they were admitted to by Reno and Benteen, would they have been subject to a court martial? The answer is obvious. Reno would have known Custer planned on flanking the Indians and he should not have left the timber. If these were the orders delivered by Sergeant Major Sharrow, or possibly a third courier, to Benteen, then his move back to the trail by Valley 3 (also referred to as No Name Creek), the time spent at the morass, his slowness in attempting to reach the Little Bighorn - which continued even after receiving Trumpeter Martin's message to hurry and join Custer - were inexcusable actions that would have led to court martial charges being levied against him.

The sighting of Custer's troops on the ridge by Reno's men as they moved down the valley had to have been well known. The Defense would realize this required a warning to the Prosecution (under overall military control) not to ask the officers any penetrating questions pertaining to such early sightings, as well as directions to the officers not to mention having seen Custer on the ridge during the move down the valley. If they did, it would have been hard for Reno to deny knowing that Custer was planning on flanking the Indians (later sightings were permissible, in fact desired, as long as Major Reno would not have been aware of them). If he had known about the early sightings (and I am sure he did), or the later ones, there is little chance they could have defended his leaving the timber, particularly at that time and under the existing circumstances.

After Captain Benteen's battalion joined forces with what was left of Major Reno's, I don't see how any objective analysis could maintain that Reno, Benteen and Wallace didn't hear gunfire coming from what had to have been Custer's two battalions. Why were they the only officers who apparently didn't hear gunfire? Was there collusion? If so, what motivated the conspiracy? Was it because the Defense realized that if shots had been heard, it would have made it that much more difficult to justify the late decision to investigate? Even with the main conspirators' failure to hear the gunfire, timing still required a third major cover-up. The question the Defense faced was how they could accomplish it.

The time Major Reno's forces moved to investigate the firing was fairly well documented as occurring after 5 P.M. If the defense was to use the July, 1876, "official" time submitted by Reno for the division of the command, the passing of the Lone Tepee, and receiving his attack orders, there would have been roughly a 3 hour time delay between Benteen's arrival on Reno Hill and their move to investigate the gunfire. There is no way this time interval could have been justified. The Defense needed to come up with a rational excuse. They could not stretch the time Reno fought in the valley (certain writers believe the time accepted is too long and represents a cover-up). Even with their lengthening of the distance traveled during Benteen's scout to the left - while stressing its difficulty, the need to wait for the packs and ammo, and the extension of the distance the packs were trailing - the time taken could not be increased to where it justified Reno's late move, using the "official" division of the command as portrayed in documents and statements made after the battle. This "official" time correlated with that used by the Indian scouts, the Sioux, Cheyenne, and the orderlies, Private Davern and Trumpeter Martin. An "official" time change had to be made. I believe the cover-up is very apparent, when examining the Court records. If there wasn't a cover-up, why weren't there questions and a demand for explanations concerning the dichotomy of "official" timing? The threat of a court martial charges against Major Reno and Captain Benteen would have been apparent to the Defense, if this time lapse could not have been modified. One might ask: What other way could the Defense have shortened this period between Benteen's arrival on the ridge and their move downstream, except by changing the "official time"?

The cover-up of orders, the early sighting by Reno's troops of Custer on the ridge, and the time change, have had many other ramifications on how the battle has been viewed. One of the most important is the "event-time-event" relationship between what Custer and Reno were doing. It shows that Custer's five companies were in action before Reno's troops retreated from the timber. If the orders, the sighting and the timing change were cover-ups, and the actual truth is what I have outlined, and the testimony confirms, then Reno and Benteen would have been blamed for the demise of Custer's five companies. This would have led to a court-martial that the army would not have wanted, which in their view justified the distortions and lies. The end justifies the means.

Many writers and commentators do not contend that Custer attacked at the ford, at a time when Indian testimony indicates he could have. When analyzed, this portrays Custer not only as inane, but lacking in courage. For him to have delayed an attack because he was waiting for Benteen, as so many have claimed, only adds to that perspective. This goes against his record and his psyche. If you examine the questions asked and not asked at the Reno Court of Inquiry concerning Custer's orders, his being sighted on the ridge, and the timing, you can easily discern how they reveal a concealment of the truth. One should then relate the effect these cover-ups have had on the common perceptions of the battle. Although many of his admirers do not seem to realize it - since their main concern appears to be showing Custer went down fighting to the last - this image has led to the denigration and degradation of Custer's character, and ability as an individual and a commander.

The following points outline a general but plausible scenario of the actions Custer planned or performed:

1. Custer planned to flank the Indians when he divided his command. The only variables were whether Benteen encountered Indians during his mission, and whether Custer was attacked while moving down Ash Creek.
2. Custer sent Benteen orders just before, or at the time, he issued his attack orders to Major Reno. The orders instructed Benteen to continue to the Little Bighorn and, if he had not located any Indians, to move down the valley in support of Major Reno. The orders to Reno and Benteen were the subject of the primary cover-up associated with the battle.
3. Reno knew that Custer planned to support him with a flanking movement, and that Benteen would also be expected to come to his aid.
4. Reno took much longer than is usually estimated to reach Ford A, cross, and reform before he was ready to charge down the valley.
5. Custer delayed his flanking movement because he was waiting to hear from Benteen. Finally he had to gamble on Benteen, and so made his move to the ridge.

6. Custer's move to flank the Indians was part of his plan, and was not prompted by any message from Girard via Cooke. In fact, Girard never carried any message, and Cooke never went to the ford with Reno.
7. Reno hadn't set up his skirmish line when the van of Custer's five companies began their move off the ridge.
8. Custer viewed the Indian village from Weir Point.
9. Custer moved down the "Gorge" or Middle Coulee to Medicine Tail Coulee.
10. As he moved down Medicine Tail Coulee, Custer received word that Benteen was back on the main trail. He then sent Trumpeter Martin with a message.
11. At that time or before, Custer placed Captain Keogh's battalion in reserve and sent them to Nye Cartwright Ridge.
12. Custer moved to Ford B while Reno was still on his skirmish line or had just moved into the timber.
13. Three and possibly four of the Crow scouts fired on the village from the bluff above the ford at the time Custer was moving toward it.
14. Custer was shot at the ford, Captain Yates' battalion retreated, the four Crows left and moved back beyond Reno Hill.
15. Curley left the three Crows to get water and met Black Fox. The other three Crows met Benteen and went to the ridge with him.
16. The retreat of Yates' battalion was disorganized and moved to the north under slight Indian pressure.
17. Keogh's battalion moved off Nye Cartwright to Battleridge, and fired on the Indians in an attempt to support the retreating Yates' battalion.
18. Only sporadic defenses were set up, and none of them were coordinated.
19. The Indians that returned after attacking Reno, coupled with those Indians already fighting Custer's companies, soon overran and destroyed them.
20. There were attempts to escape and many troopers committed suicide. Others, such as Sergeant Butler, fought until they succumbed.

These are the essential components derived from my study. Many of these points have not been understood or accepted. However, they are the only explanation which logically solve the mystery of why Custer didn't attack with his five companies. If you accept the underlying doctrine that Custer was a competent commander, with both the experience and courage necessary to lead a regiment of men, this summation of the events is a reasonable deduction of what Custer's actions encompassed. This scenario not only coincides with Custer's psyche and known ability, but has the corroborating testimony to make it a sound hypothesis.

Appendix 1: Time Table

1:20–1:35   Major Reno starts down the valley. Custer's troops seen on ridge. General Custer is on Weir Point.

1:35–1:40   Custer and lead troops move off ridge. Sgt. Kanipe sent back to packs. Reno moving to where he will set up a skirmish line. Captain Benteen at or near Lone Tepee.

1:40–2:00   Reno has established his skirmish line. Lt. Varnum sees Gray Horse Troop as they are leaving the ridge. Custer's roops pass down Middle Coulee, except for rear guard. Custer enters MedicineTail Coulee. Rees have captured Lacotah ponies and are moving toward cliffs. Slower trailing Rees have reached the ridge; Stabbed most likely gives message to rear guard. Rear guard fires on Rees driving Lacotah ponies. Kanipe meets Benteen, goes with message to Captain McDougall. A member of the rear guard or a courier inform Custer that Benteen is back on the main trail. Trumpeter Martin is sent back. Captain Keogh is placed in reserve.

2:00–2:25   Reno has moved into the timber. Custer is shot at the ford. CaptainYates' battalion halts. Commanders Yates, Custer and Smith move forward to check on General Custer, and to decide their next move. Indians leaving camp to fight Reno are turning back to Ford B. Martin sees Reno's troops entering the timber. Crow scouts flee Bouyer's Bluff toward Reno Hill and Ash Creek. Yates' battalion begins an unorganized withdrawal from Ford B. Near Weir Point, Curley passes rear guard and Rees with ponies. Other Crows are moving on east side of ridge, and join Curley near Reno Hill. Reno's battalion leaves timber. Martin meets Benteen.

2:25–2:45   Reno and some of his troops have reached Reno Hill; others are still retreating from the valley. The four Crows come across Red Bear and White Cloud; the Crows leave. Curley goes for water while other Crows meet Red Star and then Benteen. Benteen moves to hill. Most of Reno's troops have reached top of hill or are on ridge below. Many of Yates' battalion on foot and firing on Indians from Deep Coulee, Greasy Grass and West Calhoun Ridge. Some members retreat toward Keogh's command, while the main element moves to cemetery area. Bugle attempts are unable to reorganize companies. Keogh's battalion moving across Deep Coulee in support of the retreating Yates' battalion. Indians have left Reno because they have heard about the new threat from Custer's troops, and some have seen Keogh's battalion as they move across Nye Cartwright Ridge. Reno's and Benteen's troops have heard firing from Custer battlefield area. Most likely the volleys heard were from Greasy Grass or West Calhoun Ridge.

2:45–3:00   Keogh's battalion attempts to hold off Indians arriving from Reno fight. Rear concentrating on Custer's five companies. Packs arriving on Reno Hill. Troops hear gunfire from downriver. Yates' men below Last Stand Hill and near present Cemetery Area see Keogh's battalion moving to Battleridge and attempt to join them. Indians are now thick on all sides of troops. Companies are not under the control of company commanders, except for Captain Keogh and Lieutenant Calhoun.

3:00–3:30   Members, mainly of E Troop, flee ridge to near Deep Ravine. Indians overrun Calhoun's and Keogh's companies. All Indians now attacking Custer's troops. Crazy Horse and Joseph White Bull ride through remaining soldiers on Battle Ridge. Indians storm Last Stand Hill. Battle is over. Confusion exists on Reno Hill.

3:30– . . .   Non-combatant Indians join warriors on the battlefield. Wounded soldiers are killed, some bodies mutilated, shoot arrows into bodies, strip soldiers, take guns and ammunition, put on uniforms, fire guns, etc.

APPENDIXES

4:20–6:00   Captain Weir moves to contact Custer. His company follows. They see Indians still going over battlefield firing new guns, and a general celebration. Reno's other troops follow; some companies reach Weir Point and move to defensive position. Indians start toward them. Companies are ordered to retreat back to Reno Hill.

. . . –7:00   All companies reach Reno Hill and are setting up defensive positions. Indians surrounding them. Reno entrenchment battle follows.

Appendix 2

Part A: An examination of Major Reno's and Captain Benteen's statements, following the battle, with those made at the Reno Court.

Part B: How Trumpeter Martin's questioning, at the Reno Court, shows the bias of the Court in favor of dismissing the charges against Major Reno.

PART A:

One of the more interesting analysis any writer concerned with the Battle of the Little Big Horn should make is a comparison of communiques and letters made right after the battle by the two remaining battalion leaders, Major Reno and Captain Benteen, with their statements and writings that took place later. After the battle, realizing that General Custer and his five companies had been killed, what rationalizations of their actions would you expect them to have made? I think one could expect there would be an attempt to excuse their failure to immediately have gone to the aid of Custer and his men. However, the full extent of the furor, the accusations, and the searching for a scapegoat that swept the country and later resulted in the Reno Court of Inquiry would not have been realized by either participant right after the battle.

Major Reno:

What could Major Reno have desired to cover-up, and were there any glaring differences between statements he made after the battle and those made at the Reno Court?

The most obvious differences that stand out were Reno's timing estimates. These are readily apparent when reading from his official communique to the office of General Terry on July 5, 1876 and later timing used at the Reno Court of Inquiry. In his official communique Reno indicated they crossed the divide by 8 A.M., and since Indians had been seen, the division of the command took place. This would have been some four hours earlier than the Reno Court time of after 12 P.M. used for the division of the command. Reno's early time estimate could be off somewhat, but not four hours. Other earlier time statements used by Reno differed dramatically from those he later used. Particularly noteworthy are the 11 A.M. arrival at the Lone Tepee; 12:30 when he received his orders to attack; and the 2:30 P.M. time when he and Captain Benteen met on the ridge. The question for the writer to answer is why the differences? The answer for me is clear. How were they to explain what they were doing between 2:30 P.M. and at least 5 P.M. before going to aid Custer? From Reno saying, "We heard firing in that direction and knew it could only be Custer," to not having heard gunshots by the time of the Reno Court. Even waiting for the packs and the need for ammunition could not account for such a delay. Wouldn't Reno have realized the military would have expected him to immediately have gone to the aid of Custer, particularly since Captain Benteen's three companies had not seen any action?

What were other concerns Major Reno would most likely have been aware of and have wanted to cover-up? Couldn't we agree that he knew, from a military standpoint, that not attacking the Indian encampment, or certainly his leaving the timber and the way it was done, would be questioned? Also, wasn't there already the question, in the minds of officers and men, whether he or Captain Benteen was really in charge after they met on Reno Hill? In his official communique, Reno attempted to leave no doubt that he was in charge of the decisions to go to the aid of Custer, to return, setting up the defense, and his overall control of the fighting that ensued.

What Major Reno's orders were and how he attempted to carry them out would certainly be of primary importance in his communiques. In stating his orders, Reno said he was to be supported by the whole outfit, but does not say how. He needed to, and does attempt to, portray that he carried his orders out expeditiously. I definitely believe that, following the battle, he realized that he must not say he knew Custer was planning on flanking the Indians, for this would mean he should have either continued his attack on the village or not have left the timber. I differ with most others in that I believe Reno's initial attack orders indicated he would be supported by not only a flanking attack by General Custer but that Captain Benteen, if he did not find any Indians to the south, when reaching the Little Big Horn, would move in support of Major Reno. I cannot believe that although Reno's enlisted men, when moving down the valley, saw General Custer and his troops on the ridge, Major Reno and the other officers were not aware of them. As I stated, Major Reno realized he could not admit to knowing Custer was planning a flanking attack; however, one does not find in his or Captain Benteen's accounts written right after the battle that they only expected Custer to support Reno by fol-

359

lowing him into battle. This view appeared later. Major Reno's letter to General Terry written on June 27th said, "but <u>meeting</u> no support was forced back into the hills." (my underlining) Meeting does not infer that he expected his support from the rear but it does infer support from the front, or in other words, a flanking attack. I realize one should not rest the case on a one word semantic; however, I believe it does support Reno's recognition that Custer was attempting to flank the Indians. The fact that enlisted men seemed to have seen Custer, but the officers didn't, to me, is added proof of a cover-up. Major Reno should have realized by the time of his official communique, that he could not admit to knowing Custer was planning to flank the Indians, for he would not have had any military justification for leaving the timber. Compounding the picture against Reno would be the fact that at the time they retreated to the ridge they had not yet been attacked while in the timber by the Indians, nor had Reno lost any number of men.

Reno's use of the word <u>meeting</u>, in his urgent message of the 27th to General Terry, besides inferring a flanking attack as the support promised, would also imply that he had, along with his troops, seen Custer on the ridge some thirty minutes before he left the timber. The implication of this time lapse was then applied at the Reno Court with Lt. Varnum's sighting of Troop E on the ridge near Weir Point. It was used as justification for Reno's decision to leave the timber. Reno's defense brought out time and again that Reno only expected support from the rear; however, Varnum's sighting indicated Custer (whom everyone now knew had attempted to flank the Indians) had plenty of time to have attacked the Indian village while Reno was still fighting in the valley. This was not justification for Reno's leaving the timber, however, as Reno's Defense made sure the Court realized, Reno was not aware of Varnum's, or any other sighting, and they continued to stress that Reno <u>only</u> believed that Custer was planning on supporting him from the rear. Reno, of course, had no idea of where Benteen was, or his orders. Since Custer was not in sight and Reno's orders <u>only</u> said he would be supported, and there had been plenty of time for that to have happened, it left Reno with the decision to do what was best for his men. He believed the odds were too great and that he could not hold out in the timber. He would have to "charge" the Indians and attempt to reach the ridge and a more defensible position, which he then did.

Reno must certainly have realized this "charge" was not conducted as military tactics would have supported. It was necessary for Reno's Defense to emphasize, and find support for, his belief the timber could not be defended for any period of time, and, of course, the "charge" should be led by the commanding officer. Reno must also have realized that his conduct and his control of the troops, once they had gained the ridge and met Captain Benteen, was in question. This need to stress that he was in control can be seen in all of his statements. On the other hand, any complete objective analysis of officer or enlisted men's accounts would deny his assertions. To what extent Captain Benteen took over would be the only question.

Orders, sighting, and timing are primary questions any writer should be concerned with, Reno's conduct would be of a major concern primarily as it relates to Custer's orders and why there was a need for timing changes.

Captain Benteen:

In many ways, following the battle, Captain Benteen would have had more need to defend his actions than Major Reno. But, from his letters to his wife, it appeared he realized that he was considered the hero of the battle (which in many ways he was), so his writings didn't reflect his later angry accusations against General Custer. Many of these later writings and statements made at the Reno Court became vehement, rambling, disoriented and incoherent. To me, Benteen, after the battle, became increasingly aware of his failures rather than just the fact he was credited with saving Reno's forces and the recognized hero of the Reno entrenchment battle. He began to realize that he hadn't moved as fast as he could have on his excursion to the left, nor after receiving the messages carried by Sgt. Kanipe and Trumpeter Martin. As I have previously stated, I think the orders Custer gave were more extensive than either Major Reno or Captain Benteen <u>could admit to.</u> Benteen knew that outside of presenting to Reno the written orders from Custer delivered by Martin, there was no immediate attempt to question or be concerned for Custer or to carry out the orders he had received. And whether, in his subconscious or not, there would have been a recognition that underlying his failures to act was his dislike for General Custer. Possibly, at the time, he also felt justified in staying with Reno because he believed he could say that since his original orders were to support Reno, and because of Reno's condition and his belief that Custer could defend himself, his actions would be excused. In this same sense, Benteen, in realizing the military brass was not too happy with Custer, may have thought his disobeying orders would have been overlooked. However, after realizing and reflecting on the outcome of the battle, he could not have failed to recognize that if they had gone immediately to aid Custer that many of Custer's five companies may have been saved. I believe this is why one finds so many irrational remarks by Benteen - not immediately following the battle, but after the furor surrounding the battle became a paramount concern throughout the nation, and Benteen had time to reflect on his own actions. Benteen was too capable a military man not to recognize his errors and the effect they may have had. One could say his guilt made him flay out at the one he not only disliked but that he could blame, which was Custer. The explicit order from Custer, carried by Trumpeter Martin, made it necessary for him to also blame Martin for his failure to recognize the urgency of the message, and so go immediately to the aid of Custer. And as time went on he began to believe his own rationalizations.

Benteen was faced with the need to justify his slowness on the trail and why it took so long to move to aid Custer once he met Reno on the ridge. It became necessary by the time of the Reno Court to concur with Reno's claims concerning his control and conduct - support which so surprised Captain Carter and others.

Why were his actions more difficult to justify than Major Reno's? Foremost would be the fact that he had been the recipient of two messages sent by Custer stating that he needed immediate aid. Could one really say that Major Reno's rank or his predicament justified Benteen in ignoring his commanding officer's orders? Benteen had to have known that the period between when he met Reno on the ridge and when they moved to investigate the gunfire could not rationally be excused. It became necessary to blame his actions on the man he hated. Custer had sent him on a "wild goose" chase to the left. Custer did not even know where, or if, there was an Indian encampment. Custer divided his troops at a time they should have remained united. Benteen said he believed the Indian scouts, both as to where the Indian camp was, and the number of Indians they would be going against - Custer didn't. Custer didn't notify either Reno or himself as to what actions he planned to take. It was necessary to wait for the packs in order to obtain needed ammunition before moving to aid Custer, and the packs were miles behind.

Questions that come to mind: Shouldn't Benteen have hurried the packs when he received the message from Sgt. Kanipe? Didn't Kanipe tell Benteen that Custer wanted Captain McDougall to not only hurry the pack train to Custer but to cut across country and not follow the trail? Wouldn't he have told Benteen of Captain Tom Custer's addition to his orders that if he saw Benteen to tell him to come quick? This would mean that Benteen also shouldn't follow the trail but would be expected to cut straight across country. The way both Sgt. Kanipe's and Trumpeter Martin's messages were given or worded would certainly imply a knowledge, by not only Captain Benteen but Major Reno, that they were aware of Custer's plan to surround the Indian villages. If Benteen didn't already know, wouldn't Custer's messages have said something to the effect that he had moved to the north in an attempt to flank the Indians? Wouldn't Custer, if Benteen hadn't already known, have said Major Reno is attacking the Indian camp by way of the valley, but I want you to cut across country and support my attack? Wouldn't Custer more than likely have said this particularly, if his original plans had been to follow Reno into battle? In other words, the inference is that Custer needed to change an earlier order that had Benteen crossing the Little Big Horn in support of Reno. Custer was not only interested in his scouts reporting to him but in making sure his battalion commanders received and knew their orders. Reno's and Benteen's criticism that they didn't know what Custer planned was necessary for their own protection. I would surmise that Captain McDougall and Lt. Mathey had orders that once the packs neared the Little Big Horn they should wait for further orders. This is probably why Lt. Mathey spoke of a fifteen minute wait. In other words, the questions a writer should ask, and the answers I believe they would arrive at, support my belief that Benteen had to have received orders (by the Sgt. Major or a third courier) indicating Reno was being sent across the Little Big Horn to attack the Indian villages, that Benteen should cross the Little Big Horn and support him; and Custer would be attempting to flank the Indians. Custer, by the time he sent Kanipe with his message to McDougall, knew that he didn't want the packs to attempt to cross the Little Big Horn or to hold in that area, but to cut across and aid his flanking attack. On his excursion to the left, Benteen had been expected to reach the Little Big Horn and support Major Reno; however, when Custer knew he was some distance back on the main trail and now knew the location of the Indian village, one doesn't have to be a military genius to realize Custer would have wanted Benteen to come quickly and support his attack, and to hurry up the packs who should have already been moving in Custer's direction.

Did Martin's message for Benteen to hurry to Custer's aid and bring the packs solicit the desired reaction? If one was to go by Benteen's later statements that the packs were some distance back, shouldn't this have created an even greater urgency to hurry the packs? Undoubtedly yes, but, it didn't for Benteen. He said the packs were not his immediate concern, and they were in no danger from the Indians as they were protected by Benteen's battalion troop position. According to Benteen, he did not even send Martin or anyone else back to the packs with a hurry-up message. What sort of an answer was this? Custer wasn't worried about the packs' protection; what he wanted was the ammo in a position to aid his attack. Benteen's excuse and explanation for not hurrying to Custer's aid was Trumpeter Martin's response to what was taking place between Custer and the Indians. Benteen said Martin had told him the Indians were "skeddaddling" so it was not necessary to move at a faster pace or hurry to his aid. Martin saw Reno being faced by hundreds of Indian warriors and Reno's troops moving into the timber: if he used the word "skedaddling", or one of a similar meaning, it would have been in connection with the fact that Martin saw the Indian non-combatants fleeing from the villages. Indian scattering was a major worry of any army attack, so "skedaddling" should not have been a reason for Benteen not to have hurried. Since there was no denying that Benteen's battalion arrived shortly after Reno reached the ridge, and although by the time of the Reno Court, both Benteen and Reno had decided it was best not to have heard any amount of firing that would have caused concern for Custer's ability to defend himself, they still needed better reasons for their delay. The need for ammunition, and therefore the necessity to wait for the packs became the acceptable excuse. Though enlisted men and the packers indicated the packs arrived shortly after Benteen's troops, these reports had to be denied by the two major officers. Major Reno's and Captain Benteen's Defense had the packs miles behind, and even though Benteen's troops had their full supply of ammo, they could not leave Reno and the wounded. Even by creating all these necessities it was still too long a period before they went to aid Custer. What then? The time had to be changed. The division of the troops didn't take place until at least 2 hours later than earlier estimates; Benteen didn't get back on the main trail by 1 P.M. as he first stated; and no matter what time Benteen met Reno, the packs didn't arrive until after 4 P.M.

What I believe the reports following the battle bring out is that the orders received by both Reno and Benteen were more extensive then they could admit. That if Reno had only expected support from the rear, this would have been mentioned in his early reports instead of the inference and the recognition that Custer was attempting to flank the Indians. Captain Benteen, even if he hadn't known before, would definitely have known, from both Sgt. Kanipe's report and Trumpeter Martin's message, that Custer was executing a flanking attack. Any analysis of events on the 24th and 25th would substantiate that Custer knew the general location of the Indian encampment and that he would be facing at least 1500 warriors. The earlier timing when Reno's attack would have occurred, coincides with initial Indian accounts. What this brings out is that any investigation of reports made by the two primary figures following the battle and their later reports should revolve around orders, sightings, timing and a recognition of Reno's and Benteen's need to rationalize and cover-up these essential points.

PART B:

The most damaging evidence that the Reno Court of Inquiry was not impartial in their Inquiry of Major Reno, and, I believe, substantiates that there was an intentional cover-up by the Court of the orders Custer gave, can be seen in their interrogation of Trumpeter Martin. If there was one person, besides the three officers, Major Reno, Captain Benteen, and Lt. Wallace, who knew the orders given by Custer, it was Martin. It is understandable that the court would not have wanted Martin to become part of the Defense's inner stratagem circle, and believed, if necessary, they could discredit his testimony. The inner circle most likely would not have included any more officers than the three I have mentioned. However, the military knew Martin was the one person who could destroy Major Reno's Defense, and have even necessitated an indictment of Benteen. They warned Martin that he need not disclose everything that he knew, and later, I believe, pressured him to take back his answer that he took a message to Captain McDougall. His interrogation was a monumental farce, and, is the most damaging evidence against the Reno Court in recognizing that they were not attempting to determine the truth, but only to acquit Reno of the charges against him.

The basic determination of whether the Reno Court was impartial would be how they examined the underlying question of whether Custer's orders to Major Reno only said he would be supported without saying how. Captain Benteen, as could be expected, corroborated Reno by saying Custer had no plan. Shouldn't Custer's orders then have been the main focus of the questions asked of Martin? Shouldn't the Prosecution's primary concern have been in determining from someone other than Major Reno or Captain Benteen what knowledge, if any, there was of Custer's plans to flank the Indian villages and support Reno? Here again, the one person to ask was

Trumpeter Martin. When Martin just happened to say, in his testimony, that Custer gave an order to Benteen, what was the "so-called" Prosecution's reaction? Did the recorder, 1st Lt. Jesse M. Lee, attempt to find out the message? No; instead he jumped quickly to the written order that Martin received some time later from Custer. Again and again the questions concerned topography, distance and timing, and were asked in such a convoluted way as to mix up and discredit Martin. Although none of the witnesses were consistent as to timing or distance, Martin's answers were used as the Court excuse for dismissing him. Yet this was the man who could have cleared up the basic question of the inquiry; however, at the same time, he could have caused the court to render a guilty charge against Major Reno, and more than likely an indictment of Captain Benteen. Wouldn't this lack of questioning as to orders indicate the Court's fear, and more than likely their prior knowledge that Custer's orders, if revealed in there entirety, would show Custer not only planned a flanking attack, but expected initially for Benteen to have aided Reno?

The interrogation of Trumpeter Martin is the best evidence that the Reno Court was not attempting to determine whether Major Reno was guilty of the charges levied against him; instead it showed that their only concern was how to circumvent and dismiss those charges. The realization that the Court's aim was not to find out what actually happened that day should be recognized since Reno Court testimony has been used extensively in judging and condemning Custer's actions.

I will attempt to carry this line of thinking one step further in order to emphasize its importance and logic. Let us assume you were an <u>impartial</u> Prosecutor of Major Reno, and your witness was Trumpeter Martin. You know that Martin was the last white man to have seen Custer alive, that he was his orderly and had been riding next to him, and that he more than likely had heard the various messages Custer had given and received: What would be some of the questions you would ask? They would probably include some of the following: When was the Sgt. Major sent with a message to Captain Benteen? What was the message? Did Custer send any messages to Benteen at the time he gave Major Reno his attack orders? If so, what were they and who carried the messages? What were the attack orders Custer gave to Major Reno? Did those orders indicate that he was planning on flanking the Indians? Did Private McIlhargey deliver a message from Reno to Custer? If so, when and where did Custer receive the message? Do you know if Adjutant Cooke was expected to do anything more than deliver an attack message to Major Reno? Do you know if Captain Keogh went with Adjutant Cooke, and if so why? When did they report back to Custer? What was their message? As a Prosecutor attempting to find whether Reno was guilty of charges of misconduct, wouldn't you have asked Martin some of these questions? Why do you believe they were not asked? Martin gave important answers concerning the location of the packs and timing, but since Martin's answers were contrary to the desired position of the court, they proceeded to ignore them or allow Benteen's denials to suffice. Since Martin's answers as to the location of the packs were direct and spontaneous, his later claims that the court misinterpreted him would appear to reflect either military pressure (as I previously stated), or his own realization of the adverse affect they had on Captain Benteen's claims and actions.

Martin's questioning was brief, and with his dismissal the court was able to accomplish its objective and dismiss the charges against Major Reno. However, from a historical standpoint, the Courts motives and partiality was extremely damaging, for Martin was the one person – if asked the right questions – who could have shed light on what actually happened on the 25th of June, 1876. Since the right questions were not asked of him at the time or later on, we now can only speculate on the answers.

Bibliography

Government Documents

House of Representatives, Ex. Doc. No. 184, 44th Congress, lst Session. Military Expedition against the Sioux Indians.
Secretary of War – Annual Report, 1876 (44th Congress - 2nd Session).
Report on Indian Affairs, 1875.
Report of the Commissioner of Indian Affairs, 1876.

Books

Barnard, Sandy. *Digging Into Custer's Last Stand.* Terre Haute: AST Press, 1986.
Barnett, Louise, *Touched By Fire,* Henry Holt and Company, Inc., 1996.
Brady, Cyrus Townsend. *Indian Fights and Fighters.* Lincoln, Nebraska, 1971.
Brininstool, E. A., *Troopers With Custer.* New York, 1952.
Brown, Dee. *Bury My Heart At Wounded Knee.* New York, 1952.
Camp, Walter. *Custer in 76.* Ed. by Kenneth Hammer, Provo, Utah,1976.
Chiaventone, Frederick, J., *A Road We Do Not Know,* Simon & Schuster, 1996.
Connell, Evan S. *Son of the Morning Star.* Harper & Row, 1984.
Crow, Joseph Medicine. *From The Heart of Crow Country, The Crow Indians' Own Series.* Orion Books, N.Y. 1992.
Darling, Roger. *Benteen's Scout-to-the-Left.* El Segundo, Calif., Upton & Sons, 1987.
_____. *General Custer's Final Hours.* Potomac Western Press, Inc., 1992
du Bois, Charles G., *Kick the Dead Lion.* 1961.
_____. *The Custer Mystery.* El Segundo, Upton & Sons, 1985.
Dustin, Fred. *The Custer Tragedy.* Ann Harbor, Mich., Edwards Brothers, 1939.
Ege, Robert J. *Curse Not His Curls.* Ft. Collins, Colorado, 1974.
Ellison, Douglas W. *Sole Survivor.* North Plains Press, Aberdeen, S. D. 1983
Evans, David C., *Custer's Last Fight: The Story of the Battle of the Little Big Horn,* Battle of the Little Big Horn Series, Vol. 1, Upton and Sons, El, Segundo, California, 1999.
Fox, Jr., Richard Allan. *Archaeology, History & Custer's Last Battle.* University of Oklahoma Press, Norman, 1993.
Frost, Lawrence, A. *The Custer Album.* University of Oklahoma Press, Norman, 1964
Godfrey, Edward S. *Custer's Last Campaign.*
Goodman, Ron. *Lakota Star Knowledge.* Sinte Glaska College, 1992

Graham, W. A. *The Custer Myth: A Source Book of Custeriana.* Harrisburg, Stackpole Company, l953.
_____. *The Story of the Little Big Horn, Custer's Last Fight.* New York, Century Company, 1926.
_____, ed. *Abstract of the Official Proceedings of the Reno Court of Inquiry.* Harrisburg: 1954.
Gray, John S. *Centennial Campaign.* Fort Collins, Colorado, 1976
_____. *Custer's Last Campaign.* University of Nebraska Press, 1991.
Greene, Jerome A. *Evidence and the Custer Enigma.* Golden: Outbooks Inc., 1973, reprinted 1986.
_____. *Lakota and Cheyenne, Indian Views of the Great Sioux Wars, 1876-1877.* University of Oklahoma Press, Norman, 1994.
Grinnell, George Bird. *The Fighting Cheyenne.* New York, 1915.
Hans, Fred M., *The Great Sioux Nation,* Ross & Haines, Inc., Minneapolis, Minnesota, Reprinted 1964.
Hardorff, Richard G. *Markers, Artifacts & Indian Testimony.* Short Hills, Don Horn Publications, 1985.
Hinman, Eleanor H. *Oglala Sources on the Life of Crazy Horse.* 1976.
Hofling, Charles K. *Custer and the Little Big Horn: A Psychobiographical Inquiry.* Detroit, 1981.
Hoig, Stan. *The Battle of the Washita.* Lincoln, Univ. of Nebraska Press, 1976.
Hunt; Frazier. *I Fought with Custer: The Story of Sergeant Windolph as told to Frazier and Robert Hunt.* New York, Charles Scribner & Sons, 1947.
Hyde, George. *Red Cloud's Folk, A History of the Oglala Sioux Indians.* Univ. of Oklahoma, 1937.
Kidd, J. H. *A Cavalryman With Custer.* Edited by Paul Andrew Hutton, Bantam Books, 1991.
King, W. Kent. *Massacre: The Custer Cover-Up.* Custer Trail Series, Vol. III, Upton & Sons, El Segundo, Calif., 1989.
Kuhlman, Charles, A. *Legend into History.* Harrisburg, Stackpole Co., 1951.
Libby, Orrin G. *The Arikara Narrative of the Campaign, against the Dakotas, 1876.* J.M. Carroll and Company, 1920.
Linderman, Frank B. *Pretty Shield: Medicine Woman of the Crows.* A Bison Book, University of Nebraska Press, 1932, reprint 1972.
Luce, Edward S. *Keogh, Commanche and Custer.* St. Louis, 1939.
Marquis, Thomas B. *Custer on the Little Bighorn.* Reference Publications, Algonac, Mich. 1967, Revised Edition. 1986.
_____. *Wooden Leg, A Warrior Who Fought Custer.* Lincoln, Nebraska, 1962.

BIBLIOGRAPHY

_____. *Keep The Last Bullet For Yourself: The True Story of Custer's Last Stand.* Reference Publications, Algonac, Mich. 1976.

_____. *She Watched Custer's Last Battle.*

_____. *Rain-In-The-Face & Curly, the Crow.*

_____. *Which Indian Killed Custer.*

_____. *Two Days After the Custer Battle.*

_____. *Sketch Story of the Custer Battle.*

Marshall, S.L.A. *The Indian Wars.* New York, 1972.

Michno, Greg, *Lakota Noon,* Missoula Montana. Mountain Press Publishing Company, 1997.

Michno, Greg. *The Mystery of E Company.* Montana Press Publishing Co., Missoula, Montana, 1994.

Miller, David Humphrey. *Custer's Fall, The Indian Side of the Story.* New York, Duell, Sloan and Pearce, 1957.

Neihardt, John G. *Black Elk Speaks.* Lincoln, Nebraska, 1961.

Nichols, Ronald H., Ed. *Reno Court of Inquiry, Proceedings of a Court of Inquiry in the case of Major Marcus A. Reno.* Pub. Custer Battlefield Historical & Museum Assoc. Inc., Hardin, Montana, 1996.

Nightengale, Robert. *Little Big Horn.* DocuPro Services, Inc., Edina, Minn., 1996.

O'Neil, Thomas E., *Passing Into Legend, The Death of Custer,* Arrow and Trooper Publishing, Brooklyn, NY., 1991.

Overfield, Loyd J. *The Little Big Horn, 1876.* (The official Communications, Documents & Reports with rosters of the Officers and Troops of the Campaign) Univ. of Nebraska Press, 1971.

Panzeri, Peter, *Little Big Horn, 1876, Custer's Last Stand,* Reed International Books, Ltd., Copyright, 1995.

Reedstrom, E. Lisle, *Custer's 7th Cavalry, From Fort Riley to the Little Big Horn,* Sterling Publishing Co., 1992.

Ross, A. C. *Mitakuye Oyasin, "We are all related."* Published by Wiconi Waste, Denver, CO.,1989.

Sandoz, Mari. *Crazy Horse: The Strange Man of the Oglalas a Biography.* New York, 1942.

_____. *The Battle of the Little Big Horn.* New York, 1966.

Scott, Douglas D. & Fox, Jr., Richard A. *Archaeological Insights into The Custer Battle.* Norman, University of Oklahoma Press, 1987.

Scott, Douglas. D. & Fox, Jr., Richard A., Connor, Melissa A., Harmon, Dick. *Archaeological Perspectives on The Battle of the Little Bighorn.* Norman: Univ. of Oklahoma Press, 1989.

Sklenar, Larry, *To Hell With Honor, Custer and the Little Bighorn,* University of OklahomaPress, Norman, 2000.

Stands In Timber, John & Margot Liberty, with the assistance of Robert M. Utley. *Cheyenne Memories.* University of Nebraska Press, Yale Univ., 1967.

Stewart, Edgar I. *Custer's Luck.* Norman: Univ. of Oklahoma Press, 1955.

Taunton, Francis, B. *Custer's Field.* London, The Johnson-Taunton Military Press, 1986.

Taylor, William O. *With Custer On The Little Bighorn.* Viking Penguin, 1996.

Upton, Richard. *The Custer Adventure.* Upton & Sons, El Segundo, Calif. 1990.

Utley, Robert. *Custer and the Great Controversy.* Westernlore Press, Pasadena, Calif., 1980.

_____. *Cavalier In Buckskin.* Norman: Univ. of Oklahoma Press, 1988.

_____. *The Last Days of the Sioux Nation.* Yale Univ. Press, New Haven, Conn. 1963.

Varnum, Charles A. *Custer's Chief of Scouts: The Reminiscences of Charles A. Varnum.* Edited by John M. Carroll, University of Nebraska Press, 1985.

Vestal, Stanley. *Warpath.* Boston, 1934, Univ. of Nebraska Press, 1984.

Viola, Herman J., *Little Big Horn Remembered, The Untold Indian Story of Custer's Last Stand,* Rivilo Books, 1999.

Weibert, Henry & Don. *Sixty Six Years in Custer's Shadow.* Falcon Press, 1985.

Weibert, Don, *Four Days With Custer.* Citizen Printing Co., 1987.

Westfall, Douglas Paul, *Letters from the field, Wallace at the Little Big Horn,* The Paragon Agency, 1997.

Willert, James. *Little Big Horn Diary,* Upton & Sons, El Segundo, Calif., 1997.

Potomac Corral of the Westerners. *Great Western Indian Fights.* University of Nebraska Press, 1966.

Articles:

"An Indian Account of the Custer Battle," *The Flandreau Review,* Dec., 1916.

Anderson, Harry H. "Cheyennes at the Little Big Horn, A Study of Statistics." *North Dakota History,* Winter 1960.

Bardull, Tom. " Was Custer In Command Or Dead." *Pioneer West,* April, 1972.

Beardsley, J. L. "Could Custer Have Won." *Outdoor Life,* March, 1933.

Bowers, John. "The Stonewall Image." *The Quarterly Journal of Military History,* Winter, 1960.

Brown, Lisle G. "Medal of Honor Couriers." *By Valor & Arms,* the journal of military history, Vol. I, No. I, October, 1974.

Boyes, W. "Surgeon's Diary – With The Custer Relief Column." *South Capital Press,* l974.

Burdick, Usher L. "Tragedy in the Great Sioux Camp." 1936.

Burrows, Jack. "White Bull, Vestal and Custer." *Montana: The Magazine of Western History,* Winter, 1970.

Byrne, P. E. "When War Came to the Indian." *North Dakota Historical Quarterly,* April, 1932.

Camp, Walter Mason. "Notes from the Custer Battlefield: Walter Mason Camp's Interviews with Survivors of the

Little Bighorn." Edited by Kenneth Hammer, *The American West,* March, April, 1976.

———. "Camp's Lost Account of Custer's Last Fight." Edited by Dale T. Schoenberger, *Old West,* Winter, 1989.

Carroll, John M. "General Custer and the Battle of the Little Bighorn, The Federal View." *The Garry Owen Press,* 1976.

———. "Word from Beyond." *By Valor & Arms,* the Journal of American Military History, Vol. I, No. l, October, 1974.

Cole, Ralph D. "Custer, the Man of Action." *Ohio Archaeological and Historical Quarterly,* Vol. XLI, Oct., 1932.

Collins, Richard, E. "Custer's Favorite Scout." *Greasy Grass,* Vol. 13, May, 1997.

Crowell, T. V., Evelyn Sibley Lampman. "Historic Distortion – Once Upon The Little Bighorn." Reviewed by William Meyer. *The Indian Historian,* Spring, 1972.

Custer, George Armstrong. "Battling the Sioux on the Yellowstone." *By Valor & Arms,* the Journal of Military History, Vol. I, Number l, October, 1974.

"Custer Massacre." *Army & Navy Journal,* Jan. 18, 1896 (p. 342).

DeWolf, James M. "The Diary and Letters of Dr. James M. DeWolf, ...His Record...As Kept Until His Death." Transcribed by Edward Luce, *North Dakota History.*.

Dustin, Fred. "George Armstrong Custer." *Michigan History Magazine,* Vol. 30, No. 2, April-June, 1946.

Edwards, William Waller. "The Battle of the Little Bighorn." Lt. Colonel of Cavalry, USA. *Outdoor Life,* Feb. 1933.

Ellison, Douglas W. "Did Frank Finkel Survive Custer's Last Stand?" *South Dakota Magazine,* Sept. 1988.

Fox, Jr., Richard Allan. "A New View of Custer's Last Battle." *American History Illustrated,* Oct. 1993

Galbreath, C. B. "George Armstrong Custer." *Ohio Archaeological and Historical Quarterly,* Vol. XLI, October, 1932.

Garlington, E.A. "The 7th Cavalry." *By Valor & Arms,* the Journal of American Military History, Vol. I, Number l, October, 1974.

"Ghost Dog John," speech by. "Letter to John Collier – Commissioner Indian Affairs, Washington, D.C., from James Browndus." April, 18, 1940.

Gray, John S. "The Pack Train on George A. Custer's Last Campaign." *Nebraska History,* Spring, 1976.

Griffith, Paddy. "Civil War Cavalry: Missed Opportunities." *The Quarterly Journal of Military History,* Vol. I, No. 3, Spring 1989.

Hill, Louis. "With General Custer on the Northern Pacific Surveying Expedition of 1873." *By Valor & Arms,* the Journal of American Military History, Vol. I, Number l October, 1974.

Hutchings, James S. "Custer's Clay." *Corral Dust,* Wash. D. C., May, 1960.

Johnson, Rev. A.F. "Progress of Civilization Among the Oglalas – The Custer Battle." *The Flandreau Review,* Vol. I, Number 6, April, 1916.

Jordan, Robert Paul. "Ghosts on the Little Bighorn." *National Geographic,* Dec., 1986.

Maketa, Ray. "NAP: The Gray Horse of E Company." *True West,* March, 1985.

Meistrich, Ira. "En Avant!" *The Quarterly Journal of Military History,* Vol. I, Number 3, Spring,1989

Michno, Greg. "Little Big Horn Mystery Solved." *Research/Review,* The Journal of the Little Big Horn Associates, Vol. 6, No. l, January, 1992.

———. "Lakota Noon, At the Greasy Grass." *Wild West,* June, 1996.

Miller, David Humphrey. "Echoes of the Little Bighorn." *American Heritage,* June, 1971.

Mulhair, Charles. "Fatal Beauty – Major Reno and the Colonel's Daughter." *True West,* March, 1985.

Myers, Rex C. "Montana Editors and the Custer Battle." *Montana: The Magazine of Western History,* Vol. XXVI, Number Two, April, 1976.

Nichols, Ron. "Should Reno Bear the Blame." *Greasy Grass,* Custer Battlefield Historical & Museum, Assoc., Vol. 12, May, 1996.

Noyes, Lee. "Major Marcus A. Reno at the Little Big Horn." *North Dakota History,* Winter, 1961.

Owens, Harry J. "Another Survivor of the Custer Battle." *True West,* May, 1983.

Paulding, Homes. "Letters to His Mother, Surgeon at the Little Bighorn." *Montana: The Magazine of Western History,* Edited by Thomas R. Buecker.

Peterson, John. "Mark Kellogg: Dakota Enigma."

Pickard, Edwin, Private. "I Rode With Custer." Edited by Edgar I. Stewart, *Montana Magazine of History,* Summer, 1954.

Prucha, Francis Paul. "A Bibliographical Guide to the History of Indian-White Relations in the United States." *The University of Chicago Press,* 1977.

Reed, John D. "Benteen's Other Option." *Research/Review,* Vol. 5, No. 2, June, 1991.

Ryan, M. E. "Indian Scout for Custer." *True West,* Jan.-Feb., 1956.

Scott, Douglas, D. & Connor, Melissa A. "Post Mortem at the Little Bighorn." *Natural History,* January, 1987.

Sievers, Michael A. "The Literature of the Little Bighorn." *Arizona and the West,* Sept. 1976.

"Six Letters Add Dimension to Historic Puzzle." *Montana: The Magazine of Western History,* Autumn, 1959.

Spencer, Jerry, D., M.D., J.D., (CDR. M.C., U.S.N.). "George Armstrong Custer and the Battle of the Little Bighorn: Homicide or Mass Suicide?" *Journal of Forensic Science,* Vol. 28, Number 3, July, 1983.

Stewart, Edgar I. "A Psychoanalytic Approach to Custer: Some Reflections." (Analysis of Dr. Hofling's account.) *Montana: The Magazine of Western History,* Summer, 1971.

BIBLIOGRAPHY

Taunton, Francis B. "A Scene of Sickening, Ghastly Horror, The Custer Battlefield. 27th & 28th, June, 1876." *The English Westerner's Society,* 1980.

Terrell, John Upton & George Walton, "*Faint the Trumpet Sounds – The Life and Trial of Major Reno.*" (Reno testimony at Court of Inquiry,)

Turner, Frank C. "Custer and the Canadian Connections." *The Beaver Magazine of the North,* Summer, 1976.

Utley, Robert M. "The Legend of the Little Bighorn." *Corral Dust,* June, 1956.

_____. "There'll Always Be an Indian Who Killed Custer." *Corral Dust,* Wash. D.C., June 1957.

_____. "The Gatlings Custer Left Behind." *The American West,* March, 1974.

Wert, Jeffrey, D. "Custer on the Rise." *Civil War Times,* June, 1996.

White Buffalo Man, Frank, (Great Grandson of Sitting Bull). "Two Survivors of the Battle of the Little Bighorn."

Wright, Donald C. "A Different Drummer." *Soldiers,* April, 1974

"Yellow Nose Tells of Custer's Last Stand." from the Chicago Record Herald, *The Indian School Journal,* Nov., 1905.

Newspapers

duBois, Charles G. "The Custer Mystery – Excerpts." *Rapid City Journal,* Sept. 14, 1986.

Friggens, Paul. "History Buffs Still Fighting It Out With Custer." *Rapid City Journal,* June, 22, 1986.

"Indian Scout (Loneman) Kept Sioux From Being Surprised At Little Bighorn." *Rapid City Journal,* Nov. 22, 1959.

"Little Bighorn Battle Still Shrouded in Mystery." *Aberdeen American News,* Aug. 6, 1990.

"36 in Custer's Last Stand Laid To Rest 110 Years Later." *The Sun,* New York Times News Service, June 26, 1986.

Letters

Little Big Horn Survivors – Agent to Comm. of Indian Affairs. *Dept. of Interior,* 1876.

Index

Arapahoes, 158, 159
Archaeological Insights into The Custer Battle (book), analysis of, 293–300
Archaeological Perspectives on the Battle of the Little Bighorn, analysis of, 293-300
Archaeology, and battle, 5
Arikara Narrative (book), 101, 189
Arikaras, 85-90
Ash Creek. See Reno Creek

Bad Juice. See Bad Soup
Bad Soup, 167, 168, 169, 170
The Battle of the Little Bighorn (book), 140
Battle of the Rosebud, 7, 113, 117, 118, 198
Battle of the Washita, 13, 14, 252
Battleridge, 123, 126, 136, 137, 141, 144, 151, 153, 154, 155, 157, 158, 162, 163, 164, 166, 168, 179, 180, 197, 201, 213, 220, 230, 236, 238, 248, 289, 356, 357
Beard, Dewey (Iron Hail), 269; testimony of, 172-173, 184
Benteen Creek. See Reno Creek
Benteen, Capt. Frederick, 3, 4, 5, 7, 10, 14, 25, 26, 30, 33, 37, 49, 63, 68, 81, 85, 86, 87, 88, 96, 116, 121, 130, 132, 133, 135, 151, 152, 155, 194, 195, 196, 198, 199, 201, 203, 206, 209, 210, 215, 218, 221, 223, 230, 234, 235, 237, 238, 240, 246, 250, 253, 255, 257, 258, 259, 276, 278, 300, 320, 327, 328, 332, 334, 338, 340, 353, 354, 355, 356, 357; and trumpeter Martin, 65, 66, 69, 72, 78; comments on DeRudio, 59; diatribe against Custer, 45; examination of statements of, 360-362; narrative of, 72, 73; orders of, 14-15, 19; pace of movements, 40, 61; rejoin's Reno, 10, 137, 163; scout to the left by, 14–20, 35, 39, 129, 304; supports Reno at Court of Inquiry, 34; testimony re Custer, 12, 14, 27
Benteen's Scout to the Left (book), 14, 16
Berger, William (interpreter), 162
Bethune, Frank, 227
Big Belly, 85, 258
Big Foot, 119, 120
Big Nose, 273, 287
Bighead, Kate (Cheyenne), 116, 118, 156, 166, 186, 203, 204, 211, 214, 219, 220, 226, 229, 230, 231, 266, 276, 290, 298, 300, 337; testimony of, 176-
Bismarck *Tribune*, 44
Black Fox (Ree scout), 74, 85, 87, 89, 91, 92, 95, 96, 97, 99, 111, 191, 254, 255, 263, 265, 307, 308, 309, 313, 314, 315, 356
Black Hills Expedition, 66
Black Kettle, 182
Black Moon, 140, 154, 171, 269
Black Wolf, 125, 176, 276
Bloody Knife, 6, 11, 12, 26, 51, 85, 87, 257
Blummer, Joseph A., 226
Bobtail Horse (Cheyenne), 102, 115, 176, 182, 183, 184, 186, 229, 274, 276, 277
Bob-tailed Bull, 85, 87, 88
Bourke, Lt., 316
Bouyer, Mitch (interpreter/scout), 6, 11, 12, 15, 18, 47, 49, 51, 62, 63, 74, 75, 79, 85, 91, 92, 94, 97, 100, 103, 105–110, 126, 174, 175, 188, 189, 191–193, 197, 198, 205, 207, 209, 226, 236, 240–245, 247, 250, 251, 254, 260, 261, 264, 272, 273, 292, 294, 326, 330, 348
Bouyer's Bluff, 76, 88, 89, 93, 95–99, 122, 242, 247, 329, 357
Boy Chief (Ree scout), 55, 87–89, 90
Bradley, Lt., 13, 91, 101, 264
Brady, Cyrus, 13, 20, 24
Brave Wolf, 275, 285, 286, 291
Brininstool, E. A., 15
Brisbin, Gen. James, 13, 59
Buffalo Calf, 115, 186
Bull (Ree scout), 87, 88, 90
Bull-in-the-Water (Ree scout), 87, 89, 90
Butler, Sgt. James, 109, 116, 120, 138, 248, 356

Calhoun Coulee, 216
Calhoun Hill, 123, 126, 141, 154, 156, 157, 158, 164, 179, 180, 229, 237, 296, 315
Calhoun Ridge, 89, 90, 102, 145, 201, 228, 237, 238
Calhoun, Lt., 7, 127, 131, 137, 138, 148, 157, 163, 165, 168, 212, 213, 255, 335, 357
Camp, Walter, 4, 15, 20, 28, 36, 48, 51, 59, 62, 68, 75, 86, 88, 91, 92, 94, 108, 161, 191, 198, 204, 207, 208, 233, 235, 239, 241, 242, 243, 244, 256, 259, 310, 312, 333, 348; interview with Curley, 103, 104, 105, 107; interview of Trumpeter Martin, 73, 74, 76, 77, 78, 79, 81
Carter, Capt. Robert, 8, 10, 28, 33, 42, 46, 57, 129, 282, 339, 340, 345
Cartwright Ridge, 157, 164
Cavalry Journal, 11
Cedar Coulee, 4, 9, 73, 75, 76, 78, 79, 81, 83, 102, 104, 110, 194, 200, 207, 209, 210, 216, 220, 224, 232, 233, 234, 237, 240, 241, 242, 244, 246, 271, 293, 307, 327, 329; discussion of, 186-192
Cemetery Ravine, 116, 158
Centennial Campaign (book), 7, 10, 24
Century Magazine, 30
Charging (Rushing) Bull (Ree scout), 87, 88, 90
Charging Hawk, 173
Cherry Creek, 168
Cheyenne Ford, 144, 175, 216, 237
Cheyenne Memories (book), 119
Cheyenne River Indian Reservation (South Dakota), 168
Cheyenne testimony, 40, 47
Churchill, B. F., 334, 339, 342
Claymore, Mr. (interpreter), 155
Closed Hand, 119, 124
Coleman, James (trader), 101
Comes-in-Sight, 185, 275
Connell, Evan S., 95
Connor, Melissa A.; analysis of book, *Archaeological Perspectives*, 293-300
Contrary Belly, 185
Cooke, Lt. William W., 7, 11, 18, 21, 23, 24, 25, 30, 34, 35, 36, 47, 48, 49, 50, 51, 53, 57, 69, 76, 105, 130, 133, 173, 194, 202, 205, 221, 222, 223, 224, 232, 253, 254, 268, 270, 281, 282, 293, 305, 322, 326, 356
Corcoran, Pvt., 19, 61
Coughlin, 11
Cover-ups, 11, 39, 96, 116, 338
Crazy Horse, 116, 138, 146, 150, 153, 154, 157, 159, 161, 164, 166, 168, 172, 173, 174, 181, 184, 288, 296
Crittenden, Lt., 7, 127, 137, 138
Crook, Gen., 160, 162, 171, 182, 194, 198, 236
Crooked Horn, 258, 303
Crooked Nose, 119
Cross, Bill, 87, 314
Crow King (Hunkpapa), 127, 138, 140, 146, 153, 274, 284, 337; testimony of, 150–152
Crow scouts, 4, 6, 12, 13, 62, 75, 85, 91-100, 111, 130, 191, 193, 215, 219, 225, 274, 240, 247, 251, 282, 284–286, 299, 301, 305, 313, 314, 328, 329, 343, 348, 337, 356, 357
Crow's Nest, 11, 12, 13, 25, 26, 40, 41, 85, 162, 194, 217, 250, 251, 258, 282, 301, 302, 344
Culbertson, Sgt. F.A., 24, 38, 51, 215, 305
Curley (Crow scout), 4, 24, 26, 74, 78, 83, 85, 88, 89, 91, 92, 93, 96, 97, 125, 126, 162, 186, 191, 197, 198, 207, 209, 211, 215, 216, 225, 226, 227, 232, 235, 236, 239, 240, 241, 243, 245, 246, 248, 254, 256, 260, 262, 263, 265, 269, 272, 276, 281, 307, 308, 309, 314, 315, 326, 329, 335, 348, 349, 356, 357; accounts of the battle, 101-111; claims of presence at Last Stand Hill, 96; comments on Cedar Coulee, 187, 188, 189; interview by Gen. Scott, 94, 95, 96, 98, 99
Curse Not His Curls (book), analysis of, 193-199
Curtis, E., 59
Custer, Boston, 73, 77, 78, 79, 81, 192, 225, 233, 238, 239, 242, 289, 328
Custer, Capt. Tom, 7, 121, 128, 137, 166, 170, 173
Custer, Elizabeth B., 3
Custer, Gen. George A, *passim;* advised by scouts, 27; anticipates battle, 26; character of, 4, 7; develops battle plan, 10-14, 20; general outline of actions, 355; gives orders

369

INDEX

to Reno, 23; knowledge of Sioux camp, 85; orders to Reno & Benteen, 37, 39; presidency and, 4, suicide theory and, 169
Custer, Thomas, 63, 102, 107, 210, 334, 240, 259, 335, 336, 361
The Custer Controversy: A Critical Analysis (book), 342
Custer Creek, 92
Custer Hill, 204, 238, 245
Custer in 76 (book), 92
The Custer Myth: A Source Book of Custeriana (book), 14, 25, 59, 109, 129, 142, 187, 303, 319; analysis of, 220-223
Custer on the Little Bighorn (book), 140
Custer Ridge, 238
The Custer Tragedy (book), analysis of, 250–268
Custer's Chief of Scouts (book), 47, 268
Custer's Fall (book); analysis of, 269–277
Custer's Last Campaign (book), 42, 90, 129, 317; analysis of, 301–316
Custer's Luck (book), 65, 319; analysis of, 278-292, 319
Cut Belly, 119, 124

Darling, Roger, 5, 14, 16, 41, 305, 321
Davern, Sgt., 18, 20, 44, 70, 77, 82, 87, 222, 268, 280, 304, 305, 312, 334, 340, 354, 355
Davis Creek, 251
Deep Coulee, 102, 123, 138, 144, 145, 151, 153, 161, 163, 185, 186, 200, 229, 236, 237, 248, 274, 289, 295, 357
Deep Ravine, 100, 116, 148, 156, 158, 174, 179, 180, 210, 228, 229, 230, 231, 238, 276, 290, 292, 294, 296, 297, 298, 299, 357
DeRudio, Lt., 7, 24, 27, 28, 29, 36, 37, 51, 53, 54, 56, 57, 59, 105, 114, 133, 162, 179, 191, 194, 205, 224, 232, 253, 254, 257, 260, 263, 270, 344
DeWolf, Dr., 7, 57, 253
Dives Backward, 276
Dixon, Dr., 117
Donahue, Pvt., 44, 354
du Mont, Mr., 169
duBois, Charles, 5, 10
Dull Knife, 182
Dustin, Fred, 5, 11, 24, 92, 109, 110, 189, 192, 317; analysis of book, *The Custer Tragedy,* 250–268

Eastman, Charles, 5, 117, 140, 286, 331
Edgerly, Lt. Winfield Scott, 7, 10, 12, 19, 20, 21, 23, 30, 40, 41, 48, 49, 61, 67, 72, 87, 132, 133, 212, 223, 252, 279, 302, 332, 346; evaluated by Graham, 25
E-esh (Lakota Interpreter), 90
Ege, Robert J., analysis of his book, *Curse Not His Curls,* 193-199
Ellison, Douglas; analysis of book, *Sole Survivor,* 239-249
Evidence and the Custer Enigma (book), 28, 187; analysis of, 223–231
Far West (steamer), 101, 107

Farribault, Mr., 133
Fast Bull, 172
Fast Horn, 162
Feather Earring (Sioux), 94, 229
The Fighting Cheyenne (book), 124, 226
Finkel, Frank, 110, 240, 244, 246, 330
Flying By (Miniconjou), testimony of, 155–156
Flying Hawk (Oglala), 229, 286, testimony of, 154
Foley, Cpl., 164, 175, 186
Foolish Elk (Oglala Sioux), testimony of, 160–162
Ford A, 10, 23, 24, 28, 34–36, 41, 42, 44, 45, 46, 48, 51, 53, 54, 60, 92–94, 96, 129, 130, 131, 143, 199, 200, 202, 223, 253, 255, 258, 264, 280, 281, 302, 309, 314, 321–324, 342, 350, 355; time needed to cross, 29, 30
Ford B, 36–38, 41, 44, 56, 70, 74, 76, 78, 79, 81, 83, 88, 89, 90, 91, 97–99, 104, 105, 109, 122, 129, 133, 137, 144, 151, 160, 163, 164, 166, 167, 175, 184, 186, 196, 201, 208, 209, 216, 217, 232, 241, 248, 256, 266, 272, 309, 312, 314, 329, 347, 349, 353, 356
Forked Horn (Ree scout), 85, 87
Forsyth, Gen. G. A., 6
Fort Custer, 136
Fox, Richard A., Jr.; analysis of books of, 293-300
French, Capt. Thomas, 7, 40, 133, 137, 147, 255, 267, 268, 347, 350, 353
Frett, John, 19, 252, 280, 334

Gall, 62, 113, 115, 116, 146, 147, 153, 173, 174, 184, 213, 214, 227, 249, 269, 270, 274, 276, 277, 284, 289, 291; testimonies of, 125-141
Garland, Hamlin, 175
Ga-roo (Lakota Scout), 90
Gibbon, Col., 13, 91, 111, 194, 206, 212, 215, 226, 251, 264, 265, 266, 272, 292, 294
Gibson, Lt., 7, 15, 18, 19, 40, 41, 86, 305, 320, 321, 354
Gilbert, Mr. (defense counsel), 33, 34, 35, 45, 56, 60, 204
Girard, Fred (Ree interpreter), 6, 7, 11, 12, 19, 20, 23, 24, 25, 28, 29, 33, 36, 46, 47, 49, 54–56, 85, 92, 103, 193, 202, 205, 210, 221–223, 253, 255, 279, 304, 305, 322, 345, 356; testimony of, 50, 51, 52, 53
Gitchell, James, 11
Godfrey, Capt., 7, 10, 12, 13, 14, 19, 24, 25, 28 40, 42, 48, 49, 61, 82, 147, 153, 166, 169, 250, 251, 256, 259, 274, 276, 303, 305, 306, 322, 346; and Gall testimony, 129-141; and Mrs. Spotted Horn Bull testimony, 142; narrative of, 26, 30
Goes Ahead (Crow Scout), 89, 91, 92, 97, 109, 111, 186, 189, 191, 192, 207, 209, 215, 226, 255, 256, 272, 273, 276, 287, 313, 314, 331, 348
Goldin, Theodore, 15, 185
Good Bear Boy, 171, 172

Good Feather Woman, 168
Good Voiced Elk, 236
Goose (Ree scout), 85, 87
Graham, Col. William A., 3–5, 8, 10, 11, 12, 14, 24–26, 28, 29, 33, 34, 40, 42, 57, 59, 61, 68, 76, 77, 87, 102, 108, 109, 129, 142, 145, 150, 204, 232, 235, 254, 302, 310, 317, 319, 339, 345, 346; analysis of book, *The Custer Myth,* 220-223; and Trumpeter Martin, 77, 79, 81, 83; evaluation of Curley, 101
Gray Eagle, 171
Gray Horse Troop, 19, 38, 47, 56, 57, 59, 63, 68, 75, 88, 102, 105, 110, 114, 123, 129, 140, 157, 162, 167, 189, 190, 197, 200, 206, 211, 224, 230, 231, 232, 236, 247, 254, 261, 263, 270, 272, 273, 314, 357
Gray, John, 5, 7, 10, 24, 41, 42, 90, 281, 317; analysis of book, *Custer's Last Campaign,* 301
Greene, Jerome, 5, 28, 187, 191, 235, 299; analysis of book, *Evidence and the Custer Enigma,* 223-231
Griffith, Paddy, 78
Grinnell, 5, 119, 124, 173, 226, 236, 286, 324

Hairy Moccasin (Crow Scout), 89, 91, 92, 93, 97, 109, 111, 192, 215, 233, 255, 273, 276, 313, 331 interview in *Tepee Book,* 94
Half Yellow Face (Crow scout), 85, 87, 91, 101, 103, 215, 255, 256, 269, 281; joins Reno command, 92
Hammer, Kenneth, 92, 104
Hampton Indian Institute students, 349
Hardorff, Richard G., 5, 7, 128, 299; analysis of book, *Markers, Artifacts and Indian Testimony,* 232-239
Hare, Lt., 7, 18, 24, 27, 39, 46, 51, 81, 82, 85, 86, 88, 90, 132, 223, 238, 250, 290, 304, 305, 321, 334
Harmon, Dick; analysis of book, *Archaeological Perspectives,* 293-300
Harrington, Lt., 7
He Dog (Oglala), 162, 175, 179; Testimony of, 162-164, 236
Henryville, 138
Herendeen, George, 24, 51, 52, 133, 221, 307
High Backbone, 172
Hodgson, Lt., 7, 20, 34, 45, 47, 345
Holley, Francis, 146
Horned Horse, 225
Houston, Frank, 149, 150
Hughes, Capt. Robert P., 342, 343, 348
Hump (Miniconjou), 138, 146, 150, 172, 228; testimony of, 149

Ice Bear, 172
The Indian Wars (book), 131, 282
Indians, numbers of, 5, 6, 38; testimony of, 3, 6, 8, 9
Inkpaduta, 172
Iron Cedar, 135, 137, 139, 141, 147, 289
Iron Hail. See Beard, Dewey
Iron Hawk, 230, 275

INDEX

Iron Thunder (Miniconjou), testimony of, 155
Jackson brothers, 87
Jackson, William (scout), 11

Kanipe, 4, 6, 9, 19, 24, 30, 35, 39, 40, 41, 49, 59, 60, 66–70, 72, 74, 81, 87, 88, 94, 104, 105, 108, 131, 157, 174, 187, 188, 191, 193, 194, 196, 199, 200, 205, 206, 219, 225, 232, 235, 240, 252, 254, 256, 257, 259, 260, 262, 280, 297, 306, 309, 310, 312, 324, 325, 327, 332, 345, 346, 357, 360, 361; account of, 61–64
Keep the Last Bullet for Yourself (book), 231, 278; analysis of, 215-220
Keogh, Capt., 7, 21, 34, 35, 44, 47, 48, 49, 51, 53, 60, 78, 102, 120–123, 125–127, 131, 133, 135, 137, 138, 148, 155, 157, 161–165, 168, 179, 185, 201, 205, 213, 216, 217, 221, 223, 224, 226, 230, 235, 238, 248, 258, 274, 282, 289, 291, 322, 327, 335, 353, 356, 357
King, W. Kent, 5, 44, 64, 268
Kuhlman, Charles, 5, 7, 9, 10, 24, 27, 117, 129, 197, 216, 227, 229, 235, 248, 253, 270, 271, 276, 295, 299; analysis of book, *Legend into History*, 199-214; impressions of Trumpeter Martin, 65, 66, 77

LaForge, Thomas, 226, 265
Lakota testimony, 40, 47
Lame White Man (Cheyenne), 116, 118, 119, 120, 124, 172, 179, 198, 211, 290, 296
Last Stand Hill, 96, 102, 111, 120, 123, 148, 151, 153, 160, 161, 162, 166, 180, 185, 213, 214, 229, 232, 236, 238, 248, 249, 255, 264, 274, 292, 296, 298, 299, 302, 330, 357
Laudin, Reginald K., 169, 170
Lee, Jesse M., 33, 34, 36, 37, 50, 60, 77, 203, 204, 208, 354, 363
LeForge, Thomas H., 101, 264, 272
Left Hand (Arapahoe), testimony of, 158-159
Legend into History (book), 10, 227, 248; analysis of, 199–214
Liberty, Margo, 119
Limber Bones, 124
Limpy, 276
Linderman, Frank B., 99, 219
Little Big Horn Diary (book); analysis of, 317–341
The Little Big Horn, 1876 (book), 95
Little Brave (Ree scout), 85, 87
Little Sioux (Ree scout), 86, 87, 88, 90
Little Soldier (Ree scout), 86
Little Sun (Cheyenne), 125
Little Whirlwind, 119, 124
Little Wolf, 176
Logan, W. R., 297
Lone Tepee, 7, 10, 12, 18, 19, 23, 24, 25, 26, 27, 40, 41, 57, 61, 63, 72, 76, 86, 90, 91, 131, 162, 199, 200, 252, 262, 303, 305, 321, 344, 357
Lookout Point, 259
Lord, Capt. G. E., 7

Low Dog (Oglala), 150, 229, 337; testimony of, 152-153
Luce Ridge, 44, 88, 102, 107, 108, 115, 123, 126, 133, 136, 148, 158, 217, 234, 235, 236, 243, 330
Luce, Edward S., 227
Lynch, Pvt. Dennis, 61, 91, 227

Mad Wolf, 183
Magnussen, Daniel, 5, 24, 59, 60
Maguire, Lt. Edward, 204, 226, 347
Makes-Room, 168
Maps, of Custer on ridge, 80; of Custer's Route to battle area, 177; of troop movements, 43; of routes of troops, 17
Markers, Artifacts and Indian Testimony (book)
Marquis, Dr. Thomas B., 5, 101, 111, 113, 117, 119, 129, 139, 140, 146, 167, 178, 180, 181, 196, 201, 208, 211, 214, 230, 231, 235, 266, 270, 271, 276, 278, 292, 300; analysis of book, *Keep the Last Bullet for Yourself,* 215-220
Marshall, S.L.A., 131, 282, 317
Martin, Greg, 343, 348
Martin, Trumpeter, 4, 6, 7, 9, 18, 20, 24, 30, 33, 35, 38, 39, 41, 44, 57, 60, 61–63, 87, 89, 94, 96, 100, 104, 105, 110, 120, 121, 123, 130, 131, 134, 136, 144, 172, 186, 188, 189, 191–194, 196, 200, 203–205, 209, 218, 219, 220–222, 224, 232–236, 239, 240, 242, 244, 250, 252, 254, 260, 261, 266, 268, 269, 271, 272, 276, 280, 285, 287, 293, 299, 302, 304, 306, 309–312, 324, 325, 328, 334, 345, 349, 354–357, 359, 360, 361; account of, 65–84; examination of questioning of at Reno Court, 362–363; testimony at Reno Court, 40
Martini, Giovanni. See Martin, John
Massacre: The Custer Cover-Up (book), 64, 268
Mathey, 7, 14, 39, 40, 41, 61, 63, 70, 72, 92, 96, 262, 332, 342, 348
McCausland, Gen. John, 6
McChesney, Asst. Surg., 147
McClellan, Gen., 49
McClernand, Lt., 286
McCoy, Col. Tim, 158
McDougall, Capt., 5, 13, 14, 21, 26, 29, 30, 35, 39, 40, 41, 61, 63, 66, 68, 69, 70, 75, 81, 82, 85, 88, 108, 116, 132, 135, 143, 194, 196, 199, 216, 238, 246, 250, 259, 262, 288, 298, 327, 332, 333, 339, 342, 346, 357, 361
McIhargey, Pvt. Archibald, 30, 50, 86, 281, 305, 323, 324, 363
McIntosh, Lt., 7
McLaughlin, Maj., 129, 133, 141, 142, 145
Meador, Thomas, 125
Medicine Crow, Joseph, 215
Medicine Tail Coulee, 6, 34, 35, 62, 67, 68, 73, 76, 77, 81, 83, 90, 92, 96, 99, 100, 109, 110, 119, 120, 121, 125, 134, 162, 163, 172, 175, 178, 179, 182, 184, 186, 189, 191, 196, 200, 202, 208, 209, 215–219, 225, 227, 228, 233–236, 241, 243, 244, 252, 266, 271, 285, 293, 312, 356, 357
Memoirs of a White Crow Indian (book), 215
Meotzi, 186
Middle Coulee, 75, 76, 77, 78, 81, 102, 208, 209, 242, 287, 313, 314, 356, 357
Middle Ford, 213
Miles, Gen. Nelson, 10, 117, 302
Miller, David Humphreys, 5, 24, 168, 170, 172, 182, 185, 245, 300, 331; analysis of book, *Custer's Fall,* 269–277; describes Crow scout animosities, 91
Miniconjou Ford, see Ford B
Mitchell, Pvt. John, 323
Moeller, Pvt., 61
Morgan, George, 101
Morris, Pvt., 29, 61, 147, 305
Moylan, Capt., 7, 24, 28, 51, 130, 223, 235, 238, 305, 319, 323, 327, 342, 347

No Hip Bone, 215
Noisy Walking, 116, 119, 124
Nye Cartwright Ridge, , 41, 44, 79, 83, 88, 102, 107, 108, 115, 120, 123, 126, 133, 136, 138, 145, 148, 151, 154, 157, 158, 163, 166, 175, 178, 179, 185, 188, 192, 201, 213, 216, 217, 220, 226, 227, 228, 237, 239, 242, 243, 249, 266, 274, 289, 293, 330, 353, 356
Nye, Col. Elwood L., 226

O'Hara, Sgt. Miles F., 29, 193
O'Neil, Pvt. Thomas F., 29, 44, 55, 306, 354
One Bull, 114, 115, 170-172, 269, 270
One Feather (Ree scout), 87, 89
Overfield, Loyd J., II, 95

Pack-train, 7
Payne, Capt. J.S., 288
Penwell, Trumpeter, 133, 136
Petring, Pvt. Henry, 55, 56
Pine Ridge Reservation, 172
Pine, 276
Pleasonton, Gen., 49
Poland, Capt. J.S.; interviews Sioux, 153-154
Porter, Dr., 7, 24, 27, 47, 51, 133, 305
Porter, Lt., 7
Pretty Face (Ree scout), 87, , 307
Pretty Shield, 102, 172, 219, 226, 287; story of, 99-100
Pta-a-te (Lacotah scout), 90

Rain-in-the-Face, 140
Rain-in-the-Face and Curley, The Crow (book), 111
Red Bear (Ree scout), 24, 87, 90, 95, 96, 98, 256, 273, 276, 307, 313, 357; remembers battle, 89
Red Cloud, 150
Red Cloud agency, 147
Red Foolish Bear (Ree scout), 85, 87
Red Fox, 276
Red Horse (Sioux); testimony of , 147–149, 292, 337

INDEX

Red Star (Ree scout), 12, 40, 55, 87, 88, 89, 90, 101, 255, 256, 258, 259, 263, 273, 282, 302, 309, 313, 318, 344
Red Wolf (Ree scout), 87, 88, 90
Ree Indian scouts, 23, 24, 26, 47, 63, 95, 160, 162, 165, 171, 193, 222, 240, 246, 251, 279, 301, 308, 313, 345. See also Arikaras
Reily, Lt., 7, 213
Reno Court of Inquiry, 4, 8, 12, 14, 20, 25, 28, 30, 31, 33–38, 39–44, 45, 49, 50–53, 55, 73, 76, 77, 81, 130, 142, 203, 204, 208, 214, 254, 266, 267, 281, 301, 310, 311, 312, 317, 318, 322, 332, 333, 334, 342, 343, 346, 350, 353–355, 359, 360, 361; and trumpeter Martin, 65, 67, 68
Reno Creek, 7, 12, 13, 16, 18, 19, 23, 24, 26, 28, 29, 41, 44, 47, 49, 62, 63, 76, 83, 85, 92, 94, 97, 103, 110, 111, 136, 143, 162, 199, 224, 252, 256, 279, 304, 344, 348, 349, 200, 206, 207, 235, 240, 281, 306, 324, 327, 339, 357
Reno Ford. See Ford A
Reno Hill, 8, 36, 39, 40, 53, 55, 76, 83, 88, 91, 93, 99, 105, 154, 171, 190, 205, 234, 256, 265, 267, 287, 307, 310, 311, 312, 333, 355, 357, 358
Reno, 3, 4, 6, 7, 9, 29, 33, 39, 52, 55, 86, 132, 161, 199, 207, 208, 223, 240, 250, 254, 266, 267, 269, 286, 317, 321–324, 327, 340, 345, 357; accusations against, 70; and Custer gunfire, 48; attack in the valley, 125, 126, 155, 164, 165, 324, 325; Cheyenne reaction to, 113, 114; crossing of ford, 44; examination of statements of, 359; fails to support Custer, 39; movements of, 27, 28; receives orders, 20, 23, 24, 45, 220, 281; retreat of, 42
Reynolds, Charley, 6, 11, 12, 47, 50, 51, 85, 251, 258, 318
Rickey, Don, Jr., 227
Ricker, Judge Eli S., 154
Ridge B, 16
Ridge C (Gibson's Lookout), 16
Rising Sun, 276
Roan Bear, 115, 182, 186
Roe, Gen. C.F., 347
Roman Nose, 124, 150
Rosebud Creek, 7, 13, 171
Roubideaux, Louis (interpreter), 160
Roy, Sgt. Stanislas, 30, 55, 59, 75, 104
Ryan, Cpl., 28, 287, 351

Sanderson, Capt. C.K., 293
Sandoz, Mari, 140
Scott, Douglas D., 5; analysis of books of, 293-300
Scott, Gen., 4, 24, 26, 88, 89, 91, 188, 191, 215, 219, 233, 240, 265, 269, 281, 301, 331, 348; evaluation of Crow interviews, 100; interview with Curley, 103, 109, 110
Seventh Cavalry; Companies of and commands, 7; divided by Custer, 7, 8, 14
Sharpshooter Hill, 62, 93, 104, 187, 190, 220, 254

Sharpshooter Ridge, 71
Sharrow, Sgt. Maj., 16, 18, 19, 41, 66, 70, 77, 86, 88, 193, 203, 252, 278, 279, 304, 320, 328, 354
Shaw, Mr. (interpreter), 160
Shenandoah Valley, 6
Sheridan, Capt. Michael, 101, 293, 298
Sherman, Gen., 6
Sioux and Cheyenne testimonies, 113–192
Sitting Bull, 125, 126, 127, 129, 134, 140, 146, 150, 152, 165, 167, 168, 170, 171, 172, 229, 291
Sixty Six Years in Custer's Shadow (book), 175
Smith, Capt. E. W., 40, 48
Smith, Lt. Algernon E., 7, 102, 121, 128, 137, 138, 166, 173, 197, 246, 265, 329, 335, 336, 357
Soldier (Ree scout), 87, 89, 90, 246, 279
Sole Survivor (book); analysis of, 239-249
Son of the Morning Star (book), 95
Spotted Elk, 119
Spotted Horn Bull, Mrs., 133, 134, 136, 148, 208, 211, 213, 214, 219, 291; testimony of, 142-146
Spotted Rabbit, 173
Spotted Tail, 150
Stabbed (Ree scout), 15, 20, 41, 66, 86, 87, 88, 89, 90, 96, 255, 279, 328, 357
Standing Bear, 154, 163; testimony of, 157-158
Standing Rock Agency, 129, 134, 142
Stands in Timber, John (Cheyenne), 166, 170, 185, 229, 238, 274, 290, 299; testimony of, 119-125
Stewart, Edgar I., 3, 5, 6, 8, 11, 21, 24, 33, 227, 299, 319, 332; analysis of book, *Custer's Luck*, 278-292; impressions of Trumpeter Martin, 65-66, 67, 68; speculations of, 27
Strikes Two (Ree scout), 55, 87, 88, 89, 90, 95, 96
Strikes-the-Lodge (Ree scout), 87, 89, 90
Sturgis, Lt. James G., 7, 197, 211
Sundance Creek. See Reno Creek

Tall Bull, testimony of, 156-157
Tall Sioux, 120
Taunton, Francis B., 299
Taylor, William O., 342, 343, 344, 347, 349, 350
Terry, Gen., 3, 11, 13, 52, 77, 81, 111, 212, 236, 250, 266, 272, 284, 287
Thompson, Pvt. Peter, 95, 246, 309
Time analysis, 1, 7, 8, 10, 24, 25, 30, 42-44, 78, 99, 194, 301-303, 346, 350, 357-358
Time-motion analysis, 301, 315
Tullock's Fork, 264, 265, 308
Turtle Rib (Miniconjou), testimony of, 160, 186
Twin Woman, 119
Two Moon, 113, 125, 159, 182, 184, 212, 230, 236, 277, 292; comments on by Wooden Leg, 176; testimony of, 173-175

Upton, Richard, 5
Utley, Robert, 5, 8, 11, 19, 24, 34, 87, 121, 123, 301

Varnum, Lt., 7, 8, 10, 11, 15, 24, 25, 28, 37, 40, 46–49, 51, 52, 53, 56, 57, 59, 88, 94, 105, 114, 129, 140, 162, 190, 205, 223, 228, 230, 232, 233, 235, 236, 250, 253–255, 261, 263, 268, 270, 301, 302, 305, 318, 345, 357, 360; in charge of Ree scouts, 85; testimony of, 46
Vaughn, J.W., 120, 229
Vestal, Stanley, 165, 167, 170
Voss, Trumpeter Henry, 19, 66, 278, 279, 320

Walks-Under-The-Ground, 173
Wallace, Lt. George D., 7, 20, 24, 25, 28, 29, 30, 34, 35, 40, 46, 48, 49, 56, 70, 72, 81, 282, 301, 305, 318, 321, 338; actions with Reno, 45, 47
A Warrior Who Fought Custer (book), 215
Washita Battle, 182
Waterman (Arapahoe), testimony of, 159
Watts, Chip, 16, 321
Weibert, Henry, 175, 181, 192
Weir, Capt., 7, 14, 21, 30, 39, 40, 69, 87, 136, 137, 212, 338, 339, 346, 353, 358
Weir Point, 4, 8, 39, 40, 55, 56, 59, 62, 63, 67, 70–76, 79, 81, 83, 88, 91, 93, 98, 104, 116, 119, 126, 131, 132, 135, 140, 147, 151, 155, 162, 166, 187–189, 190–192, 194, 195, 198–200, 202–204, 207, 210–213, 216, 220, 225, 228, 229, 232–234, 241, 242, 244, 248, 254, 257, 259, 263, 265, 274, 287, 307, 311, 325, 326, 328, 356, 357
West Calhoun Ridge, 357
West Coulee, 209, 287
White Bear, Russell, 107, 109, 110, 189, 227, 239, 240, 331, 332, 335
White Bull, 113, 115, 116, 138, 149, 172, 181, 184, 270; testimony of, 156
White Bull, Joseph (Miniconjou), 156, 162, 173, 201; testimony of, 165-167, 168-170
White Cloud (Lakota scout), 87, 89, 95, 96, 98, 307, 313, 357
White Cow Bull (Sioux), 78, 102, 124, 158, 163, 169, 175, 182, 188, 191, 226, 245, 247, 272, 273, 276, 277, 287, 299, 315; testimony of, 182-186
White Dress (Sioux), 125
White Eagle, 87, 88, 90, 279
White Man Cripple, 159
White Man Runs Him (Crow Scout), 4, 12, 18, 24, 26, 78, 91, 94, 97, 98, 109, 111, 119, 186, 191, 192, 215, 219, 226, 233, 252, 255, 256, 259, 269, 273, 276, 281, 286, 308, 313, 331, 348; testimony to Gen. Hugh Scott, 91-92, 97
White Shield, 183
White Swan (Crow scout), 85, 91, 99, 103, 215, 255, 256, 269, 281; joins Reno command, 92
Whittaker, Frederick, 54, 266, 267
Wilbur, Pvt. James, 29, 48, 49
Willert, James; analysis of book, *Little Big Horn Diary*, 317-341

INDEX

Wilson, Sgt. James E., 101
Windolph, Pvt., 24, 28, 66, 320
"With Custer on the Little Bighorn" The First And Only Eyewitness Account Ever Written (manuscript), 343
Wolf Mountains, 7
Wolf Tooth, 61, 88, 119, 120, 121, 123, 124, 135, 154, 185, 201, 241, 274, 289, 299
Wooden Leg (Cheyenne), 119, 124, 129, 134, 138, 153, 156, 160, 161, 166, 170, 172, 180, 184, 186, 211, 212, 219, 226, 228, 229, 230, 231, 238, 249, 254, 260, 261, 263, 266, 270, 276, 290, 298, 337, 339, 351; comments on Two Moon, 176; testimony of, 113-118
Woodruff, Gen. Charles A., 256
Wright, Oscar, 348

Yates, Capt., 7, 21, 44, 102, 128, 135, 137, 145, 153, 155, 157, 162, 163, 165, 166, 173, 178, 185, 192, 209, 213, 216, 217, 223, 224, 235, 236, 237, 238, 335, 353, 356, 357
Yellow Bird, 186
Yellow Hair (Cheyenne), 113
Yellow Nose, 124, 184, 185
Young Hawk (Ree scout), 85, 87, 96, 99, 308, 313, 314

The Battle of the Little Bighorn: A Comprehensive Study
by Jack Pennington has been produced
in an edition of 1050 copies, of which
50 are specially bound, numbered and signed.
It was designed by Robert A. Clark of the
Arthur H. Clark Company, Spokane, Washington.